C0-AVH-052

France's Rhineland Diplomacy, 1914-1924

"France follows a policy of suicide. . . . For the guarantor powers the treaty is a piece of paper; for us it is an instrument of servitude. . . . C'était bien la paix boche!"

—Camille Barrère, 1919

France's Rhineland Diplomacy, 1914-1924

The Last Bid for a Balance of Power in Europe

Walter A. McDougall

Princeton University Press
Princeton, New Jersey

Published by Princeton University Press, Princeton, New Jersey
In the United Kingdom: Princeton University Press, Guildford, Surrey

Library of Congress Cataloging in Publication Data will be
found on the last printed page of this book

This book has been composed in VIP Caledonia

Printed in the United States of America by Princeton
University Press, Princeton, New Jersey

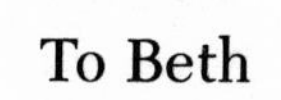

To Beth

CONTENTS

ILLUSTRATIONS

The map was drawn by Adrienne Morgan, Geography Department, University of California/Berkeley. The illustrations, from H. P. Gassier and J. Sennep, *Histoire de France, 1918-1938* (Paris: Éditions Mana, 1938), are reproduced under the copyright of S.P.A.D.E.M.

PREFACE

Few would claim any longer that reports of the death of the "old diplomatic history" are exaggerated. Yet in the half-century since Eckart Kehr challenged the basic assumptions of the historiography of international relations, no two historians seem to have agreed on the nature of the "new" diplomatic history. Instead, "functional-structuralists," "Kehrites," "socio-Marxists," "New Leftists," and "consensus" historians (which seems only to mean "none of the above") exchange harpoons barbed with accusations about the identity of ideology with methodology and the incompatibility of "critical theory" with the shibboleth of objectivity. Despite or because of this anomie, diplomatic history has never been so imaginative as in the last decade—precisely when demands for its abolition or banishment to political science have been most strident.

This monograph was originally conceived as an investigation of French involvement in the Rhenish separatist episodes after World War I. While I recognized the centrality of the reparations problem and social strife in the politics and subsequent historiography of the period, I hoped to isolate the power political and security aspects of France's German policy. The weight of the evidence, not any theoretical assumptions about the determinants of foreign policy in industrial society, led me quickly to abandon this isolated approach. Even as I understood more clearly the complex interaction of all military, political, and economic issues affecting postwar Europe, I also concluded that no approach stressing the primacy of any one factor yielded a satisfactory approximation of French policy-making and the pattern of international relations. Yet all approaches offered insights: nationalist foreign policy was in part a means of avoiding social conflict and reform at home; structural problems in industry and commerce were an important influence on political strategy; theoretical conceptions of French economic and military security and the requirements of the balance of power did emerge in part independently of domestic pressures; personality and the incoherence of bureaucratic planning did limit and direct policy formation. In short, the course of international history in this period depended as much on policy as on process.

There is not now and ought never to be *a* "new diplomatic history." To seal the study of international relations within a programmatic methodological or interpretive cell would restore the limitations imposed by the purveyors of the primacy of foreign policy and many of their critics alike. The history of international relations ought to suggest a finite realm of subject matter, but not of evidence or approach. For the subject of diplomatic history—the formulation and execution of foreign policy over time—is singularly resistant to inflexible modes of explanation. Whatever his predilections, the diplomatic historian searches in practice for the restraints and imperatives operating on policy-makers. In so doing, he is in the best position to perceive that the statesman exists in an interface between two systems—the international polity and the domestic polity, each with its own patterns of development and response, each with its social, economic, and technical imperatives. When foreign policy and its effects are viewed as the product of this interface, the assertion of a "primacy"—foreign, domestic, economic, or ideological—is revealed as artificial. Why is it necessary to deny the existence of an autonomous international balance of power system in order to acknowledge the importance—occasionally primary—of socio-economic structure and conflict, whether revolutionary or counter-revolutionary, in the formation of foreign policy in a given state at a given time? To understand the domestic roots of foreign policy *and* the role of the international political and economic system in transmitting the effects of that policy; to ask not only why the statesman chose one policy over another, but why other options were closed to him—this is how I came to view my task as I confronted the complexities of European stabilization after 1918, in which foreign and domestic politics and economics were inextricably linked.

A dissertation and first book probably constitute the most valuable learning experience of an aspiring historian. More than in any classroom or other project, it is here that the novice confronts the technical, interpretive, and stylistic problems of historical writing. It is with this deep sense of personal enrichment that I record my acknowledgments. My thanks go first to my mentors at the University of Chicago: F. Gregory Campbell, who as patient teacher and friend encouraged my pursuit of the history of international relations, and William H. McNeill, whose breadth of interpretive insight and stylistic guidance cannot be praised enough. Despite his vast responsibilities, he always makes time—hours and hours of it—for students. To have worked under Professor McNeill is a great privilege.

The most welcome help is often help unlooked-for. In the course of my research I was greatly aided by M. Jean Laloy, Directeur des Archives et de la Documentation, M. Maurice Degros, Conservateur en Chef, and the archival staff of the Ministry of Foreign Affairs in Paris; P.

H. Desneux and the archival staff of the Ministry of Foreign Affairs and Exterior Commerce in Brussels; the staffs of the Service historique de l'Armée de Terre, Vincennes, the Archives of the Senate and National Assembly, the Archives Nationales, and Institut de France, Paris, the Public Record Office, London, and the Archives Générales du Royaume, Brussels. I am also indebted to Agnes Peterson and the staff of the Hoover Institution, Stanford. Mme. Renée Duval-Deschanel kindly permitted me to view the Paul Deschanel papers, M. André Lorion the André Tardieu papers, and M. Stanislas Mangin the Charles Mangin papers.

Special gratitude is due to those friends and colleagues who were generous with advice, ideas, and encouragement. I thank Denise Artaud of the University of Paris and Jacques Bariéty of the University of Strasbourg, whose suggestions for research and lines of inquiry were invaluable. I also thank my contemporaries in the floating community of scholars in Paris: Peter Berger, Edward D. Keeton, David K. Miller, and Joel Blatt, all of whom directed my attention to materials that contributed to the final text. Charles S. Maier, Duke University, deserves mention for his friendly oral criticism and his own exemplary research in this period.

I am greatly indebted to Jon Jacobson, University of California/Irvine, and Gerhard L. Weinberg, University of North Carolina/Chapel Hill, for their careful reading of the manuscript and expert criticism. Gerald D. Feldman, University of California/Berkeley, offered valuable advice regarding revision and the innumerable details of the publishing process. I thank Émile Karafiol of the University of Chicago and Thomas C. Childers, University of Pennsylvania, for moral support beyond the call of duty, and John G. Gagliardo, Boston University, whose teaching and friendship over a decade have been my assurance that history is a worthwhile pursuit.

M. Jacques Pennès, Chevalier de la Légion d'Honneur, graciously approved the use of the "Sennep et Gassier" cartoons as illustrations. Adrienne Morgan drew the map and Peter Stern helped in preparing the index. Grace O'Connell expertly typed the final manuscript. I also thank the Committee on Research of the University of Calfornia/Berkeley for providing funds to support preparations of the manuscript. To all the above I owe the contributions of this work; errors of fact or interpretation are my own.

Berkeley, California
April 1978

ABBREVIATIONS

A.A.	Auswärtiges Amt (German Foreign Office)
A.F.R.	Armée Française du Rhin
A.G.R.	Archives Générales du Royaume (Royal Archives, Brussels)
A.N.	Archives Nationales (Paris)
A.O.B.	Armée d'Occupation Belge
B.G.	Besetzte Gebiete (occupied territories)
B.N.	Bibliothèque Nationale (Paris)
B.R.	Büro des Reichsministers
B.SS.	Büro des Staatssekretärs
CAB	Cabinet Minutes (British)
CdR	Commission des Réparations
Corr.	Correspondence (collection)
C.S.D.N.	Conseil Supérieur de la Défense Nationale
C.S.G.	Conseil Supérieur de la Guerre
D.B.F.P.	Documents on British Foreign Policy
Des.	Despatch
Dos.	Dossier
E.M.	État-Major
E.M.A.	État-Major de l'Armée
E.M.G.	État-Major Général
F.O.	Foreign Office (British)
F.R.U.S.	Foreign Relations of the United States
G.Q.G.	Grand Quartier Général
H.C.F.	Haut-Commissariat Français
H.C.I.T.R.	Haut-Commission Interalliée des Territoires Rhénans
I.F.	Institut de France (Paris)
Let.	Letter
M.A.E.	Ministère des Affaires Étrangères (French Foreign Ministry)
M.A.E. Bel.	Ministère des Affaires Étrangères (Belgian Foreign Ministry)
M.G.	Ministère de Guerre (French War Ministry)
M.I.C.U.M.	Mission Interalliée du Contrôle des Usines et Mines
Pap.	Papiers (collection)
PdC	Président du Conseil (French Premier)
Pers. Let.	Personal letter
P.R.O.	Public Records Office (London)
P.-V.	Procès-Verbal (-aux), minutes of proceedings
Rive Gauche	Left Bank of the Rhine
Tel.	Telegram

France's
Rhineland Diplomacy,
1914-1924

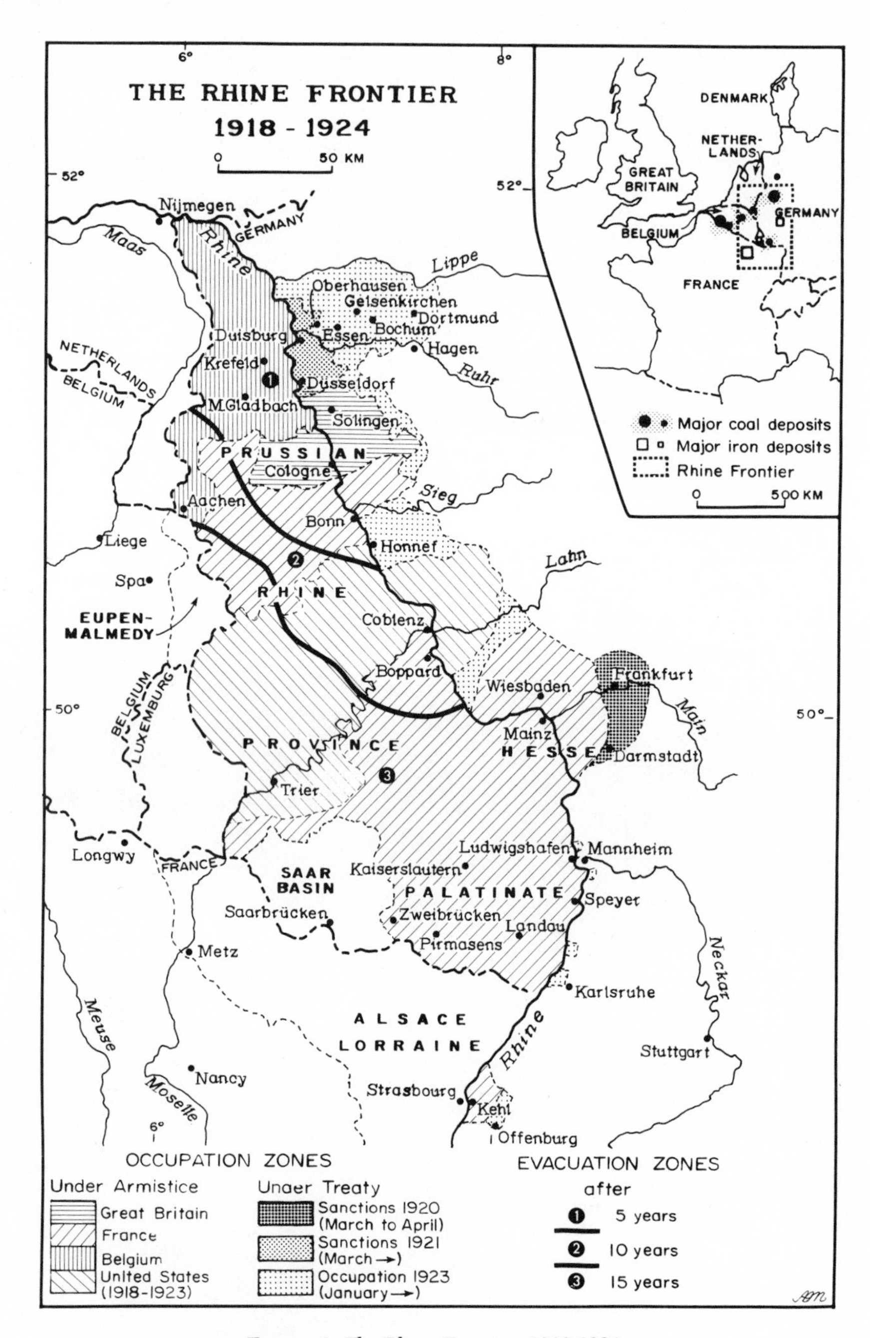

FIGURE 1. The Rhine Frontier, 1918-1924.

INTRODUCTION

"It was in 1915 the old world ended," observed D. H. Lawrence. Surely it was the casualty lists of Ypres, Champagne, and Loos, confirming the awful suspicion that the opening slaughters of the Great War were not aberrations but would be repeated again and again in hideous hyperbole, that shocked the European consciousness out of past illusion. A sense of Europe's agony, and of the victors' determination that such a war must never recur, provides the starting point for an understanding of the interwar years. As in the Atomic Age of the 1950s, the technology of destruction seemed to have outdistanced man's power for social organization, for control of his own behavior. The toys of war had become too dangerous for men to remain immature enough to use them. The leaders of the Paris Peace Conference were united in their desire to fashion a sophisticated peace, designed not to gird their states for future conflicts but to prevent them.[1]

Given the common intent of the victorious coalition, why did the Paris Peace Conference fail to restore political stability to the European continent? In part, it was because the Treaty of Versailles was not designed to be a European peace. Both Woodrow Wilson and David Lloyd George represented extra-continental empires with worldwide interests. The eclipse of Europe itself was manifested in Wilson's dream of a world system. Europe would merge into the world to be governed, not by principles derived from its own experience, but by universal intuitive principles—the Open Door, national self-determination, and collective security. The balance of power itself—and not its breakdown under the force of nationalism—was deemed responsible for the war. Frustration, not indulgence, of nationalism was the sin to avoid. Only reluctantly did the Anglo-Saxon powers commit themselves to the future defense of France—less willing yet were they to guarantee a European balance. The purpose of the German peace

[1] The concept of "hyperbolic war" is developed in Raymond Aron, *The Century of Total War* (Garden City, N.Y., 1954), pp. 19-22. These general remarks on the agency of the First World War and the role of the Paris Peace Conference in the transition from a "European" to a "world" political system are inspired in part by the judgments of Pierre Renouvin, *Le Traité de Versailles* (Paris, 1969); Helmut Rössler, *Ideologie und Machtpolitik, 1919: Plan und Werk der Pariser Friedenskonferenz* (Göttingen, 1966); Hajo Holborn, *The Political Collapse of Europe* (New York, 1951); Ludwig Dehio, *Germany and World Politics in the Twentieth Century* (New York, 1967), and *The Precarious Balance: Four Centuries of the European Power Struggle* (New York, 1962), in addition to the works cited below.

was to liquidate the war as a prelude to a new world order, not a European one.[2]

Had European politics *per se* been transcended? To be sure, from the vantage point of the second postwar era, the great tragedy of Versailles seemed to be the defection of America, which threw Europe back on its own resources and permitted the renascence of German power. But the American political defection need not have been so damaging. Just as the European balance of the nineteenth century had rested on division and balance within Germany, so the world's repose depended on balance within Europe. Yet French pleas at the Peace Conference for a weakening of Germany as a *prelude* to supranational organization were incomprehensible to the Anglo-American leaders. They suspected France of seeking hegemony, or at least believed French continental preoccupations to be antithetical to the requirements of world order. But by renouncing the balance of power, they granted Germany's preliminary war aim. The Reich had sought to escape the bounds of the continent by consolidating it, to form the basis for *Weltpolitik*. France was a power in full retreat. Throughout the interwar years, she sought, not to project continental power onto the world stage, but to focus what world power she could—colonial armies and Anglo-American alliances—onto a narrow stage, to restore balance on the Rhine. The Anglo-Americans' resistance to France's European policy, as well as the vacuity of their own world policies, determined the fragility of European stabilization in the interwar years.

Another great misunderstanding among the well-intentioned peacemakers concerned the requirements of postwar social and economic stability. Why did the Peace Conference not lay the foundations for economic reconstruction on which a political settlement could rest? Why did the Big Three fail to reconcile their own economic interests, to regulate the interallied debts to free investment capital, to stabilize

[2] For the American conceptions of the task of the Peace Conference, see above all Arno J. Mayer, *Political Origins of the New Diplomacy, 1917-1918* (New Haven, 1959), and *The Politics and Diplomacy of Peacemaking, 1918-1919* (New York, 1967); also N. Gordon Levin, Jr., *Woodrow Wilson and World Politics: America's Response to War and Revolution* (New York, 1968); Klaus Schwabe, *Deutsche Revolution und Wilson-frieden* (Düsseldorf, 1971), and the standard works on the American delegation in Paris: Ray Stannard Baker, *Woodrow Wilson and World Settlement*, 3 vols. (Garden City, 1922-1923); Edward M. House and Charles Seymour, eds., *What Really Happened at Paris, 1918-1919* (New York, 1921); Arthur S. Link, *Wilson the Diplomatist* (Baltimore, 1957); Seth P. Tillman, *Anglo-American Relations at the Paris Peace Conference of 1919* (Princeton, 1961).

The phrase "Anglo-Saxon powers" was used constantly by the French themselves to refer to Britain and the United States. I have retained it in the text in order to convey French sensitivity to the waxing power and cultural impact of the English-speaking nations.

exchange rates torn loose from the gold standard, to reintegrate Germany into the European economy without threatening the security and prosperity of the beleaguered victors? John Maynard Keynes accused the Allied delegations of having no interest in or understanding of the requirements of economic recovery. Without a reforging of prewar economic ties, Keynes held, attempts at political stabilization were chimerical. The Big Three, led in this respect by Wilson, did not agree with Keynes's priorities. They did not disinterest themselves in economic questions, but they subordinated them to political ones. Economic aid and investment would be premature unless Europe first made an end to revolution and international strife.[3]

In fact, both Keynes and Wilson failed to understand the degree to which politics and economics were intertwined in such questions as the Allied war debts, German reparations, or industrial raw materials distribution. The Big Three elected to put off economic decisions for months or years, but the terms of the financial settlement with Germany, and among the victors themselves, would determine power relationships in postwar Europe as much as the boundary settlement. Finally, the victors and vanquished alike, pressured by public opinion anxious for "business as usual," hastened to dismantle the command economies forged during the war. But the World War had clearly shown national economic strength to be the business of governments, responsible for national security and prosperity, and not of capitalists alone. At the very moment when diplomacy assumed the task of postwar economic stabilization, governments relinquished much of their power to act in this sphere.[4]

Failing to account for the degree of politicization in economic relations, the Big Three failed to agree at Paris on a strategy for the preservation of the peace they craved. Wilson envisioned a world of peaceful evolution based on international law and self-determination, backed by collective security. In combination with his Open Door economic program, this necessitated the rapid reintegration of an economically un-

[3] See Denise Artaud, *La reconstruction de l'Europe, 1919-1929*, Clio Series (Paris, 1973), pp. 9-17.

[4] The problem of economic demobilization is now beginning to attract scholarly interest. See Gerald D. Feldman, "Economic and Social Problems of the German Demobilization, 1918-1919," *Journal of Modern History* 47, no. 1 (March 1975), with comments. On the political problems and economic pressures for decontrol in France, Germany, and Britain, see the older works by Maurice Baumont, *La grosse industrie allemande et le charbon* (Paris, 1928); M. Olivier, *La politique du charbon, 1914-1921* (Paris, 1922); and Étienne Clémentel, *La France et la politique économique interalliée* (Paris, 1931). More recent treatments include R. H. Tawney, "The Abolition of Economic Controls, 1918-1921," *Economic History Review* 13, no. 1 (1943); and Susan Armitage, *The Politics of Decontrol of Industry: Britain and the United States* (London, 1969).

fettered German national state into the councils of the victors. But the American government itself refused to extend the financial aid that could have stabilized the world economy without new European sacrifices and concomitant social unrest. Instead, Wilson endorsed a punitive peace—not permanently to weaken Germany, but to serve as an example for would-be aggressors. The ambiguity of the President's public utterances led all parties in France to see in Wilson an advocate of what they considered a "just peace."[5]

Within the British delegation, Keynes and others argued for a mild peace with Germany, coupled with a general annulment of debts to promote world recovery. They represented the youthful and brilliant generation of economists in Europe and America who placed their faith in economic expertise as the technology of world peace. In their view political conflicts were trivial and ought not to interfere with the demands of "the economy"; right-thinking economists could synthesize the antidotes to war—prosperity and trade—if the poisons of political rivalry were driven or bled from the body of nations. "Expert" considerations, however, always seemed to dictate advantage for Germany and sacrifice for the bloodied victors. Why had the war been fought if German economic domination on the continent was now seen as natural and unavoidable? In the coming years, French governments fearful of, but resigned to, German recovery demanded prior political guarantees. But at the same time industrial and financial sectors in all countries invoked their importance to "the economy" to avoid the sacrifices required for European political detente.

Contrary to the Keynesian trend in the British delegation was the attitude expressed by Sir Eric Geddes, First Lord of the Admiralty: "We must squeeze the German lemon until the pips squeak." The slogan was appealing to the electorate and the policy was calculated to compensate Britain for the loss of her financial and maritime supremacy to the United States. Reacting to the echo of its own wartime propaganda, the British delegation at Paris contributed some of the harsher clauses of the treaty, particularly in reparations. But the resultant treaty was all the more problematical for the insincerity of the British contribution. After 1919 the Foreign Office and the Board of Trade sought to revive their German trading partner quickly and neutralize the French policy of "guarantees."[6]

[5] The confusion in France over the true Wilsonian attitude toward the peace with Germany is analyzed in depth by Pierre Miquel, *La paix de Versailles et l'opinion publique française* (Paris, 1972).

[6] Major works on British policy at the peace conference include Tillman, *Anglo-American Relations*; Harold I. Nelson, *Land and Power: British and Allied Policy on Germany's Frontiers, 1916-1919* (London, 1963); David Lloyd George, *The Truth About the Peace Treaties*, 2 vols. (London, 1938).

To the French survivors there was no doubt that France's contribution to the war effort had been the greatest. She had provided the battleground, a generation of men, her national treasure. The pillars of her prewar foreign policy—a disproportionately large and excellent army, the alliance with Russia offsetting Germany's demographic superiority, and the financial power that had always been the basis of French influence in a number of strategic areas—had all been swept away. French casualties were the highest per capita of any belligerent, which, given her feeble natality, increased the disparity with a "Germany of seventy millions." A shrewd, large-scale foreign investor in 1914, France now owed 22 billion gold francs to her allies. Finally, a wide swath of northern France was devastated, including important mining and industrial areas. In a war decided in a "storm of steel," underdeveloped and crippled France became largely dependent on foreign economic contributions. The French army, largest in Europe in 1919, was under pressure from public demands for a sharp cut in the term of service, from Allied accusations of militarism and calls for disarmament, and from the critical deficit in the French budget. But military force would be needed to oblige Germany to pay reparations, lest the whole cost of repairing the devastation fall to the French treasury. Peace would bring no financial respite.

Who had foreseen a war in which victory proved more terrible than all the defeats of the past? If France had regained the Lost Provinces, the war nevertheless had evolved into a desperate fight for survival. If Germany had been thrown back in the end, peace only spawned in France a consciousness of increased peril, for it had failed to destroy the aggregation of demographic and industrial power that had upset the prewar balance. Instead, a war justified by the need to preserve France's Great Power position within the European system ended with the collapse of the system itself. The price of victory was the self-sufficiency the war had been fought to preserve.

Georges Clemenceau accordingly presented a peace program narrowly European in spirit. If he sought above all to preserve the wartime alliance, it was to focus Anglo-American power on the Rhine, to maintain the balance struck in 1918. But the opposition shown by Wilson and Lloyd George to the French proposals for security, reparations, and industrial relations meant that the French program was also contradictory. Fear and recognition of France's depleted resources dictated the necessity of transforming the Western alliance into a permanent anti-German instrument. To the extent that the Allies resisted such an interpretation of the alliance, France's adherence to their liberal program was irrelevant to her security and recovery. French ambitions, drawn from an unwillingness to accept that France had fallen from the ranks of the Great Powers, demanded the deliverance of France from the trammels placed on her by the Western alliance. Given Anglo-American protection of a united Germany, France must seek alliances in Eastern Europe, use force to prevent a full revival of German strength, and resurrect a local balance of power.[7]

The Treaty of Versailles, therefore, was a product of conflicts among the victor nations and within their governments. It was a compromise among strategies for political stabilization and it charted no path at all for economic stabilization. If Clemenceau prevented immediate reintegration of the Reich at full economic capacity, he failed to win permanent material guarantees. Disarmament, reparations, economic constrictions, a fifteen-year occupation of the Rhineland—the safeguards were temporary and conditional. Above all, the treaty was self-consciously an interallied creation, dependent for its execution on continued Allied unity of purpose. As one statesman remarked, "The peace imposes Napoleonic conditions and seeks to execute them with Wilsonian methods."[8]

Since the treaty created no accepted "system" for postwar Europe, the Entente powers did not agree on an interpretation of its goals, or on the responsibility of the signatories for its execution. Allied unity did not survive the treaty's ratification. The moral strength of the political settlement depended on American association with it; all hopes for rapid economic recovery relied on American participation. With American failure to ratify, the treaty, which had already been condemned as insufficient by a wide spectrum of French opinion, became virtually *caduc*. In the wake of America's withdrawal, Britain, too, opposed reparations and hoped for political stabilization through promotion of Weimar democracy.

Given the disaffection in France with the Treaty of Versailles, and its rupture through the falling off of her allies, it would be surprising indeed if the shorthand description of postwar French policy, "integral

[7] See Renouvin, *Le Traité de Versailles; idem, Histoire des relations internationales*, Vols. 7-8: *Les crises du XXe siècle* (Paris, 1958); Jean-Baptiste Duroselle, *La politique extérieure de la France de 1914 à 1945* (Paris, 1965); *idem, Les relations franco-allemandes de 1914 à 1950* (Paris, 1967); Arnold Wolfers, *Britain and France between Two Wars* (New York, 1940); W. N. Jordan, *Great Britain, France, and the German Problem, 1919-1939* (London, 1943); Piotr Wandycz, *France and Her Eastern Allies, 1919-1925* (Minneapolis, 1962); Kalervo Hovi, *Cordon Sanitaire or Barrière de l'Est? 1917-1919* (Turku, Finland, 1975); Georges Berlia, *Les problèmes internationaux de la sécurité de la France* (Paris, 1967); Maurice Baumont, *Les questions européennes en 1919* (Paris, 1956); Jay L. Kaplan, "France's Road to Genoa, 1921-1922" (Ph.D. dissertation, Columbia University, 1974); K. Paul Jones, "Stresemann and the Diplomacy of the Ruhr Crisis, 1923-1924" (Ph.D. dissertation, University of Wisconsin, 1970).

[8] Pierre van Zuylen, *Les mains libres: La Politique extérieure de la Belgique, 1914-1940* (Brussels, 1950). The statesman was an unidentified Balkan delegate.

implementation of the treaty," accurately reflected reality. The treaty was mutilated; it held no magic for the rightist French parliament elected in November 1919. The only benefit to be salvaged from the wreck of Versailles was the right to act forcibly against Germany in case of default. Under growing pressure to exact reparations from Germany, to secure political guarantees of French security, to ensure the flow of raw materials, particularly coal and coke, needed to sustain French economic recovery, French governments grasped at their rights to sanctions, to force treaty execution, or to force a new settlement altogether.

As early as January 1920, French counsel wavered between a policy of treaty fulfillment and one of revisionism—French revisionism. The governments of the *Chambre bleu-horizon* rebelled against a treaty that left them dependent for the fulfillment of their most vital national interests on the whim of foreign powers. They struck out, tentatively at first, then with determination after the occupation of the Ruhr in 1923, to rectify the nonsettlement of Versailles. They sought to replace the security system aborted by the Allies with a material system of territorial and economic alterations within Germany. They sought to replace the clumsy and unenforceable economic regime with one that would permit French metallurgy to recover as a partner and not a satellite of German industry. They sought to force the Anglo-Americans, through economic pressure on Germany, to grant the financial settlement denied in 1919. But the goal of the various and uncoordinated policies that made up French revisionism was not hegemony, but security, and the resort to ultimate force in the occupation of the Ruhr came only after years of bluffing, pleading, and cajoling with Germany and the Allies, in an effort to secure what public and official opinion in France considered minimum guarantees. Integral implementation of the treaty was only one tactic tried, discarded, and tried again during the frustrating years of European stabilization. It was the perceived needs of the postwar French state, not the clauses of the Treaty of Versailles, that formed the basis of French foreign policy between 1918 and 1924.

Policy in the occupied Rhineland provides the most convenient focus for viewing the development of French revisionism and the interplay of revisionist policies with that of strict execution. For it was the presence of French military force on the Rhine by virtue of the Armistice and treaty that afforded French governments the opportunity to exert force against Germany. Still more crucial is the fact that the political and economic statute of the Rhineland formed the primary target for French revisionist policies. It was through political separation of the Left Bank of the Rhine that French peacemakers first sought permanent security against Germany, and that means was never fully abandoned. In France's struggle to collect reparations and to achieve a secure *modus vivendi* between French and German metallurgies, the occupied Rhineland and Ruhr provided the ideal zone for interference with German economic life. But the interdependency of the Western Allies, increased significantly by the costs of war, meant that all questions bearing on European stabilization were linked. Just as the political benefits to be sought through control of the Left Bank of the Rhine affected French policy in reparations, so did the debacle of French finances and the need for Anglo-American financial support limit French pretensions on the Rhine. Finally, faced with unanimous resistance to their demands and domestic lobbying for a Rhenish policy, French governments flirted with security through subterfuge, again in the Rhineland. Running almost silently through the years after 1919, only to burst forth in 1923 and spill onto the lofty plateau of power politics, was the undercurrent of Rhenish separatism. The abiding hope for German dismemberment best exemplifies the schizophrenic policy of France after World War I: the policy of fear and ambition.

If the Treaty of Versailles failed to supply the French with a blueprint for stabilization, neither did it charm the statesmen of the other interested powers. The British, Germans, and Americans, as well as the Belgians and the Little Entente on occasion, opposed French initiatives with their own familiar brand of revisionism: progressive liberation of Germany from the strictures of the treaty that left her vulnerable to French pressure. The process of stabilization became a struggle between strategies for revision of Versailles, not between simple execution and revision. But the French effort to achieve economic as well as political goals on the international stage through the application of state power conjured up the opposition of indigenous economic elites and sharpened domestic conflict—in France, Germany, and elsewhere—concerning the prerogatives of the state in dictating national economic policy. The heightened conflict between state and interest groups after the experience of war economies and demobilization contributed to the paralysis of postwar diplomacy.

Thus the focus of French Rhineland policy projects onto a larger screen revealing the diplomatic and social instability of the *après-guerre*. Until recently, the years after 1919 attracted little attention from historians. The war guilt question fascinated the diplomatic historians of the interwar decades; the rise of Hitler, the origins of World War II, and the Cold War dominated the historiography of the 1950s and 1960s. To understand the 1920s it was enough to demonstrate the clash of views at the Peace Conference. English-language writers sympathetic to Wilsonianism and receptive to "expert" denunciations of the peace condemned France's "harsh" German policy as destructive of efforts to fashion a "new diplomacy" and injurious to German democracy. Within the context of the Hitler and World War II debates, the 1920s were often dismissed as a kind of Indian summer of politics as usual before the Depression and the Nazi onslaught of the 1930s. They were a false truce or an era of illusions—a hiatus, rather than a comprehensible stage in the transition to a world political and economic order.[9] Only in the last five years has a new generation of historians begun the task of reëxamination of what is now revealed as a crucial turning point in European history.

Several contemporaneous developments demand a reëvaluation of the early 1920s. The first is the maturation of approaches to international relations gauging the interplay of foreign and domestic policy and of social and economic pressures in the formulation of foreign policy. One need not deny the role of personality, power politics, and the autonomous bureaucracy in foreign policy formation in order to assert the role of structural economic and domestic political forces in defining the parameters of state action. French postwar strategy cannot be understood without reference to those domestic constraints in France and Germany that precluded a German policy of fulfillment and gave France little alternative to one of coercion. A second circumstance permitting a new view of the first postwar period is the perspective offered by the European experience in the second postwar period. Not only is the observer struck by the similarity of the problems of industrial integration and security after the two wars; he is also obliged to recognize the subordination of economic interest to political preconditions in the search for secure Franco-German economic unity. The third and indispensable circumstance permitting a fresh look at this period is the availability at long last of the French diplomatic documents released by the Quai d'Orsay in 1972. For the first time we are able to examine French policy from French sources rather than filtered through those of the other powers. It is this conjunction of new approaches, perspective, and documentation that provides the opportunity and justification for this book.

The recent interest in the early 1920s began with the appearance of Ludwig Zimmermann's *Frankreichs Ruhrpolitik* in 1971.[10] Written

[9] Characterization of the 1920s as an era of "illusion" seemed especially appropriate to historians writing from the French perspective. See Jacques Chastenet, *L'histoire de la Troisième Republique*, Vol. 5: *Les années d'illusion, 1918-1931* (Paris, 1960); Pierre Renouvin, *Histoire des relations internationales*, Vol. 7 (Paris, 1957); J.-B. Duroselle, *Histoire des relations internationales de 1919 à nos jours* (Paris, 1953); René Albrecht-Carrié, *A Diplomatic History of Europe Since the Congress of Vienna* (New York, 1973).

[10] Ludwig Zimmermann, *Frankreichs Ruhrpolitik von Versailles bis zum Dawesplan* (Göttingen and Frankfurt, 1971).

from documents captured during the Second World War, Zimmermann's monograph was composed under a *Kriegsmentalität* that renders its interpretation, a one-sided condemnation of French "imperialism," untenable. Stephen Schuker's recent intense examination of the French financial crisis of 1924 and the origin of the Dawes Plan not only corrects Zimmermann's view, but provides a valuable insight into the confused and incoherent process of French decision-making. Above all, Schuker's work indicates that, just as the diplomacy of reparations must be seen within the overall context of the postwar political settlement, balance of power politics were subordinated in the 1920s to the perceived needs of the international monetary system and the politics of international finance, an interpretation suggested by Karl Polanyi over thirty years ago.[11]

The role of international finance—and financiers—in determining the political as well as economic shape of postwar Europe suggests a new look at the socio-economic origins of Germany's hyperinflation and German budgetary and foreign policy in the 1920s.[12] Ernst Laubach, Hermann Rupieper, and Gerald Feldman, among others, have demonstrated the agency of economic interest groups and the government itself in prolonging the postwar inflation that stymied both execution of the Treaty of Versailles and significant social reforms.[13] Rather than reparations undermining the German currency and social stability, therefore, German fiscal irresponsibility can be seen as sabotaging a moderate and fulfillable reparations bill. Marc Trachtenberg has demonstrated the moderation of French reparations policy at the Paris Peace Conference and hypothesized why Anglo-American historians have been blind to the evidence for so long.[14]

[11] Stephen A. Schuker, *The End of French Predominance in Europe* (Chapel Hill, 1976). Cf. Karl Polanyi, *The Great Transformation: The Political and Economic Origins of Our Time* (Boston, 1944), especially Chapter 2.

[12] On the question of continuity in German foreign policy, 1871-1945, and its domestic origins, see Klaus Hildebrand, *The Foreign Policy of The Third Reich* (Berkeley and Los Angeles, 1970), who digests the contributions of V. R. Berghahn, Fritz Fischer, Andreas Hillgruber, H.-J. Jacobsen, Bernd Martin, Hans Rosenberg, Theodor Schieder, Michael Stürmer, Hans-Ulrich Wehler, and others.

[13] Ernst Laubach, *Die Politik der Kabinette Wirth 1921/22* (Lübeck, 1968); Hermann Rupieper, "Politics and Economics: The Cuno Government and Reparations 1922-1923" (Ph.D. dissertation, Stanford University, 1974); Gerald D. Feldman, *Iron and Steel in the German Inflation, 1916-1923* (Princeton, 1977). See also Jean-Claude Favez, *Le Reich devant l'occupation franco-belge de la Ruhr en 1923* (Geneva, 1969); Karl Dietrich Erdmann, *Adenauer in der Rheinlandpolitik nach dem ersten Weltkrieg* (Stuttgart, 1966); the numerous seminal articles in Hans Mommsen, Dietmar Petzina, and Bernd Weisbrod, eds., *Industrielles System und Politische Entwicklung in der Weimarer Republik* (Düsseldorf, 1974).

[14] Marc Trachtenberg, "French Reparations Policy, 1918-1921" (Ph.D. dissertation, University of California, Berkeley, 1974). The emerging new consensus on the modera-

Balancing and in some ways transcending all these works is Charles S. Maier's comprehensive analysis of domestic stabilization in Western Europe after the war.[15] Maier seeks the response patterns of bourgeois Europe to the postwar threat of reform and revolution, and traces the transformation in the relation between state executive power, parliamentary parties, and competing domestic pressure groups. He argues for a drift away from democratic pluralism toward corporatist solutions and reveals French and German foreign policies as expressions in part of domestic conflict. The common thrust of these recent works is toward a new synthesis of this complex period of restructuring. Everyone recognized that one barrier to a stable order in Europe was the German Problem—the threat to the security and economic autonomy of the lesser states of Europe posed by the military and economic potential of united Germany. How could it be solved? A firm commitment of American power to the maintenance of continental stability was not forthcoming;[16] the "pacification" of Germany through the democratic redistribution of power in society (assuming such a linkage is justified at all) was blocked by the leverage of conservative corporatist groups. One is left with the much maligned policy of permanent restrictions on the sovereignty of the German national state—the French solution. Such coercive denial of national self-determination was anathema to historians writing in the Wilsonian tradition, yet since World War II such limitation of sovereignty as prelude to international cooperation has permitted the substantial integration of European states and helped to give the old continent its longest period of peace since 1914.

This is not the place to speculate on the wisdom or folly of past counsels, or indeed whether interwar Europe—like Humpty-Dumpty—was beyond repair. But reassessment of the century's first postwar period is nonetheless overdue. What is still lacking is an analysis of French policy toward Germany that encompasses the entire period of peacemaking through the occupation of the Ruhr; that integrates poli-

tion of the reparations bill and self-conscious German sabotaging of its fulfillment became evident through two American Historical Association conferences in Washington, D.C., December 1976: "Reparations Reconsidered" and "Problems of European Integration, 1919-1929."

[15] Charles S. Maier, *Recasting Bourgeois Europe* (Princeton, 1975).

[16] New studies of American policy toward Germany and Europe after 1918 have interred the myth of American "isolationism" but left open questions about the motives for American investment in Europe in the 1920s. Cf. Schwabe, *Deutsche Revolution*; Werner Link, *Amerikanische Stabilisierungspolitik in Deutschland, 1921-1932* (Düsseldorf, 1970); Joan Hoff Wilson, *American Business and Foreign Policy, 1920-1933* (Boston, 1971). The forthcoming doctoral thesis by Denise Artaud promises a thorough examination of American war debt and financial policy toward Europe in the 1920s.

tics, economics, and finance; and that seeks to describe French policy in its own terms. This study helps alleviate that need with a first synthesis seen from the standpoint of the power that had the most vital interest and took the first initiatives in the search for a solution to the German Problem.

·1·

BEYOND ALSACE-LORRAINE: FRENCH WAR AIMS ON THE EASTERN FRONTIER, 1914-1918

France entered the war with an offensive military doctrine but a defensive purpose. The expansionist French war aims revealed in 1919 evolved from the nature and course of the conflict itself.[1] For the strategic and economic problems that French war aims were to counter in 1918-1919 did not exist in 1914. First, the revelation of the true extent of Germany's power and intentions, next the sacrifices demanded by an unforeseen war of attrition and materiel, then the irreversible dependence on foreign economic and financial power, and finally the collapse of the dynasties in Eastern Europe and the continental order—these factors, developing gradually or only gradually perceived in the course of the war, obliged French governments to endorse war aims beyond the mere recovery of the Lost Provinces, Alsace-Lorraine. Indeed, all the needs of postwar France seemed to point to the efficacy and even dire necessity of extension of French power into Western Germany itself. There Germany's strength could be tapped and transfused into the "anemic victim of her aggression."

The French Rhenish war aims, a compendium of "traditional" desires for annexations, protectorates, and commercial strictures, were unaffected by the dissemination of Wilsonian ideals in 1917.[2] French

[1] As yet there is no study of French war aims to compare even remotely with the exhaustive research on German aims in Fritz Fischer's *Germany's Aims in the First World War* (New York, 1967), the translation of *Griff nach der Weltmacht* (Düsseldorf, 1961). Pierre Renouvin made a first examination of the problem and laid down the grand lines for future research in "Les buts de guerre du gouvernement français, 1914-1918," *Revue historique* 235, no. 477 (1966). See also Nelson, *Land and Power*; A.J.P. Taylor, "The War Aims of the Allies in the First World War," in *Politics in Wartime and Other Essays* (London, 1964); Douglas Johnson, "French War Aims and the Crisis of the Third Republic," in *War Aims and Strategic Policy in the Great War*, Barry Hunt and Adrian Preston, eds. (London, 1977).

[2] Discussion in this chapter is limited to official (i.e., governmental) war aims, and does not treat the announced programs of opposition groups such as the S.F.I.O. To be sure, the governments of Alexandre Ribot and Paul Painlevé in 1917-1918 were obliged to pay heed to the nonannexationist sentiment prevalent on the Left in the Chamber. See Mayer, *Political Origins of the New Diplomacy*, pp. 157-177, 199-214. Evidence concerning the extent and nature of war aims formulation during this period is unfortunately scanty, the bulk of the diplomatic archives having been destroyed during the Second World War. My argument for the essential continuity of French war aims is based, therefore, on the unaltered recognition of the need for extensive "guarantees" against German resurgence after the war. What form those guarantees were to take for Ribot or Painlevé is unclear, although the difference between the war aims of these cabinets and those of Briand and later of Clemenceau seems to be one of degree rather than kind.

governments tactfully concealed the extent of their claims against Germany or cloaked them in Wilsonian rhetoric until 1919. But the advent of Wilsonianism did encourage the formulation of another body of French war aims, directed not against Germany but at France's own allies. Each new loan approved or ton of coal imported to support a total war on French soil revealed to the official consciousness with growing clarity the likely condition of postwar France. Victory might be won, Germany might even be rendered harmless, but what would become of France, mangled and destitute? Demands on Germany must be matched by demands on the Allies—"war aims" of an entirely new ilk. France must be assured continued unity of purpose, financial and economic solidarity with the Anglo-Saxon powers, if she were to survive the peace. In this context, Wilson's apparent internationalism was not entirely unwelcome.

By 1918 the government of Clemenceau had developed two sets of war aims—traditional aims to be extracted from its enemy, and transcendent aims to be begged from its friends. The old requirements of peace demanded the first if European stability were to endure; the new requirements of war demanded the second if recovery were to be achieved at all. His failure to achieve either set of war aims—German disruption or Allied unity—earned Clemenceau the vitriol of his allies and his countrymen alike. But the scope and duality of French war aims were only a measure of the enormity of France's sacrifice and the sudden inadequacy of her own resources to perpetuate her status as a Great Power.

THE RHENISH QUESTION

The essential war aim, supported by the entire spectrum of French opinion, was the restitution of Alsace-Lorraine. It was a justification of the war and a rallying cry for the embattled nation. But the course of the opening battles convinced French observers that war aims had to be based on containment of Germany, whatever it might require. After the stabilization of the Western front in early 1915, the emerging "war aims bloc" in Parliament, confident of ultimate victory, argued the need for further claims against Germany. In a series of articles, nationalist deputy and *littérateur* Maurice Barrès opened the campaign for French war aims on the Left Bank of the Rhine. Postwar France would need a buffer against German aggression. The separation of the Rhineland would provide it, as well as reduce the Reich's economic and demographic strength to that of her neighbors.

Such strategic arguments quickly produced echos. But Barrès' personal contribution to the French "Rhine" literature was his justification of annexation or "organization" of the Left Bank by France on racial and cultural grounds.[3] The cis-rhenian provinces, Franco-German battleground for a thousand years, fell under Prussian control at the Congress of Vienna and had remained unquestionably German for a century. But Barrès revived the myth that the Rhineland was an unwilling captive of Berlin. The Rhenish population, being of Celtic origin, Catholic faith, and Latin culture, was antagonistic to Germanic, Protestant, and authoritarian Prussia. If given the opportunity to choose, Barrès believed, the Rhineland would opt for republican France as in Revolutionary times. In the atmosphere of war, respected French historians hastened to elaborate the myth of Franco-Rhenish affinity. Ernest Lavisse, Alphonse Aulard, and Édouard Driault were among the most distinguished who lent academic blessing to Barrès' thesis.[4] Capturing the imagination of the French Right, the military, and friends of the Church, the Rhenish myth awakened dreams of French expansion to the Rhine.

The government resisted the early calls for an enunciation of French war aims. Premier Réné Viviani instructed the war censor in February and April 1915 to forbid all published discussion of the subject. Articles concerning the peace conditions, he warned, could create an annoying movement of opinion.[5] The government certainly feared circulation of ideas that could foment agitation for a separate peace. But the opposite could also be dangerous. Propagation of ambitious ideas would invite foreign and domestic accusations of French imperialism, or lead the public to expect a peace that might prove unattainable. Silence was the only reasonable counsel.

The government extended this policy to the alliance as a whole. In October 1914 Russian Ambassador Alexander Izvolski requested an exchange of views on war aims, but French Foreign Minister Théophile Delcassé insisted it was "too early to sell the bearskin." Nevertheless, Izvolski was convinced that while French territorial ambitions did not extend beyond Alsace-Lorraine, France's essential goal was the destruction of the German Empire and the greatest possible weakening

[3] Barrès' major writings on the Rhine can be found in Maurice Barrès, *L'appel du Rhin: La France dans les pays rhénans* (Paris, 1919), and *Les grands problèmes du Rhin* (Paris, 1930).

[4] French wartime and post-armistice literature advocating the separation of the Rhineland from the Reich or the destruction of German unity appears in the bibliography. One instructive feature of the propaganda, whose authors ranged from Sorbonne professors to nationalist crackpots, is the absence of *la gloire* and national expansion as justifications. Liberation of the Rhine and restoration of European balance through prevention of German hegemony are the common themes.

[5] Pierre Renouvin, "Les buts de guerre," p. 7.

of Prussia.[6] The French ambassador in Petrograd, Maurice Paléologue, suggested informally that France might seek to extend her influence beyond Alsace-Lorraine into the Rhineland. In March 1915 the Tsar gave his blessing: "Take Mainz, take Coblenz, go farther if you judge it useful."[7] But when an interallied conference was suggested, French President Raymond Poincaré wrote Paléologue personally that "war aims ought not to be discussed. There will be a general *règlement* at the end." The ambassador responded bitterly: "When [Russian Foreign Minister Sergei] Sazonov asks me what impression the imperial confidences produce in the French government, I am forced to answer 'Je l'ignore absolument!' "[8] Paris was concerned with keeping Russia in the war while resisting her ambitious war aims. But silence served France poorly. The Gallipoli expedition obliged Russia to demand assurances that yielded an Anglo-French promise of Constantinople to the Tsar, Turkish gains for Britain, and nothing for France.[9]

The year 1915 fixed the pattern of the war of attrition. To French generals and politicians who had looked for élan to prove decisive, the real elements of modern war revealed themselves: manpower, steel and the iron and coal to produce it, and above all, money. French industry was particularly ill-suited to support the war effort. Before 1914 it was dwarfed by the metallurgies of Germany and Britain. Critics even accused French steel men of "economic Malthusianism," of seeking to limit production for private benefit. But France was sorely lacking in coal, and its richest iron regions were now in the hands of the enemy. During the war, deficiencies could be made good through interallied cooperation, and 1915 and 1916 brought unprecedented experiments in military and economic coordination. Nascent command economies gradually replaced the free market in Britain and France; the two nations pooled their resources and, in the end, fueled their war machine with the financial power of a third, the United States. But peace would come eventually, with France left more dependent than ever on foreign powers for raw materials and investment capital. How could she recoup her loss of economic autonomy?

[6] Tel. 497 Izvolski to Sazonov, 13 Oct. 1914: *Un livre noir: Diplomatie d'avant-guerre et de guerre d'après les documents des archives russes (1910-1917)* (Paris, n.d.), vol. 3, no. 1, pp. 20-21.

[7] Tel. Paléologue to Delcassé, 4 Mar. 1915: France, Archives of the Ministère des Affaires Étrangères-Paris (hereafter cited as MAE), series Paix (hereafter cited as Paix), vol. 164, no. 18.

[8] Let. Poincaré to Paléologue, 9 Mar. 1915; Let. Paléologue to Poincaré, 16 Apr. 1915: Stephen Pichon, unpublished private papers, Institut de France-Paris (hereafter cited as IF Corr. Pichon), vol. 4397, nos. 245-246.

[9] France's war aims in the Near East were eventually recognized by her major allies in a tripartite accord of April 1916, in the bilateral Sykes-Picot Accord of 9 May 1916, and in the Ribot government's St. Jean de Maurienne agreement with Italy of April 1917.

The powerful combine of French iron and steel interests, the *Comité des Forges*, was preoccupied by the coal shortage. The recovery of the Lost Provinces with the rich Lorraine iron deposits would only aggravate matters. In a postwar struggle for markets, the high price French industry must pay for coal would cripple French firms at a time when they must be seeking ever wider markets for their expanded capacity. On 28 October 1915 Secretary-General Robert Pinot testified to French industrial needs before the Senate Committee of Economic Expansion. The return of Lorraine would increase French coal and coke deficits to thirty and seven million tons per year, respectively, leaving France gravely dependent on foreign combustibles for an industry basic to national power. If, on the other hand, France found a secure source of coal, the return of Lorraine could double her steel capacity and make her the equal of Germany. He urged that annexation of Alsace-Lorraine be matched by annexation of the Saar with its rich coal deposits.[10] But Saar coal was unsuitable for coking and of little use to French metallurgy. In July 1916 the *Comité des Forges* adopted a formal resolution: "Any extension of French territory beyond Alsace-Lorraine *and beyond the Saar* could only simplify the problems that recovery of Lorraine would create for France by providing combustibles, new markets, and the transport facilities of the Rhine."[11] The failure to solve French coal problems, Pinot warned, would make France a second-rate power.[12]

The enhanced dependence of France revealed by modern war produced a reaction expressed in terms of power political war aims. The Rhineland now assumed economic as well as strategic importance. But the potentialities of the remarkable Allied cooperation also suggested themselves, and it was in 1916, before American belligerency, that French officials first considered a second approach to the problem of peace. Planning for postwar financial and economic problems fell almost by default to the French minister of commerce, Étienne Clémentel. While wartime premiers and their ministers of armaments and finance were preoccupied with the management of a total war, only Clémentel was free—at this early stage—to consider France's postwar requirements. His long tenure in office, from October 1915 to November 1919, lent continuity to French economic planning. He presciently expected little in the way of an indemnity once Germany

[10] Robert Pinot, *Le Comité des Forges au service de la nation* (Paris, 1919), pp. 206-235.

[11] Renouvin, "Les buts de guerre," p. 10 (my italics). See also Ferdinand Friedensburg, *Kohle und Eisen im Weltkriege und in den Friedensschlüssen* (Munich and Berlin, 1934), pp. 34-39.

[12] Pinot, *Le Comité des Forges*, pp. 230-235.

was beaten, and based his hopes for French recovery on the preservation of Allied economic unity. Encouraged by the success of Allied wartime cooperation in raw materials distribution, price and marketing controls, as well as mutual exchange supports, Clémentel dreamed of making these permanent features of the world economy. Although he had developed a theoretical dislike for "the anarchy of the marketplace," his plans for postwar cooperation were founded on precise judgments of French interest. The German economy must be restrained, even as her military expansion was contained; the French economy must be subsidized by her great allies if it were not to collapse upon the shock of peace.[13] These considerations led Clémentel to sponsor the Paris Economic Conference of June 1916, where the "second set" of French war aims was revealed. There the European Allies pledged to continue economic solidarity past an armistice, to act jointly against German economic resurgence and for their own reconstruction. To the extent that France must remain dependent, at least she might guarantee that her dependence would not be used against her by the enemy or by allies reverting to economic particularism.

French war aims policy shifted under the leadership of Aristide Briand, premier since October 1915. In his ministerial address, Briand confined his war aims to restitution of Alsace-Lorraine and Belgian independence, but he reversed this reticent policy in 1916. Under relaxed censorship, not only rightist papers but the *grands journaux* of Paris publicized war aims of wider scope. *L'Echo de Paris* and *Le Petit Journal* demanded annexation of the Saar. *Journal des Débats* proposed neutralization of the Rhineland, and in the *Revue des Deux Mondes*, ex-Foreign Minister Gabriel Hanotaux insisted on the dissolution of the German Reich. The idea found support in *Le Matin*, *Figaro*, and other mass circulation papers. A flood of new pamphlets appeared, going beyond those of the previous year in advocating Rhenish separation or the smashing of German unity. In the other direction, none questioned the government's program of Allied unity in peace as well as in war.[14] Allied solidarity in reconstruction—meaning cheap coal, financial relief, and restrictions on German competition—was becoming a French war aim.

Military opinion developed in accordance with the journalists'

[13] See Clémentel, *La France et la politique économique interalliée*. Clémentel's planning for the postwar period is described and analyzed in Trachtenberg, "French Reparations Policy," pp. 4-35.

[14] A member of the Senate Foreign Affairs Commission, d'Estournelles de Constant, deplored the outpouring of "imperialist" sentiment and later accused the government of having subsidized the press campaign. Note, de Constant to M. de Selves (president of the commission), 27 June 1918: MAE Paix, vol. 165, nos. 2-17.

new ambitions. In August 1916 Poincaré asked Marshal Joseph Joffre to study conditions for an armistice. He returned instead a peace program: Alsace-Lorraine and the Saar to France, three or four independent states on the Left Bank of the Rhine, the breakup of Prussia within rump Germany.[15] In October, the cabinet, military, and parliamentary leaders all gathered at the Elysée to consider French interests on the Rhine. No firm policy emerged, but whatever the solution adopted, Briand declared, France must have the major voice in its determination. But could this be achieved in the context of a grand coalition? The Belgian government-in-exile at Le Havre reacted first to the change in French policy. Baron Gaiffier d'Hestroy, ambassador in Paris, reported that Briand and the Quai d'Orsay under Director of Political Affairs Philippe Berthelot, had taken up the policy of Louis XIV. Domination of the Rhineland by France alone, he felt, meant encirclement for Belgium. Belgian interests were more in tune with the thoughts of veteran French diplomat Jules Cambon, who favored an independent Rhenish republic guaranteed by the Western alliance as a whole.[16]

The decision to air France's new ambitions and to seek Allied approval seems to have been dictated by a concatenation of pressures at the beginning of 1917. The German peace note, Wilson's request for definition of war aims, and fears about the reliability of the Russian war effort all suggested the need to press French claims By 1917, the Allies had not even recognized Alsace-Lorraine as an Allied war aim, much less French interests on the Rhine. On 12 January 1917 Briand summarized the French view on "the general directions of future accords." Alsace-Lorraine was not the only question; without guarantees the recovery of those provinces would be in vain. But England, he wrote, must recognize that French goals in the Rhineland were not dreams of conquest. "The organization of these territories, their neutrality, their provisional occupation are to be envisioned," Briand insisted, "and it is important that France, being most directly concerned, have a preponderant voice in the solution of this grave question."[17] The Rhenish question had become a diplomatic reality.

[15] Joseph Joffre, *Mémoires du maréchal Joffre*, 2 vols. (Paris, 1932), II, 253.

[16] Minute #6266, 4 Apr. 1915; Tel. #7676/2703 Gaiffier (Paris) to Beyens (Le Havre), 25 Sept. 1916; Tel. #7714/3050 Gaiffier to Beyens, 21 Oct. 1916; Tel. #7656/3020 Gaiffier to Beyens, 18 Oct. 1916: Belgium, Ministère belge des Affaires Étrangères-Brussels (hereafter cited as MAE Bel.), Classement B (hereafter cited as CLB) 348, dos. Sort de la Rhénanie, 1914-1919.

[17] Des. Briand to P. Cambon, "Projet," 12 Jan. 1917: Stephen Pichon, unpublished private papers, Ministère des Affaires Étrangères-Paris (hereafter cited as MAE Pap. Pichon), vol. 4, nos. 101-108.

The occasion for an exchange of views with Russia arose during the Allied military conference in Petrograd in early 1917. French Minister of Colonies Gaston Doumergue carried instructions that looked beyond wartime strategy. Tsar Nicholas received him on 3 February and agreed that France needed firm guarantees against Germany, given the "phony humanitarianism" of Woodrow Wilson, which he likened to that of Theodore Roosevelt at the time of the Russo-Japanese war. Doumergue responded with the French plan: Alsace-Lorraine and the Saar to France, the Left Bank of the Rhine made into independent states temporarily occupied by France. The Tsar approved and Paléologue wired Paris for authorization to conclude a written accord. Philippe Berthelot saw "only advantage in consecrating by a written accord the conversations of Doumergue with the Tsar," and he began drafting a project. It would refer in general terms to the support France and Russia would lend each other "to secure all military and industrial guarantees necessary to the security and economic development of the two nations."[18] But this was not the agreement signed at Petrograd.

Believing they had the Quai d'Orsay's approval to proceed *in situ*, Paléologue and Doumergue plunged ahead with a draft of their own that detailed precisely the French program in Western Germany. When news of the pact reached the West, there was consternation. Camille Barrère, ambassador in Rome, and Paul Cambon protested the specification of French aims, and Cambon also feared the impact the note would have in London. To make matters worse, the Russian ambassador in Paris called at the Quai d'Orsay on 16 February with instructions to negotiate a similar formula for Russia's western boundaries. The French considered their Rhineland agreement the *quid pro quo* for the 1915 Constantinople pact. Now Russia asked further concessions that posed an obstacle to an independent Poland. Paléologue insisted that he and Doumergue had promised no such exchange, but Briand and Izvolski took up the vague Paris draft promising mutual support and letters were exchanged on 10 March.[19]

Ten days later Briand fell from power. It was several months before the facts of the Doumergue mission were made known before a parlia-

[18] Tel. Paléologue to Briand, 1 and 4 Feb. 1917; Tel. Berthelot to Paléologue, 9 Feb. 1917: MAE Paix, vol. 164, nos. 63-70, 81. See also Tel. 507 Petrograd to Izvolsky, 12 Feb. 1917; Foreign Ministry Note #26 to Paléologue, 14 Feb. 1917: Friedrich Stieve, ed., *Iswolski im Weltkriege, 1914-1917* (Berlin, 1925), pp. 211-213.

[19] Note Pokrowski (Russian Foreign Minister) to Paléologue, 14 Feb. 1917; Des. P. Cambon to MAE, 17 Feb. 1917; Tel. Paléologue to Berthelot, 27 Feb. 1917: MAE Paix, vol. 164, nos. 98, 100, 119. Tel. 97-98, 101, Izvolsky to Petrograd, 10-11 Mar. 1917: *Livre noir*, vol. 3, no. 4, pp. 172-174, 186-187.

mentary inquest.[20] But by then an event of far greater impact had swallowed the war aims convention—the first Russian Revolution had ousted the Tsarist government. The provisional government's Foreign Minister Paul Miliukov labeled the exchange of letters "a mistake."[21] The French government, now headed by Alexandre Ribot, could only agree.

The French war aims initiative fared no better in London. The first French agitation for a Rhenish policy in the spring of 1915 had produced a series of worried despatches from British Ambassador Lord Bertie that prepared the British government for the eventual French demarche. By December 1916, when Asquith was replaced as prime minister by Lloyd George, British peace plans for Europe hinged on the best means of restoring a balance of power.[22] The return of Alsace-Lorraine, and some recognition of French interests in the Saar, could serve this purpose, but Foreign Secretary Arthur Balfour and Lloyd George both saw French Rhineland ambitions as a destabilizing element. Balfour preferred to restore continental balance through commitment of British power in the form of a permanent Western alliance. The entry of the United States seemed to remove the need for this unpopular step. Envisioning a European peace based on nationalism and democracy, Lloyd George counted on American power to preclude future German mischief, while French Rhine schemes became all the more dangerous.[23] Paul Cambon waited until July 1917 to recite the Briand program of January, but Balfour balked at the reference to the Left Bank of the Rhine, and showed no inclination to discuss war aims.[24]

The fall of Briand and the entrance of America into the war produced a further shift in French diplomatic strategy, but the war aims themselves continued to evolve along the lines laid down by French conceptions of their own postwar needs. On 5 June 1917 the Chamber of Deputies and Senate passed "peace resolutions." They demanded the return of Alsace-Lorraine and reparations, no more. But they were accompanied by an "omnibus clause" subject to varying interpretations. There must be "durable guarantees for peace and independence for peoples great and small. . . ." The Chamber text expected these to be

[20] The parliamentary inquest and debate concerning the Briand government's "war aims treaty" with the Tsar are summarized in Mayer, *Political Origins of the New Diplomacy*, pp. 209-214.

[21] Tel. Paléologue (for Albert Thomas) to MAE, 3 May 1917: MAE Paix, vol. 164, no. 126.

[22] See Nelson, *Land and Power*, pp. 3-26.

[23] Ibid., pp. 27-52.

[24] Des. P. Cambon to Ribot, 10 July 1917: MAE Pap. Pichon, vol. 4, nos. 122-125.

achieved through a league of nations. The Senate text did not. Publicly, Ribot and his successors Paul Painlevé and Georges Clemenceau retreated from Briand's policy and sought to assure only the restoration of the Lost Provinces "with reparations and the necessary guarantees." In his ministerial address Ribot deplored any *ésprit de conquête*. In September 1917 Painlevé claimed only Alsace-Lorraine and reparations. In January 1918 Clemenceau's foreign minister, Stephen Pichon, outlining war aims in a departmental note, made no allusion to the Left Bank of the Rhine or the Saar.[25] Had official French war aims been altered under Wilsonian inspiration and domestic anti-expansionism, or was the retreat a tactical one? In fact, there were many circumstances suggesting a low profile on war aims, of which the miscarriages with Russia and Britain were only one. American belligerency in April, the desperate campaign to keep revolutionary Russia in the war, and the French army mutinies after May 1917 all required that no further ammunition be given to those who might accuse France of imperialism.

Until the deliberations for the Armistice began, the *Union Sacrée* governments of 1917 and 1918 restricted their diplomatic initiatives to securing Allied recognition of French rights to annex Alsace-Lorraine without plebiscite. The inclusion of this aim in Wilson's Fourteen Points of January 1918 sufficed. But beneath the opaque rhetoric, French war aims continued to evolve in accordance with European political and economic upheavals. In February and June of 1917, officials of the *Comité des Forges* elaborated the dangers of postwar German economic hegemony if France's raw material needs were not met. The financial crippling of the French government, borrowing unprecedented sums at home and abroad to support the war, demanded an aggressive policy of reparations on the one hand, and an ever closer cooperation among the Allies on the other, if the French currency and standard of living were not to plummet, rendering battlefield victories illusory. France might have to look to Germany not only for annexations but for coal and capital. If references to occupation or "organization" of the Left Bank of the Rhine were dropped from French official war aims, some limitation of German sovereignty was implicit in Ribot's call for "necessary guarantees" retained in his ministerial address at the behest of Poincaré.[26] The *Manchester Guardian*, reporting Painlevé's ministerial address, lauded the abandonment of "the am-

[25] Note Pichon, 27 Jan. 1918: MAE Pap. Pichon, vol. 4, nos. 238-243. Cf. Taylor, "War Aims of the Allies," pp. 93-122.

[26] Raymond Poincaré, *Au service de la France, neuf années de souvenirs*, 10 vols. (Paris, 1926-33), IX, 78-79.

bitious program of the chauvinists relative to the Left Bank of the Rhine," but followed by reporting that Painlevé "asks that the treaty include effective guarantees to protect the society of nations against aggression."[27]

It remained until the Armistice negotiations for France's allies to discover that the "guarantees" sought by Clemenceau did not differ from those demanded by Briand. In fact, they had increased. In October 1917 the Quai d'Orsay circulated a memorandum entitled "Preliminary Note on the Reorganization of Germany." In this project the dual nature of French war aims emerged. To ensure French security, the Left Bank of the Rhine must be neutralized and the Rhenish railroads placed under international administration. To prevent postwar German economic expansion at the expense of the exhausted Allies, the German Zollverein must be shattered and the Reich restructured into a loose federal state. To achieve both of these goals, France and Britain must conclude a permanent military alliance matched by a permanent economic alliance with France's creditors, Britain and the United States.[28] The advent of Woodrow Wilson and the "changed nature of the war" did not temper French war aims, for they could not change French perceptions of their postwar requirements. The return of Alsace-Lorraine would not suffice.

ARMISTICE

The hopes engendered by America's entry into the war did not fail to affect French opinion.[29] But formulation of war aims rested with the cabinet, which in turn depended on a Chamber whose "sacred union" had become increasingly difficult to sustain. By late 1917, the convoluted process of party politics had limited Poincaré's choices for premier to Joseph Caillaux, "defeatist" advocate of negotiated peace, and Georges Clemenceau. If neither represented the war aims bloc, the

[27] *Manchester Guardian*, 19 Sept. 1917.

[28] MAE Memo, "Note préliminaire sur la réorganisation de l'Allemagne," 27 Oct. 1917: MAE Paix, vol. 67, nos. 3-6.

[29] See Ebba Dahlin, *French and German Public Opinion on Declared War Aims* (Stanford, 1933); Mayer, *Political Origins of the New Diplomacy*; and Miquel, *La paix de Versailles*. The problem of evaluating the impact of Wilsonian rhetoric on public opinion is complicated by the effectiveness of French governmental censorship during the war. Official silence on war aims deepened under the Clemenceau cabinet, whose formation preceded Wilson's Fourteen Points speech (8 Jan. 1918) by seven weeks. Dahlin argues that enthusiasm for Wilsonian idealism forced Briand's successors to retreat from his war aims initiatives. In fact there is no evidence that popular pressure affected official evaluation of France's postwar requirements. When Clemenceau revealed French demands at the peace conference, it was nationalist public opinion that he had to contend with, not Wilsonianism.

Tiger was the only man capable of uniting the embattled nation. For all Poincaré's personal distaste for his old rival, Clemenceau at least could be counted on to pursue the war *jusqu'au bout*. His performance justified expectations. Clemenceau stifled internal dissent, persecuted "defeatists," marshaled all the resources of the nation to the business of survival. Among the requisites of a policy of unity was strictly enforced silence on war aims. As his prestige and power increased with the battlefield victories of the summer of 1918, Clemenceau's secretive and authoritarian rule aggravated not only President Poincaré but the French military and political establishments as well. The most crucial point of debate as victory approached became the strategy for containment of Germany to be consecrated in the peace.

Europe was in total flux, but the epochal events of 1918 permitted Clemenceau to glimpse the shape of postwar Europe. The Bolshevik Revolution and the Treaty of Brest-Litovsk eliminated France's Russian alliance. But recent conventions with the Polish and Czechoslovak national councils committed France to a policy of collaboration with Germany's new eastern neighbors.[30] In the West, French officials all agreed on the necessity of preserving the wartime alliances with Britain, Italy, and, if possible, the United States. Prewar Europe was in dissolution, but the eradication of German military power could permit the foundation of a new balance. Clemenceau determined not to betray the soldiers' victory; but could he prepare for satisfaction of France's demands against Germany in the armistice convention while preserving Allied unity?

When Prince Max of Baden requested an armistice from President Wilson on the basis of the Fourteen Points, Wilson at first left his European allies in the dark. But the Allied general staffs had reported to their governments that the end of the German army was in sight. Accordingly, on 7 October 1918 Lloyd George, Clemenceau, and Italian Premier Orlando met secretly to discuss the basis for a cessation of

[30] To the extent that Clemenceau had the leisure to consider peacemaking during the final battles of 1918, the degeneration of Russia could only have increased the importance of a postwar French presence on the Rhine. Yet the Russian alliance did not disappear from French planning and Paris did not greet the new Bolshevik regime with undiluted scorn. Rather, Clemenceau ignored Lenin's politics in a fervent effort to encourage continued Russian resistance to Germany, even offering vast new arms shipments. After Brest-Litovsk, French policy did turn anti-Bolshevik, but even then it aimed at preserving a "large Russia" to balance Germany in the future. The Civil War forced France to rely solely on the successor states in the end, and the means to exert direct pressure on Germany in the West became vital. See Hovi, *Cordon sanitaire or Barrière de l'Est*, and the excellent, most recent analysis by Michael Jabara Carly, "The Origins of the French Intervention in the Russian Civil War, January-May 1918: A Reappraisal," *Journal of Modern History* 48, no. 3 (Sept., 1976), pp. 413-439.

hostilities. The Fourteen Points had been a useful banner under which to rally their peoples to a last effort, but they could not be permitted to interfere with fundamental national interests. Lloyd George denounced Wilson's call for freedom of the seas in war and peace, and Clemenceau grimaced at the postwar implications of Wilson's "removal of economic barriers," and "reduction of armaments." But the most direct challenge to French security aims was contained in Wilson's Four Principles and Five Particulars addresses of 11 February and 27 September 1918. How could Germany be rendered innocuous if "peoples and provinces must not be bartered about from sovereignty to sovereignty"? How could Allied cooperation be maintained if there were to be "no alliances within the League of Nations" or any "economic combinations between League members"? The armistice presented an opportunity to attack these questions.

The armistice terms were a military problem. Germany must be placed in a position from which her army would be incapable of resuming hostilities. But the military terms had a political goal: to ensure that Germany would be forced to accept whatever peace terms the Allies might impose. Most important, the armistice would play an important role in the determination of those peace terms. This meant that the Allied armies must gain through the armistice a de facto geographical and legal position that would make it difficult for the Anglo-Americans to refuse France's peace proposals. Clemenceau, Lloyd George, and Orlando unanimously agreed that the armistice terms were best left, in the first instance, to the military experts. They wired Wilson accordingly.[31]

French leaders themselves were not unanimous in their desire for an armistice. Poincaré saw German peace feelers as a trap to divide the Allies. German forces were in full retreat; the next push would carry French troops onto German soil. Anything short of total victory could jeopardize French war aims. On 7 October the President outlined his arguments to Clemenceau and Pichon. "An armistice that will sap the élan of our troops and not place us in a position to negotiate as conquerors would be a great peril," he warned. Failure to occupy Alsace-Lorraine could lead to ideas of autonomy there instead of union with France. Failure to occupy portions of Germany would give France no guarantees of German compliance with the armistice. Finally, Poin-

[31] Cf. Pierre Renouvin, *L'Armistice de Rethondes* (Paris, 1968), pp. 195-220; Keith L. Nelson, *Victors Divided: America and the Allies in Germany, 1918-1923* (Berkeley and Los Angeles, 1975), p. 91; Mayer, *Politics and Diplomacy of Peacemaking*, pp. 53-89, describes the failure of socialist and labor minorities to force public acceptance of the Fourteen Points on their governments.

caré believed that an armistice satisfying these fears was impossible, for the Germans would never sign it.[32] Clemenceau angrily reminded the constitutionally weak President not to interfere. He was fully capable of seeing France's interests for himself and he offered to resign rather than let more French sons die without need. The President submitted, but he still considered an armistice unjustifiable.[33]

Poincaré took his case to Marshal Foch, who had his own controversy with the Tiger over the bounds of their respective jurisdictions. Foch shared Poincaré's anxiety for a "war aims" peace, but he believed it could be accomplished through an armistice. The Germans were beaten and would sign anything; the Allies were the stumbling block. On 16 October he asked Clemenceau whether adequate guarantees would be included in the armistice. What were the French plans for the Rhineland, outright annexation or buffer states? Finally, would the Quai d'Orsay assign a liaison to the Supreme Command to keep him informed of the government's intentions?[34] Again Clemenceau reacted sharply, reminding Foch that political matters were outside his competence. The liaison request was denied.[35]

To Clemenceau the issue was the integrity of his authority. To Poincaré and Foch it was equally their fear that the premier did not share their estimation of "necessary guarantees," i.e., the occupation of the Rhineland.[36] But their worries were unnecessary. Clemenceau shared the view that the armistice must give France "securities in the hand, currency with which to overcome opposition at the peace conference."[37] If French demands for security and reparations—and Allied solidarity in peace—were to carry the day at the conference, then the armistice terms must point toward them. And the arguments dictating a Rhenish occupation were many: military, political, economic. All

[32] Let. Poincaré to Pichon, 7 Oct. 1918: IF Corr. Pichon, vol. 4398, no. 51.

[33] Let. Poincaré to Pichon, 8 Oct. 1918: IF Corr. Pichon, vol. 4398, no. 52; MS Loucheur, "Incident Clemenceau-Poincaré," 9 Oct. 1918: Louis Loucheur, unpublished private papers, Hoover Institution, Stanford (hereafter cited as HI, Pap. Loucheur), Box 12, Folder 10.

[34] Ferdinand Foch, *Mémoires pour servir à l'histoire de la guerre* (Paris, 1931), VII, 278. See also Jere King, *Foch versus Clemenceau: France and German Dismemberment, 1918-1919* (Cambridge, Mass., 1960), p. 13.

[35] Raymond Recouly, *Le mémorial de Foch, mes entretiens avec le maréchal* (Paris, 1929), pp. 43-45.

[36] Let. Poincaré to Pichon, 9, 10, 11 Oct. 1918: IF Corr. Pichon, vol. 4398, nos. 53-55. The feud between Poincaré and Clemenceau was of long standing. Clemenceau all but accused Poincaré of seeking a presidential despotism during the 1912 campaign. During the entire period of the armistice and peace conference, Poincaré was forced to use Foreign Minister Pichon as an intermediary between himself and the premier. Poincaré wrote Pichon scores of letters, daily during periods of crisis.

[37] Foch, *Mémoires*, p. 447. Georges Clemenceau, *The Grandeur and Misery of Victory* (New York, 1930), p. 90.

vagaries and misunderstandings could be made good, once France had a means of pressure to back up her program in Germany. Clemenceau turned around and instructed Foch to draw up the terms for an armistice. They must be the equivalent of unconditional surrender.

Marshal Foch presented his proposals to the Supreme Council as the minimum guarantees necessary to ensure that Germany could not renew hostilities. In the West he asked for occupation of the Left Bank of the Rhine and bridgeheads by Allied troops, and for a fifty-kilometer neutral zone on the Right Bank. The German army would retreat behind the neutral zone and lay down the bulk of its arms. Alsace-Lorraine would not be "occupied," but placed directly under French sovereignty. The British negotiators, led by Lloyd George and Sir Douglas Haig, recognized that Foch's program was in part political. But their resistance, based on unspoken distrust of French intentions and fear of jeopardizing German acceptance, was worn down under the pressure of Foch's military arguments. On 24 October Wilson "admitted" the Allies to his German negotiations. The next day American Commander John J. Pershing endorsed a Rhineland occupation at French headquarters at Senlis.[38] On 1 November American plenipotentiary Edward M. House, despite Wilson's expressed misgivings and the warnings of American General Tasker Bliss, also bowed to Foch's judgment. The British then gave their assent, demanding in their turn the surrender of the German fleet.[39] One element remained to complete the "preliminary peace" of the armistice. On 2 November Clemenceau introduced the question of reparations. He succeeded in persuading the Americans to accept what amounted to German recognition of an open account for reparation of all war-related damage. No economic or political details were discussed—it was in no one's interest to risk Allied unity at this point—but the armistice placed France in a de facto military position whence to defend her particular demands. It laid the foundation for the treaty edifice to be designed hastily in the months to come.

What of the Fourteen Points? Faced with British and French resistance to aspects of Wilson's program, Colonel House threatened a separate peace rather than compromise American principles. When the Entente powers refused to yield, House produced an "interpretation" of the Fourteen Points on 29 October 1918 that endorsed Britain's posi-

[38] According to Nelson, *Victors Divided*, p. 38, Pershing was at this time unaware of the political significance of the Rhine occupation.

[39] Colonel House and Lloyd George seem to have been softened by Clemenceau's promise that the French army would withdraw from the Rhine "after the peace conditions have been fulfilled" (Tel. House to Wilson, 30 Oct. 1918: *Foreign Relations of the United States* [hereafter cited as FRUS], 1918, supplement 1, vol. I, pp. 425-426).

tion on freedom of the seas and France's position on economic freedom and disarmament. But the point of principle went to House. All parties would sign the armistice with the recognition that peace would be concluded on the basis of the Fourteen Points. Wilsonianism survived as the official philosophy of the Paris Peace Conference, but it was not to provide a smokescreen behind which Germany could prepare a new expansionism. On no other basis could the Entente powers permit international reconciliation to proceed.[40]

Foch's opinion was borne out. Despite mutterings of betrayal, the German government authorized Matthias Erzberger to accept Foch's terms. Germany was given two weeks to disarm and evacuate all occupied territory, a further eight days to evacuate the Left Bank of the Rhine, three more to clear the fifty-kilometer zone. The Allied armies would follow behind, restoring Alsace-Lorraine to France, and placing the Rhineland and four bridgeheads across the Rhine under occupation. Thus, the military object of the Armistice was accomplished. But was the political object fulfilled? Did the Armistice place Germany in a position from which she could resist the eventual peace terms? Enemies of Clemenceau's peace, pointing to the effective circumvention of the treaty in postwar years, would come to answer, "No." A "premature armistice" had failed to bring Germany to its knees, to impress upon the Germans the reality of defeat. The critiques were unfair. In November 1918 an overwhelming preponderance of military force seemed all that was necessary to enforce compliance. The complexities of political and economic stabilization, the rupture of the Western alliance, much less the unprecedented maneuvers by which Germany would evade the treaty's thrusts in a thicket of economic chaos, could scarcely be glimpsed.

Another fact of the Armistice was equally pregnant. France had triumphed, but only as part of the greatest coalition ever assembled. It was unlikely that she would be so blessed if again she faced a Germany in arms. The armistice placed the original French war aims on the solid logic of *force majeure*. Conditions would never again be so propitious for ensuring that Germany's broken sword would not be reforged. Addressing the Chamber of Deputies on 5 November, Clemenceau recognized the impossibility of neglecting to take whatever guarantees were necessary to prevent another holocaust. In the same breath he assured the deputies that Allied unity would survive victory. In fact,

[40] House was convinced of the continuing integrity of the Fourteen Points. He wired Wilson that ". . . nothing will be done to embarrass you or to compromise any of your peace principles. You will have as free a hand after the Armistice as you now have" (Charles Seymour, ed., *The Intimate Papers of Colonel House*, 4 vols. [Boston, 1926-28], IV, 174).

Clemenceau's dedication to continued Allied unity, itself the expression of France's "second set" of war aims, provided the skeptical Allies with the only guarantee they needed that an armistice occupation would not prejudge the Rhine settlement. At Senlis, House had held in reserve his ultimate weapon to ensure French acquiescence to American wishes: the threat of a separate peace.[41]

The conflicts to arise between the two sets of French war aims were hinted at in the struggle over the Armistice. But France's agony was both her justification and most compelling argument for a peace whose safeguards were as material as the war's destruction, and for Anglo-American cooperation in France's economic and financial reconstruction. As Colonel House wrote confidentially to French Ambassador Jules Jusserand: "France has given the most in manpower and economic sacrifice to the cause of liberty and democracy. Indeed, France is the one country in Europe near to economic ruin from the war. She can never be in a position even to attempt world domination. Even with Alsace-Lorraine her recovery will be slow—without it, almost impossible."[42]

Given House's sympathetic view of the problems of peace that France would face, the French government permitted itself to harbor hopes that Allied solidarity would survive the armistice, whatever the eventual settlement with Germany. To Clémentel, who began in 1918 to formulate solid programs for Allied economic recovery, the German settlement was important, but contingent. The command economies of the Western belligerents must not be dismantled, but expanded into an international economy within which France could draw on Anglo-American strength in finance and raw materials. Above all, French diplomacy must prevent America from withdrawing into isolation, or Britain into imperial preference.[43] If this were achieved, German reparations would be secondary. On 19 September 1918 Clémentel presented Clemenceau with his scheme for the continuation of wartime agencies as a premier French war aim. *Mitteleuropa* might prove impossible to prevent, he wrote, but a Western economic bloc would more than balance it. On 28 September Clemenceau, Clémentel,

[41] Seymour, *Intimate Papers*, IV, 135-136. See also the discussion by Nelson, *Victors Divided*, pp. 16-24.

[42] Appendix, "Note communiquée à titre confidentiel par le Col. House," Pers. Let. Jusserand (Washington) to Pichon, 31 Jan. 1918: IF Corr. Pichon, vol. 4397, nos. 102-103.

[43] British economic planning for the postwar period has been most recently treated by Robert E. Bunselmeyer, *The Cost of the War, 1914-1919* (Hamden, Conn., 1975). Until late in the war, British economic and governmental leaders seriously considered Allied tariff unity and imperial preference as two means of blunting the German postwar challenge (pp. 34-59).

Pichon, and André Tardieu adopted the letter as the basis of postwar French economic policy. The rigor of French reparations policy would depend in large part on American willingness to subsidize French recovery.[44]

It remained for Foreign Minister Pichon, perceiving the tension between France's two sets of war aims, to counsel the French Senate three days before the Armistice that the work of peace would be no less arduous than war. "The era of difficulties begins," he said.

[44] Clémentel, *La France et la politique économique interalliée*, p. 347. Notes of the 28 September meeting may be found in the Archives Nationales, Paris, Archives of the Ministry of Commerce, F^{12} 8104, dos. Propositions des ministères, cited by Trachtenberg, "French Reparations Policy," pp. 22-25.

·2·

RHENISH SEPARATISM AND PARIS PEACEMAKING, 1919

The French peace delegation did not envision its task as one of obstruction. Clemenceau's resignation to France's new dependence obliged him to reconcile his own war aims, based on the narrow requirements of European balance, and the transcendent principles of the Wilsonian world view. The tragedy of 1919 was the incapacity of the Big Three to synthesize their geniuses. Instead, they crossed purposes, each sterilizing the creativity of the others. France's understanding of continental necessities, expressed in its security program of Rhenish separation and economic strictures on Germany, seemed antithetical to the self-determination of nations, not potentially constructive in terms of international integration and the supranational League. But prior to the Rhineland struggle in March and April 1919, the feeble League Covenant, promising no viable instrument to prevent aggression, and the shocking revelation of American economic aloofness, had already shattered illusions about the contribution the United States was willing to make to European stability. Thus, Wilsonianism proved unavailing to both sets of French war aims.

The product of Paris was a massive political compromise. In the hope of preserving American power in Europe, Clemenceau sacrificed his demand for Rhenish amputation, a demand supported by a wide spectrum of French opinion. But the complementary aim of preserving Allied economic cooperation ran counter to American principles of the Open Door and hopes for rapid rehabilitation of a democratic Germany. This, in turn, obliged France (and Britain) to pursue a "Carthaginian" reparations policy. As Allied unity dissolved steadily throughout the year, the opportunity and the domestic pressure for a renewed Rhineland policy became irresistible. The fifteen-year occupation of the Rhine won from the Allies offered post-Versailles French governments the chance to enforce or revise the decrepit treaty—for political and economic security—through direct pressure on Germany. The Rhenish question survived as France's only leverage in the struggle for European stabilization.

The course of the Peace Conference is well known. The shadowy elements in the equation were the indigenous Rhenish separatist movement, which offered a brief hope of a Rhenish policy acceptable to the Anglo-Americans, and the French military administration on the

Left Bank of the Rhine, which quietly and purposefully laid the groundwork for a continuing French Rhineland policy. Here were the links of continuity between the war aims of the previous years and the revisionism of the years to follow Versailles.

THE TIGER OF FRANCE

Georges Clemenceau's political career began in the whirl of foreign invasion and civil war of the Commune of 1871. When he accepted the prime ministry in 1917, his career reached a climax only to find itself in the same maelstrom, now whipped broader and deeper, whence it began. Again a great German army besieged the fatherland, and again France threatened to divide before the enemy. When the squat, walrus-moustached septuagenarian moved his office into the Ministry of War and announced his intention to unite France and defeat Germany, he echoed the mission of the Third Republic whose political life had so closely paralleled his own. But in war the goals and enemy were clear; peacemaking, where allies became adversaries and policies fluid and uncertain, proved more strenuous for the Tiger. His energy put to shame aides and ministers thirty years younger and an anarchist's bullet in the right shoulder did not keep him from the conference table, but the hourly combat, against his allies and constituents alike, wore down his imagination, as the strain of the Paris conference did to all trapped in its frenzy. Hopeful at the outset of placing French war aims within the context of Wilson's world view, Clemenceau by the end of the conference came to stand on stubbornness alone.

Clemenceau began preparations for peacemaking without illusions—unless it were for his faith in the power of his own personality. He shared neither the vision of the prophet Wilson nor the canny empiricism of David Lloyd George. In addition, these men were his juniors by more than a generation. He could not conceive of a paper treaty capable of reconciling nations for all time and he placed little hope in the German revolution sputtering from Berlin. He prepared to make peace with the only Germany he knew—the Germany of 1871 and of 1914. He was separated from his colleagues by age and mission. In his seventy-eighth year, he was granted the unique opportunity to erase the national humiliation he witnessed in his thirtieth year.

It would nevertheless be a mistake to define the French approach to peace as antithetical to the American.[1] On the contrary, the

[1] Ray Stannard Baker most clearly portrayed Wilson and Clemenceau as antagonists in a Manichaean struggle for the world's soul. Sir Harold Nicolson (*Peacemaking 1919* [New York, 1965], pp. 82-90) admits to a grave conflict of principle at Paris. Such conflicts could be—and were—overcome. What is unfortunate is the fact that the Big Three dele-

Clemenceau team was dominated not by old-guard politicians versed in the Old Diplomacy, but by youthful, vigorous minds raised up by the experiences of coalition warfare and a directed economy. Men like Louis Loucheur, André Tardieu, and Clemenceau's private aides Jules Jeanneney, Georges Mandel, and Henri Mordacq were more likely to be open to fresh ideas than the old guard in the military and in the Quai d'Orsay. The vitriol Clemenceau's peace attracted from these quarters attests to the Tiger's very willingness to forgo a measure of French interest and to experiment with new international forms. That he was able to do this, despite the near unanimous opposition from within, was a measure also of his unquestioned authority.

Clemenceau demonstrated his jealousy of authority against Poincaré and Foch in the Armistice debate. But his doctrine of exclusivity applied to all functionaries who shared state responsibility, and it became all the more sacred during France's fight for survival.[2] As minister of war, he retained direct control over his generals; by appointing weak men to other ministries, he reserved direction of affairs. "Pams, Nail, Pichon," the premier said of his ministers, "nice fellows. They had only one fault. They were too decent, not made for war."[3] The influence of the Foreign Ministry, already reduced by four years of war, declined further. Through special aides and commissions, like André Tardieu's in America, Clemenceau bypassed the professional bureaucrats.

Personal rule was fitted to the needs of a nation under siege, as illustrated by the Tiger's words, at once threat and promise, "Je fais la guerre!" But Clemenceau did not alter his style after the Armistice. There were no elections as in Britain after the guns fell silent. Wartime censorship continued and the government grasped tighter its cloak of secrecy. The Chamber adjourned foreign policy debate to give their chief a free hand. The war was not over for Clemenceau until France had won the peace, and that, he warned in February 1919, might prove the hardest task of all.[4]

Clemenceau's power and prestige reached a pinnacle in January 1919. Even political enemies paid him homage as *Père la Victoire*. It was precisely this exclusivity that permitted Clemenceau to negotiate

---

gations exaggerated conflicts of *interest* that prevented a coherent synthesis of the French and American approaches to reconstruction. Clemenceau showed sincere interest in the possibilities of American-sponsored international institutions, especially in the economic sphere, but Wilson identified "liberal internationalism" so closely with American national interests that his principles were prevented in practice from bearing on European needs (Levin, *Woodrow Wilson and World Politics*, pp. 148-153).

[2] Geoffrey Bruun, *Clemenceau* (Cambridge, Mass., 1943), pp. 66-68.

[3] Jean Martet, *Le Tigre* (Paris, 1929), p. 33.

[4] "La guerre est gagnée, mais . . . ," *Le Petit Journal*, 10 February 1919.

freely with his allies. Far from restricted, Clemenceau was more liberated from the pressure of public opinion, parliamentary scrutiny, and military dictates than his British, Italian, or American colleagues. The price paid for this freedom, however, was the scorn of his countrymen and universal disaffection for the peace he helped conceive. "All social activity," wrote Clemenceau, "is a resolution of forces, an association of interests in which the individual and the group cannot serve one another to advantage . . . except by a mutual thrust and counter-thrust."[5] Nevertheless, the Tiger refused to allow this process to work within his own government. By shutting out those who felt a keen desire to share in France's victory—deputies, diplomats, soldiers, the president—Clemenceau left a legacy of bitterness surrounding the compromise of Versailles. And he offered himself as scapegoat for those who argued that France had lost the peace.

French organization for the Peace Conference manifested Clemenceau's design. Scorning parliamentary leaders, especially Briand, who coveted a post as plenipotentiary, Clemenceau named personal collaborators André Tardieu, Louis Klotz, Stephen Pichon, and Louis Loucheur, and diplomat Jules Cambon as delegates. In the official breakdown of responsibilities circulated on 6 December 1918, only Eastern European and Asiatic questions fell to the Quai d'Orsay. Western European problems came under the authority of the minister of war—Clemenceau himself. Economic questions were the joint concern of six ministries, but in the breakdown problems concerning Germany, industrial reconstruction, and reparations were the responsibility of Loucheur.[6] Loucheur was the leading representative of that international class of industrialists who had come to understand, through service in wartime economic agencies, the enhanced economic responsibility of government. With connections in French heavy industry, Loucheur struggled to restructure and expand French metallurgy and to solve France's coal problem at the expense of Germany.

The Quai d'Orsay assumed peacemaking to be the vehicle for a recovery of its influence over French policy. It was not to be. In 1917 Clemenceau had left vacant the office of secretary-general of the Foreign Ministry, which served as a kind of executive-directorate of French diplomacy. Career diplomats were informants, not idea men, to Clemenceau. The "permanent fixture" at the Quai d'Orsay, Director of Political Affairs Philippe Berthelot, played only a minor role at the

[5] Georges Clemenceau, *Au soir de la pensée*, 2 vols. (Paris, 1930), II, 375.

[6] Note, "Documentation française du Congrès," 6 Dec. 1918: MAE Pap. Pichon, vol. 6, nos. 161-164.

Peace Conference.[7] Finally, with Stephen Pichon as foreign minister, Clemenceau assured that the ministry would be in the hands of a loyal collaborator subservient to his direction.[8] It was symbolic that Pichon was moved out of his own office at the Quai d'Orsay to make way for the Big Three.

THE RHINE, FRONTIER OF DEMOCRACY

Peace had come unexpectedly early. Although Clemenceau joined with the military, the Elysée, and the Quai d'Orsay in looking for a solution to French security on the Rhine, a precise formula for security remained to be drafted. The Quai d'Orsay reviewed the war aims literature for ideas. Professor Alphonse Aulard asked that peace be based on the liberty of peoples, but to Aulard this meant the organization of the Left Bank of the Rhine into an independent republic. Édouard Driault also called for a peace of nationalities, but such a peace required severing Germany at the Rhine and the Elbe. Geographer Onésime Reclus, André Sardou, and others saw the peace of Europe eternally threatened unless German unity were undone. The Foreign Ministry adopted this theme as its general conclusion: "The German and Austrian empires cannot survive in their present form and must be broken up if peace is to be assured."[9] Gabriel Hanotaux celebrated the Armistice by drafting his own suggestions for the government. The Peace of Westphalia must be the model for France; balance within Germany must be restored. "Above all, it is important that England, Belgium, and France join to solve the *Rhenish question*. . . . The populations west of the Rhine, more Celtic than Germanic, must be freed from Prussian tyranny. A prolonged occupation of the Rhine would facilitate this arrangement and perhaps lead to the dissolution of the Reich."[10]

[7] Note Tardieu, "Quelques remarques," n.d.: André Tardieu, unpublished private papers, Ministère des Affaires Étrangères-Paris (hereafter cited as MAE Pap. Tardieu), 3e versement, vol. 4. "Berthelot, tout à fait mal avec Clemenceau, n'a joué aucune rôle, d'aucune sorte, pendant les huit premiers mois de la Conférence. . . ." Berthelot was a close collaborator of Briand, who was also feuding with Clemenceau at this time.

[8] The evidence of Pichon's ineffectual ministry abounds. See, for instance, Jean Jules Henri Mordacq, *Le ministère Clemenceau, journal d'un témoin*, 4 vols. (Paris, 1930-1931), III, 118, 180-181. Pichon, whose career had been to a great degree tied to Clemenceau's, was also accused of being dominated by the Tiger during their first partnership, 1906-1909. A talented and staunchly republican statesman, Pichon suffered from apparent irresoluteness compounded in 1918-1919 by the loss of influence of the Quai d'Orsay and by his own physical strain, which brought on a complete breakdown late in 1919.

[9] MAE Memo, "Conditions de la paix," Nov. 1918: MAE Paix, vol. 165, nos. 67-89.

[10] MAE Memo, "Deux notes de M. Hanotaux," 11 Nov. 1918: MAE Pap. Tardieu, vol. 44, nos. 1-2 (italics in original).

Marshal Foch was in complete agreement. His note of 25 November 1918 provided the skeletal form for the policy given official blessing until the end of March 1919. Foch identified the security of all Western Europe with that of France. The Rhine, as Woodrow Wilson had once pronounced, was the frontier of democracy. The peace must provide for a permanent occupation of this single natural barrier by the Allied powers and for the creation of independent states on the Left Bank of the Rhine. To offset Germany's manpower superiority, the Rhenish states would be integrated into the western military bloc.[11] Foch's plans fit Clemenceau's requirements well. Never an annexationist, Clemenceau was nonetheless acutely aware of the need to prevent a return of German military power to the Left Bank of the Rhine. It was not only the Western balance that was at stake. In the hectic weeks following the Armistice a pattern of European relations evolved in French councils. If Poland and Czechoslovakia were to replace the Russian barrier to German expansion, France must have the capability to take offensive action into Central Europe. Political separation of the Left Bank would not only facilitate French military control of the Rhine bridgeheads; it would also weaken Germany substantially in manpower and industry. A similar arrangement would be considered for the east—restoration of Poland's 1772 borders and neutralization of East Prussia.[12] But the primary consideration for Clemenceau was that the Rhine occupation be an interallied operation. An international force on the Rhine showing the flags of Britain and the United States as well as France would ensure Germany's respect as well as allay fears of French annexationism among the Allies. Clemenceau deleted Foch's reference to Rhenish military service, which could never be reconciled with Wilson's principles, and adopted the marshal's note as the French position.

Foch elaborated his ideas in a second note of 10 January 1919, while Tardieu gathered supporting arguments for Rhenish separation. His *Comité d'Études*, managed by historian Ernest Lavisse, produced eighteen separate studies justifying the French program for Western Germany, and Tardieu went to work on the famous brief to be revealed to the Allied delegations—when the moment was ripe for discussion of the Rhine. As Tardieu argued in a preliminary note to Lord Balfour of 6 February 1919, Rhenish separation did not contradict the principles of the League of Nations; rather it was the necessary cornerstone of the edifice. No annexations were desired, no profit to any power, only the security of the democracies on whom the League would depend. "The

[11] Note Foch, 25 Nov. 1918: MAE Paix, vol. 165, nos. 44-51.

[12] Piotr Wandycz, *France and Her Eastern Allies*, pp. 35-36.

principles behind this measure," Tardieu concluded, "appear indisputable. It remains only to seek the best means for their realization."[13]

The best means for realization of French aims on the Rhine were the subject of some dispute. Despite French preparations, Clemenceau balked at raising the Rhenish question until four months after the Armistice, and seven weeks after the opening of the Peace Conference on 18 January. Why was the most important plank of the French peace platform left untouched until anxieties and clashes of interest had already damaged relations among the Allies? In part, the answer lies in the reasons for the delay of the Peace Conference itself: Wilson's resolution to attend, the British elections, the Christmas interlude, and Wilson's insistence on priority for the drafting of the League Covenant. But there was also the question of French tactics, and here Clemenceau and his professional diplomats parted ways. As early as 3 October 1918, Ambassador in London Paul Cambon urged immediate Franco-British consultations if France were to secure her war aims. "But a policy!" he lamented. "That requires resolution and clarity. Pichon has the perception and intelligence, but he has lost his will—he is paralyzed by fear of Clemenceau and allows those prattling imbeciles, who believe themselves made for foreign policy, to impose."[14] Tardieu courted American support, but Wilsonian principles, Cambon wrote, were the major threat to a French peace.[15] France must come to a prior settlement with England and tackle the large questions of the peace first, before the arrival in Europe of President Wilson.[16] In December, France's fiery ambassador at Rome, Camille Barrère, visited Paris to warn Clemenceau and Pichon of the dangers of delay. The foreign minister sympathized, but Clemenceau replied that Lloyd George's "capricious temperament" was an almost insurmountable obstacle to prior accord. He hoped instead to create a conciliatory atmosphere through agreement on lesser issues, and the extensive organizational efforts of Berthelot and Jules Laroche in the Quai d'Orsay failed to impress the premier. The diplomats came away worried and bitter about the Tiger's disrespect for their expertise.[17]

[13] Note, "Le rôle international du Rhin comme frontière de la liberté," 20 Jan. 1919, forwarded 6 Feb. 1919: MAE Pap. Tardieu, vol. 49, dos. 1.

[14] Pers. Let. P. Cambon to Barrère, 3 Oct. 1918: Camille Barrère, unpublished private papers, Ministère des Affaires Étrangères-Paris (hereafter cited as MAE Corr. Barrère), vol. 1, nos. 196-197.

[15] Pers. Let. P. Cambon to Pichon, 15 Nov. 1918: IF Corr. Pichon, vol. 4396, no. 150.

[16] Pers. Let. P. Cambon to Pichon, 17 Dec. 1918: IF Corr. Pichon, vol. 4396, no. 151.

[17] Note Barrère, "a.s. de la conférence de la paix," 30 Apr. 1919: MAE Pap. Barrère, vol. 2, nos. 2-9; Pers. Let. P. Cambon to Barrère, 7 Mar. 1919: MAE Corr. Barrère, vol. 1, nos. 118-121.

Clemenceau's inactivity before the opening of the Peace Conference did not stem from indolence, but from tactical differences, although his secretiveness again misled his critics. First, the diplomats had already demonstrated the dangers of their approach through a bungled attempt to play the Americans and British off against each other. On 26 November, Paul Cambon had drawn up his own negotiating plan and presented it to the British with an invitation to forge a common front before Wilson's arrival. The draft had definite virtues. It suggested the rapid formulation of the general lines of the preliminary peace with Germany, a subsequent schedule for Allied debate on pressing questions, then a congress attended by the defeated and neutral powers to negotiate a final treaty. It noted that Wilsonian principles were "insufficiently defined" to form the basis for these deliberations, and suggested that the League principles might instead draw strength from the prior terms to be concluded with Germany. But the British were cool to the idea of prior agreements, and three days later Jules Jusserand presented a similar plan, stripped of its offensive references, to the Americans. Aside from calling into question French sincerity, the demarches discredited the organizational efforts by suggesting the "federalization" of Germany as a principle to be debated. In any case, neither party responded.[18] Two weeks later, Clemenceau and Foch visited London. If this was an attempt at "prior agreement," Clemenceau showed no anxiety to initiate it. Far from attempting to engage the British cabinet in meaningful negotiations, the Tiger even contrived to be absent when Marshal Foch outlined his ideas for the Rhine to Lloyd George. The prime minister's reaction being outwardly cool, the French leaders summarily dropped the matter.[19] There is no doubt that the French drive for "organization" of the conference to come, carried on at least in part behind the back of Clemenceau, was motivated by the desire to "water down" the Fourteen Points still further before official peace talks began. They also served to "signal"

[18] Lacunae in the diplomatic documents of the Quai d'Orsay prevent a confident analysis of the genesis of these pre-peace conference demarches. See FRUS, Paris Peace Conference 1919, I, 344-354. French tactics in this period have long been a source of puzzlement. See the somewhat contradictory treatments by Nicolson, *Peacemaking 1919*, pp. 100-103, and Nelson, *Land and Power*, pp. 135-136.

[19] Cf. Nelson, *Victors Divided*, pp. 67-71, who argues that the French demarches were a blunt and clumsy attempt directed by Clemenceau himself to split the Allies prior to the peace conference. D. K. Watson, *Clemenceau: A Political Biography* (London, 1974), pp. 337-338, suggests that Clemenceau avoided the London confrontation with Lloyd George because he wanted Foch to see for himself how unsympathetic the British were to his ideas and/or because his own later proposals for the Rhine would seem moderate by comparison to those of Foch.

the Allies that France would insist on inclusion of the Rhenish question among the most vital points to be examined at Paris. But far from demonstrating a conviction that the Americans were the primary "enemy" of a French peace, they bear witness instead to confusion in the French camp on that very point, and perhaps can be understood as an attempt by the diplomatic establishment to elbow its way into Clemenceau's councils.

The absence of prior negotiation among the major victors was in part the product of Anglo-American reticence. But after the failure of clumsy French probes, the Paris government, too, came to believe that its negotiating position might be strengthened, not weakened, over time. French diplomats saw in Wilson the major stumbling block to a satisfactory peace. Clemenceau and his American expert Tardieu understood that Britain was the principal enemy of French claims on the Rhine. It would be difficult to argue for a Rhenish occupation or political separation on Wilsonian grounds, as Tardieu was attempting; more difficult still would it be to convince the British that a Rhenish policy was in their national interest. In October it had been American support that had carried the Armistice occupation over British opposition. The Armistice itself had vitiated the Fourteen Points as the strictly interpreted basis for peace, and with Wilson defeated in both houses of Congress in the November elections, his influence was problematical.[20] Clemenceau, on the other hand, had won a four-to-one vote of confidence in the Chamber to pursue a peace of material guarantees. Wilson's "mandate of humanity" must be shown up for the illusion it was, and replaced by the "noble candor" enunciated in the Tiger's Chamber speech of 29 December.

Finally, the timing of French Rhineland initiatives at the Peace Conference was determined by events in another sector altogether—in the Rhineland itself. As if to render credible all the wartime myth-making, an indigenous separatist movement had actually arisen in the occupied territories. The reports from the French armies after December 1918 suggested, first, the prudence of reserving Allied discussion of the Rhenish question; then, by the end of February, the need for immediate decision.

[20] Miquel, *Le Paix de Versailles*, pp. 37-46, supports the contention that the Democrats' electoral defeat severely damaged Wilson's prestige in the eyes of the French and British governments. In the wake of the election, a French journalist tested American opinion by writing directly to the chairman of the Senate Foreign Relations Committee, Henry Cabot Lodge, who heartily endorsed setting Germany's western boundary at the Rhine. Pers. Let. Henry Cabot Lodge to Paulin Herbin, 18 Nov. 1918: MAE Paix, vol. 165, nos. 65-66.

GAINING A FOOTHOLD I

The contrast was unmistakable in the weeks after 11 November 1918 between the discipline of the German retreat, despite hunger and defeat, and the confusion of the Allied advance. Difficulties arose not only from mines, devastation, and straggling German columns, but from command conflicts as well. Dormant antagonisms between commanders found expression in political disputation. All parties soon noted that the coming occupation was a political tool as well as a military one, and respect for the French-dominated Supreme Command quickly waned. Foch's race to the Rhine became a crawl; only by mid-December did Allied units cross the German frontier in sufficient mass to permit occupation of the Rhine bridgeheads. The physical apportionment of the Left Bank and the command structure of the occupation became important subjects of discord.

Foch circulated his first occupation plan on 16 November. He divided the Left Bank into zones corresponding to the size of the contingents each power offered to contribute.[21] The French zone was by far the largest, encompassing the entire Palatinate in the south, Rhenish Hesse, and the Prussian Rhineland as far as the Mosel. The Americans received Coblenz and its hinterland, and were flanked on the north by another French zone from Bonn to the Belgian border. Aachen and all the territory north along the Dutch frontier became the Belgian zone. This left a small island around Cologne to the British. The three major bridgeheads at Mainz, Coblenz, and Cologne would, in Foch's plan, be occupied by troops of all the powers. Within a week all the commands involved had accepted the apportionment with one exception. Sir Douglas Haig asked that the British army be left in sole control of the Cologne bridgehead "as a gracious gesture demonstrating the Marshal's satisfaction with the British contribution in the last months of the war." Foch accepted this proviso, apparently unaware that he was giving the British sole authority over the political and financial hub of the Rhineland.[22]

Foch ordered execution of his plan for 1 December, but five days

[21] Nelson, *Victors Divided*, claims that Foch had political intent in "pushing U.S. troops northeast to Coblenz" while French troops occupied the south. This cannot be demonstrated. It is true that the French command desired to secure the Saar with its own troops, but Foch's plan only succeeded in splitting the French occupation into noncontiguous parts while sacrificing the Rhineland's key political centers, Coblenz and Cologne, to the Allies. It is more likely that the Foch plan derived simply from the armistice positions of the armies, thus facilitating their advance.

[22] Note, Foch to Clemenceau, 6 Dec. 1918: France, Archives of the Ministère de Guerre, Vincennes (hereafter cited as MG), code 6N114 Renseignements Allemagne, dos. 22.

later the American division marked for the French bridgehead at Mainz had not been transferred. When Foch inquired, General Pershing responded with a sharp protest against the principle of interallied bridgeheads—a protest he had not raised in his first note of 18 November. After a week's confrontation Foch relented. By withdrawing the order for transfer of the U.S. unit, Foch satisfied Pershing's stated desire for "unity of command before the enemy," but he also surrendered his scheme for interallied occupation of all zones.[23] The military foundation was laid for a principle later written into the permanent occupation agreement: within its own zone, each occupation authority was answerable only to its own government. If the Allies were not in accord, four policies would exist in the occupied territories, not one.

On 14 November 1918 Foch created the *Service des territoires rhénans*, the first auxiliary organization and the brainchild of Generals Maxime Weygand and Jean Payot. Its duty was examination of administrative dispositions to be taken upon installation of the Allied regime on the Rhine. By mid-December it was clear that several months would pass before Allied diplomacy would determine the Rhineland's permanent status. In the meantime, Foch must forge an administrative tool for the execution of occupation policy. He expanded the *Service* into the *Contrôle-Général des territoires rhénans* and installed it next to his headquarters in Luxembourg.

At the head of the *Contrôle-Général* Foch placed an ambitious thirty-nine year-old civil servant, Paul Tirard. The son of a departmental president, Tirard graduated second in his class at the École Libre des Sciences Politiques and rose rapidly in the ranks of the Conseil d'État. His big break came in 1912 when General Lyautey appointed him his chief civilian aide in Morocco. There Tirard learned firsthand the theories and practice of military administration from the man whose deeds and writings on the subject had earned him tremendous prestige in France. In Morocco, Tirard saw how active associationist policies in economics, education, and justice, matched by paternalistic cultural programs and charities, could pacify a rebellious populace and fashion a model colony. He also gained experience as Joffre's administrator of Alsacian territories retaken in 1914. Foch's selection of Tirard for the Rhineland post was pregnant indeed, for the Rhineland was not North Africa. To Rhenish citizens sensitive to foreign occupation, the cultural arrogance of the French administration was adding insult to injury. Tirard's gratuitous efforts to spread French influence through

[23] Note, Foch to Clemenceau, 6 Dec. 1918, annex 8, 10 Dec. 1918: MG 6N114 Renseignements Allemagne, dos. 21.

careful application of Lyautey's principles only contributed to the military arrogance of his bureaucracy, with important implications for French Rhenish policy. Tirard was the man to carry out a policy of administrative infiltration and usurpation—he was not the man to foster goodwill and reconciliation between France and the Rhineland.

Economics was the key to French influence on the Rhine, Tirard advised. He admitted that the Rhineland formed an economic unity with Westphalia on the Right Bank, but he proposed to smash that powerful relationship and to integrate the Left Bank into the economy of "western Europe." He suggested a customs union between the Rhineland and the West, mobilization of Rhenish industries for the reconstruction of northern France, and a banking network free from Berlin's control. An Allied high commission would execute Allied policy under a civil chief. He would fill the latter post himself. Following close on the heels of the conquering soldier, the rapacious bureaucrat envisioned his fief.[24]

The week after Christmas 1918 Foch and Tirard debated the possible solutions to the Rhenish question. The Rhineland might remain part of Germany, with an interallied occupation as a guarantee of security. Or the Rhineland might be broken up into independent states allied to France. Tirard envisioned their regimes as resembling "self-government for a colony." The first hypothesis would preserve German economic unity and hold out the prospect of vast reparations, but the second would save France the expense of a large occupation. Either would satisfy French security needs.[25] Whatever the Allies' decision, it was the military's duty to create an administrative situation of de facto separation. For there was evidence, which the occupation authorities eagerly relayed to Paris, that the Rhineland would welcome the political separation sought by France.

WATCH ON THE RHINE

Before 1792 the Left Bank of the Rhine formed a patchwork of small ecclesiastical states, the so-called *Pfaffenallee*, a most ineffectual marchland facing powerful France. The Congress of Vienna sought to repair this chink in the German armor through its disposition of the

[24] Note Tirard, "Note sur le statut politique des pays de la Rive Gauche du Rhin," 19 Dec. 1918: MAE Pap. Tardieu, vol. 44, dos. 1 quint.

[25] Tirard, "Rapport sur l'administration des territoires occupés de la Rive Gauche du Rhin pendant l'Armistice" (hereafter cited as Tirard, "Rapport"), submitted to Clemenceau, June 1919: France, Archives of the Haut-Commissariat Français dans les territoires rhénans (hereafter cited as HCF), Archives Nationales, Paris (hereafter cited as AN), vol. 2898, pp. 30-37.

Left Bank in 1814. The Rhinelands would not recover their independence, but would be divided among trans-rhenian states more able to see to the area's defense. Thus, the misty Rhenish Palatinate in the south, a triangle of hilly massif carpeted with vineyards, fell to Bavaria. In the bend of the river south of Wiesbaden there emerged a Rhenish Hesse, incorporating Mainz. In the north, Prussia was the reluctant recipient of vast territories on the lower Rhine. Throughout the nineteenth century this artificial political integration gave rise to a number of grievances. United with Westphalia on the Right Bank, the Prussian Rhineland exploded after mid-century into the greatest industrial concentration in Europe. The Rhineland became Germany's richest jewel, and made the largest contribution to the Prussian treasury, but it received little political consideration in return. Ruled by "foreign" bureaucrats from Old Prussia, the Rhine province's liberalism and Catholicism often placed provincial leaders in conflict with the Protestant monarchist government in Berlin. The Bavarian Palatinate had similar complaints; this time it was the case of a largely Protestant province under the rule of Catholic Bavaria. Neither province enjoyed autonomy; both readily saw themselves as "cows to be milked."[26]

But Rhinelanders did not hesitate to march with Prussia in 1871. The progress and power of the Second Reich easily pushed local dissension into the background. Only after defeat and revolution in 1918 did responsible Rhenish leaders first consider severance of constitutional ties. Threats from within in the form of Socialism and Spartacism, and threats from without in the form of occupation, perhaps annexation, ignited political crisis. It was the collapse of the German war

[26] What is the *Vorspiel* to a political phenomenon such as the Rhenish separatist and autonomist movements of 1918-1919? In one sense, the war and defeat are all that is necessary to understand the political unrest on the Rhine, for without them the movement would perhaps never have arisen at all. But even with the events of 1914-1918, autonomism might not have developed were it not for a century of suppressed antagonism between the Rhine Province and Berlin. Rhenish liberalism, Catholicism, and economic particularism sufficed to make the province an uneasy subject of Berlin. Pertinent works would include Joseph Hansen, *Die Rheinprovinz, 1815-1915: Hundert Jahre preussischer Herrschaft am Rhein*, 2 vols. (Bonn: Marcus & Webers Verlag, 1917); Jacques Droz, *Le liberalisme rhénan, 1815-1848* (Paris, 1940); Herbert Homig, *Rheinische Katholiken und Liberale* (Köln, 1971); Karl Schmitz, *Der rheinische Provinziallandtag, 1875-1933* (Neustadt/Aisch, 1967); Erich Schmidt-Volkmar, *Der Kulturkampf in Deutschland, 1871-1890* (Göttingen, 1962); Wilhelm Spael, *Ludwig Windthorst; Bismarcks kleiner grosser Gegner. Ein Lebensbild* (Osnabrück, 1962); Karl Bachem, *Vorgeschichte, Geschichte, und Politik der Deutschen Zentrumspartei, 1815-1914*, 9 vols. (Köln, 1927-1968); Grünthal Günther, *Reichsschulgesetz und Zentrumspartei in der Weimarer Republik* (Düsseldorf, 1968); Rudolf Morsey, *Die Deutsche Zentrumspartie, 1917-1923* (Düsseldorf, 1966); Gerhard Senger, *Die Politik der Deutschen Zentrumspartei zur Frage Reich und Länder von 1918-1928* (Hamburg, 1932).

effort and fear of the conquerors that brought about the formation of unions for autonomy in many Rhenish towns.[27] But old grievances also surfaced. The Berlin Revolution replaced the centralizing Hohenzollerns with a Socialist government whose philosophy demanded a true *Einheitsstaat.* The Left Bank of the Rhine, in which the greatest political force was the Catholic Center party, looked with suspicion on the Ebert/Scheidemann regime. When Independent Socialist minister Adolph Hoffmann decreed strict secularization of schools in November 1918, the Rhenish autonomist movement swelled and looked to the Center party for guidance.

Behind Bertram Kastert, cleric and Reichstag deputy, one Rhenish faction called for immediate separation of the Prussian Rhineland from the Reich. Party regulars, led by Charles Trimborn, an undersecretary of state at Berlin, advocated autonomy within a federal Reich and sought to avoid hasty action. Five thousand Rhenish representatives assembled in Cologne on 4 December. Center party delegates (though not the party itself) endorsed a resolution for autonomy, but their leaders, including Trimborn, Wilhelm Marx, Matthias Erzberger, and Adam Stegerwald, held back. Liberal and Social Democratic delegates openly opposed autonomy, viewing the revolution as an opportunity to carry German unification to its logical unitary conclusion. Thus, Rhenish "patriots" seeking autonomy or separation did not speak for the whole population.

The separatist movement split. Moderates followed the Center party, looking to the prestigious mayor of Cologne, Konrad Adenauer. Ignorant of Allied intentions or the future course of events in Berlin, the Centrists chose to wait. Followers of Kastert ridiculed this as *Zentrumsschläue.* The separatist diehards found new leadership in Dr. Hans Dorten, a thirty-eight-year-old political dilettante residing in Wiesbaden. Son of a wealthy porcelain manufacturer, Dorten took a law degree from the University of Bonn and served as solicitor for the Prussian administration in Düsseldorf. He neither needed nor enjoyed his career, taking time out for two world tours before the war and resenting a promotion that took him to Berlin in 1914. Mobilized as an artillery captain, Dorten served four years before being cashiered for "violent criticism" of the Kaiser. The Armistice spared him from a court-martial, and he emerged from the war with a monomaniacal hatred for things Prussian. A somewhat foppish and insecure man, given to blaming others for his failings, Dorten was suited to lead a

[27] Cf. King, *Foch versus Clemenceau*, pp. 28-43; Erdmann, *Adenauer in der Rheinlandpolitik*, pp. 21-48; Peter Klein, *Separatisten am Rhein und Ruhr, November 1918-Juli 1919* (East Berlin, 1961).

"movement" that was, in his mind, as committed to the destruction of the "Prussian monster" as it was to loosing the spirit of the Lorelei and the cosmopolitan "génie rhénan." Whatever his personal motive—revenge, boredom, or atonement—Dorten shunned his old career and dedicated his life to the cause of Rhenish independence.

In a series of meetings with Adenauer in December and January, Dorten claimed to have won a promise from the mayor. If he could assure the adherence of both Rhenish Hesse and the French occupation, Adenauer would proclaim a *Westdeutscher Freistaat* at the Rhenish Constitutional Assembly to meet in Cologne on 2 February 1919.[28] But the crafty mayor had other intentions. Adenauer had grievances against Berlin, but at best he desired a certain autonomy for the Rhine province. Separation was a last resort to be adopted only to prevent annexation by France or Spartacism. The collapse of the major Spartacist uprising in Berlin by 15 January seemed to cancel that threat for the moment. No immediate action was called for.

French authorities became aware of the existence of separatist sentiment in the Rhineland soon after their troops crossed the frontier, but the play of factions and motivations escaped them. Rather than a reaction to defeat and revolution, French observers assumed separatism was a manifestation of the traditional complaints of the oppressed Rhinelanders, the *Musspreussen*. The movement arose in November 1918, the French speculated, precisely because the arrival of the Allies would offer the Rhineland the chance to break with Berlin. They fitted their observations into the assumptions of their own Franco-Rhenish propaganda. Thus, the French interpretation was the reverse of the truth. French policy reflected this distortion.

As *Contrôleur-Général* of the occupied territories and Foch's top administrative aide, Paul Tirard was the political and economic arm of the occupation. Intelligence from all French commands filtered through his office on the way to Paris. On 19 December 1918 he reported the existence of a Rhenish separatist movement and suggested it as an alternative to Rhenish separation via the Peace Conference. "The Rhenish people," wrote Tirard, "are in a full crisis of indecision." Their fundamental aspirations were for autonomy, but they were unsure where their best interests lay. Fear of Bolshevism and economic collapse dominated. Tirard therefore argued for an economic policy capable of convincing the population that its interests lay with the

[28] J. A. Dorten, *La tragédie rhénane* (Paris, 1945), pp. 45-46. Erdmann mentions no such "promise" in *Adenauer in der Rheinlandpolitik*. Biographical material on Dorten is derived from the Dorten Collection, Hoover Institution, Stanford; especially the letter sent by Dorten's second wife to David LePan of Ohio State University, 17 Aug. 1963.

West. If France could provide markets for Rhenish industries and create economic ties, a political solution—independent states under Allied tutelage—would follow.[29]

The Quai d'Orsay was amenable to Tirard's suggestions. Paul Cambon had already urged Paris to eschew annexations and to plan a gradual policy based on Rhineland occupation. "If we can content ourselves with a broad autonomy for the Rhineland, our influence will be able to develop and we can perhaps think of something along these lines in the future."[30] In Paris, Berthelot endorsed the idea of gradual infiltration and support for autonomist tendencies. He looked to economic as well as military measures; reparations guarantees, for instance, could include French control of Rhenish mines, forests, and customs.[31] Cambon iterated his views in December. If the French worked quietly and stressed economic ties, the Rhenish population would resume its old sentiments in regard to France, and the British could do nothing to prevent it. "Time is a gallant man," he concluded. "Let us let time work for us."[32]

When Tirard's report reached Paris, the Quai d'Orsay was quick to endorse his economic program, but it also viewed reports of indigenous separatism as a strong argument for delaying the eventual French demarche on the Rhineland vis-à-vis the Allies:

> The preponderance of Prussia has always stifled attempts at federalism in Germany. But today this powerful centralization is enfeebled. . . . Soviets organize in Prussia. The bourgeois elements of the old ecclesiastical country of the Rhine fear these developments and push for separation from Berlin. We have the greatest advantage in leaving this internal movement free to evolve and in not hastening the negotiation of the preliminaries of peace.[33]

To the men on the spot, who were anxious to aid this felicitous movement, action of some sort seemed called for. Marshal Pétain, commander of all French forces in the theater, took initiative in issuing directives to the generals on the Rhine and communicated them to

[29] Note Tirard, 19 Dec. 1918: see n. 24.

[30] Pers. Let. P. Cambon to Berthelot, 4 Nov. 1918, cited by Ludwig Zimmermann, *Frankreichs Ruhrpolitik von Versailles bis zum Dawesplan* (Frankfurt, 1971), p. 20.

[31] Notes Berthelot, "Examen des conditions de la paix," 22 Nov. 1918: MAE Pap. Pichon, vol. 6, nos. 114-134; "Frontières de l'Alsace-Lorraine et le statut de la Rive Gauche du Rhin," Jan. 1919: MAE Paix, vol. 67, nos. 64-67.

[32] Let. P. Cambon to Pichon, 18 Dec. 1918: MAE Paix, vol. 165, nos. 93-95; note, P. Cambon, "Préliminaires de paix avec l'Allemagne; clauses territoriales," Dec. 1918: MAE Pap. Pichon, vol. 6, nos. 194-197.

[33] MAE Memo, "sur le règlement de la paix," 23 Dec. 1918: MAE Pap. Pichon, vol. 6, nos. 175-187.

Foch for approval. Dorten and others sought audiences with local commanders; French officers "ought not to make advances toward civilians but to welcome those that are offered." But Pétain requested authority to go further. The Rhinelanders were insecure about their economic future, he reported, and would turn without hesitation toward France if given incentives. He also mentioned the elections for the German National Assembly scheduled for January. "We can foresee a 'French party' developing. A discreet intervention could aid incontestably." He wanted 400,000 francs for propaganda.[34]

Tirard approved Pétain's instructions and promised a propaganda program. Meanwhile, Foch appealed directly to Clemenceau for instructions. What, he asked, was the policy of France on the Left Bank of the Rhine?[35] The answers were hard to interpret. Clemenceau took action in the economic sphere, ordering his "consuming ministries" (Industrial Reconstruction, Liberated Regions, Marine) to prepare orders for Rhenish industry. It was the first example of the French desire to channel reparations-in-kind through the Rhineland for political goals. But Clemenceau refused to issue political instructions. Instead, he had Pichon reply in vague terms: "It is not to be doubted that we must take it upon ourselves to attempt in every possible way to create on the Left Bank an *état d'esprit* favorable to France. . . . Whatever the conditions that will intervene, they will bear fruit only if the Rhinelanders are not hostile to France."[36]

Clemenceau chose to remain aloof at the height of the separatist agitation in the Rhineland. Economic contacts and propaganda were long-term expedients. Clemenceau made no attempt to conspire with or support the separatist elements; the military received no mandate for involving itself in German politics. If the Tiger's goal was Rhenish separation with the blessing of the Peace Conference, his policy was sound. Intrigues with separatists would only harden Allied opposition, while an authentic autochthonous movement could strengthen the French case for separation. But the military and the French government each pursued an inappropriate policy, for the nature of the separatist activity was lost on them. The occupation authorities believed that the Rhineland would find courage to break with Germany if only given assurance of French protection and economic support. But it was in part from fear of such "protection" that the Rhinelanders considered seizing their own destiny and escaping from defeated Ger-

[34] Let. Pétain to Foch, 30 Dec. 1918: MAE Pap. Tardieu, vol. 44, dos. Organisation de l'Occupation.

[35] Let. Foch (Tirard) to Pétain, 2 Jan. 1919; Let. Foch to Clemenceau, 3 Jan. 1919: MAE Pap. Tardieu, vol. 44, dos. Organisation de l'Occupation.

[36] Let. Pichon to Clemenceau, 9 Jan. 1919, communicated to Foch, 11 Jan. 1919: MAE Paix, vol. 166, nos. 2-3.

many. Clemenceau hoped the separatist movement would develop on its own, but the very inactivity he imposed on the military slowly lulled the fears of Adenauer and other notables about annexation or other "French" solutions. With this threat evaporating, the *raison d'être* for self-imposed separation disappeared.

By mid-January 1919, when no separatist putsch or declaration arose on the Rhine, French observers began to lose faith. Tardieu insisted that Tirard send intelligence on the separatists directly to him, bypassing the Quai d'Orsay. On the fifteenth, Tardieu's military assistant, Colonel Jean Requin, gave vent to the frustration caused by Rhenish inactivity. Rebutting an optimistic report on separatist opinion, Requin scrawled: "Do not hide the fact that the elections we authorized on the Left Bank have weakened the symptoms of separatism that we observed. The Rhenish people attaches itself all the more to Germany as the Bolshevist movement appears to subside."[37]

By the end of January even the occupation's reports turned pessimistic. General Weygand confirmed anti-Prussian feeling in the Rhineland but admitted that the whole region was firmly oriented toward Germany.[38] General Émile Fayolle also noted the effectiveness of Prussian and Socialist countermeasures. "Fear of reprisals paralyzes the demonstration of a desire for rapprochement with France."[39] French authorities recognized that the retreat of revolution in Berlin and Bavaria reassured the bourgeois populace of the Left Bank,[40] but they seized on Fayolle's explanation of Rhenish passivity. Led by Tirard, the occupation advanced the theory that Prussia kept its hold on the Rhine mostly by means of propaganda and intimidation, and thus compounded the Rhenish myth prevalent in France.

On 2 February the Rhenish Constitutional Assembly met in Cologne. Instead of a declaration of independence, Adenauer's ambiguous text endorsed the principle of autonomy and called for a commission to investigate the viability of a Rhenish-Westphalian *Bundesstaat*. But the Adenauer resolution admitted creation of such a state only in

[37] Rapport, service d'administration de l'Xe Armée to Tardieu, "État d'ésprit des populations," 15 Jan. 1919: MAE Pap. Tardieu, vol. 47, dos. Renseignements.

[38] Gen. Weygand, GQG des Armées françaises de l'Est to MAE, "Résumé d'un dossier," 18 Jan. 1919: MAE Pap. Tardieu, vol. 47, dos. Renseignements.

[39] Report, Fayolle to Foch, "Rapport des VIIIe et Xe Armées," 28 Jan. 1919: MAE Paix, vol. 173, nos. 5-8.

[40] The Spartacus League led by Karl Liebknecht and Rosa Luxemburg founded the German Communist Party on 1 January 1919. A mass demonstration on 5 January developed into armed insurrection against the Ebert/Scheidemann regime and Spartacus Week followed. The complete suppression of the rebellion, culminating in the murders of Liebknecht and Luxemburg on the 15th, strengthened the Rhineland's confidence in the Berlin government. Kurt Eisner was assassinated in Bavaria on 21 February.

conformity with the constitution to be drafted by the Weimar Assembly. The commission never met, and the possibility of a Rhenish *fait accompli* under recognized political leaders vanished. Dr. Dorten and the extremists labeled Adenauer's apparent *volte-face* treasonous. They looked for other means to achieve their ends.

The events of 2 February further depressed the French. Instead of providing new impetus to the decelerating movement, Adenauer had applied the brake. The Weimar Assembly would decide the *Westfrage*, the fate of the Rhineland. And Levy Bruhl, reporter for the Peace Conference's *service de documentation*, dispelled hopes that a loosely federated Reich would emerge from Weimar. Hugo Preuss's suggestion of dividing Prussia had widespread support, but would never be carried out, Bruhl perceived, because the other states would not permit it! If Prussia were splintered, the other, weaker states would not survive it and the Reich would congeal. Total centralization would result.[41] As for the Rhenish Center party, Bruhl attributed its autonomism to fear of Bolshevism and Hoffmann's secularization decrees. The Berlin government had since retracted its education program, and separatism and autonomism accordingly declined.[42]

The French government's hands-off policy, with which the military was never sympathetic, had failed to inspire an indigenous Rhenish declaration. Foch demanded new directives. Both the timidity and the content of Adenauer's plan worried the Marshal. A grand Rheno-Westphalian state would be too strong; France was incapable of absorbing into her economy the entire Ruhr basin! The Rhinelanders must be moved to act, and to act in a way compatible with French interests. "Even before the statute of the occupation can be regulated by the conference," Foch urged, "the *Contrôleur-Général* must be in a position to orient our policy on the Left Bank. . . . A public or discreet indication of French intentions, delivered at the proper moment, alone could determine the political evolution."[43]

Again the pleas of Foch and Tirard went unanswered. Tardieu and Clemenceau judged that no action France might take in the Rhineland could aid the cause of separation through diplomacy. But by the end of February the hope for a Rhenish *fait accompli* was gone and a reevalu-

[41] Levy Bruhl to MAE, "Les rapports de la Prusse et de l'Allemagne dans le nouvelle constitution," 5 Feb. 1919: MAE series-Europe 1920-1929 (hereafter omitted: all citations for MAE followed by geographical subheading refer to series-Europe 1920-1929), Allemagne, vol. 267, nos. 10-14.

[42] Levy Bruhl to MAE, "La politique du Centre allemand," 10 Feb. 1919: Allemagne, vol. 267, nos. 59-62.

[43] Let. Foch to Clemenceau, 8 Feb. 1919: MAE Pap. Tardieu, vol. 47, dos. Renseignements.

ation was in order. Upon receipt of Tirard's monthly summation, Paris analyzed the situation. The policy of the Center was opportunistic and tended toward rupture with Prussia, not with Germany. Also, Adenauer's vision was the antithesis of the French plan for several Rhenish states confined to the Left Bank. On the other hand, the people of the Left Bank might still accept a separatist solution if it were economically advantageous. Foch's administration was at that moment fighting for an Allied policy of economic separation and orientation of the Rhineland toward the West. "The present situation in the occupied territories is eminently favorable to the solution proposed, independence, but this situation can quickly change. We have the greatest interest in seeing that the decision concerning Germany's western frontier be made as soon as possible."[44] The Allied confrontation was finally to take place.

GAINING A FOOTHOLD II

The Clemenceau government forbade intervention in German internal politics. But the Allied delegations to various control commissions were making daily decisions concerning Allied economic policy toward Germany that not only affected but previewed the political struggle soon to unfold in the *grandes salles* of Paris. Foch, Tirard, and French economic experts, seconded this time from Paris, pursued their policy of the de facto administrative separation of the occupied territories throughout the first months of 1919. They hoped to demonstrate to the reluctant Rhinelanders and the Anglo-Americans that economic ties to the West were not only possible, but could be in the interest of the Rhineland, and of the society of nations.

The basis for all interference in German economic life was the blockade, retained as a means of pressure on Germany in the Armistice and in its renewals of 13 December and 16 January. But the Bolshevik threat in Germany, thriving on the hunger and economic dislocation that afflicted the stricken Reich, soon absorbed the attention of the American experts in Europe, led by Herbert Hoover. With the creation of the Supreme Economic Council, Hoover had an institution sufficient to challenge the authority of Foch's Supreme Command. He set out to break down the Allied blockade for the purpose of revictualing Germany. But the blockade was in fact the juridical basis for French

[44] Note, "Résumé du rapport de M. Tirard," 1 Mar. 1919: MAE Pap. Tardieu, vol. 47, dos. Renseignements. Cf. Nelson, *Victors Divided*, pp. 73-75. Nelson also notes the absence of Wilson and Lloyd George from Paris after 14 February. The French may have hoped to win over Colonel House, who was considered more sympathetic to French demands, before Wilson's return.

economic action on the Rhine, and the efforts of Tirard and Marshal Foch aimed at making effective the barrier between the Left and the Right Banks. Tirard's first directives in December reduced all relations between occupied and nonoccupied territory to a minimum, especially transportation of people and goods, communication, and judicial and police matters. Laws promulgated by trans-rhenian governments were to be submitted to the *Contrôle-Général* for approval before taking effect in occupied territory. Tirard's agents oversaw tax collection and took measures to interdict export of capital. To ease unemployment, Allied committees directed distribution of raw materials, and Tirard sought markets in France for Rhenish products.

A great influx of Rhenish manufactures was bound to upset French industry. In January 1919 an interministerial conference for the Left Bank of the Rhine banned certain Rhenish imports, including steel, but they approved a long list of finished goods and construction materials. The ministers would place orders with Tirard, who would relay them to Rhenish firms.[45] On 15 January the government suspended the French tariff for certain items, granting the Rhineland favored status. French heavy industry, feeling the first effects of postwar reconversion and the desperate coal shortage that would stifle production for the next two years, favored the policy of economic detente with Western Germany. But opposition arose quickly from French commercial interests. To French small businessmen, represented by the Chambers of Commerce, the defeat of Germany should mean the elimination of competition from that quarter. They accused the steel industry of betraying the general interests of France, accused Louis Loucheur of being the "*Comité des Forges* man" in government, and called for the economic dismemberment of Germany. On 27 January 1919 the General Assembly of French Chambers of Commerce met in Paris to demand the prohibition of German exports to France.[46] The Ministry of Commerce supported their interests, and the program for economic entente with the Rhineland was stymied from within.

More to the liking of French businessmen was the reverse process. The Supreme Economic Council endorsed the suspension of the German tariff in occupied territory, thereby separating the two parts of Germany for trade purposes and creating the so-called hole in the West. Allied goods began, at first slowly, then in a torrent, to flow into occupied territory. After four years of war and blockade, French

[45] Procès-Verbal, Conférence interministerielle de la Rive Gauche du Rhin, Jan. 1919: AN HCF, vol. 2892, dos. 2E.

[46] The conflicting attitudes of French economic interests toward the eventual peace with Germany are summarized by Miquel, *La Paix de Versailles*, pp. 504-525.

wines, oil, soap, rubber, and other luxury items proved irresistible to the Rhinelanders. But the estimated six thousand French merchants who established themselves on the Rhine also took the opportunity to unload shoddy goods and war surplus in the "conquered" territories.[47] Tirard quickly formed Economic Sections to stimulate commerce. Founded on 12 January 1919, the sections were technically subject to the Supreme Economic Council, but were managed by the industrial service of Tirard's *Contrôle-Général*. The Americans and British supported a section each, in Trier (later Coblenz) and Cologne. The Belgians formed sections at Aachen and Crefeld, and the French in Mainz, Ludwigshafen, and Saarbrücken. They were meant to act cooperatively for the benefit of all Allied merchants, but the Americans and British did not encourage their work. In practice, the Economic Sections became tools of French and Belgian commercial penetration. In addition to favoring French trade, the agents, who came largely from Loucheur's Ministry of Industrial Reconstruction, compiled documentation on every industrial and agricultural enterprise of note in the occupied territories.[48] In early 1919 the work of the sections had only begun, but Tirard saw them as the vanguard of French economic and political influence. "As presently constituted, the Economic Sections are capable of rendering considerable service as long as the French army is on the Rhine. Commerce follows the flag and the opportunities here for French commerce are brilliant."[49]

The institution still lacking was a mixed commission, a joint Franco-Rhenish body designed to regularize contracts, settle disputes, and to attract the greater part of Rhenish industry to cooperate with the French. Tirard saw the need as early as November 1918, and he pushed for such a *bureau mixte* in a conversation with Tardieu in January.[50] But the French commercial invasion only stiffened official German resistance, and Rhenish initiative for a cooperative bureau was not forthcoming. Liaison with the French government arose quickly, however. The Ministry of Commerce had no objection to French exports, and Clemenceau assigned the task of guiding the Rhenish trade to the ministry's *Office du commerce extérieur*. The trade outgrew the original department and in June Tirard prevailed upon the government

[47] Ernst Fraenkel, *Military Occupation and the Rule of Law: Occupation Government in the Rhineland, 1918-1923* (London, Newark, Toronto, 1944), pp. 17-21.

[48] Voisin (director of economic services) to Tirard, 27 July 1919: AN HCF, vol. 2910, dos. 13A.

[49] Tirard, "Rapport," pp. 219-222. Tirard put French exports to the occupied territories between February and May 1919 at 600 million francs.

[50] Note Tardieu, "Conversation avec Tirard," 26 Jan. 1919; Note, Tirard, annexed to Let. Foch to Clemenceau, 8 Feb. 1919: MAE Pap. Tardieu, vol. 47, dos. Renseignements.

to create an office specifically designed to exploit the German hole in the West.[51]

The Rhenish trade was lucrative, but it did nothing to draw the Rhineland toward France. Occupation policies likely to encourage Rhenish separation from Germany were of interallied concern, and it was within the Supreme Economic Council, not within French agencies, that the issue would be decided. The Rhineland's immediate economic health depended on its access to coal and raw materials, which could come only from Germany, especially the Ruhr. As early as 13 December 1918 an interallied conference authorized certain exchanges of merchandise between occupied and nonoccupied Germany and founded a licensing commission at Trier for their regulation. Despite the hope of making the Rhineland dependent on France, Loucheur, Foch, and Tirard accepted the need for continued contacts with the Right Bank. Allied guidelines provided for importation of coal, coke, scrap iron, and manganese across the Rhine, and the German government engaged to supply the Left Bank with the materials it had received before occupation by the Allies. But the Ruhr industrialists were chary of providing materials to areas whose political status was still in doubt. By March 1919 only 50 percent of the daily coal requirements were met. In April they ceased entirely, and the arguments of the interallied committees provided a preview of the debate unfolding in Paris. The coal shortages were due to German ill will, said the French. The economic hardship of the Left Bank only reflected the imprudence of seeking Rhenish separation, said the British.

The overriding problem facing the Allied administration in Germany was revictualment, and here the Americans took the lead. From the inception of the Supreme Economic Council, Herbert Hoover fought for a lifting of the blockade, on humanitarian grounds and to stiffen Germany's resistance to the "disease" of Bolshevism. But he encountered initial apathy from the British, who had differences of their own with America over delivery of foodstuffs to Britain, and determined obstruction from the French. Apart from their policy of blockade as pressure against Germany, the French had two special interests. They feared lest Germany's gold reserves flow to America in payment for food, thus reducing capacity to pay reparations, and they hoped to scuttle Hoover's plan for common treatment of all Germany in revictualment. Favoritism in food deliveries could be a strong inducement to political change in the Rhineland. The Germans were acutely aware of

[51] Procès-Verbal, Conférence interalliée relative à l'administration des territoires occupés, lère séance, 22 Nov. and 13 Dec. 1918: AN HCF, vol. 2891, dos. 2A; Tirard, "Rapport," pp. 225-226.

this fact. Fearing that famine would drive the Rhenish population into the arms of the French, Foreign Minister Wilhelm Solf and chief of the Armistice delegation Erzberger repeatedly pleaded with the Americans to take up leadership of Allied economic policy with regard to the Left Bank. The duplicity of Germany's "poor-mouthing" is evident, nevertheless, in the fact that Berlin was purposefully holding back on foodstuffs stockpiled in unoccupied territory, in hopes of throwing the burden on the victors. Food supplies, as well as Germany's merchant fleet and the coal and coke of the Ruhr, were bargaining chips in the political struggle to come.[52]

Thus, Hoover's campaign to overcome the blockade was stalled for two months, in part by the demands of the Germans themselves, in part by the French resistance. On 21 February the French won a temporary victory. Famine within the territories occupied by the Allies would reflect badly on the Western powers, particularly the United States, which was glutted with reserves seeking a market. Also, unrest on the Left Bank could endanger the security of the troops. An interim compromise therefore created a commission to deal with revictualment of the occupied territories on an ad hoc basis and entrusted this commission to Foch's Supreme Command.[53] As Clemenceau and Tardieu made their opening moves in the Rhineland debate in Paris, the French campaign for de facto separation seemed near consummation.

Hoover retaliated quickly. Promising the French that "the assurance of regular . . . food to Germany will not affect the conditions of peace," he met privately with Lloyd George and bluntly asserted his need for British support. The following day, the eighth of March, the two of them inveighed against the French obstruction. Did the French delegate, Finance Minister Klotz, wish to be remembered as the doorman for Bolshevism? Their pressure bore fruit at the Conference of Brussels on 13 March. The British and Americans withdrew Foch's de facto control, severely limited the blockade, and unified Germany for purposes of revictualment. Under this plan, the Berlin government ordered all Rhenish foreign currency deposits to be centralized at Berlin and wrote off all Rhenish exports to the West as payment for foodstuffs. Tirard protested the decisions and succeeded in halting the outflow of hard currency, but the principle of German unity was upheld.[54]

The French judgment that the Rhenish situation was "eminently fa-

[52] See Suda Bana and Ralph H. Lutz, *The Blockade of Germany after the Armistice, 1918-1919* (Stanford, 1942), pp. 106-108.

[53] Procès-Verbal, Conférence interalliée relative à l'administration des territoires occupés, 5e séance, 21 Feb. 1919: AN HCF, vol, 2892, dos. 2D; 28 Feb. 1919, vol. 2891, dos. 2A. See also Bana and Lutz, *The Blockade of Germany*, and Schwabe, *Deutsche Revolution*, pp. 362-376.

[54] Tirard, "Rapport," pp. 59-61.

vorable" to independence, made while Foch retained control of revictualment, was premature. Hopeful that events in the occupied territories would favor their case for separation, Clemenceau and Tardieu had postponed discussion for months. Now their case was weakened: the Rhineland and the Anglo-Americans as well rallied to the cause of German unity. In the end, France must seek to carry her Rhenish policy on strategic arguments alone.

LA PÉRIODE HÉROIQUE

When the Paris Peace Conference opened on 18 January 1919 there was no question that Clemenceau intended to fight for a peace of material guarantees against German resurgence. But he was equally intent on saving Allied unity. A balance of power could be restored by weakening the preponderant power, Germany, or by a permanent increase of the forces opposing her. This could only be accomplished by an Anglo-American commitment to the Continent. This solution meant heightened tensions, for it involved an escalation of the forces pressing down on the fulcrum of Central Europe, now and in the future. But an Allied commitment to Europe would form a solid base for the very world commitment Wilson would request of all nations through the League. As Wilson himself said, "In the next war there will be no neutrals." Finally, a peace based on Allied unity was a prerequisite for France's financial convalescence and economic recovery. Thus, for Clemenceau, if not for Foch, Poincaré, and the majority of French officials, the Rhine peace was negotiable.

The first weeks of the Peace Conference served to upset the Tiger's more sanguine plans. The League of Nations, it developed, would offer little for France. Though Germany would be excluded from the institution, Wilson refused to permit the League to be used as an anti-German institution for the enforcement of the peace. Clemenceau then argued that if the League was to be an effective deterrent against aggression, it must command armed force. But again he met immovable opposition, this time led by Britain and her Dominions. Given the heady public expectations of a New Jerusalem, perhaps no document could have won approval. But when the League Covenant was made public on 15 February, it was met with universal scorn in the French press and Chamber. Public opinion leaders Jacques Bainville, Léon Bourgeois, and President Poincaré renewed their call for a peace of material guarantees, and a wave of anti-Americanism washed over Paris.[55]

[55] An analysis of the new anti-Americanism in the French press is presented in Miquel, *La Paix de Versailles*, pp. 166-206.

The League could not be a vehicle, then, either for a punitive peace against Germany or for a "constructive" Western alliance. But Clemenceau did not despair of winning Anglo-American approval for French designs. He encouraged the press in the belief of "ralliement," that by steady pressure Wilson could be brought around. Government newspapers recalled that Wilson's political position at home was weak, and that the "people" he thought to serve demanded guarantees against German revenge. If the League was to be ineffective, that very fact strengthened the French case for a Rhenish peace, and Tardieu's staff labored throughout the League debates to marshal the arguments for German dismemberment.

The root justification of Rhenish separation was its value as a security guarantee. Thus, Tardieu was compelled to show the inadequacies of other security plans, particularly that to be embodied in the feeble League. His chief aide, Louis Aubert, attacked defensive alliances as ineffective material guarantees because of the gap between the moment of attack and the arrival of aid from overseas. Without the Rhine barrier to slow up a German "attaque brusque," modern weapons could bring a German army to the Channel in a matter of days, and Britain herself would be threatened. Alliances were a psychological deterrent only.[56] The French military endorsed this analysis. France must never again be simply Britain's buffer on the Continent, she never again must provide the cannon fodder to throw up against an initial German onslaught. Foch's views are known, but in February, as the League Covenant was reaching completion, Émile Fayolle, commander of the two French armies on the Rhine, added his thoughts: "Wilson speaks of the League, but what can this hypothetical society do without a means of action? One promises alliances, but like all human things, alliances are fragile. . . . There will always come a time when Germany will have a free hand. Make all the alliances you like, but the highest necessity for France and Belgium is a material barrier."[57]

Clemenceau did not share this contempt for alliances. It was Clemenceau above all who sought to put teeth into the League; it was Clemenceau who would accept the Anglo-American pact offered in March. But the requirements of European balance, in Eastern as well as Western Europe, meant that an Anglo-American commitment must encompass the Left Bank of the Rhine, the "jumping-off point" of three

[56] Note Aubert, "Rive Gauche du Rhin: neutralisation militaire," 2 Feb. 1919: MAE Pap. Tardieu, vol. 44, dos. 2 bis.

[57] Note Fayolle, "Relative à la paix," 14 Feb. 1919: MAE Pap. Tardieu, vol. 44, dos. 2 bis.

German invasions in a century, and either guarantee or permit France to guarantee, through access to the Rhine, the stability of the new nations in Eastern Europe. If the Anglo-Americans were intent on leaving Germany intact, they must be willing to commit themselves to her containment. It was not to annex or detach the Rhineland for the cause of French expansion, it was to convince *all* the Allies to remain on the Rhine that Clemenceau pleaded his case. Out of these considerations developed the first French note to the Peace Conference on the fixing of Germany's western border at the Rhine. The carefully reasoned thirty-four page document was based on the Foch program, but was drafted by Tardieu to include all the historical, cultural, economic, and strategic reasons for its adoption. Poincaré termed the famous brief "tout à fait remarquable."[58] On 25 February 1919 Tardieu distributed the text to the Allied delegations, and the battle was joined.

The progression of events in the Rhineland negotiations of the Paris Peace Conference during the months of March and April is well known. Tardieu labeled this "la période héroique" during which he and Clemenceau stubbornly fought for and achieved a double guarantee of French security: military measures including a fifteen-year occupation of the Rhineland and a formal extension of the wartime alliance. But the strength and purpose they showed at the conference table masked a crisis in French strategy. For within the French camp, Clemenceau was the one who placed the highest value on the alliance, and his retreat from a strict Rhineland solution produced a crisis that damaged his prestige and embittered his colleagues and constituents. The reaction of the French Chamber, diplomatic corps, and military to Clemenceau's "surrender" in turn caused grave doubts among the Anglo-Americans as to the requirements of European political stabilization.

The British and Americans were content to listen in the first Rhineland conversations, as Tardieu explained the French position, and the latter came away with the impression that Rhenish independence was acceptable to the Allies.[59] But Lloyd George's policy toward Germany was predicated on a variation of Wilsonian integrationism. Although his reparations policy would turn pro-German only after the 1920 slump clarified Britain's need for rapid German recovery, Lloyd George opposed increases in French power on the continent from the

[58] Pers. Let. Poincaré to Pichon, 25 Feb. 1919: IF Corr. Pichon, vol. 4398, no. 84.

[59] Note Tardieu, "Conversations avec le Colonel House," 2 Mar. 1919: MAE Pap. Tardieu, vol. 44, dos. 1, piece 4; Note Aubert, "Exposé des motifs," 3 Mar. 1919: MAE Pap. Tardieu, vol 44, dos. 1, piece 5-3; Notes Tardieu, "Conversation Carr-Tardieu-Mezes," 11-12 Mar. 1919: MG Fonds Clemenceau 6N73, dos. Rive Gauche du Rhin.

beginning. Grasping for principles to guide him through the era of stabilization, Lloyd George looked to British traditions: opposition to the continental victor of a general war; restoration of balance; control of the seas. France, not Germany, had to be restrained, and the availability of Wilsonian ideals, which implied German unity and economic revival, only made that task easier. Finally, the German revolution was viewed differently in the Foreign Office than in Paris. The Kaiser was gone, the republic must be encouraged, not only to promote peace and recovery, but to forestall Bolshevism.

On 14 March 1919 President Wilson and Lloyd George countered French demands for Rhenish separation with the offer of an Anglo-American guarantee to fight beside France against future German unprovoked aggression. The proffered alliance represented an abrupt break with the traditions of both powers, but in the context of the war just concluded and of Wilson's visions of the postwar world, the logic of the circumstances demanded such a departure. By offering an American alliance, Wilson merely anticipated the commitment America was eventually to make to all nations through the League. To Lloyd George, Rhenish separation would be a constant irritant to peace, a "new Alsace-Lorraine." The alliance would be a balm to French fears and a harness to French ambition.[60]

Whatever the motives, the Anglo-American offer was a solemn pledge. Two days before Clemenceau had been "furious" with Lloyd George. Now he was "très ému." Returning to his office at the Ministry of War, he let Tardieu and Loucheur in on the "great secret," and explained the choice he had been given: stand alone on the Rhine against a vengeful Germany, or rely on distant allies. The following afternoon the three joined Pichon for a fateful interview. The foreign minister was skeptical of alliances. He feared lest France "turn aside from the prey to pursue the shadow," yet he did not see how the offer could be refused. Tardieu felt likewise. He saw the dangers of a permanent French occupation and believed the alliance offer must be accepted, but, he added, this solution did not preclude a return to a Rhineland policy in case of danger. Clemenceau was the most dispirited of all. France's postwar position would be tenuous at best, and the Tiger saw no potential leaders equal to the tasks ahead. In a funk, these four men charged with selecting the grand strategy for European security lacked confidence in either solution—and so they opted for both.[61]

[60] Nelson, *Victors Divided*, pp. 79-80, notes other influences bearing on Wilson's decision to offer the security pact, including "Clemenceau's obstinacy, Lloyd George's anxiety, Europe's desperation, and America's impatience."

[61] MS Loucheur, diary notes, 12-18 Mar. 1919: HI Pap. Loucheur, Box 12, Folder

Clemenceau instructed Tardieu to draft a new note. France would accept the alliances, but demand supplementary guarantees, including German disarmament, army reduction, demilitarization of the Rhine, and a postwar Allied occupation. Tardieu communicated these added demands to the British and Americans on 17 March.[62] Lloyd George offered Rhenish demilitarization only, Clemenceau refused, and after a bitter exchange the British prime minister left for London with nothing accomplished.

What had become of the once sacred Rhineland separation plans of the French government? They were not entirely abandoned. Clemenceau's team had not made a clear choice between two courses so much as a decision to keep both options open. The dangers inherent in either policy—Western alliance or German dismemberment—were evident. As early as the summer of 1918 Loucheur had foreseen such a dilemma. "If the war ends at Berlin," he wrote, "it is possible the collapse of Germany will remove for a long time the danger of the German army. If, as seems more possible, after the military success of the Entente, we are obliged to make a peace of conditions, leaving Germany the possibility of rebuilding military force, the eventual situation will become grave for France."[63] Though France's peacemakers saw the impossibility of refusing the alliances, they were unwilling to renounce hopes for a Rhenish policy that might ease the task of enforcing in perpetuity the "conditions" placed on Germany. Even as he retreated from the *separatist* plan in his response to the Allies, Tardieu invoked French intelligence of Rhenish *autonomism* and pleaded in the name of self-determination that the Big Three not frustrate the indigenous desire for autonomy from Prussia. A contemporary in-house memorandum declared:

> If the idea of fixing the German boundary at the Rhine is abandoned, then the idea of an *independent* Rhenish state must also be abandoned. But as the idea of a special military regime is retained, the idea of an *autonomous* state would best complete the overall conception. This plan, if it takes shape, would have almost all the advantages of an independent state without the inconveniences. . . . We

12. See also Louis Loucheur, *Carnets Secrets, 1908-1932*, ed. Jacques de Launay (Brussels and Paris, 1962), pp. 71-73. Note, "Objections contre la solution anglo-américaine," 16 Mar. 1919: MAE Pap. Tardieu, vol. 44, dos. 8 quart.

[62] Note Tardieu, "complementaire au sujet de la Rive Gauche du Rhin," 14 Mar. 1919: MAE Pap. Tardieu, 3e versement, vol. 5; Note, "Clauses à inscrire dans un accord entre la France, la Grande-Bretagne, et les Etats-Unis et dans la pacte de la Ligue," 17 Mar. 1919: MG 6N73 Fonds Clemenceau, dos. Rive Gauche.

[63] Note Loucheur, 27 June 1918: HI Pap. Loucheur, Box 2, Folder 1.

would thus have: a) the supplementary guarantee of our two allies; b) the special military guarantee; c) a chance of attracting toward the French sphere a region that places itself on its own accord on the margin of Germany. The movement for an autonomous Rhenish Republic would appear at first glance to re-enter the general plan of our Rhenish policy.[64]

Once the dogma of separation had been questioned, iconoclasts appeared in number. Louis Aubert broached the thought that what France required was not so much a strong defensive posture as a means of preventing a war altogether. German dismemberment would make another war inevitable and without the Anglo-Americans France would be left dependent on a river line that military technology would surely find a means to break. A fifteen-year occupation combined with the alliances, however, would guarantee that France would not stand alone and would provide time for her to "cumulate her guarantees [on the Rhine and Eastern Europe, presumably]."[65] The thoughts of the peacemaking team were swinging back to the gradualist policy first advocated by the Quai d'Orsay. Berthelot, shut out of the proceedings, now saw the opportunity to press his point. France should be content with the military guarantees contained in Tardieu's note of 17 March. "And to augment the guarantees, one must pursue, *without rupturing German unity*, the separation of the Left Bank from Prussia and Bavaria."[66] In a series of private drafts during the first days of April, Tardieu even considered reopening the whole Rhenish status question. He altered, deleted offensive passages, and in the end decided against a new Rhineland demarche, perhaps at Clemenceau's behest.[67] His note of 4 April only repeated the demand for an occupation and supplementary guarantees. A Rhenish state, independent or autonomous, would not form part of the Versailles settlement. But the renewed interest in a policy of gradual penetration, made possible by an extended occupation, pointed to a policy of revision of the treaty in the future.

The details of France's tentative change of policy did not penetrate the shroud of silence surrounding the Peace Conference, but the fact of

[64] "Note sur la suggestion présentée le 14 mars, remise le 17 mars au Président Wilson et Lloyd-George," 17 Mar. 1919: MG Fonds Clemenceau, 6N73, dos. Rive Gauche. Rough drafts can be found in MAE Tardieu, vol. 44, dos. 9ter (italics in original).

[65] Note Aubert, "fin mars" 1919: MAE Pap. Tardieu, vol. 44, dos. 15 bis.

[66] Note Berthelot, 31 Mar. 1919: MAE Pap. Tardieu, vol. 44, dos. 17 (italics in original).

[67] MS Tardieu, "Le problème politique de la Rive Gauche du Rhin," and "État d'ésprit de la region rhénane," 2 Apr. 1919: MAE Pap. Tardieu, 3 versement, vol. 4; Note Tardieu, "Les conditions d'évacuation de la Rive Gauche du Rhin," 4 Apr. 1919: vol. 49, dos. 1.

a change of strategy did; and it precipitated a second crisis in the French camp. The President of the Republic, the supreme commander, the Chamber, and the Senate all reacted predictably. They were convinced that Clemenceau was abandoning the Rhine.

Concerned about the delays in peacemaking, Poincaré demanded on 17 March to know: "Where are we going? Are the Allies to fall into military inferiority? What is the progress of the conference; what is the policy of the government?" Under orders from Clemenceau, Pichon revealed nothing. Ten days later, Poincaré asked what had become of the security program outlined in Tardieu's first note. He had heard rumors that it was given up.[68] Poincaré recalled the occupation by Germany of three French *départements* after 1871 as a guarantee of the indemnity. He wanted nothing less for France. The Rhineland must be occupied as long as reparations were due, at least thirty years. In addition, allowance must be made for the "docile" Rhenish population to carry out its desire for autonomy under French protection. When the President met with Clemenceau on 6 April, they came close to a final break. Poincaré fulminated against the Tiger's secrecy and accused him of suppressing the *procès-verbaux*. "I have the right to be informed," he shouted, "and the duty to express my opinion!"[69]

Poincaré's irritation was shared by others in government. "Pichon knows, he understands," mourned Paul Cambon, "*mais quel entourage*! Our policy is in the hands of those petty young men who speak haughtily and turn all against us."[70] By forcing France to give up the Rhine, wrote Cambon, Lloyd George hoped to assuage Germany. Nothing could be more dangerous. "I am ignorant of what has passed at Paris these last weeks," he complained, ". . . but if these hypotheses are exact, it [the British policy] contains the germs of profound misunderstandings between England and the continental allies." He urged that some system of defense on the Rhine be established.[71]

[68] Pers. Let. Poincaré to Pichon, 17 and 27 Mar. 1919: IF Corr. Pichon, vol. 4398, nos. 92, 94.

[69] Pers. Let. Poincaré to Pichon, 30 Mar. 1919: IF Corr. Pichon, fol. 4398, no. 95; Pers. Let. Pichon to Poincaré, 3 Apr. 1919: Raymond Poincaré, unpublished private papers, Bibliothèque Nationale-Paris (hereafter cited as Corr. Poincaré), N.A.F. 16013, no. 52; Pers. Let. Poincaré to Pichon, 7 Apr. 1919: IF Corr. Pichon, vol. 4398, no. 99. Poincaré added sarcastically that no *procès-verbaux* must exist or his friend Pichon surely would have provided copies. In fact, the minutes were duplicated daily by Tardieu's staff and kept by Gen. Mordacq in a special strongbox. Circulation was forbidden even to such interested parties as the foreign minister and president! See Mordacq, *Le ministère Clemenceau*, III, 207.

[70] Pers. Let. P. Cambon to Barrère, 7 Mar. 1919: MAE Corr. Barrère, vol. 1, nos. 118, 121. Tardieu, at forty-one, was the youngest delegate.

[71] Des. P. Cambon to Pichon, 28 Mar. 1919: MAE Grande Bretagne, vol. 36, nos. 100-103. The same week, Cambon wrote privately to Barrère: "The Entente is in danger. I found Pichon discouraged and lamentable." MAE Corr. Barrère, vol. 1, nos.

Marshal Foch also moved to the attack when news reached him of a change in French policy.[72] "To renounce the barrier of the Rhine," he bellowed, "would be to admit that unimaginable monstrosity of voluntarily granting Germany, soaked in the blood of her crimes, the possibility of beginning again."[73] On 6 April Foch appealed for an opportunity to address the French delegation. Clemenceau told him to wait until the peace negotiations were over; then he could offer an opinion in his advisory role. Piqued, Foch blasted Allied policy again in an interview with the *Daily Mail*, and again Clemenceau reprimanded him for insubordination.[74]

Foch then appealed to the *Parlement*, where the "war aims bloc" fretted anxiously in its impotence to guide French peacemaking. On 2 December 1918 the Foreign Affairs Commission of the Chamber had adopted a security program: no annexations, but the creation of a "special regime" on the Left Bank of the Rhine and demilitarization of the Right Bank. When Foch's peace plan was made known, a large portion of the French Center and Right accepted it without question. But the deputies had refrained from interpellating the government during the conference on the assumption that the government would accept nothing less. Now there was some doubt. On 14 April a Chamber delegation led by Radical leader René Renoult reminded Clemenceau in person that the Chamber would settle for nothing less than "immediate and material guarantees of French security," including "the organization of a solid frontier." Another deputy, André Lebey, implied in a letter to Clemenceau that the premier no longer enjoyed the full confidence of the Chamber. Lebey advised that the premier abandon his secrecy and appear before the parliament. Clemenceau refused.

Two days later the *Petit Journal*, of which Stephen Pichon himself was a political editor, reported that the British and Americans had agreed to enter an alliance with France. The article went on to quote the *New York Times*, explaining that the American president had no authority to make such a treaty. The French Senate now took initiative. Paul Doumer proposed a resolution insisting that the government

---

125-126; Des. P. Cambon to MAE, 2 Apr. 1919: Paul Cambon, unpublished private papers, Ministère des Affaires Étrangères-Paris (hereafter cited as MAE Pap. P. Cambon), vol. 6, dos. 24, nos. 8-16.

[72] The feud between Foch and Clemenceau is well known; see King, *Foch versus Clemenceau*. But their conflicts were not confined to the Rhenish issue, nor was the Rhineland debate in the French government solely, or even primarily, a Foch-Clemenceau duel.

[73] Note Foch, 31 Mar. 1919: MAE Paix, vol. 161, nos. 84-88.

[74] Let. Clemenceau to Foch, 9 Apr. 1919: MG 6N114 Renseignements Allemagne, dos. 2.

"demand instantly the insertion into the treaty of the military guarantees indicated by the Supreme Commander [Foch]." Pichon responded from the tribune on 18 April. Such a resolution would subordinate the civil power to the military and was unthinkable. He threatened to pose the question of confidence, and the senators shied from reversing a government in mid-crisis. Pichon promised that Foch would have a chance to address the Peace Conference.[75] The parliamentary revolt simmered and Clemenceau remained in control of the negotiations. But the premier's exclusivity produced a bitter fruit. The guarantees Clemenceau pursued against determined resistance were condemned by his countrymen before they were even achieved.

French officials on the Rhine were equally disappointed by rumors of Clemenceau's shift on the Rhenish question. The difference in their case was that they had the means to act on their own. When Tirard and Foch repeated their plea for instructions at the beginning of March, Clemenceau's private secretary, Jules Jeanneney, went no further than approval for the obscure "measures" taken in January. Jeanneney enclosed another note from Pichon, remarkable for its obscurity:

> It is opportune to demonstrate to the populations of the occupied territories that their prosperity does not necessarily depend on relations with the German territories of the Right Bank. . . . It remains to profit from this circumstance. The Rhenish people seem prepared to bow before the decision of the Allies relative to their fate. It is without doubt the uncertainty of their position that favors in certain circles a current of thought in the contrary sense.[76]

The French military authorities could only conclude that once again they had no instructions.

His patience worn thin by the tergiversations of Paris, General Fayolle, commander of the two French armies on the Rhine, acted on his own authority. On 10 March he ordered his army commanders, Generals Augustin Gérard and Charles Mangin, to adopt a new posture vis-à-vis Rhenish politics. Up to the present, Fayolle wrote, occupation policy had not prejudged the future, but the moment had arrived "to go a step farther and prepare the solutions that we deem favorable." He instructed the generals to encourage separatist tendencies by ap-

[75] *Petit Journal*, 14, 16, 18 Apr. 1919; Procès-Verbal, France, Archives of the National Assembly, Chamber of Deputies, Commission des Affaires Étrangères, Auditions, 18 Apr. 1919; France, Archives of the Senate, Commission des Affaires Étrangères, Auditions, 1919, pp. 1789-1800.

[76] Let. Jeanneney to Foch, 11 Mar. 1919; encl. Let. Pichon to Clemenceau, 11 Mar. 1919, cited by Tirard, "Rapport," pp. 74-75.

pealing to moral and material interests. Betraying the universal French misunderstanding of Rhenish separatism, he added: "It is necessary to allay all fears of annexation. The countries of the Left Bank will remain free to group themselves according to race, historical laws, and economic advantage, and be free to govern themselves." Plans for a unique West German republic or states encompassing both banks of the Rhine were to be discouraged. Until publication of the peace, Fayolle declared, these were the grand lines of French policy.[77]

Fayolle's orders were in defiance of the principles governing the interallied occupation. He did not inform Paris of his act, but he and General Weygand of Foch's staff did solicit approval for local involvement in Rhenish affairs. They invoked the political immaturity of the Rhenish people and told the Quai d'Orsay that precise directives were needed so that the army might respond to Rhenish "offers of cooperation."[78]

Clemenceau had not given up his hopes for a negotiated separation of the Rhineland only that frustrated generals should foment a revolution. Provocative interference in German internal politics could destroy the compromise being worked out by the Big Three. Besides, the time was not ripe. Colonel Requin, Tardieu's assistant, rebuffed another appeal from Tirard, who felt the Rhenish notables were ready to break with Germany. "No! The moderate parties only desire autonomy. This is already something, but one cannot say they are *acquis à l'idée de séparation.*"[79] Thus, the split in French councils became evident. The military sought separation, as an immediate goal. The government now would be content with autonomy, and as a long-term goal. Despairing of support from Paris, and afraid that Clemenceau was abandoning the Rhine, the generals determined to act.

With Fayolle's blessing, and unbeknownst to Paris, General Gérard in the Palatinate and General Mangin on the middle Rhine began collaboration with the diehard separatists. The months of April to June 1919 witnessed a blind race in which Clemenceau and the generals competed to finish their work before the other. Signature of a peace recognizing German unity would kill the chances of a Rhenish separatist *fait accompli*. But a putsch with French involvement might

[77] Note personelle et secrète, E. M., Groupe d'Armées, Affaires civiles #5485, Fayolle to MM les Généraux commandants les VIIe et Xe Armées, 10 Mar. 1919: Charles Mangin, unpublished private papers, Archives Nationales-Paris (hereafter cited as AN Pap, Mangin), vol. 21, dos. 3.

[78] Let. Fayolle to MAE, 30 Mar. 1919, despatched 6 Apr. 1919: MAE Rive Gauche, vol. 1, nos. 15-18. Let. Weygand to Clemenceau, 30 Mar. & 2 Apr. 1919: MAE Paix, vol. 174, nos. 10-23; MG Fonds Clemenceau, 6N73, dos. Rive Gauche.

[79] Pers. Let. Tirard to Tardieu, 6 Apr. 1919, marginal comments by Requin: MAE Pap. Tardieu, vol. 47, dos. Renseignements.

kill British agreement to the guarantees Clemenceau labored to achieve.

LA PAIX BOCHE: FRENCH SECURITY AND ALLIED UNITY

"Very well," muttered Lloyd George, "I accept." On 22 April 1919 he and Woodrow Wilson submitted to the alternate French security formula. They pledged to defend France against future German aggression and granted supplementary guarantees: German disarmament, reduction of the German army to 100,000 men, demilitarization of a zone fifty kilometers east of the Rhine. Finally, they approved a fifteen-year occupation of the Left Bank of the Rhine with four bridgeheads across the river at Cologne, Coblenz, Mainz, and Kehl. If the treaty were fulfilled, evacuation would proceed in three five-year stages. The occupation was not carried as a guarantee of security, but as a pledge of German disarmament, reparations, and adherence to the other clauses of the treaty. The Anglo-American security pacts would guarantee French security. But, sensitive to criticism that alliances were transitory, Clemenceau now drove the final nail into the treaty structure: a guarantee of the guarantee. On the very day of Lloyd George's submission, Tardieu sprung a new demand, approved by the Allies during the last week of deliberation, as Articles 429 and 430 of the treaty with Germany. If, at the end of fifteen years, the guarantees against an unprovoked aggression by Germany were not deemed sufficient by any of the Allied governments, the evacuation of the occupation troops might be delayed.

How far had Clemenceau retreated from the Foch Rhineland scheme of November 1918? He had given up a permanent Rhineland occupation for a temporary one. He had given up Rhenish separation, but he retained in the occupation the means to carry on French penetration and propaganda. Rhenish autonomy was still a possible future goal. He received the Anglo-American guarantees. But the interallied occupation itself was an alliance of sorts, since a hostile action by Germany in the west would necessarily be directed against the flags of all the Allies. What, then, was the value of the pacts? To the French, they were a declaration of permanent Anglo-French-American solidarity, committing the Allies to cooperation in the defense of the treaty, even if force were required. But the Americans and British had a different view of the arrangement. The pacts were meant to restrain France in the use of force, to permit her to be liberal in the application of the treaty. This misunderstanding was the measure of the retreat

Clemenceau had made since November 1918, and it rendered ambiguous the system under which European political stabilization was to proceed.

Clemenceau's critics within the government rued this misunderstanding. Paul Cambon feared the erosion of the Anglo-French Entente and Poincaré foresaw the isolation of France. If conflict not only with Germany but with the Anglo-Americans as well was to be avoided, the prerogatives of France and the understanding of the Allies must be clearly defined. Resigned to the alliance-plus-guarantees system, Poincaré made one last effort to secure Allied recognition of French vital interests. It is indispensable, he explained, to cite as *casus foederis* any default by Germany in the execution of the treaty of peace, and Britain must be brought to anticipate the possibility of acts of coercion by France to collect reparations. Above all, the danger would be terrible if France abandoned the territorial guarantee for alliances not yet voted by the American Senate and British Parliament. A limit to the Rhineland occupation must be set only after the pacts were in force.[80]

Poincaré peered into the future with remarkable lucidity. If the occupation did not last as long as reparations, it would encourage Germany to delay execution until the pressure disappeared, while Allied cooperation in case of German default was a dangerous assumption. Finally, the treaty's ratification of German unity was another time bomb against Allied unity. If Clemenceau wished to preserve German federalism or Rhenish autonomy as a goal of policy, then recognition of German boundaries destroyed hopes for German political evolution within the Versailles system.[81]

Poincaré seems to have foreseen the diplomatic deadlock of the postwar years. He thought of the treaty not as an abstract system, but as a workable blueprint. He asked how it would survive in practice. He expected Germany to default—precautions were taken. But he expected the British and Americans to "default" as well, if they were not brought to a common interpretation of the alliance. Was this too much to ask in May 1919? The negotiators could hardly be expected to divine the interests of their nations several years in advance, or to sacrifice future freedom of action. There was neither time nor prescience to allow the "resolution of forces, the association of interests" of Clemenceau's vision to operate on the treaty itself. Interpretation and

[80] Pers. Let. Poincaré to Pichon, 23 Apr. 1919: IF Corr. Pichon, vol. 4398, no. 102, 102 bis.

[81] Pers. Let. Poincaré to Pichon, 28 Apr. and 3 May 1919: IF Corr. Pichon, vol. 4398, nos. 105 bis, 109.

definition of the Allied commitments would be the work of five years of conferences and conflicts. The Treaty of Versailles was only a declaration of intent and it set the powers on a collision course.

The peace satisfied few in the French government, but it was the Tiger's obsession with authority and secrecy that encouraged explanations of failure in which he bore sole responsibility. One of the premier's own peace delegates, Jules Cambon, excoriated his chief for the failure to separate the Rhineland, to "undo the artificial works of the Congress of Vienna without which Prussia would never have been a neighbor."[82] Berthelot despised the practice by which the Big Three decided everything. "As often as possible we prepared notes for Pichon—they rarely left his office."[83] Paul Cambon labeled the Big Three "this trinity, which sees nothing, knows nothing, foresees nothing."[84] Camille Barrère was furious that "French ministers were shut out. Absolute secrecy, a rigorous censorship. The Rhine frontier was abandoned in unknown circumstances. This river which meant so much yesterday is *peu de chose* today. I'm told the Rhine defends nothing."[85] Barrère and Minister of Marine Georges Leygues advocated going over the heads of the Big Three to the British and American people. The justice and simplicity of the French cause could not fail to win out before the jury of peoples. "If [Clemenceau] had wished it," Barrère wrote, "England and America would have ceded on the Rhine frontier."[86] But the Tiger, he surmised, was not up to the effort, being eighty years of age and weakened by the assassin's bullet of 19 February. In March Italian delegate Baron Sonnino found Clemenceau "extremely fatigued, no longer the same man."[87]

Could France have won the Rhine frontier with a different strategy? Or could Clemenceau have won popular acquiescence in abandonment of the Rhine? If the Tiger had included the diplomatic establishment and the *Parlement* in the task of peacemaking, he could have brought

[82] Pers. Let. J. Cambon to Pichon, 26 Apr. 1919: IF Corr. Pichon, vol 4396, no. 102.

[83] Pers. Let. Berthelot to Barrère, 14 June 1919: MAE Corr. Barrère, vol. 1, no. 28.

[84] Pers. Let. P. Cambon to Barrère, 7 May 1919: MAE Corr. Barrère, vol. 1, nos. 127-128.

[85] MS Barrère, "a.s. de la Conférence de la paix," 30 Apr. 1919: MAE Pap. Barrère, vol. 2, nos. 10-21. At the height of the Ruhr/Rhineland crisis in 1923, the archival section of the Quai d'Orsay was asked to prepare an account of the negotiations for the security pact at the Paris Peace Conference. The section produced a history, but noted that no documents were found in its own files! "The ministry was left entirely out of the proceedings." MAE Paix, vol. 163, nos. 114-125.

[86] Note, Ministry of Marine to MAE, "Lloyd George et la Conférence," 4 Apr. 1919: MAE Grande Bretagne, vol. 36, nos. 119-125; MS Barrère, July 1920: MAE Pap. Barrère, vol. 2, nos. 52-53.

[87] MS Barrère, "du Rhin à la Conférence," 24 Oct. 1919: MAE Pap. Barrère, vol. 2, no. 145.

them to understand, perhaps, the extent of Allied opposition. But he would not then have been Clemenceau—and a weaker premier might not have been able to stand before the internal opposition to the course he was taking. The irony of the Rhenish question at Paris was that the only man capable of bucking the tide of French opinion and preventing the division of the West before the enemy was incapable of inspiring domestic confidence in his peace. When he left office in January 1920, even after a lengthy exposé before the Chambers, Clemenceau left bourgeois France with the conviction that the Rhine was the French peace, and that it had been abandoned.

"France follows a policy of suicide," declared Barrère. "She marches toward the abyss, and Clemenceau is responsible." With no formula for financial reconstruction, no definitive solution to the Rhenish question, the alliance was a fleshless skeleton, and Germany would be the beneficiary.[88] "For the guarantor powers," Barrère told Berthelot, "the treaty is a piece of paper; for us it is an instrument of servitude. . . . C'était bien la paix boche."

"Oui," Berthelot replied, "c'est la paix boche."[89]

The dangers inherent in the ambiguous alliance became swiftly apparent. French military collaboration with the separatists, begun after Fayolle's orders in March, reached fruition during the nervous period between release of the draft treaty of 7 May and its signature on 28 June. Although the harsh terms caused alarm in Germany and led some Rhenish businessmen to reconsider separatism, the overall response in the Rhineland was relief.[90] The Rhineland was not to be annexed or made a French satellite. Tirard noted a "severe retreat" in separatist ideas.[91] Levy Bruhl was the first to draw the proper conclusion: "Creation of a Rhenish Republic would seem to have been, in the thought of its Centrist partisans, only an artifice to avoid annexation by the enemy."[92]

To the generals in Rhineland, publication of the draft treaty meant that time was running out. General Mangin, patron of Dr. Dorten since April, complained that the treaty would leave the separatists no

[88] MS Barrère, 30 Apr. 1919: MAE Pap. Barrère, vol. 2, nos. 10-21.

[89] MS Barrère, "Traité de paix," 2 Aug. 1919: MAE Pap. Barrère, vol. 2, nos. 37-50.

[90] Henry T. Allen, *The Rhineland Occupation* (Indianapolis, 1927), pp. 189-190. There are several satisfactory accounts of the 1 June putsches: cf. King, *Foch versus Clemenceau*; Dorten, *La tragédie rhénane*; Erwin Bischof, *Rheinischer Separatismus, 1918-1924* (Bern, 1969); Erdmann, *Adenauer in der Rheinlandpolitik*.

[91] Note Tirard, "relative à la repercussion de la publication des préliminaires de paix sur la population des territoires occupées," 15 May 1919: MAE Rive Gauche, vol. 1, nos. 31-36.

[92] Levy Bruhl to MAE, "Le parti du Centre et le projet d'une République rhénane," 22 May 1919: MAE Rive Gauche, vol. 1, nos. 41-45.

legal means to proceed. On 17 May he received ten leading separatists, including Kastert and Dorten, and suggested that the only means of action was to confront the Peace Conference with a *fait accompli*. The same day, General Gérard met with twenty-one Palatine "notables," advocates of separation from Bavaria. The Bavarian prefect von Winterstein promptly arrested the dissidents and was himself expelled from occupied territory by Gérard. The *Freie Pfalz* then planned a putsch of its own.

Mangin and Dorten in the north and Gérard and the Palatine leader, Dr. Eberhard Haas, plotted their actions for the end of May. On 29 May Foch ordered all occupying forces to abandon the policy of aloofness, which only benefitted the "Pangermanist Prussian and Bavarian bureaucracies." His orders were "not to become involved in internal politics . . . but to permit no barrier to the liberty of the peoples to dispose of themselves."[93]

Clemenceau took immediate measures upon hearing of possible cabals on the Rhine. He sent Jeanneney on a fact-finding mission to discern the damage done and to forbid military indiscretions. The Weimar Assembly was threatening to reject the treaty; it must be given no encouragement to defy the Allies. Clemenceau granted that "the Rhenish populations are no doubt oppressed by Prussian functionaries," but he reminded Mangin of the limits of military authority. He ordered strict nonintervention in Rhenish affairs.[94] The next day the separatists launched their putsch.

The scenario envisioned by Haas and Dorten, working independently of each other, was farfetched. They believed that the "almost unanimous support" bottled up since Adenauer's "defection" would express itself, once a republic was proclaimed. The Peace Conference must then recognize the Rhenish states on grounds of self-determination. But the putsches were comic in their ineptitude. Haas seized the government palace in Speyer, but before he could deliver his proclamation he was dragged to the street by a crowd. Gérard's cavalry came to the rescue, but the coup was over in fifteen minutes. Dorten fared no better. His posters proclaiming the Rhenish Republic and his own provisional government ignited a general strike in protest. After an abortive effort to seize the government palace in Wiesbaden, the Rhenish Republic evaporated.

[93] Note Foch, "concernant des directives à donner aux commandants des armées d'occupation en presence de mouvements politiques éventuels dans les territoires rhénans," 29 May 1919: MG 6N73 Fonds Clemenceau, dos. Rive Gauche; Directive #3921 Fayolle to Gérard and Mangin, 30 May 1919: AN Pap. Mangin, vol. 21, dos. 3.

[94] Let. Clemenceau to Mangin, 31 May 1919: MG 6N73 Fonds Clemenceau, dos. Rive Gauche.

The 1 June putsches had ramifications in Paris out of proportion to their importance in the Rhineland. They provided a preview of the conflicts left unresolved between France and Germany, between France and her Allies, and within the French government itself. When Dorten moved on 1 June, Mangin wired Poincaré with the "good news." Poincaré urged Clemenceau to support the putsch. He saw "nothing in it to upset President Wilson," since it was an act of self-determination.[95] There was plenty to upset Clemenceau. His generals had defied him again, apparently in league with Poincaré. And the results he feared arrived quickly. On 2 June the chief of the German delegation in Paris, Ulrich von Brockdorff-Rantzau, protested venomously. France must choose, he said, between the hope of reparations or the fashioning of friendly republics, by which she would sacrifice her treaty rights.[96]

Lloyd George saw his own fears realized before the Germans had even signed the treaty. French occupation of the Rhineland, whether for one year, fifteen, or fifty, meant ceaseless intrigue and efforts at disguised annexation. Already struck by the harsher aspects of the treaty and by fear that the Germans would not sign, Lloyd George redoubled his last-minute efforts to revise the treaty in Germany's favor, including renunciation of the occupation. Clemenceau disowned the putsches, but refused to sacrifice the fifteen-year occupation. On 28 June 1919, when the German delegation signed the Treaty of Versailles, world war and peace were concluded in a spirit of suspicion and foreboding, not reconciliation and new hope.

LA PAIX BOCHE: REPARATIONS AND ALLIED UNITY

The debate over European political strategy and French security was no more important—and indeed less immediate—than the economic tasks that faced the Peace Conference. Reparations were the most emotional issue of the peace, for the solution was certain to affect the interests of every taxpayer in every nation. The moral issues also seemed clearer: the victims of German aggression were only asking restoration of the damages wrought by invasion. Surely the French taxpayer would not shoulder this burden, while the German taxpayer escaped; surely France's wealthy allies would not deny full reparation

[95] Let. Poincaré to Clemenceau, 1 June 1919, cited by Clemenceau, *The Grandeur and Misery of Victory*, pp. 223-224.

[96] Let. Brockforff-Rantzau to Clemenceau, 3 June 1919: MAE Rive Gauche, vol. 1, nos. 81-83.

in the name of the economic health of the aggressor. But to the experts at Paris the issues were rooted deeper, and as they penetrated to the wellsprings of each nation's hopes for postwar recovery, they became more and more entangled. Cross-purposes and conflicts of strategy and interest appeared that were invisible on the surface of affairs. By June 1919 the Paris Peace Conference had done with economics, and it had done very little indeed. Of all the failures of the conference, perhaps the most debilitating was the failure to take immediate economic measures. The postponement of a world financial settlement and an economic peace with Germany only weakened drastically the new German Republic, on which the Anglo-Americans counted for peace, while driving the French to forceful measures on their own economic behalf.

Clemenceau's hope for Allied unity stemmed from France's financial dependence. France owed £875 million in war debts to Britain and America and 256 *billion* francs to the Banque de France. To be sure, there were resources still untouched. The French electorate resisted direct taxation as an invasion of sacred privacy—the war had been financed almost exclusively by loans. But the conservative Third Republic rested on the pillars of financial integrity and low taxation. It was the duty of every government to achieve the first without sacrificing the second. How could this be done when wartime borrowing had all but destroyed the currency? The franc fell in value by 70 percent during the war, although Allied agreements kept exchange rates near par. When the British Exchequer withdrew support for the franc in May 1919, it fell at once to half its January rate, and the fall accelerated throughout the year. Internal inflation had already reduced the standard of living of the rentier class, which in turn was the source of capital for government finance. But peace was almost as expensive as war. France would need a large army-in-being to protect her interests in Europe and Asia, and to force reparations from Germany. Until those reparations flowed, France would be obliged to reconstruct the devastated regions herself. Finally, peace might mean the disappearance of Allied support, which had kept France afloat during her struggle for survival.

The day before the Armistice, the economically liberal *Temps* ran an editorial on the peace terms to come. It began by praising French national bonds as the solidest possible investment, for they had the first mortgage on the national wealth and labor. Their service was a sacred trust written into the annual budget. Nevertheless, French credit was in danger. The Armistice was the preface to a victorious peace, but what, asked the *Temps*, does one mean by a victorious peace? "It is a peace that assures France, especially, the victim of aggression, the reparation of all damages . . . not solely material damages and the cost of pensions, but the re-establishment of our national credit by the annual reimbursement of our war debt. This financial condition cannot be omitted. The national credit is directly dependent on it."[97]

The dual nature of French war aims emerged most clearly in the financial sphere. If Clémentel had demonstrated the need for Allied economic unity to contain Germany, it was also a domestic political necessity of the highest order for France to achieve a peace of retribution with Germany matched by a peace of harmony with the Allies. When Finance Minister Klotz presented a program including a tax on capital to the French Chamber in February 1919, the deputies "invited" the government to withdraw all such plans until German reparations had begun to flow. Klotz accordingly promised economies, and he shifted the burden of French financial recovery onto others. France would demand from Germany full compensation for war damage. France would demand from the Peace Conference firm guarantees of German payment. France would seek Allied economic largesse and continue appeals for credit abroad. The government would ask taxpayers only for what was indispensable to balance future budgets.[98] In practice, the government shied even from this. "If it is France or Germany that must be ruined," cried *Le Matin*, "let us be sure that it is Germany!" The postwar French governments faced with the task of budgetary stabilization were not free to take the necessary measures. The Chamber's Budget Commission held Klotz and Clemenceau to their promise that Germany would pay first. But the pressure from those who suffered damage in the war, the *sinistrés* of northern France, was equally irresistible. Immediate reconstruction was another sacred duty, and on 17 April 1919 the French government assumed responsibility to indemnify the cost of reconstruction to be borne eventually by Germany.

The most unbearable and seemingly unjust burden of peace was the war debts obligations. The successful deflection of these charges from the French taxpayer was, as the *Temps* had indicated, a vital peace aim of the government. "Allied economic unity" meant the reduction or annulment of the interallied debts. France had made the greatest human and material contribution to the war; surely she must not also be made to bear its financial cost. The Americans and British called for a rapid restoration of international trade, but that depended on currency stabilization and credits, which in turn depended on a war debt

[97] "Semaine financière," *Le Temps*, 10 Nov. 1918.

[98] "M. Klotz expose notre politique financière," *Petit Journal*, 19 Feb. 1919.

settlement. It was in everyone's interest to wipe the slate clean. To have peace with Germany, there must first be peace among the Allies.

The French government accordingly issued the first European plea for Allied financial unity, i.e., sharing the cost of the war, in September 1918. British Chancellor of the Exchequer Austen Chamberlain, staring at even larger debts to the United States than his counterpart in Paris, echoed the French appeal for unity in November.[99] The American government responded with phrases soon to become a refrain of postwar diplomacy: the war debts must be honored; there was no connection between reparations and war debts; there can be no single world financial settlement.[100]

The French discovered even before the Peace Conference, therefore, that Clémentel's grandiose schemes for state-directed economic cooperation, restricted to the Allied nations, were the antithesis of American policy. It is questionable to what degree Clemenceau or Loucheur expected American largesse, but both were committed to replacing free enterprise at home and abroad with a structure of controls. Both Loucheur and Clémentel promoted cartelization within France and the continuation of wartime regulation of raw materials, measures to ensure that France could speak with one voice in international economic councils. But even before the Armistice, Woodrow Wilson ordered the dismantling of the War Industries Board and only under protest did the United States participate in the continued blockade on Germany. While American consideration of Europe's immediate distress would continue for a limited period through the Supreme Economic Council, Wilson and his major economic advisors, Herbert Hoover, Bernard Baruch, Norman Davis, and Albert Rathbone, all favored a return, as hastily as possible, to free enterprise, and all opposed any long-term distinctions between the Allies and the defeated powers.[101] To the Europeans, American policy seemed narrowly nationalist, but Wilson identified American economic interest

[99] The total cost of the war to the Allied and Associated Powers was estimated at $147 billion. Of that amount $36 billion were American expenditures, including $9.5 billion in loans to the European allies. These were the war debts. Britain owed $4.17 billion to the United States, France $2.96 billion, and Italy $1.60 billion. Britain had also extended considerable sums to France, as well as to Italy, Russia, and the lesser allies. See Artaud, *La reconstruction de l'Europe*, p. 7.

[100] Denise Artaud, "Le gouvernement americain et la question des dettes de guerre, 1919-1920," *Revue d'histoire moderne et contemporaine* 20 (1963): 203-204; Georges Soutou, "Les problèmes du retablissement des relations économiques entre la France et l'Allemagne, 1918-1929," *Francia* 2 (1973): 580.

[101] Baker, *Woodrow Wilson and World Settlement*, II, 314-333, 360-375; Levin, *Woodrow Wilson and World Politics*, pp. 139-150; see also FRUS, Paris Peace Conference 1919, II, 538-546.

with that of a world market economy. European schemes for exclusivity and restrictions aroused his suspicion. His liberal internationalism demanded free trade, free access to markets, and a powerful unfettered German economy contributing to the general recovery. The victors were thus asked to sacrifice their narrow interests in behalf of universal principles; but would not America make similar sacrifices?

When negotiations for the League of Nations began in Paris, Europeans revived their hopes. Backed by an extensive Parisian press campaign, the French lobbied for a *Société Financière des Nations*, to share the burdens of economic reconstruction as the League was to do politically. To the Americans this was a disguised attempt to leave on Washington's doorstep the bill for Europe's recovery, as well as the burden of seeking to collect reparations from Germany. But without liberation from the war debts, the Europeans could hardly view with favor the economic speculations of the Americans. Colonel House's "general syndicate of reparations contributed to by all allies, enemies, and neutrals according to their capacity" met with approval on neither side of the Atlantic. Such a plan was generous to Germany, but the Europeans could permit no such generosity until the United States renounced its claim on them.

Attempts to bundle the war debt question back into the Conference through the rear door followed the early rebuffs. At the end of January 1919 the Italians took advantage of a subcommission instructed to list all outstanding financial questions other than reparations, to propose a repartition of interallied debts. When the Americans and British (who held large obligations from the continental allies) demurred, Klotz pleaded on 20 February that the idea not be rejected out of hand. On 1 March, the commission's recommendations reached the Americans. A week later, Assistant Secretary of the Treasury Albert Rathbone categorically refused to discuss the subject. What was more, the U.S. Treasury informed France that it would not consider any future advances to any governments favorable to the project.[102] It was in this atmosphere of American financial particularism that German reparations were discussed at Paris. Meanwhile, the shattering of all common cause through the removal of Allied currency supports sent the exchanges into a whirlwind. While the dollar soared, European currencies were sucked under. Continued insecurity concerning the future financial burdens of Germany and the Allies alike meant that eccentric fluctuations would characterize world finance for years.

[102] Étienne Weill-Raynal, *Les réparations allemandes et la France*, 3 vols. (Paris, 1947-1949), I, 52-59. For the motives of American war debt policy, see below, Chapter III.

Driven by nearly unanimous opinion at home (even Socialists approved of Germany's repairing the damage she had wrought) and despairing of American largesse, European peace delegations looked to Germany for the wherewithal to protect their currencies and taxpayers during the bleak years of recovery. Quickly diverging from the resolutions of the 1916 Economic Conference, the British cabinet responded to American policy, internal clashes of interest, and the vengeful mood of the electorate by dropping schemes for Allied or imperial preference and relying instead on a massive indemnity for economic security. The British insisted on the inclusion of war pensions in the reparations bill, a charge that inflated Germany's responsibilities and changed the nature of reparations from a finite material task to an endless financial fiction.[103] Instead of delivering materials for the reconstruction of France and Belgium, and ships to Britain, Germany would be obligated to hand over vast sums of foreign currency for decades. On the other hand, the British favored setting a fixed indemnity that Germany would agree to in signing the treaty and that would permit the commercialization of the German debt. The French claimed that Germany's obligation was to repair the damage, whatever the cost, and that no price could as yet be placed on it. Either approach to reparations promised mammoth difficulties. Large specie payments introduced all the problems of transfer, foreign exchange, and interest charges likely to destabilize the world's capital markets for years. Large deliveries in kind involved the problems of price, would not help to balance budgets, and would interfere with private economic interests.

Added to the Franco-British reparations controversy was the question of Germany's capacity to pay at all. The British theorized that their pensions demands would not increase Germany's burden because German transfers would be based ultimately on her capacity to pay.

[103] The tactics expressed in Britain's controversial pensions demand are still unclear. The traditional explanation has been that Britain opposed computation of Germany's bill solely on the basis of reconstruction costs, since France (and Belgium) had suffered far more material damage and would receive an inordinate percentage of German payments. Britain had suffered more "invisible" devastation in the form of lost markets and capital depreciation. But a vast increase in the British share of reparations would also give London increased influence in future Allied reparations policy, a factor that would be of great value if the British were already thinking in terms of restraining France and moderating reparations demands. But this explanation cannot confront the fact that by the end of March, when the pensions demand was pressed, the French and British negotiators had nearly reached accord on the percentages allotted to their countries regardless of the total bill. Lord Sumner had accepted a ratio of 56:28, Louis Loucheur 55:25. The reparation negotiations are treated in detail by Trachtenberg, "French Reparation Policy," pp. 36-120. British obstructionism at the Peace Conference is still enigmatic. Bunselmeyer, *The Cost of the War*. offers no new insights.

"Germany will pay to the last penny" was not an extreme program. It would, in fact, justify every sort of subterfuge by Germany to demonstrate her incapacity to pay. The French did not argue that Germany ought to pay, but that Germany *would* pay. The British recognized the right to reparations, but were not willing to ruin Germany to collect. The French were prepared to ruin Germany if necessary, for the alternative was their own ruin.[104]

Both sides were reluctant to name any figure as a total sum for domestic political reasons. Nevertheless, Lord Cunliffe and Louis Loucheur offered opening suggestions on 21 February 1919, of 480 and 800 billion gold marks, to be paid in fifty annuities. The Americans, asking nothing for themselves, felt free to suggest a sum of 20 billions before 1 May 1921, followed by 100 billion gold marks in installments afterwards. Under this coaxing, the British dropped to 190 billion and Loucheur to 160 billion. But the British still insisted on subordinating any German payments to their capacity to pay. The French responded by withdrawing their willingness to consider a "forfeiture," the fixing of a precise sum. It would take years, they claimed, to estimate the damages in northern France. On 24 March the American delegation suggested the postponement of the entire problem. A reparations commission could be created, a standing committee to determine German liabilities over the course of time.

The idea of a permanent commission did not settle the bitter and divisive controversies over postwar finances; it only permitted the victors to drag the disputes into the postwar years. Klotz and Lloyd George both offered plans toward the end of March based on a standing commission. But again the French demanded an open account while the British insisted on a solution based on German capacity to pay—even though their own inclusion of pensions had vastly increased the total bill![105] In early April the debate climaxed. The French would not agree to the principle, but admitted that the reparations commission could grant Germany reductions or even moratoria, thus accounting for Germany's capacity to pay on a de facto basis. Otherwise the Germans would use the phrase as an excuse to avoid all payment. In

[104] Rather than subordinate German payments to her capacity to pay as calculated by a committee France could not dominate, Loucheur at this point offered to return to a literal application of the Fourteen Points, which simply required Germany to make reparations, with no reference to pensions or capacity to pay. Such a "radical" suggestion was attractive to neither Lord Sumner nor the American delegate, Norman Davis. Instead, Davis urged the French to appease the British and to make further concessions in the negotiations on reparations percentages without pressing for a fixed total.

[105] Paul Mantoux, *Les délibérations du Conseil des Quatre (24 mars-28 juin 1919)*, 2 vols. (Paris, 1955), I: pp. 29-40. See Trachtenberg, "French Reparations Policy," pp. 75-77.

response, the British accused the French of seeking to use the commission to prolong German obligations indefinitely, to effect perpetual control over the German economy. The Paris debate gave first breath to remonstrances that would echo incessantly through the halls of future conferences.

On 5 April Clemenceau accepted a compromise. The German debt would be fixed by the commission, but it would not have the authority to rule on Germany's capacity to pay. German obligations would not be left to "experts" to decide; they would be a political matter between governments. Throughout April the details were filled in. The United States again retreated from any formula likely to commit America to European reconstruction, although an American delegate would sit on the commission, allowing the Europeans to claim an indirect connection between reparations and war debts. To satisfy French demands for guarantees, the commission would be empowered to declare defaults and recommend sanctions against Germany. The Belgian government received special consideration: transfer of its war debt to Germany's account and a priority of payment for Belgian reconstruction. The French petitioned for and were denied similar rights. The amount and rhythm of German payments were to be fixed by 1 May 1921, before which time Germany was to transfer 20 billion gold marks. The Peace Conference adjourned with no plan for currency stabilization, no determination of the sums owed to foreign governments by the victors or the vanquished, no philosophy on which to base postwar commercial policies, no comprehensive plan for the reconstruction of the devastated regions.

Paralyzed in part by the immensity of the financial difficulties left by the war, in part unappreciative of the need for their immediate redressment, the three major victors chose to put off stabilization. The Reparations Commission became a repository for unfinished business, guaranteeing that it would not be an impartial executor, but an arena of political disputation. The problem of transfers, untouched at Paris, was the cornerstone of the political struggle to come. The Americans recognized it: "The problem is not determining what Germany can pay, but what the Allies can afford to receive."[106] To pay reparations, Germany would have to become so strong as to pose an even greater threat to Europe than in 1914. The subcommittee's report of 7 April noted this danger, but added: ". . . if we only ask a moderate indemnity, the Germans, with their assiduousness, perseverance, and sobriety, will have it quickly paid off and can take up their former commercial tac-

[106] Memo Norman Davis to Lloyd George, 20 Mar. 1919, cited by Baker, *Woodrow Wilson and World Settlement*, III, 301.

tics, doubtless working more ardently for their own enrichment than for the repair of all they have savagely destroyed."[107]

Of what promise then was Wilson's program of German reintegration and Free Trade to Germany's competitors, particularly France? The American delegation had little influence on European economic policies, given its own unwillingness to contribute to recovery. Instead of lowering barriers to trade, Britain, France, and the successor states responded to peace with increased tariffs to defend stricken industries. For if closing western markets to German exports would make reparations more difficult, at least it would prevent the unthinkable development of German revival outstripping that of the battered Allies. The dilemma for the French government, as it viewed the wreckage of "Allied economic unity," was that France needed both reparations and German economic containment. Those tangled roots grew into a Gordian knot.

In May 1919 the Financial Committee of the Supreme Council sought to create a Financial Section in the League of Nations, so that discussion of liquidation of the cost of the war might at least continue. The American Treasury refused to participate. On 5 May Wilson rejected a plan of John M. Keynes for the linking of reparations and war debts. There remained at least the possibility of replacing the nonsettlement in the peace treaty with a fixed reparations sum, occasioned by the German observations on the draft treaty in June 1919. Lloyd George told the Empire delegations that "the time had not come for letting the Germans off of anything," but under pressure led by General Smuts he reopened the reparations questions in the Supreme Council. Loucheur showed a willingness to consider setting a fixed sum for reparations; Wilson supported the idea. But having initiated the discussion, Lloyd George now backed off.

The British reluctance to name a figure was political; neither the French nor the British cabinet relished the day when they would have "to tell the truth" about reparations expectations to their constituencies. But Loucheur offered on 5 June to set reparations "eventually" at 120 billion gold marks, again with American experts' support.[108] Wilson now proved a stumbling block. He rejected concessions made out of fear that Germany would not sign, and felt unable to press either for negotiations between the Allies and Germany on a reparations bill or for the inclusion of a reduced fixed amount. The implications of America's own financial policy precluded him from pressuring for com-

[107] Weill-Raynal, *Les réparations allemandes*, I, 85-86.

[108] P. M. Burnett, *Reparations at the Paris Peace Conference from the Standpoint of the American Delegation*, 2 vols. (New York, 1940), II, 124.

promise with Germany, lest the Allies exercise this same right concerning war debts. "Cannot understand Wilson," noted Harold Nicolson. "Here is a chance of improving the [treaty] and he won't take it."[109]

The following month, in response to European requests for American coal and foodstuffs, Herbert Hoover voiced the American opinion on Europe's difficulties. They were internal and must be solved internally. The "prewar capitalist individualism" of Europe had been destroyed in the war by the need for economic discipline and control. Now this, too, was gone, and peace had brought disorganization, labor demands, and a relaxation of effort. The crisis was one of production. But production could not increase "if political incompetence continues in blockade, embargoes, censorship, mobilization, large armies, navies, and war." Compared with these issues, the question of assistance from the Western Hemisphere was "but a minor question."[110] It was up to Europe to pull herself up by the bootstraps. But, failing American leadership, the Peace Conference left no plan as to how that might be done. As the French security settlement of Versailles offered substance without a guiding philosophy, the reparations settlement offered a philosophy without substance.

THE RHINELAND AGREEMENT, CONSTITUTION OF THE OCCUPATION

The Conference of Brussels in early March 1919 and the tough Anglo-American stand at Paris ended French hopes of an Allied-imposed Rhenish separation. But the simultaneous refusal of the Anglo-Americans to make the commitment necessary (in French eyes) to the success of their own security systems enhanced the importance of the Rhineland for France. Britain spoke of the balance of power, but shied away from Eastern Europe. The United States forced a League of Nations on Europe, but would not make the League a credible deterrent. The effect was that France was pushed toward Germany. *L'Écho de Paris* and *Le Matin*, for instance, expressed their disgust with English and American economic policies by touting relations with Germany as the only path to recovery. They spoke for heavy industrial interests, interested in peace with the Ruhr. But they also spoke for Loucheur.

[109] Nicolson, *Peacemaking 1919*, p. 358.

[110] "Memo by the Director-General of Relief (Hoover) on the Economic Situation of Europe," Supreme Economic Council Meeting XXVI, 10 July 1919: Foreign Office, E. L. Woodward and Rohan Butler, eds., *Documents on British Foreign Policy, 1919-1939* (London, 1946), 1st ser. (hereafter cited as DBFP), V, 26-31.

France could "relate" to Germany economically in either of two ways, by forceful measures to harness the German economy to work for France, or by freely negotiated cooperation. In either case, France must preserve leverage, which in turn rested on her treaty powers, and ultimately on her military presence on the Rhine. Though political goals were set aside for the moment, the French peace delegation looked again to the Rhineland. The occupation could prove to be an economic guarantee—and a "link" to Germany—as well as a political guarantee if France secured the power and right to make it so.

Since January, Paul Tirard's efforts to solidify and make permanent French economic and administrative influence in the Rhineland had proceeded apace. His *Contrôle-Général* originally consisted of three services—political, financial, and industrial. As with the Economic Sections, the industrial service was funded and staffed by Loucheur's ministry. Three more services were subsequently added to the *Contrôle-Général*: commercial and diplomatic, entrusted to an official from the Quai d'Orsay; judicial; and legislative, headed by experts in German and international law. Tirard's administrative dinosaur reached full growth.[111]

Until the month of March, when French policy changed, Tirard had sought to make feasible the creation of independent states on the Rhine. Subsequently, he reported: "The administration directed its efforts toward preparing for France the dominant place due her in whatever inter-allied control commission remained during the Rhineland occupation. The directing thought was intensification of French influence and economic action to assure *in the future* the possibility for the Rhenish people to realize their desires within the Germanic Confederation."[112] The policy of gradualism had taken over. But Tirard's measures to make the Rhineland safe for separatism commanded no respect from the British, Belgian, and American occupations. Interallied organizations already in existence required unanimity for major decisions. Tirard envisioned a new institution invested with absolute power in all four zones, capable of executing majority decisions, and chaired by the French representative. On 3 March he submitted a project for such a reorganization of Allied political power in the Rhineland. British diplomat Sidney Waterlow countered with a proposal for a council of four commissioners, equal in authority. The French objected and debate languished while the Big Three were deadlocked in Paris.

Not until 22 April did compromise on the Rhenish question and acceptance of the fifteen-year occupation permit resumption of talks on

[111] Tirard, "Rapport," p. 111.

[112] Ibid., p. 17.

the future institutional basis of Allied authority in the occupied territories. The Conference of Foreign Ministers created a subcommittee for Germany within the Supreme Economic Council and placed beneath it an Interallied Rhineland Commission. It was a temporary organ governed by two secretaries, one French and one British, and not empowered to deal with political or administrative issues. But it survived in this form for only two months. It was the embryo of the governing body given birth in the Rhineland Agreement of 28 June 1919.

The negotiations leading up to the Rhineland Agreement were refreshingly free of interallied conflict. The stuff of dissension was there in differing interpretations of the purpose of the occupation and the role of its governing body. To the British, the military presence should be passive. They envisioned small Allied contingents keeping to their barracks and interfering as little as possible with Rhenish life. Both the British and Americans insisted on a civil governing commission. To the French, such an arrangement would defeat the purpose of the occupation, which was to pressure Germany to fulfill the treaty. Despite these differences, the major debate on the occupation was carried on among the French themselves. All agreed on the need for an active occupation, but Marshal Foch opposed any suggestions of a civilian commission. The safety of the Allied armies, their operational liberty and, above all, Foch's own authority would be jeopardized under civilian administration.

The Supreme Council named a committee for the Left Bank of the Rhine on 29 May, and instructed it to draft an agreement for the fifteen-year occupation. The committee, chaired by Loucheur, took as its basis for discussion not the suggestions of Tirard nor those of Waterlow or Foch, but a letter to President Wilson from the American representative on the Interallied Rhineland Commission, Pierrepont Noyes. His plan envisioned as few troops as possible, none billeted on private property, complete freedom for the duly constituted German authorities, and a civil commission empowered to interdict German laws contrary to the treaty or endangering the security of the occupation. The only prerogative of the armies themselves would be to establish martial law if requested to do so by the commission.[113]

The occupation was to be passive, but still possess the power to act in an emergency. Discussion arose over the potentially elastic clause "security of the occupation," but the British representative, Robert Cecil, defended the wording. He agreed that it was an "omnibus

[113] Paul Tirard, *La France sur le Rhin, douze années d'occupation rhénane* (Paris, 1930), pp. 103-104.

clause" but felt it was necessary to cover unforeseen eventualities. Thus the document meant to describe a passive occupation in fact permitted Allied intervention in every aspect of Rhenish life, assuming that a majority of the commissioners agreed on a course of action.[114] The expectation that Anglo-American cooperation could block French or Franco-Belgian attempts to "misuse" the commission undoubtedly permitted Cecil's acquiescence. It was Marshal Foch, at the next meeting, who attacked the proposed commission. Witnessing the destruction of his own authority on the Rhine, Foch blurted that the power of this commission was enormous, more than any military occupation ever had! "Are you opposed to that?" Loucheur quickly interjected. "I am opposed to any commission with the right to decree in any domain whatsoever," Foch replied. This time the cool Loucheur lost his temper and reminded the marshal that the purpose of the commission was only to assure the security of his troops. "I have no need of a commission to do that!" was Foch's parting shot.[115]

The damage had been done. In the wake of this explosion, the American representative reopened the question of the future commission's powers, particularly in the economic domain. He could not accept tampering with German sovereignty in such matters as tariffs and tax collection. Loucheur was obliged to retreat, stating that such interference was certainly not the committee's intention. Foch launched his last missiles in two notes of 5 and 9 June, but following as they did the military-inspired putsches in the Rhineland, none of the three major Allies was in a mood to bow to military authority. The civil commission was adopted.[116] But the issue of the elastic clause was not settled when the committee reported on 9 June. It announced the ultimate creation of an Interallied Rhineland High Commission, composed of four high commissioners under a president, the French commissioner. The elastic clause remained, with the attached opinion that the High Commission was not to use its powers in financial or economic matters, but that the "ordinances for the protection of the treaty regime" left the door open to important extensions of the commission's field of action.[117]

The Rhineland Agreement was signed on 28 June 1919, separate from the Treaty of Versailles. The German government protested the

[114] P.-V., Commission interalliée de la Rive Gauche du Rhin, 31 May 1919: AN HCF, vol. 2891, dos. 2C.

[115] Ibid., 3 June 1919.

[116] Notes Foch, 5 and 9 June 1919: MG 6N73 Fonds Clemenceau, dos. Rive Gauche.

[117] Rapport présenté au Conseil des principes puissances alliées et associées par la commission interalliée de la Rive Gauche du Rhin, 9 June 1919: MG 6N73 Fonds Clemenceau, dos. Rive Gauche.

imprecision of the document in a series of notes throughout the summer. The Allies declined to favor the Germans with a binding interpretation of the occupation's powers, but permitted the appointment of a German high commissioner, who would act as liaison and consultant with the Rhineland Commission.[118]

Once again the unwillingness of the Allies to agree on specific interpretations of the peace settlement made inevitable future conflict among themselves and with Germany. The vague powers of the Rhineland Commission were not the result of a French plot, being first suggested by the Americans, but Clemenceau, Tardieu, and Loucheur did recognize that the Rhineland occupation was the only material guarantee of German compliance with the treaty. The occupation must be rendered a tool, a versatile tool, capable of a wide range of activities. The powers vested in the Rhineland Commission completed the program begun with military occupation seven months before. They made the occupation a guarantee.

A POINT OF DEPARTURE; THE *PARLEMENT* AND THE PEACE

Except for their brief outburst in April 1919, the Chamber of Deputies and Senate remained unassertive during the period of Paris peacemaking. But Clemenceau's secretive style only encouraged the formation of a system of assumptions about French security that ran counter to his own. The premier would have to overcome them in the parliamentary ratification debates in August and September 1919. If the Socialist Left called for a peace of reconciliation with no annexations or "disguised annexations," the Center and Right had taken for granted a peace based on the utterances of France's first soldier, Marshal Foch. But on 7 May it was clear that Clemenceau had rejected the security formula of Rhenish separation; after the putsches of 1 June, it was also apparent that the premier would take no action to help the Rhinelanders break with Prussia, a solution that, French papers claimed, the population desired. Instead, the Chamber received in the treaty a system for postwar security that it could not understand, a formula that

[118] The German protests aptly demonstrate that Berlin understood the real stakes in the debate over the Rhineland Commission. That the pleas failed to move the British and Americans indicates that the Anglo-Americans were confident of their ability to balance French influence in the Commission. American repudiation of the treaty of peace was unforeseen. See FRUS, Paris Peace Conference 1919, VI, 655, 730-734, and Alma Luckau, *The German Delegation at the Paris Peace Conference* (New York, 1941), pp. 485-489.

satisfied neither Left nor Right. When Pichon's *Le Petit Journal* called the draft treaty *Une Paix Française!* few Frenchmen believed it.[119]

The parliamentary attack directed against the security settlement was highly emotional, but disjointed and contradictory. Louis Barthou, Louis Marin, Henry Franklin-Bouillon, Charles Benoist, and other leading deputies and senators aimed their thrusts at the treaty's weak points, but could present no alternatives to rally behind. In the end, the critics knew that the treaty could not be rejected for the same reason that the terms did not satisfy them—France was only part of the alliance. Rejection of the peace would leave her alone against Germany and the Anglo-Saxon powers. The issues themselves—reliability of the security pacts, failure to destroy German unity, temporary nature of the Rhineland occupation—only reflected the new sense of France's dependence. If a French peace, the dismemberment of Germany, were impossible, then the defeat of 1871 could not be avenged nor a balance of power restored to the continent. The *Parlement* voiced its frustration in the steamy months of summer 1919.[120]

Clemenceau recognized the unpopularity of his hesitant policy in the Rhineland and the need to assuage the Chamber with promises as well as explanations. He showed deference to parliamentary opinion by postponing retribution against the culprits of 1 June, Generals Fayolle, Gérard, and Mangin, until after the discussion and ratification of the treaty. Only in October did he sack the generals, unify command of the occupation force, and place it under General Joseph Degoutte. Preparations for the defense of the treaty, entrusted to Tardieu and Pichon, reflected this need to assuage tempers. The government would find it necessary to pay lip service to the Rhenish policy so popular in the Chamber, while justifying the rejection of that policy at the Peace Conference.

The Rhenish separatist solution to French security was unsatisfactory, Tardieu wrote in July, because it would place France in perennial conflict with Germany, because it violated self-determination, and because it would impose a prolonged military effort on France incompat-

[119] The outburst of the French press against the security and reparations settlements in the treaty evidenced a profound dissatisfaction with the fruits of victory, but was tempered by the same sullen mood of resignation that cloaked the Chamber debates. See Miquel, *La Paix de Versailles*, pp. 296-313, 548-563; E. Beau de Loménie, *Le débat de ratification du Traité de Versailles* (Paris, 1945). The sharply negative reaction of the French diplomatic and military establishments has been described above.

[120] Several leading conservative *parlementaires* carried their frustrations to the general public in the coming months. The treaty had few defenders in print. Attackers included Louis Barthou, *Le Traité de Paix* (Paris, 1919); Leon Bourgeois, *Le Traité de Paix de Versailles* (Paris, 1919); Louis Marin, *Le Traité de Paix* (Paris, 1920); Jacques Bainville, *Les conséquences politiques de la Paix* (Paris, 1920).

ible with the Chamber's desire to reduce military service and cut expenditures. In addition, it would entrust the defense of France to a river line, a barrier sure to be overcome by military technology. The bond created between France and the Anglo-Saxon powers, on the other hand, was an incomparable political instrument "if we know how to make it serve us."[121] Tardieu called into existence a new balance of power in Europe of which the treaty was the charter. He papered over the risks involved in dependence on the Allies by asserting that France was the leader of the alliance. Britain and the United States would never permit Europe to absorb all their energies, but no longer could they afford to ignore Europe. "The postwar alliance will give to France an uncontested material and moral authority in the affairs of Europe, whether in regard to her friends, to the great undefined mass of Russia, or to her adversaries of yesterday."[122]

Tardieu's vision failed to impress parliamentary skeptics. The report of Louis Barthou castigated the framers of the treaty for the failure to break up the German Empire. The victory of 1871 had created it; the defeat of 1918 should end it. Such an act, Tardieu replied, was unthinkable for reasons of conscience and prudence. German unity was a fact, he said, a state of mind. To destroy it by force would make inevitable its recrudescence and a will to revenge. For France, German dismemberment would mean the abandonment of reparations and a false sense of security.[123] It was an eloquent plea, but Tardieu then sought to justify himself and Clemenceau by outlining the stubborn efforts made on behalf of Rhenish separation. He pleaded irreducible Allied opposition as the cause of the failure of the Rhine security plan! The two accounts of the Peace Conference were incompatible: had the French negotiators decided the Rhenish policy was imprudent, or did they give it up only because of Allied protest? Tardieu's image of the new Europe was also unconvincing. It assumed Anglo-American acquiescence in French leadership on the continent, which Tardieu himself knew to be chimerical, and it assumed German submission to the Treaty of Versailles.

Charles Benoist, *Rapporteur-Général* on the political clauses of the treaty, returned to the Rhenish solution as the only guarantee of French security. "Rhenish Prussia" was an artificial creation, he said, and to do away with it would not be in violation of self-determination because the Rhinelanders were of Celtic stock. Why did the French

[121] MS Tardieu, "Examen de la solution donée au problème de la Rive Gauche du Rhin," July 1919: MAE Pap. Tardieu, 3e versement, vol. 4, ch. 6, p. 11.

[122] Ibid., pp. 13-15.

[123] Ibid., pp. 19-23.

government fail to secure for them the independence they craved?[124] In the Senate Foreign Affairs Commission, Léon Bourgeois picked up the theme, asking to know why, in lieu of separation, the government did not pursue de-Prussianization of the Left Bank? Because, Clemenceau replied, France had to live with Germany. To break with the Allies in order to break up Germany was a policy of isolation.[125] It would also sacrifice the financial, economic, and military collaboration of the Anglo-Saxon powers. But had not these powers already shown their distaste for such collaboration?

The primary task of the government's defenders in the ratification debates was to turn the deputies from the idea that Rhenish separation offered a guarantee. Yet, the government also held out the prospect of a renewed separatist policy. This was its final contradiction. Pichon admitted to the Senate Foreign Affairs Commission on 14 August that the treaty did not offer all that France could desire. "If this is not the re-establishment of the frontiers of the Revolution and Empire, we nevertheless may hope in the future that these territories will return to us. . . . The wisdom of our administration will determine if we are to extend our frontiers."[126] Did the present government then have a Rhenish policy? "If so," Pichon answered, "it is in our interest not to divulge it." Tardieu continued, counseling a Rhenish policy of prudence and entente. France could "maintain that which appears useful to our cause" but only if it did not jeopardize France's rights under the treaty.[127] Pichon promised that the government would employ "all the legitimate means at our disposal to develop our activity and influence . . . but we must act with absolute prudence."[128]

On 25 August Clemenceau gave the same advice. France would be in the Rhineland for a long time. There was no need to create difficulties with America for "momentary advantages." Paul Doumer challenged the Tiger with the opinions of Marshal Foch. "Would you have annexed?" barked Clemenceau. Alexandre Ribot, the "dismantler" of Briand's war aims edifice of 1917, suggested, "One could perhaps have fashioned a protectorate." Doumer then intervened as peacemaker, grasping the drift of the premier's remarks. "Let us not be recriminatory. Let us seek to draw the best from the treaty. It is not solely a point of arrival, it is equally a point of departure."

[124] MS Benoist, "du rapport sur le traité de paix, annexé au P.-V. de la séance du 6 octobre 1919": Charles Benoist, unpublished private papers, Institut de France-Paris (hereafter cited as IF Pap. Benoist), vol. 4545, dos. 3.

[125] *Annales de la Chambre des Députés*, 24 Sept. 1919, p. 4104.

[126] P.-V., Commission des Affaires Étrangères, 14 Aug. 1919: Archives du Senat, Auditions, 1919, pp. 1873-1874.

[127] Ibid., pp. 1901-1903.

[128] Ibid., p. 1905.

"That is precisely how we must envisage it," responded Clemenceau.[129]

The last outburst of parliamentary frustration followed the news in September that the American Senate would likely refuse to ratify the treaty. The alliances with Britain and the United States, the substitution for the Rhenish security plan, would both lapse if the Senate rebelled against Wilson. Would the French government then return to its original security scheme? "If the two treaties are not voted," Clemenceau said in September, "there is an article that I myself had inserted. It says that in this case, we will make new arrangements concerning the Rhine. In consequence of that, we are prepared and all is provided for."[130] When the American Senate did refuse the Treaty of Versailles and the British grasped the opportunity to back out of their engagement to France, the Versailles security plan fell apart. The French considered it betrayal, but Clemenceau left behind the means and the justification for turning again to the Rhineland, to a policy whose dangers and shortcomings he himself had enumerated.

PEACEFUL PENETRATION

The lessons learned from the failure of the Rhenish particularist movements of 1918-1919 seemed to point to a Rhenish policy of inconspicuous encouragement for separatism and federalism and attempts to extend French influence. Practiced throughout 1920-1922 under various governments, this policy originated in the last months of the Armistice under the aegis of Clemenceau. Tirard dubbed it "peaceful penetration."

The shortcomings of the June putsches in occupied territory were unmistakable. Military intelligence reported that the separatist leaders were unknown to the great majority of the population, that they possessed little organization and no rapport with established parties and interests. The putsches were sloppy and the time ill-chosen. Finally, the plotters were discredited by their collaboration with French authorities.[131] Tirard also attributed the failure to the opposition of the Peace Conference, the resistance of Prussian and Bavarian functionaries retained at their posts by the Allies, and the opposition of the natural Rhenish leaders, the "Adenauer group." The mayor's reac-

[129] Ibid., 25 Aug. 1919, pp. 1996-1997.

[130] Note Tardieu, "Citations," Clemenceau, 23 Sept. 1919: MAE Pap. Tardieu, 3e versement, vol. 5.

[131] Capt. Bertrand (Coblenz) to GQG, 7 June 1919: MAE Pap. Tardieu, vol. 46, dos. République Rhénane.

tion to the Dorten putsch had been to lead a deputation of notables to Paris to meet with Brockdorff-Rantzau and demand amelioration of the peace terms in return for the creation of a Rhenish state. The British Colonel Rupert Ryan, political officer in Cologne, encouraged the ploy. Clemenceau refused to consider any such *marchandage*, but fears that a future separatist movement might be preempted by an Adenauer-sponsored pro-German Rhenish state remained to plague Tirard. Adenauer became suspect as a "man of the British."[132]

What is surprising is not that the French drew these conclusions from the 1919 events, but that they continued in spite of them to hope for a future Rhenish movement favorable to French interests. The military intelligence report concluded that a successful movement must have no tinge of French instigation and must win the support of party leaders. The French program must be "de longue haleine" and carried out by German agents drawn from the milieux in which they would operate: infiltration, propaganda, a broad subversive front under the direction and in the pay of the French High Commissariat. The French general staff concurred in the potential of propaganda for eliminating "the spirit of Prussianism in the Celtic Rhineland" and for expanding French culture. The general staff then proposed to Philippe Berthelot that the program of educational and political propaganda begun by the army be continued after the Armistice regime ended.[133] Berthelot approved, and met with General Mangin two weeks later to hear his account of Rhenish politics. Mangin insisted on the strength of federalist sentiment and testified that Clemenceau had shown a lively interest in it.[134]

Thus the earlier differences between Clemenceau, the career diplomats, and the military were replaced by consensus on the new Rhenish policy of France. Tirard undertook to expand the first attempts of the occupation to subsidize people, parties, and publications favoring Rhenish autonomy or rapprochement with France. Collaborators among the higher echelons of Rhenish society proved nonexistent, but by December Tirard's agents had made contact with Dr. Dorten and others whose activities Clemenceau had rued just months before. Instigated with the cautious approval of Paris, peaceful

[132] E.M.G., GQG, "Compte-rendu du 8 juin": MG 6N73 Fonds Clemenceau, dos. Rive Gauche; "Note relative à la situation à Cologne," 14 June 1919: MAE Rive Gauche, vol. 1, nos. 144-148; Let. Tirard to Tardieu, 14 June 1919: MAE Pap. Tardieu, vol. 46, dos. République Rhénane.

[133] E.M.A., 2e bureau, to Berthelot, 1 July 1919: MAE Allemagne, vol. 401, nos. 29-38.

[134] Note Berthelot, "Conversation avec le Général Mangin," 16 July 1919: MAE Rive Gauche, vol. 1, nos. 182-183.

penetration became an ongoing fact of French administration in the Rhineland.

The memory of Louis XIV, Napoleon, and the "natural frontiers" of France still fascinated nationalist circles in France, and a deep conviction of their cultural superiority permitted Frenchmen to believe that this Catholic, wine-drinking, and once-French region of Germany preferred to associate with them. If few believed in the Rhineland's desire for outright annexation by France, the view was widespread that the Rhineland was the prisoner of Protestant and authoritarian Prussia. Clemenceau and Tardieu chided the Chamber for believing that a hundred years of Prussian rule could be undone in a day, yet under their government the policy of peaceful penetration was instituted.

Tirard still saw economic measures as the best way to draw the Rhineland to France. In October 1919 he told the interministerial committee for the Left Bank that the goal of French policy was the "dislocation of Prussia." Under the Armistice, the Allies were able to place an economic barrier between the Left Bank and Germany, but the coming into force of the treaty on 10 January 1920 would restore complete German sovereignty to the Rhineland. Still, Tirard hoped, the Left Bank could be the French base of operations with Germany in economic concerns.[135] He outlined the capabilities of the Economic Sections and the possibility of reinstituting a customs barrier against nonoccupied Germany under Article 270 of the Treaty.[136] In confidential notes Tirard's economic plans ranged farther. He foresaw the possibility of economic sanctions on the Left Bank and, in a note of 29 November 1919, contingencies permitting the occupation of the Ruhr. That event alone, he prophesied, would suffice to spark a Rhenish separatist movement.[137]

Tirard did not confine himself to economics. He envisioned purchasing and subsidizing Rhenish newspapers to fashion an "indigenous" movement while matching it with French propaganda and charitable works, educational and religious activities. No aspect of the campaign that had served so well in Morocco failed to find a counterpart in the Rhineland. Furthermore, Tirard reported that Dorten had taken up a program of political action and would need money and protection.[138] For Tirard himself Clemenceau had little enthusiasm. Tirard was

[135] P.-V., conférence du 14 octobre 1919 sur le régime économique des pays rhénans: AN HCF, vol. 2892, dos. 2E.

[136] Article 270 authorized a customs barrier on the Rhine if the Rhenish populations determined it to be in their interests.

[137] Des. Tirard to MAE, 29 Nov. 1919: MAE Rive Gauche, vol. 1, nos. 272-282.

[138] Let. Tirard to MAE, 29 Oct. 1919; Let. Tirard to Clemenceau, 3 Nov. 1919: MAE Paix, vol. 167, nos. 105-111; vol. 166, nos. 107-119. French schools in the Rhineland, for

Foch's man and he operated beyond the immediate control of government. General Henri Mordacq, Clemenceau's personal aide, attests that the Tiger hesitated before naming Tirard the French High Commissioner-designate.[139] When Tirard requested regular funding for his programs of penetration, Clemenceau seized the opportunity to ensure that, if "penetration" were to continue, at least the High Commissioner would be the servant and not the master of French policy.

Funds for French propaganda in 1919 came from the budget of the occupation armies and of the French legation in Berlin. At the end of 1919 Tirard requested an allowance of his own, starting at 100,000 francs per month. Clemenceau responded with a lengthy presidential decree defining the official status of the future High Commissariat. It would receive funds and directives from the Quai d'Orsay and would enjoy no independence of policy. The decree further recognized the role Tirard's commission would play in the execution of the Treaty of Versailles: "There is no need to point out that 'ordinances to assure the maintenance and security of the military forces' is easily extended to concern everything connected with the administration of the country. This clause constitutes a weapon that must be used with the greatest care; it is one of the principal means of pressure." Tirard was instructed to report all intelligence to the Foreign Ministry and to retain close control of his agents. Policy was the government's responsibility; there were to be no initiatives from the Rhineland.[140]

The resources at Tirard's command consisted, first, of his organization. It was a simple process to transfer the administration of the *Contrôle-Général* to the newly created High Commissariat. He already possessed economic, political, and judicial staffs with a year's experience in Rhenish problems. He controlled a system of delegates distributed one per German *Kreise*, with a delegate-general for each *Bezirk*. He directed the Economic Sections, left under the High Commissariat by the presidential decree, and he would enter into the powers of the President of the Rhineland Commission on 10 January 1920.

The Allied commissions in the Rhineland were meant to be civil organizations, but Tirard drew the greater part of his administration from the occupation army. In February 1919 expansion of the *Contrôle-*

army children and for instruction of Germans in French language and culture, were supported by the Ministry of Public Instruction.

[139] Mordacq, *Le ministère Clemenceau*, III, 140.

[140] MAE memo for Clemenceau, 31 Dec. 1919: MAE Paix, vol. 166, no. 31; Tel. MAE to Tirard (Coblenz), Bruère (Cologne), Marcilly (Berlin), presidential decree, "Haut-Commissariat des Territoires Rhénans," 25 Nov. 1919, transmitted 5 Jan. 1920: MAE Allemagne, vol. 522, nos. 69-76.

Général forced personnel recruitment on a large scale. Foch and Pétain approved Tirard's suggestion that service personnel be drawn from the army as a means of retaining in service demobilized officers qualified for administrative positions. This provided a ready solution to the manpower problem, entailed less expense since a military pay scale could be adopted, and ensured discipline and security.[141] It also imbued the French Rhineland administration with a military mentality; officials looked upon the Rhineland as conquered territory and undermined the spirit of civilian government advocated by the British and Americans.[142]

The titular function of Tirard's bureaucracy was execution of the Rhineland Commission's ordinances for the protection of the occupation regime. But their duties also came to include intelligence gathering, collaboration with separatists, and advancement of French economic interests. To ensure the continued activity of the separatists, Tirard planned his first encroachment on German sovereignty. He and Foch drew up a project for amnesty to all German nationals accused of political crimes during the Armistice period.[143] Thus an inaugural act of the new Rhineland Commission would be an act of clemency, but far from fostering goodwill with the German authorities, it meant immunity from prosecution for those involved in the June putsches.

The activity of the German bureaucracy was one of Tirard's chief concerns. Since the treaty recognized German sovereignty in the occupied Rhineland, the French administration was placed in a paradoxical position. The Allied occupation, a defense of the treaty regime, was technically a support for Prussian and Bavarian authority on the Left

[141] Let. Pétain to Clemenceau, 25 Feb. 1919: MAE Pap. Tardieu, vol. 44, dos. Organisation de l'Occupation.

[142] Personnel policies of Tirard's High Commissariat were notoriously bad. Hiring procedures, to the extent they showed any discrimination, were based on cronyism and Tirard's prejudice in favor of Lyautey-trained colonial administrators. In 1922 the French employees of the Rhineland Commission produced a satirical revue as part of morale-boosting festivities. One skit portrayed two young French citizens applying for jobs in the personnel office.

Addressing the first applicant, the official asked, "Are you a *chasseur-à-pied*?"

"No, monsieur," the young man replied.

"Well, then, have you been to Morocco?"

"No, monsieur."

"The devil! I just don't know what we'll do with you. Ah! I have it. We'll put you in the press office as a translator."

"But, monsieur," the man stammered. "I don't read German."

"No matter," replied the official. "Next!"

The second applicant was asked the same questions, but being female had regretfully to reply that she was neither a *chasseur-à-pied* nor a Morocco veteran. She ended up in the steno pool despite her protests that she couldn't type.

[143] Secretary-General, conference of the peace, to MAE, 16 Oct. 1919: MAE Paix, vol. 166, nos. 103-105.

Bank. Tirard rebelled against this circumstance, insisting that French arms never be called on to defend "acts of tyranny" or to maintain a repressive regime. The institution most odious to Tirard was that of the Reich High Commissariat. It would clearly organize resistance to Allied authority, he wrote, and combat separatist and autonomist ideas. Thus Tirard prepared to do battle with Berlin, and when the treaty came into force in January 1920, he conceived of his mission as one directly opposed to the official purpose of the occupation. He had received the blessing of the government for a policy of peaceful penetration, and he had instituted an organization and tactics for its long-range execution.

Despite the legal foundation of the French Rhineland establishment, activities aimed at Rhenish political change were illegal under international law. The Treaty of Versailles and the Rhineland Agreement both recognized (the British said "guaranteed") Germany's postwar boundaries and political unity. A month after the signature of these documents, the German National Assembly at Weimar eliminated the possibility of a Rhenish autonomy within the Reich. Shunning both separatism and forceful tactics, the representatives of the Rhenish Center party went to Weimar to seek a legal path to provincial autonomy. They found allies among Bavarian and Hanoverian delegates but could not prevail against the forces favorable to German centralization. The debate on the "territorial division of the Reich" climaxed on 22 July 1919, and produced Articles 18 and 167 of the Weimar Constitution. The creation of new provinces would be possible with the assent of the interested territories. But determination of the will of the people entailed a referendum conducted under conditions that made a positive result virtually impossible. A third of the entire electorate must petition for a referendum that would then test the will of all the people in the political unit involved, not just the areas interested in autonomy. A three-fifths majority was then needed, with nonvoters placed in the negative column, for a new *Bundesstaat* to win legal existence.

The stipulations of the Constitution made legal autonomy for the Left Bank highly unlikely. The entire Prussian Rhineland would be polled together, including Westphalia on the Right Bank, with its concentration of Socialist workers. The mobilization of 60 percent of the electorate was an organizational task beyond the capabilities even of the Center party. In any case, the plebiscite would be administered by the bureaucracy of the state from which the province was seeking separation! Creation of new territorial entities could otherwise be permitted only through a constitutional law approved by the

Reichstag. Article 167 further reduced the chances of legal action. It instituted a *Sperrfrist*, a cooling-off period of two years during which no movement for a plebiscite would be entertained.

French observers and even moderate autonomist journals in the Rhineland denounced the victory of the centralizers at Weimar. Not only had the Center party permitted the defeat of true federalism, it had also joined with the Democrats and Social Democrats in the ruling coalition that governed Germany! Still the French did not surrender all hopes that the Center party might lead an anti-Prussian campaign in the future. General Staff intelligence reported that the Rhenish Center aimed at securing religious freedom and concessions from Berlin concerning administration in the Rhine province. The French must bring the Centrists to see the shortsightedness of this policy and encourage them to act against Prussia.[144]

In fact, the Center party was going through a period of factional strife. The decision to participate in the Weimar coalition, to see through the constitution and signature of the treaty, saved the Reich from chaos and possible dissolution, but collaboration with the Marxist Socialists infuriated the Center's right wing. Acquiescence on the autonomy issue was an important, but secondary, cause of internal strife. On 4 August 1919 a Centrist peasants' meeting denounced the *Sperrfrist* and the *Scheinautonomie* offered by Berlin. But French observers again misjudged such manifestations. The party leadership had no desire to abandon the German fatherland. Indeed, it had several reasons for suspending the campaign for autonomy, and distrust of French intentions and the threat posed by French occupation were among those reasons. In hoping for Centrist support for a Rhenish movement favorable to France, Tirard, the military, and the Quai d'Orsay once more plunged ahead in pursuit of a mirage.

Despite his surrender of Rhenish separatist ambitions at the Peace Conference, and despite Germany's contrary political evolution, Clemenceau agreed to keep open the option of Rhenish state-building. In the face of near unanimous criticism within the government, with a presidential election weeks away, perhaps the Tiger, in the final months of his fifty years in politics, lost confidence in his own creation. Certainly he was aware of the mood of the American Senate and the sentiment of the British Foreign Office (the first American failure to approve the treaty occurred on 19 November). The treaty system was already crumbling by the end of 1919. Lest France be cheated of her victory, Clemenceau bequeathed two policies to his successors, a

[144] E.M.A., 2^e^ bureau, to Foch, Tirard, Berthelot, "La nouvelle Article 18," 25 July 1919: MAE Rive Gauche, vol. 1, nos. 190-194.

German policy based on the Treaty of Versailles, and a Rhenish policy, based on its revision. "The Rhenish question," Tirard wrote the Tiger in the last weeks of his government, "not resolved as it could have been in 1918 and badly posed, both in Paris and in the Rhineland, during the peace conference, must enter now into its decisive phase. The constitution of a Rhenish state is an inevitable political event."[145]

[145] Tirard, "Rapport," p. 96.

•3•

RHENISH VERSUS GERMAN POLICY: THE BIRTH OF FRENCH REVISIONISM, 1920

The events of 1920 demonstrated that Europeans' hopes for rapid political stabilization and economic recovery were in vain. Strikes and domestic turmoil erupted in all nations as wartime domestic "truces" were foresworn. The new German republic and the successor states of Central Europe showed themselves to be volatile constructs, and the prestige and power of the Franco-British Entente proved insufficient to command respect for the international boundaries drawn at Paris. The Bolshevik tide reached its greatest extent in 1920, breaking only before the gates of Warsaw. The United States withdrew from the task of European stabilization through the Senate's final defeat of the Versailles Treaty in March. The French and British themselves drifted further apart as each new crisis of stabilization erupted in eastern Europe or the Near East. Finally, 1920 failed to produce any progress toward the economic and financial reconstruction of Europe. Instead of American loans, resolution of war debts and reparations, and currency stabilization, 1920 revealed a developing deadlock on these questions, while the transition from war to peace produced worldwide recession. The frantic search for solutions to the postwar malaise sharpened the conflicts among state planners, parliament, and industry—conflicts that by the end of the year had clarified the limits imposed on state action by weary taxpayers and assertive industrial lobbies alike.

For the government of Alexandre Millerand, Clemenceau's successor, 1920 was a year of testing the German government's willingness to execute the treaty of peace, and of the Allies' willingness to enforce it. It was an opportunity for the French government to experiment with the two policies bequeathed by Clemenceau: strict execution of the treaty or revisionism based on France's position of strength in the Rhineland. Millerand probed the possibilities of both policies and encountered resistance at every turn. His probes only revealed the postwar dependence of France, and the barriers, not the solutions, to her recovery.

THE INHERITORS AND THE INHERITANCE

The French electoral campaign began on 19 October 1919. Resentment bred by widespread labor agitation, the Bolshevik threat abroad, and the need for a strong military posture to enforce the peace all pointed to a victory for the Right. Further strengthening the Rightist parties was the adept leadership of Alexandre Millerand, who grasped the need for coalition politics under a new election law and engineered a grand conservative republican alliance. Promising reconstruction through social peace and a strong foreign policy, his Bloc National won three-quarters of the seats in the new Chamber, the most conservative French legislature since 1876. The presidential election followed. Clemenceau was the natural choice, but the new deputies had more grudges against him than the old. The Tiger was a man of the Left, an anticlerical, and the negotiator who abandoned the Rhine for stillborn security pacts. Aristide Briand, an old rival, rallied discontented deputies to the candidacy of President of the Chamber Paul Deschanel. Denied the nomination of the republican caucus by nineteen votes, Clemenceau withdrew and Deschanel was elected president on 17 January 1920.

Three days later Millerand formed the new legislature's first cabinet. He was a Socialist when he began his career in the 1880s, but he moved steadily to the Right, served as war minister under Viviani, and emerged in 1918 with the prestigious position of Commissioner-General of Alsace-Lorraine. A stocky, mustachioed man of sixty-one, he exhibited the zeal of a convert to nationalism and the lust for authority of a former tribune. He made revision of the Constitution in favor of a stronger executive a part of his electoral platform. In foreign policy, he was drawn by personal interest and circumstances to a preoccupation with Eastern Europe. In 1917 he wrote Foreign Minister Pichon that "a united Poland spells the death of Prussia."[1] But his German policy was not so simple. His experience in Alsace-Lorraine demonstrated to him the close economic ties existing between those regions—the "old German Southwest"—and the Rhineland and Ruhr. The economic health of the liberated territories would depend on reforging these ties. To do so without undue or dangerous advantage to Germany was the object of Millerand's quest.

The reign of Clemenceau—and the era of war government—were over. What patterns would characterize policy-making in the postwar Third Republic? There were many in France who had found the authoritarian and technocratic nature of war government refreshing. Millerand was not alone in believing that a powerful executive with a "national" base was a twentieth-century imperative from the standpoint of foreign and domestic policy. But the victory of the Bloc National was not a mandate for executive reform, or for strict conservative princi-

[1] Pers. Let. Millerand to Pichon, 28 Dec. 1917: IF Corr. Pichon, vol. 4397, no. 215.

ples, so much as the expression of widespread anti-Bolshevism and the broadening of the ranks of the moderate Right parties. The election of 1919 signaled the revival, not the eclipse, of the traditional prominence of the legislative branch in the Third Republic. But the postwar Chambers, even one as homogeneous as the Horizon-Blue Chamber, proved Millerand's contention that parliamentary pluralism was impotent to produce constructive compromise in a period of novel economic disarray and retrenchment. After 1919 the Chamber exerted constant pressure on cabinets to pursue a determined policy vis-à-vis Germany in order to avoid the task of distributing new burdens at home, but was unable to produce needed legislation to alleviate France's fiscal crisis, much less suggest how reparations could be exacted. The role of the Chamber in policy-making in the half-decade after the Peace Conference was restricted, therefore, to defining the parameters of executive flexibility. To be sure, important sectors—industrialists, unions, exporters, *sinistrés*—depended increasingly on extra-parliamentary pressure groups to influence state policy, but postwar cabinets nevertheless exhibited far-reaching independence before interest groups and the Chamber alike. Internal rifts between rival sectors of the economy had the effect of freeing the hand of state experts, even as they narrowed the range of possible policies. Despite the direct linkage of foreign and domestic issues, the official mind remained the taproot of policy; the locus of power lay within the cabinet and permanent bureaucracy of the key ministries of foreign affairs, finance, and commerce.

Millerand set a pattern for his immediate successors when he reserved for himself the portfolio of the foreign minister, ensuring the rehabilitation of the Quai d'Orsay. But it was not the ambassadorial corps, with its galaxy of first-magnitude statesmen that regained the initiative the war had taken away. Rather, two wartime practices continued: the centralization of initiative at Paris and the replacement of ambassadorial representations by grand summit conferences as the vehicle for international dialogue. Millerand also supported these trends by resurrecting the office of the secretary-general of the Foreign Ministry, dismantling Clemenceau's network of special commissions and personal aides, and perpetuating the Supreme Council. The harrowing complexity of major foreign policy issues after the war, reparations chief among them, also placed a premium on the technical expertise to be found in the undersecretariats of the various ministries. Thus, even as the Foreign Ministry regained its centrality, it was not the same establishment that had maneuvered with such success before 1914 by dint of the deftness and *ésprit* of its various diplomats. Instead, the Quai d'Orsay was becoming a bureaucracy led by politician-foreign ministers, often dealing directly with their opposite numbers and supported by a corps of technicians. But these transformations were not readily apparent when a new chamber, a new government, and the treaty of peace first entered into power. Millerand's appointment of Maurice Paléologue as secretary-general seemed to signal a return to the "good old days" of French foreign policy. "Our new chief has chosen well his *eminence grise*," Jules Jusserand wrote from Washington. "We cannot return too soon to our austere classical ideals of order."[2]

Nowhere was order more necessary than in government finance, but nowhere did the bonds of domestic politics so limit the government's field of maneuver.

The war was over, but further investment was necessary to finance reconstruction, a large standing army, and credits for the new nations of Europe. Austerity and tax increases were called for in the Finance Ministry, but imposition of a lower national standard of living as the reward for victory was politically impossible; new taxes would be difficult to effect. According to Lloyd George, Clemenceau never showed an interest in finance and was bored by figures.[3] Yet it was not the Tiger's insouciance, but the entire war finance, that had left France insolvent.

Despite Louis Klotz's promise that new burdens would not be placed on France until Germany shouldered the reparations burden, criticism of the reparations clauses of Versailles equaled that of the security settlement. In September 1919 Klotz faced the Chamber's complaints that, since reparations would not begin at once and would be strung out for decades, France would have to finance reconstruction after all.

[2] Pers. Let. Jusserand to Paléologue, 29 Jan. 1920: Jules Jusserand, unpublished private papers, Ministère des Affaires Étrangères-Paris (hereafter cited as MAE Pap. Jusserand), vol. 37, no. 215. The best general treatment of the role of French parliamentary and corporate interests in policy formation is Maier, *Recasting Bourgeois Europe*. On specific problems in French foreign policy-making the following are useful: Richard D. Challener, "The French Foreign Office: The Era of Philippe Berthelot," in *The Diplomats, 1919-1939*, 2 vols., Gordon A. Craig and Felix Gilbert, eds. (Princeton, 1953), I, 49-85, affords an overview of the French diplomatic establishment in the 1920s; Paul Gordon Lauren, *Diplomats and Bureaucrats* (Stanford, 1976), analyzes Foreign Ministry reforms and reorganization, 1906-1920; John E. Howard, *Parliament and Foreign Policy in France, 1919-1939* (London, 1948), examines the control exerted by the Chambers over diplomacy and concludes that the Parliament was neither capable nor anxious to exercise such vigilence; Elliot Fagerberg, *The Ancien Combattants and French Foreign Policy* (Presses de Savoi, 1966), and Richard Gombin, *Les Socialistes et la guerre* (The Hague, 1967), examine the attitudes of veterans' groups and the Socialist opposition.

[3] David Lloyd George, *The Truth about the Peace Treaties*, 2 vols. (London, 1938), I, 475, 499-507.

FIGURE 2. "The 'Horizon-Blue' Chamber: The Boche Will Pay! The Boche Will Pay . . . !" H. P. Gassier, 1920. © S.P.A.D.E.M. Paris 1977.

But Klotz still promised no new revenues. Instead, he instituted the notorious "double budget." The regular budget for 1919 showed a surplus of 2.2 billion francs, but it was accompanied by an "exceptional budget" of recoverable expenses slated for reparation and technically the responsibility of Germany. It threw the government 27 billion francs into deficit, and left it dependent on uncertain short-term credit. The Chamber did not fail to point out the danger of this policy, but the bourgeois majority refused to vote the direct taxation necessary to avoid it. When Socialist deputies demanded a tax on capital, the Center and Right called them "social demolishers, who seek to use the temporary embarrassment of the government to tighten the grip of the state on society . . . to realize through oppressive fiscal policies the designs of the class struggle."[4] The only means of avoiding the social im-

[4] "Le Traité de Paix avec l'Allemagne et les finances françaises," *Le Temps*, 9 Sept. 1919.

plications of bankruptcy was to "export" the crisis to Germany by strict enforcement of reparations.

Upon Millerand's accession the situation had improved little, but the franc's decline had been arrested and the doomsayers were easily ignored. The very complacency that characterized the discussion of European financial recovery at the Peace Conference served to reassure investors wandering in the unfamiliar economic landscape left by the war. The avowed policy of Britain and France was to return to the prewar gold standard and redeem state bonds at full value. In April 1920 Finance Minister François-Marsal negotiated a convention with the Banque de France under which the state optimistically pledged to repay two billion francs per year of the national debt![5] Such intentions achieved a relative stability for the franc for several years, until the hope of reparations turned sour.

The war debt obligations also did not immediately impinge on the French budget, but they hung like Damocles' sword over French policy. The Europeans possessed impressive moral arguments in favor of general cancellation, but European demarches, including a personal letter from Lloyd George to President Wilson, met flat refusals. American war debts policy resulted from theoretical and practical considerations. First, the money was not owed to the American government, having been raised by public bonds. The State Department claimed its hands were tied. Second, Wilson's cabinet invoked the political opposition to annulment, although it did nothing to alter public opinion. Third, the Treasury itself saw no advantage in debt cancellation. Secretary Carter Glass and Undersecretary Russell Leffingwell refused to let America take responsibility for European recovery. The state of economic theory did not allow a proper reading of the situation. To Leffingwell, no nation could grow rich by destroying wealth, as in war. Europe must pay her own way or the strength of the dollar would be endangered.[6]

[5] The François-Marsal Convention was a striking example of postwar financial naïveté. Repayment of the Banque de France's extraordinary wartime advances, by deflating the currency, would mean that the interest paid on the internal debt would be vastly increased. Martin Wolfe, *The French Franc between the Wars, 1919-1939* (New York, 1951), pp. 25-32.

[6] Denise Artaud, "Le gouvernement américain et la question des dettes de guerre, 1919-1920," pp. 201-229. See also the excellent articles by Melvyn Leffler, "The Origins of Republican War Debt Policy, 1921-1923: A Case Study in the Applicability of the Open Door Interpretation," *The Journal of American History* 59, no. 3 (Dec. 1972): 585-601; *idem*, "Political Isolationism: Economic Expansion or Diplomatic Realism? American Policy toward Western Europe," *Perspectives in American History* 8 (1974): 413-461; also Michael J. Hogan, *Informal Entente: The Private Structure of Cooperation in Anglo-American Economic Diplomacy, 1918-1928* (Columbia, Mo. and London, 1977), pp. 13-56.

In January 1920 the British and French governments sponsored an international financial conference. They were backed by an international businessmen's gathering organized by the neutral Dutch. It called for annulment of war debts, reduction and fixing of claims against Germany, and the opening of credits by governments, for they were "too important to be left to the normal intermediary of bankers." The Europeans enlisted the aid of American chambers of commerce, whose interests demanded the revival of transatlantic trade. But the American government was unable and unwilling to extend its own wartime economic prerogatives over private interests. Wall Street refused to open new credits until the war debts were funded and/or until Europe promised political stability. Carter Glass wrote the president of the American Chambers of Commerce that the Treasury opposed an international financial conference lest it give the impression that the United States was prepared to renew lending or annul debts. Rather the European nations must learn "to live within their resources" and reduce German obligations to a sensible figure.[7]

Millerand inherited a stopgap financial policy. His bequest in the realm of industrial reconstruction was equally insecure, for it also depended ultimately on German fulfillment of the treaty. Possessed of the iron fields of Lorraine, French metallurgy suddenly found itself with a greatly expanded potential. French steel capacity leapt from 4.7 to 9.7 million tons per year—would it vault France into the ranks of the world's premier industrial powers, or would it only bring disruption and insecurity to a conservative metallurgical structure unsuited to expansion? French experts had their doubts. The motivation for the ambitious war aims of the *Comité des Forges* had not been to expand as much as possible, but to soften the shock of whatever expansion was unavoidable with the recovery of Lorraine. During the Peace Conference it was French commerce and small business that demanded "the economic ruin of Germany" and the growth of France into a productive giant. These interests accused the *Comité des Forges* of "betraying" France by seeking entente with Germany.[8] Indeed, Robert Pinot feared the perils of overproduction and competition with Germany for markets, not to mention the struggle that would ensue for coal and coke should French and German industries be forcefully separated. Pinot had advocated continued German ownership of a share of Lor-

[7] "États-Unis: La situation financière de l'Europe," *Le Temps*, 1 Feb. 1920. Carter Glass was replaced as Treasury Secretary on 1 March 1920, by David F. Houston. Policy remained largely in the hands of Leffingwell. In any case, with President Wilson incapacitated, no abrupt change of policy could be expected.

[8] Maurice Brelet, *La crise de la métallurgie* (Paris, 1923), intro. Cf. Miquel, *La Paix de Versailles*, pp. 504-521.

raine to ease the conversion and to facilitate Franco-German cooperation.[9]

Clemenceau's policy at the Peace Conference fell between the opposing camps in France. The Tiger was determined to expel Germany completely from Alsace-Lorraine, thus rupturing at a blow the forty-seven years of integration between those provinces and the Ruhr. But he then sought to mend the rupture through a series of economic clauses designed to satisfy the needs of France's new potential. In pursuit of secure and cheap sources of coal and coke, Louis Loucheur and Clemenceau pointed to the ruthless destruction of French mines by the retreating Germans to justify annexation of the Saar, with its annual production of eight million tons. The Anglo-Americans opposed this on grounds of self-determination, but agreed to a fifteen-year French proprietorship over the mines of the basin. But Saar coal was not suitable for coking. This deficit was made good through clauses obligating Germany to deliver as reparations-in-kind 27 million tons of coal (or its equivalent in coke) per year at the German internal price.[10] Finally, to aid in the quest for markets, Articles 68 and 268 of the treaty stipulated the free passage of goods from Alsace-Lorraine and the Saar into Germany for a period of five years, with the League of Nations Council reserving the right to extend the regime. Together, these clauses entailed a French metallurgical project of mass proportions designed at once to weaken German industry and to ease the incorporation of Lorraine into French metallurgy. They promised a doubling of French steel capacity while Germany's shrank by 30 percent. But the fulfillment of the program depended from the first on the acquiescence of French industry, of the Allies, and of the powerful industrial lords of the Ruhr.

French coal and steel firms were not vertically integrated like their German counterparts, and clearly had opposite interests. Neither was favorable to the government's economic program outlined in the treaty. The coal men, represented by the *Comité des Houillères*, were threatened by massive German coal deliveries at low prices. The *Comité des Forges*, while desperate for coal, had doubts about the planned exploitation of Lorraine. Their misgivings were only heightened by the exacerbation of the European coal crisis throughout 1919 and the first

[9] Jacques Bariéty, "La rôle de la minette dans la sidérurgie allemande après le Traité de Versailles," *Centre des recherches relations internationales de l'Université de Metz* 3 (1973): 252-258.

[10] Germany was also obliged to deliver 8 million tons per year to Belgium, 4.5-8.5 million tons to Italy, and provide for Luxembourg—a total of about 45 million tons per year out of a prewar annual production of 177 millions. But Germany lost the production of the Saar and of portions of Upper Silesia.

failures of the Clemenceau government to extract coal from Germany.

During the war Paris assumed control of the price and distribution of precious coal. The price of French coal climbed quickly after the loss of mines to the Germans, and English coal, on which France became increasingly dependent, soared to 85 francs/ton, three times the 1913 figure. The Chamber responded in April 1916 with the Law of *Péréquation*, under which the government purchased all coal, equalized the price, and distributed it according to priorities. In practice, *péréquation* favored small consumers over large firms that had domestic connections and contracts. The *Bureau National des Charbons* administered the system, which, regularized under the Loucheur Plan of 1917, survived past the Armistice. The extension of controls into peacetime led to virulent demands on the part of the big firms, especially steel, for an end to *péréquation*.[11] Loucheur saw the difficulties created after the Armistice, but the need for controls was all the more necessary, given postwar shortages and the renewed price spiral.

Government policy damaged French steel in its quest for capital and markets as well. Hoping to ease the transition to peace, as armament orders ceased, Loucheur promised government purchases for ship construction and building materials. In return, he encouraged steel firms to overcome their habitual jealousy and independence and to cartelize as a preparation for peacetime. The result was the *Comptoir Sidérurgique de France*, created on 10 December 1918. But the promised government purchases did not materialize for financial and political reasons, the state continued coal distribution, and the *Comptoir* was only given the task of distributing among its members and purchasing from the government the sequestered mines and mills of Lorraine, a process that drained the industry of liquidity.[12] Thus, the government forced expansion of French heavy industry, but favored the interests of small business concerning coal and economic policy toward Germany.

The causes of the coal crisis of 1919-1920 were the dislocations of war and peace. French mines were destroyed, all nations suffered from labor shortages and unrest. Movement of coal was paralyzed by a transport crisis. Rolling stock was in short supply and maritime transport was tied up in the Atlantic and India food operations. European coal production in 1919 fell to 64 percent of prewar figures, and dependent France suffered most. In 1919 she imported 50 percent of her coal; 70 percent of that came from Britain. And once again French

[11] Olivier, *La politique du charbon*, pp. 109-122, 148-155.

[12] Rolf Bühler, *Die Roheisenkartelle in Frankreich* (Zurich, 1934), pp. 132-148; Pinot, *Le Comité des Forges*, pp. 206-235.

hopes for "Allied economic unity" were quickly crushed. The British foresaw windfall profits from Europe's difficulties and rushed their own process of decontrol. British mandatory and subsidized shipping was suspended and exports to France dropped below wartime levels, while prices climbed by mid-1919 to seven times prewar figures. The French appealed to Belgium, but the Belgian government later restricted exports because of its own shortages. In any case, English and Belgian supplies were scarcely sufficient for French needs. All parties looked to the Ruhr.[13]

The treaty offered no succor to France's immediate needs. Reparation coal deliveries would not begin until three months after the treaty was in force—in April 1920. The Armistice made no provision for coal deliveries, and French efforts to negotiate a coal for iron exchange in December 1918 broke down on the question of price. After the German peace was completed, Loucheur tried again and reached agreement with German representatives in August 1919. Germany engaged to deliver one million tons per month in exchange for amelioration of future demands, but the Germans satisfied only a quarter of their quota, pleading low production. Hugo Stinnes was already leading a press campaign against coal deliveries, convincing German opinion that they would destroy the German economy, even as Germany found coal to export to Holland and Switzerland. Pressure on the French government mounted as the French public suffered through the cold winter of 1919-1920. The coal crisis would surely bring the first test of the efficacy of the Treaty of Versailles. It was the bitterest inheritance of the Millerand government.

If the coal shortage seemed to call for harsh treatment of Germany, it also increased France's dependence on Britain, still her major supplier. Could France count on British support against the Ruhr? British ministers and industrialists looked with no more favor than their German counterparts on the prospect of a flowering of French metallurgy—and the profits were too attractive to pass up. On 1 January 1920 London suppressed its coal export licensing control and competition among French importers drove prices over 115 shillings per ton. If Germany became the major provider of combustibles to France, Britain would lose a lucrative market and a powerful means of pressure on the French government. She would be subsidizing a competitor.[14]

[13] J. Levainville, *L'industrie du fer en France* (Paris, 1922), pp. 159-178; Friedensburg, *Kohle und Eisen im Weltkriege*, pp. 185-204; Olivier, *La politique du charbon*, pp. 166-175.

[14] Brelet, *La crise*, pp. 85-91, 131-136; Bariéty, "La rôle de la minette," pp. 233-237; Olivier, *La politique du charbon*, pp. 214-217; Weill-Raynal, *Les réparations allemandes*, I, 418-422.

France could expect no gratuitous aid from her allies. Bilateral agreement with Germany met opposition from within France and depended on German goodwill, which had already proved false. There remained only a policy of force. In December 1918 Minister of Commerce Étienne Clémentel had foreseen economic inferiority for France if free competition were restored to international trade. Unrestrained inflation and loss of her own market would be France's lot, while German recovery outstripped that of the victors. Failing the maintenance of interallied economic organizations, American participation, revision or annulment of war debts, and credits for currency stabilization, Clémentel saw only one alternative: economic sanctions against Germany.[15] By the time Millerand took office, hopes of cooperation were dashed, and British policy was turning disturbingly pro-German.

FIRST FISSURES IN THE ENTENTE

The young German republic had survived the signature of the Versailles Treaty and the promulgation of its own constitution despite powerful internal dissent. Whether it could survive the execution of those two documents was questionable, and formed the basis of the postwar strategic dispute between France and Britain. The British preferred to sacrifice strict execution of the treaty to protect Weimar democracy, while the French preferred to risk injury to German republicanism rather than accept a reintegration of continental economies that would leave important sectors of the French economy structurally dependent on the Ruhr. The issue hinged on whether a political environment could be created in which renewed Franco-German collaboration could proceed on terms safe for Germany's weaker neighbors. Versailles, if implemented, could fulfill that desideratum. From the French point of view, Germany was more than capable of bearing the burden of reparations. Germany had suffered no physical damage and her industrialists were glutted with wealth. The only barrier to payment was the German will not to pay.

The French thesis found no support in Britain. The famous arguments of John Maynard Keynes seemed to demonstrate Germany's inability to make huge capital transfers or coal deliveries. The British government did not favor striking the German debt, but the Foreign Office insisted on the need to restore Germany to full productivity before burdening her with obligations. The recovery of defeated Ger-

[15] Let. Clémentel to Clemenceau, "Clauses Économiques des préliminaires de paix—principes généraux," 31 Dec. 1918: MAE Pap. Tardieu, vol. 5, dos. Questions économiques.

many, therefore, was to take precedence over that of Germany's victims.

The treaty regime was only three weeks old when Millerand proposed sanctions on the Rhine. The most tempting measure was the extension of the occupation to the Ruhr basin, only a few kilometers outside the Belgian zone and seat of 80 percent of German metallurgy. In the first meeting of the postwar *Conseil Supérieur de la Guerre*, on 31 January 1920, Millerand asked his military leaders if the French Army was capable of investing the Ruhr. According to Chief of the General Staff Edmond Buat, it would require recall of a class of reservists. "In these conditions," muttered the premier, "it is impossible to assure the execution of the treaty." Public opinion would not accept mobilization, he feared, and he ordered the general staff to form a ready reserve capable of reinforcing the Army of the Rhine at a moment's notice. Still he met opposition against military sanctions. Marshal Pétain favored economic sanctions—seizure of German revenues in the Rhineland. Poincaré, presiding as president of the Republic for the last time, insisted that Allied unity was a prerequisite to any action, especially the occupation of the Ruhr. He suggested instead the declaration that, as Germany had not begun to fulfill her obligations, the fifteen-year occupation period had not begun to run. He held to his conviction that Germany would never honor the treaty unless the occupation were to last until she did.[16]

Early in February, at the London Financial Conference, Millerand encountered the British. He had departed Paris promising the Chamber a harsh policy, including sanctions to win coal, and echoed Rhine propagandist Maurice Barrès in calling for the "moral disarmament" of Germany. In London he found that a different mood prevailed, and his belligerence was tempered by the knowledge of France's dependence on English coal. He pleaded for sanctions in vain. France had no desire to cripple Germany, he told Lloyd George, but French coal reserves had dwindled to three to six days' supply. When Millerand took Poincaré's tack of declaring that the *délais d'occupation* of the Rhineland had not yet begun to run, none of the Allies acknowledged it. As for an occupation of the Ruhr, Curzon replied that "this did not suit our book at all, and we insisted that the whole matter be referred to the Reparations Commission."[17] The French then ap-

[16] Procès-Verbal, 31 Jan. 1920: France, Ministry of War, Conseil Supérieur de la Guerre (hereafter cited as CSG), Réunions.

[17] Let. Curzon to Derby (Paris), 19 Feb. 1920: Lord Curzon of Kedleston, unpublished private papers, Public Record Office-London (hereafter cited as PRO Curzon Pap.), vol. 155, nos. 70-71. See also DBFP, vol. VII, pp. 32-37.

pealed for more British coal. The British Coal Controller promised a continuation of the set tonnage for export to France of 1.5 million tons/month, representing 60 percent of all British exports. It was not sufficient, and was not even met. English coal to France averaged 1.18 million tons for the first four months of 1920.

The Reparations Commission was not likely to be of any immediate use against Germany. Britain and Italy had each declared themselves averse to sanctions until the German productive situation was clarified. The French Chamber was losing patience. Unemployment spread in France for the lack of fuel; Paris utilities rationed heat and light; the newly recovered iron foundries of Lorraine were largely extinguished. German deliveries continued in January and February at 30 percent of the agreed levels. "It's a question of whether these are the Germans who destroyed the mines of the north and whether we are the ones to go begging for coal!" cried Amedée Peyroux in the Chamber. "Are the Boches to continue to have eight million tons a month while we, the victors, must be content with 3.8 million?" The English were soaking the French for all they could, while French officials debated endlessly. A representative of heavy industry, Peyroux accused Britain and America of enriching themselves at France's expense. He demanded that Loucheur obtain coal from Germany, while suppressing the *péréquation* system at home.[18]

Anti-British agitation spread to the press, where Britain's abuse of her coal monopoly rivaled German ill will for contemptibility.[19] The government determined to break free from Britain's restraints. Millerand based a case for unilateral action by France in defense of the treaty and for a possible occupation of the Ruhr on Section 18, Annex II, Part VIII of the treaty, which authorized, in case of default, "economic and financial prohibitions and in general all other measures which the respective governments may deem necessary." The first test of this thesis came in March.

Rightist opposition to the liberal German republic expressed itself in a monarchist putsch led by Friedrich Kapp and supported by Freikorps. In response to the overthrow of the Berlin government, workers throughout Germany proclaimed a general strike on 13 March 1920. A week later Spartacist outbreaks occurred in the Ruhr. The Kapp putsch quickly dissolved, but the republican government, reinstated, asked Allied permission to send troops to restore order in

[18] Assemblée Nationale, *Journal Officiel, débats parlementaires, Chambre des Députés* (cited hereafter as J. O. Chambre), 1920, pp. 208-213.

[19] See, for example, "Le problème du charbon," "Les difficultés de l'industrie métallurgique," and "La crise industrielle," *Le Temps*, 18 Feb., 4 Mar., and 27 Mar. 1920.

the Ruhr, which lay in the demilitarized zone. The *Conseil Supérieur de la Défense National* agreed that the integrity of the treaty was at stake. If Germany occupied the Ruhr, said Millerand, France must act, even over British objections. In fact, the incident provided a pretext for occupation of the Ruhr and seizure of German coal. But Marshal Foch introduced another consideration. Germany was in dissolution, he said, and France must not arrest this process. The struggle of parties would soon become a struggle between regions, but an occupation of the Ruhr could reawaken national sentiment. Foch urged action, but not necessarily in the Ruhr.[20]

Treaty execution, or an opportunity for favorable revision through the collapse of German unity?—Millerand was uncertain how to proceed, given the coal crisis. At first, he instructed Ambassador Paul Cambon to suggest an interallied commission to consider the German request. A second set of instructions called for an official protest against any German action in the Ruhr. Then, on 21 March the Quai d'Orsay wired a third set of instructions, suggesting Allied occupation of the Ruhr immediately following a German advance. Cambon reminded the government of Britain's intense opposition to military expeditions and of Lloyd George's sympathy for the German request. If it was coal the French government was really after, Cambon offered, let it wait until the disturbances were over to occupy the Ruhr.[21]

Again the British and French conferred in London. Lloyd George examined the German case on its merits and approved of Berlin's efforts to combat Bolshevism. Cambon yielded the point, but unabashedly admitted that larger issues were involved: the disturbances further decreased German coal deliveries, and France could not permit a breach of the Rhenish demilitarization, France's most important remaining security guarantee. Berthelot and Foch then presented compromise plans: the Germans would be given a set period to pacify the Ruhr, subject to the French army's taking guarantees. Negotiations continued for three weeks as Millerand shied from taking action in defiance of Britain. On 31 March the Senate demonstrated against his government. Foch and Poincaré both insisted on firm action.[22] Pressed on all sides, Millerand found a compromise situation—compromise among his advisors, not among the Allies. When German troops finally entered the Ruhr, despairing of Allied agreement, Millerand approved

[20] Procès-Verbal, 19 Mar. 1920: France, Ministry of War, Conseil Supérieur de la Défense Nationale (hereafter cited as CSDN), Séances.

[21] Tels. P. Cambon to MAE, 19-22 Mar. 1920: MAE Pap. P. Cambon, vol. 6, dos. 27, nos. 123-130.

[22] Notes of Allied Conferences, London, 18 and 23 Mar. 1920; Let. Derby (Paris) to Curzon, 1 Apr. 1920: DBFP, VII, 542-547, 584-591; IX, 238-241, 284-290.

occupation by the French army on 6 April of the German Maingau: Frankfurt, Darmstadt, and Offenbach. He shied from the Ruhr for the reasons suggested by Foch and Cambon. The maneuver was in defense both of the treaty and of revisionist ambitions, for Frankfurt was the link between north and south Germany; its occupation was a gesture of support for Bavarian and Rhenish particularism (see below).

The action gained neither coal nor respect. From London, Cambon described at length the disappointment of the British with the French action and suggested that the Quai d'Orsay "reflect on his words."[23] The adverse results hit Millerand like the kick of a rifle. On 8 April Foreign Secretary Curzon delivered a sharp protest and advised the British ambassador in Paris to boycott the Conference of Ambassadors.[24] The American government accused the French of contributing to German disorder.[25] More to the point, French efforts to induce general respect for the treaty only brought disrespect for her immediate coal interests. Two days after the occupation of the Maingau, Robert Pinot wrote Millerand personally informing him that the British had interdicted all coal exports for the remainder of the month. The excuse was a threatened miners' strike in response to the Coal Mines Emergency Act of 30 March. But the measure, coinciding with the interruption of Ruhr production, meant a redoubling of the crisis for French steel. Pinot trusted that the government would not sit idly by while French furnaces burned out.[26] Millerand's demarche in London received no reply until May, when the British Cabinet resumed exports but rejected special price or quota arrangements. "The French don't seem to understand that we can sell our coal elsewhere on more favorable terms." What the French seemed to want would "amount to a subsidy from the British exchequer."[27] Later in the month, at the Conference of Hythe, the British Coal Control cut France's contingent of British exports from 60 to 45 percent. The French government responded by fixing a maximum price at which British coal could be sold in French ports. French importers and British alike mocked the measure as likely to reduce imports to zero. French policy was a hostage of foreign coal.

[23] Tel. P. Cambon to MAE, 6 Apr. 1920: MAE Pap. P. Cambon, vol. 6, dos. 27, nos. 140-141.

[24] Tel. Curzon to Derby, 8 Apr. 1920: DBFP, IX, 346-348.

[25] Tel. Secretary of State Colby to Wallace (Paris), 12 Apr. 1920: FRUS 1920, II, 324-325.

[26] Pers. Let. Pinot to Millerand, 10 Apr. 1920: Alexandre Millerand, unpublished private papers, Ministère des Affaires Étrangères-Paris (hereafter cited as MAE Pap. Millerand), vol. 1, nos. 79-81.

[27] Cabinet Decisions, CAB 25/20, 6 May 1920: Great Britain, Public Record Office (hereafter cited as PRO), CAB 23/21, p. 78.

Millerand could not afford to prolong the rupture. He retreated at the Conference of San Remo, where he agreed on 26 April to evacuate the Maingau upon German evacuation of the Ruhr, and promised that France intended in the future to act only in accord with her allies. The Allied premiers then agreed to a conference to discuss reparations, disarmament, and coal deliveries. The Germans would attend, satisfying Lloyd George's assumption that only freely negotiated arrangements would be respected by the Germans. After some delays, the conference met at Spa in July 1920. The French entered as supplicants, but the German delegation failed to exploit fully the differences between the Entente powers. The general elections following the Kapp putsch were a defeat for the moderate parties of the Weimar coalition. The Left and Right gained substantially and the Social Democrats resigned from the government. Translated into foreign policy, the mood of the nation seemed to call for a tough stance vis-à-vis the Allies. But the unyielding stance only drove the French and British closer together. The denunciation of the victors by the greatest of the Ruhr industrialists, Hugo Stinnes, was especially provocative. But France still paid a price for Britain's indulgence. Germany's monthly coal obligations were reduced from the treaty-stipulated 2.25 million tons to 1.6 million. It was a 25 percent drop, though still well above the actual German deliveries: 660,000 tons in April, 964,000 in May.

The price issue involved a second French surrender. To protect Britain, Lloyd George insisted that German reparations coal be accredited at the world (i.e., British export) price, not at the German internal price. Millerand also agreed to prior payments of 13.75 francs/ton to aid the revictualment of Ruhr miners—the French Chamber found itself asked to vote credits to pay the Ruhr for a lesser amount of coal at a higher price. Finally, the Allies granted Germany a portion of the coal mined in disputed Upper Silesia and a slower rate of disarmament and demobilization. France was assured a marginally greater supply of coal at nearly triple the price borne by her British and German competitors. Those on the sidelines—Tardieu, Poincaré, Briand, and Foch, among them—castigated the French government for its capitulation.[28]

[28] The character of the debate over treaty execution is expressed eloquently in correspondence carried on by Tardieu and Poincaré between May and July 1920. Poincaré attributed France's difficulties to the peace treaty itself; Tardieu was as adamant in its defense, and laid the blame on faulty execution of the treaty. As to the policies France ought to follow, the two men were in essential agreement, but their differing roles in 1919 denied them the possibility of public or even private agreement. The same recriminations were carried on in the Chamber between the *poincaristes* and the *clemencistes*. "Correspondence avec Poincaré," May-July 1920: André Tardieu, unpublished private papers, Archives Nationales-Paris (hereafter cited as AN Pap. Tardieu), vol. 118, dos. Lettres.

The coal crisis subsided after September 1920, when reduced demand owing to the recession, the gradual resolution of the transport crisis, and increased supply destroyed the artificial price structure. The British export price fell from 96 to 25 shillings per ton by the end of 1921. But the coal crisis had placed a stamp of distrust and rivalry on the first efforts to execute the Versailles Treaty. It had pointed up the weaknesses of the Entente that Germany learned to exploit, and the weaknesses of the German government before the Ruhr industrialists.[29] The latter confirmed their veto power over German reparations policy, a fact that French officials did not fail to note. Finally, the coal crisis pointed up the constraints on the French government due to its own domestic interests.[30] The crisis over, Millerand's government hastened to liquidate French controls surviving from the war. In November 1920 Minister of Public Works Yves Le Trocquer announced the timetable for the return to economic freedom, thereby circumscribing state power to resolve by negotiation domestic and international economic conflicts. An impetus was imparted to all, industrialists and government experts alike, to despair of the treaty system and to think in terms of forceful or voluntary cooperation with Germany in continental reconstruction outside the confines of the Treaty of Versailles.

PALÉOLOGUE'S FOLLY: THE GERMAN FEDERALIST MOVEMENT

A major pillar of the security program formulated under Clemenceau was the eastern barrier he had hoped to create out of the new states between Germany and Russia.[31] But enmity between the Poles and Czechs, complicated by the Teschen dispute, frustrated French efforts. Prague stood aloof, and even moved closer to Moscow during Poland's mortal struggle against Soviet Russia in 1920. The failure of the Peace Conference to stabilize the Danubian region was just as evident in the financial collapse of rump Austria and in the continuing tension

[29] At this time in 1920, Walter Rathenau lamented: "Germany has been unburdened of her twenty-two dynasties, but instead is now divided into twenty or so industrial duchies whose potentates are absolute" (Baumont, *La grosse industrie allemande*, p. 189).

[30] Charles S. Maier, "Coal and Economic Power in the Weimar Republic: The Effects of the Coal Crisis of 1920," and Georges Soutou, "Der Einfluss der Schwerindustrie auf die Gestaltung der Frankreichpolitik Deutschlands 1919-1921," in *Industrielles System und Politische Entwicklung in der Weimarer Republik*, pp. 534-535, 545-546; Olivier, *La politique du charbon*, pp. 257-273.

[31] French efforts to forge a new "eastern barrier" against German expansion from 1917 to 1925 are analyzed in detail by Hovi, *Cordon Sanitaire or Barrière de l'Est?* and Wandycz, *France and Her Eastern Allies*.

between recalcitrant Hungary and her neighbors. Russia was still in the throes of civil war. There Millerand and Paléologue supported Admiral Kolchak in his fight against Lenin and White rivals, and discouraged Polish plans for a Ukrainian federation. They wanted to weaken Bolshevism, not Russia. Nevertheless, the settlement in Eastern Europe, far from consolidating in 1920, seemed on the verge of collapse.

Given the chaos among France's potential eastern allies, it is not surprising that conservative Frenchmen publicly rued the destruction of the Habsburg monarchy. Perhaps the best way to bring stability to the Danubian region and to create a barrier to German expansion—both military and economic—was to resurrect a confederation. To Millerand, and particularly to his secretary-general, Maurice Paléologue, this demanded a Hungarian policy. Though opposed within the Quai d'Orsay by the pro-Czech Berthelot, Paléologue pressed his plans for a Danubian confederation reconciling Hungary with those states that profited by the Habsburg defeat.[32] With this policy in mind Paléologue viewed the development of another federalism. This one involved southern Germany and the Rhineland, and it caused him to broaden his ambitions for revision, not stabilization, of the 1919 European boundaries.

Unlike the British Foreign Office, which expected to pacify Germany through preserving Weimar democracy, the Quai d'Orsay perceived little connection between forms of government and foreign policies. The Wilsonian idea that democratic governments choose peaceful foreign policies, while authoritarian regimes are aggressive, found few disciples in the French government and military. A strong and united Russia would balance Germany in the East, whether Bolshevik or tsarist, and a strong, united Germany, whether monarchist or republican, would pose a threat to France and surely come to dominate the economies of the Danubian and Balkan regions. In any case, the German revolution appeared superficial. The imperial bureaucracy, judiciary, and military remained intact. Prussia still dominated. France could not be expected to relinquish her rights to economic and military guarantees in the hope that Germany might suddenly and forever turn pacific.

The problem remained: how to preserve German weakness while permitting the German economy to support reparations? Perhaps the political *structure* of Germany could provide an answer. If Germany were divided, if a weak federal structure similar to that of the Holy Roman Empire replaced the centralizing republic, then German

[32] Wandycz, *France and Her Eastern Allies*, p. 142.

power would be diffused. General Joseph Degoutte, commander of the French Army of the Rhine, urged such a solution in January 1920: "The unitary state, which constitutes itself under the temporary form of a socialist or even bolshevist republic, or which returns to some form of monarchy, can only be fundamentally pan-Germanist. . . . Between the mortal danger of a unitary Germany and the rich promise of a federalist Germany, there can be no hesitation. *For some time yet the federalist solution will be possible; let us hasten to profit from it.*"[33]

There is little doubt that a vast majority in French military and parliamentary circles would have welcomed the disappearance of German unity, were it not for mitigating circumstances. The undoing of Bismarck's work through French military force would only ensure the destruction of Allied unity, eliminate the possibility of reparations, and impose an indeterminate burden on France. There was no guarantee that a divided Germany would remain so; Tirard and others feared that German states might feign autonomy from Berlin to escape the burden of defeat, then return to the fold after Allied demobilization. But federalism—a voluntary loosening of the ties binding "the Germanies" to Berlin—held out the prospect of a feeble central government without sacrifice of French rights. Indeed, after the Weimar Assembly completed its labors, federalist agitation continued in Bavaria, Hesse, Hanover, and the Rhineland.

As early as 25 November 1918 the French government made contact with the revolutionary Bavarian regime of Kurt Eisner through its mission in Bern.[34] Pichon was skeptical, and sent a fact-finding mission to interrogate the Bavarian representatives, who promised that Munich would lead a federalist movement against Berlin. But for this action to be effective, the Bavarians must be independent of Prussia in coal and foodstuffs, commodities that would have to come from the Allies. Pichon took his case to the Supreme Economic Council, but failed to win American and British support for favoring Bavaria, just as Foch was unable to grant special treatment to the Rhineland.[35] Eisner was assassinated in February 1919, and his successor, Johannes Hoffmann, vowed to crush revolution by recourse to Prussian Freikorps.

[33] Degoutte to MG, MAE, "Rapport mensuel de l'Armée du Rhin," Feb. 1920, cited by François-André Paoli, *L'Armée française de 1919 à 1939*, vol. 2: *La phase de fermeté, 1919-1924* (État-Major de l'Armée de Terre, Service Historique, n.d.), pp. 220-221.

[34] The Quai d'Orsay exploited as mediators Dr. Wilhelm Mühlon, a liberal German emigré in Switzerland, and the noted pacifist Dr. Friedrich Wilhelm Förster, both of whom had openly opposed Hohenzollern policies and had ties to Munich.

[35] Tel. Pichon to Clinchant (Bern), 25 Nov. 1918: MAE Allemagne, vol. 352, nos. 19-21; Tel. Haguenin to MAE, Tel. Clinchant to MAE, 26 Feb. 1919: MAE Allemagne, vol. 352, nos. 44-47, 56-57. See also Schwabe, *Deutsche Revolution*, pp. 480-483.

Symptoms of dissatisfaction with the central government in Berlin appeared elsewhere in 1919. Following the failure of his putsch in June, Rhenish separatist Dr. Dorten put his collaborator, General Mangin, in contact with the leader of the Hanoverian Guelph party, Georg von Dannenberg. Ever since the annexation of Hanover by Prussia in 1866, the Guelphs constituted a protest bloc within Prussia, seeking to recover Hanoverian independence. Dannenberg, a deputy in the Prussian Landtag, led his followers into the federalist camp, and sought a promise from France of coal and food in case of open conflict with Berlin.[36]

Clemenceau's policy toward federalism paralleled his policy toward Rhenish separatism. First, he instructed Pichon to prevent any intervention by the Quai d'Orsay in the internal politics of Germany, but hastened to add that "the French government could only view with sympathy events favorable to political decentralization that point to emancipation of certain German regions from Berlin's despotism."[37] Clemenceau then informed Mangin personally of his support for federalism, but cautioned: "At Versailles, we have dealt with the German Empire as a bloc. Only after ratification of the treaty can we recognize new states."[38]

In Bavaria, Hoffmann stood discredited by his use of troops of Prussian origin to seize control. The real power in Bavaria resided in the electoral strength of the Bayerische Volkspartei (B.V.P.), a Catholic and conservative peasants' party. A leader of the party was Georg Heim, the *Bauernkönig*, head of the Bauernbund. The French mission in Berlin reported that all Bavarian parties favored looser ties with Berlin, but that the B.V.P. would take the initiative.[39] "Los von Berlin" was the order of the day. The French minister in Bern, Louis Clinchant, was convinced of Heim's sincerity by his defiance of the national Center party and avowed intention of separating Bavaria from Prussia completely. But a kernel of doubt tempered his enthusiasm. Bavaria would hope for "consideration" from the Allies in the matter of reparations and insisted on material aid against Prussia. In addition, Heim planned a grand Alpine republic to balance the strength of north Germany. Negotiations were thought to have already begun between the B.V.P. and Austria.[40]

[36] Note Mangin, 6 June 1919: AN Pap. Mangin, vol. 21, dos. 3.

[37] Note Berthelot, "La question rhénane," 10 June 1919: MAE Rive Gauche, vol. 1, nos. 133-134.

[38] Tel. Clemenceau to Mangin, #6419BS/3, 30 June 1919: AN Pap. Mangin, vol. 21, dos. 3.

[39] Des. Haguenin to MAE, "La situation en Bavière," 28 June 1919: MAE Allemagne, vol. 352, nos. 139-145.

[40] Let. Clinchant to Pichon, 18-23 July 1919: MAE Allemagne, vol. 352, nos. 146-150, 151-154; Let. Lord Acton (Bern) to Curzon, 26 July 1919: DBFP, V, 55-57.

Dannenberg in Hanover also demanded Allied aid in disarmament and revictualment. A Guelph military formation stood ready to defend Hanoverian autonomy. Dannenberg asked that the Interallied Control Commission dissolve the Prussian garrison, but overlook his Guelph Legion.[41] Finally, a Prince Isenburg of Hesse contacted the French command in Mainz, seeking support for a Hessian autonomist movement. Isenburg was the son of an Austrian archduchess, became a "liberal" while visiting the United States, and was a personal friend of the president of the new Hessian republic. Isenburg sought to "emancipate southern Germany from Prussian hegemony and arrest the progress of Bolshevism." Hesse would recognize reparations but hoped for "adoucissements," and would follow when Dr. Heim launched the federalist movement.[42]

In the Rhineland, the indefatigable Dr. Dorten revived his small party in the latter months of 1919. As he began to receive regular subsidies from High Commissioner Tirard, Dorten altered his professed goal to one of Rhenish autonomy within a federal Reich, and drummed up scattered support from Catholic and peasant groups. In December, he coordinated his action with that of Dannenberg and Count Bothmer, Heim's "diplomatic representative." The trio met in Wiesbaden, issued a joint declaration to Tirard, and appealed to the Quai d'Orsay for support.[43] Heim also issued his first direct appeal for aid in December 1919. He promised direct collaboration with the Entente and requested the dispatch of a French plenipotentiary to Bavaria.[44] On 9 January 1920 Heim made his first move at the Center party congress in Berlin. After fierce debates over the centralizing policy of Matthias Erzberger, the B.V.P. voted 272-34 to break with the Center. The French mission in Berlin waxed enthusiastic and urged Paris to make discreet contact with Heim.[45]

Federalist ideas appealed to many segments of the German population in the immediate postwar period. Prussia was held responsible for the war by some, for the defeat by many. The "time of troubles" encouraged particularist elements in the minor states to seek the independence lost in 1866 or 1871. Serious constitutional experts felt the new republic could survive only on the basis of equality among states,

[41] Note Mangin, "Resumé de conversation tenue entre le Général Mangin et M. von Dannenberg au sujet de la question de Hanovre," 22 Aug. 1919: AN Pap. Mangin, vol. 21, dos. 2.

[42] Note Mangin, "Rapport sur le Prince Isenburg": AN Pap. Mangin, vol. 21, dos. 3.

[43] Let. Dorten to Tirard, Let. Dorten, Dannenberg, Bothmer to Bruère and MAE, 16 Dec. 1919: MAE Rive Gauche, vol. 2, nos. 9-14, 93-94.

[44] E.M.G., 2e bureau, service de renseignements d'Alsace to E.M.A., 2e bureau, #354/13, "a.s. d'un appel du parti bavarois anti-prussien," 26 Dec. 1919: MAE Allemagne, vol. 338, nos. 65-66.

[45] Let. Haguenin to Berthelot, 15 Jan. 1920: MAE Allemagne, vol. 353, nos. 64-72.

which meant the breakup of Prussia. Catholics and conservatives looked with fear and contempt on the socialist government in Berlin and the threat from the extreme Left. For all that, the number of Germans willing to rebel against the central authority or seek structural political change by illegal means was small. Overly optimistic informants led Paris to think otherwise.

The federalist movement could not be uninteresting to French authorities. A certain Catholic consciousness, especially in the military, allowed the French to view the ties binding the Catholic Rhineland and south Germany to France as more substantial than the ties binding these regions to the German national state. The true peace, as Hanotaux argued, would not rely on a balance of power between Germany and her neighbors, but on a balance within Germany itself, as after the Peace of Westphalia.[46] Four days after Millerand and Paléologue took office on 18 January 1920, the premier instructed the occupation army on the attitude to observe toward the federalist movement. Millerand wished to avoid giving ammunition to those who accused federalists of treasonous association with the French, "but it goes without saying that we must not discourage the federalists, but display a sympathy, which, if discreet, will be all the more effective."[47] Millerand's interest in federalism stemmed from the destruction of Clemenceau's security arrangement by the American Senate, from pressure emanating from the Chamber and the military, and from the lure of a weak Germany still tied to reparations and disarmament. But Paléologue, operating with a certain independence from the premier, looked also to the complementary scheme for the Danubian confederation. A renewed Danubian bloc would balance German power in Central Europe; a confederation including the south German states would balance Prussia within Germany. Thus, a Bavarian-Austrian *Anschluss* was not inconceivable, and Paléologue saw France's best interests in a revision, not a consolidation, of the 1919 settlement.

Reports from Bern attested to the growing momentum of the Bavarian federalist movement. Soon the B.V.P. would act and the other states would follow. On 16 March a reactionary cabinet under Gustav von Kahr, supposedly a "front man" for Heim, ousted Hoffmann in Munich. Success was assured, said Heim, with Allied support. Should the French government remain aloof so as not to discredit the movement, drawing on the lessons of June 1919, or was bold action called

[46] Gabriel Hanotaux, *Le problème de la paix*, quoted in MAE Memo, "Les conditions de la paix," 18 Nov. 1918: MAE Paix, vol. 165, nos. 67-89.

[47] Let. Millerand to [Minister of War] Lefevre, #215, 22 Jan. 1920; Let. Lefevre to Millerand, #12868SA/2/11, 6 Feb. 1920: MAE Allemagne, vol. 338, nos. 114-115, 149.

for? Tirard and Degoutte believed in retrospect that French inactivity in December 1918 and January 1919 had been as damaging to the Rhenish movement as the generals' involvement in June. Which lesson applied now? Paléologue chose a middle course that satisfied no one. He appointed a special agent, Émile Dard, to act as liaison between the B.V.P., the Munich government, and Paris, but he promised Heim nothing and gave Dard restricted powers.[48]

As he left for his temporary base of operations in Strasbourg, Dard received his instructions verbally from Millerand and Paléologue. Heim must be encouraged in his plans for a German Catholic confederation, but France could not agree to incorporation of Austria, a violation of the treaty, unless it were a *fait accompli*. Dard's mission would be confined to reestablishing the prewar legation in Munich. Millerand approved subsidies for Heim's movement, and Paléologue spoke of the extension of French industrial and financial interests from the occupied Rhineland into southern Germany.[49] The latter motive was another strand in Paléologue's devious web. A friend of the great steel firm Schneider-Creusot, Paléologue also planned French economic penetration of the states of his Danubian Confederation.[50]

Dard himself was skeptical. He feared that Heim's ultimate motive was incorporation of Austria into a greater Germany, in which case it made little difference whether Prussians or reactionary Bavarians held sway over Germany. His plan would also make awkward the establishment of a Rhenish state, which Dard took to be the goal of French policy.[51] Nevertheless, the months of March and April 1920 witnessed a steady increase in the contacts among the French on the Rhine and Dorten, Dannenberg, and Bothmer. Paléologue sent André Bruère, French consul-general at Mainz, to Stuttgart to examine the strength of federalist sentiment in Baden and Württemberg. For Hanover, Degoutte renewed the request to General Nollet, chief of the Allied disarmament commission, for toleration of the Guelph Legion.[52] Prince Isenberg intrigued in Darmstadt and reported to Bruère.[53]

There is little doubt that Millerand was influenced by the apparent

[48] Pers. Let. Paléologue to Clinchant, 18-19 Mar. 1920: MAE Allemagne, vol. 353, nos. 73-74.

[49] Note Dard, "Compte-rendu de la conversation avec le Président du Conseil," 19 Mar. 1920: Émile Dard, unpublished private papers, Ministère des Affaires Étrangères-Paris (hereafter cited as MAE Pap. Dard), vol. 4, dos. 1.

[50] Wandycz, *France and Her Eastern Allies*, pp. 137-138, 150.

[51] Tel. Dard to Millerand, 25 Mar. 1920: MAE Pap. Dard, vol. 4, dos. 1.

[52] Note Ernest Cramaun, ingénieur des mines, Comité militaire interalliée de contrôle, district de Hanovre, 14 Apr. 1920: MAE Allemagne, vol. 338 bis, no. 14.

[53] Note Bruère, "L'idée fédéraliste en Hesse, un mémoire de Prince Isenburg," 16 Apr. 1920: MAE Allemagne, vol. 338 bis, nos. 4-7.

acceleration of the federalist movement in his decision to occupy Frankfurt, the crucial rail center between north and south Germany. Naturally enough, Degoutte read the occupation as a signal of French readiness to move in support of Bavaria and he pressed for prompt action by Heim. But the moment chosen by Heim for the unleashing of his movement was 6 June, the date of the Reichstag elections and of Landtag elections in Bavaria. Bothmer had exposed Heim's plan on 1 April. The elections would return a great B.V.P. majority. Heim would replace von Kahr and, if agreement were reached with Paris, he would seek a pretext to break with Berlin.[54]

Paléologue responded by pledging 1.5 million francs for the creation of a "Bavarian Catholic press organization" and remitted the first 200,000 francs on 20 April.[55] The same day, he drew up a plan of action and wired Millerand, then at San Remo. All was ready for the federalist revolution, he wrote. After the June election, the French government would insist that Berlin disband the Bavarian paramilitary *Einwohnerwehr.* Heim would refuse and proclaim Bavarian independence. Dorten promised that the Rhenish revolution would follow immediately. Paléologue understood that Heim's goals included escape from disarmament and possible restoration of the Wittelsbachs, but he reasoned that "a monarchical restoration in Munich would be the best means of digging a trench between Bavaria and Socialist Prussia."[56] In Strasbourg, Dard's efforts neared conclusion. He requested an economic mission to work out the details of revictualment and French industrial penetration.[57]

Paléologue was willing to scrap strict execution of the Treaty of Versailles to reorganize all of Central Europe. He accepted Heim's Austrian goals, which dovetailed with his own Danubian ideas, and he accepted Bavarian monarchism. But he did worry that the Bavarians sought, not to break up Germany, but to unite all of Germany under Bavarian leadership. In addition, Bruère learned that the Hessian federalists would demand the evacuation of the Rhineland by France in return for their break with Berlin. The news was received with shock in the Quai d'Orsay.[58]

As the elections approached, the French authorities contrived to

[54] Note Bothmer, 1 Apr. 1920: AN Pap. Mangin, vol. 21, dos. 3 bis.

[55] "Projet" submitted by Bruère and "approuvé en principe" by Paléologue, 17 Apr. 1920: MAE Allemagne, vol. 353, no. 129; Note Dard, 20 Apr. 1920: MAE Pap. Dard, vol. 4, dos. 1.

[56] Tel. Paléologue to Millerand (San Remo), 20 Apr. 1920: MAE Allemagne, vol. 353, nos. 104-105.

[57] Note Dard, 20 Apr. 1920: MAE Pap. Dard, vol. 4, dos. 1.

[58] Tel. Bruère to MAE, "L'Allemagne fédérale et la France," 26 May 1920: MAE Allemagne, vol. 338 bis, nos. 58-59.

discover precisely what Heim planned for the future. On 1 June General Degoutte met with the *Bauernkönig* in Wiesbaden and offered a further concession. France would agree to Austrian membership in a Germanic confederation, as long as Prussia was excluded.[59] The next day Degoutte visited Paris to receive instructions; then he, Tirard, Dard, and Heim convened again on 4 June. Conforming to his instructions from Paléologue, Degoutte promised the economic and eventual military support of France for a Germanic confederation limited at the Elbe. Now Heim hesitated. Germany was not ready for the expulsion of Prussia, he said. In any case, this would mean great danger, for it would deliver Old Prussia into the arms of the Bolsheviks.[60] The federalist movement, with its long months of preparation, suddenly collapsed for Paléologue. Heim was in fact seeking a Greater Germany including Prussia and Austria, the *grossdeutsch* solution Catholics had always favored.

June 6 came and went without a rupture between Munich and Berlin, and the federalist movement, if not Bavarian particularism, disintegrated. The Quai d'Orsay had in its possession on 1 June intelligence pointing to the ultimate reluctance of Bavaria to act. Late in May von Kahr journeyed to Berlin and bargained with Chancellor Müller. Von Kahr received assurances that the Reich would respect Bavarian administrative autonomy and not force dissolution of the *Einwohnerwehr*. In return, von Kahr pledged loyalty to the Reich.[61]

Paléologue not only tolerated Heim's plan to tear up the treaty, but completely miscalculated the strength of militant federalism in Germany. The B.V.P. electoral victory did not mean a new Germany led by Georg Heim, but the consolidation of von Kahr's government. In the Rhineland, Dorten commanded nothing and there was no evidence that the Rhenish Center would follow the lead of Bavarian schismatics. In Hesse, Prince Isenburg could not even claim a party. Popular sentiment for autonomy was perhaps strongest in Hanover, which even forced a plebiscite four years later, but that land was in the least favorable position to defy Berlin. Paléologue considered the sacrifice of the most basic principles of Allied policy for a leap in the dark. It was the first manifestation of French revisionism.

French contact with Bavaria continued. Later in 1920 Dard presented his credentials to von Kahr's government and established a French mission. While the French government kept a close watch on

[59] MS Dard, 1 June 1920: MAE Pap. Dard, vol. 4, dos. 2.

[60] Des. Bruère to MAE, 1 June 1920; Tel. Paléologue to Bruère, 2 June 1920; Tel. Bruère to MAE, 4 June 1920: MAE Allemagne, vol. 353, nos. 158-160, 174-176.

[61] Tel. Marcilly to MAE, 1 June 1920: AN HCF, vol. 5271, dos. 83/9.

events in Munich, insisted that Berlin disband the *Einwohnerwehr*, and hoped for a Berlin-Munich split, it washed its hands of federalism and turned to pick up the threads of its German—and Rhenish—policy.

RHINELAND MANEUVERING

Within the Rhineland itself, 1920 was a year of consolidation during which the patterns of French, British, and German policies were set. Public resolutions of the Rhenish Center party on autonomy indicated a retreat from its position of 1919. First, the Center party would consider autonomy only in connection with the general interests of the Reich. This forbade a Rhenish movement as long as it could redound to the benefit of France, i.e., for all practical purposes, for as long as the occupation lasted. Second, the Center declared its intention to seek autonomy only through the legal means provided by the German Constitution. Third, the Rhenish party expelled from its midst all who "openly or secretly favored the separation of the Rhineland from Germany," i.e., Dorten and his followers.[62]

The Foreign Office also opposed any constitutional change in the Rhineland other than by legal means. The British feared not only the extension of French influence on the Left Bank, but also the damage a Rhenish movement could do to German political stability. Britain would remain loyal to Berlin, Tirard predicted, and if separatism threatened to succeed, the British might collaborate with Rhenish leaders to retain control of events and fashion a Rhenish Republic "safe" for Berlin. Clemenceau and Millerand both instructed Tirard to keep in touch with separatist leaders, but to avoid Adenauer. Tirard recognized, nevertheless, that the issue of autonomy would eventually be decided in Adenauer's Cologne, in the British zone.[63] In April, an officer of the British High Commission assured a German agent that British-American-German cooperation in the Rhineland Commission would block France's "special desires" on the Rhine.[64]

[62] Des. Tirard to MAE, "Rapport confidentiel sur le Congrès du Centre à Cologne," 4 Oct. 1919: MAE Rive Gauche, vol. 1, nos. 234-236.

[63] Des. Tirard to MAE, 14 Feb. 1920: MAE Rive Gauche, vol. 2, nos. 39-41; Des Tirard to MAE, 21 Feb. 1920: MAE Paix, vol. 167, nos. 67-71. This recognition was shared by the British, who were in possession of the crucial Rhenish hub. A report by the British High Commissioner designate in August 1919 advised the Foreign Office to take Dorten's movement seriously, but added that, although Rhenish leaders might favor separation from Prussia, they had no desire for cooperation with France. Let. Sir Harold Stuart (Coblenz) to Sir. R. Graham, 29 Aug. 1919: DBFP, V, 354-363.

[64] Tel. Rieth (Darmstadt) to A.A., 1 Apr. 1920: Germany, Archives of the Auswärtiges Amt, United States National Archives Microfilm (hereafter cited as AA), L1746, 5432, nos. 429856-60.

British confidence was ill-placed. The Rhineland Commission was the agency in which France's antagonists were weakest. The German commissioner was present only as an observer, and Tirard was seeking a pretext to eliminate the office altogether. The American representative was also a nonvoting observer, since the United States had failed to ratify the treaty. Pierrepont Noyes reported that the French commissioner was under pressure from Paris to pursue a "strong policy" in the Rhineland, and Noyes read Rhenish separation as the goal of France's Ruhr plans. Nevertheless, he was helpless to prevent French activities.[65] American influence in Europe could only be financial and long-term, not immediate and diplomatic. There remained the commissioners of France, Britain, and Belgium. A parting of the ways among the Allies could result in a Franco-Belgian combination outvoting the British and governing the Rhineland as it pleased.[66]

During the first year of the treaty regime, the only Rhenish inhabitants who shared France's "special desires" were the diehards of Dorten's movement. On 22 January 1920 Dorten, Kastert, and about a hundred followers joined to form the *Rheinische Volksvereinigung*, pledged peacefully to struggle against Prussian rule. Within a month, all Rhenish political parties denounced the creation as a tool of the French. Dorten's party and its organ, the *Rheinischer Herold*, subsisted on donations from his own private fortune, some local contributions, and subsidies from the French High Commissariat.

The mercurial Dorten both cultivated and resented his relationship with the French. He liked to think of himself as a Rhenish patriot, but Tirard treated him like a flunkey. Dorten flaunted his friendships with nationalist French deputies and editors, but spared no criticism for the Paris government's policy. "France ought to support us to the hilt," he declared to one reporter, "but M. Tirard is too timid. . . . We are certain of success if the French do not abandon us."[67] He demanded a Rhenish parliament, removal of Prussian administrators from the Left Bank, and the foundation of a Franco-Rhenish bank. The failure of the French to adopt these measures over British and German opposition galled the naive amateur and marked the beginning of his stormy relations with Tirard.[68]

[65] Let. Noyes (Coblenz) to Colby, 27 Feb. 1920: FRUS 1920, II, 289-296.

[66] Noyes saw clearly the danger if Franco-German antagonism, increased by Franco-British divergence, should focus on the Rhine. Noyes urged Washington to press for ratification of the Versailles Treaty and lead the way to a "European settlement." Otherwise, Europe would drift "steadily downward toward disaster." See Nelson, *Victors Divided*, pp. 144-171.

[67] Note R. Migeot (editor of *La Paix des Peuples*), "Déclarations faites par le Docteur Dorten," 1 Apr. 1920: MAE Rive Gauche, vol. 2, nos. 58-59.

[68] Pers. Let. Dorten to Mangin, 18 Mar. 1920: MAE Rive Gauche, vol. 2, nos. 50-56.

Dorten's declarations of Franco-Rhenish solidarity were an embarrassment to the French government, but they won him allies in the Chambers and in nationalist societies such as the *Comité de la Rive Gauche du Rhin* and the *Comité Dupleix*. Dorten's frequent visits to Paris to solicit money and publicity prompted English and German journals to claim that Dorten was received by Millerand himself. Even Tirard feared that the reports might be accurate and only a firm denial from Paléologue satisfied him.[69] But French efforts to claim noninvolvement with Rhenish separatism were feeble. On 23 July three Frankfurt policemen, acting on orders from their frustrated captain in the recently occupied city, seized Dorten on the street and spirited him away to answer charges connected with the putsch of June 1919. The action was clearly in violation of the Allies' amnesty for Armistice political criminals and Tirard had Dorten returned "sain et sauf" to Wiesbaden. Dorten immediately left again for Paris, where he ridiculed the "protection" the occupation afforded against German tyranny.[70]

The coming elections and the activities of the B.V.P. led Dorten to form a political party designed to draw off Rhenish Centrists dissatisfied with the party's policies. At the end of April he labored behind the scenes at the founding of the Christliche Volkspartei, then appealed through French channels to Pope Benedict XV, requesting papal recognition of the new party, dedicated as it was to the first principles of the Center party and to the struggle against Bolshevism.[71] The Pope chose not to endorse Dorten's creation and in June elections the party won a single seat. In the summer the tiny party split, delegates from Cologne and Düsseldorf rebelling against Dorten's leadership.

Why did the French authorities not wash their hands of the troublesome and ineffectual Dorten and spare themselves the denunciation of London and Berlin? First, it was not clear how large Dorten's following was. Though they were incompetent as leaders, Dorten and Kastert had, through a campaign of petitions, revealed support for autonomy among clerics, peasants, and shopkeepers in the spring of 1919. Second, abandoning Dorten would bring the vituperation of the proseparatist bloc in parliament and the military. Third, Dorten's propaganda did serve to keep the autonomy issue alive, and his movement

[69] Tel. Tirard to MAE, 6 and 11 Apr. 1920; Tel. Paléologue to Tirard, 17 Apr. 1920: MAE Rive Gauche, vol. 2, nos. 66-77, 91.

[70] Note Mangin, "Resumé d'une conversation avec M. Dorten," 6 Aug. 1920: AN Pap. Mangin, vol. 21, dos. 3 bis.

[71] Pers. Let. Dorten to His Holiness Pope Benoit XV, 16 May 1920: MAE Allemagne, vol. 316, nos. 44-47.

constituted an implied threat against Berlin. The instructions to the French authorities in relation to the Rhenish movement matched those issued for the Bavarian: discreet sympathy.[72]

On 10 March 1920 the president of the Republic, Paul Deschanel, outlined the Rhenish policy of France in an address at Strasbourg. He invoked the right of self-determination denied to the Rhinelanders in 1919, and recalled the traditional tendency of Germany toward federalism and particularism, just as the historical tendency of France was toward unity and centralization. France would aid the Rhineland to execute its rights under Article 18 of the Weimar Constitution, but sought in the meantime the creation of a Rhenish consultative committee and the elimination of the Prussian bureaucracy. This political program would be complemented by an economic one. Deschanel rued the bad impression made by "greedy French merchants, mostly Jews, who had descended on the Rhineland during the armistice." In the future, France's commercial effort would be conducted in cooperation with Rhenish industry. Finally, there was a moral program: educational projects, intellectual penetration, and charity works would not fail to foster rapprochement.[73]

The French Rhenish policy was still based on misconceptions concerning the motives and strength of autonomist sentiment in the Rhineland. By 1920 many of the threats, foreign and domestic, that contributed to its strength in 1918-1919 had disappeared. French Rhineland enthusiasts failed to understand that autonomy or federalism did not mean Franco-Rhenish friendship, despite Dorten and his Francophile collaborators. Most vital, the policy of Rhenish separation or autonomy implied revision of the Treaty of Versailles. The famous German pacifist, Helmuth von Gerlach, summed it up perceptively in April 1920:

> Separatist tendencies, or more accurately federalist tendencies, make progress on the Rhine. But it is not the sweet promises of French officers, the discourses of Maurice Barrès, or the articles of *L'Écho du Rhin* that produce this result. Rather this maladroit and brutish propaganda can only exasperate the Rhenish population and cement its sentimental ties with Germany. . . .
>
> . . . France will find herself in a most complicated situation. At

[72] Note Laroche, "Note sur la politique à suivre dans les territoires rhénans," 27 Jan. 1920: MAE Paix, vol. 167, nos. 28-32.

[73] MS Deschanel, "Discours à Strasbourg: La politique française dans les regions rhénanes, esquisse d'un programme immédiatement réalisable," 10 Mar. 1920: Paul Deschanel, unpublished private papers, Archives Nationales-Paris (hereafter cited as AN Pap. Deschanel), vol. 45, dos. 3.

> Berlin she speaks of democracy and the struggle against militarism; elsewhere, of the destruction of Prussia. At Munich she supports the monarchists and military; at Berlin she will demand the dissolution of the *Einwohnerwehr*. If France tries to play this double role, she will be quickly discredited. . . . She must settle on the principles of her German policy: unity, socialism, and peace, or separatism, military reaction, and Jesuitism.[74]

In the middle of September 1920, Millerand made a tour of inspection in the Rhineland. It prompted Sir Eyre Crowe of the Foreign Office to remark that if the French were still contemplating detachment of Rhenish Prussia, they were going the wrong way about it. "The first thing to do," said Crowe, "is to stop preaching the entirely erroneous view that the inhabitants have a natural leaning toward France."

"Such an idea is nonsense," replied Undersecretary Lord Hardinge.[75]

Nevertheless, if it appeared to French conservatives that the Rhineland had a natural leaning toward France, it was rooted in the supranational appeal of the Roman church. The Rhenish question did not fail to play a role in Franco-Vatican rapprochement. Agitation in France for resumption of diplomatic relations with the Vatican, broken off in 1905, represented a retreat from anticlericalism, but also a new circumspection in postwar France. Many felt that the "cold war" between the Third Republic and the Vatican had proven itself more injurious to France than to the Church. Benedict XV, in particular, was assumed to be pro-German during the war. There were also matters of common concern that had to be settled between Paris and Rome, such as nomination of bishops, mission support, and the status of Alsace-Lorraine, where Clemenceau appointed new bishops in 1919. Then, there was the Rhenish question. The Rhineland was largely Catholic and the home of four powerful sees: Cologne, Trier, Mainz, and Speyer. Through Rome's influence, the French hoped to win the prelates of the old *Pfaffenallee* to autonomism.

Once again, French reasoning was spurious. If the papacy were attracted to the idea of Catholic states in southern and western Germany, it would pursue this policy regardless of French desires. Insistence on France's special interests in the Rhineland would only damage the case for Rhenish autonomy. But the rapprochement proceeded

[74] Note, "Conversation avec Helmuth von Gerlach," Berlin, 15 Apr. 1920: MAE Paix, vol. 174, nos. 57-59.

[75] Minutes, Des. Harold Stuart (Coblenz) to F.O., #469, 15 Sept. 1920: PRO F.O. 371, vol. 4805, nos. 153-155.

smoothly. In January 1920 Millerand gave to veteran diplomat Jean Doulcet the mission to negotiate for a resumption of ties with the Vatican. On his side, Benedict XV declared his enthusiasm and counted on the canonization of Joan of Arc in May to win the sympathy of the French people.[76]

The Abbé Lafitte assumed the duties of France's "Catholic ambassador" on the Rhine. In March 1920 he described the importance of the Vatican for a French Rhenish policy. In the Prussian Rhineland, he began, 70 percent of the population were Catholic and docile to ecclesiastical authority. Autonomy particularly appealed to the clergy, but the anticlerical image of France damaged her chances to promote an autonomist movement. The natural antipathy of the Rhineland for Prussia could develop only if France could obtain, if not papal support, at least Rome's nonopposition to autonomy. Lafitte pointed out that three of the Rhenish sees were likely to become vacant in the near future. It was of the utmost importance that France have a hand in new appointments. But the German government, he cautioned, was negotiating its own agreement with the Vatican. The old nunciate at Munich, occupied by the Germanophile and papal favorite Monsignor Pacelli, was to be converted into an embassy at Berlin. French interest lay in seeking to preserve a separate papal representation in Munich and in counteracting Berlin's favor in Rome. The fate of the Saar, Palatinate, and Rhenish Prussia, he concluded, would be settled, not in Coblenz, but in Rome.[77]

In the course of the negotiations of 1920, Doulcet questioned Cardinal State Secretary Gasparri concerning the political aspirations of Rhenish and Bavarian Catholics. The traditional policy of German Catholicism was federalism, security from the centralizing and secularizing tendency of Berlin. Would not His Holiness find advantage in this policy again with the Reich and Prussian governments imbued with socialism? Gasparri hesitated; he offered sympathy to the desires of German federalists, but "guarded an absolute reserve concerning the Rhineland." Doulcet despaired of papal intervention in the quarrels of the Center or encouragement to Rhenish prelates to favor autonomy.[78]

Millerand had reason to be incredulous. The Center party arose

[76] Jean du Sault, "Les relations diplomatiques entre la France et la Saint-Siège," *Revue des Deux Mondes* 10 (October 1971):115-122.

[77] MAE Memo, "La question rhénane et le rétablissement des relations avec le Saint-Siège," Strasbourg, 7 Mar. 1920: Louis Canet, unpublished private papers, Ministère des Affaires Étrangères-Paris (hereafter cited as MAE Pap. Canet), vol. 123, nos. 3-9.

[78] Let. Doulcet to Millerand, 15 June 1920: AN HCF, vol. 5271, dos. 8319.

after 1871 to protect the particularist rights of Catholic Germany; Bismarck even labeled the Centrists *Reichsfeinde*. Now the moment came when the Center had the opportunity and the strength to act on behalf of the party's first principles, instilled in the 1870s by the fiery Ludwig Windthorst, yet both the Rhineland and the Vatican seemed unwilling to budge. In fact, Benedict XV followed the policy of the Center, not vice versa, and he was pleased to do so. Rather than the Reich government posing a threat to Catholics, the very survival of the republic depended on the participation of the Center party in the government. On 21 June 1920 a Baden Centrist, Konstantin Fehrenbach, became chancellor of the Reich.

The Rhenish issue was only an important sidelight of Franco-Vatican rapprochement. But in addition to the principal task of regulating the legal status of the Church in France, the French delegation continued to press for papal favor in the appointment of Rhenish bishops and for general Franco-Rhenish conciliation. In November 1920 the Chamber voted credits for a permanent French embassy at the Holy See.

COMMERCIAL RELATIONS: RHENISH POLICY OR GERMAN POLICY?

The conflict between treaty execution, dependent on Allied and German cooperation, and revision through direct Franco-Rhenish solutions also extended to the vital problem of Franco-German commercial relations. Clemenceau had expelled German business from Alsace-Lorraine, but the industrial areas of eastern France and western Germany enjoyed a symbiosis that France, especially, could not afford to snap. Not only the smelting coke for Lorraine *minette*, but the markets for the semi-finished products of Lorraine had been provided by Germany. The Clemenceau government recognized this and provided for the resumption of raw materials and merchandise exchange, but through coercive treaty clauses, not through the natural play of markets. More problematical were reparations-in-kind, earnestly desired by a government strapped for cash, but opposed by domestic producers and unions with whom German goods would be competing. Finally, there was the hope that Germany would again become a good customer for French luxury goods. But on whose terms would Franco-German intercourse take place? Only a prosperous Germany could pay reparations and buy French goods, but a prosperous Germany would pose a renewed threat, and if French recovery became narrowly dependent on German prosperity, the Germans would have the leverage to throw off reparations entirely. If France could find the necessary financial and diplomatic support in England and the United States, she could "escape her present embarrassment, and recover without having to offer a hand to Germany."[79] But France had not found Anglo-American support, and the United States informed France that it viewed the role of the Reparations Commission as "avoiding policies which will prevent German economic recovery." American and British stabilization policy aimed at a democratic, but economically potent, Germany.[80] But German policy, the Quai d'Orsay feared, would seek to split the Allies and make France come to Germany, while the French government "must seek to obtain the maximum in reparations with the minimum of German economic power."[81]

French commercial policy was in the hands of one of the finest products of the prestigious École Libre des Sciences Politiques. A tireless master of administrative detail, he was also possessed of a strikingly agile and imaginative mind. Jacques Seydoux, forty-nine years old in 1920, with twenty-seven years in the Quai d'Orsay, was named undersecretary for commercial relations in May 1919. He held the post until crippling arthritis and overexertion brought inactivity, then retirement. Seydoux's industrious intellect imposed itself on all who dealt with him, from Colonel House and Herbert Hoover to Briand and Poincaré. Overshadowed in accounts of French diplomacy by the mystique of Berthelot, Seydoux provided much of the creativity in the Foreign Ministry. If his thought was governed by any consuming ambition, it was not the destruction of Germany, but the bridling of the industrial might of France's powerful neighbor as the necessary prelude to inevitable economic cooperation. Clemenceau's government had envisioned two means of leverage for France in her dealings with Germany, but one was conditional and the second proved imaginary. The first was France's power under the treaty to impose sanctions should Germany default, but this leverage depended on the cooperation of France's fellow nations on the Reparations Commission. The second was French possession of the iron of Lorraine, which France presumably could trade for German concessions in markets and raw materials. But by 1920 the Ruhr seemed to be getting along without French ore. Finally, two other factors weakened the French negotiating position: the critical state of French metallurgy and the Rhenish policy pursued by Millerand's government.

[79] Tel. MAE to Delevaud (Stockholm), "a.s. des relations économiques entre la France et l'Allemagne," 16 Dec. 1919: MAE Allemagne, vol. 522, nos. 39-44.

[80] Tel. Colby to Wallace (Paris), 14 Apr. 1920: FRUS 1920, II, 382-383.

[81] Tel. MAE to Marcilly (Berlin), "Questions économiques," 14 Jan. 1920: MAE Allemagne, vol. 522, nos. 82-86.

Millerand and Seydoux concluded that if they could achieve a level of control over Rhenish economic prosperity by channeling French orders for German reparations-in-kind, lumber, cement, tools, etc., through Rhenish industry, French political influence in the Rhineland would be vastly increased. Tirard, Foch, and Loucheur had expressed the same hope the year before. Now Poincaré, who accepted the presidency of the Reparations Commission after stepping down as president of the Republic, and Tardieu from the Chamber also demanded a Rhenish orientation to French economic policy.[82] But this added consideration in commercial negotiations on the French side weakened the chances of striking a bargain with Berlin for massive and rapid deliveries-in-kind, and was overly sanguine, given the Reich government's complete recovery of its commercial sovereignty upon the coming into force of the treaty on 10 January 1920. The first act of the Berlin government was to resurrect the German tariff barrier, closing the "hole in the West." Berlin also regained control over import-export licensing, ending the boom in Franco-Rhenish trade.[83]

Initial contacts in March between a German delegation under Heinrich Göppert and a French one headed by Seydoux made no progress. Seydoux protested that the new German commercial regime not only eliminated the preference enjoyed by France, but actively discriminated against French merchants, contrary to Articles 264-267 of the treaty.[84] The French took their case to the Allied Conference of Ambassadors and over British resistance won the conference to an investigation of the German commercial regime. On 29 April Göppert turned conciliatory. He requested resumption of talks on a much broader scale, envisioning a commercial treaty and regulation of reparations-in-kind, and hinted at the possibility of iron for coal exchanges.[85] Talks began on 20 May.

Seydoux was troubled by France's weak position. Despite the investigation of German licensing, a return to the boom of the Armistice period was impossible. Any attempt to accord special treatment to Franco-Rhenish trade would meet energetic resistance from London

[82] J.O., Chambre, 6 Feb. 1920, p. 137.

[83] Like all other German laws, the tariff decrees had to be approved by the Rhineland Commission before having legal force in the occupied territories. The process of examination and approval of the decrees permitted Tirard to delay a final closing of the "hole in the West" until April.

[84] Tel. Seydoux to Marcilly, 27 Mar. 1920: MAE Allemagne, vol. 522, nos. 124-130; Tel. Derby (Paris) to Curzon, 24 Mar. 1920; Tel. Curzon to Stuart (Coblenz), 24 Mar. 1920: DBFP, IX, 244-246.

[85] Tel. Millerand to St. Quentin (Berlin), 29 Apr. 1920: MAE Allemagne, vol. 522, nos. 160-165.

and Berlin.[86] But the industrial conflict within France weighed most heavily. On 15 May Seydoux met with French steel men. Léon Levy discounted the German need for Lorraine iron. The Ruhr imported from Sweden and in any case would avoid becoming dependent on France. Levy reported that French steel mills were operating at 30 percent capacity, while the Germans had already returned to 60 to 65 percent. It was France that needed an iron for coke deal, not Germany.[87] But French small industrialists opposed any plan likely to introduce German competition. They worked through the Ministry of Commerce for a policy of sanctions against Germany to extract financial reparations and opposed reparations-in-kind. Finally, there was Seydoux's hope that reparations orders could be centralized on the Left Bank, instead of distributed by the Berlin government. "We must create a special grouping for the Left Bank of the Rhine, basing our argument on the de facto situation of the occupation."[88]

Such a development did not seem out of the question, for on 1 April Tirard wired exciting news to Seydoux: a great grouping of Rhenish industrialists had formed for the purpose of turning Rhenish industrial might to the task of French and Belgian reconstruction. It called itself the *Rheinische Zentralstelle für Lieferungen* and Francophile elements, including Dorten himself, supposedly aided in its formation. Three weeks later Tirard verified that the society represented an important part of all Rhenish industry, promised prompt delivery of quality materials, and guaranteed that all orders would be distributed to firms based in the occupied territory. It also, of course, fulfilled French desires to favor the Rhineland and cultivate particularism.[89] Seydoux hesitated to deal with an organization that appeared too good to be true, but the appearance of German countermeasures seems to have changed his mind. First, Göppert's sudden demarche at the Quai d'Orsay appeared designed to stay French action in the Rhineland with the offer of a broad agreement with Berlin. Second, Tirard reported a

[86] Note Seydoux, "Situation de la Rive Gauche du Rhin," 6 May 1920: AN HCF, vol. 3185, dos. Q1a5.

[87] Notes Seydoux, "Réunion avec les délégués français," and "Négociations allemandes—conversation avec M. Léon Levy," 19 May 1920: MAE Allemagne, vol. 522, nos. 184-189.

[88] Note Seydoux, "Reconstitution des regions liberées—collaboration allemande," 14 Apr. 1920: AN HCF, vol. 3208, dos. Q1Be2f.

[89] Let. Tirard to Seydoux, #1698HC/22, 22 Apr. 1920: AN HCF, vol. 3208, dos. Q1Be2f. The Rheinische Zentralstelle also provided Tirard with an opportunity to expand his bureaucratic empire by making his own economic service the liaison between *sinistrés* and Rhenish industry. Seydoux did not fail to perceive Tirard's administrative interest in the matter.

week later the creation in Frankfurt of a rival industrial organization by the German government, ostensibly to absorb the Rhenish group.

Seydoux conferred with the ministries of commerce and industrial reconstruction. He advocated separating the questions of deliveries-in-kind and a commercial accord so that Berlin could not maneuver France into a sacrifice of her freedom of action in the question of reparations. France must avoid German efforts to unite all German industry into a single bloc for the distribution of French reparations orders.[90] Seydoux now recommended negotiations with the *Zentralstelle* and Millerand dispatched a mission on 19 May. The French experts deliberated with the agents of the *Zentralstelle* for two months and prepared a broad provisional accord before the truth emerged. The *Rheinische Zentralstelle* was an instrument of Berlin. At the time of the opening of the Spa Conference, the Rhenish delegates suddenly killed their talks with the French by demanding unrealistic price levels and conditions of sale. The Office of Industrial Reconstruction withdrew its mission and attacked the ill will of the Rhenish negotiators.[91] The official negotiations also broke off in July. Seydoux and Göppert agreed to form joint subcommittees for the study of metallurgy, textiles, and chemicals, but the two sides were no nearer settlement than in January. Three months later Tirard discovered that the *Zentralstelle* was created at the behest of the German government, which hoped to secure from France a reparations agreement on extremely favorable terms by seeming to hold out the promise of Franco-Rhenish collaboration. The particularist nature of the organization and its flirtations with Dorten were eyewash.[92]

A similar pattern of events surrounded an organization created by Dorten at Wiesbaden, the *bureau mixte* advocated by Tirard and Seydoux in 1919. André Bruère at Mainz reported that Dorten's group could serve as liaison between the *sinistrés* and Rhenish industries. Rallying Rhenish industry to cooperation with France would, Bruère hoped, provide the final impetus to the federalist movement then entering its decisive weeks.[93] On 10 May, the same day as he named the *Zentralstelle* mission, Millerand directed Bruère to hasten Dorten's ef-

[90] Note Seydoux, "Négociations avec l'Allemagne," 12 May 1920: MAE Allemagne, vol. 522, nos. 180-183.

[91] "Note verbale de l'Office de Reconstruction Industrielle pour le Rheinische Zentralstelle," 12 July 1920: AN Pap. Mangin, vol. 21, dos. 3 bis.

[92] Let. Tirard to Seydoux, #525/s ATRP, 12 Oct. 1920: AN Pap. Mangin, vol. 21, dos. 3 bis.

[93] Let. Bruère (Mainz) to French Embassy Berlin, 2 May 1920; MAE Memo, "Vue de M. Bruère," 8 May 1920: MAE Paix, vol. 168, nos. 12-15, 20.

forts to gather a Rhenish delegation for the *bureau mixte* and to begin operations. "We have the greatest interest," he wired, "in arranging a first meeting for the *bureau mixte* as soon as possible."[94]

After the collapse of the *Zentralstelle*, the *bureau mixte* came to nothing. It remained in existence for months, handled some French orders, and channeled funds to Dorten for political purposes, but it could never serve as the vehicle for Franco-Rhenish economic cooperation. The French *comptoir d'achats*, also located in Wiesbaden, handled the task of making French purchases in the Rhineland while the deadlock with Berlin on a general commercial plan persisted.

THE DRIFT TOWARD SANCTIONS

Efforts to provoke a federalist reorganization of Germany, to win papal support for an autonomous movement on the Rhine, and to create a special economic relationship between France and the Left Bank were all manifestations of the Rhenish policy as practiced under Millerand. But the Paris government required that future Rhenish political change be in addition to, and not in lieu of, French treaty rights. For the financial reparations so vital to France could come only from Berlin through strict execution of the treaty. When the Peace Conference debate on reparations was carried over into 1920, however, the French met the same constellation of forces as in the coal crisis. Should liability or capacity to pay be the basis of discussion; should a global sum be set or an open account? Lloyd George and Italian premier Nitti pressed for an early decision concerning Germany's total obligations. Only then could the German government hope to find credits. At San Remo Millerand fought the proposal and presented instead the Avenol plan, calling for three billion gold mark annuities, with deferred determination of the total bill. He also called for linkage of war debt and reparation payments. Lloyd George promised not to demand funding of France's debts to Britain, but postponed an overall financial settlement in hopes of a change in American policy.[95] At Hythe in May, Millerand agreed to accept a global sum in return for a promise of immediate payments from Germany. He obliged by lowering the French estimate from the 240 billion suggested at the Peace Conference to 120 billion. The conciliatory move brought screams of protest from French

[94] Tel. Millerand to Bruère, "Bureau mixte franco-rhénan de Wiesbaden," 10 May 1920: AN HCF, vol. 3208, dos. Q1Be2f.

[95] Weill-Raynal, *Les réparations allemandes*, I, 537-542. See also "Notes of a Meeting of the Heads of the British, French, and Italian Delegations," San Remo, 18 Apr. 1920: DBFP, VIII, 10-18.

politicians and newspapers. Poincaré resigned from the Reparations Commission in a grand *coup de théâtre*.

But any reparations depended on German compliance, and the Germans pleaded an incapacity to make any large capital transfers, let alone three billion per year. The British government, under the impact of Keynesian arguments, showed sympathy rather than alarm at the German attitude. Internal pressures in France and Germany demanded that both countries must get large sums of money quickly. Once this was accomplished, the French would not be so immoderate or the Germans so intransigent. But this required large Anglo-American operations of credit, chances for which seemed remote, as well as prior acceptance of a total sum by both France and Germany.[96]

Following the Senate's defeat of the Treaty of Versailles in the spring, Washington seemed to pay less and less attention to Europe's problems. The press of elections and Wilson's illness contributed to this neglect. As Clémentel had foreseen, France would have to look to Germany, not to the Anglo-Americans.[97] But large specie payments required German recovery as a prerequisite; payments-in-kind would only stimulate that recovery, assuming the Germans could be made to pay at all. How then could German industry be controlled? Perhaps sanctions could provide the answer. The Reparations Commission could assume powers over the German economy, mused Seydoux, as it had already in Austria. Control of government monopolies, supervision of German taxation: these measures could guarantee payments despite German ill will and British aversion to military force, and leave France "free to pursue our German policy."[98]

To Lloyd George, sanctions were anathema. In the first half of 1920 the threats to German democracy from Right and Left, and later the developing unemployment and inflation in Britain, meant that barriers to German economic health would only compound Europe's difficulties. Millerand's forswearance of unilateral action meant that British cooperation was needed in any effort to enforce reparations. At the time of Spa, the Quai d'Orsay's Jules Laroche speculated that the British Prime Minister would aid France in her quest for coal to avoid an occupation of the Ruhr. This would suffice, since "money cannot always buy coal, but if France receives coal, money will follow."[99] In

[96] "Note on the German Situation by Mr. Waterlow," and Minute by Lord Hardinge, 5 July 1920: DBFP, X, 267-269.

[97] For American policy in late 1920 toward Europe in general and the Rhineland occupation in particular, see Nelson, *Victors Divided*, pp. 174-181, and Link, *Die amerikanische Stabilisierungspolitik*.

[98] Note Seydoux pour le PdC, "Paiement de la dette allemande," 5 June 1920: MAE Pap. Millerand, Réparations I, nos. 50-53.

[99] Pers. Let. Laroche to Barrère, 19 July 1920: MAE Corr. Barrère, vol. 3, no. 67.

fact, France needed both money and coal, and the collapse of coal prices after Spa loosened the tie between them in any case. Millerand and Lloyd George departed Spa with plans for another conference, at Geneva, to negotiate a compromise. But in the wake of the French coal "surrender," the French Senate rebelled, and Millerand found excuses to scuttle the conference. With the British resisting force and the French parliament demanding results, French experts turned their attention to developing a plan that had a reasonable possibility of German support. "The German government," Seydoux recognized, "is too weak to make German industry and finance accept anything but a policy of tenacious resistance." Thus the eventual plan must be acceptable to German business.[100] Millerand himself favored any plan likely to encourage Franco-German industrial collaboration. But could any arrangement acceptable to the titans of the Ruhr contain guarantees acceptable to France?

The closing months of 1920 gave further evidence of Berlin's inability or unwillingness to fulfill her obligations. Of the twenty billion gold marks to be transferred before May 1921, Berlin had managed only about two billion. Coal deliveries remained at less than 50 percent of the Spa requirements. Seydoux assumed that reparations-in-kind would have to replace capital transfers for the time being. But here again the "Annex IV" system of deliveries in the treaty was insufficient. Working through the Reparations Commission, it was cumbersome and created disputes. Seydoux again called for a Franco-German agreement based on a *bureau mixte*.[101] François-Marsal, backed by the *Comité des Forges*, suggested expanding an agreement to include cooperation between French and German metallurgies. Perhaps the entire reparations dispute could be settled directly without interference from London.[102] But payments-in-kind, repeated Seydoux, was the best means to permit German recovery. "It is in our interest to keep the system from expanding too much."[103]

Millerand summoned his economic experts, including Seydoux, the new French delegate to the Reparations Commission Louis Dubois, and François-Marsal, to a policy debate on 23 October. Geneva had been scuttled, but London and Berlin spoke of convening an experts'

[100] Let. Seydoux to Dubois, 18 Nov. 1920: AN, Archives of the French Delegation to the Reparations Commission, AJ[5]321, dos. 321, cited by Trachtenberg, "French Reparations Policy," p. 197.

[101] Note Seydoux pour le PdC, "Critique du document allemand #3," 12 July 1920: MAE Pap. Millerand, Réparations I, nos. 71-72.

[102] Let. François-Marsal (minister of finance) to Millerand, 11 Sept. 1920: MAE Pap. Millerand, Réparations I, nos. 122-124.

[103] Note Seydoux, "Problème des réparations," 15 Oct. 1920: MAE Pap. Millerand, Réparations I, nos. 219-243.

conference in Brussels as soon as possible. The majority opinion opposed trusting the new German demarche. Negotiations must be avoided until the Reparations Commission had fixed the total debt. But Seydoux dissented and, given Millerand's support, his counsel carried the day. Millerand despaired of "integral implementation" of the treaty, especially in cooperation with Britain. It was in the French interest to come to terms with the Germans as soon as possible. The hopes thus placed in a new experts' conference formed the basis for the Seydoux Plan for reparations-in-kind eventually worked out at Brussels.[104] The sense of urgency was genuine, for the alternative to a direct Franco-German accord, Seydoux told Dubois, was the occupation of the Ruhr: "It is a violent solution, but it will settle everything. We will become the masters of Germany, independent of England, and an industrial power of the first rank. There are many in France who consider it the only solution, but it is full of risks internal and external. Before it is turned to, all avenues of conciliation must first be exhausted."[105]

There were many, especially in the military, who looked to the Ruhr occupation as the only means of satisfying French needs. But lesser sanctions were available in the Rhineland. Tirard had seen the possibilities during the Armistice, Loucheur had them in mind while negotiating the Rhineland Agreement. In the latter months of 1920, the Quai d'Orsay's legal consultant Henri Fromageot and François-Marsal pointed out the possibility of exploiting mines, forests, industry, government monopolies, and customs receipts on the Left Bank of the Rhine.[106] Tirard had already prepared studies for the transformation of the Rhineland Commission into an agency for the execution of reparations. He envisioned a separate customs regime for the Left Bank, collection of revenues, and control of raw materials by the Allies.[107] Thus French Rhenish policy, under the pressure of the more immediate reparations crisis, had taken a turn from the effort to win Rhenish hearts through propaganda and paternalism to one of military and economic pressure. But sanctions remained a back-up policy while the experts convened at Brussels to formulate a structure for repara-

[104] Georges Soutou, "Die deutschen Reparationen und das Seydoux-Projekt, 1920/21," *Vierteljahrshefte für Zeitgeschichte* 23, no. 3 (July, 1975):237-270. For the considerations behind the Seydoux Plan, see p. 247.

[105] Let. Seydoux to Vignon (personal secretary to Millerand), 25 Oct. 1920: MAE Pap. Millerand, Réparations I, nos. 271-273.

[106] Let. François-Marsal to Leygues, 16 Oct. 1920: MAE Pap. Millerand, Réparations I, nos. 245-248.

[107] Note Tirard, "Étude sur les moyens des représailles économiques à tirer de l'occupation en cas de non-exécution par l'Allemagne," 30 Mar. 1920: MAE Paix, vol. 167, nos. 163-166.

tions based both on Germany's capacities and the particular interests of the Allies. The unproductive year drew to a close.

By the end of 1920 the foreign policy of Millerand and Paléologue showed few successes in Europe. German disarmament was incomplete and reparations were not forthcoming. Spa had shown that France could purchase British cooperation only at the cost of part of her treaty rights. The occupation of Frankfurt, Millerand's display of independence, was a knife in the water. In Catholic Germany and Central Europe, Paléologue's federalist schemes misfired. Paléologue's dalliance with Budapest had only precipitated the formation in August of the Little Entente, directed against Hungarian and French revisionism. In the Rhineland, the French policy of favoring separatism only aggravated the Allies and Germany without winning the support of the indigenous population, the Center party, or the Vatican. In one area alone could Millerand point to a great victory, and that was in Poland.

The military conflict with the Red Army turned against the Poles in early summer. By mid-August the Russians were threatening Warsaw. As they advanced, "all Germany began to boil up." The defeat of Poland could mean the union of the Russian and German armies, the partition of Poland, the destruction of Versailles.[108] It is not surprising that during these months a curious ideological invention called National Bolshevism produced a brief panic in the West. Haunted by the specter of a German-Russian coalition, French and British officials perceived in National Bolshevism a conspiracy of revenge against the Entente. Newspapers in France printed lurid scenarios of Cossack hordes led by the Prussian General Staff crushing Poland, then bursting across the Rhine. Even British Rhineland Commissioner Arnold Robertson feared the "alarming growth" of National Bolshevism in Germany, though he blamed the "French policy of pin-pricks" for its strength.[109]

Lloyd George displayed contemptuous indifference during the crisis on the Vistula and frivolously advised the Poles to accept Soviet peace conditions imcompatible with Polish independence. But French vital interests were at stake. Millerand sent General Weygand to advise the Poles, and Pilsudski's counterattack on 16 August crushed the Russians. A truce on favorable terms was concluded in October. The Polish victory made heroes of Millerand and Weygand, while British prestige suffered. France, it seemed, had helped to save Europe.

In September 1920 Millerand resigned as premier to become presi-

[108] Wandycz, *France and Her Eastern Allies*, pp. 161-162.

[109] Pers. Let. Robertson (Coblenz) to Campbell, 16 Aug. 1920: PRO Curzon Pap., vol. 155, no. 152.

dent of the Republic. Paul Deschanel was a sick man. A fall from a speeding train, followed by fits of bizarre behavior, forced his retirement. Like Poincaré before him in 1913, Millerand entered the Elysée determined to preserve his control over policy. Characteristically he chose a malleable place filler, Georges Leygues, as premier, while at the Quai d'Orsay Berthelot replaced Paléologue as secretary-general. Leygues's four months in office were an interlude. In lieu of the defunct Geneva Conference, he agreed to the meeting of experts at Brussels scheduled for December 1920, and described the new drift in French policy: the German industrialists must be brought to accept the inevitability of reparations, and be given a stake in their execution. To achieve this would be Seydoux's task at Brussels.[110]

The Battle of Warsaw had preserved for the Entente the dominant voice in European stabilization, but that process was not much advanced. The measured pace of international politics indicated that 1921 would be the year of confrontation over reparations, hence a year of decision for France: treaty execution or forcible revision, German policy or Rhenish policy?

[110] See Soutou "Die deutschen Reparationen," pp. 240-249.

·4·

SANCTIONS, FULFILLMENT, AND THE EROSION OF THE ENTENTE, 1921

The first year of the treaty regime had been one of disappointment for France. A posture of rigid insistence on every jot and tittle of the Versailles Treaty had been revealed as empty, and the economic vagaries of the postwar world demanded instead diplomatic imagination and experimentation. The burden of initiative fell heaviest on France. Despairing of British support for integral implementation of the treaty, but rejecting the cabalistic revisionism of the previous year, the French government in 1921 tried the opposite approach toward restoration of a European equilibrium. For January 1921, like the January before and the one to follow, saw a new government in France. Led by Aristide Briand, France returned to a policy based on the Treaty of Versailles, in cooperation not with Britain, but with Germany herself. It was the policy of fulfillment, of European stabilization based on Franco-German detente, and it was made possible by the momentary liberation of France from dependence on British coal and diplomacy. The deepening recession reduced Britain's leverage in Western Europe, while the pacification and growth of French influence in Eastern Europe improved France's continental position. Briand had reason to hope that the Treaty of Versailles might yet provide a basis for secure prosperity. But such were the fears raised by Briand's detente strategy that it was not viewed at home or abroad as responsible and predictable, but as a dangerous departure.

The year 1921 was the turning point of the postwar struggle, for the failure of Briand's initiatives drove both France and Germany to reliance on policies of ultimate intransigence and revisionism. Briand could renounce the Rhenish policies and cease threatening Germany's territorial integrity; the Wirth government could promise reparations and economic cooperation. But neither could promise domestic acquiescence in their programs. The German inflation, stimulated by the resistance of German economic elites to fulfillment, and the opposition of French interests fearful of German competition undermined political initiatives. Finally, Briand's designs of 1921, like his Rhineland schemes of 1917, were too grand for his inescapable ally Britain. The wreck both of sanctions and fulfillment seemed to force the conclusion that by no means could France draw profit from Versailles—London and the Ruhr would not permit it.

ARISTIDE BRIAND AND THE POLICY OF FORCE

The turn of the new year saw Europe frustrated by an economic anomaly that has since become a pattern of postwar malaise: simultaneous inflation and recession. If the slump hit hardest at Britain, where unemployment would reach a staggering peak of two million, or 17.9 *percent*, by the end of the year,[1] recovery prospects seemed dimmest in France, where the lack of basic raw materials and markets, resistance to government controls, and support for deflationary policies crippled production. The French Chamber reconvened in a sullen mood, and it quickly overturned the uninspiring Leygues government. Millerand's surrogate was out. On 13 January 1921 Raoul Peret was elected president of the Chamber. "The country watches impatiently," he told the deputies. "It would that it perceived more distinctly the positive consequences of the peace." President Millerand called on Peret, then on René Viviani, to form governments. After their refusal, he selected Briand to confront Lloyd George in the next Supreme Council, and demand forceful sanctions.

Briand's twelve months in office in 1921 comprise a peculiar period in his long and spectacular career. Compared with his record of international reconciliation in the later 1920s, Briand's sanctions policy of 1921 appears uncompromising and bellicose. But to contemporaries, aware of Briand's expansionist war aims, his economic separation of the Rhineland in the spring of 1921 fulfilled expectations, while the later rapprochement represented by the Wiesbaden Accords were a departure. In fact, Briand's cabinet of 1921 bracketed a transition in his career; it came near to being a transition in the politics of continental Europe.

Briand was fifty-eight when he returned to form his seventh ministry. Perhaps the most deft performer of the Third Republic's balancing act, he combined fervent republicanism with an equally potent social conservatism. Like Millerand, he began his career as a Socialist and moved to the Center, making his peace with the industrial and financial leaders of the *Gauche républicaine*; unlike Millerand, he never felt comfortable in the role of nationalist. Despite his later reputation as a visionary, Briand was a weather vane, shifting with the breezes of opinion and laboring to make the best of whatever climate obtained. *Rebus sic stantibus* could have been his motto. If he was not the symbol of international good will in 1921 that he later became, it was because the Bloc National, unlike the Chamber of 1924, did not require such a

[1] United Kingdom, Board of Trade, *Statistical Abstract for the United Kingdom*, no. 71 (London, 1928), p. 79.

symbol. The promise of Versailles with all that went with it—an end to inflation, tax stability, export advantages, security—had not been fully betrayed. To be sure, Briand harbored a profound aversion to war, but so did most survivors of the Great War, including the hawkish politicians of the Right. They differed only on the means of preventing its recurrence. If Briand's strategy shifted in late 1921, it was under the realization that France could not escape dependence on Germany *and* Britain, and must therefore play the role of catalyst in a grand process of international integration. But the very fact that he was a man of consensus meant that he was incapable of imposing on his own countrymen the reforms and austerity that might have increased France's leverage in bargaining for secure international collaboration. The imagination and mellifluous oratory with which he ornamented the councils of Europe were inadequate to the chores he set for France and Europe.[2]

Briand's collaborator in the Quai d'Orsay was Philippe Berthelot. Three years younger than Briand, with thirty-two years in the Foreign Ministry, Berthelot was secretary-general, a post he held, except for two years of eclipse under Poincaré, until 1933. The Briand/Berthelot team was a complementary combination. Where Briand preferred personal diplomacy, Berthelot governed from his desk "like a pasha." Where Briand favored the grand gesture and the big stage of international conferences, Berthelot worked prodigiously at the daily business of diplomacy, spinning the webs of policy throughout the embassies of the world. Their keynote was style, but their initial policy was determined by the irony of France's postwar position: she was the victorious supplicant. Briand favored a harsh policy toward Germany, and Millerand selected him to carry it out.

During the last week of Leygues's ministry, the Brussels experts reported. They unanimously endorsed the Boulogne figure of three billion marks per year for German payments, and called for removal of all barriers to legitimate German commerce. Reparations-in-kind must consume a large percentage of German liabilities, regulated by the Plan Seydoux. The latter called for direct contact between the *sinistrés* and German manufacturers, with Berlin guaranteeing reimbursement of German firms with a standing fund of paper marks. The Allies would pay in part for German deliveries in hard currency, which in turn

[2] There is currently no biography of Briand in English. The standard treatment is Georges Suarez' massive and sympathetic *Briand, sa vie, son oeuvre, avec son journal et de nombreux documents inédits*, 6 vols. (Paris, 1938-1952). Recent works stressing Briand's role as precursor of European integration are Maurice Baumont, *Briand, Diplomat und Idealist* (Göttingen, 1966), and Ferdinand Siebert, *Aristide Briand, 1867-1932* (Zurich, 1973).

would facilitate financial reparations. A *bureau mixte* would serve as intermediary. Finally, the Plan Seydoux permitted Germany to deliver finished goods, while the Allies would purchase raw materials with a portion of the proceeds retained by Berlin. The German industrialists were therefore given a stake in reparations, and the prospects of general acceptance seemed favorable.[3]

By the time Seydoux had produced this polished proposal, however, it was clear that the Germans had again negotiated in bad faith. While holding out hopes of an accord to Paris, they had sought to draw Brussels and London into a common front with the hope of returning to the global sum solution—and winning a substantially lower figure than those discussed in 1920. Instead of endorsing the Plan Seydoux, to run for five years, Berlin now torpedoed the experts' initiatives and promoted government-level talks on the total bill. The prospect of Franco-German industrial talks was also broached, only to collapse under the veto of Stinnes, Kloeckner, and the other Ruhr magnates. Opinion also began to swing back in France. The Treaty of Versailles required determination of Germany's total debt by 1 May 1921. Unless a provisional accord were to lead to final financial and industrial arrangements, it might only result in sacrifice of French rights under the treaty. Germany's bizarre maneuvers did not engender optimism. In the end, the Plan Seydoux fell victim to Berlin's misguided hope of enlisting London and perhaps Washington in a campaign for wholesale revision of the treaty.[4]

At the Conference of Paris, 24-29 January 1921, German obstruction persisted. They balked at the proposed annuity of three billion gold marks and demanded in return the retention of Upper Silesia, the disputed industrial area slated for plebiscite under the treaty. Lloyd George took up these German complaints, but did not go so far as to favor massive reduction or elimination of reparations. In fact, American war debt policy and German export competition made the existence, if not the execution, of reparations in line with British interest. Lloyd George would work for agreement on a global sum, but for annuities low enough so as not to threaten the integrity of the mark. Content to rely on the testimony of economic experts and devoted to European economic recovery, he failed to view the German inflation as a political problem.[5]

With the failure of the Plan Seydoux, Briand quickly resorted to the policy of sanctions debated over the previous months. He agreed to a reduction of the German annuities from three billion to two billion

[3] Soutou, "Die deutschen Reparationen," pp. 254-256.

[4] Ibid., pp. 256-258.

[5] Weill-Raynal, *Les réparations allemandes*, I, 587-592.

with a 12 percent *ad valorem* levy on German export receipts. In return, Lloyd George adopted in principle three Allied sanctions, should the Germans fail to give satisfaction on reparations or disarmament.[6] The sanctions would herald a return to Rhenish policy. First, the Allies would declare that the fiteeen-year *délais d'occupation* on the Rhine had not yet begun to run. Second, they would undertake an occupation of German territory, perhaps part of the Ruhr. Third—and this was a novelty, Briand declared—they would create a separate customs regime on the Left Bank of the Rhine. But the sanctions failed to impress the impatient *Parlement*. Former Finance Minister Louis Klotz and future Finance Minister Charles de Lasteyrie attacked the sanctions as a thinly veiled surrender. They echoed Poincaré's call for a Rhine occupation lasting as long as reparations—forty-two years according to current calculation.[7] Ten days later Briand defended himself before the Senate Foreign Affairs Commission. There he faced none other than Poincaré, returned to his Senate seat and elevated to the chair of the prestigious commission.

Poincaré distrusted the plan of Paris. Like the treaty itself, it was a time bomb against Allied unity. When pressed, Briand admitted that Lloyd George had not even initialed the sanctions agreement. How could he be sure that the prime minister would honor them? Briand also withdrew his statement, under Poincaré's cross-examination, that the Rhenish customs regime was a "novelty." The treaty itself provided for such a sanction, yet Briand made it sound outside French treaty rights. The very logic of the sanctions policy was that it permitted French economic control in the occupied territories *without* violating the treaty. Briand only considered the customs sanction special, he explained, "because of the important consequences that could result."[8] Economic separation of the Rhineland could lead to political separation.

Sanctions were the inevitable result of the failure of the treaty to regulate at a blow the security question and the economic obligations of Germany. Only sanctions could ensure Germany's political and military good behavior while her economic power permitted reparations over time. In theory, the German government would be left with no other path toward recovery of its full sovereignty than fulfillment. If Berlin still resisted, then sanctions might also engender a revisionist solution: permanent loss of German sovereignty in her richest, most strategic province.

[6] DBFP, XV, 102-109.

[7] J.O. Chambre, 8 Feb. 1921, pp. 351-367.

[8] P.-V., Commission des Affaires Étrangères, 18 Feb. 1921: Archives du Sénat, Auditions, 1921, pp. 11-38.

Prior to becoming premier, Briand's information on the Rhineland had come from newspapers, confidants of Dorten, and the appeals of the Chamber's "Rhenish bloc": Barrès, Alsacian Abbé Wetterle, and others. Once in power, Briand found himself the object of other special pleaders. Tirard and General Degoutte recounted their views of the Rhenish question and demanded support for separatism and federalism. Tirard even denied the contradiction between peaceful penetration and forceful sanctions. The only barrier to Franco-Rhenish cooperation, he believed, was the insecurity of *French* industrialists who lived by narrow protectionism. If French firms gained an interest in Rhenish industry, their fears would disappear. Tirard also urged a French diplomatic offensive on the Rhenish question. The failure of the 1919 Anglo-American security pacts justified renewed consideration of a permanent occupation of the Rhineland as a substitute guarantee.[9]

Briand did not discard these ideas as long as the German government resisted treaty execution. Like Millerand, Briand suspected that the only sanction terrible enough to ensure German compliance was the occupation of the Ruhr. But almost as effective would be the political pressure on Berlin resulting from an increase in French control in the Rhineland. Thus, Briand's Rhenish policy was cloaked in the German policy. Instead of competing, the two approaches complemented each other. By giving Berlin reason to fear Rhenish separation, Briand could best assure German treaty execution as the lesser evil. He revealed his thoughts in secret session before the Senate Commission: "We can establish a *cordon sanitaire* between Germany and the Rhineland. We have the means of expelling the Prussian functionaries who oppress the Rhineland and put obstacles before the real affinities that exist between the French and Rhenish peoples. All these solutions can yield results. It is in this sense that we can act and be assured that the German government will be sensitive, extremely sensitive." Lastly, there was the occupation of the Ruhr, "that land of which everyone speaks." But that course involved risk and sacrifice, and Briand meant to try all other paths before resorting to it.[10]

[9] Des. Tirard to MAE, "Situation dans les territoires rhénans," 1 Jan. 1921: MAE Rive Gauche, vol. 3, nos. 43-61.

[10] P.-V., Commission des Affaires Étrangères, 18 Feb. 1921: Archives du Sénat, Auditions, 1921, pp. 105-107. Briand concluded wistfully, as if remembering 1917 and speaking his thoughts aloud: "The delicacy of our situation is that there is only one power in Europe capable of a military operation, and that is France. If she wished, France could undertake the conquest of Europe. This is perhaps the sole instant in history when she could be mistress of the world! If France wished to march across Europe, nothing could resist her."

"But France will not wish it," replied Alexandre Ribot.

"Indeed," said Briand, "but that is the tragedy of the situation."

RHENISH POLICY IN THE ERA OF CONFRONTATION

Briand received support for his policy of sanctions as the best that could be achieved in tandem with Britain. The means were clear. But what of the ends, beyond the immediate goal of "engaging" the German government to a reparations bill? Were the sanctions a temporary expedient or could they bring about a final settlement of some kind in security and in raw materials distribution? Would they prod the new American administration to "return to Europe" with loans or debt annulment? Would they free France from reliance on either Anglo-Saxon power by making Germany amenable to bilateral pacts? Briand did not have a precise scenario at the Conference of Paris. The following months before the 1 May deadline would perhaps indicate the best course to follow.

Poincaré did have a plan. He envisioned cooperation with Germany once that nation had accepted defeat. That Germany was unlikely to disburse the entire reparations bill, however many billions it contained, did not disturb him. Once Germany recognized her obligation, then negotiations could ensue between France and Germany, with France in the strong bargaining position she had earned.[11] Poincaré attacked the Allied inactivity that allowed the firms of Krupp, Thyssen, Stinnes, and others to augment exports and profits while French firms made little headway toward regaining 1913 levels of production. The German government complained of bankruptcy and inflation, yet individuals grew wealthy. But Poincaré realized that an equitable distribution of the war's financial burden depended on prior Franco-British collaboration: "Never has unity among the Allies been more indispensable, for never has German ill will been more evident, more systematic, more audacious."[12]

Poincaré's was an ambitious plan, for it involved securing detente with Germany while preserving entente with Britain. Marshal Foch, whose influence was great in the early months of Briand's cabinet, rejected such subtle diplomacy. He looked for sanctions to ensure French security and reparations without recourse to cooperation with anyone. The sanctions would bring about the fulfillment, not necessarily of the treaty, but of Foch's own Rhenish policy: "The [economic] separation of the Left Bank will give new impetus to the Rhenish separatist elements. We can thus expect with more assurance than at present the constitution of an independent Rhenish state easily drawn

[11] Note Vignon, "Poincaré a dit à Cheysson il y a 12 jours," 20 Jan. 1921: MAE Pap. Millerand, vol. 46, nos. 125-126.

[12] Raymond Poincaré, *Histoire politique: Chroniques de Quinzaine* (Paris, 1921), pp. 234-241, 297.

into our sphere of influence. The political and military importance of such a development needs no explanation."[13]

At Coblenz, Tirard believed the moment ripe for a diplomatic initiative. He urged Briand to propose formation of an autonomous Rhenish state in the Supreme Council, while Lloyd George seemed willing to pursue a harsh German policy. General Degoutte at Mainz wavered in his attitude. He believed that the Reich was only held together by threats from abroad and that sanctions could arouse German national feeling. If, however, the French became masters of the German economy, then they could force a solution to the Rhenish question. "The customs sanction makes no sense," he wrote, "unless it leads to economic, then political autonomy for the Rhineland."[14]

Although senators and deputies, soldiers and bureaucrats saw what they wanted in the government's policy, Briand and his experts occupied themselves with the immediate task of preparing execution of the sanctions while struggling to maintain Allied unity. A simple solution existed for the first problem, if the Allies were prepared to renounce their resolution of June 1919 that the Rhineland Commission was not to interfere with the German economy. On 29 January 1921, the day of the Paris accords, Tirard submitted a plan for an Allied customs regime in the Rhineland under the control of his commission. Any alternative mode of execution was prohibitively expensive, requiring transplantation of an entire financial administration to the Rhine under the authority of the Supreme Council or Reparations Commission, all to protect the innocence of the body at Coblenz. Would Britain nevertheless refuse to permit the Rhineland Commission to become an executor of the treaty's economic clauses? Berthelot feared it would be so. Seydoux also doubted Lloyd George's acquiescence. He approved Tirard's project but suggested that the question of administering the customs sanction be postponed until the Conference of London in March.[15] He wondered, as did Poincaré, whether Lloyd George's "promises" were sincere. Tabling the question was not the way to find out; the failure to consult in advance would again cause friction later.

Rather than present the Germans with another "Diktat," the Con-

[13] Let. Foch to Briand, 16 Feb. 1921; Note Foch, "Note sur l'application des sanctions," 19 Feb. 1921: MAE Allemagne, vol. 230, nos. 78-81, 89-98.

[14] Rapports mensuels de l'Armée du Rhin, Degoutte to MG, MAE, Jan.-Mar. 1921: MAE Rive Gauche, vol. 63.

[15] Project Tirard, "Accord entre les puissances alliées pour l'application de la sanction #3 par la résolution de Conférence Interalliée de Paris du 29 janvier, 1921": MAE Pap. Millerand, vol. 41, nos. 22-25; Note Seydoux to Berthelot, 31 Jan. 1921; Tel. Berthelot to French chargé Berlin, 9 Feb. 1921: MAE Rive Gauche, vol. 110, nos. 2-3, 6.

ference of Paris invited a German delegation, led by Foreign Minister Walter Simons, to prepare counterproposals on reparations. The French, still nervous about fixing any global sum, had spoken of 200 billion gold marks. The British hoped to talk them into accepting half of that. But Simons' proposals of 25 February suggested a total German debt of 30 billion.[16] It was patently unacceptable; even Lloyd George feigned indignation. He confided to Belgian Foreign Minister Henri Jaspar that they must seek to preserve both the Briand and Feuerbach governments in power, but that it might prove impossible, given the German attitude. The Germans must be forced to bargain in good faith. Once they had accepted their debt, all parties could work for amelioration. "Under the influence of the English industrial crisis and the arrogance of Simons," noted Jaspar, "Lloyd George has decided to display firmness vis-à-vis Germany."[17]

In fact, Lloyd George was in a difficult position. The basis for Franco-German peace remained an industrial raw materials exchange; Lord Kilmarnock reported new efforts toward such a solution in early March. But it was precisely the solution that Britain feared most. Stinnes, Vögler, and others were alleged to be in contact with Schneider-Creusot. American bankers encouraged the idea with talk of loans.[18] Even if such rumors, which wafted intermittently across the Channel, were spurious, they perpetuated British industrial fears of an independent continental consortium. Failure to conciliate the French could drive them into the Ruhr, where they might make their own peace with the German industrialists. Conciliation meant sanctions of some variety. Renewed Franco-German strife might produce new windfall profits for British coal, but they could also alienate the United States and lead to French intrigues for Rhenish separation.[19]

Lloyd George had little choice but to rally to Briand's analysis that "as long as the Allies refrained from force, they would face a German government with which they could not deal." The Fehrenbach cabinet had not won industrial backing; it was too weak to overcome domestic

[16] Recent research by Sally Marks, Marc Trachtenberg, and Stephen Schuker, presented in the A.H.A. session "Reparations Reconsidered," 27 Dec. 1976, indicates both the moderation and the viability of the London Schedule of Payments. Gerhard Weinberg, a commentator at that session, reminded us that there never was a question of whether reparations would be paid. It was simply a matter of who would foot the bill. By avoiding payments fully within the capability of the Reich economy to make, the Germans shifted the burden of reconstruction and pensions onto the taxpayers and savers of France, Britain, and the United States.

[17] Note Jaspar, "Conversation ce matin entre M. Lloyd George, M. Theunis, et moi," 25 Feb. 1921: Henri Jaspar, unpublished private papers, Archives générales du Royaume-Brussels (hereafter cited as AGR Pap. Jaspar), dos. 205.

[18] Let. Kilmarnock (Coblenz) to Curzon, 3 Mar. 1921: DBFP, XVI, 474-476.

[19] Memo by Mr. Waterlow, F.O., 28 Feb. 1921: DBFP, XVI, 470-473.

resistance to the treaty. Lloyd George tumbled to a policy of sanctions on 1 March, but Poincaré's fears were realized: Lloyd George sought to strike all the Rhenish sanctions and replace them by one of his own choosing, a 50 percent levy on German exports to Allied nations, which protected Britain against dumping. Briand and Foch demanded the other extreme, occupation of the Ruhr, but in the end accepted a triple procedure: occupation of the Ruhr ports of Düsseldorf, Duisburg, and Ruhrort; the Rhenish customs regime under Allied direction; the 50 percent export levy.[20] The sanctions increased French flexibility. They could serve as a means to force German capitulation and/or as levers for the extension of French Rhenish policy. And in the event that Berlin resisted the reparations schedule now to be worked out by the Allies, Briand still held in reserve the military's plan: full occupation of the Ruhr, with or without Britain.

ALLIED BRINKMANSHIP; GERMAN CAPITULATION

Whatever the German government's response, the Allies would have to envision ultimate solutions to the problems of European recovery: a means for the Germans to discharge their debt, German economic recovery within a framework guaranteeing French security, settlement of markets and raw materials distribution among European metallurgies, currency stabilization and a return to the gold standard. In the end, Europe passed through crisis only to reach a fragile modus vivendi in the spring and summer of 1921. In the Rhineland, too, these months were crisis-ridden, but the inception of policies of fulfillment in May brought only a lull, no permanent solution, to the Rhenish question.

Both the *clemencistes* with their demand for rigorous treaty execution and the Rhenish bloc in the Chamber registered dismay at the half-measures of 7 March, while Poincaré admonished the government for dropping the extension of the Rhineland occupation. What was more, the British were delaying execution of the Rhenish customs sanction in hopes that an agreement with Berlin would intervene. In any case, as Berthelot admitted, the sanction would not alter German tariff rates—there would be no new "hole in the West."[21] Only the oc-

[20] "British Secretary's Notes of an Allied Conference," 1 Mar. 1921: DBFP, XV, 225-237.

[21] Note Berthelot, "Réponse aux questions posées par M. Poincaré dans sa lettre du 12 mars, 1921," 14 Mar. 1921: MAE Allemagne, vol. 232, nos. 9-14. Berthelot retorted that the extension of the *délais d'occupation* had not been dropped, but that the Allies had only chosen "not to notify Berlin of the sanction since it did not constitute an immediate source of pressure."

cupation of the Ruhr ports went ahead on schedule on 8 March, but even this aroused British suspicions. Briand felt it necessary to assure London concerning French motives. France envisaged neither annexation nor autonomy for the Rhineland, he declared; France had no ulterior motives.

When Briand faced the Senate Foreign Affairs Commission in secret session, he rested his defense on the need for Allied unity. "In the Rhineland, for example, we must act with prudence, for we encounter resistance stemming from our past imprudence." The British shied away from the customs barrier, which could lead to full Rhenish separation.[22] As weeks passed, it appeared that Lloyd George had no intention of implementing the sanction, and Tirard reported grave opposition to an Allied customs regime from the British delegation on the Rhine.[23] British officials echoed Adenauer's propaganda that the sanction would ruin German industry, while Lord Kilmarnock reported a conversation with Gustav Stresemann, who branded French militarism as "the greatest peril which menaces Europe today."[24] Briand wired London frantically in hopes that Ambassador St. Aulaire could pin down the British.[25] It was no use.

The reasons for British dawdling were legion, of which fear of French Rhine schemes was only one. Lloyd George was preoccupied by a long-expected miners' strike that aggravated the industrial crisis and brought about a reorganization of his cabinet on 1 April. Implementation of a sanction disruptive to German industry was impolitic. Seydoux also suspected the influence of Britain's Germanophile ambassador in Berlin, Lord D'Abernon, and of the London financial establishment.[26] The City attributed Europe's recession to the huge outstanding debts that America alone could alleviate. It might prove difficult to terminate a policy of sanctions once begun; Europe's instability would drag on, discouraging American involvement. Finally, Briand's patience was exhausted. On 16 April, six weeks after the sanction was declared, he insisted the British permit commercial separa-

[22] Commission des Affaires Étrangères, 23 Mar. 1921: Archives du Sénat, Auditions, 1920, II, 43.

[23] Tel. Tirard to MAE, 9 Mar. 1921: MAE Allemagne, vol. 231, nos. 1-3; Let. Tirard to Briand, 15 Mar. 1921: MAE Pap. Millerand, Réparations III, nos. 73-76.

[24] Let. Kilmarnock to Curzon, 19 Mar. 1921: DBFP, XV, 500-508.

[25] Tel. Briand to St. Aulaire, "Question des sanctions," 24 Mar. 1921: MAE Rive Gauche, vol. 110, nos. 162-164; Tel. Peretti to St. Aulaire, 24 Mar. 1921: MAE Allemagne, vol. 232, nos. 193-197.

[26] Tel. Seydoux to principal European posts, "Opinions des représentants américains, anglais, et italiens à Berlin sur les sanctions," 1 Apr. 1921: MAE Allemagne, vol. 233, nos. 8-9; Jacques Seydoux, *De Versailles au Plan Young, réparations, dettes interalliées, reconstruction européenne* (Paris, 1932), p. 47.

tion of the Rhineland, alluding in an apparent non sequitur to the sympathy of the American government to Allied policy.[27] Four days later, the prime minister relented. Tirard's officials, escorted by smart *chasseurs à pied* in horizon blue, took possession of German customs houses on the Left Bank of the Rhine.

American opinion was of great concern to the Europeans. The inauguration of a new president rekindled hopes for an American *deus ex machina*, dispensing generosity to a broken continent and removing the need for a policy of force against Germany. The British had postponed responding to the invitation to consolidate and fund their war debt, in order to test the waters in Washington. But far from appearing conciliatory, the new administration took a harder stand than the ousted Democrats.[28] If the United States insisted on Britain's recognizing her debt of £800 million, London would also be obliged for her own protection to force German recognition of her debt to Britain.

French perceptions of American opinion drew on firsthand knowledge. As anxious to promote American involvement as Lloyd George, Briand sent René Viviani on a special mission to Washington early in March. His ostensible purpose was to congratulate President Harding on his inauguration. Nevertheless, in conference with Secretary of State Charles E. Hughes and Undersecretary H. P. Fletcher, Viviani explained that the Treaty of Versailles had been a grave disappointment for France. Sanctions did not mean that France was militaristic; they only bespoke her desperation. France was bankrupt without reparations, and had reached the limit of her borrowing potential. She could never desire conflict, after her losses in the war, but she must have her due. Hughes volunteered nothing, but he did agree that Germany ought to be forced to acknowledge her responsibility to pay to the limit of her ability.[29]

The German government also looked to America in the early months of 1921. The German ambassador protested that Allied militarism threatened to wreck the German republic, and asked American mediation. But the time was not ripe, as William Castle of the State Depart-

[27] Tel. Briand to St. Aulaire, 16 Apr. 1921: MAE Allemagne, vol. 233, nos. 126-127.

[28] Minutes, CAB 72(20), 17 Dec. 1920; Minutes, CAB 37(21), 10 May 1921: PRO CAB 23/23, pp. 256-258, CAB 23/25, pp. 252-253. The British war debt difficulties were complicated by the nature of the bonds held against London by the United States. They specified the right of the American government to insist on conversion of the bonds into a consolidated long-term debt. The American Treasury requested this conversion, but the British hesitated, for this would require funding and permit placement of the bonds on the open market. This in turn would kill hopes for a blanket annulment. Britain did not possess the same rights vis-à-vis her continental debtors.

[29] "Memo by the Undersecretary of State," Interview held in the office of the Secretary of State, 30 Mar. 1921: FRUS 1921, I, 964-967.

ment noted: "The Germans believe that our selfish trade interests will urge us to let Germany off from reparations payments. They cannot see far enough to realize that even our selfish trade interests will be better served by the economic revival of all of Europe, possible only through real reparations payments, than through a rapid revival of German prosperity at the expense of world prosperity."[30]

On 3 May the American government responded to the German demarche, formally declining the German request for mediation and loans.[31] The United States was passively approving whatever measures the next Supreme Council might deem necessary to force its will on Germany. It also meant that France and Britain must stand together or admit their inability to command respect in the Ruhr. But respect paid no bills, and a desultory sanctions policy indifferently pursued by Britain was unlikely to lead to final solutions. Parliamentary majorities might be appeased, but could France ever escape her new dependencies? The French expert on Germany, Émile Haguenin, who had resided in Berlin since the Armistice, alone extrapolated the postwar diplomatic alignments and economic forces in an effort to glimpse the shape of final agreements. The only hope for prosperity, he believed, lay in the closest cooperation with German industry, a cartel that could only end in German domination. "La France est un pays fini," he mourned. She could survive only by "hanging on to the hem of the garment of German prosperity."[32]

Briand was not ready to admit that France would fall from the ranks of the Great Powers. The occupation of the Ruhr was in reserve. Despite its risks, financial and diplomatic, the government and military looked to it to solve all the difficulties of postwar France. The victory of 1918 had failed to bestow security and social peace on France, for its cost was too great. So the Briand government, stymied from meaningful reform at home, went in search of another victory abroad. The General Staff eagerly pressed planning for the Ruhr venture, producing new operations plans in January and February 1921, executing the occupation of the ports in March, then adopting revised plans for the encirclement of the Ruhr basin on 9 and 23 April.[33] Briand did not

[30] Note Castle, 25 Mar. 1921, cited by Link, *Die amerikanische Stabilisierungspolitik*, p. 57. For an analysis of the internal pressures behind U.S. war debt policy in this period, see Leffler, "The Origins of Republican War Debt Policy," pp. 586-596.

[31] Tels. Dresel (Berlin) to Secretary of State, 20-21 Apr. 1921; Memo Fletcher, "Conversation between the Secretary of State and the British and French Ambassadors," 25 Apr. 1921; Tel. Hughes to Dresel, 2 May 1921: FRUS 1921, II, 40-55.

[32] Let. Kilmarnock to Curzon, 19 Mar. 1921: DBFP, XV, 500-507.

[33] General Joseph Degoutte, *L'Occupation de la Ruhr*, rapport personnel et secret (Düsseldorf, imprimerie de l'Armée du Rhin, July, 1924), p. 9: MG, Service Historique.

shrink from the challenge; Millerand summoned him to carry out precisely this policy, if necessary.

American aloofness necessitated some sort of Allied pressure on Germany, but Lloyd George had not changed his opinion of a Ruhr occupation. Briand labored to reassure Lloyd George about French motives, but his efforts were compromised by conflict in yet another corner of Germany. The vital industrial area of Upper Silesia was the second most productive metallurgical area left to Germany, but it was a racially mixed region wedged between Germany, Poland, and Czechoslovakia. Under the treaty, an interallied force occupied the area in anticipation of a plebiscite to decide its union with Germany or Poland. On 20 March 1921 the voting took place, showing a clear majority for Germany. But Upper Silesia, the Quai d'Orsay argued, was not indivisible—the vote in the industrial communes was split and the area ought to be partitioned. The Foreign Office, pledged to support the German cause, pointed to French policy as proof that Paris cared nothing for reparations, and sought instead to weaken Germany by every means available. But Briand would not yield. The viability of his Polish ally and the interests of several French financial groups that had already invested in the region rode on the outcome of the Upper Silesian dispute.[34] After 2 May it turned violent. A Polish miners' strike sparked an uprising of Polish mobs left unchecked by the French

[34] Did the French merely "sell" their services to the highest bidder? In 1920 Ambassador Charles Laurent had made contact with German metallurgical firms in Upper Silesia on behalf of French industrial interests. The Germans hinted at special rights for France should the territory remain in German hands. But the Poles were more than willing to grant similar concessions, and held out the prospect of a military alliance as well.

The question bore on whether Franco-German cooperation in Upper Silesian metallurgy could have provided the catalyst for metallurgical cartelization on a national level. Would France opt for certain military advantages in the long-range balance among France, Germany, and Poland at the price of a possible solution to the mortal problem of Franco-German industrial antagonism? It is precisely in this direction that Georges Soutou has carried his recent research, published as "La politique économique de la France en Pologne (1920-1924)," *Revue historique* 251 (January-March, 1974):85-116. Soutou concludes that the French government, pressed by Millerand and numerous industrial (especially Schneider-Creusot) and financial interests, did envision its Upper Silesian policy as a means of leverage aimed at forcing German industry as a whole into a posture of cooperation with French industry. That the policy was duplicitous and contradictory was only a result of French weakness. Briand did not wish to sacrifice his close ties with Poland unless a Franco-German agreement were certain—he also feared antagonizing Britain too openly. His successor, Poincaré, also hoped for an industrial accord with Germany, but he insisted that the Quai d'Orsay retain direction of the enterprise, a measure of state interference that the French businessmen involved would not accept. Thus Upper Silesia failed as a bridge for collaboration—although the sincerity of the German negotiators was also suspect. At every point, the French government was forced into a staunch pro-Polish stance in public, while struggling privately for accommodation at the expense of Poland.

occupation. While Lloyd George and Briand groped for a common policy on reparations, the Silesian crisis damaged their respective credibility.[35]

Briand also encountered resistance from an unexpected corner, Brussels. The Belgian government found itself in an insecure position at home and in a far more precarious position abroad than either Britain or France. A tenuous balance existed in postwar Belgium between the Catholic, Francophonic, and bourgeois elements and an opposition coalition of Socialists and Flemings. The latter groups opposed the use of force against Germany; occupation of the Ruhr could spark a crisis threatening the existence of the small monarchy. Belgium rested between two continental powers, each a potential threat to her political integrity. French control of the Rhineland and Ruhr, unrestrained by Allied participation, could leave Belgium surrounded and her economic independence compromised. Nevertheless, Belgium was least able to support reconstruction. Belgian statesmen all viewed their task as one of mediation between Britain and France, to restrain French Rhineland policies, but encourage Britain to force reparations from Germany.

As early as 26 February, French Ambassador Pierre de Margerie reported Belgium's hesitancy. The Belgian defense minister feared occupation of the Ruhr would "open a veritable hornets' nest."[36] From Paris, Belgian Ambassador Gaiffier d'Hestroy reported that French sanctions policy aimed at separation and domination of the Left Bank of the Rhine. While a truly independent Rhineland would serve Belgian security, he wrote, a Rhenish state occupied by France would pose a grave danger.[37] Foreign Minister Jaspar responded by offering to host Allied talks prior to the Conference of London, lest differences arise of which Germany would be the sole beneficiary.[38] Belgian Premier Carton de Wiart also searched for an alternative to occupation of the Ruhr. He encouraged his representative on the Reparations Commission, Léon Delacroix, to promote Allied-German industrial talks, with a reduction of the German debt as an incentive. In mid-April Carton de Wiart himself played host to a German delegation. Under these circumstances, Briand hardly welcomed Belgian mediation. He snubbed

[35] The best diplomatic account of the Upper Silesian dispute is F. Gregory Campbell, "The Struggle for Upper Silesia," *Journal of Modern History* 42, no. 3 (September 1970): 361-385.

[36] Tel. Margerie (Brussels) to MAE, 26 Feb. 1921: MAE Allemagne, vol. 230, no. 99.

[37] Tel. #2434/1164/PF Gaiffier to Jaspar, 11 Mar. 1921: MAE Bel., Correspondance Politique, France, 1921.

[38] Tel. Briand to Margerie, 7 Apr. 1921; Tel. Margerie to MAE, 10 Apr. 1921: MAE Allemagne, vol. 233, nos. 50, 64-66.

Jaspar and chose to confront Lloyd George alone.[39] The meeting took place at Lympne on 23-24 April.

At Lympne Lloyd George played his final cards. He denied that occupation of the Ruhr would be a useful sanction. It would be expensive, unpopular, unremunerative, and would only destroy Germany's capacity to pay and drive her to extremism. Briand and Berthelot held firm, for the situation at the London Conference to come would be the reverse of that at Spa the previous year. This time it was Britain that suffered most from industrial crisis. During the short postwar boom British metallurgy expanded recklessly. When the artificialities of the 1919-1920 market were exposed, the British collapse was precipitous. Instead of windfall coal profits, the miners' strike of April to June 1921 dealt a lasting blow to Britain's superannuated steel firms. For Baldwin's and United Steel, the dividends paid in 1920 would be their last for a decade.[40] Lloyd George had little leverage this time. In fact, he had reason to welcome a Ruhr operation if it yielded the results—coal and reparations—that Briand promised. He did not think it would, but he feared a Franco-German combination even more. American opinion of the European crisis was the most crucial, he attested, but Briand recalled that American opinion was "far from disapproving, or blaming the Allies for the employment of force." On the other hand, if France and Britain abdicated from the struggle, they would yield to America the preponderant role in Europe.[41] That prospect worried British finance, but a corollary of American stabilization policy—free recovery for Germany—worried France as much. Neither ally was prepared to abdicate as a Great Power, and this fact drove them together for one last time.

The Reparations Commission succeeded in producing a total reparations bill and schedule of payments for Germany by 28 April. The plan fixed the German debt at 132 billion gold marks. The first annuities were set at two billion, plus 26 percent of the value of German exports. The debt was divided into three bond series: A bonds totaling 12 billion marks, the first to be redeemed; B bonds of 38 billion; and the virtually worthless C bonds totaling 82 billion. Once again, France had sacrificed substance for form, for Briand yielded his claim that Germany still owed twelve billion gold marks before 1 May 1921, in return

[39] Note Seydoux, "Conversation avec MM Delacroix et Bemelmans," 13 Apr. 1921: MAE Pap. Millerand, Réparations III, nos. 179-183; Tel. Briand to Margerie and St. Aulaire, 20 Apr. 1921: MAE Allemagne, vol. 233, nos. 143-146.

[40] See J. C. Carr and Walter Taplin, *History of the British Steel Industry* (Cambridge, Mass., 1962), pp. 346-365.

[41] "Notes of a Meeting held at Belcaire, Lympne," 23-24 Apr. 1921: DBFP, XV, 453-573.

for British recognition of the long-term debt. For the French, the debt was to relieve their budgetary crunch as well as prevent German resurgence, economic or military. For all the Allies, the German debt existed to be written off against their debts to each other and to the United States.

The Conference of London opened on 1 May. Before British and Italian hesitation and Belgian attempts at compromise, the French held their ground. Millerand wired Briand that France must not allow the conference to replace a Ruhr occupation by a lesser sanction. On 2 May he ordered mobilization of the class of 1919.[42] Three days later the Allies delivered an ultimatum to Berlin: accept the reparations plan or face an interallied occupation of the Ruhr. The Fehrenbach cabinet, its policy in shreds, resigned, while the Army of the Rhine, 130,000 strong in March, surpassed 250,000 men and concentrated on the Left Bank opposite the Ruhr.

Another Baden Centrist, Joseph Wirth, formed a cabinet in Berlin on 10 May. But in expectation that he would become chancellor, Gustav Stresemann had requested British support on Upper Silesia in return for acceptance of the ultimatum. The invasion of the disputed zone by Polish irregulars coupled with Allied demands for German disarmament threatened the German hold on the area. An Anglo-German compromise, first suggested by Lord Kilmarnock on 19 March, now seemed the way out. Lloyd George promised to work for the deliverance of Upper Silesia and on this basis Wirth accepted the London schedule of payments.

To many in France, the German capitulation was a great disappointment. The events of the spring had strengthened France's legal position in two invisible ways: Britain had tacitly recognized the legality of a Ruhr occupation and had consented, through the customs sanction, to a vast increase in the powers of the Rhineland Commission. But the immediate rewards were just as invisible. "Paris was worth a mass, the Ruhr is well worth a signature," observed General Degoutte. "If France obtains only a signature, French prestige in Germany will suffer a rude blow. To this people that respects only force, we give,

[42] Tel. Millerand to Briand (London), 1 and 2 May 1921: MAE Pap. Millerand, vol. 48, nos. 47-51, 86-87. The French cabinet had also ordered preliminary industrial and technical planning in anticipation that the occupation of the Ruhr would yield not only reparations, but also a broad-based Franco-German metallurgical accord. See Let. Mercier to Loucheur, "Affaire de la Ruhr," 23 Apr. 1921: Ernest Mercier, unpublished private papers, Hoover Institution—Stanford, Box 1, Folder 17. Strategies for economic control of the Ruhr are discussed in Note Foch #4821, Comité Militaire Allié de Versailles, 12 Apr. 1921: MAE Allemagne, vol. 233, nos. 94-100; Note Foch, "Projet d'occupation de la Région Industrielle de la Ruhr," 20 Apr. 1921: MAE Pap. Millerand, Réparations III, nos. 184-195.

once again, proof of our weakness."[43] The London plan made no provision for coal deliveries beyond that of Spa. It would not benefit the French treasury for the moment, because the first billion marks would go to Belgium under a priority and to Britain for unpaid occupation costs. No reparations-in-kind procedure was provided for. A Committee of Guarantees would oversee German finances, but it lacked the authority to limit German fiscal sovereignty. Above all, there was nothing to prevent the Germans from destroying their ability to pay through wasteful budgets, unchecked inflation, and export of capital.

Again André Tardieu held forth in the Chamber. Fulminating in his familiar liturgical style, Tardieu voiced the frustration of bourgeois France at the results of the sacred Entente:

> Since your arrival, M. le Président du Conseil, since the Conference of Paris, you have constantly retreated under the pretext of unity with Great Britain.
>
> You conceded the principle of a fixed sum of reparations, i.e., a reduced German liability.
>
> You conceded by accepting a figure which you yourself considered a great sacrifice of our true rights.
>
> You conceded by instructing your Reparations Commission delegate to accept a figure less than half the French demand.
>
> You conceded by renouncing the payment of twelve billion marks due by 1 May.
>
> You conceded by renouncing the sanctions. . . .
>
> Messieurs, I believe that another policy is possible for France—it is the role of the deputies to insist upon it.[44]

The *clemencistes* of the Chamber hinted at a new departure for France—a policy independent of Britain. The Briand government took note of the possibilities, but not without an equally strident *caveat* from Poincaré. The constant retreat of France was indeed due to the exigencies of coalition politics, wrote Poincaré in the *Revue des Deux Mondes*, but this did not necessitate isolation. Rather, the situation cried out for a fresh understanding with Britain, for an alliance devoid of the seeds of future conflict such as had plagued the Entente since 1918.[45] But for the moment, given the Rhineland, Upper Silesia, and other difficulties, a new accord seemed neither popular nor possible.

Despite its shortcomings, the reparations agreement was the last

[43] Pers. Let. Degoutte to Barthou (Minister of War), 12 May 1921, cited by Paoli, *L'Armée Française*, p. 236.

[44] J. O. Chambre, 19 May 1921, pp. 2304-2319.

[45] Poincaré, in *Revue des Deux Mondes*, 1 June 1921.

stone in the treaty edifice, and Wirth's Reichstag pledge to a policy of fulfillment seemed to promise a new era of reconciliation. But detente between France and Germany would only intensify the distrust flashing sporadically, but more frequently, like lightning bolts between the opposite poles of London and Paris. There were no illusions in the Foreign Office. At the height of the May crisis, Sir Eyre Crowe thought "the Germans will be very foolish if they do not agree to Allied terms and so avoid the occupation of the Ruhr." Lord Curzon, who would help see to it that Franco-German rapprochement would not come about, replied, "It will come—sooner or later."[46]

RHENISH POLICY: PEACEFUL OR FORCEFUL PENETRATION?

During his tenure as premier, Millerand pursued both the Rhenish and German policies bequeathed him by Clemenceau. Briand also shied from a decision between the two courses during his first months in office.[47] His problem was made more complex by the existence of two Rhenish policies occasioned by the continuing measures of peaceful penetration and by the implementation of Rhenish sanctions. Briand's first consideration of Tirard's activities in January and February 1921 led to no new instructions. Tirard continued to receive a monthly allowance of 1,136,000 francs, of which about 20 percent was budgeted for propaganda, subsidies for separatists, and Economic Sections. He also supported several French language publications, cultural and religious activities promoting Franco-Rhenish amity, and charities such as the *soupes populaires*. The German government countered with its own propaganda, but was especially irritated by the Economic Sections, which it considered agencies for industrial espionage. Since Berlin regained control of import licensing, they could do little to aid French trade and even French merchants saw them as benefiting only Rhenish exporters. In December 1920 the German ambassador in Paris asked that the "economic services" of the French Rhineland High Commissariat be dissolved. Sections now existed in nine cities, com-

[46] Minutes, Des. #636 D'Abernon (Berlin) to F.O., C8737/416/18, 24 Apr. 1921: PRO FO 371, vol. 5970, nos. 16-18.

[47] That a duality existed in French policy toward the treaty and toward Germany was evident to the Chamber and the public. An article in *Le Temps* of 15 Jan. 1921, entitled "Les Deux Routes," delineated the paths Frenchmen saw for themselves. The article quoted a German financier as saying: "During the next ten years, France will be absorbed with a policy *à la mode*, a narrow and sterile policy of territorial ambitions on the Rhine. We Germans will develop our industry and commerce and become again, with the United States and Great Britain, masters of the economic world. Then the roles will be reversed and France will be ruined."

prising 27 officers and 67 clerks. Seydoux admitted that they were illegal under the Rhineland Agreement, but he joined Berthelot and Tirard to insist on their retention. A solution was found by transferring the Economic Sections to the French consular corps, defusing the German protest.[48]

In the case of the Franco-Rhenish *bureau mixte* Seydoux and Louis Loucheur took the opposite attitude. They still favored employment of such an institution for de facto contracts between French purchasers and Rhenish industrialists. But when the government experts began to take Dr. Dorten's *bureau mixte* seriously, Tirard and the head of the French *comptoir d'achats* labored to convince them of the tactlessness of encouraging Dorten and his front man Dr. Boeker in their enterprise.[49] In any case, the customs sanction of April 1921 made the body unnecessary by giving the Allies control over German licensing on the Left Bank.[50] Tirard downplayed the disruption the customs barrier was causing to Rhenish industries, and hoped to lure them into connections with France. For a month after the German capitulation of 11 May 1921, Briand attempted to preserve the new powers won for the Rhineland Commission by the sanctions of March.

Foreign observers clearly saw the contradiction—which Tirard brazenly denied—between peaceful penetration and sanctions. Nevertheless, German resistance to French penetration stiffened after the sanctions. As one German official reported, French behavior only served to defeat the purpose of Franco-Rhenish rapprochement. The "overbearing authoritarianism of Tirard, motivated by the desire to increase his own jurisdiction and power," and the "arrogant displays of the military" merely fostered hatred. The use of colored troops, seizure of public buildings and goods, and the selective justice dispensed by the French all told against peaceful penetration. But, the German noted, over a period of time the population of the Left Bank might "get used to" the occupation and accept the French presence as the normal state of affairs. This resignation was what the German government labored to prevent.[51]

[48] Note Hermant (Secretary-General, French Rhineland High Commissariat), #9583ATRP, 27 Feb. 1921; Note Voisin (Director of Financial Service), #8408FC, 4 June 1921: AN HCF, vol. 3032, dos. FiBb/3; Des. Tirard to Leygues, 10 Dec. 1920; Note Seydoux for Laroche, 11 Jan. 1921; Note Seydoux for Peretti, 21 Jan. 1921: MAE Rive Gauche, vol. 200, nos. 7-14.

[49] Note Voisin, #4652EC/22, 17 Nov. 1920: AN HCF, vol. 3208, dos. QiBe2f.

[50] Note Hermant, #838ATRP, 11 Apr. 1921; Let. Tirard to Seydoux, "Achats en territoire occupé pour la reconstruction," #1376EC/7, 15 Apr. 1921: AN HCF, vol. 3208, dos. QiBe2f.

[51] Report Lerchenfeld (Darmstadt) to Simons, "Die französische Politik im besetzten Gebiete," 15 Feb. 1921: AA, Bureau des Reichsministers (hereafter cited as BR) 3058,

Tirard attributed the Rhineland's resistance to French penetration to the tyrannical influence of the Prussian administration. He hoped to expel the Prussians and his first target was Reich Commissioner Carl von Starck. In March Tirard accused him of directing resistance to the occupation and urged Briand to demand abolition of the office. In this he was unsuccessful, although he persuaded the British and Belgians to join in replacing von Starck.[52] In return the German government agreed to disband the *Pfalzzentrale*, a Bavarian *Abwehr* organization in Heidelberg that fomented resistance to the French in the Palatinate.

During the first half of 1921, then, the policies of peaceful and forceful penetration operated simultaneously. But the failure of rapprochement and "separatism by suggestion" became abundantly clear. Hopes for an indigenous Rhenish movement had always hinged on the attitude of the Center party. One rationale behind support of such nonentities as Dorten was that Rhenish autonomist sentiment might arise after the two-year *Sperrfrist* lapsed in August 1921, if only the issue were kept before the public. But the results of the Rhenish Center party congress, held in Cologne in January 1921, forced even Tirard to admit that his Moroccan-style paternalism was ineffective. At the behest of the Prussian and Reich governments, the Center tabled the issue of autonomy, not only during the *Sperrfrist*, but as long as the Allied occupation lasted. It cited the impossibility of true autonomy as long as French troops remained on German soil.[53] Finally, in March, all Rhenish political parties joined in a denunciation of the sanctions. "Economic separation is only a prelude to political separation or annexation. . . . Whatever happens, remain Germans, remain faithful to the Reich!"[54]

1469, nos. 602894-909. German anti-French propaganda took on an especially ugly character regarding the presence of colonial troops in the occupation. German propaganda fabricated numerous tales of "incidents" in which France's "black savages" assaulted German women on the street. Extensive investigations by General Degoutte's staff, as well as impartial inquiries by the American occupation designed to satisfy American public opinion, demonstrated that the black troops (who were in fact mostly light brown-skinned North Africans) had as good or better a disciplinary record as the native French troops. Although the inclusion of colonial troops in the French occupation was certainly impolitic, especially given the French desire for rapprochement with the Rhineland, it was not done out of a desire to humiliate the Germans, but for reasons of economy. See Keith L. Nelson, "The 'Black Horror on the Rhine': Race as a Factor in Post-World War I Diplomacy," *Journal of Modern History* 42, no. 4 (December 1970):606-627.

[52] Let. Laroche to Tirard, 25 Mar. 1921; Tel. Briand to Tirard, 30 May and 1 July 1921: MAE Rive Gauche, vol. 240, nos. 34-35, 69-72, 116. The new Reich commissioner, Prince Hermann von Hatzfeld-Wildenburg, was a career diplomat with experience in Washington. Tirard judged him to be "cosmopolitan" and not of the "Prussian bureaucratic" stamp.

[53] Tel. Tirard to MAE, 14 Jan. 1921: MAE Rive Gauche, vol. 26, nos. 23-25.

[54] Tel. Tirard to MAE, 9 Mar. 1921: MAE Rive Gauche, vol. 94, nos. 29-30.

The news from the Vatican was no better. In March the French envoy to the Holy See, Jean Doulcet, confirmed his suspicions about the Vatican's German policy. "The papacy is proud that predominately Protestant Germany is governed by Catholics of the Center party," he reported, "and opposes anything that would diminish the number of Catholic deputies in the Reichstag." As for the Rhenish sees, Monsignor Pacelli worked against the French in the selection of a successor to the aged Bishop of Mainz despite his assurances to the contrary.[55] Briand entrusted a final plea on behalf of Franco-Rhenish "Catholic solidarity" to the chaplain-general of the Rhine Army, Paul Rémond. In late June, Rémond met twice with the Pope and spoke at length with Cardinal Gasparri. "The Holy Father deigned to respond that he approved of the policy of M. Tirard and would instruct Msgr. Pacelli to inform them [the Rhenish prelates] accordingly." But when Rémond returned to the Rhine, the Rhenish bishops ignored his demarches. A diplomatic protest at the Vatican only confirmed French fears. Weimar Germany had won the battle for the Church.[56]

Peaceful penetration was self-defeating, for its failure stemmed from the original fallacious assumption about the nature of the separatist movement of 1918-1919. If the mass of Rhenish shopkeepers, vintners, and peasants and the notables led by Konrad Adenauer were to consider autonomy as a plausible policy, it would only be when the Rhineland again found itself between the Scylla of French expansion and the Charybdis of German internal collapse.

Almost as a mockery of the myth of Franco-Rhenish affinity, agents of the Rhenish Independent Socialist party perpetrated an incredible hoax in the weeks surrounding the capitulation of 11 May. They approached Dr. Dorten with news that the Social Democrats and Independent Socialists had decided to support separatism lest the Ruhr magnates and their government flunkeys throw the burden of reparations onto the workers. When they produced documents signed by Wilhelm Sollman and Eduard David, Dorten was convinced. He dispatched the papers to General Mangin in Paris with the message: "Tell the general that the hour has come!"[57] Mangin delivered the documents to the Quai d'Orsay, where the incident necessitated a personal conclave between Millerand and Briand before they ordered French

[55] Let. MAE to Doulcet, 12 Jan. 1921; Let. Doulcet to Briand, 26 Mar. 1921: MAE Rive Gauche, vol. 103, nos. 13-18, 47-49.

[56] Let. Rémond to Msgr. Ceretti (nuncio in Paris), 7 Oct. 1921; Let. Rémond to Canet, 2 July 1921; Let. Briand to H. Cambon (chargé at Vatican), Oct. 1921: MAE Pap. Canet, vol. 23, nos. 69-72, 67-68.

[57] Note Colonel Pellerin, "Résumé de divers conversations avec M. Dorten," 21-24 Mar. 1921: MAE Rive Gauche, vol. 26, nos. 119-125.

authorities to ignore the whole affair. Experts exposed the forgeries, but not before military intelligence, eager to encourage a separatist policy, claimed to discern a "definite movement in favor of a Rhenish workers' state under French protection!"[58]

Tirard continued his propaganda through 1921 and beyond, but illusions of Franco-Rhenish affinity were dead to all but those within France who had succumbed to the myths of Barrès.[59] French influence on the Rhine would be based on the pressure occupation authorities could bring to bear on the Rhenish economy, but in the summer of 1921 Briand even began to question the value of sanctions as he shifted his sights from London to Berlin.

RHENISH POLICY IN THE ERA OF FULFILLMENT

Following the German capitulation, Briand and Berthelot rebelled against their dependence on Britain. As long as France was forced to act in concert with Lloyd George, Allied unity would be purchased with French concessions. For the moment at least, the German government pledged to respect the treaty, and Berthelot sought to make full use of the "moral and material authority" of victorious France to construct a web of ententes in Central and Eastern Europe. France would come to terms with Germany, escaping Britain, and assure her security through a continental constellation dedicated to the preservation, not revision, of the treaty boundaries. The new independence

[58] MG, 2e bureau, to MAE, "Constitution d'une République Rhénane et les syndicats ouvrières," 26 May 1921: MAE Rive Gauche, vol. 26, nos. 126-128. The agent who spoke to Dorten was Herr Worms, an Independent Socialist. He confessed on 3 June to having forged the documents. The false association of the Social Democrats with Worms's plot was designed to win Dorten's confidence and the interest of the French, but the true motive of the hoax remained unclear, unless it was merely to discredit the occupation. Rumors of a "revolutionary movement" were rooted in fact, however. At this time the U.S.P.D. was in a process of dissolution, the Left Wing merging into the new German Communist party.

[59] Propagandists for Franco-Rhenish cooperation and a Rhenish Republic organized after 1918 into a number of societies, none of which had any direct impact on events in the Rhineland. The *Comité de la Rive Gauche du Rhin*, the *Comité Dupleix*, the association for Rhenish-Alsacian unity, led by the editor of the *Revue d'Alsace et de Lorraine*, Michel Klecker de Balazuc, and other rightist-oriented publicity groups met on a regular basis, published occasional tracts, and lobbied friendly editors of large-circulation newspapers and *parlementaires*, but did not undertake the sort of direct action in the Rhineland carried on by Belgian Rhine propaganda groups. They did, however, serve as a modest source of funds for Dorten's movement. Klecker de Balazuc's monthly reports on the Rhenish question from 1920 to 1923 provide excellent examples of the Franco-Rhenish dogma and the critiques leveled at the Paris government for its failure "to apply itself to the emancipation of the Left Bank of the Rhine and the orientation of Germany toward federalism." The reports were collected and published under the title *La République Rhénane* (Paris, 1924).

displayed by the Quai d'Orsay was not solely the product of devious calculation—it rode the crest of a great wave of anti-British feeling. Even moderate journals that acknowledged the dangers of isolation blamed Britain more and more for the unending tergiversations of Allied policy. The fruits of victory were still out of reach, and "It is Great Britain's fault; Great Britain bears the responsibility."[60] On 24 May Briand himself mounted the podium to deflect the deputies' frustrations across the Channel. Isolation was not possible for great peoples, he said. As alliances dissolve, new ones are formed. This did not mean that France would dissolve the Entente—over Upper Silesia, for instance—but Briand openly praised the policy of Chancellor Wirth, while warning Lloyd George that "France has the force to justify her confidence and *sang-froid*."[61]

Briand shared Millerand's concern for an organization of Europe on principles of continental balance. But federalist schemes were unnecessary. Under Briand's cabinet, France's *barrière de l'Est* matured. Berthelot personally favored the Czechs and distrusted Pilsudski's Poland, but the forces drawing France and Poland together after the Battle of Warsaw were irresistible. Following the conclusion of the Franco-Polish pact in February 1921, Briand threw off all pretense of a common Entente policy in Eastern Europe. He attempted to turn the Little Entente to advantage by disavowing the Hungarian policy and strengthening French ties with Czechoslovakia, Rumania, and Yugoslavia. In the Near East, Briand again departed from Entente policy by sending Franklin-Bouillon to Ankara to negotiate a separate peace with the defiant Nationalist government of Mustapha Kemal. Finally, the French and British clashed most seriously concerning the partition of Upper Silesia. French opinion could not countenance denying a rich industrial region to ally Poland in the name of German national unity, particularly when the dominant nationality in the key communes appeared to be Polish. The British argument—that Weimar democracy and pacifism would be strengthened should the Allies gratuitously deliver up more industrial power to Germany—seemed absurd. The Silesian crisis simmered throughout the summer of 1921, exposing like none previously the fundamental divergence of French and British postwar strategies.[62]

[60] "Les Deux Politiques," *Le Temps*, 2 May 1921.

[61] J. O. Chambre, 24 May 1921, pp. 2355-2365.

[62] The British were at a loss to understand Briand's intransigence on Upper Silesia. As Kaplan, "France's Road to Genoa," pp. 214-215, aptly points out, French policy not only severely damaged the chance for future Franco-British cooperation against Germany, but also handicapped the initiatives toward Franco-German cooperation, for Briand had also to contend with the pro-Polish sentiment his public stance encouraged in the Chamber. In the end Briand's willingness to grant the Germans continued industrial

Lloyd George's resistance to French independence began in the one area where he retained some leverage, in the Rhineland. By opposing Briand's efforts to retain the sanctions, Lloyd George hoped to recover his influence in Berlin. On 11 May Lord D'Abernon promised the Germans that the sanctions of March would now be dropped, given German acceptance of the Allied ultimatum. The French protested vehemently. Director of Political Affairs Peretti de la Rocca explained that the sanctions were a response to German defaults in disarmament and war criminal prosecution as well as reparations. Until all was made good, the sanctions must remain.[63] Seydoux was unsure about the best course to take and urged that no decision be made until the Committee of Guarantees was fully operative. But France must never evacuate the Ruhr ports, for these were "the keys to the Ruhr." Briand agreed and Peretti gave the appropriate instructions.[64]

When the question of sanctions was raised, London, Brussels, and Berlin all opposed French policy. But it was an empty attack that Lloyd George orchestrated, for Briand had adopted a new course. After two months, the sanctions had done little for France. Tirard's men sat in customs houses and collected stacks of paper marks that only went to pay the operation's in-country expenses. If the Rhineland was to become a "reparations province," a cow to be milked by Paris instead of Berlin, more and broader measures would be necessary. The clearest benefit lay in control of commercial licensing, but "the economic separation of the Rhineland," as General Degoutte pointed out, was just not happening.[65] The other sanction was of even less use. While the British Parliament quickly passed the Reparation Recovery Act to exploit the 50 percent levy on German imports, the French never applied the sanction. The Chamber voted a project of law on 21 April, but the government never issued the appropriate decrees. The Ministry of Commerce feared that Berlin would discriminate against France and not reimburse German merchants subject to the levy, killing Franco-German trade altogether. Instead, Briand used his executive

---

control if only Poland were given a "sovereignty of appearances" over the industrial area, expressed in a confidential meeting with the German chargé on 5 August 1921, testified to his desire only to "save face." See Campbell, "The Struggle for Upper Silesia," p. 380. Furthermore, a relaxed public stance on Upper Silesia would not necessarily have fostered Franco-British or Franco-German solidarity—it would have demonstrated the effectiveness of Anglo-German cooperation, precisely the combination Briand sought to discredit.

[63] Tel. Peretti to St. Aulaire, "Réparations: sanctions de Londres," 17 May 1921: MAE Allemagne, vol. 234, nos. 96-98.

[64] Note Seydoux, "Réparations: Maintien des sanctions de Londres," 12 May 1921: MAE Allemagne, vol. 234, nos. 58-61.

[65] Rapport mensuel de l'Armée du Rhin, Degoutte to MG, MAE, June 1921: MAE Rive Gauche, vol. 63.

powers to raise the general tariff on German goods to four times the legal minimum as a measure of protection and in hopes of making a reparations-in-kind agreement attractive to Berlin.[66]

The Quai d'Orsay began to look beyond the immediate question of the sanctions and to weigh the long-term costs and benefits of the policy. Seydoux's thoughts had been evolving since March, and now he spoke freely against all Rhenish policies. To be sure, there were political considerations involved, but the present policy was a barrier to reconstruction, the greatest drain on the French budget. "That which France can and must pursue," Seydoux posited, "is a system facilitating delivery of German products to the devastated regions. Whether they come from occupied or nonoccupied territory is irrelevant."[67] The sanctions could be used as bargaining tools only, for the retention of the Allied licensing committee at Bad Ems.[68] Otherwise, France must return to cooperation in reparations-in-kind to complement the London schedule of payments. The economic Rhenish policy must be abandoned in favor of Franco-German fulfillment of the treaty.

These suggestions made sense to Briand and Berthelot. Both had been staunch supporters of a Rhenish policy before and after the war, but wartime reveries gave way to practical politics. Berthelot's European strategy sought to make all continental nations dependent on France—perhaps he could also make Germany dependent. If the Weimar Republic relied on foreign policy successes to preserve itself against extremism, let it be France, not England, that granted those successes. On 11 July the Chamber debated the French military budget. It was an occasion to examine German disarmament, Upper Silesia, and other issues bearing on French security. André Lefèvre, former minister of war, called for *une politique française*, for an end to concessions. Briand responded with a declaration of independence. France still sought Allied solidarity, "but if the demands of this solidarity compromise the vital interests of France and of her security, then solidarity would no longer be possible. We have the right and the duty to assure our national existence. All our allies must understand this."[69]

The year before, an independent policy had meant freedom for France to act on the Rhine. Now it meant liquidating the causes of suspicion between Paris and Berlin. Briand answered Tirard's pleas for an intensified Rhenish policy with clear rejection. "I cannot urge you enough," Briand wrote Tirard, "to exercise the broadest circumspec-

[66] Weill-Raynal, *Les réparations allemandes*, II, 11-12.

[67] Note Seydoux for Laroche, "Note au sujêt du maintien des sanctions de Londres," 25 June 1921: MAE Rive Gauche, vol. 111, nos. 145-153.

[68] Note Seydoux, "Question des sanctions," 7 July 1921: MAE Allemagne, vol. 234, nos. 170-177.

[69] J.O. Chambre, 11 July 1921, pp. 3385-3399.

tion in the relations you have with Rhenish personalities. It would be preferable if your attitude were one of absolute disinterest." As for the imminent expiration of the *Sperrfrist*, Briand warned that "a plebiscite resulting from our efforts would immediately appear as an imposition to the Germans and even the partisans of Rhenish autonomy would vote against it."[70]

Briand and Seydoux now returned to the policy of early 1920, that of seeking direct commercial and deliveries accords with Berlin. For France, it meant abandonment of the Rhenish political goals that had helped defeat the previous year's efforts, and the risk of British disfavor. Briand now accepted the first, and the end of the coal crisis and the German fulfillment policy meant that he could risk the second. For Germany, bilateral accords called for the will to accept reparations, a will that the threatened Ruhr occupation had temporarily created. The Wirth government could look to cooperation with France as a means of protecting its sovereignty and economic growth. Seydoux looked ahead to an era of economic entente, not only between governments but between industries. He called for an end to discrimination on both sides and a series of private exchanges of raw materials and manufactures.[71] On 12 June 1921, Louis Loucheur encountered a German delegation led by the Minister of Reconstruction Walther Rathenau at Wiesbaden, and Franco-German conversations resumed. Rathenau demanded the lifting of the Rhenish sanctions and complained disingenuously that French luxury imports were responsible for Germany's balance of payments problems, but he accepted Loucheur's refusal to link their talks to disarmament and Upper Silesia. There were also initial differences on the machinery for pricing and placing orders, but both sides showed a willingness to bargain. An accord could be reached.[72]

Opposition from expected sources arose quickly. From Brussels, Pierre de Margerie reported the alarm of Foreign Minister Jaspar. Just as Paris suspected Carton de Wiart of seeking a "separate peace" with Germany in April, Brussels now feared a French renunciation of Allied unity.[73] The British were even more suspicious. Expecting a new Franco-German clash over the retention of sanctions, in which they

[70] Let. Briand to Tirard, 29 July 1921: MAE Rive Gauche, vol. 26, nos. 154-155.

[71] Note Seydoux, "Réparations en nature," 9 June 1921: MAE Pap. Millerand, Réparations IV, nos. 6-16.

[72] P.-V., "Entrevue à Wiesbaden 12 et 13 juin entre Rathenau et Loucheur": HI, Pap. Loucheur, Box 7, Folder 7; P.-V., "Négociations franco-allemandes," négociations franco-allemandes, 28-30 June 1921: MAE Pap. Millerand, Réparations IV, nos. 65-68, 99-105.

[73] Note Seydoux, "Réparations en nature," 2 July 1921; Let. Margerie to Briand, "Observations de M. Jaspar," 9 July 1921: MAE Pap. Millerand, Réparations IV, nos. 107-118, 159-162.

would play the role of German advocate, the Germans were discussing voluntary acceptance of new burdens directly with France! Were the French and Germans contemplating cartelization? Were the French offering concessions on Upper Silesia? Were the Germans merely seeking to widen the cleavage between the Allies? Lord Curzon and British reparations delegate Sir John Bradbury protested that a grand deliveries-in-kind scheme would weigh too heavily on Germany during the delicate first years of fulfillment and establish a virtual priority for the devastated regions of France, a boon denied by the Paris Peace Conference and three conferences since. Finally, Curzon protested French "desertion" of the Allies.[74] It was hardly a credible performance. When the threat from Paris was one of force, Britain had counseled negotiation, and had always favored reparations-in-kind over capital transfers. But now Curzon witnessed both France and Germany recovering their freedom of action and he paraded opposite opinions. When the principle of international economic cooperation came to imply Franco-German rapprochement, national interest penetrated the internationalist façade of British policy.

In August Briand played host to the Supreme Council in Paris. Germany had paid the first installment of the London plan, £50 million in May, and was in the process of transferring the second £50 million due by the end of August. But far from stimulating mutual concessions, the conference exposed the shocking degree to which Paris and London had drifted apart. Briand and Lloyd George made no progress toward a solution to the Turkish war, they clashed on disarmament, and almost broke over Upper Silesia. The financial settlement, distribution of the German monies transferred since May, yielded nothing for France. Only in the area of sanctions was accord reached. The 13 August resolution promised the disappearance of the Rhenish customs sanction and the levy on German exports, but the occupation of Ruhr ports would remain. Allied authorities in the Rhineland retained a committee of observation to ensure a nondiscriminatory commercial licensing policy. Thus Briand turned to account all of Seydoux's recommendations. Finally, the French government would adopt these measures only if the German government recognized the legality of the sanctions taken. If it did so, the Allies would lift the sanctions on 15 September.

Berlin was not ready to surrender again. Faithful execution of the London plan had earned more liberal treatment than this, Wirth believed. Recognition of an Allied "committee of observation" would set

[74] Let. Bradbury (Reparations Commission) to Blackett (Treasury), 8 July 1921: DBFP, XV, 711-713; Let. Cheetham (British Embassy, Paris) to Briand, 16 July 1921: MAE Pap. Millerand, Réparations IV, nos. 165-166.

a dangerous precedent, perhaps leading to Allied control of German finances and the "Turkification" of the Reich. The Germans waited until 14 September, then informed the Quai d'Orsay that Germany could not accept the added stipulations of the 13 August plan. In keeping with the spirit of Wiesbaden, they offered another compromise. In return for sacrifice of the licensing committee, the German government would guarantee France a certain volume of trade, as it had done in a recent accord with Italy.

The offer showed the limits of bilateral collaboration. For all Briand's desire to negotiate a deliveries accord, he could not do so at the price of his general guarantees of respect for the financial and commercial clauses of the treaty. Renunciation by France of her means of coercion was tantamount to renunciation of Germany's obligations. No agreement, no matter how generous, was worth anything to France if left to German goodwill for execution. Wirth and Rathenau could not promise that the next German government would respect their pledges, nor could they enforce German domestic compliance even while they remained in office. Thus Berthelot replied to the German offer that the two questions could not be linked. The 13 August accords were of interallied concern and commercial accords were the business of Paris and Berlin alone.[75] The 15 September deadline passed and the sanctions remained. Berlin looked to Lloyd George, but the latter could hardly desert a plan that he himself had helped to formulate. Lloyd George again lost face in Berlin and the Germans accepted the 13 August plan on 20 September. The Supreme Council hastily met and lifted the Rhenish customs regime on 30 September.

The liquidation of sanctions cleared the way for the Franco-German compromise on reparations-in-kind hammered out during the summer. The key concession offered by Loucheur was the abandonment of the Rhenish commercial policy as practiced under Millerand and Briand. Seydoux explained: "M. Loucheur is prepared, in cooperation with M. Tirard, to study means of satisfying the legitimate interests of Germany. We have no intention of intervening in the economic regime of Germany, nor of seeking self-serving favoritism on the Left Bank of the Rhine."[76] Tirard, in fact, was not at all prepared to cooperate—he fought the drift of negotiations tooth and nail. But the Rhenish policy was in disrepute. On 6 and 7 October 1921 Loucheur and Rathenau signed the Wiesbaden Accords. They envisioned German deliveries to France on a large scale, a practical means of rebuilding the devastated regions, to relieve the French budget and public opinion, and to lower

[75] Tel. Berthelot to St. Aulaire, 15 Sept. 1921: MAE Allemagne, vol. 235, nos. 72-73.

[76] Note Seydoux, "Négociations économiques avec les Allemands," 15 July 1921: MAE Rive Gauche, vol. 112, nos. 25-36.

the cash payments required of Germany. In the background the French retained the political tool of the 132 billion mark debt, and the Germans escaped the immediate danger of force or loss of sovereignty in the occupied territories.[77]

The Accords were the culmination of the fulfillment policies of both France and Germany. As such, they represented the French hope of fostering the Franco-German economic integration that most experts considered inevitable in a manner safe for the potentially weaker partner, France. It was also a program conceived and negotiated by French politicians, not businessmen; thus, Wiesbaden repeated the pattern of events surrounding the Seydoux Plan of 1920-1921.[78] Seydoux recognized that the Accords were directed against Britain, insofar as they removed reparations-in-kind from the hands of "the Allies," and looked beyond the immediate agreement to the Franco-German industrial cartel to follow. But eventually Seydoux projected a Western European condominium that would ensure stability through European integration on terms acceptable to battered France, and then turn as a bloc toward the reconstruction of Soviet Russia.[79] In effect, he endorsed the grandiose schemes Lloyd George would soon produce at Cannes and Genoa. The only difference was that rapid redevelopment of German economic strength must be preceded by the forging of adequate safeguards, lest "European integration" become a euphemism for *Mitteleuropa*. Political rapprochement must precede economic.

But the Wiesbaden Accords quickly became a dead letter. On 21 October 1921 the Reparations Commission pleaded incompetence to rule on the political reservations raised by the British and Belgians—from Washington, Herbert Hoover feared that the Accords might lead to

[77] The Wiesbaden Accords would have increased significantly the reparations received by France during the first years of the London Schedule of Payments. But the in-kind deliveries would be above and beyond the common payments made by Germany to the Reparations Commission. Strictly speaking, the Accords did not constitute a priority for France unless the deliveries damaged Germany's ability to meet future scheduled payments to other countries. France would receive no more than 7 billion gold marks of merchandise in five years, and no more than 35 percent the first year. This would mean an additional 950 million gold marks per year over the 450 million per year already allotted her. The French argued that, aside from hastening repair of the devastated regions, the Accords would facilitate specie payments to the Allies by reducing France's share, and would help to keep German goods off British, Belgian, and Italian markets. See Weill-Raynal, *Les réparations allemandes*, II, 38-39.

[78] The Seydoux Plan had made eminently good sense, but it had stimulated vigorous opposition from French and German industries. Faced with the difficulty of execution without cooperation from private interests, the French and German cabinets took the easiest way out of constructive initiatives that threatened to undermine their domestic support—they retreated into intransigence. For the denouement of the Seydoux Plan, see Soutou, "Die deutschen Reparationen," pp. 261-270.

[79] Note Seydoux, "La politique de la France à l'égard de l'Allemagne et de l'Angleterre," 1 Aug. 1921: MAE Grande Bretagne, vol. 47.

"disorganization of the world market." The British advised the Germans to stall and it was not until the spring of 1922 that all governments and the Reparations Commission sanctioned the French government's bold initiative of the previous year. By then the isolation of France in the Supreme Council had brought results far more serious than Briand or Berthelot had expected. Yet the decisive blow came from within France and Germany. The Chamber first rebelled against Briand by refusing to ratify the 13 August financial accord. That France should receive nothing of the first billion was unacceptable. The British Foreign Office disgustedly wondered if France meant to subordinate ratification to British acceptance of Wiesbaden.[80] The French cabinet indeed favored such a *marchandage*, but it was not to be, for the Chamber also refused to ratify the Loucheur-Rathenau Accords. French manufacturers were irreconcilable, calling the Accords "a national danger."[81] The Chambers of Commerce joined the opposition and stirred up public opinion against the etatist solution to reconstruction. Through their influence, they stymied approval of the detente worked out by the politicians.[82] Finally, even the promoters of that detente began to think better of bilateral accords. For Loucheur and the mercurial Seydoux noted bitterly that German economic interests, too, were mobilizing to slay not only the Wiesbaden Accords, but the entire policy of fulfillment. Germany was backsliding. Perhaps France could not afford isolation after all.

THE FAILURE OF FULFILLMENT

The Wirth government did not take up fulfillment with any hope of giving total satisfaction to France. Rather it was resigned to fulfillment as the lesser of evils. Joseph Wirth, a liberal Catholic and former mathematician, realized the internal opposition to the policy, but hoped to convince the Allies through good faith that there were limits to German capabilities. Not by protests and obstruction, but by a show of honest effort would Germany win revision of the treaty. But the effort had to be so feeble to satisfy domestic opposition that the façade of sin-

[80] Memo by Mr. Wigram "on recent developments in reparations," F.O., 29 Sept. 1921: DBFP, XV, 778-780.

[81] Camille Didier, "Un danger national. L'Accord de Wiesbaden au point de vue de l'industrie et des sinistrés français," *L'Usine*, September-November 1921.

[82] See the industrial and commercial attacks on Wiesbaden in *Journée Industrielle*, 25 Oct. 1921 and 25 Jan. 1922. A sober, balanced judgment of the Accords from the point of view of French business was drafted by deputy Désiré Ferry. "Rapport fait au nom de la Commission des Affaires Étrangères chargée d'examiner le projet de loi relatif à la ratification des accords concernant les prestations en nature à provenir d'Allemagne." Ferry criticized the etatism of Wiesbaden but recognized that after the war experience no one could maintain that the state had no legitimate economic role.

cerity was difficult to maintain. Wirth's partner in fulfillment was the A.E.G. magnate, Walther Rathenau. This brilliant man directed military raw materials procurement in the first years of the war and wrote prolifically on the problems and potential of national and world economic organization. He was a Jew and a member of the Democratic party, facts that earned him enemies on the Right from the moment he agreed to enter politics. But he shared the chancellor's analysis of Germany's plight. The government could not hope to obtain credit until it demonstrated a will to comply, to the best of its ability, with a schedule of payments. Only then could it perhaps default without inviting French economic or military advances on the hostage Rhine.[83]

But Wirth was impuissant when it came to making the necessary demands upon the industrial and commercial classes. The magnates of the Ruhr, the directorates of the great German banks, the shipping tycoons of the Hansa towns—these economic power groups acquiesced in fulfillment as a useful political slogan, but they refused to permit Berlin to enforce the fiscal sacrifices necessary to support payments. Indeed, the continuing inflation fed by the Reich's unbalanced budget stimulated German trade and multiplied the wealth of those with the power to take advantage of it. Geared for social and economic instability since 1918, the Ruhr industrialists especially profited from inflation while blocking fiscal reform. Borrowing constantly to finance expansion and capital purchases, then repaying their debts in inflated currency while their products undersold competitors abroad, many Ruhr firms became industrial dinosaurs. Expansion was matched by accelerated vertical integration. The concentration of *Mines-Usines* provided protection against coal shortages; the very size and power of the conglomerates made the Ruhr a bulwark against the feeble attempts at nationalization. Finally, vertical integration permitted profit-juggling on a grand scale, concealing the true financial state of the Ruhr firms and frustrating efforts at tax collection. Stinnes and Kloeckner especially capitalized on inflation, but the combined power of the Ruhr meant that Berlin was incapable of forcing the necessary reforms, despite impoverishment of the German middle class and the bankruptcy of gov-

[83] Wirth and Rathenau made this clear in a series of speeches in June, following the "capitulation." They were designed to reassure German opinion and rally support for their policy of detente. Fulfillment *policy*, they explained, did not constitute *fulfillment* (a fact with which Poincaré would have agreed), i.e., it was a tactical move. See David Felix, *Walther Rathenau and the Weimar Republic* (Baltimore, 1971), pp. 80-81; Ernst Laubach, *Die Politik der Kabinette Wirth 1921/1922* (Lübeck, 1968); Erich Eyck, *A History of the Weimar Republic*, 2 vols. (New York, 1962), I, 183-187; Ludwig Zimmermann, *Deutsche Aussenpolitik in der Ära der Weimarer Republik* (Göttingen, 1958), pp. 101-103.

ernment.[84] Between April and September 1921 government receipts totaled 15 billion marks, expenses 38 billion. The result was foreordained. In May 1921 the pound was worth 245 marks, already twelve times the prewar ratio. But by the end of August the mark had slipped to 325. Germany clearly could not fulfill reparations for long if present financial practice continued.

Seydoux explained the problem of German finance, as did most Frenchmen, by reference to the inability of the Berlin government to force its will upon industrialists and financiers. Wirth was forced to finance reparations by inflation, while coal taxes in Germany remained lower than in any Allied country. Railroad rates in Germany were a quarter of the French rates. Instead of taxing the great *Konzern* of the Ruhr and the shipping giants of Hamburg and Bremen, the government was subsidizing them for treaty losses! Indirect taxes were substantially lower than in Allied countries, and duties and customs lagged behind inflation. No effort was made to control export of capital or sale of foreign currency in Germany. The German government, through will or weakness, was systematically favoring big business while destroying its own currency. It was not the insatiable demands of the Allies that fed German inflation, but the absence of fiscal responsibility in Berlin.[85]

By the end of August it was already clear that Wirth's "fulfillment" policy would degenerate into one of "beggar my neighbor." Berlin had been unable to fund her second installment out of receipts and had dipped into Reichsbank reserves and juggled short-term loans. Loucheur fumed when he witnessed how well-meaning British and American observers were seduced by German cries of poverty, even as they resisted the Wiesbaden Accords that would have alleviated the transfer problem. Nor would British and American banks extend the capital necessary to stabilize the mark even as they willingly extended credit to Stinnes. "France is accused of weakening German democracy," wrote Loucheur, "or seeking to 'Turkify' the Reich and create causes for new wars. But if the democratic government cannot reform itself, then what is wrong with our taking guarantees? It must be understood that there is simply no other means of getting paid."[86] It

[84] On the Ruhr's favorable attitude toward the postwar German inflation, and its frustration of government attempts at currency control, see Feldman, *Iron and Steel in the German Inflation*, pp. 210-279, 285-286; Laubach, *Kabinette Wirth*, pp. 84ff; Baumont, *La grosse industrie allemande*, pp. 182-189.

[85] Seydoux, *De Versailles au Plan Young*, pp. 62-69.

[86] Note Loucheur, "La faillite de l'Allemagne," 10 Sept. 1921; P.-V., "Questions des Réparations. Réunion chez le Président de la République," 27 Oct. 1921. In order to demonstrate Germany's feeble fiscal effort, Loucheur divided per capita fiscal burdens

seemed that even a well-intentioned government in Berlin could not execute the treaty. The assassination of Matthias Erzberger, the "traitor" who had signed the Armistice in 1918, armed German activities in Upper Silesia, and the continued militarism of von Kahr's Bavaria also contributed to the conclusion, which many Frenchmen were all too willing to adopt, that democracy had not altered the locus of power within Germany. The Rightists and industrial magnates still governed German policy.[87]

The British could not deny certain of the French arguments concerning the source of Germany's financial difficulties. But it did not conclude that strict Allied control of the Reich budget was the solution. German goodwill could hardly be expected while France took every opportunity to weaken the German economy. The solution in Upper Silesia was a case in point. In October 1921 the League of Nations Council, to which the Allies had referred the dispute, finally pronounced on the partition, granting a large portion of the industrial region to Poland. The German response was immediate and bitter. Fulfillment seemed to offer the Germans little.

Lloyd George desired above all to keep Wirth in office and to refrain from new demands. But the force of the French argument remained: the German problem was political, not financial. Adenauer himself explained this in May to the British commissioner in Cologne. He would have accepted the chancellory, he said, if certain conditions had been met: return to a nine-hour day, an end to the Reichstag's socialization hearings, power to select his ministers from any party. Only a nearly dictatorial government, pledged to preserve the social status quo, could enforce strict taxation, repress geographical and economic particularism, and fulfill the treaty.[88] In other words, for Germany to make the effort needed for reparations, a centrally directed command economy would have to be restored. But the civil authorities in Germany were even less powerful vis-à-vis their own economic elites than were Entente governments. In any case, it was not the civil government so much as the army that had directed Germany's war mobilization. Given Adenauer's cogent analysis, what was France to do?—permit an authoritarian, perhaps military regime to regain control of a

---

by the average daily wage for government employees. France's tax burden represented 30 days' labor, Britain's 40 days', and Germany's only 18 days'. Note Loucheur, "Sur la situation financière de l'Allemagne et la question des Réparations," 1 Nov. 1921: HI Pap. Loucheur, Box 5, Folders 3, 13.

[87] For a discussion of the failure of German fiscal reform, see Maier, *Recasting Bourgeois Europe*, pp. 249-272.

[88] Des. #195 Robertson (Coblenz) to F.O., C10270/416/18, 18 May 1921: PRO FO 371, vol. 5970, nos. 183-184.

centralized Germany? The issue never came to a test. Weimar Germany was permitted to stumble along, with the Ruhr magnates hiding beneath the cloak of British diplomacy, which was meant to shield German democracy.

The Committee of Guarantees was meant to observe German finances. In June it proceeded to Berlin to exercise a triple control: control of German export statistics, control of customs, withholding of foreign currency totaling 25 percent of German exports. In practice, the guarantees were worthless. The Committee could not staff every customs house, so it relied on the German bureaucracy for the statistics it was supposed to validate. Furthermore, the receipts were in

FIGURE 3. "Insolvency: The German Ambassador Pays an Official Visit to the Elysée." J. Sennep, 1921. © S.P.A.D.E.M. Paris 1977.

paper marks and the Reich showed great reluctance in converting them, since a quarter of the hard currency received would go to the Allies. Forced sale of marks only served to drive their value down further. The Committee of Guarantees made a gloomy report in October. The receipts expected from German exports were not forthcoming, though the totals for German exports were higher than predicted! The Germans were holding back, while the deficit meant the direct German transfers due in November 1921 and January 1922 would have to be increased, not reduced. Finally, German industrialists reacted with as much vehemence to the Wiesbaden Accords as did their French counterparts. In a series of meetings in November, industrial groups led by Stinnes and Hugenberg exercised their "veto" power over Berlin reparations policies by refusing to back the government's supportive credit action, and the short-lived detente between the Wirth government and the Ruhr came to an end.[89] Instead, the government's impending bankruptcy, and Britain's show of displeasure with France, encouraged Berlin to replace fulfillment with a new attempt at treaty revision.

The French also began looking for alternatives to the London schedule. The Germans could not enforce reforms, and, with their present powers, neither could the Allies. Loucheur drew up a new scheme, a far-reaching synthesis of old and new ideas, descriptive of the turning point reached in the reparations tangle. He urged Allied control of German finances, regulation of foreign currency circulation, application of the Wiesbaden Accords, an immediate loan to be contracted abroad by German *industrialists*, and Allied participation in German business through *stock transfers* under title of reparations.[90] It was an interesting departure. Loucheur did not give up hopes of Franco-German cooperation; indeed he looked ahead to the post-1945 solution of mixed ownership of the industrial belt straddling the Franco-German border. Arnold Rechberg, the independent-minded German potassium czar who favored Franco-German rapprochement, had proposed such a solution to reparations at the time of the May Conference of London. A certain percentage of stock in German firms could be transferred to France, thus liquidating at a blow the German debt and the problem of industrial integration. At the time, Loucheur balked at such a solution. Stock transfers would form an adequate

[89] Laubach, *Die Politik der Kabinette Wirth*, pp. 120-121; Maier, *Recasting Bourgeois Europe*, pp. 258-267.

[90] Note Loucheur, "La faillite de l'Allemagne," 25 Sept. 1921: MAE Pap. Millerand, Réparations IV, nos. 221-239; Note Seydoux, "Départ de la CdR pour Berlin," 5 Nov. 1921; Note Loucheur, "Situation financière de l'Allemagne et la question de réparations," 9 Nov. 1921: MAE Pap. Millerand, Réparations V, nos. 5-14, 25-46 (my italics).

guarantee of a regular schedule of payments, but they were dangerous as a *means* of fulfillment. Loucheur demanded that France be given firm majority interest (65 percent share) in German firms, lest French assets remain vulnerable to the Ruhr's directorial caprice.[91]

Whatever the ultimate solution, French leverage had been severely reduced by the failure of fulfillment. Barring a unilateral military operation against Germany, new pressure could be brought to bear on Germany only through cooperation with Britain. Seydoux too declared that "Europe cannot remain at peace if we are not in accord with England. We must liquidate as soon as possible all the differences that now separate us." Otherwise, Britain would isolate France, support Germany in default, and France "would be forced to use violence to break the Anglo-German entente."[92]

Briand's policy was a shambles. Fulfillment was a gamble that the Weimar parliamentary system could reconcile its constituencies to the price of continental stability—respect for, and only very gradual liberation from, the Treaty of Versailles. The gamble lost, and the price of renewed Franco-British cooperation would be high, perhaps higher than the French parliamentary majority would accept. At the very moment when Briand regretted his independent stance and looked again to London, Lloyd George sprang his long-prepared counterattack. The scene was the Washington Conference on Naval and Far Eastern affairs. Soon after the conference opened, Briand, who insisted on attending in person, was isolated. The particular defeat for France, reduction of her naval tonnage to parity with Italy, was humiliating, but the circumstances of the defeat were disastrous. The Franco-British Entente registered no vitality. On 25 November Lord Curzon spoke up, warning France of the dangers of isolation and urging her to heed the "conscience of the world." Although the "world opinion" so highly prized by London and Washington had not spared France four years of desolation, even with all the world in her camp, France alone had not the power to ignore it. Meanwhile, Stinnes himself visited London for industrial talks. He reached no agreements, but it was then that Lloyd George developed his grand design for enlisting German aid in the reconstruction of Russia. Walther Rathenau next made a pilgrimage to London, seeking an international loan to be matched by a moratorium. Montagu Norman, director of the Bank of England, put Germany's credit at zero, owing to the priority of reparations claims on her. This argument only strengthened the case for a

[91] Tel. St. Quentin (Berlin) to MAE, 5 Mar. 1921; MAE Memo, "Participation de l'industrie allemande aux Réparations," 10 Mar. 1921: MAE Allemagne, vol. 460.

[92] Note Seydoux, 29 Nov. 1921: MAE Pap. Millerand, Réparations V, nos. 113-116.

moratorium, a fact that the British government hastened to recognize.[93] On 15 December Chancellor Wirth informed the Reparations Commission of Germany's inability to meet the 15 January payment. The state was bankrupt, and requested the interruption of the London schedule of payments. Briand had not much time to revive the Entente.

Early in December the French ambassador in London, the Comte Beaupoil de St. Aulaire, raised the prospect of a Franco-British pact. He was alarmed at the deterioration of the Entente and took initiative to replace it with an alliance. The agreement would have to be broad, encompassing all the outstanding issues between the two nations and the general problem of security as well. The idea of such an alliance had existed ever since the British retreat from the 1919 pact, but the time had never been right. In May 1921 the British Cabinet, attributing French sanctions policy to security considerations, debated the wisdom of offering a security pact. Winston Churchill spoke against it at that time. Instead of allaying French fears, he thought a pact would embolden the French in the Rhineland.[94] Precisely the opposite analysis occurred to Jules Laroche, chief of the Quai d'Orsay's European subdivision. Disaster would follow if France and Britain did not find common ground, but a full alliance, without previous compromise in all disputes, would condemn France to vassalage.[95] But now both premiers deemed St. Aulaire's initiative felicitous and met in London in mid-December. To an inscrutable Lloyd George, Briand proposed an alliance much broader than that of 1919—a pact reconciling French and British interests all over the world. Briand and Berthelot pressed ahead with a draft.[96]

If the security question had not heretofore been the preoccupation of the French governments, it was because the Rhineland occupation was an ideal temporary guarantee. The efforts to balance Germany through disarmament, sanctions, and alliances with successor states in Germany's rear all served French security for the immediate future. But if France and Britain were now to consider permanent security solutions as part of a grand alliance, then the Rhenish question, set aside while Briand experimented with fulfillment, must again be broached.

The security pact with Britain, wrote Berthelot, must include "an

[93] "Memorandum respecting the German financial position," enclosed in Des. D'Abernon to Curzon #1332, C22141/508/18, 16 Nov. 1921: DBFP, XV, 808-809; see also Felix, *Walther Rathenau*, pp. 110-114.

[94] Minutes, CAB 40(21), 24 May 1921: PRO CAB 23/25, pp. 282-284.

[95] Pers. Let. Laroche to Barrère, 25 Aug. 1921: MAE Corr. Barrère, vol. 3, no. 78.

[96] MAE Memo, "Conversation: Lloyd George et Briand," 21 Dec. 1921: MAE Grande Bretagne, vol. 69, nos. 43-47.

extension of French rights in the Rhenish regions. The special situation of the Rhenish regions ought to be recognized in the guarantee given by England to France." Permanent safety for France, and for the successor states that relied on her, meant a *paix rhénane*, nothing less. But Britain would never agree to a permanent French presence on the Rhine, warned St. Aulaire. He suggested instead the execution of Article 18 of the German Constitution under the aegis of the Entente as an acceptable path toward Rhenish separation. This London might agree to, but never a permanent French occupation.[97] Briand recognized, however, that an Allied-imposed plebiscite was bound to fail. The key issue in his mind was whether Britain would accept as *casus foederis* any German violation of Articles 42-44 of the Treaty of Versailles, the demilitarization of the Rhineland. That was where French interest lay.

At London, in December, Briand carried out the preliminaries. He recognized the failure of fulfillment and renounced his independence. As for reparations, all parties acknowledged again that loans to Germany were the only means of rapid German stabilization. Briand, Loucheur, and Lloyd George worked on the Chequers Plan for a comprehensive financial settlement. But it was a pipe dream based on annulment of war debts, vast loans to Germany over the next seven years, repartition of the A and B reparations bonds to accord a priority to France, and a substantial reduction of German payments until 1930.[98] In such circumstances, Allied unity would be easy, but the plan depended again on American financial succor. It was not forthcoming, so Briand and Lloyd George shouldered their responsibility to heal Europe alone. They postponed a response to the German moratorium request and tabled security negotiations until their next meeting. It would be at Cannes, in January. There the solidity of the Entente—or the price for its solidification—would be revealed.

[97] Des. St. Aulaire to Briand, 28 Dec. 1921: MAE Grande Bretagne, vol. 69, nos. 56-63.

[98] "British Secretary's Notes of a Meeting between Mr. Lloyd George and M. Briand," 20 Dec. 1921: DBFP, XV, 768-772. See also Weill-Raynal, *Les réparations allemandes*, II, 86-96. On 22 Dec. 1921, Briand and Lloyd George also struck a bargain on the leftover disputes concerning the 13 August and Wiesbaden Accords. With guarantees and emoluments on either side, Briand accepted the division of monies according to the 13 August pact and Britain accepted the reparations-in-kind accord. The trade-off was ratified at Cannes in January 1922 (DBFP, XV, annex 3 to no. 111). The Poincaré government ratified the financial distribution in March 1922, but the Wiesbaden Accords, as has been noted, were tabled by the French Chamber. On the Chequers Plan, see Maier, *Recasting Bourgeois Europe*, pp. 276-281.

·5·

POINCARÉ AND DIPLOMATIC DEADLOCK, 1922

After two years of unrelenting criticism—of the treaty, the Allies, German ill will, and French policies—Raymond Poincaré accepted the responsibility of power following a crisis of confidence in Briand's leadership. It would be up to the Treaty of Versailles' most piercing critic to decide between fulfillment and revisionism. He did not prejudge the issue. In his first six months in office Poincaré tried every acceptable means of ending the deadlock concerning reparations/war debts, security, and heavy industry. But the definition of "acceptable" was in the hands of substantially the same parliamentary majority that had dumped Briand for seeming to be too flexible in the quest for accommodation. The deputies of the Bloc National felt that a firmer stand, more credible under Poincaré, would succeed somehow in imposing the French point of view, born of financial desperation, on the Allies and Germany. French industrial leaders saw their plight worsen in the first half of 1922, and they too looked to their traditional tribunes, Millerand and Poincaré, to force cooperation on the Ruhr. But they themselves, like the Chamber, were as intractable as ever toward political detentes purchased with economic concessions. Finally, the French diplomatic position inherited from Briand was the weakest since 1919: Germany in default, Britain hostile, America aloof, with France unable to afford concessions on any one issue until the others were settled. The compendium of interest groups in France thus expected more from Poincaré, but gave him less to work with. Far from anxious to resort to force, Poincaré explored the peaceful paths to agreement with Britain, Germany, and the United States. Only after these nations proved unwilling to execute the treaty or otherwise satisfy French vital interests did the premier seriously consider a Ruhr occupation and revision of an unfulfillable treaty.

THE NEW TEAM

On 4 January 1922 Lloyd George arrived at Cannes. He brought with him a draft of a Franco-British security pact. In return for a British guarantee of French security, he expected from Briand a willingness to compromise in other areas and to cooperate fully with the prime minister's new plan for European economic reconstruction. Failing American financial aid, and pressed by domestic unemployment attributable to depressed foreign markets, Lloyd George hatched a scheme for a grand economic conference to open the markets of Eastern and Central Europe, particularly Russia. Invitations would be extended to the U.S.S.R. and Germany, thus reintegrating the outcasts into the society of nations, and to the United States. If Briand did not oblige, the British cabinet expected the fall of the French government. Poincaré, although a hard-liner, was a vocal supporter of the Entente, and might prove easier to deal with.[1]

Lloyd George proposed a nonreciprocal defensive pact in case of unprovoked aggression by Germany against France. He offered no military convention, and suggested a duration of only ten years, during which France would occupy the Rhineland in any case. Most important, the draft only "affirmed the common interest" of the Allies in Articles 42-44 of the Treaty of Versailles and promised "consultation" if the Rhineland demilitarization were violated.

Briand rejected the offer on 8 January, emphasizing the importance of the Rhenish clauses for the containment of Germany in the west and the east. Briand also sought to engage the British to defend the status quo on Germany's eastern borders.[2] The Foreign Office concluded that "what France would like is a guarantee against Germany while remaining free to pursue an anti-British policy in every country of the globe!"[3] On 10 January the British cabinet met again. The broader pact urged by Briand was unacceptable. It was meant to tie Britain to France's plan for "continental hegemony." Britain must have a free hand regarding Germany. In addition, there was Lloyd George's economic scheme to consider. "Germany is to us the most important country in Europe, not only on account of our trade with her, but because she is the key to Russia." German reconstruction of devastated Russia under Entente supervision could provide for European commercial recovery and reparations at the same time.[4]

Briand accepted, by way of improving the general atmosphere at Cannes, the principle of an economic conference. But his apparent desire for rapid rapprochement with Britain was his undoing. President Millerand, the conservative press, and Briand's rivals in the Chamber,

[1] Minutes, CAB 93(21), 16 Dec. 1921: PRO CAB 23/28, pp. 269-276; Aide-Mémoire Regarding Conversation on Anglo-French Relations Between Mr. Lloyd-George and M. Briand on 4 Jan. 1922: HI Pap. Loucheur, Box 5, Folder 13.

[2] Note Briand to Lloyd George, "Exposé des vues du gouvernement français," 8 Jan. 1922: MAE Grande Bretagne, vol. 69, nos. 134-140.

[3] Campbell and Villiers, Minutes, 9 and 10 Jan. 1922, Des. #39 Hardinge (Paris) to F.O., W/193/50/17, 5 Jan. 1922: PRO FO 371, vol. 8249, nos. 198-200.

[4] Minutes, CAB 1(22), 10 Jan. 1922: PRO CAB 23/29, pp. 1-6.

among them Tardieu and Poincaré, expressed their alarm. A notorious press photograph of Briand being given a golf lesson by Lloyd George seemed to epitomize the degree to which the French premier had fallen under the other's sway. Millerand and Poincaré, in the name of the Senate Foreign Affairs Commission, demanded that the premier renounce any engagements he had taken and return immediately to Paris to explain his policy.[5] Briand was in an apparent cul-de-sac. He could appeal to the Chamber and perhaps win a vote of confidence. But the price of British cooperation would be high, and if he returned to a policy of force against Germany, he would be tying his career to the fortunes of the French Right. On the other hand, to be chased from office in defeat would hardly advance his career either. On 12 January he defended himself before the Chamber with customary eloquence, then promptly resigned. Thus he was not forced from office, but departed as a martyr to the cause of entente. His return to power three years later, after a Left-Republican electoral victory, was neatly prepared.[6]

Raymond Poincaré constituted a ministry on 15 January 1922. He had himself patiently prepared a return to power. The refusal to seek reelection as president, the resignation from the Reparations Commission, the return to the Senate were all steps away from the "prison" of the Elysée toward the real power of the premier. He used his prestige as wartime president and his access to print and podium in 1920 and 1921 to criticize the treaty and its haphazard execution. But the principal target of his journalistic and oratorical missiles was Germany, specifically the arrogant industrialists of the Ruhr who subverted reparations, drove Allied goods from world markets, and encouraged revanchism in Germany. The theme of his critiques, as in 1919, was guarantees. Security and raw materials were equal parts of the problem of the continued imbalance between French and German potential power. But it was through reparations that France could legally take action. The problem of reparations, Poincaré stated in his ministerial declaration, dominated all others.

Poincaré was sixty-one when he became premier for the second time and foreign minister. He was three years older than Lloyd George and, like his British counterpart, had entered politics as a deputy at the age of twenty-seven. The influences on Poincaré's life have often been discussed. He was a Lorrainer. At the age of ten he watched Prussian *Pickelhauben* bob up and down the main street of his home town, Bar-le-Duc, and the desire for recovery of the Lost Provinces certainly imposed itself on his politics. But his enemies would accuse him of obses-

[5] Tel. Millerand to Briand, with marginal notes by Loucheur, 10 Jan. 1922: HI Pap. Loucheur, Box 5, Folder 13.

[6] Suarez, *Briand*, V, 390-406.

sion, of having plotted the war from 1912 to 1914. He was a lawyer, and he exhibited in his diplomatic style the attention to textual detail and the deductive mind befitting the advocate. But his detractors considered him nothing more than the provincial lawyer, unable to see beyond his own petty and nationalist arguments to the larger issues of a broken continent. The criticisms are inaccurate, for Poincaré's nationalism and professional discipline balanced each other. To be sure, he revered solemn treaties and respected precision above all, but the purpose of treaties was to define relationships. If they failed in that purpose through imprecision or ineffectiveness, it was the duty of statesmen to revise or replace them. Versailles defined the context of Poincaré's diplomacy; it was not an end in itself. His career was built on crises—the war, the Ruhr occupation, the financial panic of 1926. Hence, to the Left he was eristic, "Poincaré-la-guerre." But to the Right he was a symbol of order and stability, precisely the man to restore confidence in a crisis.[7]

Poincaré was short and jaunty, possessed of energy and endurance, and thrusting from his chin was a short triangular beard. When aroused, his uneven eyes pierced menacingly, and his countenance turned Mephistophelian, dangerous and grim. He spoke often in public, but he lacked the magniloquence of a Briand. His style was halting, his content predictable. A staunch Republican and conservative bourgeois, Poincaré chose voluntary eclipse during the Dreyfus Affair lest he be forced to take a stand damaging to the centrist. Yet he raised Catholic eyebrows by wedding a divorcée. In 1903 he became a senator and in 1912 rose to premier, then to the presidency, on a platform of military preparedness. He entered the war with "hearty high spirits" but could not have been unaffected by the government's flight to Bordeaux in August 1914. His presidential septennium launched him into the postwar period as the most prestigious politician in France.

During his last days as premier, Briand spoke of the need to create a united Europe, lest the Old Continent surrender leadership to the new giants on her flanks. Poincaré did not deal in the currency of dreams, yet he perhaps understood better than Briand the preconditions for such unity: the weakening of Germany and assurance of political and economic security for the lesser nations of Europe. Like de Gaulle after him, and with more justification, Poincaré envisioned

[7] Despite his stature as one of the towering politicians of the Third Republic and his complex personality, Raymond Poincaré has attracted few biographers, none in English. Sisley Huddleston's *Poincaré—A Biographical Portrait* (London, 1924) was a topical and popular sketch of the British government's current arch-rival, and is a compendium of clichés. What insights can be painfully pried from the life of this fascinating political introvert are offered by two of France's leading historians, Jacques Chastenet, *Raymond Poincaré* (Paris, 1948), and Pierre Miquel, *Poincaré* (Paris, 1961).

European cooperation through gradual steps, with French rights carefully protected. It is dangerous to attribute specific schemes to Poincaré; as his friend Jacques Bardoux admitted, he was by nature a critic, not a creator. But Poincaré certainly understood that France could not remain a Great Power in juxtaposition with a unified Germany, except by close alliance with the Anglo-Saxon nations. She must have Germany divided, or her sovereignty curtailed or balanced by an integrated Western bloc. Like Tardieu, he hoped to make France the continental "cutting edge" of such a bloc. But by 1922 Britain had abandoned France, and the United States had abandoned Europe. What remained then of the compromise of 1919? Poincaré is considered the symbol of the will to execute the Treaty of Versailles, but he entered office clearly dissatisfied with the treaty. As a blueprint, it was a failure.

Poincaré's ascendency brought changes in the Quai d'Orsay. Briand had quietly ignored a scandal in which his collaborator, Philippe Berthelot, was involved. Now Poincaré seized on the pretext to rid himself of the powerful bureaucrat.[8] The premier chose to be his own foreign minister and his own secretary-general. Director of Political Affairs Emmanuel de Peretti de la Rocca became Poincaré's top professional assistant. Peretti was a conservative aristocrat, fiercely anti-Bolshevik and anti-German. His advancement at Berthelot's expense and Poincaré's personal rule over the ministry would tend to win little sympathy for the tandem from career diplomats. Poincaré, like Clemenceau, kept his own counsel. But he worked through the Quai d'Orsay, resisted conference diplomacy, and promised a strong policy. Only in the dark days of late 1923 would the ministerial and diplomatic team begin to lose confidence in their chief.

The Chamber's right wing and the national press cheered Poincaré's timely appearance, while German journals reported that "in the Rhineland, the separatists rejoice." Official reactions to Poincaré were more realistic. Lord Hardinge, British ambassador in Paris, applauded Poincaré's expressed hope for a reforging of the Entente, but he feared that the fickle Chamber would make concessions difficult.[9] The Belgian

[8] Berthelot had attempted to use his office to promote foreign loans for his brother's failing Banque Industrielle de Chine. In a fit of vindictiveness, Poincaré planned to preside personally over Berthelot's hearing. Peretti talked him out of the indiscretion, but a council of his peers condemned Berthelot to inactivity for a period of ten years. The British Foreign Office noted the strict sentence with amusement, predicting that Berthelot would be back in short order. The forecast was accurate, but as long as Poincaré remained in office, Briand's powerful collaborator was out. See August Felix Charles de Beaupoil, comte de St. Aulaire, *Confession d'un vieux diplomate* (Paris, 1953), pp. 601-607.

[9] Des. #130 Hardinge to F.O., W457/50/17, 13 Jan. 1922: PRO FO 371, vol. 8249, nos. 274-278.

ambassador concluded simply that Poincaré would follow Briand's policy—he had no other choice.[10] In February Walter Rathenau confided to the new British Rhineland high commissioner, Lord Kilmarnock, that he was pleased to notice no increase in French chauvinism since the change.[11] Cognizant of his image, Poincaré sought to project himself as a moderate. He announced his intention to rely on no parliamentary majority, to choose his ministers from various parties, and to return to a kind of *Union Sacrée.* Despite a vote of confidence of 472-107, the fiction of a national government was impossible to preserve. The Left offered an alternative to the hard-line foreign policy of the governments of the *chambre bleu horizon*. Led by Léon Blum, the Socialists called for disarmament, collective security, and a generous reparations settlement worked out by all the powers. They attacked Poincaré as the *porte-parole* of narrow nationalism.[12] But at the moment the ex-wartime president embodied the mood of bourgeois France. Millerand turned to Poincaré just as Poincaré had chosen Clemenceau in 1917, because he could be counted on to see the struggle through to the finish.

POINCARÉ VERSUS LLOYD GEORGE: SECURITY DEADLOCK

The change of government did not determine a sharp change in French policy. Poincaré had not altered his opinion that the Allied occupation of the Rhineland should last as long as Germany owed reparations, or that the fate of the Rhineland was the crux of the security issue. But his first concern, in 1922 as in 1919, was with the dangerous divergence between Britain and France on the interpretation of their roles in the execution of the peace settlement. His fears had been realized. The 1919 security pacts had collapsed, and French governments were forced to drag Britain reluctantly behind in attempts to extract reparations. Instead of achieving their goals, France and Britain had only destroyed Allied harmony and given Germany new reason to defy the treaty. The new premier would try to secure an Allied agreement devoid of the seeds of future misunderstanding.

The two dominant figures of the early postwar years, Poincaré and Lloyd George, met privately in the British embassy in Paris on 14 January 1922. The French premier-designate reviewed the inadequacies

[10] Des. #530/250PF Gaiffier (Paris) to Jaspar, 14 Jan. 1922: MAE Bel., Correspondance Politique, France, 1922.

[11] Des. #38 Kilmarnock (Coblenz) to F.O., C2724/336/18, 21 Feb. 1922: PRO FO 371, vol. 7520, nos. 121-123.

[12] Richard Gombin, *Les socialistes et la guerre*, pp. 39-44.

of the British draft treaty. A security pact must be reciprocal, it must be accompanied by a military convention, and it must run much longer than the ten years proposed. In response, Lloyd George alluded to the other problems left unsettled at Cannes: Tangier, Turkey, reparations. Poincaré agreed that a pact would be untimely until the governments found the bases for worldwide accord.[13] The prime minister returned to the cabinet in London. The British government decided to let the French make the next move.[14]

The central importance of the Rhineland in the security duel became clear at once. Tirard noted the failure of Poincaré to mention the need for a clause concerning Articles 42-44 in his conversation with Lloyd George,[15] but the reminder was unnecessary. Poincaré had already locked horns with the Belgian government on the same point. In 1920 the Belgian government acted on its newly won escape from the neutrality treaties of 1839 by concluding a defensive alliance with France that specified the Rhineland as the optimal field of defense. Now the Belgians seized the occasion to negotiate a similar pact with the British. But the proposed Anglo-Belgian pact that came under French scrutiny did not specify violation of Articles 42-44 by Germany as *casus foederis*. The French premier protested that such a hiatus would violate the 1920 accord and damage his negotiating position with London.[16] On 23 January 1922 he released his own draft for a pact calling for a British guarantee of Rhineland demilitarization and Anglo-French collaboration "on all questions of a nature to endanger general peace or threaten the order established by the peace treaties." It included reciprocity (a concession to French pride), a military convention, and it would run for thirty years.[17]

The British foreign secretary, Lord Curzon, explained his reaction in a candid memorandum. He admitted *in camera* that he indeed considered the eastern frontier of France as the British frontier also. But he despaired of French good faith. It would be foolish, Curzon wrote, to expect the French to honor an alliance when they could not respect an entente. There could be no pact unless all other questions were first settled to British satisfaction.[18] The French ambassador, St. Aulaire,

[13] MAE Memo, "Conversation entre Poincaré et Lloyd George à l'ambassade anglaise," 14 Jan. 1922: MAE Grande Bretagne, vol. 69, nos. 210-216.

[14] Minutes, CAB 2(22), 18 Jan. 1922: PRO CAB 23/29, pp. 11-12.

[15] Des. Tirard to MAE, 17 Jan. 1922: MAE Grande Bretagne, vol. 69, nos. 221-223.

[16] Tel. Poincaré to Margerie (Brussels), 20 Jan. 1922: MAE Grande Bretagne, vol. 69, nos. 269-270.

[17] Tel. Poincaré to St. Aulaire (London), "Projet français," 23 Jan. 1922: MAE Grande Bretagne, vol. 70, nos. 27-28.

[18] Memo Curzon, "On the question of an Anglo-French Alliance," 28 Dec. 1921: DBFP, XVI, 860-870.

reported that Curzon would give in on reciprocity and an extension to fifteen or twenty years, but Parliament would never engage to defend the Rhineland against German reoccupation or the status quo in Eastern Europe. "You conceive of an alliance as mechanistic," explained Curzon, "with every circumstance, possible or impossible, accounted for. We see it as organic. The project of M. Poincaré is static; mine is dynamic."[19]

The pact was important to the new French premier. Just as Briand's later exploits have hidden the nationalistic policy he pursued in 1921, so has Poincaré's Ruhr policy led historians to overlook his dedication to the Entente. But the British had to be educated to believe that Germany, not France, was the major continental threat. Public opinion in France expected a security pact; Poincaré even reinforced that opinion with a government-inspired press campaign. He was aided by the work of the *Association France-Grande Bretagne*, an organization subscribed to by most of the political and business luminaries, which publicized the danger of Russian-German cooperation and agitated for a close Western alliance.[20] Once the press campaign was in full swing, Poincaré made his pitch in London. He was prepared to make concessions.

The length of the pact might be shortened, the formal military convention might be sacrificed, the clause on consultation might be made the subject of an exchange of letters instead of a part of the pact, but on one point he would not budge. Poincaré instructed St. Aulaire to use the concessions to secure above all a British guarantee of the Rhenish demilitarized zone.[21] His demarches went unanswered. On 9 February St. Aulaire informed Paris bluntly that the British were stalling. The cabinet had not even seen the French counterproposal and Curzon warned the French "not to risk the pact by seeking to ameliorate it beyond the possible."[22] The stumbling block was the British unwillingness to guarantee the status quo in Eastern Europe, or accept a permanent French presence on the Rhine, which, in the view of the Foreign Office, meant French continental hegemony.

Unable to make progress through official channels, Poincaré countered by sending his personal friend Jacques Bardoux to London. His

[19] Tel. St. Aulaire to Poincaré, 27 Jan. 1922: MAE Grande Bretagne, vol. 70, nos. 70-79; St. Aulaire, *Confession*, pp. 614-615.

[20] On the press campaign and Association France-Grande Bretagne, see Kaplan, "France's Road to Genoa," pp. 140-141.

[21] Tel. Poincaré to St. Aulaire, 29 Jan. 1922: MAE Grande Bretagne, vol. 70, nos. 109-112.

[22] Tel. St. Aulaire to Poincaré, 9 Feb. 1922: MAE Grande Bretagne, vol. 70, nos. 219-220.

report was even gloomier than St. Aulaire's. The industrial crisis obsessed the nation; new political commitments to the continent were unpopular. The prospect of Russian-German ties only led the Foreign Office to consider intensifying its own overtures to Moscow, while the Left Liberal and Labour opposition leaned even more toward such a course.[23] The cost of a British guarantee would be, at the very least, French submission to Britain's Genoa plans. But Poincaré was in no mood to participate in Lloyd George's resurrection of Germany and the Soviet Union without assurances of French security and reparations. It was not enough that the British prime minister planned to gather at Genoa all the victorious powers to compromise French rights. This time delegations from Germany and Russia would be present. No largesse could be expected from the outcasts, both of whom owed the Allied nations large sums of money. The Bolsheviks refused to recognize the wartime and prewar tsarist debts or to make good on Allied property lost during the civil war. The only possible result of the economic conference, in Poincaré's mind, would be injury to France should the discussion turn to reparations, security, or disarmament. As for Russia, British and French policies had diverged ever since the Armistice.[24] The Anglo-Russian Trade Agreement of May 1921 was as much of a "betrayal" to France as the Franco-Turkish accord had been to Britain. But the inability of France and Britain to agree on the terms with which they would approach the Soviets, and their fear that German-Russian economic contacts would escape their control, only served to drive the defeated powers together. The British also encouraged rumors in the pre-Genoa period to the effect that the French were secretly negotiating their own modus vivendi with Moscow, rumors that only infuriated Poincaré and damaged chances for accord on either Russia or security.[25]

Poincaré was intent on emasculating Lloyd George's program. On 5 February he insisted that no discussions take place at Genoa that bore in any way on the peace treaties. Next, he sought to delay the conference, insisting on the need for extensive preparations. He appealed to the Americans to support this request, if not decline to attend al-

[23] Kaplan, "France's Road to Genoa," pp. 142-143.

[24] See Richard H. Ullmann, *Anglo-Soviet Relations, 1917-1921*, 3 vols. (Princeton, 1972); Louis Fisher, *The Soviets in World Affairs* (New York, 1971); Piotr Wandycz, *France and Her Eastern Allies*.

[25] The Quai d'Orsay was evidently not trying to "steal a march" on Britain and Germany. Certain officials and businessmen surely viewed Russia as a natural anti-German ally and potential economic partner, but progress was stymied by the Soviet repudiation of Tsarist debts and by Poincaré's efforts to reforge the Entente by playing up the German-Russian danger. Cf. Kaplan, "France's Road to Genoa," pp. 160-170, and Wandycz, *France and Her Eastern Allies*, p. 258.

together. He asked that the invitation list be expanded to include all of France's Eastern European collaborators. Finally, he insisted that all discussion with the U.S.S.R. be subordinated to Moscow's acceptance of strict prior conditions. In response, Lloyd George openly accused Poincaré of sabotage.[26] But the telling blow to his fanciful economic construct came from Washington.

The American government was skeptical of Lloyd George's schemes. He seemed to be bypassing the unsolved problems of reparations and political stability in order to promote a grandiose plan for reconstruction. The United States would not be drawn in. "Currencies cannot be stabilized until inflation has stopped," wrote Herbert Hoover, "and inflation cannot be stopped until government budgets are balanced, and government budgets cannot be balanced until there is a proper settlement of reparations."[27] The Europeans would doubtless seek leniency on the war debt question. If they could promise political stability and removal of barriers to commerce, the United States would consider participation. That, however, would require "disillusioning" the French on the fundamental economic question—reparations. Finally, Lloyd George's schemes for an international consortium to develop Caucasian oil violated the principle of the Open Door and the interests of Standard Oil. Secretary of State Hughes concluded that American involvement in European affairs would come, not through government, but through private American investment. He declined the invitation to Genoa.[28]

Poincaré, of course, hoped his attack on Genoa would bring Lloyd George around on the security issue.[29] When the two premiers held a surprise meeting at Boulogne on 25 February, Lloyd George deplored the Anglo-French discord, "the worst since Fashoda." In parting, he admitted that he was prepared to consider the security question. Poincaré took this as the expected cue.[30] Bolstered by intelligence that the British War Office desired military collaboration with France in any case, he authorized St. Aulaire to drop the demand for a military convention, concluding: "It would be possible to make this concession if we had assurance that it would facilitate acceptance by the British gov-

[26] Tel. Montille (London) to MAE, 6 Feb. 1922: MAE Pap. Millerand, Gênes 2, nos. 5-6.

[27] Memo Hoover to Harding, "Memorandum on the major questions before the proposed economic conference in Europe," 21 Jan. 1922, cited by Link, *Die amerikanische Stabilisierungspolitik*, p. 107.

[28] Ibid., pp. 108-114.

[29] Tel. Poincaré to St. Aulaire, 17 Feb. 1922: MAE Grande Bretagne, vol. 70, nos. 239-240.

[30] Procès-Verbal, "Conversation entre M. Poincaré et M. Lloyd George à Boulogne sur mer," 25 Feb. 1922: MAE Pap. Millerand, Gênes 2, nos. 169-200.

ernment of Article 2." This was the clause of the draft treaty concerned with Rhenish demilitarization. On this point no concession was admissible.[31]

Poincaré and Lloyd George pursued their diplomatic standoff through March. At the end of the month Lloyd George denied before the Cabinet that he was seeking to use the pact to threaten or to blackmail France, but he "believed it would be useful to reserve the pact to bring pressure on France in connection with reparations and the treatment of Germany generally."[32] French resistance to the Genoa Conference was equally adamant. Great hopes had been nurtured in Britain and Russia, wrote Seydoux. If the French government did not take a position at once concerning Russia, it would be faced at Genoa, as at Washington, with a *fait accompli*. A British-German consortium would control the incalculable resources of Russia and the spoils of the war would go to the enemy.[33]

The conference finally opened on 10 April 1922. Poincaré sent Louis Barthou, minister of justice and personal crony, in his place. Barthou was ordered to prevent any discussion potentially injurious to French treaty rights. He could make use of the Belgian and Eastern European delegations to block any British attempts to make concessions to Germany or Russia.[34] Barthou was successful; the conference was a disaster. None of the prior conditions for success obtained, and Lloyd George therefore summoned the outcast nations to the European council under circumstances that could only enhance German and Russian prestige. With the Western powers unable or unwilling to extend a helping hand to devastated Russia without insistence on major prior concessions, the Soviets had no recourse but to turn to Germany. On the German side, Baron Ago von Maltzan, head of the eastern section of the Foreign Office, had been pushing for detente with Moscow. Walther Rathenau, now foreign minister in Wirth's reorganized cabinet, surrendered to Maltzan's pleadings. The two European pariahs came together on 16 April when Rathenau and Soviet Foreign Affairs Commissar Georgi Chicherin signed an accord at Rapallo, a coastal town a short drive from Genoa.

To the Western powers, the "bombshell" of Rapallo was a defiant statement of disinterest in collective economic recovery. It was widely

[31] Tel. Poincaré to St. Aulaire, 4 Mar. 1922: MAE Grande Bretagne, vol. 70, nos. 250-251.

[32] Minutes, CAB 21(22), 28 Mar. 1922: PRO CAB 23/29, p. 343.

[33] Note Seydoux pour le PdC, 17 Mar. 1922: MAE Pap. Millerand, Gênes 4, nos. 102-105.

[34] Note Poincaré to Barthou, "Instructions," 6 Apr. 1922: MAE Pap. Millerand, Gênes 5, nos. 2-14.

assumed that the pact, which settled financial and economic questions left over from the war, included secret military clauses. In fact, Russo-German military cooperation had already begun with Chancellor Wirth's knowledge. The 1920 panic over National Bolshevism took on verisimilitude. On 24 April Poincaré responded with a speech at Bar-le-Duc: "The events at Genoa singularly confirm all that we have known of the attitude prevalent in the Reich. . . .[This pact] consecrates the rapprochement that tomorrow can represent a direct menace to Poland and even an indirect menace to ourselves." The Genoa Conference was a British idea, he concluded, and Frenchmen attended only because of the previous government's promise. Poincaré called for immediate dissolution of the conference.[35] The Franco-British duel since January had been a struggle for retention of initiative in European affairs. Now it seemed that initiative had passed from the hands of both Western powers. Poincaré instructed Barthou to block any possible accord with Russia,[36] and on 19 May the grand conference dissolved, having accomplished nothing but the planning of an experts' conference on Russia later in the year.

The disastrous results of Lloyd George's personal policy (Lord Curzon strongly opposed the Genoa idea) led Poincaré to believe that the prime minister might now be willing to see the French side of things. On 2 May, St. Aulaire began looking for an opportunity to reopen the security talks. The need for a public affirmation of the Entente was all the more necessary now, wired Poincaré, and the French argument for common defense of the Rhine made all the more sense.[37] But this time it was the French premier who underestimated his British rival. Poincaré's assertion of independence made it imperative that Britain not make concessions until other matters were put to rest. Again Poincaré unleashed the weapon of public opinion. The Entente's worst fears regarding Genoa had been realized, yet Lloyd George still resisted the logic driving France and Britain together! Instead, he received Wirth and Rathenau during the last days at Genoa for private conversations. Why, asked *Le Temps*, was Britain seeking entry to the Russo-German entente? "But as the price of entry, what can Britain offer? Financial support to Russia and political support to Germany, to the common profit of German and British industry. Against whom is this policy di-

[35] MAE Memo, "Discours de Poincaré à Bar-le-Duc," 24 Apr. 1922: MAE Pap. Millerand, Gênes 5, no. 88.

[36] Tel. Poincaré to Barthou (Genoa), 9 May 1922: MAE Pap. Millerand, Gênes 7, nos. 24-26.

[37] Tel. Poincaré to St. Aulaire, 2 May 1922: MAE Grande Bretagne, vol. 71, no. 37; Tel. Poincaré to St. Aulaire, 11 May 1922: MAE Pap. Millerand, Gênes 7, no. 104.

rected? Against France, inevitably."[38] But Poincaré's repeated démarches went unacknowledged. Two weeks later Lloyd George told his cabinet: "I do not think M. Poincaré puts much stress on the conclusion of a pact."[39] The prime minister ignored the rapping at the door. The last French mention of the pact came as late as 28 July 1922, but the British had dropped the notion until further notice.

The failure to reforge the Entente in early 1922 stemmed from the conviction of both governments that the other's policy was determined by ulterior motives. But Lloyd George was clearly unprepared to satisfy the French craving for security on the Rhine, a concession that could only stem from the assumption, which Lloyd George did not share, that Germany was still the paramount continental threat. On his side, Poincaré did not do all that he could to dispel British fears of French imperialism during the first months of 1922. Not only did he refuse to make economic concessions, but he also chose to take up again the French Rhineland policy, a fact that could not fail to influence the Foreign Office. A security pact was designed to make French adventures in Western Germany unnecessary, not to make Britain a partner in them.

RETURN TO THE RHINELAND

Poincaré recognized clearly the weakness of the French bargaining position. France had many needs, financial, economic, and military, which only Germany and her former allies could meet, but little in the way of currency to purchase foreign cooperation. The only solid sacrifice Poincaré could make was the evacuation of the Rhineland, or the renunciation of France's right to use that occupation to take sanctions against Germany. But such a sacrifice would eliminate the only guarantee he possessed that Germany would honor her agreements. Force or the threat of force against Germany was his only means of pressure also against Britain and the United States.

Why did Poincaré revive the flirtation with Rhenish separatism? It was a veiled threat, surely—a constant reminder to Berlin and London of the stranglehold France had on the Reich. It was a bluff, and it kept the issue of separation before the public so that France might point to an indigenous movement, should the Rhenish question impose itself in the future. It satisfied French nationalists and so removed one source of criticism from that powerful quarter. It was consistent with the assumption that German democracy was a sham, that only territorial

[38] "Les Pactes et les Actes," *Le Temps*, 6 May 1922.

[39] Minutes, CAB 29(22), 23 May 1922: PRO CAB 23/30, pp. 85-98.

guarantees sufficed to secure France against invasion. But as is often the case when many rationales can be offered in explanation of a single phenomenon, none is convincing. Poincaré did not press for a showdown in the Rhineland so much as he merely refused to halt the advance of French activities there. In the standard practice of statesmen groping by several paths toward an uncertain goal, he wished to keep his options open. Poincaré was not obsessed by the Rhineland as were those who saw only past glories and the geographical felicity of the "natural boundaries." But he was affected enough by the mystique of the Rhine to preserve hopes for a future Rhenish state.

Tirard and Degoutte wasted no time in thrusting their old programs at the new premier. Degoutte again predicted the dissolution of Germany from its own centrifugal forces and urged Poincaré to support federalism.[40] Tirard called for a new customs regime, control of railroads, and new currency for the Rhineland. He renewed his plea for the suppression of the Reich commissioner and the expulsion of the Bavarian and Prussian functionaries. He advocated, in fact, a complete revision of the Rhineland Agreement and justified it by Article 432 of the treaty, which left it to the Allies to "make whatever arrangements relative to the occupation which they deem necessary, and which Germany engages to observe."[41]

Tirard backed his case for expulsion of the Prussian functionaries with some striking figures. He reported that 60 percent of Rhenish customs officials and 40 percent of the teachers were originally from nonoccupied Prussia.[42] In fact, this practice dated back 250 years in the Prussian administration and was a prime tactic in centralized state-building. But Tirard saw it as despotic and began invoking the Rhineland Commission's power to veto administrative appointments. Berlin and the Allies in Coblenz began a quiet struggle. One after another the German government nominated officials hailing from Silesia, Brandenburg, or East Prussia, and one by one Tirard rejected them. On 3 March Poincaré extended his full approval.[43] It seemed that France was finally responding to the argument that the Rhineland would flee from Germany once the Prussian stranglehold was broken. To British observers, it was only another example of the French "policy of pinpricks."

[40] Rapport mensuel de l'Armée du Rhin, Degoutte to MAE, Jan. 1922: MAE Rive Gauche, vol. 64.

[41] Tel. Tirard to MAE, 2 Jan. 1922; Tel. Tirard to Poincaré, "Secret: politique rhénane," 12 Mar. 1922: MAE Rive Gauche, vol. 5, nos. 116-118; vol. 6, nos. 33-40.

[42] Report, Comité de renseignements et de Sûreté, 13 Dec. 1921: MAE Rive Gauche, vol. 6, no. 113.

[43] Tel. Poincaré to Tirard, 3 Mar. 1922: MAE Rive Gauche, vol. 6, no. 6.

The signs of the new French initiatives on the Left Bank sparked a British response. The immediate cause for discord was a notorious legal battle involving Joseph Smeets, the disreputable leader of the *Rheinische Republikanische Volkspartei.* Smeets favored total separation from Germany and received money from Tirard, but his tiny movement operated mostly in the Belgian zone of occupation. In fact, Smeets's foreign contacts and most of his support were Belgian; he was especially close to the expansionist *Comité Politique National Belge* of Pierre Nothomb. Smeets was of working-class origin, the type of street politician and petty tyrant that was common in the chaotic cities of postwar Germany. He was an Independent Socialist at the end of the war and even served on the Cologne Workers' and Soldiers' Council, where he followed the anti-separatist line. He left the party in 1919 and apparently seized on separatism as a vehicle for his ambition. He ruled his separatist party council with an imperiousness that brought many defections. The Rhenish Republicans aimed at winning the proletariat, promising revolution through separatism. Hence, Smeets was in ideological but not actual competition with Dorten's Catholic bourgeois movement.

In December 1921 German government agents arrested Smeets on a charge of libel against the president of the Reich, Friedrich Ebert. Tirard immediately intervened to secure his release with the support of Briand, who was obliged to pacify angry nationalist deputies in the French Chambers.[44] Berlin protested, but the Conference of Ambassadors upheld the authority of the Rhineland Commission. The British government took the opportunity to question the motives of the French government, and in March 1922 the British ambassador in Paris informed Poincaré that in the future His Majesty's Government would entertain protests from Berlin concerning the conduct of the Rhineland Commission.[45] It was an empty gesture. As long as France and Belgium stood united in the Coblenz commission, Britain could not prevent it from being made a tool of their policy on the Rhine.

The Smeets issue dragged on throughout 1922 and, in the end, Lord

[44] Des. Briand to Margerie, 7 Dec. 1921; Let. Briand to Maurice Barrès, 7 Dec. 1921: MAE Rive Gauche, vol. 26, nos. 193-195. Smeets's arrest stemmed from his journalistic characterizations of German public figures. He accused the Leipzig police prefect of "boundless cowardice and blundering" and of being "hundsgemein und nichtswürdig." President Ebert was "a fattened pig who has pains to carry his huge belly and rolls of lard in the neck," "dick und schwabbelig wie heisse Blutwurste. . . ." Ebert was a "bloated replacement for the Hohenzollerns, idolater of the pipe and bottle, representative of the Republic of Merchants." Smeets also accused Ebert of having violated his own ration quotas during the hard winter of 1918-1919. Although Smeets's defamations were scandalous, the arrest was clearly political—similar attacks from the Right went unpunished.

[45] Let. British Embassy Paris to MAE, 9 Mar. 1922: MAE Rive Gauche, vol. 200, no. 108.

Kilmarnock refused to defer to the Franco-Belgian majority for the purpose of preserving a semblance of Allied unity. By a two-to-one vote, Smeets was released permanently. The majority decisions on Smeets and an ordinance integrating the Rhineland into the Western European time zone comprised the first public display of disunity in Coblenz. The Foreign Office simply concluded: "The French have made perfect fools of themselves over this miserable creature."[46]

The British campaign against French power in the Rhineland found another issue to pursue, that of the financial burden the Rhineland Commission represented for a Germany struggling to pay reparations.[47] On 10 March 1922 the Supreme Council created a committee to investigate the possibility of reducing the expenses of the occupation. Thanks to the Franco-Belgian majority, the committee's report was tame. The president of the Conference of Ambassadors, Jules Cambon, ruled that each Rhineland commissariat was free to dispense its budget as it pleased: "If the German government wishes to reduce occupation costs, let it abolish the Reich commissariat!"[48] In fact, the cost of the Rhineland Commission was tiny compared with the military expense of the occupation, but the British pressed their point. Poincaré rightly interpreted the issue as "a maneuver against the services of the French High Commissariat and generally against French influence in the Rhineland." But at this point the French received a rude surprise. The Belgians suddenly adopted the British point of view, arguing that each commissariat within the Rhineland Commission was subject to the will of the Allies as a whole. Thus the financial dispute was a test case. The French wished to be able to pursue their Rhenish policy without interference. The British wished to be able to restrain the French, but to conduct a separate policy in pivotal Cologne. The Belgians were in the middle. Deathly afraid that France might come to dominate the Rhineland alone, the Belgians would have to participate in any French adventures. They wished to impose Allied unity, to avoid British obstructionism or French *faits accomplis*. Poincaré chose

[46] Note Tyrrell, 7 Sept. 1922: PRO FO 371, vol. 7521, no. 181.

[47] Disputes over occupation costs dated back to the very inception of the post-treaty occupation in June 1919. At that time, France proved conciliatory and accepted reimbursement of occupation costs from the Germans at a lower per capita rate than the other powers, her occupation force being by far the largest. In 1921 occupation costs were politicized by German inability to meet the bill and led to conflict between the European Allies and the United States, which had politely permitted the Allies to recover expenses first, then found itself with no means of recovering its own costs when the Germans pleaded straitened circumstances. The 1922 dispute described here was not primarily a financial issue, but a British political offensive against France's Rhineland "establishment."

[48] MAE Memo, "Déclarations de M. Cambon, président de la conférence d'ambassadeurs," 5 Apr. 1922: MAE Rive Gauche, vol. 200, no. 119.

to avoid a showdown. He refused to subject the French commissariat to the scrutiny of an interallied enquiry, but he would agree to certain economies and to individual investigations by each nation.[49] The issue was a red herring—per capita, the French occupation was the most frugal of all—but it served to reveal the central position that the Belgian delegate would play in a showdown in the Rhineland Commission.

British protests and enquiries had only a nuisance value. But the Foreign Office also sought a real alteration in the balance of power on the Rhine. Once again, it looked to the United States. American troops still occupied a small enclave centered on Coblenz; they were a tiny vestige of the great expeditionary force that crossed the Atlantic in 1918. The rump occupation remained, even after the signature of a peace treaty between Germany and the United States in August 1921.[50] The first suggestion that America, instead of gradually pulling out altogether, should seek full participation on the Rhineland Commission came from Walther Rathenau. In February 1922 the German minister also suggested that England might seek to increase its own troop levels, to recover the Bonn sector transferred by Britain to France in 1920. The British were wary. Rathenau's suggestions were clearly another attempt to promote disunity in the Allied camp. In addition, Kilmarnock had spoken with the American commander, General Henry Allen, who announced Washington's intention to continue reduction of troop levels. Allen nevertheless shared British hopes that the American flag would remain on the Rhine.[51]

It is a measure of the importance that the Foreign Office attached to the Rhenish balance of power that, despite the signs that it would fail, Curzon acted on Rathenau's suggestions.[52] Miles Lampson, newly promoted chief of the Foreign Office Central European division, described the British attitude: "All the arguments from our point of view are in favor of the Americans remaining. One of the chief ones is that it puts a brake on French activities in the Rhineland."[53] But American

[49] Memo Secretary-General of the Conference of Ambassadors to Laroche, 28 June 1922; Let. Hardinge to J. Cambon, 5 July 1922; Tel. Tirard to MAE, 25 July 1922: MAE Rive Gauche, vol. 200, nos. 260-261.

[50] The multiplicity of reasons—often contradictory—behind the continued American presence in the Rhineland from 1918 to 1923 is the subject of Nelson, *Victors Divided.*

[51] Des. #38, Kilmarnock to F.O., "French Policy in the Rhineland," C2724/336/18, 21 Feb. 1922: Des. #43, Kilmarnock to F.O., "United States Participation in Administration of Rhineland," C2848/336/18, 23 Feb. 1922: PRO FO 371, vol. 7520, nos. 121-123, 128-131.

[52] Tel. #259, F.O. (Waterlow) to Geddes (Washington), 6 Mar. 1922: PRO FO 371, vol. 7520, no. 133.

[53] Minutes, Des. #93, Ryan (Coblenz) to F.O., C4769/336/18, 28 Mar. 1922: PRO FO 371, vol. 7520, nos. 182-185.

influence was to be moral only, and on 20 March President Harding chose to honor his campaign pledge by promising to have all U.S. troops home by July. On 7 April the former American commissioner, opponent of separation, and architect of the Rhineland Commission, Pierrepont Noyes, attacked Poincaré for the provocative Rhenish policy, which, he said, endangered world peace. General Allen appealed to Washington for a reconsideration of Harding's position, citing the "impartial and moderating influence" of the American presence.[54] His appeal was quickly seconded by all the Allied governments, including the French. America's sudden announcement had surprised everyone. To the British and Germans, the presence of an American observer (Noyes until May 1920; Allen thereafter) served as a moral, if not legal, check on France's putative ambitions on the Rhine. To all parties, especially the French, the American toehold in Europe preserved the hope that Washington might reverse its policy and take an active (i.e., financial) role in European stabilization. Pressure from Secretary Hughes sufficed for the moment. On 3 June he wired Berlin that the American flag would remain in Coblenz, but that the occupation would be cut to a bare thousand men.[55] The United States was ultimately committed to bringing the troops home, not to deeper involvement in a sticky European affair, and Washington refused full participation on the Rhineland Commission. Troop cuts continued and where doughboys moved out, *poilus* moved in.

The British government also tried Rathenau's other suggestion—increase in the British zone of occupation. Foch and the French delayed, then refused to hand back the extra territory voluntarily relinquished by Britain in 1920. British initiatives in opposition to French influence in the Rhineland, therefore, all met with failure. If the French held Belgium to the line, they would be in a position to rule the occupied territories as they pleased.

THE ANTICS OF DORTEN AND SMEETS; BELGIAN AND GERMAN INTERFERENCE

The advent of Poincaré also signaled an increase in the activity of the separatists under Dorten and Smeets. But in dealing with their Rhenish puppets the French authorities did not have things all their own way. The leaders were men of no prestige or ability. It is safe to assume that a large minority of their followers were agents or informers

[54] Tel. Allen (Coblenz) to Secretary of State, 24 Mar. 1922: FRUS 1922, II, 213-214.

[55] Tel. Hughes to Houghton (Berlin), 3 June 1922: FRUS 1922, II, 218. See Nelson, *Victors Divided*, pp. 197-200.

for Berlin. Their movements were thoroughly discredited; newspapers referred to them as creations of the French and Belgian authorities. If their rallies and publications kept the autonomy issue before the Rhenish people, they also destroyed the possibility of normal citizens, much less civic leaders, associating with it. The German government could not have done a better job than Tirard himself in having separatist and autonomist ideas labeled as treasonous. Finally, and most dangerously, the separatists were uncontrollable.

The principal problem posed by Smeets's Rhenish Republicans was the movement's close connection with Belgium. The Brussels government was favorable to separatism in 1919, supported the French Rhineland program at Paris, and ordered the Belgian military to encourage separatism in its zone. But as important to Brussels as the expulsion of Prussian power was the prevention of a solidification of French power there. A Rhenish Republic under French domination, according to postwar premiers Paul Hymans, Carton de Wiart, and Paul Theunis, Foreign Minister Henri Jaspar, and Ambassador Gaiffier d'Hestroy, would pose a serious threat to Belgian independence. The small and struggling state, weakened by internal strife, would be encircled by France.[56]

After Versailles, the Belgian government neglected to rescind its instructions concerning support of separatism until July 1921, when Briand also called a halt to French Rhenish initiatives. But by then the government's attitude did not determine events in the Belgian zone. The Belgian high command emerged from the war with the same jealousy for authority as the French. Despite the protests of High Commissioner Rolin-Jaequemyns, the character of the Belgian occupation was harsh and aggravating, while certain Belgian officers took it upon themselves to collaborate with the separatists. Also operating independently of government was the *Comité Politique National Belge*. After the Peace Conference, its leader, Pierre Nothomb, broke with the government and began execution of a private policy in the Rhineland.[57]

[56] These brief remarks concerning the Rhenish policy of the Belgian governments after 1918 summarize the evidence of many notes and telegrams over the period 1915-1923 to be found in the archives of the Belgian Foreign Ministry, dossiers CLB 348, CLB 349, and CLB 351.

[57] Foreign Minister Hymans was interpellated in the Belgian Senate concerning the activities of Nothomb and the C.P.N.B. in 1919. He admitted that Nothomb had had an intimate relationship with the Foreign Ministry during the war and peace conference, but that the "semi-official" relationship was ended. Hymans defended the government's right, however, to continue to welcome information from private citizens on important foreign political issues. *Annales Parlementaires de Belgique*, Sénat (Brussels, Imprimerie du Moniteur belge), 7 Oct. 1919, pp. 703-704. See also Tel. Gurney (Brussels) to Curzon, 10 Oct. 1919: DBFP, V, 662-663.

Smeets himself resented Belgian direction as much as French, but Nothomb's men, in collusion with certain military officers, kept up steady contact with various shady figures associated with the *Rheinische Republikanische Volkspartei* and its splinter groups. The increase in Belgian influence alarmed Tirard. According to his informants, the Belgians sought to win Smeets to a Rhenish state north of the Moselle under Anglo-Belgian influence. The agricultural and sparsely populated Palatinate would be left to France.[58] Poincaré wired Brussels to learn the intentions of the Belgian government. Pierre de Margerie, the French ambassador, spoke to Foreign Minister Jaspar personally. "Certainly we can desire only one thing," said Jaspar candidly, "the de-Prussianization of the Rhineland." As for Pierre Nothomb's organization, Jaspar disowned its activities but would not say whether the government viewed its plans favorably.[59] France, it seemed, had no monopoly on intrigue.

Dr. Dorten did not get along with Smeets. To Dorten, Smeets was a gutter opportunist, a rabble-rouser and a revolutionary. His movement openly advocated separation from Germany while Dorten's *Rheinische Volksvereinigung* claimed to want only autonomy. To Smeets, Dorten was precisely the type of Catholic bourgeois he despised, effete, monocle-sporting, and wealthy, who saw the Rhenish movement as a means to cheat the workers of their revolution. Under these circumstances, the first French-inspired attempt to unite the two movements in February 1922 failed utterly. To make matters worse, Dorten had rushed again to Paris as soon as Poincaré was installed as premier, inspiring German and British papers to claim that Poincaré had granted the separatist a long audience. This time the irritated Peretti de la Rocca surveyed all the offices of the Foreign Ministry to determine if anyone had received Dorten or a man called Dahlen, which, according to the *Sûreté*, was the Rhinelander's present alias. On 24 February Poincaré wired Tirard, expressly denying that Dorten had been entertained by the French government and insisting that the prestigious *Frankfurter Zeitung* publish a denial.[60]

Poincaré's problems with Dorten had only begun. While seeking to evade French control, Dorten nevertheless asked for more money. Prussia was spending 30 million marks per year on its hate campaign

[58] Tel. Tirard to Poincaré, 2 Feb. 1922: MAE Rive Gauche, vol. 27, nos. 177-180.

[59] Des. Margerie to Poincaré, 8 Feb. 1922: MAE Rive Gauche, vol. 27, nos. 198-200.

[60] Note Peretti for Poincaré, 21 Feb. 1922: MAE Rive Gauche, vol. 27, no. 238; Tel. Poincaré to Tirard, 24 Feb. 1922: AN HCF, vol. 5270, dos. 83/7. Poincaré's denial was not necessary where the German government was concerned. The German ambassador in Paris wired Berlin that Poincaré was too cautious to take up with Dorten personally. Tel. Mayer (Paris) to A.A., 27 Feb. 1922: AA BR 3058, 1469, no. 602978.

against France, Dorten claimed, but he received only 50,000 per month from Tirard, despite his need to support a "cadre of forty thousand."[61] More disturbing was Dorten's continued connection with Bavarians, left over from the federalist days of 1920. Dorten was even using French money to help support Bavarian monarchists grouped around Prince Rupprecht! Tirard visited Paris in March and received verbal instructions from Poincaré to investigate Dorten's use of subsidies and, in effect, to "straighten him up." Dorten's own lieutenant willingly confided his chief's plan to increase aid to the Bavarians if the French granted him more money. Tirard informed Paris that he would reprimand the insolent puppet and, if he refused to take orders from Coblenz, cut off his subsidy altogether.[62]

Remonstrances were in vain. Instead of toadying to Tirard, Dorten fell readily under the influence of a young Frenchman named Paul Hocquel. Hocquel had been an employee of the French High Commissariat after being fired from General Mangin's civilian staff in 1919 for "indiscretions and bad character." Indiscriminate employment practice was a notorious feature of Tirard's administration. Hocquel undertook to collaborate with Dorten, claiming to be an agent of Tirard, and when the latter heard of it Hocquel was again dismissed. But the adventurer could not be gotten rid of so easily. Hocquel succeeded in charming Dorten's wife and through her won a position in the council of the *Rheinische Volksvereinigung*, as well as a suite in the Wiesbaden villa.[63]

Hocquel proceeded to attack the French High Commissariat through Dorten's contacts in the Parisian press, accusing the French authorities of ignoring and even hindering the Rhenish movement. Poincaré now suggested that perhaps it would be better "to disengage ourselves little by little, in order to avoid being compromised by Dorten's intrigues."[64] As if in answer, Hocquel wrote Poincaré in April to attack the "machinations and abominable intrigues" of Tirard.[65] The exchange marked a virtual break between Tirard and Dorten, although the former still urged Poincaré not to give up entirely on Dorten. "It would not be useless for us to continue to support him," he wrote in May. But close collaboration would not begin again for over a year.[66]

In fact, the French were trapped by their own folly. Even if Tirard

[61] Note Mangin, "Conversation avec le Dr. Dorten," 1922: AN Pap. Mangin, vol. 21, dos. 3 bis.

[62] Tel. Tirard to Poincaré, 11 Mar. 1922: MAE Rive Gauche, vol. 27, nos. 256-258.

[63] Des. Tirard to Poincaré, "Information demandée par le PdC," 3 and 6 Mar. 1923: MAE Rive Gauche, vol. 206, nos. 15-36.

[64] Tel. Poincaré to Tirard, 16 Mar. 1922: MAE Rive Gauche, vol. 27, no. 261.

[65] Pers. Let. Hocquel to Poincaré, 26 Apr. 1922: MAE Rive Gauche, vol. 206, nos. 2-3.

[66] Tel. Tirard to Poincaré, 16 May 1922: MAE Rive Gauche, vol. 28, nos. 11-13.

did drop Dorten, his antics would still be attributed to French inspiration by the Germans and British. By controlling the purse strings, Tirard might hope to exercise some restraint on the man. To French nationalists, a break with Dorten would only confirm Hocquel's accusations that the commissariat was abandoning separatism. By 1922, then, barring a complete reversal in France's German policy, there was no choice but to suffer the unruly puppets, though the strings controlling them had passed to other hands, or become hopelessly tangled. In the meantime, Poincaré's Rhenish policy, from which he was partly unwilling and partly unable to escape, only increased the resistance he would meet from London and Berlin in security and reparations.

BANKERS' COMMITTEE: REPARATIONS DEADLOCK

While Lloyd George and Poincaré practiced their unconstructive maneuvers, the reparations question remained in limbo. Rathenau appeared at the Cannes Conference to appeal for a moratorium on the very day Briand left for Paris. As an expedient, the Reparations Commission granted Germany a conditional postponement of the January and February installments, and the German government engaged to submit a currency and budget reform plan to the Commission.

As Poincaré and his advisors considered the problem during the early months of 1922, present circumstances and past lessons forced them to admit what many had suspected since 1919: that Europe could not recover fully, nor Germany pay reparations, without American loans. Following his predecessors, Poincaré favored also a massive deliveries-in-kind program, but resistance from all sides blocked such schemes. Complicating matters were the Allied war debts. Legally, there was no connection between the indemnity owed by Germany and the contractual debts owed by the Allies to each other and to the United States. But the connection became undeniable to Europeans when one suggested the advisability of reducing or eliminating German payments. If Germany were let off the hook for all or a good part of her burden, or if she were permitted to fulfill it "in-kind" only, the net effect would be that the victorious nations would be left with an "indemnity" greater than defeated Germany's. Finally, a favorable trade balance that would facilitate payment of the war debts was prevented by American tariff policy. American protectionists, like their French counterparts, demanded cash payments and barriers to imports. Stung by the recession, Congress passed the Emergency Tariff Act in May 1921, followed by the Fordney-McCumber tariff of September 1922, the highest in American history.

Until 1921 London and Paris ignored their debts to the United

States in hope that they would go away. But the creation by Congress of the World War Debt Funding Commission in February 1922 bespoke an ever tougher American stance. The French government, it seemed, was unfairly caught in an Anglo-American struggle for world financial supremacy—the United States could not favor France without favoring Britain. This the American Treasury refused to do. Under the circumstances, Paris could not afford to consider reduction of Germany's theoretical debt. There remained the lone hope of putting the German government in a position to pay. This would require budgetary reforms to stabilize the mark and loans to mobilize the reparations debt. Since the only likely source of capital was America, European governments again looked across the Atlantic.

On 2 February 1922 Poincaré instructed the French delegate on the Reparations Commission, Louis Dubois, on the necessity of forcing German financial reform if Germany were to appear as a sound field for investment. Let the Allies respond to Germany's moratorium request by removing a portion of her fiscal autonomy. Short-term solutions, which only resulted in the reappearance of the reparations problem and controversy among the Allies, would no longer suffice. "This is why we must study the possibility of a grand solution based on exterior loans, which alone can solve, pragmatically and positively, the problem of reparations." But, Poincaré added, such an operation would have to be carried out without injury to the treaty or to the London schedule of payments.[67]

Poincaré's last proviso hid no ulterior motive—he was only protecting France's guarantees and responding to the deadlock in interallied debts. Minister of Finance Charles de Lasteyrie and Jacques Seydoux agreed that the 132 billion gold mark reparations bill was of value only when placed against the war debts. Germany could never pay it all, and would not pay at all, it seemed, except under force or threat of force. But it was equally clear that Franco-British cooperation in coercion would not last five years, much less fifty. Thus, the London plan based on scheduled redemption of the A, B, and C bonds was defunct. There remained a solution based on loans, but German credit was zero. Two developments could improve it: currency stabilization and/or reduction of Germany's total debt. If France were to allow a reduction in the reparations debt, however, there must be an equal reduction in war debts.[68]

[67] Let. Poincaré to Louis Dubois (Reparations Commission), 2 Feb. 1922: MAE Pap. Millerand, Réparations VI, nos. 16-20.

[68] Note Margerie (chef-adjoint du cabinet, ministère des finances) to de Lasteyrie (minister of finance), "Note sur le problème des réparations," 19 Feb. 1922; Note Seydoux, "Paiement des réparations par l'Allemagne," 4 Feb. 1922: MAE Pap. Millerand, Réparations VI, nos. 70-81, 21-26.

The reparations problem resolved itself into one of attracting American capital under conditions acceptable to the victorious, but beleaguered, powers. Poincaré called a reparations council of war in his office on 4 March. Present were Louis Dubois, de Lasteyrie, Seydoux, and their assistants. Europe had come to a critical turning point, the premier maintained. The German debt must be mobilized if serious conflict were to be avoided. Thus, the Reparations Commission must adopt: (1) immediate solution for the 1922 payments, perhaps a temporary reduction; (2) Allied control of German government finances; (3) foreign loans encouraged by that control; and (4) realization of a system of reparations-in-kind.[69] This was scarcely an extreme program, but it assumed Anglo-American tolerance of the nullification of German fiscal sovereignty. The American observer on the Reparations Commission, James Logan, viewed Poincaré's moderation as evidence of France's financial difficulties, which were exacerbated by the "tactful pressure" being applied by New York banks with respect to short-term credits. Logan predicted that the "sane elements" in France would "realize that when the question comes up of Germany's borrowing foreign money, the conditions and amounts of such loans will not be dictated by the politicians but by the fellow who is going to lend the money."[70] American bankers were to dictate to France her German policy; moderation would serve Poincaré poorly.

Dubois proceeded to execute the French plan. The Reparations Commission reduced Germany's 1922 obligations on 21 March, but judged the Wirth government's tax reform to be unsatisfactory. The Committee of Guarantees would proceed to Berlin to investigate directly. In return, the German government offered reforms and new taxes promising 40 billion paper marks.[71] The next step was acquisition of loans. The post-Genoa malaise was broken on 24 May, when there convened in Paris an international bankers' committee to discuss the prospect of loans for Germany. It opened with less éclat than the Conference of Genoa, which Lloyd George had dubbed "the greatest gathering of European nations ever assembled," but the bankers' conference boasted one delegation absent at Genoa. It was a delegation of private American bankers, and it was led by J. P. Morgan.

Poincaré is accused of having sabotaged the Bankers' Committee just as he did the Conference of Genoa, his purported goal being the prevention of any settlement that might restrain him from occupying the

[69] P.-V., "Réunion tenue dans le cabinet de M. le PdC," 4 Mar. 1922: MAE Pap. Millerand, Réparations VI, nos. 141-150.

[70] Pers. Let. Logan (CdR, Paris) to Benjamin Strong (Chairman, New York Federal Reserve Bank), 17 Mar. 1922: James A. Logan, unpublished private papers, Hoover Institution—Stanford (hereafter HI, Logan Papers), Box 2.

[71] Weill-Raynal, *Les réparations allemandes*, II, 148-150.

Ruhr. It cannot be denied that Poincaré saw the potential benefits of a Ruhr occupation, but he also understood the risks. Just as the interpretation of Poincaré's 1923 policy as "force for the sake of force" ignores the many problems other than reparations faced by France—coal, war debts, security—so is it a mistake to ignore the financial tightrope trod by the French government, with its double budget, and the intense emotionalism of the seemingly dry issue of financial reconstruction. France had made her contribution to victory in lives and in devastation. Could not her great allies, especially America, accept the financial burden? Or was France to be cast, by the parochial nationalism of her comrades, into the ranks of the defeated powers? When Poincaré asked British and American financiers to annul French war debts, or to provide capital for German reparations without a diminution of French rights, he was only asking for a settlement most Frenchmen considered just. The failure of the Bankers' Committee was due as much to the intransigence of the British and American governments, themselves subjected to popular pressure, and to Berlin's inability to force austerity measures, as to Poincaré's stubborn defense of French rights.

The maneuverability of the French government was also severely limited following the debacle of Genoa. Germany had dealt the Allies an unforgivable "slap in the face," while Britain responded by demanding more concessions of *France*. French finances continued to deteriorate under the double budget. Instead of solace from America, France received the official call for consolidation and funding from the World War Debt Funding Commission on 21 April, and Morgan's firm in New York warned that if the French banked on future debt revision, "they shall wait in vain."[72] An atmosphere of hope nevertheless pertained. On 25 May André Tardieu rose in the Chamber and addressed a dramatic appeal to the committee. It was a personal and collective catharsis: no longer did Clemenceau's draftsman hold up the Versailles Treaty as a viable structure for peace and prosperity. Instead, Tardieu proclaimed the triple crisis that France and Europe faced: an industrial crisis, born of the war's destruction and plaguing all nations with unemployment and depressed markets; a political crisis, stemming from the failure of the Anglo-Saxon powers to underwrite European security, which only encouraged "certain forces" to work for revolution and revenge instead of reconstruction; a financial crisis, the legacy of the Peace Conference's failure to regulate the interallied debts and fix the amount and method of German reparations. The Peace Conference

[72] Maier, *Recasting Bourgeois Europe*, p. 289. Logan nevertheless believed Poincaré would have to accept the bankers' demands for a reduction and moratorium for Germany. Pers. Let. Logan to Herbert Hoover, 2 June 1922: HI Logan Papers, Box 2.

was largely to blame, Tardieu admitted, but the time for recriminations was past. "Let us not think," he implored, "that mere invocation of the treaty will suffice to bring immediate solutions to all difficulties present and future. Life must go on, even as a river flows." Solutions to these more profound problems would not be found in the clauses of the treaty. They could only be found in the participation of the United States in European stabilization.[73]

The Bankers' Committee received a limited mandate from the Reparations Commission. It was to examine the conditions for issue of an international loan to Germany, but it did not have the authority to consider solutions prejudicial to the Treaty of Versailles or the London Schedule. Yet the non-French delegates unanimously agreed that for a stabilization loan, not to mention a grand reparations loan, to succeed, a moratorium and reduction in Germany's total debt were mandatory. J. P. Morgan understood the difficulties the French government would have in reconciling itself to such a measure, but the reduction was necessary. As for the French debt to the United States, Morgan recommended that Paris inform Washington frankly that it was incapable of paying. Given Washington's constant calls for disarmament and France's inflated defense budgets, such an appeal was unlikely to have effect. Nevertheless, Morgan insisted that "it will be necessary, in the United States and in France, to look facts in the face."[74]

Morgan was sincere. As far as he was concerned, "the war debts did not exist," and he considered the Anglo-French Entente "the pivot of civilization." But he could not speak for the American Treasury nor it for him. Morgan could not promise an annulment of war debts, nor could he promise American participation in a German loan unless Europe showed signs of recovering political stability. This meant amelioration of the German financial position and renunciation of further acts of force by the Allies. Accordingly, the committee requested on 1 June that its mandate be extended. Six days later the Reparations Commission responded affirmatively, but over the protest of the French delegate. Without the assent of Germany's principal claimant, the bankers, considered further discussion fruitless and adjourned.

Poincaré braved the foreign backlash. As much as he was convinced of the need for a grand loan to "prime the pump" of German reparations, he could not accept it in return for further sacrifice by France.

[73] J.O. Chambre, 24 May 1922. See the summary and interpretation in "Les interpellations sur Gênes," *Le Temps*, 25 May 1922.

[74] Renseignement Mauclère, "Comité des banquiers," 8 June 1922: MAE Pap. Millerand, Réparations VII, no. 204.

Belgian delegate Émile Delacroix believed that Morgan could have brought substantial influence to bear in Washington on the debt question. He considered Poincaré's action unfortunate.[75] The French premier did expect a loan eventually, but the Anglo-Americans were still demanding a *quid pro quo* that he could not abide. The loan must wait until France was no longer a supplicant, until her bargaining position was improved.[76] Did Poincaré undermine an excellent opportunity to "bring America to Europe"? In fact, the hope for later American debt concessions was shaky. Financiers and merchants along the East Coast had lobbied in Washington for a "flexible" war debt policy to no avail. More telling still was the German attitude. Hugo Stinnes rallied the Ruhr to oppose the idea of a stabilization loan. Stinnes feared the loss of the export advantage Germany enjoyed owing to the steady inflation of the mark. A stable currency, he said, would be "ein nationales Unglück." The German ambassador in Washington and Rathenau himself were skeptical of the Committee's work—they did not want loans unless accompanied by a great reduction in the German debt.[77] Thus, the Morgan offer in Paris was such that expanding the mandate could only damage French interests—but it made Poincaré appear to have exploded the Committee.

Peaceful progress was blocked by the failure of the Bankers' Committee. All parties had come to accept the impossibility of massive capital transfers except through the mechanism of American loans to Germany. Now the irreconcilability of national interests seemed to smash that last hope for settlement. A new determination became evident in every capital, as governments searched for new tactics or leverage to shift the balance. On 16 June 1922 the British cabinet launched a new policy to strengthen the defenses and sharpen the bite of British policy in the coming confrontation with France. Britain would consolidate its debt to the United States. Economic recovery, reasoned Lloyd George, would only follow a reparations settlement, which in turn must follow a debt settlement, given French policy. Recognition of the war debts, as painful as it was, would free America's hand and give to

[75] Tel. Margerie to MAE, 12 June 1922: MAE Pap. Millerand, Réparations VII, nos. 245-248.

[76] Note Seydoux, "Visite de M. Delacroix," 23 June 1922: MAE Pap. Millerand, Réparations VII, nos. 290-296. The Belgians favored pressing instead for a small loan to Germany permitting stabilization of her currency, but stood firm on no debt reductions or moratoria.

[77] Link, *Die amerikanische Stabilisierungspolitik*, pp. 129-135. Britain supported Germany in this position throughout early 1922. Memo prepared in the British Treasury, "German Reparations: The Need for a Readjustment of the Present Schedule of Payments," 16 Nov. 1921, communicated to Berlin, Apr. 1922: AA RM 3243, nos. K603155-158.

the British government a powerful form of leverage against Paris, since both nations held large credits from France. Hopefully, by September a British delegation would proceed to Washington.[78] Brussels, too, showed new resolve in the face of Anglo-American intransigence. To be sure, the small ally's policy aimed ultimately at reforging the Western Entente, but she could not purchase unanimity at the cost of her treaty rights, and it was Britain that questioned those rights. A portion of British opinion or the bankers of the City and Wall Street, proclaimed one Belgian deputy, must not be permitted to dictate Belgian policy. Foreign Minister Jaspar responded in Parliament that if Western interests clashed, the defense of Belgian interests would come first. Premier Theunis seconded him: "Our need for reparations is an indisputable fact. It is as indisputable as the indissolubility of the interests of France and Belgium. To renounce reparations, messieurs, would be a policy of suicide."[79] Unless the Anglo-Saxon powers overcame their egotism, Belgium would follow France's lead.

Finally, the French government displayed its new determination by recourse to the threat of French revisionism. The Chamber and Senate proved skeptical of any arrangement by which Germany would receive a grand loan and thus stabilize her exchange and obtain credit first among the ex-belligerents. In competition with the loan idea, there arose again the notion of sanctions—not this time as a means, but as an end in itself. The inspiration for the Chamber's new resolution came from the president of the Finance Commission, Adrien Dariac. Vexed by the failure to collect reparations, and by the resultant French budgetary deficits, Dariac toured the occupied territories and returned on 28 May 1922 to submit his report.

Far from being a conservative and objective document as reports from financial experts are wont to be, Dariac's recommendations outlined a program of semi-permanent French military and economic domination of the Rhineland and Ruhr. The Ruhr, he showed in figures, was not the heart of German industry; it *was* German industry. It was controlled by a handful of immensely powerful men whose holdings compared favorably with the entire French industrial plant. Dariac saw the occupation of the Ruhr as the only guarantee that could satisfy both French reparations and coke needs. As for the Left Bank of the Rhine, Dariac parroted the briefings he had received from French authorities. The Rhenish people desired autonomy and the French occupation sought conciliation, but fifteen years counted for little in the life of a nation. If France were to free the Rhineland and draw it to the

[78] Minutes, CAB 35(22), 16 June 1922: PRO CAB 23/30, pp. 216-221.

[79] *Annales Parlementaires de Belgique*, Sénat, 8 and 13 June 1922, pp. 607-623.

West, the French army must remain on the Rhine for decades. As an aid to Rhenish autonomism, Dariac advocated introduction of a Rhenish currency, a customs barrier, and the expulsion of the Prussians.[80]

Ten days after Dariac submitted his confidential report, Poincaré went before the Senate Foreign Affairs Commission and broached for the first time the prospect of a Ruhr occupation. It bore no connection to the Dariac report, which was parliamentary in origin and effect. Rather, the decision to occupy the Ruhr if necessary was the result of years of observation while France came no nearer to solution of her various postwar problems. Only the occupation of the Ruhr could break the resistance of German industry and give to France a sound guarantee that could then be traded off for permanent solutions. If attempts to rebuild the Entente and provide for German reparations had reached a deadlock by June 1922, so had the attempt at industrial rapprochement. The plight of French heavy industry had become as critical and as demanding of prompt initiative as the problem of international finance.

CRISE DE LA MÉTALLURGIE: INDUSTRIAL DEADLOCK

The French government's metallurgical program of 1919 was coherent but unrealizable. It provided for a tremendous increase in the iron and steel capacity of French industry, but, of all the components of a large and healthy metallurgy, only an iron source had been safely acquired. The rest—coal and coke, markets, and capital—would have to be obtained through execution of the treaty or by the energy and sacrifice of Frenchmen themselves. Experts in France and Germany had thought the wisest course to be retention of many Lorraine enterprises by their pre-Armistice owners, the Ruhr magnates.[81] But if French industrialists were conservative in their approach, seeking above all to avoid *bouleversement* and overextension of their industry, the government concerned itself with the political and military interests of France, especially with the necessity of a powerful heavy industry in the waging of modern war.

The complete break effected by the peace treaty between Lorraine and its former partner, the Ruhr, meant that the work of renegotiating

[80] Report Dariac, 28 May 1922: MAE Rive Gauche, vol. 6, nos. 192-219.

[81] Robert Pinot, *Le Comité des Forges au service de la nation* (Paris, 1919), p. 220; "Denkschrift uber Elsass-Lothringen als Rohstoffgebiet," A.A. #17, Rep. 330 Berlin Staatsarchiv, cited in Bariéty, "Le rôle de la minette," p. 250; Maier, "Coal and Economic Power in the Weimar Republic," pp. 530-534.

the structural relationship between French and German metallurgy had to start from scratch. That such renegotiation should end favorably for France was difficult to doubt in 1919, given the losses and obligations thrust upon Germany. But German industrialists showed no sign of seeking agreement for raw materials exchanges, price controls, or market division. This was perplexing in itself to French producers as the world slumped through the postwar depression of 1920-1921. But more troubling still was the continued depression of French metallurgy, compared with the steady German rate of recovery. Defeated and amputated, Germany seemed to be rebounding, while victorious France spoke of the "crise de la métallurgie." What had gone wrong?

The most important deficit for French forges was that of coke, but no less asphyxiating was the deficiency of capital. After 1918 the German government advanced huge sums to private business in compensation for its losses resulting from the peace treaty. Thus, the Ruhr magnates confronted postwar competition with the means for a capital *masse de manoeuvre*. In France, precisely the opposite occurred. French metallurgists were obliged to distribute among themselves and purchase from the government the liberated mines and mills of Lorraine. Furthermore, the government prevailed upon French finance and industry to buy up German enterprises of the Saar for political reasons. French industry was drained of capital at the very moment when reconversion from wartime production was necessary and world competition for markets revived.[82]

The Ruhr magnates took full advantage of their sudden liquidity to modernize and expand the industrial base left to Germany, now concentrated almost entirely in the Ruhr. But the losses suffered in coal and iron still had to be made good. The first expedient was simply not to execute coal deliveries. This tactic sufficed to win a lowering of the monthly quotas at the Spa Conference and then a concession on price. This raised the reparations credited to Germany for each ton of coal delivered and broke the delicate equilibrium worked out at Versailles between German and English coal on the French market.[83] Since the Ruhr no longer had a stake in the fate of Lorraine, the Germans had no impulse to execute the Spa Accords faithfully. In 1913, the Ruhr consumed 19.5 million tons of coal and shipped 9.7 million tons to its subsidiaries in Lorraine. In 1922 the Ruhr consumed 22.6 million tons, while delivering only 6.3 million tons to France, Luxembourg, and Belgium!

There remained the quest for iron to feed the forges of the Ruhr. The most obvious source was Sweden. In 1913, 11 percent of Ger-

[82] Bariéty, "Le rôle de la minette," pp. 253-258.

[83] Ibid., pp. 263-265.

many's iron was mined there; in 1922, 28 percent. Second, iron deposits in Central Germany discovered or exploited more intensively during the war added considerably to German supplies. Third, there was recovery of scrap iron. Not only domestic sources, particularly rich during the period of disarmament, but foreign imports helped lessen the Ruhr's dependence on Lorraine. Derelict and decrepit ships from England, the ruins of Russia, imports from the Low Countries, even the old factories of the Ruhr, torn down for modernization, were fed back into the furnaces. German metallurgy used 3.5 million tons of scrap per year after 1919, while importing only 2.8 million tons of ore from Lorraine. Despite their wartime oaths that annexation of the Briey-Longwy ore fields were indispensable to German industry, the Ruhr magnates admitted as early as November 1918 that they could dispense even with the Lorraine fields, and that the French would be far more dependent on the Ruhr than vice versa. No wonder it seemed to French observers, Poincaré among them, that Germany was winning the peace, and that German claims of bankruptcy were fraudulent.[84]

While German industry raced upwards toward its prewar production levels, basing itself on the internal market and on foreign markets won thanks to the depreciation of the mark, French industry foundered. Lack of coke and capital barely permitted established forges, much expanded during the war, to stay in operation, and rendered them incapable of exploiting the Lorraine iron. The latter, being high in phosphorus, demanded even more coke than higher-grade German or Swedish ore. The limitations of the French market demanded foreign outlets if French industry was to dispose of its production. But the high price it was forced to pay for combustibles destroyed the competitiveness of French metallurgy in the export trade.[85] Following the coal crisis, the cost/price squeeze continued; coal prices dropped, but so did finished iron and steel prices, to less than 40 percent of their 1920 level![86] Under these circumstances, it would not profit the French firms to develop Lorraine's industry even if they possessed the means to do so. As it was, Germany continued to default on her coal and coke deliveries throughout 1921 and 1922, and to fill the hoppers bound for her rival with as much brown dust as quality coal.[87] By the end of 1922,

[84] Feldman, *Iron and Steel*, pp. 84ff, 203ff; Guy Greer, *The Ruhr-Lorraine Industrial Problem* (New York, 1925), pp. 18ff; Bariéty, "Le rôle de la minette," pp. 269-270.

[85] Levainville, *L'Industrie du Fer en France*, pp. 159-199.

[86] Carr and Taplin, *History of the British Steel Industry*, p. 347.

[87] The Office Français des Houillères Sinistrés had to refuse 30 percent of the reparations coal delivered in July 1922 because of its poor quality. In August, the figure rose to 63 percent! Weill-Raynal, *Les réparations allemandes*, II, 275-278.

47 percent of French furnaces were extinguished for lack of coke and markets, steel production was 64 percent of its 1913 level, and French firms defaulted on the payments owed to the government. What was to be done?

The Wiesbaden Accords represented the first official move toward an industrial understanding between the two rivals. But the Briand and Wirth governments had acted in conciliation, just as Clemenceau's had acted in ambition, without consulting the industries involved. The insistence on prior political agreements that did not necessarily serve the interests of the industrial circles hampered the movement toward private economic agreements. Poincaré took office, therefore, at a time of industrial crisis for France. Despite his Germanophobia, he did not reject out of hand the idea of negotiation with Germany. He was too perspicacious to weaken France's international position unduly by eliminating one path of possible progress on grounds of personal distaste. Rather, Poincaré was willing to experiment during his first months in office in the matter of heavy industry as in the other outstanding problems of France. Like Briand, he carried on the initiatives on two fronts, governmental and private negotiations, but he did not subordinate one to the other. On 1 February 1922 Seydoux began a push for the revival of the Wiesbaden Accords. He looked on the recent promotion of Rathenau to foreign minister as a favorable development and hoped that resistance from French industrialists to a reparations-in-kind plan could be overcome. One reason for the failure of the 1921 accords, Seydoux felt, was that they were too etatist. He sought to replace the system whereby orders for materials were centralized in Paris and Berlin with a system allowing free disposition of orders by the French firms themselves. He hoped thereby to avoid the practice of the German government of passing French orders to inferior manufacturers, saddling the French with shoddy goods and saving the best for export.[88]

From Coblenz, Paul Tirard favored the same policy, but for different reasons. He had not lost his conviction that French influence in the Rhineland could best be spread by economic measures. The abandonment of the Rhenish policy in the Wiesbaden Accords had been distasteful, but with Poincaré in power, he hoped for a return to the policy of commercial favoritism for the Rhineland.[89] Indeed, Poincaré circulated Tirard's report of January 1922, emphasizing the

[88] Note Seydoux, "Accord de Wiesbaden," 1 Feb. 1922: MAE Pap. Millerand, Réparations VI, nos. 2-5.

[89] Report Tirard, "Situation générale dans la Rhénanie au début de 1922," 19 Jan. 1922: MAE Rive Gauche, vol. 5, nos. 192-225.

FIGURE 4. "M. Poincaré Passes to Action." H. P. Gassier, 1922. © S.P.A.D.E.M. Paris 1977.

conclusion that "it is absolutely necessary for the development of our influence on the Left Bank of the Rhine to secure the most business possible for the Rhineland."[90]

The Reparations Commission had given to Belgium a mandate to negotiate her own accord with Germany, which produced the Bemelmans project of 27 February 1922. The plan restored freedom to the commercial relations between Belgium and Germany for the purposes of reparations, but granted Berlin a right to veto any individual transaction. This proviso did not suit France's purposes; otherwise the project was attractive.[91] When the Reparations Commission gave Paris the go-ahead to negotiate, an accord based on the Belgian one was initialed in Berlin within a week. Details were left for future talks but it seemed that Wirth's government again desired an amicable agreement with France. Then came April, and with it came Rapallo, Poincaré's Bar-le-Duc speech, and news of the most serious French attempt to date to come to terms with German industry.

Under pressure of the metallurgical crisis in France, Poincaré had to consider the advantages of a Franco-German accord worked out between the industrialists themselves for European metallurgical cooperation. For all his enmity toward the masters of the Ruhr, in March 1922 Poincaré blessed approaches made by French industrialists to sound out the Germans on a raw materials and markets agreement. A group of French firms executed the demarche through the intermediary of Upper Silesian interests with whom they had made contact since the occupation there in 1919. The great captains of the Ruhr then convened to forge a common policy toward the French initiatives. The Germans noted that all the economic leverage was theirs, but that a Franco-German steel cartel would be subject to military and political pressure as long as French troops remained on the Rhine. They deemed that they had nothing to gain from bargaining with France, and that time was on their side. The conference, led by Fritz Thyssen, agreed to consider any definite French proposals, but to set as prerequisites for an accord the evacuation of the Rhineland and the Saar.[92]

Five weeks later French industrialists made a firm proposal for partition of raw materials and markets, and price regulation. Once again, the Ruhr magnates met and reviewed the lack of any compelling reason for concluding an agreement at the present time. The new Lorraine

[90] Note Poincaré, containing Tirard report of 19 Jan. 1922, 6 Feb. 1922: MAE Rive Gauche, vol. 115, nos. 7-8.

[91] Tel. Tirard to Poincaré, 7 Mar. 1922: MAE Rive Gauche, vol. 27, nos. 250-252.

[92] "Notes prises pendant la réunion du 21 mars, 1922," R13, I/261, folios 158-159, Bundesarchiv Coblenz, cited in Bariéty, "Le rôle de la minette," p. 273.

enterprises ran large deficits. The French saw their only salvation in a general rise in world iron and steel prices and in a guaranteed market, all of which could come only through a cartel with Germany. But the Ruhr was surviving and even expanding without French iron. Once again, the answer came back: no agreement before evacuation of the Rhineland and Saar.[93]

France had an army on the doorstep of the Ruhr. The German response was an act of defiance in the face of French military power, an economic Rapallo. Still, Poincaré fared no better with Berlin. After the promising beginnings in the wake of the Bemelmans project, the reparations-in-kind pact foundered, then died. The Gillet-Ruppel Accord, signed on 6 June, excited little interest on either side of the Rhine. Though Poincaré had extended Briand's promise to refrain from favoring Rhenish industries for political goals, and Berlin agreed to create a standing fund of marks to ensure reimbursement to German firms, the accord suffered a similar fate to the Plan Seydoux. Neither official rapprochement nor the goodwill of nonpolitical experts could replace the fears and ambitions of national states and industries. Berlin saw French efforts to deal with West German industry, as did Prussian Minister of the Interior Carl Severing in March, as a means of prying the Rhineland away from Germany.[94] But Ruhr industry was simultaneously rebuffing French advances by holding out for political concessions to Germany! Belgium and Britain again showed displeasure with the Gillet-Ruppel Accord, and French commerce, in the wake of the Bankers' Committee and the Ruhr's cold shoulder, forsook cooperation and hinted at occupation of the Ruhr.[95] Once again, the French Cabinet was isolated, and Poincaré no nearer a solution than in January.

During the first half of 1922 Poincaré pursued agreements in security, reparations/war debts, and heavy industry, and met the same response everywhere he turned: sacrifice your treaty rights, relinquish your freedom of action, then perhaps you will find us willing to bargain. Stripped of those rights, France would be without leverage in international affairs, the military and financial appendage of the Anglo-Saxon states. The alternative was to make use of France's military power and relative domestic stability—indeed, parliamentary en-

[93] "Notes prises pendant la réunion du 27 avril 1922," R13, I/261, folio 154, Bundesarchiv Coblenz, cited by Bariéty, "Le rôle de la minette," p. 274.

[94] Let. Severing to A.A., 21 Mar. 1922: AA, Abteilung Besetzte Gebiete (hereafter cited as BG), L1476, 5342, 430379-81.

[95] The French Association Nationale d'Expansion Économique met in early June and passed unanimously a resolution calling for "forceful means" in response to German bad faith. *Journée Industrielle*, 1 June 1922. On the Gillet-Ruppel Accord, see Weill-Raynal, *Les réparations allemandes*, II, 145-150.

thusiasm for advance. The only sanction likely to produce the triple result needed was occupation of the Ruhr. If it was inevitable, as Lord Curzon lamented, then it was due as much to British, German, and American policy as to the French.

In 1919 Britain and the United States recognized France's rights to reparation, security, and industrial growth. By 1922 those powers had reneged on their obligations and allowed Germany to do the same. To the French nation, motivated to a degree by ambition, but conscious of the tremendous sacrifices made on behalf of the common victory and clutching profound fear of German revenge, the policy of her former allies seemed betrayal. Poincaré could drift with the tide of British and German revisionism, or strike out boldly on his own. But, by June 1922, he could no longer remain stationary.

·6·

FRANCE AT THE RUBICON: THE RUHR DECISION, 1922

During the last half of 1922 Poincaré found himself under increasing pressure from President Millerand and the Chambers to achieve results, to break the diplomatic deadlock, if necessary to occupy the Ruhr. Yet the premier was intent on following Briand's advice from 1921, to try every other tactic first, justify himself abroad and at home, and thus minimize the risks accompanying a Ruhr occupation. The French cabinet and military proceeded with preparations for the ultimate sanction, while Poincaré tried once more to wean the British and Germans away from their demands for French concessions. By autumn the premier had little to show for his efforts at conciliation, but the preparations for confrontation, both military and political, were well advanced. The cabinet elected to take the plunge. But the process of preparation concerned the means; what of the ends of the Ruhr occupation? Was it to force execution or revision of the Versailles Treaty? On these questions the French government was mute. Frustrated and under pressure, the French had chosen conflict, but the scale and nature—even the aims—of the conflict they had chosen were hidden from them.

RUHR PREPARATIONS I

Raymond Poincaré went before the Senate Foreign Affairs Commission on 7 June 1922. The Commission's mood reflected that of a great part of the National Assembly, of the government, and of the nation. They applauded the independence the premier had shown and his announced readiness to return to a policy of sanctions. But Poincaré did not appeal to the senators' aggressive mood. There were only three means for reparations to be discharged, he said. The Wiesbaden Accords would have permitted large-scale deliveries, and Poincaré considered the Chamber's blockage of them unfortunate. He called for support for reparations-in-kind and warned that the government must be able to control domestic industry. "I insist on this point," he declared, "because whenever and wherever I can use coercion vis-à-vis our own industry, I shall frankly do so. . . . Our industries must face reality. If they persist in this opposition, they will make it extremely difficult to liquidate the German debt."[1] A second means of payment, continued Poincaré, was by German transfer of foreign currency obtained by a highly favorable balance of payments. No Allied government wished to encourage German exports on such a scale. There remained the third solution based on loans. Even as his adamant stance was undermining the Bankers' Committee, Poincaré assured the senators that such a grand loan to Germany was a *fatalité*, the only means for Germany safely to acquire the necessary capital to make reparations payments.

The problem was to secure the necessary loan for Germany without having to make unilateral sacrifices to purchase American and British cooperation. How could France find the leverage, Poincaré asked in secret session, to support her position in the international marketplace? The answer was in military force. The occupation of the Ruhr would raise the necessary fears in London and Washington, as well as in Berlin, to make those governments cede. "One must not believe," continued Poincaré confidentially, "that the occupation will be an *opération blanche*—it will scarcely show a profit." The Ruhr would be a political guarantee designed to make Germany and the Allies "transigible."[2] In this connection, the very suspicions leveled at French policy would work in its favor. Britain would rather satisfy French demands than see France entrenched on both banks of the Rhine.

The key to the reparations question for the French premier was the German fiscal problem. As long as France insisted on full reparations payment, the Germans would continue to inflate their currency. But if reparations were reduced or a long moratorium granted to permit currency stabilization, the German tax burden would become the lightest in Europe! The following year Poincaré expressed this frustration to St. Aulaire in London:

> The day Germany desires it, the day when the government will balance its budget, an easy task for a nation without military expenses or any internal debt, the German taxpayer will be the most unburdened and enriched in the entire world. This situation preoccupies us, but it seems not to preoccupy England. The English view is only for the present, the unstable mark and the chronic instability of world markets. They do not think of the future and foresee the truly frightful danger not only for France and Belgium, but for Eng-

[1] P.-V., Commission des Affaires Étrangères, 7 June 1922: Archives du Sénat, Auditions, 1922, pp. 8-9.

[2] Ibid.; see also Denise Artaud, "À propos de l'occupation de la Ruhr," *Revue d'histoire moderne et contemporaine* 17 (March 1970): 1-21.

> land and all of Europe. An economic hegemony will suddenly appear and Germany will have won the objectives she expected from a victorious war.[3]

Poincaré's vision of apocalypse may have been exaggerated, but it was true that if Germany's debt were reduced without a war debt annulment, France's per capita debt would be higher than Germany's. Poincaré was not interested in German currency reform unless it was part of a grand scheme of reparations, capable of overcoming the German political barriers to fulfillment. Having won no sympathy from any quarter, Poincaré now promised to take action. He told the Belgian ambassador in July 1922, "I will propose a short moratorium subject to guarantees. If England refuses, I will act alone. The German industrialists conspire to destroy the mark. They hope to ruin France."[4]

Preparations for the Ruhr had already begun. In fact, they began at the time of the advance of the Allied armies in December 1918, but this fact does not prove that the Ruhr occupation was plotted from the Armistice. To be sure, many ambitious Frenchmen saw the Ruhr occupation as a panacea. General Degoutte made only a slight overstatement when he claimed that "in the eyes of all, the Ruhr constituted the *gage par excellence*."[5] But the existence of military contingency plans is hardly evidence of immutable governmental intent. The first Ruhr planning stemmed from the desire to find an alternative to a march on Berlin, should the German government refuse to sign the peace treaty. Until 1921 plans for a Ruhr operation continued to rest on the assumption that an advance into the basin would be a response to German refusal to disarm. Although the Millerand government was sensitive to France's coal shortage, the Ruhr occupation was still envisioned as a military act of pressure.

The plan developed by Marshal Foch for the Briand sanctions policy was of another order. The occupation planned for May 1921 was to have been primarily an economic operation aimed at direct exploitation of the Ruhr mines and cokeries, necessitating a host of soldiers and technicians. By 1922 thinking on the Ruhr had been raised to a more sophisticated plane. A Ruhr occupation would aim at indirect exploitation, hence would not require nearly so many men as provided for in 1921. The operation would not be unduly expensive and would yield at

[3] Tel. Poincaré to St. Aulaire, 29 June 1923: France, Government Publications, *Documents relatifs aux notes allemandes du 2 mai et 5 juin, 1923, sur les réparations* (Paris, 1923), p. 52.

[4] Tel. #8874/4092/PCA Gaiffier (Paris) to Jaspar, 25 July 1922: MAE Bel., Correspondance Politique, France, 1922.

[5] Degoutte, *L'Occupation de la Ruhr*, intro.

least enough cash and coal to pay for itself, thus satisfying French taxpayers. In the aftermath of the Rapallo treaty, the French military took up the task of detailed planning. Minister of War André Maginot visited the occupied territories and General Degoutte responded with a report on the subject of a Ruhr occupation. Its goal, he posited, was to pay for itself, no more, no less. To Degoutte, as to Poincaré, the Ruhr would be a political guarantee. "The ideal is to leave the Ruhr in the hands of its present owners and to interest them in the success of our efforts."[6] Tirard complemented Degoutte's report a week later with his own. The Rhineland, he pointed out, could be made to support the Ruhr operation through seizure of German customs, mines, and forests on the Left Bank. As in 1921, the Rhineland would become a "reparations province." Degoutte followed with a second plan on 18 May, specifying the military and civilian forces required for the encirclement and management of the Ruhr.

These first efforts stimulated the interested ministries of Paris. Minister of Public Works Yves Le Trocquer appointed Inspector-General of Mines Émile Coste to form three industrial services necessary to oversee control of Ruhr production. Coste met with members of the Ministry of Finance, with General Weygand, Marshal Foch, and Le Trocquer, and all gathered with Tirard on 29 May. Coste outlined the measures to be taken in the Ruhr. He spoke against an economic separation from Germany, arguing that France could probably not succeed in stifling Germany by such means and it would surely antagonize all parties. Rather, the occupation must see to it that prescribed coal deliveries were made to the West and that fiscal exploitation was carried out. All sorts of government revenues were open to confiscation in the Ruhr, Coste noted, but the greatest plum was the *Kohlensteuer*, a tax of 40 percent on every ton of coal mined in the region.

The first discussion on the nature and goals of a possible Ruhr occupation took place beneath the top levels of government, but they ended in agreement on principles that dovetailed with Poincaré's conception as revealed in the Senate secret session. First, the entire Ruhr basin would be occupied—no half-measures such as the seizure of the Ruhr ports in 1921. Second, no direct exploitation of the Ruhr would be attempted such as was planned in 1921. Third, a number of financial measures would be taken to provide immediate income, particularly collection of the *Kohlensteuer* and sanctions on the Left Bank of the Rhine. Fourth, the Ruhr would not be evacuated upon German ac-

[6] Report Degoutte, "Rapport sur les modalités d'exploitation de la Ruhr," to Foch and MG, 2 May 1922: ibid., pp. 36-37.

ceptance of some new Allied reparations plan, but would continue to be held as a guarantee of German compliance.[7] It would constitute a political hostage.

Preparations went no further for the moment. The Reparations Commission had granted Germany a respite for 1922, and sanctions were not an immediate possibility. But it seemed only a matter of time on 24 June, when Europe was swept out of the doldrums by the assassination of Walther Rathenau. In Germany it precipitated a republican backlash of an intensity surpassing that following the murder of Erzberger, and Chancellor Wirth proclaimed openly that the enemy within was to found on the Right. But in France, news of the assassination was another reminder that no German government had the power, even if it possessed the will, to fulfill the treaty of peace.

DEADLOCK CONFIRMED IN BERLIN AND LONDON

On 12 July 1922 the Hague conference on Russia broke up in failure and once again the Allied powers turned their attention to Germany and reparations. On the same day, Poincaré and Lloyd George received a program for their next encounter in the form of the German formal request for a full moratorium deposited with the Reparations Commission. The event was not unexpected, an admission by Wirth that the policy of fulfillment was dead—assassinated, General Degoutte believed, by the same forces that had eliminated its chief exponent. Until January 1923 the subject of Franco-British debate would be the conditions under which a moratorium could be granted, the final phase of the process of bluff and dare leading to the Ruhr.

Poincaré had refrained from giving his blessing to the first Ruhr preparations in May, and by the first week in July Foch still lamented: "The great shame is that we have no plan. If we had one, strong, clear, and practical, England could do nothing but accept it."[8] The premier was not so certain of British acquiescence, but he saw now the need to invoke the Ruhr occupation—at least as a threat—if France's antagonists were to be made to yield. On 12 July, the same day as the German request, the French council of ministers deliberated. Poincaré ordered the reconstitution of the Ruhr Committee of 1921, composed of interested ministerial and military figures. He gave the go-ahead for Ruhr planning, and asked for reports by August.

[7] P.-V., Meeting of 29 May 1922: ibid., pp. 47-50; Note Seydoux, "Rapport de l'inspecteur général des mines," 30 May 1922, cited in Zimmermann, *Frankreichs Ruhrpolitik*, pp. 81-82.

[8] Zimmermann, *Frankreichs Ruhrpolitik*, p. 83.

But Poincaré's second initiative at the 12 July council reflected instead his stubborn attachment to Briand's advice: exhaust all other policies before gambling on the Ruhr. True to his promise to the Senate, Poincaré had arm-twisted and cajoled French industrial cliques to lift their opposition to reparations-in-kind. The Gillet-Ruppel Accord was approved by the Reparations Commission on 27 June, and the French government followed by insisting that the *sinistrés* organizations and manufacturers resolve their differences. The result was creation of a *Comité Consultatif des Prestations en Nature*, permitting reconstruction firms to place orders freely in Germany, but authorizing the Comité to issue stop orders on purchases that could have been made in France.[9] The creation of this mechanism did not settle the power struggle between state and industry, and within industry, on the guidance of national economic policy. But it would begin the dismantling of French barriers to the flow of German goods—if the Germans would dismantle theirs. Thus, even as Poincaré ordered Ruhr preparations, he also approved, with Seydoux's support, a new appeal to Berlin for encouragement of deliveries-in-kind. "I insist most strongly on the urgency of this demarche," he wired Berlin, "and on the necessity of receiving the German government's acceptance without delay." Poincaré hoped to implement the accords by 20 July, only a week away.[10]

The Wirth government and portions of German business were not averse to industrial deliveries and accords, but only if they would indeed pacify France. Unfortunately, Poincaré needed financial reparations as well and spoke of guarantees and sanctions in case of German default or a moratorium. But without a moratorium and perhaps an Allied loan granted without strings, Wirth could not hope to rally business support for stabilization of the mark. The cabinet presented a program in July 1922 designed to satisfy the Reparations Commission: import restrictions, an internal loan to the government, currency reform. But the Ruhr, led by Stinnes and Kloeckner and in alliance with the Reichsbank, rejected the plan. Wirth turned to the Reichstag and sought a political means to break the deadlock through a Grand Coalition. The state could take emergency measures in the economy but only with a two-thirds majority. The concessions demanded by the Social Democrats (control of the Reichsbank) on the one hand and the

[9] *Journée Industrielle*, 22 July 1922. See also Hermann Rupieper, "Industrie und Reparationen: Einige Aspekte des Reparationsproblems 1922-1924," *Industrielles System*, pp. 582-592 (see pp. 588-589); Weill-Raynal, *Les réparations allemandes*, II, 290-291.

[10] Tel. Poincaré to Chargé Berlin, 12 July 1922: MAE Pap. Millerand, Réparations VIII, nos. 15-16.

industrial Deutsche Volkspartei (end of the eight-hour day) on the other precluded a coalition.[11] The inflation in Germany continued unchecked, and Berlin instead concentrated on shoring up its diplomatic and political defenses against the expected French "offensive" in the occupied territories. The Gillet-Ruppel Accord went into operation on 20 July, but few orders were passed and it led to no broader negotiations. Franco-German political initiatives were sterile.[12]

Not only did Berlin expect France to return to a sanctions policy, given the German failure to stabilize the mark, but the separatist movements of Dorten and Smeets showed a new vitality. Leo Deckers, one of Smeets's lieutenants, reportedly was forming armed separatist *Stosstruppen.*[13] A corroborative piece of evidence suggested that the French High Commissariat had secretly arranged for the separatists to bear arms "for self-protection." In the Palatinate, Tirard proclaimed martial law to quell disorders following the Rathenau murder, but he prolonged the special decrees after the pretext had disappeared.[14] Contemporaneous with these reports was the publication by a Munich newspaper of the "Eichhorn documents," which exposed French involvement in the Speyer putsch of 1919.[15] These events combined to produce a rash of rumors in July 1922 to the effect that the separatists were "on the march," that the French planned another coup in the near future.

The separatist activity was harmless. Both Dorten and Smeets were preparing for their annual congresses, which were held on 10 July at Boppard and on 23 July at Aachen. But the Berlin government feared violence and increased the number of *Schutzpolizei* in the occupied territories. The real danger of Rhenish political change, as seen from Berlin, was not a French-inspired putsch, however, but that Britain might agree to Rhenish autonomy in a compromise to save the Entente. The period of uncertainty came to a climax when Gustav

[11] Maier, *Recasting Bourgeois Europe*, pp. 293-302; Rupieper, "Politics and Economics," pp. 104-137.

[12] Weill-Raynal, *Les réparations allemandes*, II, 293-302. French industry continued to attack the Gillet-Ruppel Accords, pointing to the preponderance of finished goods, especially machine-tool, in the first orders placed in Germany. Poincaré insisted that "certain French industrialists have perhaps pushed the defense of their interests too far." To stimulate orders under the Accord, he lowered the French tariff on German goods from the peak level achieved under Briand, and was accordingly lambasted by the *Journée Industrielle.*

[13] MAE Memo, "Traduction d'un officiel document allemand du 13 juin, 1922," MAE Rive Gauche, vol. 28, no. 110; Report Schellen to A.A., 7 July 1922: AA BG L1544, 5632, no. 469179-81.

[14] Let. Poincaré to Dard (Munich), 27 July 1922: MAE Allemagne, vol. 350, no. 203.

[15] Des. Tirard to Poincaré, 9 Aug. 1922, relative to articles published by *Münchner Neueste Nachrichten*, 20-22 July 1922: MAE Rive Gauche, vol. 28, nos. 136-144.

Stresemann, deputy and head of the Deutsche Volkspartei, rose to challenge the government's "complacency" on the Rhenish question. Was it not true that the British attitude had changed? asked Stresemann. He cited a conversation with the British delegate in Cologne, who suggested that Lloyd George might favor a plebiscite. He also expressed concern over the American retreat from Rhenish affairs.[16]

The Reich cabinet answered Stresemann's challenge with further assurances. The Wilhelmstrasse had been aware of the utterances of Mr. Piggot in Cologne and stated that the rumors were unfounded. Nevertheless, the *Auswärtiges Amt* wired London the same week to inquire once again about Britain's Rhenish policy. The Foreign Office told the German ambassador that Lloyd George intended to hold firm against Poincaré.[17] Despairing of the internal reform necessary for rapprochement with France, the impotent Berlin government again placed its hopes in the effectiveness of British diplomacy.

During the interval between 12 July and the opening of the Conference of London, Poincaré set out to devise a plan of constructive guarantees that he would demand in return for granting a moratorium. Le Trocquer reminded Poincaré of the plight of French metallurgy and judged the only guarantee worth taking was the Ruhr itself. If the present trend continued, he warned, Germany would have the power to extinguish French metallurgy entirely. "It is absolutely necessary that we *possess* the Ruhr coke. . . . We must demand the cession of German mines capable of producing the coke we need."[18]

In his turn, Jacques Seydoux repeated the prognosis he had offered at the reparations "council of war" in March. Stabilization of German finances followed by external loans was the only hope for priming the pump of German reparations. But Seydoux recognized also the need for deliveries-in-kind, a coal-for-iron agreement, and a settlement on steel prices and markets. On the financial side, France could not accept a moratorium without constructive pledges. For this purpose a sanctions policy must be taken up and the Rhineland made into a reparations province. The Allies should receive proprietorship of German mines, forests, dye factories (95 percent of which were in the Rhineland), and customs receipts for the duration of the moratorium and as guarantees for any loans the Berlin government could contract.[19] Poin-

[16] Aufzeichnung, 20 July 1922: AA BG L1544, 5632, nos. 469184-87.

[17] Tel. Sthamer (London) to A.A., 27 July 1922: AA BR 3059, 1469, no. 602998.

[18] Note Le Trocquer to Poincaré, 26 July 1922: MAE Pap. Millerand, Réparations VIII, nos. 166-172.

[19] Note Seydoux, "Question des réparations," 24 July 1922: MAE Pap. Millerand, Réparations VIII, nos. 191-201.

caré combined these suggestions into a far-reaching plan of constructive guarantees, an alternative to occupation of the Ruhr by France. Lloyd George would be loath to agree to such an increase in Allied control over the Rhenish economy, but the alternative, Poincaré hoped, would appear to him far worse.[20]

Even before the opening of the Conference of London, Poincaré suffered a rude blow from across the Channel. The new war debts policy enunciated by Lloyd George in the cabinet in June now burst upon the French consciousness with even more impact than Lloyd George had intended. He had delayed the offer to the United States for consolidation and funding of the British war debt pending the outcome of a new and accelerated fall of the German mark in June and July. By the end of July he said, ". . . it is time we asserted ourselves."[21] Acting on the prime minister's intent, but without consulting Lord Curzon, who was absent from London recuperating from illness, Lord Balfour issued the ill-fated declaration of 1 August 1922.

His Majesty's Government, the Balfour note declared, was prepared to abandon all rights to German reparations and all claim to repayment of Allied debts, provided this renunciation formed part of a general plan of international financial rehabilitation. Britain would fund her debt to the United States, but invited Washington to liberate her from that responsibility so that Britain could liberate her own debtors. The note was meant to be constructive, the first direct effort by Lloyd George's government to break the financial deadlock, but it was impolitic, as Curzon noted with regret when he returned to his post. The American reaction was indignant, as befitted the putative victim of moral blackmail. The note untactfully implied that Washington's greed was the only barrier to world recovery. To the French, the note seemed to be directed at them. Whatever the American response, the British would increase their own financial and moral leverage vis-à-vis France. The "Shylock" accusation only tied the hands of Secretary of State Hughes, precluding American concessions, and the note exacerbated the suspicions between Britain and France on the eve of the London Conference.

Poincaré arrived in the British capital on 7 August with a veritable ultimatum. He demanded expropriation by the Reparations Commission of the state-owned mines of the Ruhr, thus satisfying French coal needs. On the Left Bank, he called for the Rhineland Commission to take control of the state forests and 60 percent of the dyestuff industry.

[20] Let. Poincaré to Dubois, "Question des réparations," 3 Aug. 1922: MAE Pap. Millerand, Réparations VIII, nos. 191-201.

[21] Minutes, CAB 42(22), 25 July 1922: PRO CAB 23/30, pp. 347-364.

Finally, the Allies were to reinstate the customs barrier surrounding the Rhineland and the Ruhr ports and levy a 26 percent duty on German exports. To ensure the execution of the budgetary reforms still uneffected by Berlin, the Allies would assume direction of the Reichsbank.

After an early skirmish for Belgian and Italian support, Poincaré found the British willing to bargain. Lloyd George accepted the export sanction and the Belgians and Italians also approved of the mines and forests sanctions. But the British stopped short at the customs barrier. If Poincaré persisted in his demands for economic separation of the Rhineland, Lloyd George announced, it would mean the rupture of the Entente. Poincaré reported to Millerand that France could acquire "some guarantees, but certainly not all that we have asked."[22]

Millerand convoked an impromptu council of ministers. Seydoux, Laroche, and Finance Minister de Lasteyrie urged the sacrifice of the customs barrier to preserve Allied unity, but the prevailing mood in the rump council, in which Millerand's determination set the tone, was firm. A short-term agreement no longer interested the president; the Ruhr had been held in reserve long enough. On 10 August, Millerand urged Poincaré to hold to his program.[23] Lloyd George convened his Cabinet on the same day. The British ministers were unanimous in their opposition to Poincaré's "ultimatum." As in Paris, the voice of the Foreign Office spoke for accommodation. Lord Curzon said that it would not do to drive the French into the Ruhr, where Belgium would have to follow, and still not achieve French cooperation in Turkey and elsewhere. But Curzon had no practical suggestion as to how France might be appeased. The cabinet rejected Poincaré's plan and, in effect, dared him to occupy the Ruhr.[24]

Poincaré relaxed his stance on the Ruhr customs line and the dye factories in defiance of Millerand, but negotiations faltered. The French president expressed delight at the prospect of a break. Millerand had come to consider France's economic power more important than the Entente, and if a break with London would leave France free to act, he was willing to accept the consequences. He wired Poincaré that he was pleased and hardly surprised at the outcome of the conference.[25] Poincaré was not pleased. His concessions had shown him to

[22] Tel. Poincaré (London) to MAE for Millerand, 9 Aug. 1922: MAE Pap. Millerand, vol. 50, nos. 162-163.

[23] Tel. Millerand to Poincaré (London), 9 and 10 Aug. 1922: MAE Pap. Millerand, vol. 50, nos. 170-172; vol. 51, nos. 26-28.

[24] Minutes, CAB 44(22), 10 Aug. 1922: PRO CAB 23/30, pp. 397-415.

[25] Tel. Poincaré (London) to MAE for Millerand, 12 Aug. 1922; Tel. Millerand to Poincaré (London), 12 Aug. 1922: MAE Pap. Millerand, vol. 51, nos. 113-114, 120.

be in sympathy with Seydoux and Laroche, not with Millerand. But Lloyd George's firm stance gave the French premier and the conservative men of the Quai d'Orsay new resolve. On 14 August, when the Conference of London broke up in failure, Poincaré wired Millerand to convoke another council of ministers. As an afterthought, he sent another wire five minutes later. This one went to the minister of war: "Urgent! Please return to Paris at once and convoke Marshal Foch and General Degoutte."[26]

RUHR PREPARATIONS II

"LE 'DEADLOCK' CONTINUE!" announced *Le Temps* upon Poincaré's return from London. Lloyd George had shown himself "more obstinate than ever," and the semi-official journal feared that it was becoming clear that the British government no longer saw any logic in the Entente with France but instead sought entente with Germany. This was "sad and dangerous and could lead to the very result British policy has sought to avoid: French hegemony is impossible, so German hegemony must result." Was this inevitable? Not if European reconstruction, blocked by Anglo-American policy, could proceed, but German hegemony would "develop naturally and in accord with modern ideas if all nations were afflicted or menaced with the same economic ruin."[27] The stakes were clear to Germany's continental neighbors. Integration was inevitable, but without Anglo-Saxon support for the weaker states led by France, the only possible outcome of economic chaos and conflict was domination of all by united Germany. Britain must be brought to understand.

Poincaré's sense of urgency was anticipated again by his ministerial and military team. The Ruhr committee met under the direction of Seydoux on 9 and 10 August, and upheld the principles agreed upon in May. Degoutte believed that the Ruhr industrialists, being self-interested businessmen, would bow to *force majeure* and prove anxious to come to terms after an occupation of their mines and factories. Émile Coste, slated to lead the technical contingent in the Ruhr, was not so confident. The committee had considered, for instance, a substantial increase in the *Kohlensteuer*, and expected the Ruhr magnates to submit to such confiscatory measures. Coste argued that the occupation must seek to avoid undue disturbance to the German internal market if it expected cooperation from the Germans. Despite this

[26] Tel. Poincaré (London) to MAE for Millerand, 14 Aug. 1922; Tel. Poincaré to Maginot, 14 Aug. 1922: MAE Pap. Millerand, vol. 51, nos. 132-134.

[27] "LE 'DEADLOCK' CONTINUE," *Le Temps*, 15 Aug. 1922.

warning, the committee still planned a 25 percent increase in the tax. It did not expect German resistance on a large scale. The French did not envision a German policy of suicide.[28]

On 15 August Poincaré arrived in Paris and received a briefing on where things stood. He also sought to temper optimism. France did not have a free hand in Western Germany—there were diplomatic aspects to consider. With the co-agency of the Allies, a success in the Ruhr would be difficult to achieve; without it, almost impossible. Belgian support, at least, was indispensable.[29] More vital to the launching and success of a Ruhr operation than impeccable military and technical planning was the acquisition of comrades-in-arms. Despite Millerand's willingness to jettison the Western alliance and face Germany alone, the Ruhr would be a diplomatic problem.

What was the financial prognosis for the Ruhr occupation? The potential weakness of the franc was a weapon for France's adversaries. Reconstruction of the devastated regions was a task of national honor—that financial burden must be maintained. France's large standing army, including expensive contingents in Turkey and Syria, drained the treasury but was necessary if France was to be able to pressure Germany at all. If the taking of the Ruhr entailed further long-term investment without return, it could push France under instead of Germany. De Lasteyrie bluntly informed the premier that he was disturbed by France's steadily deteriorating financial position. The government desperately needed a rapid reparations settlement; otherwise it would be forced to present a tax program to the Chambers "staggering to French public opinion."[30] If a Ruhr occupation were undertaken, it must pay its own way.

Seydoux projected a highly favorable financial balance in a report of 19 August. He estimated the cost of extending the occupation and Tirard's financial services to the Ruhr at 300 million francs per year. In return, Seydoux expected 450 million gold marks from the *Kohlensteuer* alone. But he assumed full production in the Ruhr, and a rise in the tax from 40 to 50 percent *ad valorem*. Taxes on other industries would yield from 200 to 300 million gold marks, and customs and export duties would yield the same. Thus the cost would equal about 100 million gold marks and the receipts from 850 to 1,000 million gold marks. In addition, the French government would expect cession of

[28] "Conférence relative aux mésures économiques et financières éventuelles à envisager en cas d'occupation du Bassin de la Ruhr," 9 Aug. 1922: MAE Ruhr, vol. 3, nos. 147-149; Degoutte, *L'Occupation de la Ruhr*, pp. 50-52.

[29] Note Vignon, "Dispositions à prendre," meeting of 15 Aug. 1922: MAE Pap. Millerand, vol. 53, nos. 139-142.

[30] Pers. Let. Logan to Strong, 28 July 1922: HI Logan Papers, Box 2.

the state mines of the Ruhr capable of producing 12.6 million tons of coal per year.[31] Assuming the Ruhr would work under full steam for a foreign power, the occupation would be the guarantee par excellence.

Poincaré was not sanguine about the financial return to be expected from the Ruhr, as evidenced by his warning to the Senate commission not to look for a favorable balance, but he evidently expected to break even. It was left to the finance minister to worry. De Lasteyrie found Seydoux's thumbnail sketch to be wildly unrealistic. He protested to Poincaré on 24 August, warning against the danger of being hypnotized by such estimates. Seydoux's incremental expenses—over and above the burden of the present Rhineland occupation, for which Germany might suspend payment after a Ruhr occupation—did not take into account the care of the population. The pittance allotted by Seydoux for revictualment could explode into a figure of 100 million francs monthly if the French were forced to feed and heat the population of the Ruhr. Seydoux's receipts, de Lasteyrie pointed out, assumed full production. The expenses could very well be gigantic and the receipts negligible if the masters of the Ruhr chose not to cooperate. "Everything," de Lasteyrie warned, "depends on the attitude of the German authorities and their reaction to the measures of the occupation."[32] But if Seydoux erred on the side of optimism, Poincaré considered de Lasteyrie too pessimistic. He instructed Degoutte to draw up military plans.

DIPLOMATIC PREPARATIONS AND ALTERNATIVES

The Balfour note and London Conference prepared the way for the final confirmation of the financial deadlock on 23 August. In April the American Congress' World War Debt Funding Commission had begun to turn the screws on its European debtors. In response, Poincaré made a personal appeal (as J. P. Morgan had suggested) to Secretary of State Hughes by letter in July. "France came out sorely tried from a bloody conflict . . . ," he pleaded, and "since the peace, France has done all in her power to improve this difficult situation." But the insignificant reparation received from Germany threw the burden of reconstruction—already 90 billion francs—on the French budget. France had not considered demanding repayment from her own overburdened debtors; could not the United States show the same understanding? In sum, France was incapable of payment, and insistence

[31] Note Seydoux, "Note sur la Ruhr," 19 Aug. 1922: MAE Pap. Millerand, vol. 53, nos. 181-193.

[32] Pers. Let. de Lasteyrie to Poincaré, 24 Aug. 1922, cited by Zimmermann, *Frankreichs Ruhrpolitik*, pp. 85-86.

upon it by America, especially "if any reduction of our credit with Germany were one day imposed on us by circumstances," would involve France's ruin and a "scandalous revenge of the nations that have fought against our common ideal of liberty. . . ."[33] Hughes's cold and uncompromising reply of 23 August stood in brutal contrast to Poincaré's impassioned appeal. Hughes was "constrained to believe that the path to this full economic recovery through an early and practicable settlement [of reparations] is the one which alone can lead to the prosperity which the friends of France so much desire. . . ."[34] But it was clear by the end of August 1922 that France was given little incentive to pursue that "practicable settlement" by Germany, or Britain, or the United States.

No firm decision to occupy the Ruhr had been made, but Poincaré had to continue preparations for that eventuality. The first diplomatic arena was the Reparations Commission. Wirth's opponents in Germany had blamed his fulfillment policy for the depreciation of the mark, but the calamitous fall of the summer of 1922—during virtual moratorium—seemed to explode that myth. The mark was still under 350 to a dollar on 24 June, the day of Rathenau's death, but it soared to 670 by the end of July, 2,000 by the end of August, and it showed no sign of stabilizing. To Poincaré, the collapse reflected nothing but the ill will of German government and industry. He directed a report from Tirard to the Reparations Commission to support his point of view.

The Rhenish economy, Tirard observed, was booming, monetary crisis notwithstanding. The internal market had never been better. To be sure, the inflation, which had sent bread up to 137 times its prewar price, had already ruined the rentier class. But industry and commerce were unaffected. Germany suffered from inflation, Tirard concluded, only because certain powerful elements of society desired not to prevent it.[35] A moratorium, Poincaré argued, was unnecessary for the restoration of German finances. If Berlin refused to balance its budget, the continued productivity of the German economy must provide the guarantee of reparations deserved by France. To ensure a majority opinion on the Reparations Commission favorable to France, Poincaré instructed his embassy in Belgium to begin pressuring the Belgian government to oppose a moratorium and to approve an occupation of the Ruhr.[36]

[33] Let. Poincaré to Hughes, 19 July 1922: FRUS 1922, I, 404-405.

[34] Let. Hughes to Poincaré, 23 Aug. 1922: FRUS 1922, I, 412-413.

[35] Report Tirard, "Rapport sur la situation économique dans les territoires occupés," 10 Sept. 1922: MAE Rive Gauche, vol. 7, nos. 112-174.

[36] Let. Poincaré to Dubois, 10 Sept. 1922: MAE Rive Gauche, vol. 7, nos. 110-111; Tel. Poincaré to Chargé Brussels, 14 Sept. 1922: MAE Pap. Millerand, Réparations IX, no. 21.

The French chargé at Brussels reported that Léon Delacroix, the Belgian delegate, approved of a declaration of default rather than a moratorium, but that the Belgians could not promise to participate in pledge-taking. Poincaré countered by threatening to act alone; he hoped the Brussels government would recognize its own interests.[37] Belgian Premier Paul Theunis feared an irrevocable split between his senior partners, Britain and France, but he feared unilateral action by France most of all. The Belgians continued to display nerves throughout September 1922. On 3 October Delacroix visited Seydoux and admitted his government's desire to follow the French lead, if only it could be sure of Poincaré's intentions.[38]

A surprising development then intervened to give Poincaré pause. During August and September 1922, with the Ruhr occupation becoming more likely, the president of the Alliance of French Reconstruction Associations, Senator Marquis de Lubersac, concluded with none other than Hugo Stinnes a 1.5 billion mark private contract for deliveries of construction materials under the Gillet-Ruppel Accord. Poincaré envisioned two possible sequels: a governmental accord for deliveries-in-kind and a private agreement between French and German industrialists.[39] Had the prospect of a Ruhr occupation softened the attitude of Stinnes, "king of the Ruhr"?

The Stinnes-Lubersac accords raised the customary doubts in French industrial circles, but were more bitterly attacked in Germany than in France. Stinnes seemed to be cooperating with the French now for private profit where he previously blocked Berlin's attempts to cooperate by way of treaty fulfillment. When Poincaré again instructed his ambassador to urge rapid amplification of any of the five accords negotiated since 1921 into a comprehensive plan for repair of the devastated regions, the German government procrastinated. On 6 October, after three French demarches, the Germans announced their unwillingness to consider promoting reparations-in-kind until conclusion of a financial settlement.[40]

Stinnes' accord with Lubersac was a signal of his desire, shared by Siemens and Silverberg, to promote industrial peace between France

[37] Tel. Jaunez (Brussels) to Poincaré, 15 Sept. 1922: Tel. Poincaré to Juanez, 16 Sept. 1922: MAE Pap. Millerand, Réparations IX, nos. 88-91.

[38] Note Seydoux pour le PdC, "Réparations—au sujet de M. Delacroix," 3 Oct. 1922: MAE Pap. Millerand, Réparations IX, nos. 88-91.

[39] Georges Suarez, *Herriot, revue, corrigée et augmentée suivie d'un récit historique de R. Poincaré* (Paris, 1932), p. 215.

[40] Note Ministère des Travaux Publics, cabinet du ministre, 28 Dec. 1922: MAE Pap. Millerand, vol. 52, nos. 1-6. See also Weill-Raynal, *Les réparations allemandes*, II, 298-302.

and Germany. But he had not altered his terms. As he told the Reich Economic Council two months later, he hoped to exploit his strength and the desperate plight of French metallurgy to grant the French the gigantic trust they desired, but to ensure that it submitted to German direction.[41] Fearing precisely such a development—if France threw in her lot with Germany, she could expect no succor from Britain—and unable to bring French industry to a common position, Poincaré now saw nothing but political embarrassment in private industrial talks. Working through Émile Mayrisch, a Luxembourgois industrialist, Stinnes attempted to arrange a personal meeting with the leading French steel magnate, Eugene Schneider. Three dates were set, the first being 28 September; three times Schneider failed to appear. It was now clear to French political authority that only a Ruhr occupation could give France the bargaining position of a victor, not a supplicant. Poincaré quashed the planned rendezvous.[42]

The deadlock in the Reparations Commission gave Poincaré the opportunity to rid himself of the French delegate Louis Dubois, who had become "tainted" by his association with the body of international experts, and to replace him with a personal collaborator.[43] Once again, he called on Louis Barthou. The first week in October also saw a change in the French ambassadorial alignment. Upon the retirement of Charles Laurent, the difficult post of ambassador to Germany went to Pierre Jacquin de Margerie, previously in Brussels. A younger man, the fifty-year-old Georges Herbette, replaced him in Belgium. It was Herbette's first embassy, and he inherited the delicate task of preserving Franco-Belgian cooperation in an undertaking in which mutual suspicion, not trust, seemed to keep the governments in tandem.

On 13 October Poincaré summoned a reparations council to examine the British note to the Reparations Commission that recommended granting Germany a four-year moratorium without guarantees. Belgian and Italian support would be needed to prevent consideration of such a plan. Poincaré resolved to court that support by presenting an alternate plan based on Allied control of German finances.[44] Seydoux was charged with its formulation, but the Quai d'Orsay's expert frankly

[41] Jean-Claude Favez, *Le Reich devant l'occupation franco-belge de la Ruhr en 1923* (Geneva, 1969), pp. 28-31; Rupieper, "Politics and Economics," pp. 130-143; Feldman, *Iron and Steel*, pp. 329-330.

[42] Bariéty, "La rôle de la minette," pp. 275-276; Poincaré in Suarez, *Herriot*, p. 221.

[43] In return, Dubois complained that the premier constantly made him a scapegoat for unpopular decisions before French opinion, and refused to be "an automaton of Poincaré's will" (Pers. Let. Logan to Hoover, 29 Sept. 1922: HI Logan Papers, Box 4, Folder 2).

[44] P.-V., Réunion tenue chez M. le PdC, "Examination du note Bradbury," 13 Oct. 1922: MAE Pap. Millerand, Réparations IX, nos. 119-124.

admitted a lack of comprehension of his chief's tactics. Seydoux had been pulling when many others pushed toward a Ruhr occupation. Now, when Seydoux himself had come to regard it as inevitable, Poincaré seemed to be backing off. Seydoux had a proclivity for being out of phase with the prevailing opinion in government. It was too late to rehabilitate German finances, he said, the mark was past saving. What if the British accepted Poincaré's limited project? Would not France lose her pretext for direct action? A comprehensive plan, such as that of August, would guarantee a British refusal and France would be left free to act.[45] No longer a restraining force, Seydoux now became a leading exponent of the Ruhr occupation throughout the decisive months.

Poincaré would soon put Seydoux at ease concerning his doubts about French policy. The premier did not intend to grant a moratorium without guarantees. But for the moment he did show signs of renewing his hope for a common Allied policy toward Germany. Even if the British would not participate in a Ruhr occupation, Poincaré preferred to cover his flank, and a rare opportunity now opened to him to foster Franco-British cooperation. Lloyd George was no longer Poincaré's rival. There was a new government in London.

TURKISH TROUBLES; BONAR LAW AND MUSSOLINI

The British and French, always at odds in the Near East concerning oil concessions and the borders of their mandates, also failed to forge a common policy on the Turkish revolution and the Graeco-Turkish war. When Mustapha Kemal declared the National Pact and the creation of a revolutionary government in Ankara in January 1920, the Treaty of Sèvres had not even been signed by the sultan in Constantinople. France, Britain, and Italy maintained an occupation force at Chanak on the Asian side of the Dardanelles, but Lloyd George welcomed Greek Premier Venizelos' offer to resist Kemal with a Greek army. In 1921 the Greeks swept deep into Anatolia, penetrating to within two hundred miles of Ankara.

Despite the Greek invasion, the revolutionary government solidified its control in the interior of Turkey. Briand made the first move to accommodate Ankara. A French mission reached accord with Kemal on boundary questions in October 1921, and France adopted a position of benevolent neutrality toward the Turks. The obvious antagonism

[45] Note Vignon, "Réparations," 19 Oct. 1922: MAE Pap. Millerand, Réparations IX, no. 140; P.-V., "Réunion du 18 octobre 1922 sous le présidence du PdC": MAE Allemagne, vol. 476, nos. 17-25.

stemming from their divergent Turkish policies helped to weaken the Entente during Briand's tenure, but the military situation had stabilized and several attempts followed under Poincaré to mediate between the belligerents. Greece was determined to uphold the Treaty of Sèvres, to retain Smyrna, and talks never began.

On 26 August 1922 the period of stability ended violently. Kemal's general offensive overwhelmed the Greek lines as resistance turned to retreat, then to rout. Two weeks later the Turks entered Smyrna while British and Greek ships evacuated thousands of Christian refugees. By 21 September the Turks had approached the neutral zone, which included the Allied bases at Chanak and Constantinople. The neutral zone guaranteed free navigation in the Straits; its defense was the primary concern of Lloyd George's Turkish policy. On 16 September Lloyd George announced his intention to go to war to resist a Turkish advance into the neutral zone. The French and Italian response to the crisis was also rapid. On 21 September they withdrew their detachments from Turkey.

There was little London could do after the French "desertion" but stick to its guns and petition Poincaré to restrain the Turks, drunk with victory. Ailing Lord Curzon undertook a personal mission to Paris to seek cooperation. Having placed France in the position of appellee for a change, Poincaré obliged Curzon by joining in an Allied invitation to Greece and Turkey to commence peace talks. The cease-fire took place on 11 October, and the Conference of Lausanne opened on the twenty-fourth.

The overthrow of the peace settlement and war scare in Turkey, in addition to Lloyd George's handling of the Irish question and the spectacular failure of his economic schemes, proved to be too much of a strain on the Liberal-Conservative coalition that had ruled Britain since 1916. A revolt of the Conservatives ousted Lloyd George, and the Tory government of Scotsman Bonar Law emerged from the ensuing elections with a comfortable majority. Curzon remained in the Foreign Office.

The dominant statesman of the immediate postwar period thus disappeared. What had Lloyd George tried to accomplish since the war, and what had he achieved? Faced with the unfathomable complexities of worldwide upheaval—new nations, new social and political threats, economic disorganization—he found guidance in the traditional strategy of Britain: control of the sea, financial supremacy, balance of power. But naval parity and financial dominance had already passed to the United States, and Lloyd George's attempts to resurrect German power on the continent preceded stabilization itself. Finally, his German policy was based on a gross miscalculation of the long-term power ratio between France and Germany.

Why did Lloyd George seem to take Germany's side, even as early as during the Armistice deliberations? But that is our traditional policy, Lloyd George answered. He would play the middle man, the self-proclaimed friend of both France and Germany. It was this method, rather than Lloyd George's goals, that introduced an antagonistic element in postwar relations. "He decided to go in one direction," observed Harold Nicolson, "while pretending that he was going in another." He reassured the French concerning the Entente, but openly demonstrated his belief that the two nations shared no interests. His refusal to satisfy French demands for an explicit security guarantee removed Britain's potential influence for peace. His haste in supporting Germany against France in all questions except when British interests were at stake forfeited the mediatory value of England's position. Unable to depend on the British in any given situation, the French and Germans both were driven to defend the extreme of their points of view. The insincerity of Lloyd George's methods even estranged him from Curzon, who valued "knowledge and precision," and believed in intervening only when that intervention was decisive. Curzon presented no ideas for Europe's rapid political and economic stabilization, but he, like Poincaré, was suspicious of conciliatory gestures devoid of substance, of self-proclaimed "internationalism," and of grand conferences. These were the fundamental elements of Lloyd George's method.

Perhaps the British government's own domestic restraints prohibited Lloyd George from assuming a more constructive stance. The enhanced influence of the Dominions and the exhaustion of the British public precluded bold initiatives and commitments. Certainly Britain's fiscal policy, more responsible than either France's or Germany's, and the economic malaise after 1920 forced all British politicians to concern themselves with economic rehabilitation at the expense of long-range security considerations.[46] Given the need to drag behind him a reluctant electorate, perhaps Lloyd George's theatrics were necessary for any activist foreign policy. But Britain's very weakness precluded the kind of "decisive intervention" desired by Curzon. Unable to intervene to procure what he considered the just demands of France and Germany, Lloyd George only managed to prevent the two continental powers from settling their own differences. In his defense, he would point out that while in office he had kept the Turks out of Constan-

[46] Gordon A. Craig, "The British Foreign Office from Grey to Austen Chamberlain," *The Diplomats*, I, 15-48.

tinople and the French out of the Ruhr, both of which incursions quickly followed after his departure. Critics retorted that Lloyd George's policy made these developments inevitable.

Poincaré held out hopes for the Tory government. The Conservatives had always expressed an attitude harsher toward Germany than the Liberals. Bonar Law might come around to a policy of guarantees short of a full Ruhr occupation, and if he refused he might at least be counted on not to oppose a French action openly. A week after the British change, another Allied government fell, to be replaced by a regime likely to favor a strong German policy. On 29 October 1922 Benito Mussolini led his sixty thousand blackshirts into Rome and prevailed upon Victor Emmanuel to appoint him head of Italy's government. More interested in his foreign policy than his politics, the Quai d'Orsay was pleased to discover that the Italian Fascist would support the declaration of a default by Germany and the seizure of productive guarantees.[47]

The events of September and October 1922 strengthened Poincaré's hand. The diplomatic constellation he considered necessary for a Ruhr operation was taking shape. That very fact led him to hope for the last time that the Allies might agree on a plan of guarantees without resort to a military operation. Nevertheless, the "economic bloc" of the French government, led by Millerand, increased its pressure for an immediate occupation of the Ruhr. Poincaré found himself being rushed to the Rubicon, not only by the intransigence of foreign governments, but by the determination of his own colleagues and the increasingly desperate plight of the French economy.

THE DECISION IS TAKEN

Maurice Bokanowski performed an unpleasant duty in the Chamber of Deputies on 22 October 1922. He was the *rapporteur-général* of the Finance Committee, and he was forced to remind his colleagues of some ugly truths. Once again the government proposed a budget severely imbalanced by the charges of reconstruction. Even if the government were able to finance this deficit with new credits, the service of the French national debt would place an intolerable burden on future budgets. The practice of the double budget had to cease. Taxes were already 360 percent of the 1914 level, but did not suffice. France recognized the need for sacrifice, but asked what sacrifices Germany offered. The per capita fiscal burden in Germany was 306 francs; in

[47] See William I. Shorrock, "France and the Rise of Fascism in Italy, 1919-1923," *Journal of Contemporary History* 10, no. 4 (Oct. 1975), pp. 591-610.

France it was 558. This was unconscionable and in violation of the Treaty of Versailles. To be sure, a cancellation of the interallied debts would lower significantly the total debt of the French government (which also was higher per capita than Germany's), but it would have no direct effect on French finances, since Paris resisted American appeals to fund the war debts. But the least reduction of Germany's obligations, if she could be made to pay at all, would contribute cruelly to French financial weakness, for the cost of reconstruction could not be avoided. Reparations, Bokanowski concluded, must be paid.[48]

It was true that war debts had no immediate financial significance. But their existence was a political fact of the utmost importance, for European resistance to their funding blocked the flow of American capital to Europe. Instead of ignoring the debt question, the French and German governments both participated in diplomatic offensives on the question, abetted by America's own embassies. From Berlin and Paris, Ambassadors Houghton and Herrick pleaded with Washington to reconsider its intransigent position, arguing that European recovery and the resulting political stability and commerce would more than compensate the United States. "God has been good to America," Houghton implored. "He has made it possible for us to create and pile up wealth. I believe most humbly that He has given our people also the vision, once the essential facts are laid before them, to use any necessary part of this wealth to bring about a real and, it may be, a lasting peace among the four great nations involved." Chief of the Western European division of the State Department William Castle echoed these sentiments, seeing cancellation of the debts as "the only way I can see of really winning the war." The pleas were in vain, and the offensive came to an end on 7 November, when Hughes and Ambassador Herrick informed French Ambassador Jusserand and Poincaré, respectively, that war debt policy was up to Congress and that reparations and Europe's political tensions must be settled first in any case.[49] The Americans could not make the first move.

Poincaré answered Bokanowski's complaints in the Senate on 9 November. He defended his patience and reluctance to resort to force by insisting that coercion against Germany would be of far more moral and financial value if it were interallied. He also denied that France was in financial trouble, and applauded the postwar efforts to match deficits with deflationary policies and so avoid the dreadful inflation afflicting

[48] J.O. Chambre, 24 Oct. 1922, pp. 2794-2811. See also "Les finances et la France," *Le Temps*, 23 Oct. 1922. The French definition and arguments for "fiscal justice" were strikingly outlined by the anonymous Alpha, "Reparation and the Policy of Repudiation," *Foreign Affairs*, Sept. 1923, pp. 58-60.

[49] FRUS 1922, II, 160-183.

Germany. But that inflation, Poincaré hastened to add, was the work of the German industrialists who opposed all monetary and fiscal reform.[50] Nevertheless, the strength of the French franc depended on the credibility of her attempts to force reparations.

The month of November 1922 was a nervous one for the French premier. Heralded as the champion of French rights ten months before, Poincaré was now under increasing pressure to end his efforts at accommodation and take the plunge into the Ruhr. A Chamber chorus led by Tardieu challenged the premier to live up to his promise, and in print Tardieu suggested that Poincaré lacked the courage to occupy the Ruhr.[51] Poincaré found himself increasingly isolated within his own government. Maginot, backed by Foch and Degoutte, urged immediate military action, and rumors circulated that the minister of war was next in line for the premiership. Even the Quai d'Orsay, voice of prudence, despaired of peaceful settlement in reparations and heavy industry. Peretti and Seydoux went into the camp of the activists. Finally, President Millerand made known his own intentions, and Poincaré concluded, "If I do not undertake the operation myself, another will be found to do it, and do it less well."[52]

Given the mood of the government, it is logical to ask whether Poincaré could have executed any other policy even if the new British government had accepted his August program. A complete surrender by the Tory government might have pulled the rug from under the advocates of military action. But Bonar Law proved unwilling to purchase a postponement of the Ruhr occupation at the price of French domination in the Rhineland. It is probable that Poincaré himself did not hope for British acquiescence so much as for British neutrality, while France (and presumably Belgium) acted out the drama of the Ruhr. It was this achievement of neutrality which Millerand's precipitousness threatened, and for which Poincaré labored during his month of hesitation.

The British showed no signs of yielding on the question of guarantees, and Lord Hardinge, ambassador in Paris, even held out hopes of Poincaré's fall from power. He failed to intimate that any replacement would probably be more intractable still.[53] But more substantive than

[50] J.O. Sénat, 9 Nov. 1922, pp. 1312-1330.

[51] MS Tardieu (weekly newspaper columns, 1922-23): AN Pap. Tardieu, vol. 42, dos. Journalisme. On 30 November 1922, Tardieu wrote, "La vérité, ce n'est pas du tout que Poincaré soit présentement decidé à tirer des coups de canon et à envahir la Ruhr; c'est qu'il cherche à nourrir sa popularité en compensant le néant des résultats par l'énergie des paroles."

[52] Chastenet, *Les Années d'Illusion*, p. 101.

[53] Des. #2551 Hardinge to F.O., W9078/4/17, 1 Nov. 1922; Des. #2949 Phipps (Paris) to F.O., W1026/4/17, 18 Dec. 1922: PRO FO 371, vol. 8247, nos. 228-230, 283.

hopes for a cabinet crisis was the fear that France was out to escape the guiding hand of Britain and to use her independence to destroy Germany. The French were perfectly right, Lord Curzon told the cabinet, that Germany had brought on its own financial ruin, but the French did not seem inclined to do anything about it. Curzon favored a reparations/debts settlement, but would not accept Poincaré's terms.[54]

An untimely exposé by the *Manchester Guardian* did nothing to aid Poincaré's attempts to reassure the British. The Dariac report of the previous May was leaked to the British press. Francophobe journals expressed shock at this new revelation of the extent of French imperialist designs on Germany: seizure of the Ruhr, separation of the Rhineland, economic hegemony. Ignoring the fact that its obstructionism had contributed to French "chauvinism," the Foreign Office only saw the exposé as justification for its policy. Miles Lampson concluded: "I trust that the Dariac Report is already a little out of date."[55]

Negotiations in the Reparations Commission proved fruitless. Louis Barthou took the Commission to Berlin early in November for an enquiry into German finances. A body of international experts, including John Maynard Keynes and the Swedish economist Gustav Cassel, delivered a decidedly pro-German report, holding that Germany could undertake currency stabilization, but that a moratorium would be necessary and a revision of the reparations bill advisable. The German government took the opportunity to petition anew for a moratorium on 13 November. Seydoux concluded from an interview with William Tyrrell that the British were stalling for time, hoping for political unrest in France.[56]

The British and German governments looked to the Conference of Brussels, scheduled for early December, to put together the compromise unachieved in August at London. But they had delayed once too often, and both governments now lost control over the drift of opinion in Paris. On 20 November Foch showed up with a comprehensive program of reparations, security, and raw materials policy: not just an operational plan, but a political strategy. France would declare that the Rhineland occupation would continue until France was granted adequate security guarantees. The occupation of the Ruhr would give to France the bargaining power to negotiate a satisfactory metallurgical settlement with the Ruhr, and provide a guarantee to bargain for a satisfactory reparations/debts plan.[57]

[54] Annex IV, CAB 64(22), 1 Nov. 1922: PRO CAB 23/32, pp. 15-24.

[55] Minutes, Des. #956 Addison (Berlin) to F.O., C17385/336/18, 13 Dec. 1922: PRO FO 371, vol. 7523, no. 82.

[56] Note Vignon, "Conversation Seydoux—William Tyrrell," 8 Nov. 1922: MAE Pap. Millerand, Réparations IX, nos. 204-206.

[57] Note Foch, 20 Nov. 1922, cited in Zimmermann, *Frankreichs Ruhrpolitik*, p. 88.

The following day Seydoux presented his own Ruhr logic. The French government could accept no stabilization plan that was not linked to a plan of reparations, which in turn meant a loan to Germany. Such a plan was impossible without American intervention, which subordinated loans to the settlement of war debts. This intervention would arrive, predicted Seydoux, but not for two years or so, until the American economy slumped and Washington sought to reopen the European market. In the meantime, France must take the opportunity to seize guarantees in Germany. "We have an interest in fortifying the German economy only if it is so tightly fettered by reparations that it cannot escape us, only if we are no longer menaced by German economic or political hegemony. We must never lose sight of the rapid growth of German population." Seydoux saw two possible outcomes to a Ruhr occupation. Either the Ruhr magnates would submit, in which case French and German industry could cooperate under circumstances safe for France, or the Germans would resist, in which case the French would disinterest themselves in the fate of the Reich and form a new regime in the Rhineland. The Left Bank, he expected, would be eager to join with France to escape anarchy. The German chauvinists would reap a bitter reward for their resistance.[58]

The German government knew nothing of this new determination. It had reason to be pleased with the outcome of the experts' investigation. But President Ebert feared for the future. Determined to prepare Germany for a possible struggle requiring unquestioned unity, he invited Chancellor Wirth to expand his cabinet into a national government. The well-intentioned maneuver backfired. The Social Democrats refused to cooperate with Stresemann's party of business and industry and deserted Wirth. After eighteeen months in office, the government of fulfillment resigned. Rising to replace it was the "business ministry" of Dr. Wilhelm Cuno, wartime director of the national grain authority and successor to Albert Ballin as director of the Hamburg-Amerika line. He had recently become a Centrist, being Catholic, but was never a sincere republican. Cuno pledged to follow "the policy of 13 November," referring to the moratorium request, and the French saw his advent as further evidence of the degree to which Berlin had fallen under the influence of the industrialists.

On 23 November Poincaré held a grand meeting attended by Finance Minister de Lasteyrie, Seydoux, Peretti, and Barthou. The special guests were Paul Theunis, the Belgian premier, his foreign minister Henri Jaspar, and Ambassador Gaiffier d'Hestroy. The Belgians considered the United States to be the last hope for a peaceful settle-

[58] Note Seydoux pour le PdC, "Question des réparations," 21 Nov. 1922: MAE Pap. Millerand, Réparations X, nos. 22-31.

ment. Would the Allies join in posing again the question of the interallied debts? Poincaré would agree to an "even trade": annulment of Germany's "C" bonds for annulment of French war debts. Such an offer was highly unlikely—it would liberate France while leaving Germany owing some 50 billion gold marks. The Belgians then referred to a last offer made by J. P. Morgan. The American financier made it known that he would consider loans if the French government officially solicited an interview with him, if Germany were granted a five-year moratorium, and if the Allies renounced future sanctions. Morgan's terms were not only unacceptable but distinctly insulting, coming from a foreign private citizen.[59] Caught between the demands of men like Stinnes and Morgan, Poincaré rebuffed Theunis' call for more negotiations and asked if the Belgians were prepared to seize guarantees in Germany.

Jaspar and Theunis avoided answering directly. They had come to inquire precisely what Poincaré had in mind by "guarantees." Did the French government envisage a modification of the occupation of the Rhineland? asked Theunis. Poincaré enumerated the fiscal measures planned for the Left Bank and alluded to the possibility of expelling the Prussian functionaries. Did Poincaré plan to replace the inflated mark with the French franc in the Rhineland? Poincaré thought this dangerous, but considered it possible to create a new, stable, Rhenish currency. "One will ask if you pursue a policy of annexation or separatism from Germany," offered Theunis. Poincaré replied forcefully: "We have not the least thought of annexation, but to have a Rhineland without Prussians is something else." He hoped that the Allies would march with him into the Ruhr, but he would act alone if necessary.[60]

Poincaré's will was now fixed. Four days after the meeting with the Belgians, on 27 November 1922, the cabinet convened at the Elysée. Millerand presided and Foch was present. Only one voice spoke for a policy of negotiation. It was that of Finance Minister de Lasteyrie. Everything depended on the German response, he repeated, and therefore the Ruhr occupation could not escape being highly risky. It could be a cakewalk or it could bring financial and political ruin. If Poincaré shared these fears at the time, he chose to sublimate them. The occupation of the Ruhr, by committing France to a large and risky investment and incurring the displeasure of the Anglo-Americans, could end in the collapse of the franc. But to admit defeat, to give up reparations,

[59] Tel. Herrick to Hughes, 13 Oct. 1922: FRUS 1922, II, 165. Poincaré refused to see Morgan despite the pleas of de Lasteyrie. Pers. Let. Logan to Strong, 24 Nov. 1922: HI Mogan Papers, Box 2.

[60] P.-V., réunion chez le PdC, 23 Nov. 1922: MAE Pap. Millerand, Réparations X, nos. 40-52.

would have the same effect. France was losing her Great Power status and all choices were ill.[61] The council of ministers put the question, and decided conclusively that France would occupy the Ruhr basin as soon as German default was declared.

Poincaré had not considered the occupation of the Ruhr as an immediate possibility until June 1922. Thereafter he remained watchful for signs that the operation might prove unnecessary, but steadily prepared for the day when he would have to undertake it. He seems to have resorted to wishful thinking about the financial consequences, as well as the potential for revolutionary chaos following economic disruption in the Ruhr. These would result only if the Ruhr magnates chose to resist and risk losing everything. That Poincaré did not believe they would do. Of necessity, therefore, the French government made a classic strategic error: it based its decision on assumptions about the enemy's intentions, not on his capabilities.

Poincaré did worry about the diplomatic aspects of such a bold initiative, especially since his plan was not to force a new peace on Germany but to use the political guarantee of the Ruhr to bargain with his allies. His preparations had gone well; the diplomatic situation at the end of 1922 was not unfavorable. Most important for Poincaré perhaps was the knowledge that if he refused to occupy the Ruhr he could be replaced. By remaining in power, at least he could impose his own strategy on the Ruhr policy and call the Entente back into existence when the British showed themselves to be flexible. Added to those elements were the man's emotional drives, rarely externalized—his frustration at British disloyalty and American selfishness, his hatred for the lords of the Ruhr. After months of lucid analysis and unremunerative mental labor, Poincaré gave in, probably with relief, to the simplest course—open conflict. As on 1 August 1914 Poincaré did not want the conflict, but he did not do all he could to prevent it, and he welcomed it when it came.

RUHR PREPARATIONS III

The cabinet's decision of 27 November meant that the final frantic Allied meetings in December 1922 and January 1923 were strictly *pro forma*. Plaintive hopes for Allied accord turned to acrid denunciations of both the British and the Germans as the Parisian press kicked off a

[61] Insight into the postwar monetary dilemma facing France and Belgium was offered by Belgian Foreign Minister Jaspar while defending the Ruhr policy before the Belgian Senate in January 1924. The Belgian and French francs were in collapse, the defeat of the Ruhr policy was in sight:

press campaign preparing the public for the occupation of the Ruhr. The theme of the campaign in the pages of *Le Matin*, *Le Temps*, and others was threefold. The German government was interested solely in protecting private interests; the French budgetary situation and the imminent peace in Turkey (removing French leverage on Britain) meant that time was not on the side of France; France would receive only what she could seize on her own. In this spirit the French Cabinet met again on 3 December and Poincaré demonstrated an obstinacy markedly in contrast to his attitude prior to the Ruhr decision. He rejected de Lasteyrie's draft of a plan to present to the Allies and he repudiated his own August plan. The finance minister protested that France had to offer *some* plan, and Poincaré then impatiently recited his scenario: "We are going to demand the liquidation of the interallied debts. We will be told that this is impossible. Next we will demand loans for Germany. This, too, will be labeled impossible. We will then return and effect our own policy. Under these circumstances, it is useless to talk of figures. What we require is a political plan."[62]

The long-awaited Brussels Conference never came off. Without some measure of prior agreement among the participants, the conference would only be conspicuous in its failure. So it was at London, on 9 December 1922, that the French and British premiers went through the motions of bargaining. Millerand reminded Poincaré not to tolerate British maneuvers to gain time. Any delay now would only give Germany time to prepare for a showdown.[63] The conference divided on 12 December.

"*M. Jaspar.*—I can therefore conclude that our policy in the Ruhr has fulfilled its object as a means of pressure on the [German] government and the great industrialists."

"*M. Volckaert.*—What has all that cost us?"

"*M. Jaspar.*—I was expecting that! (*laughter*) Have you, M. Volckaert, had to vote one centime for the expedition of the Ruhr?"

"*M. Volckaert.*—We *have* paid, because for a year the fall of our franc has rendered living more expensive for all Belgians (*exclamations and laughter on the Right*)."

"*M. Jaspar.*—Have you forgotten what I've told you so often: it is Germany which makes us pay more, not the Belgian government?"

"*M. Volckaert.*—Pardon! The collapse of the franc dates from the occupation of the Ruhr."

"*M. Jaspar.*—*Allons donc! Do you imagine that the Belgian and French francs would have been maintained if Germany had continued the policy she followed prior to the occupation of the Ruhr?* What an error that would be!" (Italics mine.)

Thus the occupation of the Ruhr was a considered gamble. It exposed the French and Belgian currencies to considerable risk. Not to do so might have exposed them to greater risks. *Annales parlementaires de Belgique*, Sénat, 16 Jan. 1924, pp. 255-256.

[62] P.-V., réunion tenue dans le cabinet du PdC, 3 Dec. 1922: MAE Pap. Millerand, Réparations X, nos. 214-218.

[63] Tel. Millerand to Poincaré (London), 11 Dec. 1922: MAE Pap. Millerand, vol. 51, nos. 159-160.

The Cuno government followed with an eleventh-hour effort to introduce the United States into the European equation. Foreign Minister Rosenberg believed that security obsessed French policy-makers, and the German ambassador in Washington discussed his own fears with Secretary of State Charles E. Hughes. Poincaré, he said, was seeking indirect annexation of the Rhineland through advancing military and economic control there. If he succeeded, it would mean prolonged political crisis in Europe.[64] Hughes listened sympathetically to the German proposal: an international committee of experts, including Americans, to regulate reparations, and a nonaggression pact offered by Berlin to run for thirty years, and accompanied by a proviso that war could be declared by signatories only after a national referendum.

Poincaré ignored the German proposals. In his view they were a transparent attempt to win world sympathy and cast France as an aggressor. Of what value was a guarantee pact that made France's security dependent solely on German goodwill? Poincaré could hardly be interested unless the pact involved Britain and/or the United States. Hughes showed no sign of returning to the policy of Wilson, and the British also were unenthusiastic about the German security offer.[65]

The last two weeks of December brought daily conferences among the ministerial and military chiefs responsible for the execution of the Ruhr policy. Meanwhile, Poincaré pressed his Belgian and Italian allies. Theunis resisted the idea of a military seizure of the Ruhr. If all else failed, he would have to participate to retain some influence in Paris, but he preferred sending an interallied technical mission to the Ruhr. The Italians shared this preference, and Seydoux was not sure of Italian backing for a military advance.[66]

The attitude of France's potential partners precipitated a final flurry in the planning for the Ruhr. Concerned above all for the diplomatic soundness of French policy, Poincaré considered the advantages of a nonmilitary mission to the Ruhr. On 22 December, General Denvignes presented his plan for the 45,000-man Ruhr occupation, expecting approval. But General Destiker suggested cutting back this force to two divisions, about 18,000 men. Émile Coste then asked why soldiers were needed at all. Germany would not dare to court disaster by attacking unarmed civilians. He believed a nonmilitary occupation

[64] Tel. Wiedtfeld (Washington) to A.A., 19 Dec. 1922: AA BR 3058, 1469, no. 603069; Memo Hughes, "Conversation with the German Ambassador," 12 Dec. 1922: FRUS 1922, II, 186-187.

[65] Memo Hughes, "Conversation with the French Ambassador," 21 Dec. 1922: FRUS 1922, II, 206-207.

[66] Note Vignon, "Visite de M. d'Amelio à M. Seydoux," 20 Dec. 1922: MAE Pap. Millerand, Réparations X, nos. 279-281.

would reassure the Ruhr industrialists whose cooperation was so vital. A Ruhr policy, he said, would require twenty-five technicians, no more! Destiker agreed with Coste's analysis. The presence of troops, not their absence, would cause incidents.

On Christmas Eve another meeting opened with Poincaré urging that the diplomatic ramifications of every French act be analyzed. In this spirit he welcomed Coste's plan. The premier said he favored detachment of a skeleton force not meant to occupy the Ruhr but only to act as escort for the engineers. Now Maginot protested, insisting that the full military advance had already been adopted at the Elysée. Seydoux reminded the war minister of the real issue: if France went in without troops, she would have allies accompanying her. The same could not be guaranteed for a military advance. General Destiker then voiced the opinion of Marshal Foch. Small contingents would be worse than none at all; their presence would be provocative, but they would be unable to defend themselves. The problem was indeed diplomatic, but not as Seydoux had stated it. If the British accompanied the French into the Ruhr, there would be no danger in any case. If France marched alone, it would be necessary to send many troops or none at all.[67]

The campaign for allies bore its first fruit in the Reparations Commission. German failure to fulfill the 1922 timber deliveries provided a pretext for a declaration of default. The Belgians and Italians voted with the French, and Poincaré had his mandate. The question remained how he was to use it. Peretti, Seydoux, and then Poincaré came around to Foch's opinion on the use of troops. Poincaré would invite the British to participate in a nonmilitary Ruhr operation. If they refused, France would send in an army. On 29 December Seydoux summarized the measures prepared for the Left Bank. The Rhineland Commission would take over customs, forests, and state mines. The Bad Ems Allied licensing regime, a relic of the 1921 sanctions, would control foreign currency in the Rhineland. But these measures would be effective only if Belgium cooperated.[68] The nature of the Ruhr policy was still in doubt as the year closed.

The German demarche in Washington finally bore fruit on 29 December. In a speech delivered to the American Historical Association at Yale, Secretary of State Hughes called for the creation of an international committee of experts to regulate reparations. Overlooking the fact that financial experts had shown a striking tendency to support

[67] P.-V., "Conférences—opération de la Ruhr," 24 Dec. 1922: MAE Pap. Millerand, Réparations X, nos. 304-316.

[68] Note Seydoux, 29 Dec. 1922: MAE Pap. Millerand, vol. 52, nos. 22-26.

their own nations' interests over the last four years, Hughes believed that an independent panel of economists could point the way to German financial recovery, loans and reparations, and the reestablishment of the gold standard, which, according to Benjamin Strong, governor of the New York Federal Reserve Bank, was the keystone of prosperity and democratic institutions.

Hughes recognized that the war debt question was also a barrier to international recovery, but the political mood of the United States, he said, precluded an immediate solution to this problem. So it was necessary for the Europeans to make the first gesture, settle reparations, and then appeal to America with the promise of political stability. Hughes's speech won few plaudits in France. The American had not recognized that European governments were also obliged to respect public opinion, and he ignored the indissoluble link between economics and politics in the reparations question. Poincaré knew perfectly well that Hughes's procedure—a committee of experts, restoration of German finances, a grand loan—was the only possible path to a settlement. He said as much throughout 1922, and he would accept such a plan ten months later. But in December 1922 France's bargaining position was too weak to permit a general settling of accounts.

Bonar Law, Poincaré, and representatives of Belgium and Italy convened at Paris on 2 January 1923. The British proposed a four-year moratorium for Germany. Poincaré offered a two-year moratorium subject to guarantees, including a nonmilitary occupation of the Ruhr. No pretense at bargaining was made, and a German delegation, waiting outside with a plan of its own, was not even heard. The French and British premiers issued an amicable statement announcing their mutual attachment to the Entente and their parting of the ways on reparations. Poincaré had not won Britain to a common policy; he had won British neutrality. Belgian Premier Theunis, stunned by a British challenge to the Belgian priority, announced his intention to act in conjunction with France, dragging his king and foreign minister along with him. He deemed that the need to restrain a potentially dangerous French Rhineland policy and to seek reparations for Belgium was more immediate than his internal problems. The Italians would support France in the taking of guarantees, sending a team of engineers to the Ruhr.

Late in the evening of 3 January 1923, the French council of ministers reacted to the events just transpired. At 3 A.M. on 4 January the order went out to the military to execute the plan for full military occupation of the Ruhr on 11 January.

THE RUHR, THE RHINELAND, AND FRENCH SECURITY

Did Poincaré elect to occupy the Ruhr for reparations or for security? This blunt question has gone unsettled for half a century, partly because of the political and historiographical weight it carried, partly because it oversimplifies a complex causal problem. First, it is impossible strictly to separate reparations and security. The war revealed to French leaders both the economic foundations of national security and the responsibility of government for their maintenance. Reparations were both an essential component of French recovery and a harness on Germany. Left unrestrained, the Reich could threaten France by its superior capacity to produce for war and by its ability to weaken French productivity through competition. In this sense, the Ruhr occupation was clearly motivated by the drive to make France "viable" in the political economy of postwar Europe.

But French security planners did not think only in terms of economic potential for war or "economic war." Their fear of German revenge was predicated on the demographic imbalance between the two peoples, and on the belief that Germany would hardly renounce economic or political expansion because of its democratic constitution. Wilson and Lloyd George recognized France's claim to permanent security guarantees, but the defeat of the 1919 pacts reopened the security question. It is tempting, therefore, to interpret the decision to occupy the Ruhr and expand French control in the Rhineland as a plot, not to collect reparations, but to separate the Rhineland from Germany or otherwise to replace the defunct Versailles settlement with a territorial guarantee of French security in a narrow military/political sense.

This interpretation of French policy found many exponents in Britain and Germany. Miles Lampson had "no doubt" that the ultimate object of French policy was separation of the Rhineland. William Tyrrell agreed and felt that Britain should remove the cause of French aggressiveness by granting a new security settlement. Nevertheless, Lord Curzon insisted that a security pact must not intervene to prevent the coming Franco-German crisis, but must follow in its wake.[69] Rather than seeking to prevent a Ruhr confrontation, therefore, Curzon was reconciled to it.

German interpretations of French policy showed the same conviction that Paris was motivated by security considerations in the Rhineland. Dr. Silverberg, the industrial lobbyist, saw also the inevitable "understanding" to come between French and German metallurgies.

[69] Minutes, Memo of Mr. Headlem Morley, "French Policy Regarding the Rhineland at the Peace Conference," 10 Aug. 1922: PRO FO 371, vol. 7521, nos. 172-176.

Konrad Adenauer was most fearful that a Ruhr occupation would destroy the Reich by placing control of German coal in French hands. He was prepared to form a Rheno-Westphalian state to pacify the French, but the offer, he added, would have to come from Berlin.[70] On 10 December 1922 Wilhelm Marx, Centrist leader and future chancellor, proclaimed: "The French policy seeks the Rhine as a frontier and the annexation of the Left Bank. If such is Poincaré's will, it is because those to whom he owes his power demand it. But we will oppose it with all our energy and with the profound consciousness of our rectitude."[71] Were Marx's fears justified? Was Poincaré intent on forcing the separation of the Rhineland through pressure on the Ruhr? Here we encounter a second oversimplification: the assumption that Poincaré's policy—to the extent that he had a clear idea of means and ends at all—was "French policy," an expression of the combined wills and pressures bearing on French official decision-making. Individual political decisions are unfortunately not so easily reducible, nor does examination of the domestic inputs into French policy reveal even a rough consensus. Rather, French security thinking in the years after Versailles suffered from a kind of governmental anarchy. Just as the political power never coordinated its economic policies with the desires of French industrialists, neither did a unity of purpose, or even a constructive dialogue, characterize the relationship between government and the military elite concerning long-range security planning.

Following the Armistice, Marshal Philippe Pétain assumed control of the postwar organs of national defense. The *État-Major de l'Armée* replaced the *Grand Quartier Général* as the organ of planning and execution, and it fell to the direction of Pétain's chief collaborator, General Edmond Buat. In January 1920 the old *Conseil Supérieur de la Guerre* (C.S.G.) was revived and given the mission of advising on all matters concerning military preparedness. The liaison between these planning organs and the ministerial *Conseil Supérieur de la Défense National* was vested in the vice-presidency of the C.S.G. and commander of French armies. From 1920 to 1924 this position was held by Pétain.

Entrusted with the development of concepts on which to base the

[70] Des. #355 Ryan (Coblenz) to F.O., C17232/99/18, 14 Dec. 1922: PRO FO 371, vol. 7490, nos. 65-66.

[71] Tel. Genoyer (Düsseldorf) to Poincaré, "Discours de M. Marx," 14 Dec. 1922: MAE Allemagne, vol. 316, nos. 313-317. Similar statements abounded in the weeks before the Ruhr occupation. Ex-Chancellor Wirth proclaimed, for example, "The noblest goal of German policy can only be the recovery of national liberty and the conservation of the Rhineland for the Reich." Des. Tirard to MAE, 8 Jan. 1923: MAE Allemagne, vol. 387, nos. 77-78.

future defense of France, Pétain evolved the doctrines of "inviolability of territory" and the continuous front. Both were designed to prevent another German flanking movement and the loss of valuable industrial areas, as had happened in 1914. But Tardieu and his advisers had already found reason to doubt the wisdom of a static defense by April 1919. They rejected the ultimate value of a Rhine barrier, but Pétain pushed ahead with plans for a static defense based on a system of fortifications within France herself.[72] Ignoring the pace of technological and tactical advance, Pétain and Buat based their theories on the assumption that France would again face the German army of 1918, an infantry army versed in the tactics of infiltration. Their ideas were adopted as the order of the day by Minister of War André Lefèvre in his general instructions of March 1920.

Violent opposition to Pétain arose in the C.S.G. meeting of 17 May 1920. Marshal Foch challenged the concept of inviolability of territory as precluding offensive operations, which were necessary if France were to hold the Rhine and come to the aid of Poland and Czechoslovakia. Supported by Marshal Joffre, he ridiculed Pétain's "fortified fields of battle" on the border as a new Wall of China.[73] Pétain contended that the Rhineland occupation would indeed be a firm guarantee for fifteen years, but he insisted that planning look ahead to the period when France would no longer possess this safeguard. Even the mobilization plans drawn up by Buat's general staff after 1920, while paying lip service to the offensive into Central Germany, emphasized the rapid formation of a continuous front and gave second priority to the assembly of a *masse de manoeuvre*.[74]

Pétain's defensive attitude, as well as his leadership in postwar planning, rested primarily on his 1914-1918 experience, but it also was compatible with the public's demand for a sharp decrease in the term of military service, hence in the size of the active army. Foch attacked the planned reduction in the term of service to eighteen months, and eventually to one year, to which the general staff and postwar governments were committed. But his demands for a large standing army in

[72] A report produced by Clemenceau's own Ministry of War in April 1919, entitled "Valeur stratégique des rivières," provides an interesting example. The study concluded from the experience of the 1914-1918 war that river lines were no surer a defense than positions without natural advantage. What mattered was the amount of *prior* organization accomplished in the defensive position. While the report exploded Foch's Rhine theory, it supported Pétain's ideas concerning the value of permanent fortifications along the French border. MG Fonds Clemenceau, 6N73, dos. Rive Gauche du Rhin.

[73] P.-V., CSG, 17 May 1920: MG, CSG, Réunions. On French strategy debates in the 1920s, see P. E. Tournoux, *Défense des frontières, Haut-Commandement-Gouvernement 1919-1939* (Paris, 1960); Judith Hughes, *To the Maginot Line* (Cambridge, Mass., 1971); Paoli, *La phase de fermeté*.

[74] Paoli, *La phase de fermeté*, pp. 161-167.

perpetuity were unpopular. After several years of debate, during which one minister of war resigned in protest, Poincaré's cabinet presided over the passage of the Law of Eighteen Months in 1922 and 1923. The smaller army would seem to prohibit an offensive posture.

In the minds of many deputies, cutbacks in manpower made all the more vital the maintenance of the French army on the Rhine. On 14 December 1920 the president of the Chamber's army commission addressed a letter to the general staff that expressed this belief: "The fate of the peace is in the hands of France. If she possesses an unshakeable will that war will not recommence, it will not. *For no one can oblige us to leave the Rhine* if the treaty is not particularly observed. The Rhine is the guarantee of peace."[75]

French defensive strategy was the subject of dispute but of infrequent coordination among factions in the military and the government and between the military and political establishments. The debate came to a second climax in the C.S.G. in May 1922. Millerand presided passively while Pétain fought off the attacks of Joffre and Foch against his Wall of China. If the national territory were to be inviolate, Pétain concluded, there must be fortifications. They must be built on French soil, not in the temporarily occupied Rhineland, and they must be begun at once.[76] The concept of fields of battle was the direct antecedent of the Maginot Line. At the time of the occupation of the Ruhr, the problem had been entrusted to a special committee on the organization of frontiers. It was originally headed by Joffre, but Pétain forced Joffre's resignation from the chairmanship in August 1922, and brooked no opposition to his defensive strategy.

Pétain did not speak for the whole army, nor for the government, whose responsibility included security guarantees of a political nature. Thus, the governments of Millerand, Briand, and Poincaré carried on their Rhenish policies, Eastern European policies, and negotiations with Britain in cooperation, not with the general staff, but with Marshal Foch, Supreme Allied Commander, and with the French Army of the Rhine. General Degoutte was the champion of security through dismemberment of the German Reich. He saw the occupation of the Ruhr as the vehicle for this change. If the Reich dared resist the move to the Ruhr, economic catastrophe would result and France would leave trans-Rhenian Germany to its fate. The Ruhr would be the best guarantee of reparations and security.

How much of Degoutte's forecast did Poincaré share on the eve of

[75] Let. Lt. Col. Fabry, président de la commission de l'Armée de Terre, to E.M.A., submitted in defense of a project by M. Landry, interim minister of war, 14 Dec. 1920, cited by Paoli, *La phase de fermeté*, pp. 93-96 (italics in original).

[76] P.-V., CSG, 22 May 1922: MG, CSG, Réunions.

the Ruhr occupation? What was the connection between French Rhine and Ruhr policies? Throughout 1923 Poincaré never ceased to discount the question of security in speeches and diplomatic notes. France had occupied the Ruhr for reparations and had no ulterior motives. Technically, Poincaré was truthful. He was never annexationist, but he knew full well that the Ruhr occupation and its concomitant measures on the Left Bank would involve an inevitable change in the balance of political power in the Rhineland. Seydoux had projected the direct control over the Rhenish economy to be exercised by France. Poincaré himself admitted to the Belgian premier that Rhenish economic unrest following a Ruhr occupation might lead to a new Rhenish currency, the expulsion of Prussian functionaries, and the creation of a "neutral" Rhineland. If the Ruhr occupation were to solve the reparations and heavy industrial difficulties of France, it could well produce the requisite security settlement also. Whatever the outcome, it was sure to bring French Rhenish policy to a climax.

Thus, the Ruhr occupation was an expression of many "French" policies, all of which to some degree intertwined. It offered the prospect of breaking the deadlocks in finance, industry, and security, which had frustrated in one way or another all the bureaucracies and economic sectors in France, all of whom could make a case that their special interests represented the cause of national security. Poincaré may indeed have had Rhenish separation as an ulterior motive in January 1923, but it does not follow that this was the primary goal of the Ruhr occupation. If the "economic bloc" in the government considered an industrial settlement as the first priority, and if certain of the military hoped for territorial security guarantees, Poincaré was obsessed first with the French financial crisis. He was neither soldier nor bureaucrat, but politician, sensitive as much to the mood of the rente-holding middle classes and the Chambers they elected as to the special pleadings of corporatist interest groups. To be sure, Poincaré, along with Degoutte and Seydoux, believed that the Rhineland would be forced to abandon its ties with Germany only if open conflict or profound economic disruption resulted from the Ruhr occupation. But Poincaré could not tell any more than the optimistic Degoutte or the pessimistic de Lasteyrie what turn events would take after 11 January 1923. The premier's apparent lack of concern over the possible financial investment involved in a Ruhr operation implies that he did not expect serious German resistance. Without resistance there would be no chaos and no pressure on the Rhineland to abandon Germany. Certainly, Poincaré the diplomat never intended to impose separation by military force. He never de-internationalized security and reparations. The only settlement France could afford was an internationally recognized settlement. Poincaré could hope for an internationally recognized Rhenish state, but he could not be sure of it in January 1923. It was the German passive resistance to come, not the initial occupation of the Ruhr, that raised the stakes in the Ruhr and in the Rhineland.

·7·

ECONOMIC WAR ON THE RHINE AND RUHR: THE STRUGGLE OF POSTWAR REVISIONISMS, 1923

Jacques Seydoux had feared that France might be forced to use violence to break an Anglo-German entente. The Franco-Belgian occupation of the Ruhr in January 1923 was that act of violence, made necessary by the French insistence that German recovery was intolerable except within a political structure assuring French military and economic security. But the Treaty of Versailles, which France ostensibly was upholding, died in the Ruhr. German passive resistance escalated the economic struggle, making it desperate and expensive. The French responded with a seizure of all governmental authority in the occupied territories in the effort to overcome the general strike. On the basis of that position of strength, French planners returned to revisionism, to the vision of a new peace settlement that would guarantee financial security through a just reparations/war debts agreement, and that would afford permanent and secure sources of raw materials for French heavy industry. But the Ruhr struggle also brought the climax of the French Rhineland policy, the revisionist approach to security that had tangled, sometimes intertwined, with the policy of treaty implementation since 1919. Could France isolate the questions of reparations and security, and win a "Rhenish solution" to security while influencing the Anglo-Saxons to satisfy French reparations demands? Poincaré was intent on preserving the Entente, but he was under pressure to capitalize on France's newly won hegemony on the Rhine. The victory over German resistance did not bring unity among the quarreling factions in France. Instead, the apparent liberation from the restraints of Allied diplomacy enhanced the conflict within the government and between the state and domestic interest groups as to the form a final settlement should take. Ends and means became confused, and Poincaré's Rhenish and German policies reached fruition in the same hectic months, when the shape of postwar Europe was at stake.

RESISTANCE AND RIPOSTE

On 8 January 1923, 179 troop trains disrupted normal service on French and Rhenish railways. Two days later, two infantry divisions, a cavalry division, a Belgian detachment, the engineers of the Interallied

Control Mission for Factories and Mines (MICUM), and an Italian technical team awaited the order to advance into the Ruhr. Simultaneously, seventy-five miles upriver, another troop movement took place. The last American companies embarked for the Channel ports, consummating the withdrawal of the United States occupation, and the French took possession of Coblenz.[1]

General Degoutte's spearheads enveloped the western half of the Ruhr basin and invested Essen on the morning of 11 January.[2] Hours ahead of the French, the German *Kohlensyndikat* fled to Hamburg with its records of the taxation and distribution of Ruhr coal. The Rhineland Commission calmly decreed the dissolution of the organization and transferred its functions to the MICUM. Before the Chamber, Poincaré defended his policy at length, not to inform the deputies or French opinion, he said, for they understood, but to educate the world on the German danger. The British moratorium plan, aside from throwing out the Treaty of Versailles and leaving the reconstruction burden fully on France, would permit Germany rapidly to reestablish her industrial hegemony in Europe. He warned the deputies not to expect considerable returns in the wake of the occupation. "Perhaps England was right," admitted the French premier, "when she says our hopes are vain. It is possible we deceive ourselves—we make no pretense of infallibility. But in these last months, between England and France, I will not ask you who has been deceived more often." Poincaré received a vote of confidence, 452 to 72.[3] By 15 January, the entire Ruhr valley was in French and Belgian hands.

The first reports from the Ruhr seemed to justify French optimism about the German reaction—there was no resistance, and the mine proprietors declared themselves ready to cooperate in coal deliveries.

[1] The final U.S. pull-out both was and was not a reaction to the French intention to occupy the Ruhr. On 8 Jan. 1923, Secretary of State Hughes informed Jusserand in Washington that America would evacuate from Germany in case of a Ruhr operation, but the day before the American Senate had already passed a resolution demanding the return of American forces from the Rhine. The resolution was but the culmination of a long campaign by Democrats and isolationist Republicans to withdraw the American forces in Germany. Memo Hughes, "Conversation with the French Ambassador," 8 Jan. 1923: FRUS 1923, II, 47. For a discussion of the "Last Phase" of the American occupation in Germany, see Nelson, *Victors Divided*, ch. 10.

[2] The best source for the military planning and execution of the Ruhr occupation is probably General Degoutte's own secret publication, *L'Occupation de la Ruhr*, published by the press of the French Army of the Rhine, and found in the Archives of the Ministry of War, Vincennes. Also see Paoli, *La phase de fermeté, 1919 à 1924*, previously cited. For the origins of the German passive resistance, see Favez, *Le Reich devant l'occupation*; Rupieper, "Politics and Economics," pp. 210-231; Feldman, *Iron and Steel*, pp. 351ff; Paul Wentzcke, *Ruhrkampf, Einbruch und Abwehr im rheinisch-westfälishchen Industriegebiet*, 2 vols. (Berlin, 1930-1932), I, 217-227.

[3] J.O. Chambre, 11 Jan. 1923, p. 16-20.

To be sure, the national press in Germany denounced the invasion and the Reichstag proclaimed a "national front" against the enemy, but Chancellor Cuno limited himself to moral demonstrations. The occupation was illegal and contrary to the treaty, Berlin announced. Any supporting measures taken by the Rhineland Commission would be in violation of the Rhineland Agreement. The disruption of the German economy would only destroy Germany's ability to fulfill reparations. There could be no negotiation until evacuation of the Ruhr, and the German ambassadors in Paris and Brussels were recalled.[4]

Moral demonstrations Poincaré expected and could abide, but passive resistance in the economic sphere, beginning spontaneously in the occupied territories, paralleled the formal protests. The German coal deliveries commissioner ordered cessation of reparations deliveries at once, and Ruhr miners and rail workers voted overwhelmingly to resist foreign exploitation. Spontaneous strikes confounded the MICUM in its first efforts to move coal. The German administration in the Ruhr and Rhineland appealed to Berlin for instructions. On 16 January, Cuno's cabinet took a decision. Confident now of receiving local support, it ordered noncooperation in all matters concerning execution of reparations.

Passive resistance spread quickly. One by one, union locals or individual mines and plants stopped production, bent on proving to the hated French that they could not mine coal with bayonets. By 25 January, the industrial kingdoms of Stinnes and Thyssen shut down completely. The strike spread to the Rhineland, where railroads were abandoned or sabotaged, preventing transportation of combustibles and threatening the revictualment of the French army. The complex economy of Western Germany simply and suddenly ceased to function. The MICUM engineers were helpless to fulfill their program and their leader, Émile Coste, abandoned Essen and returned to France.

Coste informed the French council of ministers of its bitter choice: give up attempts to exploit the Ruhr and settle for a military occupation alone, or undertake the entire administration of the occupied territories, including direct operation of the Rhine-Ruhr rail net and mines and cokeries. The hopes for a Ruhr operation without massive investment were quashed. Minister of Finance de Lasteyrie had foreseen this possibility, but he took little comfort from the accuracy of his prediction—it would be his job to finance the Ruhr "war effort."

[4] The German cabinet met on 9 January and agreed to resist an occupation of the Ruhr with the support of the Social Democrats, but once again the Ruhr industrialists stymied the government. Only after the scope of the national outrage became clear did the industrialists fall into line and cancel their agreement with the French on 15 January. The government then assumed leadership of passive resistance.

The council of ministers, with Marshal Foch in attendance, decided on 26 January to send Yves Le Trocquer, minister of public works, and General Maxime Weygand to judge the situation firsthand. Their report confirmed Coste's analysis, but voiced what was the general opinion in Paris: retreat was unthinkable, the victory of 1918 was at stake. General Jean Payot, the military transport expert, suggested a Régie or administration of all the railroads in occupied territory managed, and worked if necessary, by Allied personnel. Once the railroads were running, the coal and coke stockpiled in the Ruhr could be delivered. A fraction of French furnaces could be kept burning and a short-term return eventually shown for the occupation.[5] In the long run, France would have to depend on a German capitulation, the end of passive resistance. But the government was confident that Germany could not support a nonproductive Ruhr for long without financial ruin and the risk of political disintegration. The Germans had raised the stakes by their resistance; if France proved equal to the task of "making the guarantee productive," then this far costlier victory might still be worth the price.

On 4 February, Poincaré wired Tirard in Coblenz to accept the gauntlet thrown down by Germany. He would decree the economic separation of the Ruhr and Rhineland from nonoccupied Germany. On the same day, President Millerand wrote to Camille Barrère: "In the Ruhr, our affairs proceed well. We have decided to hold on. Everything is there, *et la raison, une fois de plus, finira par avoir raison*."[6]

The Ruhr commanded the attention of the world. The struggle there seemed the heart of the issue: two great nations, each making potentially suicidal sacrifices in the hope that the other would crack first. But the most serious and potentially permanent alteration in the German polity was taking place, steadily and without *éclat*, on the Left Bank of the Rhine. French control of administration and economic life of the Rhineland was the firm base supporting the Allied position in the Ruhr. As the British had feared ever since the American failure to ratify the peace treaty, the Franco-Belgians had seized control of the Rhineland Commission in Coblenz. The purposely vague delineation of the powers of the Commission made by the interallied committee in June 1919 now permitted the French and Belgians to order life as they pleased in the occupied territories. Except for refusing to execute the Commission's ordinances in Cologne, the British were helpless. And ordinances poured out of Coblenz, passed by Tirard and the Belgian high commissioner Rolin-Jaequemyns over Lord Kilmarnock's absten-

[5] P.-V., meetings of 25 and 28 Jan. 1923, cited by Zimmermann, *Frankreichs Ruhrpolitik*, pp. 104-106.

[6] Pers. Let. Millerand to Barrère, 4 Feb. 1923: MAE Corr. Barrère, vol. 3, no. 221.

tions. The civil and unobtrusive Rhineland Commission designed by the American Pierrepont Noyes became a political tool of immense power.

At first, Tirard proceeded to carry out the limited program of "productive guarantees" drawn up in December 1922: seizure of the coal tax, customs receipts, and domainial forests on the Left Bank. These were only sanctions, but they soon gave way to a host of ordinances that would, by the middle of the year, make the Rhineland Commission the repository of virtually all legislative, executive, and judicial authority in the Rhineland. Although Tirard had certainly lobbied for such measures since 1920, he instituted them now, not in fulfillment of a grand scheme, but as day-to-day responses to German resistance.

The Rhineland Commission declared itself solely responsible for all distribution of coal on the Left Bank, granting itself life and death powers over Rhenish fuel-consuming businesses. In February, all shipping materials and vehicles were ordered subject to Allied sequestration; export of any merchandise into nonoccupied territory required a license from Coblenz. Export of fuels, coal and its by-products, iron and steel products, machine parts, agricultural goods, and fertilizers was prohibited. When German customs personnel as well as railroad workers and public service employees refused to respect the ordinances, Tirard took the opportunity to fulfill his long-standing desire to expel the Prussian administration from the Rhineland. Any German functionary interfering or refusing to cooperate with any Allied measure was removed with his family on four days' notice. The 350 families reported expelled by Tirard on 12 February were the tiny vanguard of the forced exodus to come. The Quai d'Orsay inquired of Tirard what measures would be taken to replace these officials. Tirard responded that they would not be replaced. Allied officers would administer customs.[7] On 20 February, Tirard dismissed *en masse* every German customs employee remaining on the Left Bank.

The boundary between occupied and nonoccupied territory was to be sealed. The paucity of Allied troops and officials made it impossible to cover the circuitous boundary, with its four "humps" over the Rhine. On 25 February, General Degoutte ordered the bridgeheads closed. French troops occupied the strips of territory on the Right Bank lying between the bridgeheads of Cologne, Coblenz, and Mainz, and the postwar occupation in Germany reached its greatest extent.

By March 1923 incidents of sabotage and "active resistance" to Allied efforts to operate railroads and utilities brought the administration

[7] Tel. Peretti to Tirard, 12 Feb. 1923; Tel. Tirard to MAE, 13 Feb. 1923: MAE Rive Gauche, vol. 8, nos. 74-78.

of justice to Tirard's attention. German courts were not cooperating in the prosecution of saboteurs. In consequence, the Rhineland Commission specified that no German prisoner could be transferred outside of occupied territory. Allied military courts would try saboteurs, and the penalty for railroad sabotage was death. Finally, to prevent German courts from taking reprisals against collaborators, the Rhineland Commission extended complete immunity to all Allied and German personnel in the service of the Rhineland Commission, the army, or the Régie. German judicial sovereignty in the occupied territories was shattered; Berlin's protest had no effect.

The German refusal to undertake reparations of any kind left the Reparations Commission with no choice but to declare a general default on 29 January 1923. The Rhineland Commission responded by declaring itself competent to seize all German government property on the Left Bank. The Franco-Belgians took over taxation and licensing of the Reich's alcohol monopoly on the Rhine and controlled all navigation on internal waterways. Trucking and all movement of goods within occupied territory became subject to Franco-Belgian licensing. Firearms, airplanes, radio transmitters, and carrier pigeons were already outlawed under the Rhineland Agreement. Circulation of German citizens within the Rhineland was closely regulated, with the army and *Sûreté* on the lookout for Berlin's agents. Movement between occupied and nonoccupied territory was periodically terminated entirely. Tirard even alerted Paris of the danger of tolerating the *Jugendherbergen*, the German youth hostels! In its effort to overcome the passive resistance, the French occupation made life in the Rhineland intolerable.[8]

The absolute power assumed by Franco-Belgian authorities precipitated a scramble among the various agencies—MICUM, the armies, Rhineland Commission, Régie—for control of the bureaucratic machinery in the Rhine/Ruhr complex. In February, Le Trocquer and Weygand again journeyed to Düsseldorf, where Degoutte had relocated his headquarters, to discuss centralizing authority. Degoutte then returned to Paris to plead his case in person, and the council of ministers appointed him overall commander of the Rhine and Ruhr. Poincaré instructed Tirard and the MICUM accordingly, and expressed the hope that all French agencies would work in close coopera-

[8] A complete list of the Rhineland Commission's ordinances with French and German texts was published by Werner Vogels, ed., *Die Verträge über Besetzung und Räumung des Rheinlandes und die Ordannanzen des Interalliierten Rheinland Oberkommission in Coblenz* (Berlin, 1925). See also MAE Rive Gauche, vol. 214, for P.-V. of commission meetings and ordinances, and the chronicle of French administrative measures in the occupied territories, in Wentzcke, *Ruhrkampf*, I, 188-216.

tion.[9] The Rhineland Commission had no authority in newly occupied territory in any case; Degoutte promulgated Tirard's ordinances in the Ruhr as military decrees. Such unity of control was imperative if the extremely volatile arena of conflict was to be policed and incidents and contradictory policies prevented. As it was, incidents were unavoidable: the incarceration of Krupp and other world-famous businessmen, the fusillade ordered by a panicky lieutenant threatened by crowd violence, the assaults of German terrorists on collaborators and French nationals. But such outbursts of violence were surprisingly uncommon, given the passion and suffering engendered by the confrontation. Ideally the occupation was a surgical operation aimed at particular industrial and governmental elites in Germany. It was not, as the French never tired of repeating, a blow against the German people. General Degoutte succeeded in imposing discipline on French and Germans alike, but the centralized control of the Ruhr campaign emanated not from Düsseldorf, but from Paris. Emulating Clemenceau's brand of leadership, Poincaré himself kept a tireless and constant vigil at his desk, sifting information, reevaluating the situation on an hourly basis, and reviewing even the most detailed of measures instituted on the Rhine and Ruhr. He had to overcome dissension within French ranks and German resistance, but he had also to contend with his reluctant allies.

The greatest French outlay of funds and manpower was for the Régie. But the organization of the Régie, on which so much depended, produced the first crisis of collaboration between France and Belgium. The passive resistance was as much of an unwelcome surprise to Brussels as to Paris, and the debate over emergency measures exposed for the first time the basic differences in strategy between the two partners.[10]

Theunis' political position in Belgium was the opposite of Poincaré's in France. Instead of being surrounded by advisors pressing him to occupy the Ruhr, Theunis was the driving force behind Belgium's Ruhr policy. Instead of enjoying a secure parliamentary majority, Theunis relied on a flimsy coalition in the face of determined opposition. Finally, the escalation of the struggle against Germany now gave him as much reason to fear victory as defeat. His apprehension over the scope of French ambitions in Western Germany increased daily as the occupation solidified its hold on Rhenish life. If the French indeed in-

[9] Tel. Poincaré to Degoutte, 13 Feb. 1923, cited by Paoli, *La phase de fermeté*, p. 280.

[10] Tel. #1065/541PLA Gaiffier (Paris) to Jaspar, 22 Jan. 1923: MAE Bel. Correspondance Politique, France, 1923.

tended to dominate a separated Rhineland, thus encircling little Belgium, then Theunis must use whatever leverage he had to restrain his ally.

The thesis which the Belgian government adopted was that no Allied action in Western Germany was meant to be permanent. All guarantees were to be envisioned as pledges to be redeemed by Germany when she again took up reparations. Rolin-Jaequemyns attempted to impress this thesis on the Régie, proposing a temporary rail administration on which the Belgians would have equal authority.[11] But the Belgian government was in no position, in February 1923, to display independence. The Belgian franc was slipping on foreign exchanges, and the French government undertook to purchase Belgian loyalty by approving a 50 million franc loan in mid-February. As for the Régie, the French would be putting up the vast majority of capital. Thus, Rolin-Jaequemyns was obliged to accept the French plan. The Régie would be an Allied administration, not a formal company, instituted to ensure rail service for an undetermined period of time. The director would be French, although the Belgians would retain some autonomy in their own zone. On 1 March the Rhineland Commission officially created the Régie. Getting the trains rolling would be more difficult.

While the rail strike paralyzed the Franco-Belgian occupation in the first months of the Ruhr struggle, the British zone around Cologne formed an island of relative tranquillity. It could not escape the economic distress of the contiguous regions, but its British occupiers could choose not to enforce the ordinances passed in Coblenz. Thus, when the French found imperative the use of an important trunk line that traversed a corner of the British zone, they petitioned the British through diplomatic channels.

The Foreign Office responded to the French request with sarcasm. The other trunk line to the Ruhr had carried twenty-six of the thirty-six daily trains from the Rhineland to the Ruhr before 11 January. Surely that number would suffice now, the British replied, knowing well that few, if any, trains were getting through to the Ruhr.[12] The French request was serious. Poincaré even instructed Tirard to postpone the planned dismissal of the Reich Rhineland commissioner, an act that would irritate London, until a rail settlement could be reached.[13] The laborious negotiations that followed were the first test of British "neutrality." On instructions from London, local British authorities were

[11] Tel. Tirard to MAE, 24 Feb. 1923: MAE Rive Gauche, vol. 126, nos. 210-211.

[12] Minutes, Note St. Aulaire to F.O., C2329/313/18, 6 Feb. 1923: PRO FO 371, vol. 8711, nos. 1-5.

[13] Tel. Poincaré to Tirard, 16 Feb. 1923: MAE Rive Gauche, vol. 241, no. 57.

not to permit any action that could be construed as support for the Franco-Belgian "pledge-taking." The resulting Godley-Payot Accord of 3 April 1923 allowed ten freight trains bearing reparations coal and two providing revictualment to pass daily through the Cologne zone, but no troops, functionaries, or dependents.[14] Paris then freed Tirard, on 17 April, to crown his policy of expulsions by terminating the mission of the Reich commissioner.

Britain was stymied for the moment. Bonar Law had wished the French *bonne chance*, but he would not aid Poincaré against Germany. He wished neither to seal the destruction of the Entente, nor to encourage German resistance. Public opinion in Britain was divided. Labor blamed French militarism for aggravating Europe's troubles and unemployment, but British coal interests benefited handsomely from the elimination of Ruhr competition, while the continental crisis eased the pressure on Britain's depressed steel industry. Still, British industry feared the Franco-German metallurgical combine that might result from the Ruhr struggle, whatever its outcome.

The British government weighed other considerations. It did not wish to break openly with France while Turkish negotiations continued in Lausanne. Curzon also hesitated to favor Berlin directly following the renewed declaration of German-Soviet solidarity in January 1923. But the position of neutrality between Paris and Berlin was untenable. The very dissociation of Britain from the Franco-Belgian policy could only encourage the desperate German government. The assurances of Britain's ambassador, Lord D'Abernon, contributed to the German conviction that Britain would not stand for a French "victory" in the Ruhr. The conviction was substantiated by the British decision to maintain its isolated occupation force in the Rhineland, much to the relief of the German government. Curzon and Bonar Law could only hope for a break in the intransigence of one side or the other, or for a stalemate permitting reparations to return to the conference table.

It was inconceivable to Poincaré that the Reich could hold out for long with its industrial heart excised. Nevertheless, the fact of the resistance required a decision as to French tactics. On 22 February, Poincaré presided over a council of war. Two points of view clashed in the meeting. General Degoutte emphasized the chaos obtaining in the Ruhr, and the growing strength of Communists with whom his agents were in contact. Political and social unrest was what the Ruhr barons feared most—France must exploit this fear by exercising the most intensive and immediate military pressure on the Ruhr. He could create conditions so intolerable and volatile that the German authorities

[14] Weill-Raynal, *Les réparations allemandes*, II, 392.

would give in rather than risk revolution. The second strategy was that of Marshal Foch. He warned that Degoutte's plan would only create the military, financial, and diplomatic problems the government sought to minimize. France should reject extreme solutions and concentrate on railroads and coal. If necessary, the MICUM could occupy mines and cokeries, recruit Polish laborers, who were numerous in the Ruhr, and undertake direct exploitation. Once coal was moving, France would not need to hurry an end to passive resistance. This fact, more than any other, would convince Berlin that resistance was useless. The government adopted Foch's plan. The Ruhr struggle would be won, not by war and revolution, but by defeating Germany's defensive tactics—the passive resistance would be overcome.[15]

INCREASED AMBITIONS

Raymond Poincaré addressed a convocation of French journalists on the evening of 4 February 1923. His remarks were predictable: Europe's problems were attributable to German ill will, France was forced to seize the Ruhr guarantee, which would create in Berlin a will to pay. While preparing his remarks, however, Poincaré had written the following summation: "It is false to claim that we seek even a single centimeter of German territory. It is false because we seek only our reparations and security, and we are resolved to establish them on indestructible foundations."[16] Officially, Poincaré would not admit any connection between the Ruhr occupation and the security issue. Privately, the French government understood well that the Ruhr policy, by removing the need of concessions in reparations, opened the way to a security settlement as well. But before the occupation, French estimates of the rewards of the Ruhr undertaking, just as the estimates of its cost, had been unclear. To be sure, Poincaré had a reparations plan in mind: German financial reform, loans to Germany, and guarantees of German payment. But what form those guarantees would take, and what solution might be found for France's metallurgical plight, were undelineated. As the investment made in the Ruhr skyrocketed, so did the expectations of French planners.

Jacques Seydoux now emerged as one of the most ambitious of French advisors. Events in the Ruhr had completely changed the situation, he wrote. The Versailles Treaty was dead, and if the Germans did not capitulate there was no need for France ever to relinquish what

[15] Note Hermant #4018s, "Compte-rendu pour M. Tirard; réunion du 22 fevrier," 22 Feb. 1923: AN HCF, vol. 3231, dos. Q4a4/2.

[16] MS Poincaré, "Adresse devant les journalistes," 4 Feb. 1923: BN Corr. Poincaré, N.A.F., vol. 16044, nos. 7-9.

he termed the "compact rhénan." France now controlled a territorial bloc extending fifty kilometers on to the Right Bank of the Rhine. France need only tend this garden on the Rhine and permit the rest of Germany to go to seed. France should agree to abandon the "compact rhénan," according to Seydoux, only in return for permanent cession of the mines of the Saar, complete payment of the "A" and "B" reparations bonds, and a Franco-German metallurgical agreement of fifty years' duration. France would evacuate the Ruhr in three stages as reparations were paid. Only after complete evacuation of the Ruhr would the Rhineland evacuations begin. A permanent Allied rail management in the Rhineland would provide a security guarantee. Never again would Germany use the Left Bank as a staging area for the invasion of France.[17]

On 6 March 1923 Seydoux presided over the interministerial Ruhr committee, convened to discuss the terms of eventual settlement. Inspector Guillaume spoke for the Ministry of Public Works, proposing that the coal-rich Saarland and Rhenish railroads be neutralized in perpetuity. But the best security guarantee, according to Guillaume, would be the creation of a Rhenish state, detached from the Reich and entrusted to the League of Nations. French troops would remain in the Rhineland for an indefinite period after the evacuation of the Ruhr, the bridgeheads being the last to be liberated. Marshal Foch concurred with this plan.[18]

Thus, the goals of the Ruhr occupation quickly became meshed with French goals in the Rhineland in the minds of many leading advisors. Louis Loucheur, always an exponent of a Rhenish solution to French security, called for political separation of the Rhineland from Prussia, on 18 March. He did not favor economic separation—France was incapable, he said, of absorbing the Rhenish economy.[19] A week later, Poincaré himself revealed his thoughts to the Belgian ambassador. "We will remain in the Rhineland for thirty years," he said—until Germany had completed reparations—"and we will control the railroads. If the Rhinelanders seek autonomy, we won't interfere, but to encourage it would be against our goal."[20] Yves Le Trocquer's report emphasized as usual the metallurgical question. "The twentieth century is the century of steel," he said, "and any nation dependent on another for its steel is dominated by it." He advised permanent cession of the Saar and the state mines of the Ruhr. But French-owned mines

[17] Note Seydoux, 16 Feb. 1923: MAE Pap. Millerand, Réparations XI, nos. 127-155.

[18] P.-V., réunion du comité interministeriel, "Propositions à faire à l'Allemagne," 6 Mar. 1923: MAE Pap. Millerand, Réparations XI, nos. 165-172.

[19] Tel. Hoesch (Paris) to A.A., 19 Mar. 1923: AA BR 3058, 1470, no. 603385-87.

[20] Tel. #4110/1945PCA Gaiffier to Jaspar, 24 Mar. 1923: MAE Bel., Correspondance Politique, France, 1923.

in Germany were worthless without security guarantees. Le Trocquer saw control of the Rhine/Ruhr railroads as the answer: "the best of neutralizations."[21]

Rhenish separation or permanent French control in the area had become a serious alternative in the French government's negotiating plan. From Clemenceau's abandonment of security through separatism in March 1919, the government had come full circle. Interest in a Rhenish state received an impetus from the *Conseil Supérieur de la Défense Nationale*, which took initiative in studying the overall benefits and drawbacks of an independent Rhineland. Pressed by Poincaré, the secretary-general, General Bernard Serrigny, circulated a top secret questionnaire to the various ministries seeking opinions on the political, economic, diplomatic, military, and cultural aspects of a number of conceivable Rhenish policies.[22] General Degoutte's contribution to the study consisted of a repetitive call for the destruction or federalization of the German Reich. Like Foch, he considered permanent occupation of the Rhine to be the ultimate guarantee, but he recognized diplomatic exigencies by assuming that military occupation beyond fifteen years would doubtless prove impossible. "Thus, strenuous effort during the fifteen years toward a federalist reorganization of Germany" was indispensable. A Rhenish state by itself would be no guarantee. "Only a federalist Germany in which the states are truly differentiated will cease to be a danger."[23]

General Serrigny, Tirard, and Charles Brugère, Poincaré's *chef du cabinet*, all agreed that the Rhenish state to come must remain within the Reich, for the population would not accept total separation. But the state would have to be autonomous in customs, monetary, and financial matters, militarily neutral, and internationally guaranteed. For the moment, Brugère concluded, the best policy was to continue the process whereby Rhenish life fell increasingly under Franco-Belgian control.[24] Peretti de la Rocca, Poincaré's top aide in the Foreign Ministry, was nonetheless skeptical of so blasé a discussion of carving up one's powerful neighbor. The Rhine was German, he wrote, despite the myths of Maurice Barrès. Any implication or initiative by France concerning separatism would suffice to kill the idea. "We must apply the recommended measures with the greatest prudence and give the im-

[21] Note Le Trocquer, "Note concernant les negotiations eventuelles avec l'Allemage," 31 Mar. 1923: MAE Pap. Millerand, Réparations XI, nos. 222-223.

[22] Let. Serrigny to Brugère, 26 Mar. 1923, "Questionnaire, présidence du conseil: Organisation de la Rhénanie," 26 Mar. 1923: MAE Rive Gauche, vol. 29, nos. 257-264.

[23] Let. Degoutte to Serrigny, 20 Mar. 1923, cited by Degoutte, *L'Occupation de la Ruhr*, annex, pp. 2-9.

[24] Rapport du MAE, préparé par M. Brugère, 30 Mar. 1923: MAE Rive Gauche, vol. 29, nos. 266-269.

pression that the Rhenish movement is happening all by itself." The principal problem on Peretti's mind was the diplomatic one. On Brugère's report he scribbled: "Admirable projet, si l'Angleterre n'existait pas!"[25]

Poincaré shared Peretti's concern for British opinion. He could not afford to attempt Rhenish separation through ultimatum or coup, but he nevertheless desired to create a de facto situation in the Rhineland that Britain would be unable to ignore. An ideal beginning would be the creation of a separate Rhenish currency. The idea of a Rhenish money went back to Tirard's musings in 1919, but the currency situation on the Left Bank had never before been so critical as to offer a pretext for such a serious curtailment of German sovereignty. Soon after Poincaré's accession, a flurry of interest attended Cologne banker Carl Stein's suggestion of a Franco-Rhenish bank to help finance reparations-in-kind.[26] The idea appeared again after August 1922, in response to the severe fall of the mark. Reich printing presses could not keep pace and there was a shortage of currency in the occupied territories.

Finance Minister de Lasteyrie reviewed the possible solutions to the currency crisis. France could introduce the franc into the Rhineland, but such a move would violate the government's strict policy on export of francs, as well as meet with Allied opposition. France could create a Rhenish currency to exist alongside the mark, but the stronger currency would quickly disappear and nothing would be gained. Finally, the government could aid in replacing the mark with a new Rhenish money based on gold and foreign currencies. Politically, this was the ideal solution, but it would require Rhenish investment. De Lasteyrie refused to permit any new currency backed by the French government or tied to French exchange rates.[27] In December 1922, the finance minister elaborated. Monetary separation of the Rhineland would not be possible "in the present economic and political regime." Poincaré took this to mean that a Rhenish currency must await the economic separation of the Left Bank.[28] Occupation of the Ruhr and reinstallation of the Rhenish customs barrier fulfilled this proviso.

Projects circulated freely for a Rhenish gulden, thaler, or franc in January 1923. In Coblenz, Tirard met with Rhenish bankers; in Paris,

[25] Note Peretti, "Contribution à l'étude de l'organisation d'un État rhénan," 30 Mar. 1923: MAE Rive Gauche, vol. 29, nos. 270-279.

[26] Let. Poincaré to Tirard, 16 Jan. 1922; Des. Tirard to Poincaré, 19 Jan. 1922: MAE Rive Gauche, vol. 5, nos. 182-190.

[27] Note Hermant #1267ATRP for Tirard, 29 Aug. 1922: AN HCF, vol. 3231, dos. Q4a4/2.

[28] Note Hermant #3567/s, "Compte-rendu pour M. Tirard," 1 Dec. 1922; Let. de Lasteyrie to Seydoux #2753SA, 2 Dec. 1922; Let. Seydoux to Tirard #957, 11 Dec. 1922: AN HCF, vol. 6383, dos. 32b.

de Lasteyrie with French bankers. By 26 January, Tirard, his financial advisor Giscard d'Estaing, finance ministry representative M. Tannery, and agents of three French banks settled on the principles for a Rhenish currency: three million francs starting capital, no gold backing but a fixed exchange rate of ten French centimes backed by treasury bonds and other hard assets.[29] De Lasteyrie was beside himself when he heard of the agreement. The planned issue was tied to the course of the franc, leaving the franc open to disastrous speculation. Poincaré added political objections. A new currency must be an interallied project, with at least Belgian participation. He suggested, however, a "provisional guarantee" by France. De Lasteyrie vetoed the project.[30]

There was nothing for it but to satisfy the finance minister's conditions. Poincaré instructed the embassy in Brussels to find some Belgian banks willing to support a Rhenish bank of issue and he wired Tirard to find Rhenish banks willing to put up gold. But the bank project was temporarily abandoned at the end of February. De Lasteyrie and Giscard now insisted that a new money would entail a completely new fiscal system in the occupied territories, and prior evidence of public acceptance. In effect, the Rhenish bank would have to follow, not precede, Rhenish autonomy.[31]

Despite his conservatism concerning the bank, de Lasteyrie shared in the wave of increased ambitions in the months following the Ruhr occupation. He subordinated evacuation of the Ruhr to complete payment by Germany of the "A" and "B" bonds, and desired complete annulment of the war debts. For security, he envisioned de-Prussianization of the Rhineland, permanent French occupation of the bridgeheads, and maintenance of the Régie.[32] On 12 April Seydoux combined all the plans presented in the past months into a negotiating project. France would proclaim that the fifteen-year occupation of the Left Bank had not yet begun to run, that the railroads of the "compact rhénan" would be neutralized and managed by an interallied company. The Rhineland would become an autonomous state and be placed under League surveillance. Finally, this neutralization would not prevent the French army from acting against Germany in case of German aggression in the east.[33]

[29] P.-V., réunions "pour l'étude de la question monétaire," Coblenz and Bonn, 25 and 26 Jan. 1923: AN HCF, vol. 6383, dos. 32b.

[30] P.-V., réunion au ministère de finance, 27 Jan. 1923: AN HCF, vol. 6383, dos. 32b. In January 1921, Poincaré was quoted in *Le Matin* as observing that any premier who did not also hold the Finance Ministry portfolio was not master of his own policy!

[31] Note Hermant #4029/s, 24 Feb. 1923: AN HCF, vol. 6383, dos. 32b.

[32] Note de Lasteyrie, "Note sur les réparations," 11 Apr. 1923: MAE Pap. Millerand, Réparations XI, nos. 239-247.

[33] Note Seydoux, "Note faite avec consultation d'Aron; projet d'accord," 12 Apr. 1923: MAE Pap. Millerand, Réparations XI, nos. 248-267.

Whatever the precise solutions adopted, the French government had drawn one conclusion from the unforeseen bitterness of the Ruhr struggle: Versailles was dead; depending on the outcome of the Ruhr occupation, either French or Anglo-German revisionism would take its place. For a few brief months in early 1923, the obstructionist British had removed themselves from the equation. Belgian influence was discounted. France was alone against Germany, and the ferocity of the struggle as well as its expense induced the French officials who had faced years of frustration to dream of a new peace settlement. But once again priorities were left unresolved. What if France's allies refused to recognize her demands, even after an "unconditional surrender" by Germany? What if France were still obliged to make concessions to purchase international recognition of her revisionist schemes? Finally, could the government rely on the acquiescence of the financiers and industrialists both at home and abroad who would have to execute its plans? Would the intentions of mid-1923, unlike those of 1916 and 1917, survive the pressures of peacemaking?

The Quai d'Orsay's Jules Laroche wrote:

> I feel that the Germans will cede before the end of April. That will be the critical moment. We must remember 1918 and bungle neither the armistice nor the future accord, which will have to contain all the necessary guarantees, but also hasten the return to normal relations with Germany. We need a conqueror's peace, but not a fanatic's peace, for we must also be able to re-establish relations with England. We cannot lose sight, alas, of our feeble natality and the terrible menace if we remain isolated against Germany.[34]

Given the awareness of Poincaré, as well as of Peretti and Laroche, that France could not afford to go it alone even in triumph, Britain retained some influence over affairs. France's increased ambitions formed, not an ultimatum, but a negotiating plan. Thus it was that Poincaré made his first soundings of British opinion in April 1923, to see if Britain had become "flexible."

FIRST SOUNDINGS IN LONDON AND BRUSSELS

Neither the initial occupation of the Ruhr nor the German resistance had proven to be decisive. But Poincaré was anxious to discover the impact that the French intention to overcome German resistance was having in London, and what solutions to reparations, war debts, and security the British might now be brought to accept.

[34] Pers. Let. Laroche to Barrère, 8 Mar. 1923: MAE Corr. Barrère, vol. 3, no. 81.

The mission to England would have to be unofficial. In the council of ministers of 17 March 1923, Poincaré asked Le Trocquer to speak to Louis Loucheur, presently out of government. Five days later, Loucheur agreed to go to England "on holiday," and to interrogate the British government. The inspiration for Loucheur's mission has been attributed to Millerand, who gave his personal blessing to the envoy on 28 March, and was rumored to be considering Loucheur as a replacement for Poincaré. Loucheur himself and Belgian Ambassador Gaiffier both attest that the mission was taken on Poincaré's initiative. In fact, Loucheur himself had begun urging talks with London soon after the Ruhr occupation. He was personally pessimistic about the costly struggle and viewed a rapid joint solution with Britain as the only means of salvaging the situation. He himself apparently proposed a secret mission to London and won approval from Millerand and Poincaré.[35]

The French had reason to believe that the British might prove more flexible on the question of the Rhineland's future than they had in the past. The Lausanne Conference made Britain temporarily dependent on French good will. Elsewhere in Europe, the anti-German bloc was holding together. Lithuania's occupation of Memel, disputed since the Peace Conference, and the Polish occupation of Vilna, created a crisis atmosphere at the Quai d'Orsay and the Foreign Office, but France's eastern collaborators tolerated the Ruhr policy.[36] Mussolini did not approve of the extraordinary measures taken in response to the passive resistance, and the Italian observers ceased to identify with Franco-Belgian ordinances. But the Italian display of independence did not turn to Britain's advantage. Mussolini attempted briefly to mediate between Paris and Berlin, appealing to the Germans with talk of a "continental bloc" against England. Poincaré was irritated by such irresponsible behavior, but it did no damage to his position vis-à-vis Britain. Support for Mussolini in his subsequent Fiume and Corfu adventures, and regular delivery of Italy's share of German coal, assured a friendly demeanor in Rome.

[35] Loucheur, *Carnets*, pp. 116-118; Tel. #5529/2540PF Gaiffier to Jaspar, 26 Apr. 1923: MAE Bel., Correspondance Politique, France, 1923. Loucheur elaborated on his plan for a London mission in January, then took credit for proposing the actual trip in April in conversations with James Logan. Pers. Let. Logan to Hoover, 26 Jan. 1923: HI Logan Papers, Box 4, Folder 3; Pers. Let. Logan to Strong, 3 May 1923: ibid., Box 3.

[36] Despite cautious support for France's efforts to extract reparations and security guarantees from Germany, Eduard Beneš, Czech foreign minister, was nevertheless unhappy with the dislocation that the Ruhr occupation caused in Germany. Above all, the Czechs feared the degeneration of German internal disorders into armed conflict and the possible reappearance of an authoritarian regime in Germany. Especially perplexing to Poincaré was the insistence of Czechoslovakia and Poland on continuing coal shipments to Germany during the passive resistance, which contributed to Germany's ability to prolong the struggle against France. F. Gregory Campbell, *Confrontation in Central Europe: Weimar Germany and Czechoslovakia* (Chicago, 1975), pp. 117-133.

Plans for neutralization of the Rhineland had circulated before in Britain, but they appeared now with more meaningful names attached. Robert Cecil, co-drafter of the League of Nations covenant, called for demilitarization of the Rhineland and its administration by the League. Railroads and police would be internationalized.[37] General Spears seconded the idea. M.P. David Lloyd George suggested neutralization of the Rhineland in return for Allied evacuation. The French and German governments denounced such a trade: the French would not hear of premature evacuation; the Germans demanded neutralization of French border territories as well.[38] But a consensus on Rhenish political change seemed to be emerging in the spring of 1923.

Loucheur met first with Ramsay MacDonald, leader of the parliamentary opposition. On reparations and war debts they were "près de compte," but MacDonald offered "enormous resistance" on the Rhenish question. The Conservatives Stanley Baldwin, chancellor of the exchequer and future prime minister, and Bonar Law were also taken aback by the new ambitions revealed in Loucheur's negotiating plan. It called for the stabilization of German finances through a 500 million gold-mark interior loan underwritten by industry. Germany would then finance annual reparations payments of 3.5 billion gold marks with the aid of 40 billions in exterior loans guaranteed by customs and rail receipts and 25 percent shares of industrial stock. The Ruhr would be evacuated progressively according to German payments. Finally, Loucheur's trial balloons on French security included an autonomous neutralized Rhenish state with international railroad control and a League of Nations gendarmerie.[39] Time and again Bonar Law responded with the query: But will Germany accept it? Nevertheless, Loucheur returned to France with the conviction that the hour was propitious for Franco-British negotiations. The judgment was not wholly optimistic—Loucheur also carried back Bonar Law's warning that Britain's ambiguous stance could not last indefinitely. Soon he would be forced to adopt a clear policy.[40]

Upon his return, Loucheur discovered that his journey had instead made negotiations impossible. Perhaps Poincaré never intended that

[37] Tel. Sthamer (London) to A.A., 20 Mar. 1923: AA BR 3058, 1470, no. 603388-89.

[38] "Neutralisation de la Rhénanie," *Le Matin*, 28 Mar. 1923.

[39] Documents of the Loucheur mission can be found in HI Pap. Loucheur, Box 7, Folder 2. See especially Let. Loucheur to Poincaré, 4-5 Apr. 1923; Note Loucheur, "Texte que j'avais en mains pour discussion avec Bonar Law," 4 Apr. 1923. Excerpts are published in Loucheur, *Carnets*, pp. 118-121.

[40] Note Loucheur, "Résumé envoyé au PdC, copie au Président de la République," 10 Apr. 1923; HI Pap. Loucheur, Box 7, Folder 2. For British reaction to Loucheur's proposals, see F.O. Memo, "Situation in the Occupied Territories and the Position of the Reparations and Security Questions," 17 Apr. 1923: PRO FO 371, vol. 8729, nos. 8-30.

Loucheur should succeed as trouble-shooter, but the wave of undesired publicity concerning the "pilgrimage" to England not only called into question France's determination in the Ruhr, but also engendered a panic in Brussels.

Having thrown in his lot with France in order to retain a measure of control over French policy, Theunis now had reason to fear that Poincaré was going over his head without consultation. Rather than pursuing negotiations, then, Poincaré and Peretti denied that any mission existed, and assured the Belgians that "France will not weaken or act except in concert with her Belgian ally."[41] The French premier then explained his actions to his (somewhat confused) ambassador in London: "It would certainly be desirable, if the thing is possible, to be in accord with England *before* the German capitulation. On the other hand, if we are not certain of accord, it would be better to await the capitulation. A *fait accompli* will without doubt render England more conciliatory."[42]

Loucheur's mission set Belgian nerves on edge because it seemed to violate the promised solidarity between the Ruhr partners. The increased ambitions of the French pulled the two governments farther apart. The passive resistance had been unfortunate for Belgium. There were ambitious Belgians who saw their country as a future force in European affairs. The drive for aggrandizement and economic independence had led Brussels to renounce the neutrality treaties of 1839, to seek annexation of Luxembourg, to free the river Scheldt from its long suffocation at the hands of the Dutch, and to foster Rhenish separatism independent of the French. Since 1919, Belgium had enjoyed much of the influence and prestige of a Great Power, thanks to her mediatory role between Britain and France. But the occupation of the Ruhr had forced Belgium's hand and destroyed her leverage. Theunis had envisioned an easy advance into the Ruhr, a rapid capitulation by Germany, and evacuation. Instead he was caught in a struggle of great cost and unforeseeable duration in which the stakes had risen far above his intentions.

It was imperative for Poincaré to keep the Belgians in line, but the tiny monarchy was in the throes of internal unrest. The government's refusal to fund a Flemish university at Ghent rallied Flemish opinion against the government; talk ranged from rebellion to secession. As the Ruhr operation became the Ruhr crisis, Socialists and Flemings at-

[41] Tel. Poincaré to Herbette, Très Urgent, 7 Apr. 1923: MAE Bel., vol. 59, nos. 111-113.

[42] Tel. Poincaré to St. Aulaire, Urgent, 14 Apr. 1923: MAE Pap. Millerand, Réparations XI, nos. 268-270.

tacked the government's militarism, "which threatened German democracy." There was also the financial debacle. The government dared not call for massive credits, but further reliance on French financial support only increased Belgium's subservience to French policy. Theunis' interest was to end the Ruhr struggle as quickly as possible, then to negotiate a moderate settlement not too favorable to France or to Germany. In particular, he sought to uphold the principle that no Allied measures on the Left Bank or in the Ruhr were to be permanent.

In the middle of May, Ambassador Gaiffier communicated his government's misgivings to Jacques Seydoux. Poincaré's project was more political than economic, he said, and the progressive evacuation of the Ruhr as Germany paid the "A" and "B" bonds was draconic. They would be in the Ruhr for twenty-five years, or never leave at all! Theunis could be reversed, he warned, and be replaced by an anti-Ruhr government. Where would France be then? Finally, said Gaiffier, "La Ruhr coûte horriblement cher, et nous n'en tirons rien." Seydoux discounted Gaiffier's fears. Germany would yield soon, he promised; it was necessary only that France and Belgium agree on a negotiating plan beforehand.[43]

Two weeks later, Poincaré renewed the invitation to Belgium to settle on a statement of goals. He spoke of making the Régie and the Rhenish customs control permanent, and of a Rhenish currency. "It is not at all a question of augmenting the pressure already in our hands," Poincaré said in rebuttal to Belgian demands for maximum pressure, "but one of giving the population the impression of the *duration* of our presence there."[44] This was precisely what Theunis sought to avoid. He wanted to tighten the screws on Germany to hasten the end of the Ruhr agony, but he could never admit the permanence of French control in the Rhineland.

On 6 June 1923, the French and Belgians held a grand meeting in Brussels. But instead of providing the stage for a showdown on goals, the conclave degenerated into an artificial show of unity. First priority was to force an end to German resistance, the conference declared; the ultimate goals were ignored. Poincaré was pleased to win Belgian support to the bitter end, and in Peretti's mind Theunis displayed the veneer of solidarity to reinforce his shaky government.[45] After the vic-

[43] Note Seydoux, "Visite de l'ambassadeur de Belgique à M. Seydoux," 17 May 1923: MAE Pap. Millerand, Réparations XII, nos. 131-136.

[44] Tel. Poincaré (redaction Seydoux) to Herbette, 29 May 1923: MAE Pap. Millerand, Réparations XII, nos. 217-220.

[45] Note Vignon, "Réunion de Bruxelles, 6 juin," 7 June 1923: MAE Pap. Millerand, Réparations XII, nos. 281-282.

tory was won, the French reasoned, they could ignore or accommodate the Belgians. The Belgians, in their turn, waited to assert their independence and scuttle France's more ambitious schemes in Western Germany.

PASSIVE RESISTANCE

As Poincaré had predicted in November 1922, the German government did not have a prepared response in case of occupation of the Ruhr. The general strike in the occupied territories began locally; after it had clearly won public support in the Rhine/Ruhr and elsewhere, the government endorsed it. But the effectiveness of the passive resistance as a diplomatic weapon is debatable; its domestic ramifications were disastrous. It delayed the international financial settlement sought by all parties, and during that delay it inflicted the sorrows of economic collapse, political insecurity, and social upheaval on every German citizen. By giving the Franco-Belgians the choice of brutal repression or surrender, the resistance determined the despotism of the occupation regime in 1923. By completing the collapse of the German mark, it did unfathomable damage to traditional social values and drove thousands into extremism. By destroying German productivity, it permitted the undoing of the progressive social legislation of 1919 by Stinnes and the great industrialists. Above all, it threatened German unity itself.

The first proffered justification of the passive resistance was diplomatic. The Wilhelmstrasse hoped to rally world opinion against France and the Ruhr occupation. Once isolated, France would have to relent. But this strategy clashed with the German government's own assumptions. For years it had held up France as an expansionist power seeking not reparations but the dismemberment of the Reich. When Poincaré occupied the Ruhr, the government declared its assumptions proven. But if the "chauvinist clique" was indeed in control of French policy, then it would merely welcome the resistance as a pretext for the use of force against Germany. As it was, the resistance gave Poincaré the excuse and the need to adopt measures of coercion beyond the "taking of productive guarantees."

Passive resistance was an effective means of financial pressure on France, but it involved terrible risk. The critical German error was in the evaluation, not of French policy, but of British and American policy. Cuno hoped that Germany's courageous resistance would force the Anglo-Americans to intervene before France had won a victory in the Ruhr. Poincaré knew that Britain would wait for the end of German resistance to see what France would do with the victory. As long as

Poincaré made it clear that he had not deinternationalized reparations and security, then he could be sure that Britain would not intervene during the Ruhr struggle itself. The passive resistance was wide of the mark. Logic demanded that the German government bring the whole matter to a conference as soon as possible. Resistance only exposed Germany to the disasters the government sought to avoid. German acquiescence and moral indignation following a Ruhr occupation would have put the burden of concession on France. Given Secretary of State Hughes's New Haven policy, the compromise settlement achieved in 1924 might have come about without the tragedy of 1923.

Unfortunately, the diplomacy of passive resistance was not the most pertinent factor in the situation. Cuno's ratification of resistance also stemmed from internal pressures, from the necessity to preserve the Weimar Republic itself in the face of an irresistible wave of national feeling. The cabinet had neither the power nor the desire to ignore the popular indignation released by the Ruhr occupation. A policy of apparent submission would have substantiated for many the Rightist thesis that the Republic was a regime of traitors, unable to defend Germany against foreign and domestic foes. Finally, submission before the Franco-Belgians, even if it won for Germany the immediate diplomatic support of the Anglo-Americans, would have destroyed the myth, assiduously touted since 1919, that Germany was incapable of supporting reparations.

The helplessness of Cuno's government in January 1923 derived from the presence not only of the German Right, but of the Left in the vanguard of the passive resistance. "This combat," announced the Social Democratic party, "to which we enlist millions of men of the German working class, must be directed against the true enemy, the criminal blindness of the Poincaré government."[46] The spontaneous resistance by German laborers expressed their nationalism as well as their antipathy to militarism. It stemmed from a visceral hatred and defiance of the bayonets of men in the same uniforms they had faced in the trenches five years before. Ambassador Pierre de Margerie cursed the perverse resistance that meant an unnecessarily bitter struggle, perhaps Germany's suicide. "The decadence and degeneration of this people is unmistakable; it is possessed of no will." Their very act of resistance was an act of indolence, devoid of imagination. The government was not its own master. Without the support of business, it was paralyzed.[47] But the fatalism de Margerie deplored in Berlin was

[46] *Verhandlungen des deutschen Reichstages*, 25 Jan. 1923, vol. 357, p. 9501.

[47] Pers. Let. Margerie to Peretti, 21 Mar. 1923, cited in Zimmermann, *Frankreichs Ruhrpolitik*, pp. 155-156.

equally apparent in Paris. The French still insisted that the resistance, like all previous German policies, was a ploy of the industrialists and power brokers. Its very "inevitability" contributed to the bitterness with which the Ruhr struggle was fought.

The initial measures of German resistance gave way to the general enabling ordinances of 15 May 1923, the *Notgesetz*. As in wartime, the government took control of transport, revictualment, and raw materials. It undertook relief for the functionaries expelled from occupied territory, extensive espionage and *Abwehr* operations in the Ruhr and Rhineland, propaganda, and reimbursement for private property lost to the occupation. But the charters of the passive resistance were the Düren agreement of 12 February 1923, concluded with the Rhenish employers and labor organizations, and the Steel Finance agreement of 14 April. Under these plans, the employers and government agreed to pay the full salary of workers on strike against the occupation, while the Reichsbank extended short-term paper mark credits to Ruhr industry. The measures meant the likely destruction of the German currency, but without them there could be no general strike. Special agencies organized to deal with the immense task of managing the unemployment relief. Funds had to be smuggled into the occupied territories and distributed clandestinely to avoid confiscation by the French. Private associations from all over Germany contributed, the foremost being the *Rhein- und Ruhrhilfe*. The atmosphere and institutions of total war returned to Germany in 1923.

The pillar of resistance was the unemployment relief. The crack in that pillar was the financial insolvency aggravated by four years of "passive resistance" to French reparations demands. The German floating debt in 1914 was 29 billion gold marks. In January 1923 it was 1.8 trillion. The budget for 1923 predicted a deficit of 13 trillion paper marks, or 877 billion gold marks. A further collapse of the mark was inevitable even without the passive resistance, but it meant that the Reich could meet the cost of resistance only by means of the printing press. Currency in circulation reached 22 trillion paper marks in June, 1.2 quadrillion by August. De Margerie's indictment of Germany was half right. The resistance of the German population to the French incursion was an act of will, determined and directed. But the resistance of the government and its policy of monetary suicide was born of the perverse unwillingness of Germany's social and economic elites to share the burden of Germany's defeat. Reparations were an impossibility, not because Germany was bankrupt, but because they would require tax reform and reallocation of fiscal responsibility—social change unpalatable to the upper economic strata. Inflation and inflammation of national spirit against France were weapons of social conservatism; the burdens of defeat were distributed, not according to which social groups were best able to bear them, but according to which were least able to resist. As during the war, the latter consisted of those groups least organized to defend their interests. The irony of the German inflation was that it was not big business or organized labor, or even the unorganized poor, who had little to lose in any case, but the amorphous "middle class," whose values otherwise sanctified social discipline and patriotism, who suffered most from the national resistance.

The destruction of the German currency convinced British observers that no reparations would be forthcoming until the German financial debacle, for which they blamed the Ruhr occupation, was overcome. But in terms of the resistance itself, inflation was the barometer indicating the steady collapse of German pressure on France. Self-strangulation could not proceed for long before national disintegration replaced national unity. The shortage of money in the Rhineland was such that hourly and salaried employees could not always purchase their fundamental needs even if the shaken economy were able to provide them. The extreme Left made alarming progress in the Ruhr. A Communist uprising in May, tolerated for a while by General Degoutte, hinted at one possible result of the Reich policy. Unless collapse of the mark could be halted at some point, the Rhenish laborer might rebel, or go over to the French. Degoutte welcomed this eventuality. "The day Berlin is no longer able to finance the resistance, the patriotism of the Rhine and Ruhr populations will cease to have a hold on them." They would turn to France in search of work and food, and the battle would be won.[48]

The Cuno government made two half-hearted attempts to arrest the fall of the mark. It could not hope to improve the deficit because of the scissors effect of the resistance: the longer the strike, the greater government expenses and the smaller the tax receipts. There remained only the application of the Reich gold reserves. In February 1923 the Reichsbank began buying marks on foreign exchanges and the mark doubled its value in two weeks. But at that early stage the effect of the unemployment payments had not been felt. The mark tumbled again. In April and June the Reichsbank again dipped into its reserves, but these attempts were undercut by German businessmen themselves, who took the opportunity to dump their own holdings in marks. Inflation accelerated, hastening the end of the German government's ability to resist.[49]

[48] Report Degoutte #11336/D, 5 July 1923, cited by Degoutte, *L'Occupation de la Ruhr*, annex, pp. 17-18.

[49] Seydoux, *De Versailles au Plan Young*, pp. 129-135; Favez, *Le Reich devant l'occu-*

In the occupied territories, the passive resistance was experiencing another defeat. It proved incapable in the long run of preventing the French from "making the guarantee productive." To be sure, the first months had been costly and unremunerative for the Franco-Belgians, but the impossibility of retreat translated itself into an organizational effort of immense proportions in which French technocratic talents displayed themselves to best advantage. Before the occupation of the Ruhr, the French and Belgians were receiving 64,500 tons of coal per day. They received 39,000 tons total for the three weeks following 11 January 1923. This was coal "captured" by the army and ready for transport. After the Brussels Conference of 13 March, Poincaré ordered occupation of certain mines and cokeries. Through the efforts of Allied technicians and volunteer workmen, the occupation began slowly to remove coal from the Ruhr. Thousands of volunteer railroad men entered the Rhineland after 1 March to do the work of the 28,000 German rail workers on strike and expelled by Tirard. From the low point of a handful of trains per day, service picked up. Freight service was matched by the recovery of passenger service. General Payot proudly noted that 250,000 passengers rode the struggling Régie in March, and 1.5 million in June, despite Berlin's appeals for a boycott. Once the French survived the first chaotic months and began making progress toward normalization in the occupied territories, the passive resistance was doomed.

Except for an abortive attempt to revive the call for a committee of experts, Cuno's first diplomatic initiative was the German note of 2 May.[50] His proposals to the Reparations Commission disappointed

---

pation, pp. 211-219; Eyck, *History of the Weimar Republic*, pp. 242-246. On the profiteering of Ruhr industrialists, especially Stinnes, from the German inflation, see Baumont, *La grosse industrie*, p. 337, and the massive research presented by Feldman in *Iron and Steel in the German Inflation*, ch. 6.

[50] The conduct of the public diplomacy of the Ruhr occupation and international exchanges concerning a possible settlement have been often treated. See Zimmermann, *Deutsche Aussenpolitik* and *Frankreichs Ruhrpolitik*; Eyck, *History of the Weimar Republic*; Renouvin, *War and Aftermath*; Duroselle, *Histoire diplomatique de 1919 à nos jours* (Paris, 1957) and *Relations franco-allemandes*; R. B. Mowat, *A History of European Diplomacy, 1914-1925* (London, 1927); Weill-Raynal, *Les réparations allemandes*; Bergmann, *Der Weg der Reparationen*; Rufus C. Dawes, *The Dawes Plan in the Making* (Indianapolis, 1925); Favez, *Le Reich devant l'occupation de la Ruhr*. Making use of recently available German documents are the dissertations by Jones, "Stresemann and the Diplomacy of the Ruhr Crisis," and Rupieper, "Politics and Economics." Publication by all the governments concerned of the official exchanges of notes during 1923-1924 provided the documentary foundation for the standard narrative of events. See especially Belgium, MAE, *Documents diplomatiques relatifs aux réparations* (Du 26 décembre 1922 au 27 août 1923); France, MAE, *Documents Diplomatiques. Documents relatifs aux notes allemandes des 2 mai et 5 juin sur les réparations*; France, MAE, *Documents diplomatiques. Réponse du gouvernement français à la lettre du gouvernement britannique du 11 août 1923 sur les réparations*; Germany, AA, *Aktenstücke zur Reparationsfrage*

even Lord Curzon. The Germans threatened to continue the passive resistance until all the "illegally occupied" territories were evacuated and the Rhineland returned to full German sovereignty. The note repeated the German offer of 30 billion gold marks, but insisted also on a foreign loan and a four-year moratorium. To pacify French security fears, Cuno only iterated his offer of a Rhine guarantee. It was a bluff, pure and simple. Under pressure from the political Right and industry, the Berlin government once again was obliged to negotiate in bad faith. The cabinet agreed that it dared not offer a figure that France might accept.[51] Instead, Cuno hoped to split the French and Belgians and bring Britain and the United States, unofficially represented in Berlin by the banker Fred I. Kent, into open opposition to France.[52] But the demand for evacuation of the Ruhr gave Paris the excuse it needed to eschew negotiations. Poincaré replied by placing a sole and immutable condition on negotiations: the complete cessation of passive resistance. He adhered to General Degoutte's estimate that a true end to passive resistance meant repeal of all resistance decrees, recognition of the legality of the Ruhr occupation, the Régie, the MICUM control, and the expulson of functionaries, as well as resumption of reparations.[53] An end to passive resistance, to the French, meant economic unconditional surrender.

The British scolded Cuno for his note of 2 May, but they also urged Poincaré not to be so precipitous in his rejection of the German offer to negotiate. Bonar Law's government itself had nothing to contribute, and the prime minister, deathly ill, resigned on 22 May. His replacement was Stanley Baldwin, who, together with Curzon, the fixture in the Foreign Office, protested French actions on the Rhine, and clung to neutrality. The final conclusion of peace between Greece and Turkey on 26 May did not alter their mood.

Cuno refused to resign at the behest of his foreign minister, Frederic Hans Rosenberg, although it was clear that he was not the man to break the diplomatic deadlock. Instead, the chancellor presided over efforts to draft a second note, one that might force Britain to break with

---

von 26. Dezember 1922 bis 7. Juni 1923; Great Britain, Parliament, House of Commons, *Correspondence with the Allied Governments Respecting Reparations Payments by Germany*.

[51] See Rupieper's sophisticated treatment of the politics of reparations under Cuno in "Politics and Economics," pp. 277-296.

[52] Ibid. Rupieper has examined for the first time important American source material revealing the extent of the participation of unofficial American emissaries in the diplomacy of the Ruhr crisis prior to the end of passive resistance.

[53] Let. #2225/SAT Degoutte to Poincaré, 4 May 1923: Degoutte, *L'Occupation de la Ruhr*, pp. 344-347.

FIGURE 5. "Defiance: 'You tell those who have sent you that I am here by force of bayonets and I will not depart but by the will of the people.' " H. P. Gassier, 1923. © S.P.A.D.E.M. Paris 1977.

Paris, should Poincaré maintain his intransigent stance. His efforts were seconded by Fred Kent, who visited Montagu Norman in London to gauge British financial opinion, and by the British ambassador D'Abernon. But the group he most needed to please were the industrial cohorts of Stinnes. Internal opposition brought Cuno to the brink of resignation by mid-May, but the *Centralverband deutscher Industrieller*, in return for domestic concessions, and Stresemann's Deutsche Volkspartei threw their support behind a second demarche on 25 May. The result was the German note of 7 June. It did not mention the Ruhr occupation or passive resistance. It offered fixed annuities, guaranteed by tax receipts and the Reich railroad system. In return, Germany must be granted a loan and a two-year moratorium.

The German government knew that the British, given their participation in the note's composition, would not reject the offer out of hand. If Poincaré was adamant, he would be drifting closer to isolation. But how quickly could the wheels of diplomacy be made to turn? The German situation could only become more desperate and the choice between perseverance and surrender might soon disappear. Given the impossibility of internal reform, hence of meaningful German offers, the fate of the passive resistance was in the hands of the Allied governments. But diplomatic pressure was not the Reich's only weapon. The Ruhr cost France dearly, too, and as the Ruhr struggle entered its fifth month, the French premier began to encounter signs of impatience at home.

THE HOME FRONT

Lord Hardinge's prediction at the end of 1922 that Poincaré's government was on the verge of collapse proved embarrassingly false. The erosion of the Bloc National and the slippage of Chamber support for Poincaré that the British ambassador perceived were genuine but not far enough advanced to pose a threat to the government. France was embarked on an effort requiring solidarity and determination, and Poincaré's redundant but effective oratorical and press campaigns served to turn most dissatisfaction against the foreign foe.

In his first post-Ruhr appearance before the Senate Foreign Affairs Commission on 4 February 1923, Poincaré sought to discount the crisis created by passive resistance. The Memel controversy was more critical, he insisted, and he offered the prevarication that the German resistance had been foreseen. The Ruhr was in the able hands of General Degoutte, Belgium was a solid ally, and even Bonar Law would "sincerely do everything possible to aid France without breaking with his own majority." But Poincaré could not hide the fact that the Ruhr operation would require far greater expenses than anticipated. He urged his countrymen to shoulder the sacrifices with grim determination and to expect great rewards. "Results will come slowly but inexorably," Poincaré told the Chamber commission in March. "Germany's systematic resistance has only retarded events."[54]

If a firm majority backed Poincaré in the Chambers, there was evidence that his opposition was making progress in the nation at large. The Socialist and Radical parties intensified their assaults on Poincaré-la-guerre. Léon Blum invoked the "universal conscience," which now

[54] P.-V., Commission des Affaires Étrangères, 4 Feb. 1923: Archives du Sénat, Auditions, 1923; P.-V., Commission des Affaires Étrangères, 19 Feb. and 4 Mar. 1923: Archives de l'Assemblée Nationale, Auditions, 1923.

clearly pointed to France, not Germany, as the disrupter of tranquillity and international cooperation. The Ruhr was ruinous for France, perhaps fatal to German democracy.[55] Slowly public opinion began to question this unrewarding and unending struggle. It was enough that the nerves of an exhausted nation must bear another test of will with her mightier neighbor, but signs of impending national insolvency raised doubts among Poincaré's own middle-class constituency. The Ruhr expenses began to drive down the value of the franc on foreign exchanges, and the worst burst of domestic inflation since 1919 made *la vie chère* a more immediate topic than the Ruhr. The inflationary horror in Germany was all the example Frenchmen needed to question the wisdom of an expensive foreign adventure.

Attacks on Poincaré from the Right lost their impact after the occupation, but Tardieu, for one, did not let up. "This is a struggle without grandeur," he wrote, "carried on by timid wills."[56] The unproductivity of the Ruhr venture, not the occupation itself, aggravated the Center-Right majority. The long-awaited act had not brought the instant rewards expected, but rather more requests for sacrifice and patience. It was this mood that Poincaré prepared to dispel when he went before the Senate commission in secret session in May to ask for credits. Armed with charts and pointer—like a young businessman—Poincaré explained the expenses incurred in the Ruhr and justified the new demands. The funds allotted for military and economic sanctions had been exhausted in the first two months of the Ruhr struggle. The major expense was the Régie, costing 82 million francs so far. Another 32 million had been advanced for April and May. The government now estimated an additional requirement of 167 million francs, of which 128 million were the responsibility of France. But the worst was over, Poincaré argued. Total receipts from the Rhine and Ruhr sanctions were an estimated 35.4 million francs. Coal was moving, daily tonnages having grown from 1,000 in February to over 11,000 in May. (It was still just 28 percent of the amount specified by the Spa Accords.) Finally, the Régie was beginning to show receipts—22 million francs and growing.

The financial exposé was necessary to combat incipient restlessness in the National Assembly. Debate was bitter—Tardieu accused the government of making the Ruhr "the Verdun of the peace battle," but the vote was predetermined. Only the Socialists dared refuse further credits in the national emergency, and the Chamber discussion turned to political strategy. Blum and the Socialist Vincent Auriol suggested

[55] Gombin, *Les Socialistes et la guerre*, p. 50.
[56] MS Tardieu, 29 Mar. 1923: AN Pap. Tardieu, vol. 42, dos. Journalisme.

that Poincaré intended to stay in the Ruhr forever. Not at all, replied Poincaré. The goal of the Ruhr policy was to force international loans to Germany without a reduction of the reparations debt. Once provided with loans, Germany would be able to pay rapidly and liberate the Ruhr. The Ruhr was a reparations guarantee only; the Rhineland was the security guarantee. The Régie, Poincaré added, could be considered a permanent organization.

Auriol then penetrated to the heart of Poincaré's international finance policy: "Concerning the interallied debts, you make a reduction in Germany's reparations dependent on an annulment of the war debts. Why then don't you deal with this matter? Why have you not negotiated with England?" Poincaré shot back, "Because I *have* negotiated with England and the United States for a long time on the debts and have obtained, as you know, no favorable response from either." Each nation stuck to its interest, he said, but through the Ruhr occupation he was seeking to make the Americans "reflect." As for security, Poincaré repeated in conclusion, that would be decided on the Left Bank of the Rhine. The Ruhr was a matter of reparations only.[57] In the first half of 1923, Poincaré could thus impose his own definition of the Ruhr occupation on his foreign and domestic opponents and allies. But behind the government's rigid stance there were as many differing interpretations of the Ruhr policy as there were interest groups in France. The Chamber, the newspapers, the military and the Rhenish bloc, the steel and coal interests held various priorities. Those differences would clash seriously and challenge Poincaré's control over policy after the present need for unity disappeared.

The passive resistance had not succeeded in intimidating the French government or parliament, but the 50 million francs per month added to the budget were only the visible cost of the Ruhr. Indirect costs included the loss of the modest, but tangible reparations-in-kind from Germany, the forced importation of English coal and other goods at inflated prices made even worse by the franc's decline in purchasing power, and the vast loss of production in French industry. The occupation of the Ruhr had not been a project of the *Comité des Forges*. The steel interests were no more pleased with the early results of the operation than were those responsible for the government budget. Instead of ensuring the flow of reparations coal from Germany, the Ruhr action stopped it almost completely. By March over half of all French furnaces were blown out.

Occupation of the Ruhr did raise hopes that the German indus-

[57] P.-V., Commission des Affaires Étrangères, 17 May 1923: Archives de l'Assemblée Nationale, Auditions, 1923.

trialists might prove amenable to an industrial accord favorable to France, but the hopes were in vain. Stinnes and his cohorts had just elected to follow their workers into passive resistance when French steel demarches were made in January 1923, and they were in no mood to bargain. While French industrialists enjoyed a bit of *Schadenfreude* from knowing the Germans were as badly off as themselves, they derived no benefit from the Ruhr occupation. A struggle resulted within the *Comité des Forges* between those openly opposed to the government's policy and those who stuck by the effort to overcome passive resistance. It brought about the replacement of Eugene Schneider, a Poincaré supporter, by François de Wendel, an advocate of negotiation, as head of the *Comité*.[58] But the shift in mood could not alter government policy. Industrial interest groups in the Third Republic did not enjoy the "veto" over state policy exercised by their German counterparts. Incipient technocracy, represented by men such as Loucheur and Le Trocquer, ensured a certain respect for the needs of "the economy" above politics. But an industrial agreement with Germany would not be purchased at the cost of the financial settlement required by the masses of small investors who elected the parliamentary majority. As long as Poincaré retained his overall control, the first priority of the Ruhr incursion was relief for the postwar French budget.[59]

Domestic policy was another concern for the French premier in the late spring of 1923. Troubles arose because of Poincaré's neglect of internal affairs and because of his attempt to straddle the line between Right and Left. Tardieu had asked him in January 1922 with what majority he intended to govern. Poincaré answered, "I did not dabble in party politics when I occupied the Elysée, and it is not to dabble now that I became premier." But while the president was technically above parties, the premier was not.[60] Poincaré's foreign policy angered the Left, his refusal to replace certain Leftist prefects angered the Right. A proposal to alter the election law worried all parties. Prosecution of Royalist or Communist hooligans was unpopular with one wing or the

[58] Favez, *Le Reich devant l'occupation*, pp. 158-159.

[59] See Maier, *Recasting Bourgeois Europe*, for the conflict between traditional parliamentary pressures on the government and those of corporate interest groups. As Maier himself notes at times, one must be cautious about generalizations concerning the hypothesized advance of "corporatist solutions" to the postwar difficulties of continental Europe. There is a certain continuity in France, Germany, and Italy between the prewar and the postwar period. Corporatist politics had been characteristic of the German economic-political structure ever since the 1870s, while in France pluralistic parliamentarism survived even the experiences of war and reconstruction to a degree. At the climax of the postwar crisis in later 1923, Poincaré was still much more independent of his corporatist lobbies than his counterparts in Germany and Italy.

[60] MS Tardieu, 6 June 1923: AN Pap. Tardieu, vol. 42, dos. Journalisme.

other. The budget was a perennial source of ammunition for malcontents. The issues were trivial, but the political situation was similar to that in the summer of 1919—an authoritarian government had been in office for a year and a half, a long tenure in the Third Republic, and it was preoccupied with foreign affairs. General elections loomed less than a year away. By June 1923 the Chamber was growing anxious, and called the cabinet before it to defend its domestic policy.

Poincaré responded with a masterful speech on 15 June. He dismissed the petty critiques, denounced extremism of all varieties, and recalled his thirty-seven years of staunch republicanism. The result was a 200-vote majority, secure, but down from the 380-vote majority achieved in January. Most notable were the forty abstainers, including Briand, Loucheur, and Louis Klotz. There could be no fiction of *Union Sacrée*, even at the height of the Ruhr struggle. Poincaré came to depend more and more on the Right.

While the Ruhr policy was castigated by the Left, and criticized by factions in the Center and in industry, it was also questioned by elements of the Right for being too lenient. Why should France continue to display tact and respect for legalities when she possessed the means of destroying Germany? The *Action Française* called for a Carthaginian peace: "Dissolve Germany or Die!" was one headline; "Annexation! Annexation!" was another. The *Éclair*, *Écho de Paris*, and *République Française* all demanded separation of the Rhineland. The political editors of those papers, as well as Stephen Lausanne of *Le Matin*, were all members of the *Comité de la Rive Gauche du Rhin*.[61] The new wave of pro-separatist propaganda created an uncomfortable situation for Poincaré, arguing as he was his limited intentions abroad while probing for a weakness in the British resistance to a Rhenish state. As during the Great War, strict silence on war aims was imperative. American observer James Logan felt that "the French, when the time comes for negotiations, will be more conciliatory than the press would lead us to believe today. . . . The ultimate policy is unknown—the only man who does know is Poincaré, who keeps it to himself."[62]

PLAYING WITH FIRE: SEPARATISM REKINDLED

The French government had come to include some permanent curtailment of German sovereignty in the Rhineland in its private statement of goals. What role was the heretofore insignificant separatist

[61] Leo Böhmer, *Die rheinische Separatistenbewegung und die französische Presse* (Stuttgart, 1928), pp. 42-52.

[62] Pers. Let. Logan to Strong, 9 Mar. 1923: HI Logan Papers, Box 5.

movement to play in the events to unfold during and after the passive resistance? As of January 1923 Poincaré showed little interest in it. Economic pressure and the winning of Britain to a Rhenish security solution would be the means for the desired changes in the Rhineland. But the collapse of German governmental power in the Rhineland sufficed to awaken separatism from its lassitude of 1920-1922. It recreated the chaos that obtained when separatism first arose in 1918, and it made of the movement a possible agency of Rhenish political change.

Tirard was predictably the prime advocate of intensified French support for the Rhenish separatists, although his continuing feud with Dr. Dorten, more than ever under the influence of Paul Hocquel, proved to be a nuisance. The occupation of the Ruhr was heralded by separatists, but Dorten, for one, chose this moment to flee from the front lines. He removed himself to Cannes and awaited an invitation to Paris. He expected Poincaré to come to him.[63] Tirard interpreted this self-exile as an act of cowardice. To expose himself in Germany during the first weeks after the occupation, when German national feeling ran high, would be risky for Dorten. Indeed, vandals broke into Dorten's printing office in Coblenz and smashed the presses with sledges. Tirard felt compelled to pursue the perpetrators of the outrage. He arrested a German judge who released one suspect for lack of evidence, and seized the equivalent of 5,000 francs from the municipal treasury to replace the machines. But Dorten refused to take up his propaganda—he would wait for France "to consolidate her hold" on the Left Bank.[64]

Joseph Smeets's reaction to the Ruhr occupation was the opposite. He placed himself and his *Rheinische Republikanische Volkspartei* at the disposal of the Allied authorities. Despite daily threats on his life, Smeets propagandized among workers and informed for the French and Belgians. His loyalty was his undoing. Governments could not retain a monopoly of violence amidst conflict that touched every individual's daily life on the Rhine. On the evening of 17 March 1923, a man burst into Smeets's office in Cologne. He fired four shots, wounding Smeets in the head and killing his brother-in-law. Fleeing past Smeets's terrified sister, the assassin exploded through a glass door and disappeared into the crowd. Surgery saved Smeets's life, but left him incapacitated. The German yellow press boasted that when the surgeon opened the Francophile's skull, a tricolored butterfly fluttered out.

[63] Pers. Let. Dorten (Cannes) to Mangin, 2 and 11 Feb. 1923: AN Pap. Mangin, vol. 22, dos. 3.

[64] Tel. Tirard to Poincaré, 2, 11, and 30 Mar. 1923: MAE Rive Gauche, vol. 29, nos. 231-236, 238, 282-286.

One way or another, German resistance had put the two separatist leaders *hors de combat*. Nevertheless, Tirard expected the movement to grow as life became more difficult during the passive resistance. For the moment he agreed with Dorten—the French ought to concentrate on consolidating their hold on the Rhineland. "But whatever our reserve regarding the diplomatic situation," he added, "the Rhenish question appears to me to remain an element of pressure against the Reich that we ought not to neglect." Poincaré agreed, authorizing continued contact with separatist leaders and development of the movement.[65]

Two months later, following the Loucheur mission and the first exchange of notes on reparations, Poincaré elaborated on his view of the Rhenish question. "The problems of reparations and even of our security," he wrote Tirard, "depend far less on the form of government or administration that is established in the Rhineland, than on the conditions that we will succeed in imposing."[66] Whether it was Adenauer's or Dorten's or Cuno's Rhineland mattered little. What interested Poincaré were the conditions: permanent Allied occupation, demilitarization and international or League guarantee, Allied control of the railroads. It was not likely that an uprising by separatist rabble would win the support of the people, but an active movement could help to pressure Adenauer and the Berlin government to make the concessions France demanded.

The chaos in occupied territory in 1923 led to a proliferation of separatist organizations. It also brought a further erosion of Tirard's control over the movement as a whole. The Belgian government held to its policy of favoring Rhenish separatism but opposing any development that could lead to a Rhineland dominated by France alone. Thus, Brussels sought to splinter separatism, to create several Rhenish states. After sharp disputes between the Belgian occupation and the Brussels government, the latter came to define Belgian policy as benevolent neutrality. Smeets had protested the insufficient protection offered by Belgium only five days before he was shot. After the attack, Belgian High Commissioner Rolin-Jaequemyns and his agents transferred their interest to Leo Deckers, the Rhenish Republican renegade who was rumored to have desired armed rebellion the year before.[67]

[65] Tel. Tirard to Poincaré, 2 Mar. 1923; Tel. Poincaré to Tirard, 8 Mar. 1923: MAE Rive Gauche, vol. 29, nos. 231-237.

[66] Tel. Poincaré to Tirard, 24 May 1923: MAE Rive Gauche, vol. 30, no. 243.

[67] Let. #340910 Rolin-Jaequemyns to General Rucquoy (commander Belgian occupation army), 6 Mar. 1923; Let. Belgian delegate Aachen to Rolin-Jaequemyns #2796, 20 Mar. 1923; Let. E.M., 2e bureau, A.O.B. to Rolin-Jaequemyns, 26 Mar. 1923; Let. #1403e Rolin-Jaequemyns to General Rucquoy, 30 Mar. 1923: MAE Bel., HCITR 51, dos. 4.

The Belgian government was not alone in its interest in Deckers and his new *Rheinische Unabhängigkeitsbund*. Pierre Nothomb of the *Comité Politique National Belge* and his military conspirators seized on Deckers as the main instrument of their intrigue. The Rhineland represented troubled waters, and no authority, French, Belgian, or German, could prevent others from fishing there.

In 1923 the separatist campaign also spread to the Ruhr. Always quick to get his hand in where bureaucratic authority was at stake, Tirard sent a personal agent to Düsseldorf to accompany the army as it advanced on 11 January. His man was Paul Valot, a young and eager state servant drawn from Tirard's bureau of press and information in Coblenz. He was to coordinate French press releases and propaganda in the Ruhr, and to report daily to Tirard. Poincaré meanwhile also ordered the creation of a press bureau in Düsseldorf and selected André François-Poncet to direct it. François-Poncet, in the early stages of a distinguished governmental career, had fulfilled the same function at Genoa the year before. On 21 January, Poincaré asked that Valot's independence be suppressed, then requested his recall. But Tirard fought for his liaison in the Ruhr and, in the end, Valot stayed and proved valuable. Le Trocquer even asked Valot confidentially to keep him advised of the Ruhr situation after a visit there in March.[68]

In December 1922 Valot was almost alone in predicting that a German general strike would greet an occupation of the Ruhr and he feared it might defeat the French operation.[69] After five months in the Ruhr, he considered political intrigues to be "obsolete formulae." Richelieu, he said, would ignore Dorten and Smeets, and he told Marshal Pétain in June that there was no region more German than the Rhine and no province more hostile to separatism.[70] Yet a week later Valot was writing Tirard enthusiastically about the founding, in cooperation with François-Poncet, of a new separatist journal in Düsseldorf. This time they had found a German collaborator worthy of French confidence and capable of making separatism a veritable force in the struggle against passive resistance. The man was Joseph Friedrich Matthes, a thirty-seven-year-old "revolver-journalist" and adventurer.[71]

Matthes was of lower middle-class origin, and he was clever, ruthless, and opportunistic. Like Smeets, he was a scavenger-journalist and confidence man, living off the suffering and insecurity afflicting postwar

[68] AN HCF, vol. 4331, dos. 98/27.

[69] Pers. Let. Valot (Mainz) to Tirard, 13 Dec. 1922: AN HCF, vol. 4331, dos. 98/27.

[70] Let. Valot (Düsseldorf) to Tirard, 8 and 15 June 1923: AN HCF, vol. 4331, dos. 98/27.

[71] Let. Valot (Düsseldorf) to Tirard, 21 June 1923: AN HCF, vol. 4331, dos. 98/27.

Germany. He roamed the country, starting up newspapers and dodging lawsuits, until he found his way to Düsseldorf in 1923. He won a position in François-Poncet's service and used his access to French supplies to run a black market in tobacco. He edited the daily *Nachrichtenblatt* issued by the French press bureau. In June Matthes conceived of a new Rhenish newspaper and separatist movement. With the aid of the French authorities, who were in a position to sustain unemployed and down-and-out residents of the stricken north Rhenish cities, Matthes quickly built an organization that dwarfed those of Dorten and Smeets.

Matthes found an able coadjutor in the person of Wilhelm von Metzen, who contributed "respectability" to his *Frei Rheinland* movement. Before the war von Metzen held an army commission, then a middle management position in Krupp's. Fired for defrauding fellow employees, he took revenge by feeding information about the giant organization to the Socialist leader Karl Liebknecht. Both being unscrupulous and not untalented, Matthes and von Metzen showed themselves capable of mass action and collaborated loyally with the French press bureau. Valot concentrated his efforts on the *Frei Rheinland*, abandoning the relics of Smeets's group and leaving Dorten to be dealt with by none other than Poincaré himself.

On 3 April 1923, Dr. Dorten surfaced in Paris. His visit was a journalistic event of embarrassing proportions. Most of the *grands journaux* hailed his mission, others questioned his activities, but all gave circulation to his ideas. The *Éclair* and *Écho de Paris* called for deliverance of the Rhineland and Palatinate from their German overlords and criticized the weak-willed government policy. Jules Sauerwein interviewed Dorten for *Le Matin*, the journal closest to Poincaré, and Tirard, who had gone to such lengths to support the eccentric Dorten, found himself attacked for having "deserted the separatist." Dorten proclaimed, "I have come to Paris to discover yes or no, if I can go forward. I await an answer."[72]

The government carefully ignored Dorten's presence in Paris, but foreign newsmen made capital of his visits with distinguished Frenchmen. On previous trips, Dorten had met with Marshals Foch and Joffre, General Fayolle, future president Paul Doumer, and others. Now he pleaded his case before Louis Loucheur (Loucheur's impression: "médiocre") with the aid of the Rhine propagandists Jacques Bainville, Klecker de Balazuc, and Léon Daudet. Journalists and nationalist organizations fêted Dorten for over two months. The excitement subsided gradually, only to erupt again on 24 June, when

[72] *Le Matin*, 11 Apr. 1923.

the British *Observer* stunned the Quai d'Orsay by publishing a secret document pilfered directly from Tirard's files in Coblenz. It was a report from the Marquis de Lillers, Tirard's agent in Wiesbaden, recounting French involvement with Dorten over the previous four years. It disclosed the French role in the 1919 putsch, the French subsidies, the *bureau mixte* episode of 1920, the Bavarian royalist connection, the feud with Tirard, and the Hocquel affair. For the French government the exposé was mortifying. Dorten's continued presence in Paris was intolerable.

Days after the *Observer* incident, Poincaré received a deputation from the *Comité Dupleix*. The premier denounced Dorten as a Prussian spy, an agent provocateur, and denied any connection between him and French policy.[73] The next day Dorten received an unexpected solicitation from Maurice Bunau-Varilla, confidant of Poincaré and owner-publisher of *Le Matin*. He claimed to bear a message from the premier himself. Bunau-Varilla assured Dorten that Poincaré was a friend of Rhenish particularism, but considered Dorten to be a general without troops. If Dorten could prove that his following really existed, the French government would provide unlimited support. On these terms, would he promise to quit Paris at once? In that case, replied Dorten, his mission was fulfilled. He would go home and raise the Rhineland. On 28 June 1923 Dorten embarked for Wiesbaden.[74]

Bunau-Varilla's ploy to rid Paris of Dr. Dorten had implications far more injurious to French policy than the *Observer* scandal. Poincaré was certain that Dorten had few followers to call forth. It could do no harm to allow him to operate.[75] Dorten had little in the way of a movement, it was true, but Matthes' organization had grown. Passive resistance had created a *Lumpenproletariat* of restless unemployed, vagabonds, and criminals in every town in the occupied territories. There were thousands ready to join any movement, especially if it held promise of easy meals, political thievery, or just the excitement of packing a revolver and being "in" with the authorities. Poincaré was not sending Dorten back to oblivion, but to a merger with Matthes, to

[73] Let. Dorten to Louis Marin (president of the Chamber of Deputies), 18 June 1923: AN Pap. Mangin, vol. 22, dos. 2; Let. Klecker de Balazuc (president of the *Comité de la Rive Gauche du Rhin*) to Poincaré, 28 June 1923: MAE Rive Gauche, vol. 31, nos. 114-122.

[74] Dorten, *La tragédie rhénane*, pp. 133-144. Documentary evidence of Dorten's account of Bunau-Varilla's visit is to be found in MAE Rive Gauche, vol. 31. Bunau-Varilla was a dedicated collaborator of Poincaré and had placed himself at the statesman's disposal on several occasions. He did visit Dorten on 26 June because he bore a return note from Dorten that Poincaré then forwarded to Tirard.

[75] Tel. Tirard to MAE, 12 July 1923; Tel. Poincaré to Tirard, 16 July 1923: MAE Rive Gauche, vol. 31, nos. 175-176, 186.

a movement instructed to "show its strength," one that the French would find increasingly difficult to control.

In the Rhineland, German papers "exposed" a plot, attributed to François-Poncet, to proclaim the Rhenish Republic on Bastille Day. The rumor was false, but it had a kernel of truth. The Düsseldorf press bureau, using Matthes' *Frei Rheinland* as a base, now undertook to unite all the separatist parties. It was the only means to assure French control over a movement whose every act had diplomatic ramifications. That unity of control was precisely what the Belgians feared most.

THE END OF PASSIVE RESISTANCE

Receipt of the German note of 7 June exposed the developing divergence between Paris and Brussels. The Ruhr struggle was quickly becoming mortal—"total victory" by either side was what Belgium sought to prevent. Furthermore, the Belgians were petrified of a final break between Britain and France. The new moderate offer from Germany, therefore, was an opportunity to renew serious negotiations among all parties and to de-escalate the conflict. In particular, Premier Theunis sought to impose consideration of the "Belgian plan" of reparations worked out by himself and Léon Delacroix. The plan envisioned a total German obligation of 50 billion gold marks guaranteed by pledges similar to those offered in the German note. It was easy for Brussels to write off the German "C" bonds, since Belgium, alone among the powers, had been liberated from her war debts. Poincaré could not countenance such an offer, but when he again sought general rejection of the German note, Brussels refused to join him. Needless to say, London also urged negotiation and Curzon began his attack on France on 13 June by inquiring of Poincaré precisely what he expected to achieve in the Ruhr.

In a series of heated exchanges Poincaré and Theunis failed to agree on a formula for their response to Germany. With Socialist and Flemish agitation at a peak, Belgian business frantic over government finance, and Communist gains in the nearby Ruhr, the mood of the Brussels leadership was gloomy. Delacroix confided that he saw no possible solution to the European crisis until "that happy day when M. Poincaré would fall." Instead, the Belgian cabinet fell on 15 June, but Theunis survived to form a new government. The Belgian premier now insisted that if France could not be brought to negotiate, the uneasy allies might at least seek to hasten the end of German resistance. Thus the German note only caused an intensification of pressure on the Rhine. The Rhineland Commission responded with another flurry of ordinances. In protest, the Reich and state governments had ceased to submit their new laws for the Rhineland Commission's ratification. Tirard overcame this by declaring the Commission to be the supreme legislative authority in the Rhineland, enacting or ignoring any law on the books in nonoccupied Germany. The French and Belgians also tightened the cordon isolating the Rhineland and further restricted the list of exportable goods. In addition, all customs would henceforth be paid in sound foreign currency, not paper marks, and a 25 percent surcharge was added to the rates. In early July the Rhineland Commission again stiffened the sentences for resisting or inciting resistance to execution of any ordinance. All cases of sabotage or injury to Allied persons or property would be tried in military tribunals. The number of expelled functionaries reached 16,300, and the total number of exiles from occupied territory climbed toward the ultimate figure of over 100,000.

Intensification of pressure coupled with increased exploitation of the Ruhr was to force Germany to end the passive resistance, but this struggle against Germany was not the only engagement. While an end to passive resistance would greatly strengthen Poincaré's hand, it was to London and Washington that he looked for a sign of "flexibility." The taking and holding of guarantees in Germany, he told St. Aulaire, would not by itself solve the reparations problem. The Ruhr was a political guarantee. "It is the problem of the interallied debts that prevents our putting a figure on the total amount we demand from Germany. The solution to this problem is entirely in the hands of Britain and the United States."[76] It was the Anglo-Saxon powers who withheld their capital from bankrupt Europe; it was they who must yield in the end. Poincaré told the British ambassador that France would continue the struggle to the bitter end, if necessary. But this would bring Germany to certain ruin, protested Lord Hardinge. Yes, replied Poincaré, a crisis was doubtless inevitable.[77]

Lord Curzon attempted to respond to Poincaré's warning during the exchanges concerning the German note of 7 June. Convinced that France was obsessed with security alone, Curzon attempted to renew consideration of a security pact. His tactic was to offer a *marchandage*, satisfaction of French security fears in return for concessions on reparations. But the ploy had not worked at Cannes and it was even more ineffectual now that Poincaré had invested so much to avoid the need

[76] Tel. Poincaré to St. Aulaire, 12 June 1923: MAE Pap. Millerand, Réparations XIII, nos. 32-37.

[77] Note Vignon, "Visite de l'ambassadeur de l'Angleterre à M. Poincaré," 24 June 1923: MAE Pap. Millerand, Réparations XIII, nos. 139-140.

for concessions. Poincaré instructed St. Aulaire in forceful language not to permit a connection between reparations and security:

> We have *never* considered the Ruhr from the standpoint of security. It is the Rhine, the bridgeheads and railroads, that offer us security. We will speak of that in a general *règlement*, but the question of the Ruhr is distinct.
>
> If, however, Lord Curzon wishes to enlarge the discussion, let him speak of the interallied debts, which are in fact the key to the whole problem.[78]

Poincaré's scheme was ambitious: victory in the Ruhr, a new "peace conference" afterwards, separation of the issues of reparations and security, the Ruhr and the Rhineland. But his position depended, as Peretti pointed out, on Belgium. If the Belgians pulled out or sought premature settlements, French leverage would dissolve. Another fall of the Belgian franc set off the debate in Paris. Seydoux insisted that France continue to support the Belgian currency, while financial experts pleaded France's inability to take on new responsibilities. Poincaré intervened with a personal appeal to his minister of finance, and this time de Lasteyrie, on 24 July, granted the premier's wishes.[79] But the Belgians wanted more than a loan. Foreign Minister Jaspar informed French Ambassador Herbette that Theunis would surely fall from power if the Allies did not form a common German policy. He pleaded that France and Belgium bargain together with England. "The little country that is Belgium," he explained, "cannot survive without accord between England and France. If Paris and London are not constantly preoccupied with our existence, we disappear from the map of Europe."[80]

Theunis had one reason for optimism. In July he was visited by another unofficial envoy of the United States. Following the 7 June note, John Foster Dulles had traveled to Berlin in anticipation of negotiations prior to a German collapse. After a month, with the Allied responses not forthcoming, Dulles toured the Western capitals. Theunis told him that Belgium was "uncomfortably" yoked to France and sought a way out of a conflict tending toward unconditional surrender. Dulles then saw Loucheur in Paris and returned convinced

[78] Tel. Poincaré to St. Aulaire, "Réparations, conversation avec Lord Curzon," 9 July 1923: MAE Pap. Millerand, Réparations XIV, nos. 100-103.

[79] Note Seydoux, "Franc belge," 23 July 1923; Let. Poincaré to de Lasteyrie, "Question du change en Belgique," 24 July 1923: MAE Pap. Millerand, Réparations XV, nos. 39-41, 57-58.

[80] Tel. Herbette to MAE, "Conversation avec M. Jaspar," 24 July 1923: MAE Pap. Millerand, Réparations XIV, nos. 45-53.

that the interallied debts were the stumbling block. But State Department policy relegated all American intervention to European political stability. Dulles urged Theunis to bring France and Britain together, while imploring the Germans to make serious attempts at budget stabilization and pacification of France. But Poincaré continued to insist on unconditional cessation of passive resistance, and obstructionists in Germany blocked conciliatory policies. Dulles left Europe in failure.[81]

The last week of July 1923 was the most strained period yet in Franco-Belgian relations. Theunis walked the tightrope, refusing to make a common response with France to the German note unless Britain could also be brought to participate. When Poincaré ignored Theunis's request for a personal meeting for several days, a split seemed imminent. Finally, they worked out a compromise: all three powers would respond separately to the Germans. Theunis' response to Berlin made a reference to security and was more conciliatory in tone, but the Belgians remained opposed to negotiation prior to the end of passive resistance.[82]

In a separate note to Britain, Poincaré protested Curzon's attempted introduction of security questions into the matter of the Ruhr and reparations. He reminded Curzon that it was Britain, not France, which had terminated the security pact talks in 1922.[83] But pressure was increasing on Poincaré also. President Millerand sent his personal secretary to the Quai d'Orsay on 4 August to urge a French diplomatic initiative. Something must be done, said Millerand, to capitalize on the Ruhr occupation. The metallurgical crisis preoccupied him. But Poincaré resisted. He was supported in these nervous weeks of summer, the hottest in Paris in decades, by Peretti, who "reminded Poincaré daily of the need to hold on until victory was won." To negotiate directly with Germany would incur the wrath of Britain, but France dared not negotiate with Britain until her leverage was won in the Ruhr.[84]

From Berlin, Pierre de Margerie also advised that Poincaré negotiate with the Germans. A gesture from France could topple Cuno

[81] Rupieper, "Politics and Economics," pp. 313-331.

[82] Tel. Poincaré to Herbette, "Réponse à la note anglaise," 25 July 1923: MAE Pap. Millerand, Réparations XIV, nos. 61-64; Tel. Herbette to Poincaré, 26 July 1923: MAE Belgique, vol. 59, nos. 149-152; Tel. Peretti to Herbette, 29 July 1923; Note Vignon, "Conversation avec Peretti," 30 July 1923: MAE Pap. Millerand, Réparations XV, nos. 141-144, 162-164.

[83] Tel. St. Aulaire to MAE, 31 July 1923; Tel. Poincaré to St. Aulaire, 1 Aug. 1923: MAE Grande Bretagne, vol. 53, nos. 193-197; vol. 54, no. 10.

[84] Note Vignon, "Conversation avec Peretti," 4 Aug. 1923: MAE Pap. Millerand, Réparations XV, nos. 263-264.

and end the resistance, he wrote. One fact was certain: an end to the unemployment relief by Berlin meant the end of resistance. A new government would be free to take this step.[85] What kind of gesture did he have in mind? Perhaps a public declaration, answered de Margerie, assuring the German people that France was not bent on destroying the Reich. On 12 August 1923 Poincaré made two gestures that he hoped would satisfy the ambassador's request. First, he released the French Yellow Book on reparations, explaining French Ruhr policy and emphasizing his limited aims. Second, he altered his customary Sunday speech, setting aside his familiar attack on German ill will for an appeal to Germany to end the fruitless resistance and participate in a settlement fair to all parties.[86] The following day, 13 August, Chancellor Cuno resigned—not in hopes of French altruism, but because the Reichstag finally repudiated his suicidal tactics.

By August the policy of passive resistance had brought about what seemed the final collapse of the mark. After a few more weeks the resistance would be physically impossible to sustain. But the social and political unrest engendered by the chaos surpassed even the supposed ambitions of the French as the most immediate threat to the German republic. Hitler's National Socialists grew from a puny splinter party to a local power in Bavaria, and rightist terror organizations such as the *Oberland* and *Blücher* corps paraded their strength. It was only a matter of time before such groups, which originally directed their hatred against the French, turned their violence inward. The climate of international economic conflict and militarism also proved favorable to the growth of communism in the Ruhr and in major cities. Strikes and riots erupted all over Germany. Socialists and Communists in Saxony and Thuringia joined in common defense organizations and formed coalition governments. In the Rhineland, separatists demonstrated under French protection and Berlin could no longer be sure of the patriotism of the common Rhenish burgher or peasant in a situation fast becoming intolerable.

The Reichstag convened after its recess in the first week of August. Its first priority was to reassess the strong medicine of passive resistance, which was killing the healthy cells of the body politic along with the invaders. Final efforts at strengthening government finance through internal loans fell short of their targets as big business, especially heavy industry, made inadequate subscriptions. By the end of

[85] Tel. Margerie (Berlin) to MAE, 8 and 9 Aug. 1923: MAE Ruhr, vol. 26, nos. 77-78, 101-102.

[86] Tel. Margerie to MAE, 12 Aug. 1923; Tel. MAE to Margerie, 13 Aug. 1923: MAE Ruhr, vol. 26, nos. 145-153, 168.

July the government no longer had access to the foreign currency necessary to purchase foodstuffs—it was the end of the line. Inevitably preoccupied with the issue of urban revictualment, the Social Democrats lost confidence in Cuno's "business ministry." On 11 August they withdrew their support for the government.[87]

In desperation, President Ebert turned to Gustav Stresemann, head of the conservative Deutsche Volkspartei. Stresemann was only forty-five when he won his struggle to enter the republican government as a minister. A staunch monarchist in 1919, he had organized the remnants of the old National Liberals into a business-oriented party deceptively labeled the People's Party. But the logic of the international situation and the violence and irrationality of the German Right convinced Stresemann that monarchical restoration was an undesirable goal. Furthermore, the early collapse of the Weimar coalition meant that his ministerial ambition was not fanciful. In 1920 his party gained in strength and respectability, its campaign touting Stresemann as a man "im Geiste der Grossen," another Bismarck or Hindenburg. By 1923, the bourgeois politician had maneuvered himself into a position where he could be selected as chancellor of the German Reich. Such had never happened in the aristocratic empire. This fact, more than any other, won Stresemann to the republic.[88] He came to power at a time when his Bismarckian qualities were sorely needed. But it was a lesson of Lenin that he first applied: to move two steps forward, it would first be necessary to take one step back.

Stresemann ended the boycott Cuno had placed on the French embassy. He was eager to talk to the French, to see if Poincaré was willing to make concessions to purchase an end to the passive resistance. He had the support of de Margerie, of Louis Barthou in the Reparations Commission, and of the Belgian government, all of whom regarded Stresemann's government as the last chance for a peaceful settlement between France and Germany. Stresemann opened a dialogue with the Belgians, and on 1 September he offered a reparations settlement and a security pact, a mutual guarantee of frontiers among all the "Rhine-interested" powers. His primary concern was to receive in return a guarantee of German sovereignty in the occupied territories.

Poincaré reacted to Stresemann's overtures with more vehemence

[87] Cuno was overturned at the very moment when he had finally begun to make progress in reconciling business interests to the need for reforms. But he was pleased to be free of the responsibilities of power and returned with relief to the shipping business. On his fall, see Maier, *Recasting Bourgeois Europe*, pp. 356-373; Rupieper, "Politics and Economics," pp. 332-404.

[88] Henry A. Turner, *Stresemann and the Politics of the Weimar Republic* (Princeton, 1963).

than he had to Cuno's defiance. He insisted that the Belgian government reject out of hand the German proposals. Stresemann's demarches were only an attempt to bargain before the end of passive resistance, and the fact that he offered so much indicated that the end would come soon.[89] De Margerie, in turn, was forced to inform Stresemann that the French government did not recognize the German approach, since the passive resistance had not terminated. The French ambassador feared that failure to grant Stresemann a success might mean the collapse of the German democracy. But Stresemann had no choice but to surrender. Moderate industrialist Otto Wolff, who had met secretly with Degoutte and his economic advisor General Denvignes, told the chancellor that morale was on the verge of collapse. By late August he was joined by Stinnes and Vögler. To appease labor, wages were now indexed and the hyperinflation was no longer beneficial to industry.[90] This change of heart represented a significant achievement. Though at great cost, France had destroyed the value of the inflation for the Ruhr and thus removed the primary barrier to German financial stabilization.

Stresemann was equally unable to turn the resistance to the government's account. His furious efforts of August and September had been meant to rally Curzon to an anti-French line. The new chancellor was stunned and embittered by Britain's inertia. His misconception was the same as Cuno's in January—Britain would not intervene to prevent a French victory, but would wait to see what France would do with it. Poincaré confidently warned that "Germany is at the turning point. If she persists in her methods, she will call down disasters for which we will not be responsible." Given British and American inactivity, Stresemann's one inroad—his successful solicitations in Brussels—could have little effect. After a sharp quarrel with Poincaré, Theunis rejected Stresemann's offer to negotiate on 21 September 1923.[91]

Failure to exact a price for German capitulation meant that the German surrender would have to be unconditional. As in 1918, it was the only means left to save the Reich. Capitulation was a desperate act, but not one born of desperation. Stresemann foresaw the internal

[89] Tel. Herbette to MAE, 4 Sept. 1923; Tel. Poincaré to Herbette, 5 Sept. 1923: MAE Pap. Millerand, Réparations XVI, nos. 257-261.

[90] Feldman, *Iron and Steel*, pp. 395-398.

[91] Note Laroche, "Questions des réparations," 12 Sept. 1923; Note Laroche, "Visite du chargé d'affaires de Belgique," 13 Sept. 1923; Tel. Poincaré to Herbette, 19 Sept. 1923; Tel. Poincaré to Margerie, 21 Sept. 1923: MAE Ruhr, vol. 28, nos. 157-158, 169-170; vol. 29, nos. 51-62, 100. Concerning Stresemann's attempt to exact concessions for the end of passive resistance, see Jones, "Stresemann and the Diplomacy of the Ruhr Crisis," pp. 92-140.

backlash that could develop after an end to resistance and he was prepared for it. On 26 September 1923 he and President Ebert proclaimed the cessation of passive resistance and the revocation of the edicts supporting it, "to preserve the life of the nation and of the state." Surely now Poincaré would negotiate.

THE COMMITTEE OF EXPERTS

But Poincaré did not negotiate. Instead of responding to Stresemann's declaration with an ultimatum or bilateral "peace talks," he ignored the appeals from Berlin and concentrated on local efforts to "make the guarantee productive." He permitted the psychological moment to pass. The French premier's behavior in the critical weeks following the cessation of German resistance was a vexation and a mystery to his comrades and rivals alike. For months Poincaré had subordinated negotiation to a German capitulation, and now, the day after the German surrender, he wired his European ambassadors that nothing had changed. In later months and years his French critics seethed when they contemplated how this great chief had thrown away the costly victory and thereby lost for France the peace she deserved. How can this inactivity be explained?

Poincaré's first response was to analyze the German capitulation. We must remain calm, he instructed, and modify nothing until Ruhr workers and magnates themselves have restored production and deliveries to France. Only then would General Degoutte's definition of an end to resistance be fulfilled. Only then would France have the bargaining tool she required. "It goes without saying that these conditions for a true end to resistance are independent of the general *règlement* of reparations that will come later and be the work of all the Allies."[92] Poincaré recognized that Stresemann's action was only a change of tactics, and he resisted his colleagues' impulse to cry victory. This time Poincaré was in the position to block any "premature armistice" through which the Germans might escape the perception and consequences of defeat.

So Poincaré stuck to his program. Over Belgian protests he informed General Degoutte that France could not be content with declarations. "We need realities and it is in the occupied territories that we shall look for them. There will be no negotiation with Berlin until deeds have been done in the Rhineland and Ruhr."[93] Poincaré thus gave De-

[92] Tel. Poincaré to Brussels, Coblenz, Düsseldorf, 27 Sept. 1923: MAE Ruhr, vol. 29, nos. 211-212.

[93] Tel. Poincaré to Degoutte (Düsseldorf), 1 Oct. 1923, cited by Degoutte, *L'Occupation de la Ruhr*, p. 447.

goutte the go-ahead to receive delegations of industrialists and negotiate the MICUM accords, which would become the symbol of France's "victory" over the passive resistance. Short-term contracts with the industrialists themselves would consummate the Ruhr policy. An international settlement based on France's new position of strength would follow. Poincaré ignored Stresemann's demarche because he had no business to do with Berlin.

Poincaré's refusal to name his terms nonetheless infuriated Millerand and perplexed de Margerie, St. Aulaire, Degoutte, and Seydoux. A crisis in the victors' camp was the premier's bitter October harvest. But it was no more than what Poincaré had foreseen when he decided to stay on in December 1922 and to lead France into the Ruhr rather than entrust it to less cautious men. Now he threatened to resign rather than force terms on Germany in defiance of France's allies. "Do you want me to break with England?" he asked his critics. Poincaré did not behave like a conqueror after the end of passive resistance because he awaited a sign, not from Germany but from Britain. Far from considering only France's parochial interests on the continent, Poincaré was sacrificing an opportunity to crush the concentrations of power represented by the Ruhr and the Reich in favor of the international stabilization he knew to be in France's, as well as the world's, best interest. Stresemann could not solve the problem of the interallied debts and the weakness of the franc. The Franco-British Entente would not survive a Franco-German separate peace—and Britain, Poincaré knew, would not hesitate to use its financial superiority to ruin an overly ambitious France. To be sure, Poincaré's ambitions had increased markedly since the previous autumn as the Ruhr struggle escalated. He had reason to hope for British acceptance not only of a suitable reparations/debts plan, but of a Rhenish security solution as well. But security was a separate matter, and in reparations Poincaré held fast to his procedure enunciated in June and November 1922.

The agency to provide the groundwork for the eventual settlement, Poincaré had already decided, would be the Reparations Commission. He explained to Seydoux on 18 August 1923 that "a committee of experts named by the Reparations Commission could render the double service of 'saving face' for England and researching the terms of future arrangements without anyone being compromised by it."[94] Now that passive resistance was over, all that remained was for the United States and Britain to renew their offer of December 1922 for convocation of such a committee.

[94] Note Vignon, "Conversation avec Seydoux," 18 Aug. 1923: MAE Pap. Millerand, Réparations XVI, nos. 178-179.

The first hopeful signs came from across the Atlantic. On 2 August Calvin Coolidge succeeded to the presidency upon the death of Warren G. Harding. The new administration had an ideal opportunity to alter American policy on war debts or possible loans. The arrival of American Treasury Secretary Andrew Mellon in Europe on a fact-finding mission was a good omen. On 19 September the first clear sign of an end to the "mésentente cordiale" took the form of a visit by Prime Minister Stanley Baldwin to Paris. Presumably a nonofficial call worked into Baldwin's return trip from a spa in Savoy, it could hardly be anything but a political event of the first magnitude. For the first time since January, French and British premiers met face to face—and it was Baldwin who had come to Poincaré.[95]

Baldwin announced Britain's readiness to make generous concessions in the matter of the interallied debts and to revive discussion of a security pact. Thus, Britain would still try to connect reparations and security to force French concessions. Baldwin also offered a veiled warning about the consequences of unilateral French action against Germany. Speculation against the French franc, he pointed out, was an unfriendly act of which Britain had not been guilty. Poincaré replied that German passive resistance was to be blamed for all Europe's troubles. He assured his British counterpart that the eventual solution to reparations would be reached by *all* the Allies together.[96]

A provocative speech by Lord Curzon before British Empire representatives interrupted the march of events early in October. Poincaré's old enemy accused the French of seeking the destruction of the German Reich. But Curzon's speech served only as a final warning to Poincaré not to use his victory in the Ruhr for such a purpose. Far from being close to a break, as the Germans hoped, France and Britain now pursued compatible reparations policies. The British cabinet had already decided to make the demarche Poincaré had awaited since January. On 13 October, the British ambassador in Washington invited the Americans to participate in a reparations committee of experts.[97]

The only piece missing from the tableau was American. As Poincaré had guessed, the Americans, too, had not intervened or done anything to prolong the German resistance, but they "watched intently developments following the German surrender." Two days after the British

[95] The "surprise visit" had of course been prepared. This time the Belgians were notified and consulted before the tête-à-tête with the British. See Note Loucheur, "Visite de M. Delacroix," 28 Aug. 1923: HI Pap. Loucheur, Box 12, Folder 4.

[96] MAE Memo, Poincaré-Baldwin interview, 19 Sept. 1923: MAE Pap. Millerand, Réparations XVII, nos. 15-34.

[97] Minutes, CAB 47(23), 26 Sept. 1923: PRO CAB 23/56, pp. 253-254; Aide-mémoire Chilton (British chargé in Washington) to Hughes, 13 Oct. 1923: FRUS 1923, II, 68-70.

demarche, Hughes informed the British that the United States was "entirely willing" to take part in a reparations conference and to cooperate in an "appropriate financial plan for securing such payments."[98] The same day Poincaré charged Ambassador Jusserand to request such participation on behalf of France. Why had the French government not agreed when Secretary of State Hughes recommended an identical procedure in December 1922? Because, Peretti explained to the ambassador, it would have been useless to examine Germany's capacity to pay until Germany acquired a will to pay. The Ruhr occupation and defeat of the passive resistance had induced such a change in the German attitude. It had also given France a *position acquise* she had not enjoyed ten months previously. "We know," Peretti wrote, "at what point the cooperation of the United States will be necessary. It alone possesses the capital to be made available when credit operations again become possible." Moreover, he continued, the question of loans was linked to the question of the debts that the United States held against Germany's creditors. Jusserand must urge the American government to take those "reasonable and energetic measures that alone can save Germany from chaos and reëstablish durable peace in Europe."[99]

The American proposal declared America's "great interest in the economic situation in Europe and readiness to promote economic stability." Secretary Hughes suggested either an international conference or a Reparations Commission enquiry, and requested the Europeans to state their preference. Poincaré examined the proposal and asked specifically whether it was the result of American or British initiative. It was, he was told, a British initiative. Armed with this indication of the "flexibility" he had pursued for eighteen months, Poincaré guided the proposal through the French council of ministers on 25 October.[100] He announced: "The French government had made known on many occasions how desirous it is of American collaboration in the examination of reparations. . . . The Reparations Commission can therefore designate within the limits of its powers an experts' commission as M. Hughes envisages. . . . The French government is disposed to request the cooperation of the American government."[101]

A month of discussion would follow during which Poincaré ensured that the powers of the experts' committee were carefully defined. But his acceptance launched the Allies and Europe on the path of financial

[98] Aide-mémoire, Hughes to Chilton, 15 Oct. 1923: FRUS 1923, II, 71-73.

[99] Tel. Peretti to Jusserand (Washington), 15 Oct. 1923: MAE Pap. Millerand, Réparations XVII, nos. 153-156.

[100] Tel. Hughes to Whitehouse (chargé in Paris), 24 Oct. 1923: FRUS 1923, II, 79-83.

[101] Tel. Poincaré to St. Aulaire, 25 Oct. 1923: MAE Pap. Millerand, Réparations XVII, nos. 220-222.

reconstruction. Poincaré could not accept a committee of experts in 1922 because France lacked the leverage to prevent a settlement so injurious to French rights as to leave France inferior to Germany economically and financially—as she already was demographically. Such a settlement would make of France a financial and political hostage of the Anglo-Saxon powers. The occupation of the Ruhr, Poincaré hoped, gave France the leverage to avoid such a settlement. To be sure, the struggle against Germany had increased French isolation and her financial vulnerability. But the experts, too, must bow to political realities and grant France an acceptable compromise on reparations/war debts. If they resisted for a time, France might remain in the Ruhr—Poincaré was seeing to it that the guarantee became self-supporting.

Poincaré's advisors did not all agree with or even grasp his policy after the launching of the Committee of Experts. Why did Poincaré not name his terms at once and extract them from defeated Germany, instead of withholding his goals and entrusting his victory to an undefeated and unsympathetic Allied committee? "Millerand and Foch and several cabinet members all pressed in vain for him to seize the hour," testifies St. Aulaire, who was himself ordered back to his post on pain of dismissal when he went to Paris in October to urge negotiations. He advanced several explanations for Poincaré's policy: respect for the Treaty of Versailles, desire to conciliate England, a move to escape the tyranny of the Bloc National in preparation for the 1924 elections. In the end, St. Aulaire suggests that Poincaré succumbed to the depression and aimlessness that afflicts man after a long and difficult accomplishment; that he suffered, in fact, an eclipse of the will.[102]

General Degoutte held Poincaré's "paralysis" responsible for the defeat of the entire Ruhr policy, by February 1924. But Degoutte's own analysis of Stresemann's prospects offers another interpretation of the premier's policy. France could force a very favorable settlement on Stresemann, but if his government then fell, France would be left with a scrap of paper. If, however, France ignored Stresemann, Germany might fall into social and political chaos. This policy was also dangerous, leaving France with heavy responsibilities for the future.[103] Poincaré did ignore Stresemann, making plausible the conclusion that he had adopted Degoutte's second policy, that he wished to promote German disintegration by every means possible.

French historian Jacques Chastenet offers four reasons for Poincaré's rejection of direct exploitation of his victory. He respected the treaty,

[102] St. Aulaire, *Confession*, pp. 672-675.

[103] Note Degoutte, 29 Aug. 1923, cited by Degoutte, *L'Occupation de la Ruhr*, annex, pp. 46-56.

feared a final break with Britain, was acutely worried about the financial weakness of France, desired to appeal to the Left, which was sure to gain strength in the 1924 elections. These explanations all serve to expose the logic of the circumstances in which Poincaré was obliged to make a momentous decision. But they fail to emphasize the continuity of the premier's strategy from June 1922 to October 1923. Poincaré never de-internationalized reparations. A military man like Degoutte saw only the opportunity to destroy the enemy utterly. But the diplomat is careful always to leave an "out," to his enemies, his allies, and above all to himself. The length and cost of the Ruhr struggle seemed to justify a bolder move, but Poincaré clung to his plan because he recognized that financial stabilization could not take place without the Anglo-Americans. Financial disaster for France would be the epilogue of any other policy.

On the question of Germany's future, Poincaré's own desires conflicted. Surely Poincaré would have welcomed a return of Germany to *Kleinstaaterei*, in the abstract. But a fragmented Germany would pay no reparations and require decades of armed vigilance by France. The Rhenish question was another matter. As Poincaré announced every Sunday for months, the Ruhr episode had nothing to do with security, but the Rhineland did, and it had not failed to be affected by the Ruhr struggle. As the summer of 1923 turned to autumn, the separatist movement initiated four years before seemed genuinely to be approaching fruition. Britain opposed any alteration of Rhenish political status. If Poincaré demanded such a solution of Stresemann, he would sacrifice British tolerance. And if Germany fell into chaos, for whatever reason, the British would hardly fail to blame the French Ruhr policy and accuse France of seeking to destroy the Reich. If, however, by economic catastrophe and the threat of armed separatism, the Rhenish notables and Berlin government themselves could be brought to accept Rhenish autonomy and material guarantees of French security in their province, the British could hardly refuse.

The Ruhr involved reparations, the Rhineland security. This oft-stated policy represented a lucid and long-prepared calculation on the one hand, and a fatal miscalculation on the other. While going out of his way to respect interallied procedures in the Ruhr, Poincaré permitted a course of events most aggravating to Britain to play itself out in the Rhineland. He erred in thinking that he could separate reparations and security for diplomatic purposes, and once again the French Rhenish policy would spoil France's patient struggle for a just and lasting postwar settlement. By the time Poincaré recognized the Anglo-

American offer as the sign he had awaited, events in the Rhineland had already escaped his control.

WILDFIRE SEPARATISM

In accordance with Bunau-Varilla's instructions to "show his strength," Dorten staged the first of his grand demonstrations on Sunday, 29 July 1923. Tirard was ignorant of any directives from Poincaré to aid Dorten, as Bunau-Varilla had promised; Dorten took this to mean that he had been "betrayed" again. But Tirard needed no special instructions—the separatist movement had been his charge since 1919, and the assistance he now offered created Dorten's spectacle. It was held in the Festsaal of Coblenz and was attended by six thousand Rhenish "delegates" transported by special trains of the Régie. The rally benefited from the protection of French security agents and the hall itself was arranged for by Tirard. Dorten's collaborators were in attendance, but Matthes's *Frei Rheinland* members outnumbered them ten to one.

The Festsaal was packed on 29 July; the crowd spilled into the street. Banners of green-white-red, the Rhenish republican colors, festooned the walls. Crass but sentimental renderings of the "Rhenish Hymn" served to create a heady atmosphere. The flamboyant correspondent Jules Sauerwein described the rally for Parisian readers, indulging in the exaggeration and distortion that characterized French perceptions of the Rhenish movement. The convention invoked in him ". . . a violent emotion of joy, stupor, and shame: joy at witnessing the magnificent power of the Rhenish movement; stupor before the thousands who traveled cross-country and risked reprisals by riding the Régie; shame that this man who has raised six thousand delegates has been suspected of having no partisans by the Prussians and, alas, by the French." Dorten cried before the assembly: "For three months I labored in Paris, but was only asked, 'Where are your men?' " Gesturing to the crowd, he intoned, "My men are here!" The audience thrice shouted, "Hoch der rheinischen Republik!" and swore to create a Rhenish state.[104]

Dorten tried to take advantage of the publicity following the rally by requesting from Poincaré the immediate creation of a Rhenish currency and a Rhenish *Beirat* to assist in governing the Left Bank. If his demands were not met, Dorten threatened to resign from the move-

[104] Dorten, *La tragédie rhénane*, pp. 145-151; *Le Matin*, 30 July 1923; Tel. Tirard to MAE, 2 Aug. 1923: MAE Rive Gauche, vol. 32, nos. 5-7.

ment. Tirard and the Düsseldorf press bureau had long since transferred their hopes to Matthes, but the Parisian Rightist backlash and the appearance of a "defeat" for French policy made jettisoning Dorten unattractive. In fact, the French were somewhat surprised by the separatist showing, and certainly willing to be seduced. Tirard convinced Dorten that retirement was unwise; he must exploit the first success with more rallies.

After 29 July Poincaré considered that the Rhenish movement might be of value as a means of pressure against Berlin and the Rhenish Center party. He entered into direct communication with Paul Valot, who now pursued the task of uniting the various separatist organizations into a *Vereinigte Rheinische Bewegung*. On 6 August, the second great rally convened in the Tonhalle in Düsseldorf. Matthes was the leading figure. This time *Le Matin, L'Écho de Paris, L'Homme Libre, L'Intransigeant, L'Action Française*, even the official *Temps* and *Journal des Débats* extolled the Rhenish movement or called for a Rhenish Republic. Momentum began to build. Matthes's partner von Metzen spoke secretly to Dorten, promising a position of equality in the directorate of a united movement if he would merge. In mid-August Tirard's services and the *Frei Rheinland* orchestrated a convention of five thousand at Bonn. Dorten and Matthes mounted the podium together and announced the unification of their movements.

Poincaré quickly wired Tirard to approve of the measures taken with Dorten. But he must not be permitted to return to Paris under any circumstances: "The Rhenish movement must be led by Rhinelanders with no hint of our patronage. This is the essential condition of durable success."[105] Poincaré was perfectly correct, but even if the French were innocent of involvement in separatism, foreign critics would accuse them of it. As it was, French involvement was glaring. Only an abrupt change in the will of the Rhenish people and constituted leaders would suffice to win for France a Rhenish state with a measure of legitimacy.

Smeets's Rhenish Republican party met in München-Gladbach on 26 August, and for the first time there was violence. A crowd agitated by "nationalists" attacked the separatist gathering. Local police and Belgian troops restored order. Two days later Matthes addressed a rally in Cologne. The pattern was well developed by this time. Each week the separatists informed Tirard of the site of their next Sunday's meeting. Tirard arranged for the Régie's "separatist specials," for the

[105] Tel. Poincaré to Tirard, 18 Aug. 1923: MAE Rive Gauche, vol. 32, nos. 54-55. General Mangin took care to see that Poincaré understood the import of the separatist "triumphs" (Let. Mangin to Dorten, 5 Aug. and 8 Oct. 1923: HI Dorten Collection).

leasing of a hall, and for security. Matthes's followers, substantially the same ones every week, would then be notified of the arrangements. The traveling show gave the impression of a numerous and widespread following. On 9 September the Matthes/Dorten movement held a rally at Trier with eight thousand reportedly in attendance. Smeets's group met the same day in Bonn, numbering three thousand. Tirard reported "indisputable progress in recent weeks for the idea of Rhenish independence."He regretted only that the Smeets group remained aloof."[106]

A week later Tirard's regret vanished. Before a crowd of ten thousand in the Aachen Westpark, Dorten, Matthes, and the disabled martyr Smeets shared the platform. The German chargé in Paris saw it as an ill omen. Poincaré, Foch, and Tirard now considered the Rhenish Republic prepared, he believed, and a proclamation would follow soon.[107] The following Sunday, 23 September, the separatist specials delivered their human cargo to Wiesbaden, Dorten's base of operations. The last stop would be in Matthes's headquarters, Düsseldorf. There, it was rumored, the Republic would be proclaimed.

The day of the Wiesbaden rally, Tirard came into possession of a note that Matthes had secretly confided to the press bureau. Matthes had completed unification of the movement, it read, which was just inasmuch as he claimed a following of 140,000 while Dorten and Smeets had only 15,000 between them. Matthes counted on two million partisans in all, mostly in rural areas. The vanguard of the movement was the *Rheinlandschutz*, armed "patriots" who would protect the Rhenish state against Prussian reprisals. Dorten himself admitted that Matthes's revolver and club-toting brigades were composed of "disparate elements," but that Matthes had imposed discipline upon them. When the time came for the putsch, separatists would strike at 5 A.M., seizing public buildings in selected cities. Matthes asked the French and Belgians to disarm the German police, close the frontier, and observe a benevolent neutrality (*sic*).[108] The day of the putsch had not been set, but rumors circulated that it would come off on Sunday, 30 September, at Düsseldorf.

The rumor was false. The great rally was planned for that city on Sunday afternoon, but not a putsch at 5 A.M. Yet the same rumor reached the ears of the German authorities. Düsseldorf's expelled *Regierungspräsident*, operating out of Elberfeld, ordered the

[106] Tel. Tirard to Poincaré, 13 Sept. 1923: MAE Rive Gauche, vol. 32, nos. 112-115; Let. #2070ATRP Tirard to Poincaré, 18 Sept. 1923: AN HCF, vol. 5268, dos. Séparatisme rhénan.

[107] Tel. Hoesch to A.A., 22 Sept. 1923: AA BR 3058, 1470, no. 603636.

[108] Tel. Tirard to Poincaré, 24 Sept. 1923: MAE Rive Gauche, vol. 32, nos. 150-155.

Schutzpolizei (Schupos) to disperse the assembly at all costs. Orders from the German police kept the streets of the city clear of bystanders on 30 September. The morning was ominously quiet. Shortly after noon, train after train arrived at the main station debouching separatists. The growing and disorganized mass rolled through the streets toward the Hindenburg Wall, site of the rally and only a few blocks from the barracks where Schupos and police had taken up their watch.

At 3:45 P.M. Matthes and von Metzen ascended some theater steps overlooking the crowd, estimated at thirty thousand. As Matthes began his speech two shots sounded and a band of Schupos appeared on a side street. They advanced toward the square, moving from tree to tree, firing revolvers. The separatist guards, permitted by the French to bear arms in violation of the Rhineland Agreement, retreated across a corner of the square before returning the Schupo fire. A portion of the crowd was trapped in a cross fire. In the ensuing melee atrocities were committed by both sides. By the time French cavalrymen arrived to restore order, there were ten dead and eighty wounded, including two Frenchmen. Both the German and French press took full advantage of the propaganda material and the Düsseldorf clash inevitably became known as Bloody Sunday.

The result for the *Vereinigte Rheinische Bewegung* was momentary paralysis. Dorten responded with outraged letters to Poincaré and General Mangin. Urged to show his strength, Dorten had led his followers into ambush and massacre at the hands of the Prussian state police—just kilometers from General Degoutte's own headquarters! It was a day of shame for France, he wrote. Dorten decided the only course of action was to call a halt to mass demonstrations. But he did not sacrifice hopes for a putsch. Indeed, the moment seemed most propitious. "We must act!" Dorten wrote Mangin. "M. Poincaré, in whom all hopes reside, is in the process of losing the Rhineland. Prestige! Prestige and action, not doctrinaire reflection!"[109]

Matthes, not possessed of Dorten's sensibilities where bloodshed was concerned, was delighted by Bloody Sunday, evidence of Prussian brutality. He told reporters that the incident had doubled the strength of separatism. Peretti also recognized the possibilities. The order went out to Tirard and Degoutte to "exploit the incident to our best interests."[110] But Poincaré himself was ambiguous. Paul Valot had frankly

[109] Let. Dorten to Poincaré, 1 Oct. 1923; Let. Dorten to Mangin, 1 Oct. 1923: MAE Rive Gauche, vol. 32, nos. 184, 192; Let. Dorten to Mangin, 3 Oct. 1923: AN Pap. Mangin, vol. 22, dos. 3.

[110] Tel. MAE to Degoutte, 2 Oct. 1923: MAE Rive Gauche, vol. 32, no. 204.

admitted to the premier two days before that the majority opinion on the Left Bank was anti-separatist. The unpredictability of the movement also worried Poincaré, but he limited himself to expressing doubt that the separatist movement could ever bring about a positive result, lacking the adhesion of the majority of the population.[111] Having expressed this opinion, it was foolish for Poincaré to permit further collaboration with separatism, but an abandonment of the movement would have aroused the vitriol of a good portion of the Chamber. The Allies were coming together to form the Committee of Experts; the MICUM negotiations proceeded. But, instead of restraining Poincaré on the Rhine, the French Ruhr victory heartened French deputies and other Rhine enthusiasts concerning separatism's chances. Poincaré's very moderation in the handling of the end of passive resistance made it hard for him to suppress the separatists even had he ardently desired to do so. But a miscarriage of the movement could mean a grave defeat.

The occupation authorities had sought to prevent such a miscarriage by uniting all the parties under French control. But a unified separatism under French aegis was precisely the development the Belgian intriguers feared most. Pierre Nothomb, Colonel Leopold Reul, and others of the *Comité Politique National Belge* watched in frustration while the French monopolized the movement through Matthes. For Belgium the stakes were high. A French-dominated Rhineland meant encirclement and eclipse for Belgium, while a partitioned Rhineland could mean Belgian security and aggrandizement. But there remained to Belgium only the tiny organization of Leo Deckers with which to work. Following Bloody Sunday, Reul met with Deckers and together they attempted to win Matthes away from the French. Matthes refused to defect.

In mid-October, Reul called a council of war at the home of Lieutenant Peters. Deckers and his aide Herr Dietz represented the *Rheinische Unabhängigkeitsbund*. The moment for action was at hand. Poincaré's true goal was annexation, alleged Reul. He promised Deckers revictualment, regular wages for his "troops," and two thousand Belgian carbines. The Belgian government, he promised, would support the movement. Deckers was to march on the night of 20-21 October. Aachen was chosen as the site for the putsch.[112]

[111] Let. Valot to Poincaré, 28 Sept. 1923: AN HCF, vol. 4331, dos. 98/27; Tel. Poincaré to London, Berlin, Brussels, Rome, 3 Oct. 1923: MAE Rive Gauche, vol. 32, nos. 220-221.

[112] Tel. Tirard to Poincaré, 9 Nov. 1923 (testimony of Peters): MAE Rive Gauche, vol. 35, nos. 251-255; Note Davignon for Jaspar, 23 Oct. 1923: AGR Pap. Jaspar, dos. 240, Folder 2 ("Action du Comité rhénan français et du Comité de Politique Nationale"), pièce 3.

Over a week before, on 4 October, the Belgian government had hinted to the French ambassador of the possibility of a Rhenish putsch. Poincaré was incredulous. The chiefs of the Rhenish movement had shown no facility for action in the past, and he considered it premature to exchange views on the possible future configuration of the Rhineland.[113] He did not guess at a plot unconnected with Matthes's movement, and he said French authorities would "give the Rhenish people every opportunity to make manifest their sentiments and to protect them against Prussian reprisals."

On 19 October Belgian Ambassador Gaiffier telephoned the Quai d'Orsay with an urgent message: the Belgian government had just been informed of the possibility of a Rhenish Republic being declared in the Belgian zone. What was the French government's attitude? Peretti took the call and replied, truthfully, that the French government had no intelligence of an imminent putsch.[114]

The next day the same sequence of events took place. Gaiffier now had information directly from the Belgian commander, General Rucquoy. There were from 2,000 to 2,500 separatists standing ready to seize the government in Aachen that very evening. Peretti refused to take the hint. Perhaps he was unaware of Deckers' organization, or perhaps he took Rucquoy's intelligence to refer to the putsch Matthes had now scheduled. On 20 October the Düsseldorf press bureau reported that Matthes had appeared three days before with the following report: "Messieurs, we have decided to strike the decisive blow." Had the date been fixed? Yes, replied Matthes, it was set for the last Sunday in October. He asked that M. Poincaré be informed.[115] That would be 28 October.

On the evening of 20 October, Pierre Nothomb telegraphed to Deckers the single word "Marchez!" Deckers and his armed followers rode into Aachen in the early hours of 21 October and quietly took possession of the municipal buildings. When day broke, Deckers proclaimed the Rhenish Republic. The conflagration had begun.

[113] Tel. Poincaré to Jaunez (Brussels), 17 Oct. 1923; Tel. Poincaré to Degoutte, 17 Oct. 1923: MAE Rive Gauche, vol. 33, nos. 33-34.

[114] Note Peretti, "Coup de téléphone de l'Ambassade belgique à M. Peretti," 20 Oct. 1923: MAE Rive Gauche, vol. 33, nos. 49-50.

[115] Note François-Poncet for Poincaré, 20 Oct. 1923: MAE Rive Gauche, vol. 33, nos. 57-62.

·8·

CONFLAGRATION: RHENISH SEPARATISM, 1923-1924

Poincaré had steered France and Europe through ten months of crisis. With daily, even hourly, attention to all aspects of the Ruhr struggle, he had endeavored to keep direction and initiative in his own hands, to apply or relax pressure when needed and to minimize the risks of a provocative policy. But his control in the French-dominated Rhineland itself had proved imperfect. Poincaré received the news of the separatist putsch with shock and confusion, but French deputies, generals, and journalists reacted to it with enthusiasm. In response to their pressure and to his own revisionist ambitions, Poincaré cast his lot with violent separatism. He believed he could isolate the questions of reparations and security, the battle in the Ruhr and the battle in the Rhineland. This one error sufficed to cancel out much of the diplomatic leverage won during ten months in the Ruhr.

Intellectually, Poincaré had been revisionist ever since the peace treaty took shape in April 1919. By the time he assumed office it was clear that the treaty failed to satisfy the security, metallurgical, and financial needs of France. He had foreseen the discord that would attend French efforts to enforce the treaty, and he deplored it. The greatest exponent of the Entente, Poincaré was obliged to strain it to the breaking point. A "man of the nineteenth century," economically "liberal," he was forced to lead the etatist attack against the prerogatives of private industry, both French and German. The most diligent defender of economic stability and the integrity of the franc, he exposed both to the wildest risks. Having overcome with great effort and political risk the demands of the majority of his advisors that he force a "new peace" on Germany after the end of passive resistance, Poincaré perhaps was not able to defy them again and to crush the untimely separatist putsch. While entrusting French reparations demands to the Committee of Experts, he elected to pursue his revisionist security program *in loco*, to seek a *fait accompli* the Allies must then recognize. In so doing, he ensured the demise of the paralytic Versailles system—for a failure of French revisionism now meant the certain victory of British and German revisionism in postwar Europe.

THE REVOLVER REPUBLIC: FRENCH RESPONSE TO SEPARATISM

Information about the Aachen putsch trickled into Coblenz, and thence to Paris, throughout the day of 21 October. The Quai d'Orsay had ignored the blunt warnings offered by the Belgian ambassador and was caught off guard. Poincaré earnestly desired the *paix rhénane*, a solution to French security based on alteration of the political or military status of the Rhineland, but only if it could be legitimized at the conference table. Separatist violence offered slim hope of such legitimization, but Poincaré and Tirard had been under constant pressure from the French Right for not having supported separatism enough! Now the dalliance with Matthes and Dorten as a means of pressuring Berlin had exploded into open conflict, and one sparked by the Belgian torch. Rather than act impulsively, Poincaré and Peretti chose a middle course. They ordered Tirard to prevent German police from acting if the movement should spread to the French zone. French authorities were to observe a "benevolent neutrality."[1]

While French correspondents rushed their banner stories to Parisian presses, rhapsodizing on the long-awaited Rhenish Republic, French authorities worked swiftly to regain control over the uprising. In Düsseldorf, Paul Valot of the French press bureau met with Matthes and von Metzen and pondered the origin of the Deckers putsch. Was it a plot to destroy separatism by a premature outbreak, or the ill-conceived action of zealots? They agreed that there was no choice but to launch a separatist movement in the French zone at once. "Under no circumstances," Valot said, "must the Aachen drama be allowed to play itself out in isolation." Whatever the Belgians' motives, "every effort must be made to regain the initiative, to submerge this isolated action in the flood of a general insurrection."[2] Von Metzen personally damned Deckers as a traitor to the Rhenish causes, for their organization was not really prepared for a widespread insurrection. In Wiesbaden, the Marquis de Lillers informed Dorten of the Aachen events and summoned him to meet with Tirard in Coblenz the following day. There the united separatists would plan their riposte.

On the evening of 21 October the French government still retained freedom of action. The origins of the putsch were not yet clear, but the fact that it took place in the Belgian zone left the French at liberty to

[1] Tel. Tirard to MAE, 21 Oct. 1923: MAE Rive Gauche, vol. 33, nos. 77-84; Let. #2439 Crewe (Paris) to F.O., C18931/129/18, 25 Oct. 1923: PRO FO 371, vol. 8685, nos. 101-103.

[2] Des. Valot (Düsseldorf) to Poincaré, 24 Oct. 1923: MAE Rive Gauche, vol. 33, nos. 253-257.

disown the movement. It was Poincaré's last opportunity to save himself from a gambit whose end results could not be foreseen. But the Belgians seemed to be supporting the movement, he wired Tirard and his embassies, and the movement would surely spread to the French zone. He left the decision to the men on the spot. Tirard took this to mean that he could unleash Dorten and Matthes in the French zone. On the morning of 22 October he told Dorten that "the French government has the intention of joining the initiative taken by the Belgians; the instructions have already been given by Poincaré."[3]

While Valot and von Metzen debated strategy, Matthes traveled to Aachen to effect a union with Deckers. He hoped to incorporate the Aachen group into the united movement, the avoidance of which had been the very logic of Deckers' putsch. Deckers agreed to associate himself with the "provisional government" to be formed, but he would retain leadership of his north Rhenish state centered at Aachen. Having achieved this settlement, Matthes reported to Valot and loosed his *Rheinlandschutz* battalions on the unhappy towns of the Left Bank of the Rhine.

Two movements expanded simultaneously on 22 October. Leaving a detachment at Aachen, Deckers' men piled into trucks and invaded Düren and Krefeld, raising the green-white-red banner and proclaiming the Republic. Matthes' ruffians seized public buildings in Trier, Rüsselheim, Ems, München-Gladbach, and a host of smaller towns. In Aachen itself, German police made their first appearance, rushed the occupied Rathaus, and were disarmed by Belgian troops. Police in other towns suffered the same fate. Riots occasioned some separatist actions and even French newspapers admitted "regrettable incidents" of violence and pillage. Revolver-toting rowdies and ex-convicts posing as "authorized representatives of the Rhenish Republic" requisitioned the meager food supplies left to Rhenish cities after ten months of economic collapse.

The seizure of Bonn and Duisburg, and the installation of the provisional government at Coblenz went ahead the next day. It was also the day when the Quai d'Orsay received its first intelligence concerning the origins and motives of the Aachen putsch. With Tirard's blessing, Matthes and Dorten proclaimed themselves co-directors of the provisional regime. Matthes became plenipotentiary for the middle Rhine, and Dorten for Rhenish Hesse and "the south." Deckers was granted

[3] Tel. Poincaré to Berlin, London, Brussels, Rome, Washington, Coblenz, and Düsseldorf, 21 Oct. 1923: MAE Rive Gauche, vol. 33, no. 94; Dorten, *La tragédie rhénane*, p. 166.

his north Rhenish state in the Belgian zone, but Matthes was already planning his ouster.

Despite the seeming success of the separatist troops in the urban centers of the Left Bank, Tirard showed concern for the future of the movement. The separatists had a government, he reported on 23 October, but they commanded no obedience from municipal administrations. It was not only a question of loyalties; the separatists were incapable of organizing an administrative effort. "Their incompetence will quickly lead to their expulsion if abler men do not take their place."[4] In the meantime, the French officials themselves inherited the task of keeping public services functioning and preserving order.

The burden separatism might place on France was evidenced most clearly in what otherwise was the most exciting victory yet for the wildfire spread of separatism—the proclamation on 23 October of an autonomous Palatine republic at Speyer. Separatism in the Bavarian Palatinate differed from the Matthes/Dorten variety by commanding support and justification beyond immediate relief from the hardships of the passive resistance and its aftermath. Palatine peasants and vintners suffered from what they considered exploitative taxation, the *Zwangswirtschaft*, by which Bavarian bureaucrats obliged peasants to sell the government a portion of their crops at fixed prices. The politics of the Munich government also found few sympathizers in the Palatinate. The Rightist von Kahr spoke again of Bavarian separation from the Reich and monarchical restoration, while "the Bavarian Mussolini," Adolf Hitler, threatened to install an authoritarian regime. The French delegate-general in Speyer, General de Metz, took advantage of the discontent to rally several Palatine leaders, including a veteran of Kurt Eisner's government, Johannes Hoffmann, and Dr. Franz Josef Heinz-Orbis of the Palatine *Freie Bauernschaft*.

The Palatine insurgents turned at once to France for material aid. Tirard authorized withdrawal of foodstuffs from the French occupation stores and appealed to Paris for instructions. This time Poincaré was forced to define the limits of benevolent neutrality. He was willing to provide aid only if certain that the movement served French interests. What was a socialist like Hoffmann doing at the head of a separatist movement? *Vorwärts* interpreted the movement as directed against Munich, to preserve the Palatinate's ties with Berlin should Bavaria secede. Poincaré accordingly vetoed financial support until the Speyer government made clear its intentions. "Lacking any sound informa-

[4] Tel. Tirard to MAE, TRÈS URGENT, 23 Oct. 1923: MAE Rive Gauche, vol. 33, nos. 167-173.

tion, how am I to know where the truth lies?" he asked. When Tirard protested, Poincaré continued: "Your telegraphic intelligence has proven contradictory and unintelligible."[5] In Speyer, General de Metz transferred his hopes from the inscrutable Hoffmann to peasant leader Heinz-Orbis.

The first three days of the Rhenish insurrection had been days of maddening anxiety for the Quai d'Orsay. Incoming information was confusing, events defied direction. Three separatist movements now existed where the French had hoped for one. Despite the official policy of neutrality, French authorities were thrust more and more to the forefront by their efforts to compensate for the separatists' incompetence. Finally, on 24 October Paul Valot submitted a lengthy report to Poincaré on the state of the separatist struggle. Revolutionary separatism was not the French goal, he wrote, rather an autonomous Rhineland within a democratic Reich. Nevertheless, French and foreign opinion linked the separatist outbreak to French policy, and a defeat for the movement would be interpreted as a personal defeat for the premier. This was why he gave Matthes approval to follow up the Deckers putsch with a full-scale rebellion. "It was necessary to make the best of a bad situation and turn all our efforts to pulling the bogged separatist cart out of the ditch." Valot admitted that Belgian "duplicity and personal ambition" were responsible for the premature outbreak at Aachen, but he believed the game might still be saved. Above all, the separatists must avoid "comic opera demonstrations," concentrate on public services, and then, having given an impression of permanence, invite the constituted parties of the Rhineland to collaborate. The battle would be won with potatoes, not bullets.[6]

Matthes was helpless to carry out Valot's strategy. His *Rheinlandschutz* recruits scurried to and fro, breaking into public buildings, raising flags, and terrifying the populace. There were setbacks, since the lack of indigenous support required unreliable garrisons to be left in each town. Police demonstrations sufficed to drive some invaders away. München-Gladbach was lost temporarily when the garrison looted shopkeepers, then vanished. Elsewhere, Deckers' movement foundered in the Belgian zone and no separatist activity at all took place in the hostile British zone. Especially vexing for Matthes was General Degoutte's refusal to permit separatist agitation in the Ruhr. Degoutte's immediate concern was the ongoing negotiations with the

[5] Tel. Tirard to MAE, 25 Oct. 1923; Tel. Poincaré to Tirard, 25 Oct. 1923; Note Poincaré, 26 Oct. 1923; Coup de téléphone, de Metz to Tirard, 26 Oct. 1923: MAE Rive Gauche, vol. 33, nos. 21-30, 36, 60-76, 260-261.

[6] Let. Valot to Poincaré, 24 Oct. 1923: MAE Rive Gauche, vol. 33, nos. 253-257.

Ruhr magnates for a return to order and productivity. He would not tolerate interference from petty insurrectionists.[7] Dr. Dorten provided the final source of irritation for Matthes. Fleeing from administrative responsibility, he preferred to hobnob with French journalists and, on the advice of his wife and of his shadow Paul Hocquel, advocated a complete break between the Rhenish Republic and the French commissariat.

Despite the patent impossibility of radicating a separatist movement in inhospitable soil, Matthes did not despair. He would move on Düsseldorf, he told Valot on 30 October, oust Deckers from Aachen, and surround the British zone. He could then force Cologne's adherence through a "war of pin-pricks."[8] He was not aware that at that very moment the French government was deciding that Cologne's adherence was easily worth the sacrifice of Matthes' entire movement.

Tirard entrained for Paris on the evening of 29 October and attended a strategy conference with Peretti and Poincaré the next morning. Tirard spoke only of the danger and precariousness of the separatist movement. French delegates maintained order and municipal services, while the Rhenish people compounded their hatred for brigands who pillaged under French military protection. The "provisional government" was only a façade. If it did survive for any length of time, Berlin might cut off all unemployment relief for the occupied territories, throwing a burden of 50-100 million francs on the French treasury. If a Rhenish state was to emerge from the chaos, responsible Rhenish leaders must be brought in to take control. For this, at least, there was hope. Tirard told Poincaré that he had been contacted during the past week by various notables. Adenauer himself had requested an audience.

Poincaré issued precise instructions this time. Tirard should engage the Rhenish notables with the goal of striking a bargain on creation of a legitimate Rhenish state. Total independence under the auspices of the League of Nations was his maximal program, but he repeated that the conditions that the Rhineland could be brought to accept were more important than the form of the state itself. He wanted a separate Rhenish budget, parliament, railroads, and diplomatic representation. French security and reparations rights under the treaty must remain unchanged. Finally, Poincaré urged speed, not only because of the diplomatic inconveniences of such negotiations, but because the im-

[7] Tel. Tirard to Degoutte, 22 Oct. 1923: MAE Rive Gauche, vol. 33, nos. 131-133; Let. of Comité Politique Nationale Belge, 26 Oct. 1923: AGR Pap. Jaspar, dos. 240, folder 1, piece 1.

[8] Let. Valot to Poincaré, 30 Oct. 1923: MAE Rive Gauche, vol. 34, nos. 201-205.

mediate leverage that Tirard possessed—the lawless separatist movement—could not preserve even its façade for long. Tirard feared that the notables and separatists would be chary of dealing with each other. That was of no consequence, replied Poincaré. The separatists could be abandoned at any time.[9] Tirard returned to the Rhineland with a clear mission, but its success depended in part on the durability of his puppets' regime.

COUNTERATTACK: BRITISH AND BELGIAN RESPONSE TO SEPARATISM

The initial Belgian policy toward the Aachen putsch was officially "strict neutrality." This translated itself in practice into military protection for Deckers' north Rhenish state, the key to Belgian strategy. The Belgian military, cabinet, and private intriguers all hoped to fashion a federalized autonomous Rhineland in which British and Belgian influence would balance the French. While the Belgian authorities and conspirators, led by Colonel Reul, struggled to maintain the de facto situation, Foreign Minister Jaspar tried to capitalize quickly on Deckers' movement by soliciting talks with London and Paris for a common solution to the Rhenish question. Belgian loyalty to France, preserved by carrot and stick throughout the long Ruhr struggle, disappeared when Rhenish separatism came to the fore.

On 24 October Jaspar sent identical demarches to his allies announcing that "political consequences of the separatist movement, if it succeeds, ought to be examined by the Allied governments in common." Poincaré exploded at this "premature action." He characterized the issue as an internal German problem and refused to discuss it with the British. Above all, he castigated Jaspar for acting without prior consultation. Jaspar's reply was appropriately curt: the Belgian government had chosen to demonstrate that in a question as important as the creation of a new state on her frontier, Belgium could only have an independent policy, and that a solution must be formulated *à trois*, not *à deux*.[10] The Belgian game was exposed. If the French insisted on directing the separatist movement, the Belgians would enlist British support to defeat them.

The Belgian demarche in London failed to stimulate a British statement of position. Since 20 October the Belgian ambassador had men-

[9] P.-V., "Entretien Tirard/Peretti/Poincaré," 30 Oct. 1923: MAE Rive Gauche, vol. 34, nos. 188-198.

[10] Des. Poincaré to Jaunez (Brussels), 24 Oct. 1923; Tel. Jaunez to MAE, 25 Oct. 1923: MAE Rive Gauche, vol. 33, nos. 225-226; vol. 34, nos. 4-8.

tioned the separatist movement in hopes of receiving a precise response, but three times the Foreign Office had refused to discuss a "hypothetical situation." On the morning of 23 October, Sir Eyre Crowe hosted a Foreign Office conclave to formulate a Rhenish policy. His Majesty's Government, it was decided, would hold to the formula that "any change [in the Rhineland's status] brought about by the regular means provided for in the German constitution could not be objected to." Thus, separatism and de facto autonomism were anathematized. Only a Berlin-supported autonomy for the Rhineland would find tolerance in London.[11]

The failure of the Belgian government to promote an exchange of views between the Allies meant a crisis for Belgian policy. Agents of the Belgian *Sûreté* made contact in Aachen with the local British consul, seeking support for Deckers' regime. But the goal of the British agents, as Brussels realized after Curzon's message of 23 October, was to induce the Belgians to eject Deckers. Colonel Reul and Lieutenant Peters, the plotters responsible for the putsch, resisted the efforts of their own government's political agents and prevailed upon Deckers to break off relations with the British consul. This engendered a lively protest from the chief inspector of the Belgian *Sûreté* and a clash within the government.[12]

Colonel Reul left Aachen for Brussels on 26 October and explained to the government why the preservation of Deckers' regime was crucial. His north Rhenish state was the only guarantee against complete French domination on the Left Bank. It was Reul who had defended Deckers' interests during the Matthes visit on 21 and 22 October. Once aware of the British opinion, however, Jaspar lost interest. If a Rhenish Republic were to come about, it would only be achieved through a general security arrangement with Britain and Germany. As for separatism, Belgian ambitions reverted to prevention of French Rhenish ambitions. Jaspar began searching for an excuse to liquidate separatism in the Belgian zone.

The Quai d'Orsay did not anticipate Brussels' wavering. Instead, it prepared for London's negative reaction to Rhenish separation. But on what grounds could Paris defend the movement? This question had lurked behind French revisionist endeavors ever since 1919; never had the question been squarely confronted. On the morning of 25 October, *Le Temps* attempted to do so. It turned over its headline editorial to an

[11] Note Cadrogan, "Separatist Movement in the Rhineland," 24 Oct. 1923: PRO FO 371, vol. 8685, no. 61.

[12] Note Nothomb pour M. Renkin, 27 Oct. 1923: AGR Pap. Jaspar, dos. 240, folder 1, piece 2.

impassioned appeal on behalf of "NOTRE POLITIQUE RHÉNANE." The Rhenish movement was legitimate and spontaneous, the editors argued; its very disorganization bore witness to the fact! But how can change in the Rhineland come about? Will those who favor autonomy (i.e., the Adenauer group) oppose those who seek independence? Will Berlin be free to crush the Rhineland's hopes by force? All depends on the attitude of the Allied powers. In France, two extreme opinions have been expressed. One urges us to use the Rhenish Republic to "correct" the Treaty of Versailles. Another urges us to think only of the treaty and to desert the Rhinelanders in their hour of need. "Why," asked *Le Temps*, "ought France and Belgium to concern themselves with events on the Rhine? Is it solely because they have signed the Treaty of Versailles? Is it solely because their policy must evolve as a function of the treaty . . . ?" To be sure, no one suggested that France and Belgium ought to overthrow treaties by fomenting revolution. But "France and Belgium are not only signatories of the treaty. They are also neighbors of the Rhineland, and the Rhenish country, under the domination of Prussia, has served as the staging area for invasion of France and Belgium." Thus there was a higher imperative than the sacredness of treaties. "France and Belgium, as immediate neighbors, have therefore the natural and inalienable right to take interest in changes affecting the Rhineland. What is more, they have the obligation not to remain indifferent to Rhenish demands. . . . To practice a policy of non-intervention would be to intervene in favor of Berlin against Rhenish liberties!"

The impassioned defense of French revisionism ended with a burst of fireworks designed to illuminate the policy of its chief opponent. The British government had been dominated until now by industrialists and merchants who had joined forces with German industry. They had opposed a Rhineland Republic and all reparations as well. But the creation of such a state, with its powerful industry—if not tied to Berlin—would actually serve British interests by promoting reconstruction under conditions of "fair competition."[13] Thus, the unofficial medium of the press pleaded the French case for treaty revision. The Treaty of Versailles assured neither European security nor economic prosperity. The Rhenish movement afforded the Allies an opportunity to correct the errors committed since the Armistice. But the French policy was too revolutionary: it implied the legitimacy of a "sphere of influence" within the borders of another Great Power. How else was the intrinsic imbalance of the European order to be redressed? It was a concept at

[13] "NOTRE POLITIQUE RHÉNANE," *Le Temps*, 25 Oct. 1923.

once too modern and too reactionary and it could only exacerbate the righteous anger the Rhenish episode produced in London.

Following the acceptance of the Committee of Experts by France on 25 October, the British government dropped its reserve. Curzon informed High Commissioner Lord Kilmarnock that only duly constitutional change was tolerable, hence the Rhineland Commission had no business taking any action or engaging in any negotiations with German citizens. On 30 October Curzon instructed his ambassadors in Paris and Brussels to make known in the strongest language Britain's opposition to the events taking place on the Left Bank: "His Majesty's Government feel it incumbent upon them, as signatories of the Treaty of Versailles, to call the serious attention of their Allies to the grave consequences which would follow the setting up of independent sovereign states carved out of territories within the existing frontiers of Germany."[14] French, not German, revisionism was now the antagonist. Thus it was now Britain, not France, that took refuge in the letter of the treaty. But even more serious than the British policy was the effect it would have in Brussels.

The French-supported separatists themselves provided the excuse Jaspar sought to rid himself of the embarrassment of insurrection in the Belgian zone. Matthes chose the evening of 1 November to carry out his planned "absorption" of Deckers' territory. Informed of Matthes' plan and unsure of Belgian support, Deckers fled. The Rathaus fell into the hands of the police. In the night of 1-2 November, 1,500 of Matthes' men debarked from Régie trains in the Aachen station. At dawn a cache of weapons was produced and they moved against the fourteenth-century Rathaus. The defenders held off repeated assaults by training fire hoses on their assailants until the separatists killed the water pressure by opening the hydrants in the vicinity. By noon, the Schupos surrendered, and two hours later a Belgian military detachment arrived. The separatist victors cheered. But Rolin-Jaequemyns was also in the city that afternoon, returning from Brussels where he and Jaspar had consulted. Finding Deckers gone and the town in the hands of French-supported separatists, he ordered the Belgian commander to disarm and expel Matthes' rowdies, and to clear the Belgian zone of Rhenish separatists.

Jaspar explained, in response to the shocked protests of France and

[14] Tel. #215 F.O. to Kilmarnock (Coblenz), 31 Oct. 1923; Tel. #361 F.O. to Crewe (Paris); Tel. #114 F.O. to Wingfield (Brussels), 30 Oct. 1923: PRO FO 371, vol. 8685, nos. 204-205, 26-27. The U. S. State Department also warned France that "pushing matters to a point of disintegration . . . will destroy hope of adequate reparations payments and prove in the long run a futile reliance for French security" (Tel. 397 Hughes to Paris, 25 Oct. 1923: HI Logan Papers, "Secret Letters," vol. 10, p. 372).

the Belgian Right, that his policy had not been incoherent or inconsistent. Belgium had declared her neutrality in the face of a genuine display of separatist sentiment on the part of residents of the Belgian zone (Deckers' putsch), but this new invasion had been the work of rabble drawn from the Ruhr (Matthes' men). It was the responsibility of the Belgian authorities to restore order and Rolin-Jaequemyns had done his duty.[15] What Jaspar failed to add was that Deckers was safe for Belgium, Matthes was not.

Poincaré was livid at this new and harmful display of Belgian independence. He ordered Ambassador Herbette to warn Jaspar of "the risk the Belgian government is running in its path of the last several weeks, pursued in a spirit of fierce independence vis-à-vis France."[16] The expulsion of the separatists from the Belgian zone left them isolated in the French zone, and left Poincaré alone in the defense of an insurrection he had not instigated, but for which he was primarily responsible. Four years of attempted subversion, sustained by an indefensible cultural arrogance as well as legitimate fears, ended by poisoning France's victory in the Ruhr, by doing serious harm to the diplomatic position that victory had established.

In the Rhineland itself, the loss of the Belgian zone was balanced by the recrudescence and expansion of Palatine separatism under Heinz-Orbis. On 5 November his partisans seized the government building of Kaiserslautern, where the French disarmed the police, and the movement spread to Kirchheimbolanden and Germersheim. On the same day, Matthes moved south, anxious to regain momentum after the defeat at Aachen. Palatine villages fell one by one to the Revolver Republic. Rural burgermeisters, some voluntarily, some under threat of expulsion, declared adherence to the autonomous government. But the spread of separatism to the limits of the French zone could not offset the diplomatic defeat represented by the British protest and the Belgian defection.

Poincaré responded to the British note on 2 November, denying French involvement in the separatist movement and questioning why the spontaneous creation of new states in Germany should require a general revision of the Treaty of Versailles. The following day Poincaré opened a desperate campaign to achieve a bilateral settlement with Belgium on the political future of the Rhineland. But Ambassador Herbette's repeated demarches in the following weeks bore no fruit.

[15] Discours Jaspar, 20 Nov. 1923: MAE Belgique, CLB 351, "Occupation de la Rhénanie, 1922-24," dos. 2.

[16] Tel. Herbette (Brussels) to MAE; Tel. Poincaré to Herbette, 2 Nov. 1923: MAE Rive Gauche, vol. 35, nos. 13-24, 27.

Jaspar told him that Belgium would remain neutral; in Paris, the Belgian ambassador told Peretti that Brussels was now solely interested in reparations.[17] In Coblenz, Rolin-Jaequemyns recognized the separatists as a de facto government only for the purpose of maintaining order. He would not register its decrees.[18]

Lord Curzon asserted again on 10 November that establishment of a Rhenish Republic meant the sacrifice of reparations by France. Poincaré knew this was true unless Belgium could be won back to separatism, or unless the Berlin government and Rhenish notables formed a new state legally. On 13 November he thought his pleas in Brussels were taking effect. Belgian Ambassador Gaiffier declared himself "ready to begin conversations on the subject of the regime in the Rhineland." Peretti eagerly accepted. Two days later, Jaspar wired from Brussels that Gaiffier had misunderstood his instructions—the Belgian government would negotiate *à trois*, with Britain, or not at all.[19]

French hopes for a diplomatic understanding on the Rhineland dissolved. There remained the possibility of direct negotiations with Rhenish notables. It was the identical tactic to that followed in the Ruhr: negotiations with local authorities for the creation of a de facto situation that the experts would then have to take into account. France still had the means, he told Tirard, "to make the Germans accept as complete a limitation as possible of German sovereignty in the new state."[20]

VERSCHLEPPUNGSPOLITIK: GERMAN RESPONSE TO SEPARATISM

The end of the passive resistance threw Germany into a state of internal siege. Reich authority ceased to exist in the occupied territories, commanded little obedience from the Leftist governments of Saxony and Thuringia, and now met open defiance from Bavaria. On 26 September Munich had declared a local emergency and von Kahr assumed "extraordinary powers to prevent one faction [the Nazis] from committing a stupid act." The Berlin government's power to direct the economic life of Germany was equally curtailed. On the black market, the German mark approached its final November low of 4.2 trillion to the

[17] Tel. Herbette to Poincaré, 4 Nov. 1923; Note Peretti, "Visite de Baron de Gaiffier à M. Peretti," 3 Nov. 1923: MAE Rive Gauche, vol. 35, nos. 129-130, 102-104.

[18] P.-V., H.C.I.T.R., 5 Nov. 1923: MAE Rive Gauche, vol. 217, séance 207, p. 5.

[19] Note Peretti, "Visite de Baron de Gaiffier," 13 Nov. 1923; Note Peretti, 15 Nov. 1923: MAE Rive Gauche, vol. 36, nos. 53, 105-106.

[20] Tel. Poincaré to Tirard, 8 Nov. 1923: MAE Rive Gauche, vol. 35, no. 227.

dollar. Stripped of capital resources, Berlin also faced the responsibility of financing a return to full productivity in the Ruhr.

The German Reich entered its most serious crisis since 1918. Stresemann was prepared for a showdown between Right and Left, but his resources were limited. In the last analysis, the fate of the republic depended on the loyalty of the army, and of its chief, General von Seeckt. Should Bavaria or Saxony defy Berlin openly, von Seeckt's reaction could save the republic or plunge it into civil war. Prudently, Stresemann elected to defer the showdown with the Right. On 13 October the Reichstag granted the government full powers to deal with the financial crisis. Two days later the government announced its intention to scrap the old currency and replace it with the *Rentenmark*, an ingenious currency valued in gold, but backed by mortgage bonds on Germany's national wealth. The date for the opening of the Rentenbank was a month hence—15 November. Stresemann then turned his attention to Saxony, only to receive the news on 21 October that an Allied-supported separatist movement had erupted on the Left Bank of the Rhine.

The German government responded as Cuno's did in January, with ineffectual protests in Brussels and Paris. But Stresemann understood that his real adversaries on the Rhine were the Rhenish notables themselves. Their first responsibility was to their home provinces. It was not through disloyalty or personal ambition that the leaders of the Rhenish Center and economic committees now approached Berlin with requests for a mandate to act freely vis-à-vis the occupation. Rather it was the result of near starvation in the Rhineland and of the impotence of the Reich government to improve the lives of millions of its citizens. Poincaré refused to talk to Berlin. The Rhenish leaders must be allowed to talk with the French, if only to prevent a hunger revolution or French domination.

Konrad Adenauer occupied the obvious position of leadership in the Rhineland. He was Mayor of Cologne, the province's leading city. He was president of the provincial committee, the Landtag's executive organ. He was chairman of the Landbank administrative council, of the Rhenish council of cities, and of the Prussian state council. He led a delegation of Rhenish leaders to the city of Hagen on 25 October to confront Stresemann. The meeting proved to be an exhausting duel between sincere and desperate men forced to debate from different points of view in a common search for the lesser evil. Adenauer denied having any desire to separate the Rhineland from Germany or Prussia, but the ties between the Rhineland and Berlin had been removed one by one until the Reich no longer possessed a single means of influencing events in the occupied territories. Stresemann's news that the relief payments would also have to be terminated to protect the *Rentenmark* only added strength to Adenauer's argument. The Rhenish leaders must be permitted to find a *modus vivendi*, just as were the Ruhr industrialists with the MICUM.

Stresemann replied to Adenauer with evidence drawn from foreign capitals. German Chargé von Hoesch reported from Paris that the putsch had taken the French government by surprise and that separation was not its first priority. Ambassador Sthamer in London promised that Britain would not tolerate an illegal Rhenish state. These were reasons to resist the French, not negotiate. Karl Jarres, eminent Mayor of Duisburg, even advocated a temporary "abandonment" of the Rhineland while German finances recovered. This *Versackungspolitik* could earn Germany a wholesale revision of the treaty.[21]

Stresemann chose a middle course. He would permit a delaying action in the Rhineland while the international situation clarified itself and pressure could be brought to bear on France. There was no sense in rushing events to a conclusion while the Reich stood in its weakest posture. He would grant Adenauer a limited negotiating autonomy in order to sound out Tirard on French demands, and he promised temporary continuation of relief payments to the distressed Rhineland. It was a *Verschleppungspolitik*, a policy of calculated delay and deception. Given Germany's plight in the last week of October 1923, Stresemann could not have chosen better. On 29 October he opened his counterattack on the enemies of Reich authority. A Reichswehr division marched into Saxony and the Reich procured the resignations of the Communists from the Saxon government. In the following days, both Britain and Belgium announced their immutable opposition to the French brand of separatism. Germany began to recover.

Following the Hagen conference, Adenauer returned to Cologne to assume direction of a Committee of Fifteen, supposedly representative of the Rhineland as a whole, but in fact dominated by Cologne. On 26 October delegates from the Fifteen and the Rhenish Economic Committee, led by Adenauer, banker Louis Hagen, and union leader Heinrich Mayer, petitioned Tirard for an audience. The French high commissioner refused to see them. Aware that Tirard mistrusted him, Adenauer resorted to middlemen. But Tirard's political aide Colonel d'Arbonneau told the emissaries that the Committee of Fifteen was an inadmissible body, owing to the preponderance of Cologne, and that

[21] Erdmann, *Adenauer*, pp. 87ff.

Adenauer himself was *désagréable*. He said the French goal on the Rhine was the shaping of an independent neutral state like Switzerland. Peretti at the Quai d'Orsay approved, characterizing total separation from the Reich as the ideal solution.[22] On 28 October, Adenauer tried again with Cardinal Schulte, Archbishop of Cologne. Tirard received him personally, but Schulte came away with the impression that the French wished to back the separatists and eschew negotiation.[23]

Then came 30 October, and the Paris conference between Poincaré and Tirard. Only men such as Adenauer, it was decided, could consummate Rhenish autonomism. Tirard returned to Coblenz with instructions that "we ought to take it upon ourselves to make the interested parties adopt the conditions that constitute our guarantees." Tirard must receive Adenauer at once.[24] The French were now ready, but the Germans were not. Tirard had to wait until mid-November for his first session with Adenauer.

The issue of Germany's future wavered like sea water caught between the tide and opposing winds. The events of the past week gave Stresemann further reason to doubt the wisdom of permitting negotiations in the Rhineland. Not only the British and Belgian actions, but the incompetence of the separatist movement and French acceptance of the Committee of Experts all pointed to ultimate defeat for French Rhineland ambitions. A concerted diplomatic attack might suffice to deliver the Rhineland. On 5 November Stresemann sharply protested the occupation's tolerance and even support of treasonous activities. He formally opposed any change in the Rhineland's political status.

Suddenly, on 2 November, the question of Germany's very survival eclipsed the Rhenish struggle. The Socialists in the German cabinet resigned, leaving the government without a majority or emergency powers. With his hands thus tied, Stresemann watched the Bavarian crisis erupt before him. On 8 November Adolf Hitler led his

[22] Tel. Tirard to MAE, 27 Oct. 1923; Note Peretti pour Laroche, 28 Oct. 1923: MAE Rive Gauche, vol. 34, nos. 127, 59.

[23] Tel. Tirard to MAE, 28 Oct. 1923: MAE Rive Gauche, vol. 34, nos. 144-145; Erdmann, *Adenauer*, pp. 112-116.

[24] Upon Tirard's return to Coblenz, Poincaré wired details on what the "conditions" ought to include. Using the Treaty of Westphalia as a model, he envisioned a Rhenish state represented solely in the Reichsrat—legislative power would reside in the Rhenish Landtag. The state would enjoy its own foreign representation and receive foreign emissaries. It would possess a separate customs regime, railroad administration, educational system, and civil bureaucracy. The Rhineland would have its own budget based on internal resources and would pay no federal taxes. Finally, the Rhenish Republic would be exempt from military duty and Rhenish citizens would be forbidden to serve in Reich forces. Des. Poincaré to Tirard, URGENT, SÉCRET, 6 Nov. 1923: MAE Rive Gauche, vol. 35, nos. 188-189.

brownshirts into the Bürgerbräukeller in Munich, kidnapped von Kahr, and declared a new national German government. President Ebert transferred the Reichswehr minister's authority to von Seeckt himself. But the army chief had declared that Reichswehr would never fire on Reichswehr. Would he oppose a march on Berlin by Bavarian army units? The next day von Kahr's government disowned Hitler, and a national showdown was avoided. Hitler and Ludendorff led the Nazis in a march on the Feldherrnhalle, where they were dispersed by the fire of loyal police. The constitutional struggle between Munich and Berlin was not settled, but the immediate threat to the republic abated.

Stresemann and the cabinet turned their attention back to the occupied territories. Two days before the Rentenbank opened, on 13 November, the government appointed Hjalmar Schacht to the post of national currency commissioner. Schacht could not make the mortgage currency succeed if subsidies were continued to unproductive Rhineland-Westphalia. But the cabinet was split. Karl Jarres, now minister of the interior, urged immediate suspension of all payments. Stresemann wanted to continue them for a brief period, to buy time for his diplomatic offensive. The minister of labor protested any abandonment of Rhenish relief; it would "throw the Rhineland into the arms of France."[25]

Stresemann's opinion prevailed. He informed the Committee of Fifteen that the *Rentenmark* could not be used to support Rhenish unemployed. Reich relief would cease on 27 November. In that case, Adenauer replied, the Rhine province must be granted administrative and economic freedom. But the Reichsrat representatives of the German states rebelled at this prospect. "We must, to a certain extent, leave the occupied territories to their fate," said Prussian Minister-President Otto Braun. "It is impossible to grant such broad powers to a local commission." The Reich dared not abandon the Rhineland to save the *Rentenmark*! shouted Adenauer in reply. The Rhineland was surely worth three new currencies. The Committee of Fifteen intended no separation, he continued, but it must have the freedom to deal with the French, to avert starvation. Stresemann compromised again by renewing the committee's mandate to negotiate, but upholding the decision to halt relief payments in two weeks.[26] Although Jarres's extreme solution was rejected, the Rhenish press still accused Berlin of pursuing *Versackungspolitik*. The Reich was jettisoning its richest province in order to save the rest.

[25] *Auszug aus den Protokollen über die Sitzung des Reichkabinetten*, 12 Nov. 1923: AA Referat D—Rheinland, L1766, 5664, no. 515686.

[26] Ibid., nos. 515687-89.

Tirard received Adenauer on 14 November. What did the Rhenish patriot hope to accomplish? If Adenauer harbored private notions about a grand West German state taking its place beside Prussia and Bavaria in Reich councils, never did he contemplate separation from Germany. When the threat of foreign annexation or internal revolution arose in 1919, and again in 1923, Adenauer left open the possibility of Rhenish autonomy to pacify France, but he always considered political change through constitutional processes only. He spoke eloquently of his views on autonomy in an interview with the socialist *Le Peuple* on 31 October. A buffer state was impossible, he believed, and would guarantee neither French security nor European peace. Only a community of interest between France, Belgium, and Germany could assure peace between those nations. "A Rhenish Republic," he said, "*presupposes* a unified France-Belgium-Germany." Political coordination must follow economic integration. Poincaré's view was exactly the opposite. Given the imbalance of power on the continent, Germany must first be made incapable of mischief through economic restraints and, if possible, mitigation of her demographic superiority through territorial change and/or military controls. Only then could France seek closer ties with Germany without fear.

In the 14 November meeting Adenauer told Tirard that the rumors making him a man of the British were inexact. He spoke of a far-reaching economic entente between French and German industry and a formula for Rhenish autonomy fulfilling most of Poincaré's conditions. Tirard suppressed his enthusiasm and told Adenauer that he would study the problem. "It was an excellent time," he concluded, "for the Rhenish people to take their destiny in their own hands."[27]

The committee planned its next move for 23 November. The delegation sent to Tirard would have the mission of prompting Tirard to reveal France's true goals, and of suggesting that a Rhenish state was not really in the interest of any party. They would propose the Moldenhauer plan, calling for an indigenous administrative directory to govern the Rhineland for five years. The Rhineland would not constitute an autonomous state.[28] Tirard was disappointed upon hearing of these plans. He wired Poincaré to expect little from the next meeting since the committee's proposal would probably be "notoriously insufficient."[29]

Tirard's rejection of the Moldenhauer plan on 23 November coincided with the final signature of the MICUM accords by the Ruhr in-

[27] Tel. Tirard to MAE, 15 Nov. 1923: MAE Rive Gauche, vol. 36, nos. 95-98.

[28] Erdmann, *Adenauer*, pp. 136-146.

[29] Tel. Tirard to Poincaré, 24 Nov. 1923: MAE Rive Gauche, vol. 36, nos. 318-319.

dustrialists and the fall of Stresemann's government. The result was that the Committee of Fifteen broke up in disagreement, to be replaced by a Committee of Sixty elected by Rhenish-Westphalian Reichstag deputies. This "mini-parliament" never displayed any initiative and Adenauer remained the Rhineland's leading spokesman. But for the moment, his position was ambiguous.

Poincaré was becoming impatient, and pressed Tirard to pin down the Rhinelanders. On 29 November, Tirard handed Adenauer a document entitled "Principles for the Foundation of a Rhenish State," which outlined the French conception of a suitable autonomy. Adenauer rejected the principles and added that any political settlement in the Rhineland would have to be accompanied by a general reparations and economic agreement. This would require abandonment of her allies by France, and doubtless substantial economic concessions as well.[30] It was practiced *Verschleppungspolitik*. Poincaré's impatience now turned to anger. What had become of the grand autonomous state Tirard attributed to Adenauer two weeks before? Tirard replied that Adenauer was speaking *à titre privé* at that time. His ideas were unofficial. Poincaré pointed out that the progressive collapse of the Matthes/Dorten government made it "indispensable that a conclusion be reached in the shortest possible time in the interviews with Rhenish representatives."[31]

The Reichstag had reconvened on 21 November to decide the fate of Stresemann's government. The end of passive resistance had alienated the Right; agitation for an end of the eight-hour day and the Saxon purge offended the Left. The Social Democrats found a face-saving solution. They would vote no-confidence against Stresemann, then join in supporting a new government of similar composition, with Stresemann retained as foreign minister. Thus, Stresemann resigned as chancellor after only a hundred days, martyred for the unpopular decisions he had taken for preservation of the republic and the Reich. It took eight days for the Reichstag to accept a new cabinet, headed by Wilhelm Marx. The choice was ideal from the point of view of the Rhenish crisis. Marx was a respected jurist, a moderate Centrist, and a native Rhinelander. No man was better suited to induce additional sacrifice from the Rhineland without suspicion that he was abandoning the province. The Reichstag voted him an enabling act valid until 15 February 1924.

The standpoint of the new government became readily apparent to all but the French. On 4 December Marx told the Reichstag that "in

[30] Erdmann, *Adenauer*, pp. 150-151.

[31] Tel. Poincaré to Tirard, 3 Dec. 1923: MAE Rive Gauche, vol. 37, nos. 140-141.

the face of attempts at separation, the Reich government, in accord with the state governments, remains absolutely attached to its ties with the Rhineland and Ruhr." The cabinet instructed Foreign Minister Stresemann to intensify diplomatic efforts against France, and forbade all further negotiations between Rhenish and French representatives.[32] This resolution satisfied Stresemann, now opposed to further dealings with Tirard, though Marx was not quite ready to abandon the policy of dalliance. He authorized Adenauer confidentially to continue stringing the French along. But there was no possibility of Berlin ever accepting Rhenish political change. The decision came at a time when Poincaré was at the height of optimism. He had every reason to believe that the economic foundation of Rhenish autonomy, a Franco-Rhenish bank of issue, was finally to be a reality.

DEFEAT OF THE RHENISH NOTENBANK

French hopes for a successful conclusion to the negotiations for Rhenish autonomy based themselves largely on negative pressures: economic hardship and the separatist threat. One positive development toward autonomy that the French government could participate in was the creation of the Rhenish gold note bank. Ostensibly a measure to alleviate the financial disorder accompanying the collapse of the mark, the monetary separation of the Rhineland from the Reich would clearly be a political event of the greatest importance. Depriving Berlin of the right to coin money for the Rhineland would make the constitution of an autonomous Rhenish fiscal system and government unavoidable. In 1922 German industrialists had demanded political concessions from France in return for economic cooperation. Now it was the French government that hoped to extract political concessions from the occupied territory in return for the capital needed to restore the Rhenish economy and social stability.

The first attempts to create a new Rhenish currency in the months following the occupation of the Ruhr collapsed because of the ineluctable opposition of Finance Minister de Lasteyrie. But Poincaré kept the issue before de Lasteyrie, emphasizing the political stakes involved.[33] By June 1923 the currency shortage in the occupied territory resulting from the runaway inflation and from French efforts to block importation of marks from nonoccupied territory stimulated a new round of discussion on possible monetary solutions. "We consider only our own treasury and the foreign exchange repercussions of suggested meas-

[32] *Kabinettprotokol*, 5 Dec. 1923: AA BG L1476, 5343, no. 430973-78.

[33] Let. Poincaré to de Lasteyrie, 23 Apr. 1923: AN HCF, vol. 6383, dos. 32b.

ures," complained Seydoux. "Instead we must pursue a grander financial policy."[34] Poincaré agreed wholeheartedly, and on 16 June he ordered de Lasteyrie to prepare a project in accord with occupation officials.[35]

Tirard and Degoutte each submitted projects based on the issue of gold bonds, which would neither threaten the course of the franc nor imply replacement of the German mark. But de Lasteyrie held to his policy of the spring: "A Rhenish solution to the monetary problem distinct from a general German reform supposes a solution to the *political* problem of the Rhineland and the existence of a Rhenish budget. . . ."[36] Pending a permanent solution to the currency crisis, Tirard and Rolin-Jaequemyns adopted a policy of *Notgeld* in the late summer. Rhenish municipalities and large employers would be permitted to issue local emergency money valued in paper marks. General Degoutte opposed any amelioration of Rhenish economic distress until the capitulation of the German government, but Poincaré sided with Tirard. The hardships of the occupied territories, he explained, must be attributable only to the German resistance, not to French policy.[37] Accordingly, scores of banks and businesses on the Rhine issued their own currency, thereby preventing regression to a barter economy and producing souvenirs for future generations in the form of colorful "Krupp money" or "Triermarks" in denominations of a hundred million, or one billion.

Tirard did not give up on a Rhenish bank. He set out to design a scheme that de Lasteyrie could not refuse. In September he met with a member of the Barmer Bankverein of Mainz who expressed interest in funding a Rhenish currency, and mentioned possible support from the great Darmstädter and Dresdner banks. De Lasteyrie took notice. But no progress could be made on the Belgian front. Consistent with his policy that no Allied measure taken in consequence of the passive resistance was to be permanent, Premier Theunis refused to consider a Rhenish bank. Instead, he emphasized the role of *Notgeld* and agreed to the issue of *bons de la Régie*, valued in francs and redeemable in the services of the railroads. Theunis insisted also that the Régie money

[34] Note Dayras, "Seydoux dit . . . ," 16 June 1923: MAE Pap. Millerand, Réparations XIII, no. 103.

[35] Marginal Note, "Instructions de M. Poincaré," note pour le PdC, "Pays rhénans: question de la monnaie," 16 June 1923: MAE Pap. Millerand, Réparations XIII, nos. 104-105.

[36] Let. #0766ATRP/FC/3 Tirard to Poincaré, 5 July 1923; Note Giscard #1341OFC/3 pour M. Tirard, 16 July 1923; Let. Ministère des Finances, section de l'Allemagne, to Poincaré, 22 Aug. 1923: AN HCF, vol. 6383, dos. 32b.

[37] Let. #32329/F Poincaré to Tirard, "Politique monétaire en territoire occupé—émission de Notgeld," 13 Aug. 1923: AN HCF, vol. 6383, dos. 32b.

have no political significance. This caution was unnecessary—the bonds quickly followed the mark toward worthlessness. But it should have warned the Quai d'Orsay of Belgium's eventual attitude toward a currency scheme.[38]

The outbreak of violent separatism on 21 October and the imminent cessation of Reich relief breathed new urgency into the currency question. Adenauer's close collaborator, Louis Hagen, now contacted Tirard and expressed his willingness to take the lead toward a gold-based Rhenish currency. Hagen was a Rhenish patriot, not averse to autonomy, and immediately interested in restoration of Rhenish prosperity. He was president of the Cologne Chamber of Commerce and one of the most influential businessmen in the Rhineland. His consortium of Cologne banks was so self-sufficient that Tirard feared lest Hagen embark on a currency solution by himself, without Allied participation. A French financial expert hurried to Cologne.[39]

Poincaré leaped at this unlooked-for opportunity and, given Hagen's security, French banks also took an interest. The Société Générale Alsacienne was a natural candidate, and the Banque Nationale de Credit and Lazard Frères also spoke up. Having received Berlin's mandate to negotiate at the Hagen conference, Louis Hagen visited Coblenz on 3 November. He would not do business with the rabble separatists, he told Tirard, and the latter replied that the separatists were of no consequence. "I and my government are agreed in beginning negotiations with you and a small circle of Rhinelanders."[40]

Poincaré ordered Tirard to produce a finished project as soon as possible. The new *Rentenmark* was due for issue on 15 November. The Rhineland Commission could veto the law creating the Rentenbank or refuse the importation of the currency into occupied territory, but only with Belgian cooperation. Should the *Rentenmark* prove a success, moreover, extended delay in introducing a legal and stable currency would force world opinion against France. The race was on. Tirard instructed his representative in Cologne to press Hagen to complete a plan. On 9 November Hagen declared himself ready to proceed. Three days later the German ambassador in Brussels excitedly wired Berlin that Belgium would support introduction of the *Rentenmark* into the Rhineland.[41] In Paris, Poincaré rejoiced that

[38] Tel. Poincaré to Jaunez, 14 Oct. 1923; Tel. Poincaré to Herbette, 16 Oct. 1923; Tel. Tirard to MAE, 19 Oct. 1923: MAE Ruhr, vol. 30, nos. 188-189; vol. 31, nos. 11-12, 74-80.

[39] Tel. Coblenz (de la part de M. Schweisguth) to MAE (pour de Lasteyrie), 29 Oct. 1923: MAE Rive Gauche, vol. 107, no. 183.

[40] Erdmann, *Adenauer*, pp. 118-119.

[41] Note #281ZW/3 Délégué Cologne to Tirard, 9 Nov. 1923: AN HCF, vol. 6383, dos. 32b; Tel. Boediger (Brussels) to A.A., 12 Nov. 1923: AA BR 3058, 1470, no. 603819.

some private Belgian banks had been found to contribute capital to a Rhenish bank. On 14 November, Schweisguth prepared the French proposal: initial capital of 25 million gold marks, reduction of the Rhenish share to less than 50 percent, with the French share 30 percent. On 17 November, de Lasteyrie gathered agents of the French banks ready to participate. Poincaré pressed for an immediate conclusion.[42]

On 18 November the Rentenbank law came up for discussion in Coblenz. Tirard struggled to buy time for the creation of the Rhenish bank, pleading before his colleagues that the *Rentenmark*, not supported by gold, would only increase the monetary chaos on the Left Bank. He prevailed upon Rolin-Jaequemyns to postpone a decision on the Rentenbank, but could not prevent Allied approval for circulation of the *Rentenmark* in occupied territory. In Paris, Seydoux was worried. He believed the *Rentenmark* to be stillborn and that a Rhenish bank could not come in time to promote economic recovery before spring. With the cessation of Reich relief payments, France could be left with the responsibility for supporting a stricken Rhine and Ruhr all winter.[43]

Hagen and Adenauer understood the situation as well as Seydoux. On 25 November they presented their case before Hjalmar Schacht and the officers of the Reichsbank. For three hours the Rhinelanders pleaded for the recognition by the Reichsbank of Rhenish *Notgeld* as a means of seeing the Rhineland through the crisis without having to resort to French aid. "A storm of supplications, appeals, and threats" was Schacht's description of the meeting, but he stood firm in defense of the *Rentenmark*.[44] Hagen resigned himself to the alternative—creation of the Rhenish currency.

At this high point of French hopes, on 26 November 1923, Poincaré boasted before the Senate foreign affairs commission that the bank negotiations were "très avancés." He predicted an agreement within three days, perhaps a week, with the capital furnished largely by the Rhinelanders themselves. The bank of issue, he added, would lead to rapid success in the political talks as well.[45] Suddenly problems arose, manifestations of the contradictions within the entire French Rhineland policy. By depending on Rhenish and Belgian participation and

[42] Tel. Poincaré to Herbette, 17 Nov. 1923: MAE Rive Gauche, vol. 108, nos. 3-4.

[43] Note Vignon, "Conversation avec Seydoux," 23 Nov. 1923: MAE Pap. Millerand, Réparations XVIII, nos. 255-256.

[44] Hjalmar Schacht, *Confessions of the Old Wizard*, trans. Diana Pyke (Boston, 1956), pp. 170-171.

[45] P.-V., Commission des Affaires Étrangères, 26 Nov. 1923: Archives du Sénat, Auditions, 1923.

German and British acquiescence in the bank scheme, Poincaré was seeking separatism by grace of his very enemies and rivals. French capital alone was far from sufficient, and now that the bank scheme was near completion the opposition rallied to prevent it.

Britain delivered the first blow. On 30 November the French invited City banks to participate in the Rhenish venture, which would oblige the Foreign Office to tolerate the scheme. But the Foreign Office's negative opinion toward a Rhenish bank only buttressed the position taken by the president of the Bank of England, Montagu Norman. He asked the government not to encourage a Rhenish bank nor to recommend British participation. Monetary separation of the Rhineland, he wrote, was the prelude to economic and political separation.[46]

The second blow came from Belgium. Fearing a ploy by the Germans to entice French capital to aid in German recovery, French Finance Minister de Lasteyrie insisted that the Allies receive a majority interest in the Rhenish bank. But Schweisguth and Tirard discovered during the final round of negotiations that the Belgian government absolutely refused to accept a plan granting the Allies a majority, implying, as it did, a permanent French control in the Rhineland.[47] On 4 December, Rolin-Jaequemyns announced his firm instructions to join with Britain in refusing registration by the Rhineland Commission of the Rhenish bank unless it provided for a Rhenish majority interest and had the blessing of the Berlin government.[48]

The final blow to the Rhenish currency came from Berlin. The new Marx cabinet protocol of 5 December, which denounced Rhenish autonomism, did not ignore the bank issue. "The Reich and Prussian governments," it stated, "have considerable reservations about the planned Rhenish bank. Under no circumstances must there be a currency separation between occupied and non-occupied territories."[49] Louis Hagen was still prepared to go ahead, despite Berlin's attitude, but there was no available procedure for the bank's creation. Berlin refused to authorize it; the Belgians and British refused to permit the Rhineland Commission to register a bank without that authorization.

[46] Let. Montagu Norman to Niemeyer (Treasury), 14 Nov. 1923: PRO FO 371, vol. 8689, no. 70.

[47] Tel. Tirard to MAE, 25 Nov. 1923: MAE Rive Gauche, vol. 108, nos. 32-34; Conversation Peretti/Seydoux, "Banque d'Émission en Rhénanie," 27 Nov. 1923: MAE Pap. Millerand, Réparations XVIII, nos. 305-306; Let. #45356/s Seydoux to Tirard, "Banque d'Émission dans les territoires occupés," 28 Nov. 1923: AN HCF, vol. 6383, dos. 32b.

[48] Des. #310xiv, Ordre #822 Jaspar to Rolin-Jaequemyns, 15 Nov. 1923: MAE Belgique, HCITR dos. 100, "Banque d'Émission"; Note Seydoux, "Banque d'Émission dans les territoires occupés," 4 Dec. 1923: MAE Rive Gauche, vol. 108, nos. 53-56.

[49] *Kabinettprotokol*, 5 Dec. 1923: AA BG L1476, 5343, no. 430973-78.

The best hope for forcing a subsequent political alteration in the Rhineland gradually dissolved. Negotiations might continue, but the common front against France precluded consummation, and the imminent collapse of the French franc delivered the *coup de grâce.* Meanwhile, the negative pressure on the German notables, the separatist movement of Matthes and Dorten, was dissipating itself in dissension and incompetence.

DISSOLUTION OF RHENISH SEPARATISM

The *Vereinigte Rheinische Bewegung* had been a formidable threat in French hands while it remained potential. The unprepared insurrection following 21 October only demonstrated the weakness of separatist sentiment on the Left Bank, while the separatists' criminal behavior increased the hatred much of the population felt for the French. Separatism had degenerated into open extortion. But the terror and chaos, hence the pressure on Adenauer and Berlin, could last only as long as the separatists could prolong their regime. As the Reich itself showed signs of survival, the Rhenish movement steadily collapsed.

By the first week in November, Rhenish tricolors flew above public buildings in all the major towns of the French zone. But these displays and occasional requisitions were the only evidence most citizens had that the provisional government existed. In a few towns local officials agreed to cooperate with the separatist cadre on a de facto basis, but for the most part the separatists enjoyed no more public cognizance than an unmentionable disease. The French deplored separatist violence, but did nothing directly to prevent it. Tirard requested only that Matthes exercise discipline upon his followers.

Armed clashes were inevitable. The greatest "patriotic battle" took place on 16-17 November. A large separatist band from Bonn left the city, depleted of rations, on a foraging expedition into the countryside. Some German peasants ambushed the column of trucks at a narrow gorge in the Siebengebirge region near Bad Honnef. According to German reports, the peasants were armed only with rocks, staffs and pitchforks, yet blocked the road and massacred over two hundred separatist brigands. It brought a frantic wire from Poincaré, demanding to know what damage had been done to the movement. Tirard's investigation revealed that the peasants in fact had firearms and that separatist losses were fourteen killed and seven wounded. The battle had little significance, Tirard concluded, beyond demonstrating the unpopularity of the separatist regime.[50]

[50] The fact of the separatists' criminality is hard to escape, although French journals tended to attribute the outrages to "certain elements," while attesting that the majority

The French Army of the Rhine attempted to keep a low profile during the separatist days, but local commanders and even general officers were confused by their instructions. The army was to remain neutral except to preserve order. But which side was to be dispersed in case of "disorder"? Should police be treated differently than rioters? At one point General Mordacq told Tirard bluntly that the situation was far from precise and that he had always been a man of precise situations. If the government wished to separate the Rhineland, why did it not order the army to execute that policy?[51] This failure, not only by the army but by a good portion of the French press and parliament, to understand the delicacy of the Rhenish question was a source of frustration for Poincaré. A military protectorate was out of the question, yet the premier was not entirely free to dump the separatist movement in the Rhineland at any time after the first rally of 29 July without bringing upon himself the fury of the French Right.

Even with military protection, the fiction of a separatist government was impossible to preserve. The temperamental and jealous chiefs proved irreconcilable. Within a week after the putsch, Dorten and Matthes exchanged accusations and divided authority geographically to avoid one another, Matthes presiding in Coblenz, Dorten in Wiesbaden, then Bad Ems. The taking of Mainz, across the river from Wiesbaden, exemplified the random advance of the movement and enmity between leaders. Dorten told General Mordacq on 4 November that he intended to incorporate Mainz into his area of influence with fifteen hundred men. The same afternoon, two agents from Coblenz claimed authorization to lead two thousand men into Mainz for Matthes' government. Mordacq later learned that the "Matthes men" were independent adventurers in search of a fief, and that Dorten had no troops at all.[52]

Dorten and Matthes came to a final break on 7 November. Deprived of all authority, Dorten returned to Bad Ems, where he idled away the following weeks with a scheme for a Rhenish bank involving former French Finance Minister François-Marsal. When Poincaré and Tirard pressed him to reveal the banks he had enlisted, he could name none. For the last time Dorten resorted to his stock excuse, betrayal. "I remain on the field of battle," he wrote General Mangin, "but they are

---

were Rhenish patriots. But Tirard's own investigation of the separatists holding the Rathaus in Wiesbaden, for instance, revealed a former bookie, a gigolo "on leave" from his mistress, a thief convicted on twenty counts, another on thirteen counts, an ex-policeman fired for debts, an abortionist, and over twenty others with prison records. HCITR, Bureau d'Information, 18 Nov. 1923: MAE Rive Gauche, vol. 36, nos. 186-197.

[51] Jean Jules Henri Mordacq, *La mentalité allemande, cinq ans de commandement sur le Rhin* (Paris, 1926), pp. 198-199.

[52] Ibid., pp. 201-203.

double-crossing me. Secret powers support Matthes. We will lose everything if I cannot take control."[53]

By mid-November the first permanent separatist losses occurred. Smaller villages expelled their garrisons or the ruffians tired of occupying buildings and disappeared in search of plunder. On 19 November the crippled Joseph Smeets left for Lorraine to convalesce. A week later the true chiefs began to defect. Foreign Minister von Metzen of the provisional government announced his resignation in disgust with the movement's impotence. On 29 November a band of Matthes' own *Rheinlandschutz* burst into his office with carbines and ordered the dissolution of his cabinet. Matthes blamed it on Dorten and German agents. The next day he quit Coblenz for Düsseldorf to begin again with a new organization, and returned to obscurity.

Dorten seized the opportunity of Matthes's fall to declare himself president of the Rhenish Republic. But Tirard told him on 4 December that the game was up. Soon Adenauer's group would assume control of the Left Bank, Tirard said, and Dorten ought to cease all activity. But Dorten and his coterie indulged in one last caper. In the small hours of 10 December three bandits intercepted a German vehicle running paper money across the frontier. They wounded the driver and made off with 240 trillion marks. It took the *Sûreté* three days to solve the crime and trace it to Paul Hocquel and Dorten's men. Tirard had Hocquel arrested, and even now the Parisian press demanded Tirard's recall for this "betrayal."

By the first week of December the separatist movement was played out. In Paris, the French government came under fire for having permitted the defeat. Poincaré promised rapid results from the Adenauer negotiations, while delicately dodging responsibility for the separatist fiasco. The movement had been spontaneous, he told the Senate commission in secret session, hence chaos was unavoidable. The lawless gangs had only been strengthened by their ability to dupe certain Parisian circles into thinking them consequential. It was "evident" that the French government could not embrace a German political movement openly, said Poincaré, but the result of neutrality "naturally" was that extremists took advantage of the situation. Still, he sought to appease the senators. Rhenish autonomy was inevitable, he said. Even Britain and Belgium were coming to view as impossible a return of Reich influence to the Left Bank. "Here is how I see the future. We remain in the Rhineland as long as the treaty is not executed. At that time, what will prevent us from making the Rhineland autonomous

[53] Pers. Let. Dorten to Mangin, 2 and 10 Nov. 1923: AN Pap. Mangin, vol. 22, dos. 3.

and placing it under the League of Nations?" The Anglo-American defection from the 1919 security settlement entitled France to another guarantee. "Consequently," the president of the commission replied, "our security vis-à-vis Germany consists of the Rhine." Poincaré answered ambiguously, "The guarantee is to be where we are."[54]

In the Rhineland General Degoutte renewed his attacks on separatism. The French government was wasting its efforts on "tainted individuals who quarrel among themselves and whose bands multiply their acts of brigandage." Even Tirard wearied of the feckless putschists. There was nothing left of the movement but its flags. He would press his contacts "with the sane, serious, honest elements of the population."[55] Then, on 5 December 1923 France's greatest Rhenish propagandist, Maurice Barrès, died in bed, entrusting Rhenish liberties to Poincaré and Millerand. His passing marked the spiritual death of the French Rhineland policy.

Three weeks later Dr. Dorten asked Tirard for permission to quit, and requested 450,000 francs to settle his affairs. Even at this juncture Poincaré had his eye on the effect a final collapse would have on the Adenauer talks. He approved continuation of Dorten's monthly subsidy of 100,000 francs, and ordered Tirard to keep a separatist government in existence, whomever it might contain. But Dorten and Tirard were well rid of each other. On 28 December 1923 Dorten made a farewell speech in the Kurhaus at Bad Ems. Fifty persons responded. On 1 January 1924 Dorten retired from the Rhineland to his villa in Nice. Rhenish separatism departed with him.

ASSASSINATION OF PALATINE SEPARATISM

The Palatine separatist movement differed from its counterpart in the Prussian Rhineland in two significant ways. Rhenish separation from moderate socialist-governed Prussia would have been a treasonous blow to the factions that struggled to preserve German democracy. The Palatine movement sought deliverance from reactionary Bavaria, the center of German monarchism and particularism. Second, the Rhenish movement depended entirely on the French and suffered from incompetent leaders and disreputable membership. The Palatine movement had a measure of legitimate support in the countryside. Al-

[54] P.-V., Commission des Affaires Étrangères, 26 Nov. 1923: Archives du Sénat, Auditions, 1923.

[55] Note Degoutte, 20 Nov. 1923, cited by Degoutte, *L'Occupation de la Ruhr*, annex, pp. 68-85; Let. Tirard to Poincaré, "Situation du mouvement séparatiste," 14 Dec. 1923: MAE Rive Gauche, vol. 37, nos. 327-335.

though French aid was just as important, it was a far more likely enterprise than the Rhenish charade, and Poincaré steeled himself to fight the Palatine battle to the bitter end.

In November 1923 Heinz-Orbis's peasants assured a measure of separatist control in the countryside while Matthes' invasion seized the cities. But the key to the preservation of the regime was money, to meet a government payroll and to take over unemployment relief. General de Metz, the French delegate, requested 300,000 francs per week in aid, a subsidy Poincaré was politically and financially incapable of granting.[56] For the time being, the regime persisted through ad hoc contributions from the coffers and supply dumps of the occupation. By December, the last rural *Kreisen*, Frankenthal, Pirmasens, and rural Zweibrücken had fallen to autonomist forces. Tirard announced that the former Bavarian regime had collapsed utterly. It was not an exaggeration, as most of the Bavarian officials had been expelled during the passive resistance. But that administration had not dissolved; it regrouped across the river in Heidelberg, former Palatine capital with a history of depredation at the hands of Bavarians and the French. There the Bavarians prepared their counterstroke under the direction of Ritter von Eberlein, chief of the *Obersicherheitsbüro* for the Palatinate. French intelligence connected Eberlein with the paramilitary Rightist organizations *Treuhand* and *Oberland*, and with "a certain Captain Göring of the *Sturmabteilung*."

The French treasury could not subsidize the Speyer government, and Heinz-Orbis himself desired to organize a normal fiscal regime. But his decrees for raising revenue, like any other German law, would not be valid unless registered by the Rhineland Commission. On 24 December Heinz submitted decrees calling for a tax on capital to found a stable currency, creation of an unemployment fund, and repression of the currency black market. The struggle thus moved to Coblenz, where British pressure could be brought to bear. Tirard defended his point of view skillfully. Registration of the decrees would not imply recognition of the government, he said. Besides, over 600 of 650 municipal and rural burgermeisters had expressed their allegiance to the autonomists. In the interests of public order alone, the Rhineland Commission should permit the government to function. Miles Lampson and Sir Eyre Crowe judged this latest French gambit outlandish and preposterous, but Tirard did convince Rolin-Jaequemyns. Insisting that this action did not amount to recognition, he agreed to vote with France for registration on 2 January 1924.[57]

[56] Tel. Tirard to MAE, 16 Nov. 1923: MAE Rive Gauche, vol. 36, nos. 134-136.
[57] Minutes, Des. #1273 Kilmarnock to F.O., C22363/129/18, 27 Dec. 1923: PRO FO

The British riposte was swift. Curzon asserted that the Palatine movement was artificial and that the "declarations of adherence" were secured by threats. The British ambassador prevailed on the Brussels government to suspend execution of the 2 January decision pending an interallied enquiry. In Coblenz, Lord Kilmarnock invoked Article Six of the Interallied Memo of 13 June 1919, which permitted a delegation to delay enactment of any majority decision of the Rhineland Commission for one week. The Palatine situation would be reexamined. Poincaré and Curzon concentrated their pressure on Brussels.[58]

On 6 January 1924 the Rhineland Commission perforce suspended the Palatine decrees, but refused the British request for an enquiry. Curzon was determined. On 9 January he notified the Quai d'Orsay that a British officer had been ordered to depart the following morning for the Palatinate to conduct his own investigation. Would the French government dare impede his mission? Poincaré nearly panicked. The effect of such a unilateral violation of an Allied power's zone would be disastrous for French prestige and the government's domestic standing. He beseeched Curzon to turn from this "gravely incorrect act at the expense of our *amour-propre*."[59]

Suddenly the situation in the Palatinate was overturned. On the evening of 9 January 1924 five German nationalists, reputedly *Oberland* agents under Eberlein's direction, paddled quietly across the Rhine, traversed the streets of Speyer, and entered the sedate hotel dining room where Heinz and four other members of the autonomous government were seated. They shot Heinz three times in the head, then emptied their pistols into his table mates. The apparent leader stooped to make certain Heinz was dead, another cut the lights, and the five assassins retraced their steps, escaping into nonoccupied territory. They left six dead and three wounded.[60]

The shocked commissioners in Coblenz agreed unanimously to postpone consideration of the decrees until the altered situation be-

---

371, vol. 8691, nos. 206-298; Tel. Tirard to MAE, 2 Jan. 1924: MAE Rive Gauche, vol. 38, nos. 213-215.

[58] Tel. #4 F.O. to Crewe (Paris), C91/91/18, 4 Jan. 1924; Tel. #1 Grahame (Brussels) to F.O., C213/91/18, 5 Jan. 1924: PRO FO 371, vol. 9770, nos. 208-212, 246; Tel. Poincaré to Herbette, 5 Jan. 1924: MAE Rive Gauche, vol. 38, nos. 261-262.

[59] Tel. Poincaré to St. Aulaire, 9 Jan. 1924: MAE Allemagne, vol. 351, nos. 45-46.

[60] *Le Matin*, 11 Jan. 1924. Eyewitness account by British journalist G.E.R. Gedye, *The Revolver Republic* (London, 1930), chap. 13. The assassins themselves directed a letter (if genuine) to the French delegate in Ludwigshafen, claiming that they represented *Oberland* and "thanking God that justice had been done." They promised not to rest until "the last of the brigands and traitors is laid in the ground." Interrogation by French agents in April allegedly revealed the names of the murderers and the fact of their direction from Heidelberg. MAE Rive Gauche, vol. 44, nos. 117-121.

came clear. The center of the struggle was still Brussels. "The Belgians," the Foreign Office noted, "are wobbling again." In Paris, the council of ministers made a decision. France would continue to press for registration, using the assassinations as proof of the need for haste, but would consent to an interallied enquiry "in the interest of truth." The conciliatory act did not budge the British. Sir Eyre Crowe practically chased St. Aulaire out of the Foreign Office, threatening to pull Britain out of the Rhineland Commission if the French continued to abuse the institution.[61] The British government also ordered its minister in Munich, Robert Henry Clive, to proceed to a Palatine investigation regardless of French *amour-propre*. Poincaré now abandoned political strategy—the Palatine movement was beyond resurrection—and fought for personal and national pride. He ordered General de Metz to appoint a French officer to accompany Clive, while he assigned a *Sûreté* agent to enter the British zone "to investigate nationalist organizations harbored there."

While Clive was in the Palatinate, the question of the decrees came up again in Coblenz. Tirard's funds had run out. Unless the decrees were passed, the Speyer regime would collapse. But the Belgian government, under the strain of the cross fire between its two great allies, suffered total paralysis, refusing to take any action on any issue in the Rhineland until France and Britain settled their differences. On 20 January Clive announced his conclusions: the Palatine autonomist movement was a sham, 75 percent of the separatists were outsiders, and the statements of adhesion were invalid. Frenchmen and autonomists protested the Clive conclusions, but action through the Rhineland Commission was impossible. Unless Poincaré approved regular subsidies, he must make an end to the Palatine movement.[62] But the French franc was now in collapse on foreign exchanges, having finally succumbed to the pressure of postwar deficits exacerbated by the Ruhr struggle. Not only were further financial efforts impossible but so was any policy trying the patience of London. With Tirard's reluctant cooperation, the Rhineland Commission proceeded gradually to the formation of an interallied control committee for the stabilization of the Palatinate and its return to Bavarian sovereignty.

After Clive left the Palatinate, the terrorists returned. Two men fired eight bullets into a former separatist administrator and three men assassinated a separatist burgermeister in Frankenthal. The Allies would have to restore order by main force. Poincaré's determination now flagged. The Palatine adventure was a costly failure, his own

[61] Tel. St. Aulaire to Poincaré, 11 Jan. 1924: MAE Allemagne, vol. 351, nos. 61-62.

[62] Tel. Tirard to Poincaré, 25 Jan. 1924: MAE Rive Gauche, vol. 40, nos. 114-115.

robust health fell prey to a severe virus, and a new and unfriendly prime minister governed in London. On 21 January 1924, the day of Lenin's death, the first Labour government under Ramsay MacDonald came to power in London. The two premiers exchanged conciliatory letters, agreeing on the need to set aside differences and to restore Franco-British cooperation in European reconstruction. Together they worked out details for the joint Palatine control commission. But the new relationship could not prevent a last echo of the bitterness, hate, and violence that characterized the separatist episodes of 1923-1924.

Pirmasens, just kilometers from the French border, was in a state of anarchy. Germany had cut off all relief to the province, the Palatine decrees were dead, and now French subsidies had ended. Gangs of unemployed roamed the streets in search of bread and plunder. Nationalist provocateurs mingled with them. The separatist garrison occupying the government building in the town square was a natural target for frustrations. In the early evening of 13 February, a crowd of several hundred attacked the prefecture, was met with revolver fire, and resolved to burn out the hated separatists. In the deepening dusk the mob succumbed to the primitive madness accompanying fire and social violence. As separatists leaped from the flames, they were shot or hacked to death. Fire and battle lasted past midnight. The nearest French garrison, stationed in Speyer, arrived the following morning in time to drag fifteen bodies from the ashes. The separatist conflagration perished in the flames it had itself kindled.

FRENCH AMBITIONS AND THE COMMITTEE OF EXPERTS

Strictly speaking, Poincaré honored his pledge to Stanley Baldwin not to exploit Germany's desperation by forcing bilateral reparations agreements on Berlin. Dealing instead with local authorities—Adenauer and Hagen on the Rhine, Stinnes, *et al.* in the Ruhr—he sought to create de facto situations that the Committee of Experts would incorporate into its conclusions. Reparations Commission delegate Sir John Bradbury judged that Poincaré hoped to have a Rhenish Free State in being by the time the experts convened, "so as to help France out of their inevitable mess at that time."[63] But instead of strengthening French defenses against the Anglo-American forensics to come, the Rhenish debacle played itself out to the defeat of French revisionist plans, while Poincaré's self-imposed limitations dictated non-negotiation with Berlin.

[63] Tel. L-23 Logan to Washington, 27 Oct. 1923: HI Logan Papers, "Secret Letters," vol. 10, p. 374.

It was the German government that had capitulated, but it was with the Allies on the one hand, and the Ruhr magnates on the other, with which the French had to negotiate. After 25 October 1923, a month of hard bargaining ensued during which Poincaré labored to specify the competence and area of enquiry of the expert bodies to be summoned by the Reparations Commission. He insisted on the same guarantees which the Bankers' Committee of June 1922 had refused to accept: that no alteration could be made in Germany's total bill nor a moratorium granted. The experts were not to question whether Germany could pay, only how. This stipulation was once again made necessary by the prior refusal of the United States to permit the experts to examine the question of interallied debts. France was on the defensive throughout November. The Belgian defection on the Rhine was matched by Premier Theunis' independent policy on reparations. Going over to the British side, the Belgian delegation to the Reparations Commission favored a mandate for the experts as broad as necessary to ensure American enthusiasm for the vehicle.

The isolation of France in the Allied camp became disturbingly clear following the illegal return to Germany of the exiled Crown Prince on 11 November. This act, approved by Berlin, ridiculed the Treaty of Versailles and, in other circumstances, would have provided Paris with a pretext for Allied sanctions. Instead, Poincaré's insistence that Germany be punished by the resumption of military control inspections met a solid wall of mistrust. A French threat of unilateral action even drove the Belgians, who were far from pleased with the German provocation, into opposition. The British solemnly threatened to pull out of the Interallied Military Control Commission. Poincaré retreated and the Allies resigned themselves to the despatch of an anodyne scolding to Berlin. A week later, on 29 November, Poincaré gave in to his united opposition on the Reparations Commissions as well. A broad mandate was granted to two experts' committees. The first would investigate means for German financial stabilization as a prelude to resuming a reparations schedule. The second would seek to restore exported capital to Germany. Together they formed the Dawes Commission under financier Charles G. Dawes of Chicago.[64] To be sure, these men would rule on the degree of success to be granted to France in the wake of the Ruhr occupation. But that fact did not necessarily register a defeat for France. Poincaré had planned as much and, if his campaign to specify

[64] On the formation of the Dawes Commission, see Dawes, *The Dawes Plan in the Making*; Weill-Raynal, *Les réparations allemandes*; Bergmann, *Der Weg der Reparationen*; Jones, "Stresemann and the Diplomacy of the Ruhr Crisis"; Rupieper, "Politics and Economics."

more closely the limits of the mandate was unsuccessful, the delay engendered by his bickering launched the committees at the moment when France's bargaining position had been stunningly improved. The giants of the Ruhr had just come to terms.

The Ruhr in French hands was first and foremost a political guarantee. But to be credible the Ruhr pledge had to support itself, and not constitute a drain on the French treasury. Poincaré's bargaining power now rested on France's ability to remain in the Ruhr for as long as necessary. His first concern in the autumn of 1923 was to make the guarantee productive. Various German industrialists had approached the MICUM as early as July, but Poincaré, while welcoming the demarches, cautioned that no accords could be reached without cessation of passive resistance.[65] After Stresemann announced that step in September, Poincaré pressed for intensive local negotiations. Passive resistance would truly end when all the proprietors of the occupied territory had resumed production and reparations deliveries. All stocks seized would remain in French hands, all mines and cokeries would continue under MICUM supervision. The *Kohlensyndikat* would not be reconstituted and export licensing control, railroads, and customs would remain in Allied hands.[66] With these guidelines, General Degoutte received representatives of German firms in October.

Hugo Stinnes, Albert Vögler, and Florian Kloeckner "went to Canossa" on 5 October, and talks began at Degoutte's Düsseldorf headquarters. Stinnes still hoped to bargain and sought to unify all the great local *Konzern* for this purpose. But industrial unity could not survive the pressures of social disintegration that threatened if economic regularization were not rapidly achieved. It also suffered interference from Berlin, where Stresemann refused to recognize the right of local businessmen to negotiate in the name of Germany. The first defector was Otto Wolff of the Rheinstahl and Phönix works, who signed an accord with Degoutte on 12 October. Stinnes was then hard put to keep his Commission of Six together, but he hoped to entice the French with a broad economic accord, which he assumed to be their primary goal. Poincaré refused to permit French industrialists to enter the discussions, or to consider broad metallurgical arrangements purchased with concessions in reparations. The MICUM treaties must involve only the return to work. Stinnes did have another means of leverage: if the Ruhr were unable or unwilling to resume work and Berlin ceased relief payments, the burden of supporting the Ruhr

[65] Tel. #405 Poincaré to Degoutte, 25 July 1923, cited by Degoutte, *L'Occupation de la Ruhr*, p. 409.

[66] Tel. #473-80 Poincaré to Degoutte, 1 Oct. 1923, cited by Degoutte, pp. 447-448.

population would devolve on France. It was the theory behind the *Versackungspolitik*—the French treasury could not afford to "purchase "Western Germany in this manner.

Poincaré had other difficulties with the negotiations in course. How would the Ruhr payments—both in-kind deliveries and cash from the *Kohlensteuer*—be accredited? Technically, they would be "reparations," but if they went to the common Allied pool administered by the Reparations Commission, the receipts from the Ruhr could not be set off against the costs of the French occupation, and the French treasury would not be spared. Stresemann blocked agreement by refusing to compensate the Ruhr for any payments *not* directly credited to reparations. Once again the interests of the state collided with private interests to forestall Franco-German accord. Once again the governments were obliged to retreat. Both Poincaré and Stresemann accepted a compromise worked out between the French expert Paul Frantzen and the Ruhr whereby all payments but the coal tax would be counted as reparations, and even the coal tax would eventually be credited after France no longer needed to cover its occupation costs.[67]

There remained the general desire of Stinnes to win reparations concessions for Germany in return for a metallurgical agreement with France. Stinnes' threat to break off negotiations was largely a bluff, and Poincaré responded with a bluff of his own. He wired Degoutte that if Stinnes did not sign the accords as they stood, French troops should seize new coal mines chosen from among Stinnes' holdings.[68] Stinnes elected to give way, and to carry on his economic offensive in spite of the surrender. On 23 November, he signed the MICUM Accords. They provided for an unconditional return to work; 21 percent of the Ruhr's output would flow to the west. Passive resistance had truly ended.

Now that French demands were satisfied, Stresemann again attempted to enter into negotiations with Poincaré. He desired talks on all questions bearing on reparations, but French Ambassador de Margerie quickly informed him that this was still impossible. Reparations, after all, were of joint Allied concern. Poincaré insisted that Franco-German exchanges must deal solely with local questions on the Rhine and Ruhr. A return to economic stability in the occupied territories was the only matter in which Poincaré might have anything to gain from Berlin. In this connection, German Chargé von Hoesch met with the premier for the first time in eleven months. The Rhenish situ-

[67] Erdmann, *Adenauer*, pp. 79-80; Weill-Raynal, *Les réparations allemandes*, II, 478ff; Feldman, *Iron and Steel*, pp. 411ff; Wentzcke, *Ruhrkampf*, II, 192ff.

[68] Tel. Poincaré to Degoutte, 22 Nov. 1923: MAE Ruhr, vol. 32, nos. 74-78.

ation could be quickly improved, he suggested, if France permitted the introduction of the *Rentenmark* and the return of German functionaries expelled by Tirard. Poincaré politely labeled such solutions unacceptable and, at the end of December, ruled out any return of Berlin's influence to occupied territory.[69] France and Germany still had nothing to discuss.

Poincaré had much to discuss with the representatives of French and German metallurgy. Now that the MICUM Accords were operative and reparations in the hands of the Allied experts, perhaps French industry could finally use the leverage gained by the victory in the Ruhr. But the Ruhr struggle had not confined its damage to the German industry; it also led to the temporary extinction of French productivity. While the Ruhr barons were in a weak bargaining position as compared with 1922, the French were not in a strong position. If the government were willing to sacrifice its reparations position for a bilateral accord with the Ruhr, and if French industry could for once display a unified and aggressive front, a sound basis for Franco-German integration might have been laid. But Poincaré was not ready to ignore the budget—and the interests of French rentiers and taxpayers—on behalf of industrial groups, while those groups again succumbed to faction and timidity. The failure of France to achieve a satisfactory coal and steel settlement in 1923-1924 was the clearest indication of her internal weakness and international dependency.

After the rejection of the French industrial demarches of January 1923, the two metallurgies, French and German, suffered in separation. By December 1923 an opportunity arose for a renewal of ties. Stinnes had failed to extract concessions in return for the MICUM Accords. Now, instead of demanding French evacuation of the Rhineland as in 1922, Stinnes sought to avoid a permanent French presence in the Ruhr. Under these circumstances, he again considered collaboration. There was another motivation. Failing access to the *Rentenmark*, and failing a Rhenish bank, the Ruhr had no choice but to seek the capital to fund the return to work from foreign sources. The "return to work" was financed to a great degree by Dutch capital, but Stinnes and others in the Ruhr took the surprising step of offering blocks of stock for sale abroad. The prospects were exciting. The French government saw an opportunity to promote Franco-German industrial cooperation and improve the relative standing of French industry. If France could

[69] *Le Matin*, 16 Dec. 1923; Note Peretti, "Visite de M. Hoesch," 31 Dec. 1923: MAE Rive Gauche, vol. 38, nos. 199-200; Tel. Margerie to MAE, 31 Dec. 1923: MAE Ruhr, vol. 33, nos. 316-320. The *Rentenmark* did not circulate in occupied territory despite the Rhineland Commission's approval. The Reich government feared seizure of *Rentenmark* by the French.

legally obtain a stake in the Ruhr, a permanent relationship might be forged to which Britain could not object. All that was needed was industrial and financial cooperation.

Following the replacement of Schneider by Wendel in the *Comité des Forges* during the summer, the French steel lobby was dominated by those who favored, not dainty purchases of minority stock, but a comprehensive industrial plan exacted from the Ruhr by force. The shortage of liquidity in French steel again hampered expansion through investment, and the industrialists were impatient with Poincaré's insistence on protecting the reparations settlement at all cost. Late in October the *Comité des Forges* directorate met to formulate a plan for the exploitation of France's victory in the Ruhr. One faction demanded, not the sale, but the cession of German stock in mines and factories to French firms. Another envisioned a permanent customs barrier between the Ruhr and the rest of Germany, thus forcing Ruhr coal westward at reasonable prices. Both desired the cession to France of the German state coal mines.[70]

Secretary-general Robert Pinot combined the various industrial schemes and submitted them to the government in mid-November. The stock sales, which had been approved by a cabinet council at Poincaré's request, were dead. Furthermore, Pinot now demanded the acquisition by France, not just of German stock, but of a majority or total interest in German firms, something the Germans would never accept voluntarily. Without prior agreements on price, markets, and raw materials, Pinot argued, minority participation would leave the French at the mercy of the German directorates. The same sad theme sounded from the Rue de Madrid: integration without guarantees meant domination by the vastly more powerful Germans. Poincaré could hardly be unsympathetic: he had used the same argument against the British and Americans since 1919. Only when France was assured of independence in coke through control of German mines could French industry bargain as equals.[71]

Jacques Seydoux recognized the difficulties inherent in the steel industry's plans. It meant renewed conflict with Britain, renewed conflict between the state and industry in France and, finally, it meant renewed and crippling conflict within French industry itself. The bitter fight over coal distribution, only put to rest with the dismantling of the *Bureau National de Charbon* and *péréquation* system in 1921, would reemerge. French coal interests represented by the *Comité des Houillères* would not tolerate the creation of permanent "domestic" compe-

[70] Maier, *Recasting Bourgeois Europe*, p. 408.
[71] Note Seydoux, 14 Dec. 1923: MAE Pap. Millerand, Réparations XIX, nos. 172-173.

tition with their own mines. The chairman of the *Houillères*, Henri de Peyerhimof, favored the original plan for minority shareholding in German industry and had even sent an agent to the Ruhr to negotiate. The government was in the middle. Its only goal, Seydoux explained, was to end French dependence on England and Germany for combustibles, but all paths were blocked.[72]

French industrial lobbies did not have the leverage vis-à-vis government exercised by the Ruhr. But the state in France was just as helpless to force policies on the industrial elites. Poincaré's ministerial committee appointed the experts Inspector Guillaume of the Ministry of Public Works and industrialist Paul Frantzen to prepare a compromise plan for Franco-German integration. They made their recommendations on 22 December: (1) cession of Ruhr mines producing 3,268,000 tons of coke per year; (2) permanent French control of Saar mines; (3) accord between Ruhr and Lorraine for coke and iron exchange; (4) recognition of the above by the German government; (5) continuation of reparations coal deliveries with the above capital transfers credited to Germany's reparations account. The government approved the ambitious blueprint, but efforts to bring together French steel and coal interests were in vain. Pinot and Peyerhimof, old rivals within a French metallurgical structure lacking vertical integration, refused to yield. The coal men forbade majority participation in German mines; the steel men would permit nothing less.[73]

The government's failure to forge a common policy in cooperation with the French industrialists themselves led back to the idea of a governmental agreement with the Ruhr magnates. Stinnes was willing to talk, but his plan for a Franco-German industrial community of interest as a substitute for reparations found little favor in late December 1923, with either Stresemann or Poincaré. For a short time the so-called Rechberg plan seemed to hold promise. Arnold Rechberg, a German industrialist friendly with French deputy Paul Reynaud, was one magnate who inspired trust in Paris. He had worked for a Franco-German-Polish understanding during the Silesian dispute, was fiercely anti-Soviet, and blamed the Rapallo policy for the Ruhr occupation. Now he envisioned a settlement so favorable that Millerand renewed his pressure on the government to settle with Germany directly. Rechberg suggested a grand solution to reparations and metallurgical relations through the transfer to France of a 30 percent interest in the

[72] Note Seydoux pour Peretti, 10 Dec. 1923: MAE Pap. Millerand, Réparations XIX, nos. 134-135.

[73] Note Seydoux pour le PdC, 22 Dec. 1923; Notes, "Attitude du Comité des Houillères," and "Charbon allemand," 8 Jan. 1924: MAE Pap. Millerand, Réparations XIX, nos. 230-233; XX, nos. 41-46.

entire German industrial plant. As in all industrial schemes originating across the Rhine, a great iron and steel cartel would follow, "a huge trust from Normandy to Silesia able to cut world metallurgical prices by 20 percent—a trust of ten million tons of steel! "This is a dream," Seydoux noted, "that must tickle the German imagination. It is why we must negotiate in a manner to conserve the direction and not be placed in tutelage."[74]

The Rechberg plan, too, was incapable of moving the two nations together. As 1924 began, the separatist movements collapsed, the French franc began its descent, and German finances, thanks to Hjalmar Schacht, were in the process of stabilization. Chancellor Marx, Stresemann, and Stinnes himself thought better of such concessions as Rechberg proposed, though Stinnes asked for French evacuation of the Rhine and Ruhr in exchange. By mid-January, Berlin repudiated the Rechberg plan and urged Stinnes of the need to break off negotiations with the French until after the experts' report.[75] In Paris, Poincaré came to the same conclusion. French industrialists could not agree; the franc was in collapse. It would not do to offend Britain, whose financial power could be used to buttress or destroy the French currency. Poincaré wrote Robert Pinot that nothing could be decided before the report of the experts.[76]

Poincaré's insistence on postponing industrial talks until the settlement of the Ruhr and reparations issues boded ill for business. What leverage would France retain in the eventual negotiations if she first liquidated her Ruhr victory? One answer lay in the commercial advantages bestowed by the Treaty of Versailles. The privilege of free export to Germany accorded to Alsace-Lorraine for a period of five years was due to terminate in January 1925. The fight for extension of that privilege produced a second clash between the state and private interests in France. If the French government deemed an extension of the right of free exports to Germany to be necessary, it was obliged to notify the League council before 1 January 1924. On 25 October 1923 Lucien Dior of the Ministry of Commerce, backed by industrial interests, insisted that the government seek an extension: "I know the measure envisaged will encounter opposition from the other treaty signatories," he wrote Poincaré, "but that is the work of diplomacy."[77]

[74] Eberhard von Vietsch, *Arnold Rechberg und das Problem der politischen Westorientierung Deutschlands nach dem ersten Weltkrieg* (Coblenz, 1958), pp. 73-89; Note Seydoux, 18 Dec. 1923: MAE Pap. Millerand, Réparations XIX, nos. 215-218.

[75] Erdmann, *Adenauer*, pp. 159-180; Note Weyl, "Entretiens avec MM. Schacht et Stresemann les 9. et 10. janvier 1924": HI Pap. Loucheur, Box 12, Folder 22.

[76] Let. Poincaré to Pinot, 24 Jan. 1924, cited by Zimmermann, *Frankreichs Ruhrpolitik*, p. 252.

[77] Let. Dior to Poincaré, 25 Oct. 1923: MAE Pap. Millerand, vol. 14, nos. 21-33.

Poincaré needed no additional problems at this time, especially ones requiring that he ask favors from Britain or Germany. The League council would only expand the debate to concern reparations. The problems would be solved, he told Dior, through a Franco-German commercial agreement before the privileges lapsed in 1925.[78]

Dior refused to drop the issue. He represented a powerful Chamber bloc in turn acting for a bloc of French manufacturers and exporters. Seydoux privately registered fear of the lobby's intrigues and suspected that Dior's undersecretary and "Wendel's man" in government, Daniel Serruys, sought to replace him as the architect of French economic policy.[79] Poincaré cannily permitted the deadline to pass before pacifying Dior with tardy demarches to the League council. Then he lowered the boom, upbraiding Dior for placing private interests above the national interest.[80] The French government was not the pawn of pressure groups, but neither was it master of them.

Reparations, metallurgy, commerce—all these questions would now stay unresolved until after the Committee of Experts made its report. There remained security. One important condition Poincaré hoped to impose on the Rhineland during the separatist debacle was permanent Allied control of the railways. The French government had reached a consensus during formulation of these increased ambitions that control of Rhenish railroads was an excellent and realizable guarantee of security. The Régie could be transformed into an international society or concession, with 45 to 50 percent of the shares in French hands.[81] Poincaré mentioned such a scheme in the French Yellow Book on reparations.

Projects abounded for the constitution of a railroad company in the autumn of 1923, but again the British were quick to register their opposition. Britain would not participate and, if a railroad company were founded, would demand autonomy for the British zone.[82] The Belgians, too, announced opposition to any permanent Allied presence in the Rhineland unless the British participated. Then, in mid-December

[78] Note Seydoux, "Affaire de l'Article 280," 22 Nov. 1923; Note Vignon, "Conversations avec Seydoux—Relations commerciales avec l'Allemagne," 24 Nov. 1923: MAE Pap. Millerand, vol. 14, nos. 64-71; vol. 13, no. 72.

[79] Let. Dior to Poincaré, 26 Nov. and 12 Dec. 1923; marginal note Vignon, 30 Nov. 1923: MAE Pap. Millerand, vol. 14, nos. 78-88, 101-113.

[80] Let. Poincaré to Dior, "a.s. de l'Article 280," 16 Jan. 1924 (drafted 4 Dec. 1923): MAE Pap. Millerand, vol. 14, nos. 89-94.

[81] Note Seydoux, "Chemins de fer—organisation proposée," 1 June 1923: MAE Pap. Millerand, Réparations XII, nos. 236-239; Projects Bréaud, "Constitution d'une Société de Gérance à substituer à la Régie des chemins de fer rhénans," 15 Aug. and 16 Sept. 1923: AN HCF, vol. 6411.

[82] Let. Poincaré to Tirard, "Les chemins de fer rhénans et l'Angleterre," 29 Oct. 1923; Let. Crowe to St. Aulaire, 22 Oct. 1923: MAE Rive Gauche, vol. 127, nos. 141-143.

1923, Finance Minister de Lasteyrie sounded his tiresome refrain. The French government must avoid all engagements concerning the Rhenish railroads; France could not afford to invest a centime.[83] Finally, the German government and the Reparations Commission were the only bodies competent to grant a rail concession on German soil. This scheme, too, would have to await a decision from the experts' committee as the planning body for the Reparations Commission.

Thus, the French "victory" over Germany after the occupation of the Ruhr rested totally in the hands of a small group of international experts. This was due partially to design, and partially to the dissensions and weaknesses, financial and structural, in the French postwar polity. In his moderation Poincaré was unwilling to make Germany over by armed force. The result was that the Committee of Experts was the only agency capable of granting de jure status to the de facto position Poincaré had won for France in the Rhineland and the Ruhr. Just as France was forced to accept a treaty in 1919 dependent for its execution on other uncooperative powers, so was she obliged to consign French revision of that treaty to the same powers, with one addition: the United States of America. France *had* brought America to Europe without prior concessions to Germany. Whether future concessions could be avoided would depend on the experts' commission. What did Poincaré expect from these men?

Poincaré gave his delegate on the Reparations Commission his guidelines on 3 December 1923. The experts could not envision the diminution of the German debt in any way. They were not to consider Germany's capacity to pay at some future date, as after a moratorium, but at the present moment. The experts were to take into account the present situation in the Ruhr, including the MICUM Accords. If the committees overstepped their limits, the French delegation must withdraw. In addition, there were several particular points on which France expected to be favored. The Rhenish railroads must be constituted as an Allied company. Certain mines of the Ruhr must be transferred to French ownership under title of reparations. The customs regime for the Left Bank of the Rhine must be maintained. Finally, the experts must study German financial reconstruction in light of a Rhenish bank of issue. The limits of the experts' mandate were precise, Poincaré concluded, but its scope was vast.[84] Poincaré's "legalism" can

[83] Note Vignon, "Conversation avec Seydoux," 15 Dec. 1923: MAE Pap. Millerand, Réparations XIX, nos. 176-177.

[84] Let. Poincaré to Barthou, 3 Dec. 1923: MAE Pap. Millerand, Réparations XIX, nos. 77-88.

thus be put in perspective. He refused to use his army in the Ruhr to settle directly with Germany, for he would thereby sacrifice Allied recognition. A metallurgical accord would preclude Anglo-American support for a reparations/war debts accord, or a security agreement. The Ruhr occupation was intended to liberate France from her triple postwar crisis, but through the only means that would make the eventual peace legitimate—an international conference. This was the program of French revision of the Treaty of Versailles. France's ability or inability to "stand pat" in the Ruhr until it was granted would determine its realization or renunciation.

Could Poincaré honestly expect the Allied experts to rubber-stamp this program? Even now Degoutte urged prior settlement with Germany lest the experts double-cross France and snatch away the fruits of victory.[85] But the issue hinged on French financial stability, on France's ability to defy the Anglo-Americans until satisfied with their proposals. The insecurity of the franc, the result of the crushing burden of 1914-1918, of the French distaste for large, direct taxation, of the burdens forced on France in 1923 by the passive resistance, destroyed this ability, and made France, even at the moment of triumph, as dependent as ever on London and Washington.

Seydoux had come to the conclusion, as early as November 1923, that the battle was won, but the war lost. He confided in the young Jean Monnet: "The English will try to block us in our German policy. . . . We have nothing to expect from the Allies." By December events had only confirmed his pessimism. The long struggle was almost over, and the veteran reparations warrior became reflective:

> There is no use hiding the fact that we have entered on the path of the "financial reconstruction of Europe." We will not deal with Germany as conqueror to vanquished; rather the Germans and Frenchmen will sit on the same bench before the United States and other lending countries. We will be given conditions, perhaps disarmament, evacuation of the Ruhr. Once engaged in this path, Poincaré will be unable to stop. Failure to procure the grand loan now would be a catastrophe for our credit, the death blow to the franc. If Poincaré elects to change course, he must step down, for events cannot be stopped.[86]

[85] Note Vignon, 21 Dec. 1923: MAE Pap. Millerand, Réparations XIX, no. 219; Let. Degoutte to Poincaré, 29 Dec. 1923: MAE Ruhr, vol. 33, nos. 291-300.

[86] Note Vignon, "Conversation Seydoux/Monnet," 5 Nov. 1923; Note, "Emprunt en Amérique—prémières reflexions de Seydoux," 27 Dec. 1923: MAE Pap. Millerand, Réparations XVIII, nos. 62-64; Réparations XIX, nos. 267-269.

DEFEAT OF RHENISH AUTONOMISM

In the German cabinet protocol of 5 December 1923, the Marx government satisfied Stresemann and the opponents of negotiating autonomy for the Rhenish leaders. The French government did not get the message immediately. Correctly informed about the friction between the Cologne group and Berlin concerning relief payments, Poincaré expected Adenauer to be anxious to come to terms with Tirard in the first weeks of December. Instead, Adenauer made another trip to Berlin. Marx approved of Stresemann's emphasis on diplomatic pressure against France, but he saw the need to buy more time by continuing *Verschleppungspolitik* on the Rhine. Consequently, he told Adenauer to keep the autonomy bait before the French—and not to inform Stresemann that he had the chancellor's approval.[87]

The French were in some confusion. Tirard reported in the wake of a 12 December meeting with Adenauer that Marx was "not at all unfavorable to the idea of Rhenish autonomy." At the same time, de Margerie wired from Berlin that the Stresemann faction had won out and that talks would be broken off.[88] Poincaré concluded that German policy had not changed, that Stresemann desperately sought to open government-to-government communication to barter for concessions. He instructed Tirard to inform Adenauer that no such ploy would succeed. If he (Adenauer) wished to improve the lot of the Rhineland, he must work through the French authorities on the spot.[89]

Adenauer still subordinated creation of a Rhenish state to the standard quid pro quo, a complete Franco-German economic settlement. In December he joined forces with Stinnes. The industrial giant had failed twice to interest the French in a metallurgical arrangement in return for a reparations deal, and he now did so in connection with Rhenish autonomy. He spoke on 13 December of an exchange of coke for iron, to be followed by an exchange of corporate shares to form a Franco-German community of interest. Poincaré saw in it another maneuver to swallow French industry. "Cooperation, yes," he answered, "but reparations first, and above all with security."[90]

The French premier permitted himself one last burst of optimism in response to the mediatory labors of Vincent Arnaud. Formerly attached to the French embassy in Berlin, Arnaud had met privately

[87] Erdmann, *Adenauer*, pp. 162-163.

[88] Tel. Tirard to MAE, 12 and 15 Dec. 1923; Tel. Margerie to MAE, 15 and 17 Dec. 1923: MAE Rive Gauche, vol. 37, nos. 261, 336-342, 348-352; vol. 38, nos. 13-15.

[89] Tel. Poincaré to Tirard, 24 Dec. 1923: MAE Rive Gauche, vol. 38, no. 120.

[90] Erdmann, *Adenauer*, pp. 159-162.

with Adenauer several times to free the Rhenish leader from the stigma of dealing with the French High Commissariat. The two men had discussed a plan for a Rhenish *Bundesstaat*, to be justified by evacuation of the Rhineland by France and reparations concessions. Poincaré encouraged the talks, though he hoped to whittle down the concessions demanded to an acceptable level—and to postpone their execution.[91] Adenauer and Tirard confronted one another again on 27 December. This time they agreed quickly on the principle of an autonomous and unified Rhenish state. But Tirard refused to link the Rhenish question with reparations. "France cannot view reparations and German economic recovery with a favorable eye until her security is guaranteed." It was the standard French position toward Germany: political security must precede economic cooperation. But the inability of France to force a prior political settlement, the essence of the French Rhineland policy, bespoke the failure of French revisionism. The Rhinelanders held out for real political and economic concessions designed to free them from a recurrence of French sanctions. Agreement was impossible.

Adenauer concluded his meeting with Tirard by introducing a new difficulty. He insisted that the Rhenish state be created according to the Weimar Constitution. Since a plebiscite was impossible, this would require passage of a *Reichsgesetz* with the approval of Prussia and the Reich![92] When Adenauer next confronted the German government, Marx and Stresemann told him that an economic accord with France, not to mention a Rhenish state, was unnecessary. Hjalmar Schacht had gone to London. The business he would do there would save the *Rentenmark* and German unity. There followed a series of meetings with the French industrialist Ernest Weyl, a friend of Millerand. Stresemann assured Weyl that Germany was prepared to pay reparations, and suggested a pact on Rhenish demilitarization, hopefully guaranteed by Britain. His proposals were the kernels of the Dawes Plan and Locarno Rhineland Pact of 1924-1925. But through Weyl, Stresemann learned of the ruse played on him by Marx in permitting Rhenish negotiations past 5 December. On 16 January 1924 he vented his spleen in a letter to the chancellor, condemning the activities of Adenauer and Stinnes.[93] Franco-Rhenish negotiations terminated, and with them the hopes for Rhenish autonomy.

German tactics had worked magnificently. Adenauer refused to en-

[91] Ibid., pp. 162-167.

[92] Let. Adenauer to Arnaud, 28 Dec. 1923, enclosed in Let. Arnaud to Poincaré, 8 Jan. 1924: MAE Rive Gauche, vol. 38, nos. 305-311.

[93] Erdmann, *Adenauer*, pp. 175-179.

gineer Rhenish autonomy in defiance of the German government. Stinnes refused to offer a metallurgical agreement without concomitant solution of reparations. The German government refused to sanction any privately negotiated political or economic agreements at all. Tirard had been kept occupied and hopeful throughout the crucial months of separatism and German financial weakness. Now the crisis was past. On 10 January 1924, Adenauer revealed his true feelings to Weyl: a Rhenish buffer state was of no use to France and would contribute no reparations. An autonomous Rhineland firmly attached to the Reich would be a moderating and pacifist influence, which would be reinforced by the creation of a community of interest between France and Germany through joint ownership of the industrial belt spanning the border. He understood French security fears, but concluded prophetically that "no treaty can guarantee that France will not be molested."[94] A week later, Adenauer raised his veil before the Rhenish council of cities: "We are slaves governed by foreigners. The Rhenish question is nothing other than the question of French security. It can only be resolved by the Entente governments themselves."[95] The next day, he visited Tirard, at the latter's invitation, for the last time. The Stinnes negotiations must be carried on through government channels; he did not mention political change.

Stinnes himself made contact with Seydoux. But in February 1924 he fell ill and died two months afterward. From Berlin, de Margerie reported that "the entire German foreign policy seems aimed at reinstalling German authority in the occupied territories."[96] One final industrial initiative completed the failure of reconciliation in the post-passive resistance period. This one came from the *Comité des Forges*. His previous plan scotched by the coal interests, Secretary-General Robert Pinot attempted to promote a renewal of ties with German steel. After 12 February 1924 he met several times with a Stinnes agent and offered a four-point program: (1) cession by Germany of mines capable of producing 4.5 million tons of coke per year; (2) exchange of an additional 2.5 million tons for Lorraine iron; (3) a commercial agreement for additional German import of Lorraine iron; (4) an international steel cartel comprising France, Belgium, Germany, and Britain.[97]

[94] "Conversation avec le Dr. Adenauer," 10 Jan. 1924, remis par M. Weyl: HI Pap. Loucheur, Box 12, Folder 15.

[95] "Compte-rendu . . . sur le meeting de la Städtevereinigung," 18 Jan. 1924: MAE Rive Gauche, vol. 40, nos. 242-250.

[96] Tel. Margerie to Poincaré, 16 Feb. 1924: MAE Rive Gauche, vol. 42, nos. 150-152.

[97] P.-V., Pinot/Léon-Levy/Oberscheid, 12 Feb. and 5 Mar. 1924: HI Pap. Loucheur, Box 5, Folder 13; Note Pinot pour le PdC, "Accord avec les industriels des pays oc-

Pinot's plan asked no political concessions from either side. But by the time the governments came to consider the plan two weeks later, they judged negotiations to be untimely. The very economic sense of Pinot's plan made it unattractive. Both continental nations now placed their hopes in Britain, whom it would not do to offend. Stresemann and Seydoux each counseled discretion on the part of their respective governments.[98] On 28 February, Lord D'Abernon even protested formally the private talks between French and German businessmen. Economics had become thoroughly politicized.

The German government did not succeed in maneuvering successfully through the nervous months after the end of passive resistance solely by delaying tactics and reliance upon the patriotism of Rhenish leaders. The achievement that made the delaying tactics ultimately effective was the phoenix-like financial recovery of the Reich. The temporary "miracle" of the *Rentenmark* and its replacement by a gold currency permitted the Reich to "buy back" the Rhenish provinces placed in pawn after the end of unemployment relief.

Marx's cabinet inherited three tasks in December: preservation of the *Rentenmark* through confidence-restoring fiscal measures; replacement of this expedient as rapidly as possible by a gold currency; prevention of the establishment of a Rhenish bank. The government acted with alacrity. On 7 December it promulgated the first extraordinary ordinance calling for personal, direct taxes to put funds at the immediate disposal of the Reich.[99] Next, Marx tackled the Rhenish bank, in limbo since the British and Belgian refusals to register a bank in the Rhineland Commission. He imposed a number of conditions on Louis Hagen for Reich approval of a Rhenish currency: German monetary unity must not be broken; the Rhenish bank must be subordinated to the Reichsbank; it would receive only a five-year mandate, with the Reichsbank retaining the right to repurchase the Rhenish bank at any time. Under these conditions, a Rhenish bank would only be a French investment in, and aid to, German economic recovery! Hagen in-

---

cupés," 15 Feb. 1924; Note Pinot pour Millerand, 10 Mar. 1924: MAE Pap. Millerand, Réparations XXI, nos. 119-120, 270.

[98] Erdmann, *Adenauer*, p. 182; cf. Maier, *Recasting Bourgeois Europe*, pp. 415-416.

[99] The Marx government's success in rallying industrial and financial support for these stabilization measures was due in part to the gradual realization by those sectors of the danger faced by Germany if chaos continued in the occupied territories, partly because the hyperinflation had ceased to benefit industry and the overextended conglomerates were threatened with disaster unless the deflationary crunch could be met gradually, and also because of the political groundwork laid by Cuno and Stresemann. By mid-December 1923 the Marx cabinet enjoyed broad bipartisan support for its stabilization efforts, provided they were successful. See Maier, *Recasting Bourgeois Europe*, pp. 381-387, 400-402.

formed Tirard of these conditions on 26 December, then met with Marx two days later. He obtained no significant alteration of the conditions.[100]

Despite the new taxes, which increased government revenues 284 percent in December, only 27.5 percent of the budget was covered. On 22 December the second emergency fiscal ordinance appeared, and the Reichsrat appointed Hjalmar Schacht as successor to the suddenly deceased president of the Reichsbank. Schacht was now sole authority over German finances; he left a week later for London. The reception he received there would determine the success or failure of German recovery efforts.

Schacht met with Montagu Norman of the Bank of England on New Year's Day 1924. The two men were engaged in the same pursuit, to stop French ambitions on the Rhine and to promote European stabilization. Schacht had an American mother, spoke English fluently, and was anxious to court the favor of this powerful and eccentric Britisher. He hoped the Dawes Commission would cooperate in German stabilization (i.e., recommend American loans), but in the meantime the German crisis must be bridged. He planned a gold discount bank with 200 million gold marks' worth of foreign currency to replace the temporary *Rentenmark*. Half of the capital he could raise in Germany, the rest he hoped to borrow from the Bank of England.

The following day Norman asked Schacht about the Marx government's opinion of the attempt to found a Rhenish bank of issue. "The Reichsbank's attitude is entirely clear and unequivocal," answered Schacht. "It is definitely opposed to any project that seeks to restrict its own supreme power in matters of currency within the German Reich." Satisfied that no Franco-German separate peace was in the offing, Norman presented him with pledges, not for 100 million, but for a half *billion* gold marks. British capital would go to Berlin, not Cologne.[101]

While Germany thus obtained the wherewithal to place her financial recovery on a golden foundation, the capital in France for the Rhenish bank floated away. The French franc succumbed to the constant and increasing government deficits, and to the clear unwillingness of British and American capital to arrest the franc's fall in light of the provocations perpetrated by Poincaré in the Palatinate during January 1924. Victory over the passive resistance in September, seeming to promise quick returns for France, and Poincaré's cooperation in formation of

[100] Tel. Tirard to MAE, 26 and 29 Dec. 1923: MAE Rive Gauche, vol. 108, nos. 99-103.

[101] Schacht, *Confessions*, pp. 179-187.

the Committee of Experts only helped stave off the inevitable. Poincaré recognized the vulnerability of France in this regard when he eschewed the opportunity to "name his terms" to Germany. But the failure of France to hide her involvement in the separatist episodes helped produce the result he had sought to avoid. By December the franc began slipping. Tirard attributed it to German speculation. Francs spent in the Rhineland found their way to Cologne and were dumped on exchanges in blocks. Tirard had information that London had contributed £500,000 to the operation.[102] In any case, it was "foreign speculators" in the Paris Bourse itself who led the assault on the French currency.

Seydoux and the president of the Chamber finance commission also paid lip service to the British conspiracy theory, but they recognized that the French budgetary deficits and resistance to tax increases were immediately responsible for the collapse. On 14 January 1924 the franc tumbled to 96.11 against the pound. The dollar had been worth thirteen francs before the Ruhr occupation. It now was worth twenty. Poincaré renounced new expenses and instituted an austerity program while asking authority for a "double décime," a 20 percent increase in all taxes. He called for the majority that had sustained him for two years "to rally to me and form the square to repulse assaults on the franc." *Le Matin* screamed, "To Vote Against Poincaré Is to Vote Against the Franc!" Nevertheless, the "double décime" aroused irate opposition, and did not pass both houses until mid-March. Poincaré's austerity measures sustained the currency for a time, but February brought a new fall. The dollar reached twenty-nine francs, and the government was helpless to restore its monetary independence. It must appeal, after all, to Anglo-American finance, and relinquish ambitions in Germany beyond what the Committee of Experts would grant. France had reached too far.

Louis Hagen told Tirard at the end of January that Schacht's success precluded further discussion of a Rhenish bank.[103] In Paris, Poincaré's team, which had been breaking up ever since the end of passive resistance, rebelled against him. With the exception of the signature of the MICUM Accords, France had won no victories since September. But the defeats piled up: separatist disasters, the bank failure, mines and railroads stalemates, German recovery, and now the fall of the franc.

[102] Let. #4053ATRP/FC/3 Tirard to Poincaré, 20 Dec. 1923: AN HCF, vol. 3232, dos. Q4a5/6. See Maier, *Recasting Bourgeois Europe*, pp. 459-472, especially p. 460, n. 104.

[103] Tel. Poincaré to Tirard, 16 Jan. 1924; Tel. Tirard to MAE, 31 Jan. 1924: MAE Rive Gauche, vol. 108, nos. 126, 133-134.

FIGURE 6. "The Masseur: Poincaré: 'Is it regaining its strength?' DeLasteyrie: 'Alas, chief, it's I who am losing mine!' "
N. B.: "Baume de Fierabras": a "Cure-all." H. P. Gassier, 1924. © S.P.A.D.E.M. Paris 1977.

On 12 January 1924 the inter-ministerial Ruhr committee discussed the plight of victorious France. Despite the enormous investment, France had won no bargaining tool except the "productive guarantee" represented by the MICUM Accords, and even the recovery of Ruhr productivity depended on financial support offered by Berlin, and ultimately by Britain. Four months previously Rhinelanders shunned worthless marks in favor of francs. Now the situation was reversed and the occupation was becoming vastly more expensive. The inter-ministerial Ruhr committee recommended an end to adventure. "Everything points to the absolute necessity of halting the present crisis and supporting the franc."[104]

The Dawes Commission held its first meeting in Paris on 13 January 1924, the day after the committee's report to the French cabinet. Poincaré staked his hopes on the experts and considered the wisdom of cutting his losses through hastening Allied and German reconciliation. France and Germany had fought like gladiators in the ring to the point of mutual exhaustion. Victory might have meant independence from the Anglo-American spectators for either of the continental contestants. But neither had won a victory, and France and Germany both now looked up from the pit, beseeching grace and succor.

THE END OF AMBITION

Poincaré's efforts to secure a permanent alteration of the power relationship between France and Germany through political and economic weakening of Germany had come to nothing. Unwilling to adopt a stance wholly independent of the Anglo-Americans in part because of continued financial vulnerability, Poincaré entrusted the issues of the Rhenish bank, railroads, and Ruhr mines to the Committee of Experts. By the end of January 1924 he began to realize that the experts were unlikely to view his petitions favorably. Poincaré first abandoned the bank scheme, then despaired of a mines transfer. But he still hoped for permanent Allied control of Rhenish trade, the abandonment of which, the anchor of French Rhenish policies since the Armistice, "would produce a deplorable impression in the Parlement." He also insisted on the retention of Rhenish railroad control, an "indispensable guarantee of security."[105]

[104] Note Seydoux, "Le Comité interministériel de la Ruhr," 14 Jan. 1924: MAE Pap. Millerand, Réparations XX, nos. 128-130.

[105] Note Poincaré on margin of Note Seydoux, 21 Jan. 1924: MAE Pap. Millerand, Réparations XXIV, nos. 54-65.

Even these last special pleas of France were fast losing their force. Stresemann, supported by Britain, threw his entire effort behind the concept of German economic unity as a prerequisite for reparations. Schacht himself visited Paris in the third week of January 1924, and informed Seydoux that the experts would throw out Poincaré's demands. Schacht and Seydoux agreed that an American loan was the first priority, then a Franco-German commercial agreement. But peace could not triumph, Schacht believed, until Poincaré was gone. He echoed the sentiment of the premier's crony Jacques Bardoux: Poincaré had a critical, not a constructive mind.[106] Seydoux now despaired of the entire French Rhine/Ruhr program. He even considered the planned railroad company an unnecessary expense. One by one, Poincaré's teammates deserted him. Foch and General Destiker, the rail expert, denied the value of the Régie as a military guarantee. Charles de Lasteyrie and Yves Le Trocquer, ministers of finance and public works, berated the investment involved in an Allied rail company. Even Minister of War André Maginot no longer considered a railroad control indispensable.[107] Poincaré was out of touch; it was time for other, more conciliatory men to take charge.

In February the franc underwent its second collapse. A new round of austerity measures was politically impossible. Poincaré had tightened the belt once; to do so again would be an admission of the failure of the Ruhr policy. More immediate would be the effect on the general elections in May. The only hope for a temporary stabilization was through Anglo-American support. Peretti de la Rocca and Jacques Seydoux, the two top permanent officials in the Foreign Ministry, drafted a lengthy memorandum for the French ambassador in London. It was a veritable political testament, and preparatory to the time when these men must carry on after Poincaré's fall. The two experts sent the note directly to Millerand for approval, bypassing the premier, thence to London, on 18 February 1924.

The Committee of Experts, Seydoux's draft began, would soon produce a solution to Europe's troubles. For the first time in four years Germany understood the necessity of accepting and executing a reasonable plan of reparations—it was the consummation of the Ruhr policy. As for France, her financial situation precluded an indefinite wait for settlement. France sought three goals: (1) immediate accord on reparations, permitting France to balance her budget and repair the

[106] Note Seydoux, "Conversation Seydoux-Schacht," 24-25 Jan. 1924: MAE Pap. Millerand, Réparations XXIV, nos. 85-92, 97-98.

[107] Note Vignon, "Conversation avec le Général Destiker," 1 Feb. 1924; Note Seydoux, "Question des chemins de fer—Régie," 4 Feb. 1924: MAE Pap. Millerand, vol. 21, nos. 2-5, 25-32.

devastated regions; (2) settlement of war debts so that payment would be contingent on the amounts received from Germany; (3) security guarantees, perhaps through the League of Nations. These were not unjust demands, and Seydoux concluded in frustration: "Express this point of view with urgency to the British government. I am sure an accord can be reached, and the British might then abandon their campaign of perpetual unification against France of all the forces of Europe. For they will finally be convinced that we have never had the idea of pursuing a policy of encirclement or dislocation of Germany."[108]

With this appeal to Ramsay MacDonald, the French government effectively surrendered its former ambitions. The following day a temperamental Poincaré found himself isolated in the council of ministers on the rail issue.[109] On 22 February the experts concluded that German rail unity was imperative for German economic health. The implication for France was clear—three days later Peretti hosted an interdepartmental meeting to begin anew the examination of French security. No politicians were present, only permanent officials and military officers. Instead of ambitious plans for dismemberment of Germany or Anglo-American military conventions, the French government would be reduced to asking for something—anything—in return for evacuation of the Cologne zone of occupation, set for January 1925.

A month later, on 17 March 1924, Peretti hinted to the British ambassador that Poincaré was desirous of reopening negotiations for a Franco-British security pact.[110] His policy had come full circle. Meanwhile, the results of the new security study confirmed the mood of defeat in the French capital. Assistant Director for Political Affairs Jules Laroche now judged that Rhenish autonomy *per se* was not a security guarantee. What mattered was the effectiveness of the Rhenish demilitarization. "The most effective guarantee," he believed, "would consist of the conclusion of pacts between the interested nations." He wanted a defensive alliance with Britain, a nonaggression pact with Germany, and international guarantees of Germany's eastern boundaries.[111] The military technicians agreed that Rhenish autonomy was insufficient: "Whatever solution may evolve, it would be illusory and

[108] Let. MAE (redaction Seydoux/Peretti) to St. Aulaire, 18 Feb. 1924: MAE Pap. Millerand, Réparations XXIV, nos. 157-162. See Pap. Millerand, vol. 21, nos. 33-44, for information on the composition of this letter.

[109] Note Vignon, "Conseil du Cabinet," 19 Feb. 1924: MAE Pap. Millerand, Réparations XXIV, nos. 163-169.

[110] Tel. #173, 175 Phipps to F.O., C4545, 6/1288/18, 17 Mar. 1924: PRO FO 371, vol. 9813, nos. 23-28.

[111] MAE Memo, service de la Direction Politique, "Étude des Garanties de Sécurité," 21 Feb. 1924 (distributed 28 Mar. 1924): MAE Pap. Millerand, vol. 41, no. 57.

dangerous to sacrifice firm guarantees for the creation of an autonomous Rhenish state."[112] The French no longer had the stomach for separatism.

The abrupt turnabout in Franco-British relations bore fruit in mid-March. The second collapse of the franc reached a climax on 8 March, with the pound equal to 117.54 francs. The following day, a Sunday, Millerand summoned an extraordinary council of ministers. There Poincaré reluctantly agreed to solicit Anglo-American support for the French currency. On 13 March New York and London threw their weight behind the franc. Morgan alone contributed $89 million to the effort of the Banque de France. The franc immediately rebounded to 92.25 against the pound, and reached 62.15 by mid-April. But the French currency, and foreign policy, were hostages.

The electoral campaign in France moved into full swing during these weeks. While Poincaré had reversed the tide of devaluation, his policy of force against Germany and defiance of Britain was judged a failure. To an electorate weary of war and international discord, the platform of the Bloc National was unattractive. Millerand desperately put aside the traditional neutrality of his office in order to campaign for the Right. He feared the Cartel des Gauches under Radical Edouard Herriot would "sacrifice the Ruhr victory and plunge France into deeper financial doldrums." But the anti-government trend was unmistakable. Presented with a pensions bill on 28 March, the Chamber of Deputies revolted and defeated the finance minister by seven votes in a vote of confidence. Millerand asked Poincaré to form a new ministry. Hoping to recover lost political ground, Poincaré sacked all his ministers but two—Maginot and Le Trocquer, the spokesmen for military and metallurgical might. But the Left had taken a lesson from Millerand's 1920 tactics, and conducted a skillful coalition campaign against the government.

On 9 April 1924 the Dawes Commission spoke. It recommended a loan of 800 million gold marks for the stabilization of a German gold currency and the resumption of reparations payments, one billion gold marks the first year, rising to 2.5 billion. The German payments would be guaranteed by a lien held by the Reparations Commission on the entire German rail system and by the receipts of government monopolies and customs. The experts heralded the advent of American capital to Europe—the loan would only be the first of many—but they endorsed unequivocally the economic unity of Germany. The original and narrowest of Poincaré's Ruhr policies, that of forcing America to

[112] Note Generals Debeney and Destiker, "Note sur les garanties de sécurité," 20 May 1924: MAE Pap. Millerand, vol. 41, nos. 65-87.

finance reparations and reconstruction without a moratorium or reduction of the German debt, was a success. But that limited policy had been engulfed long before in the flood of increased ambitions resulting from the escalation of the Ruhr struggle. Those ambitions were unsatisfied.

Three days after the Dawes report became public, Stresemann accepted it as a basis for a reparations accord. In Paris there arose another controversy *in camera* between Poincaré and almost everyone else in the government. Poincaré was reluctant to approve a plan that could be termed, at best, a Pyrrhic victory. He was especially piqued by the total silence on the war debt issue in London and Washington. To be sure, the Dawes Plan did not seek a reduction in the German debt, so France retained her bargaining tool in the war debt question, but Poincaré preferred to settle the two problems simultaneously.[113] Seydoux agreed that America's unwillingness to deal with reparations and debts together was troublesome, but he saw no course for France but integral acceptance of the experts' report.[114]

The finance ministry singled out the loan as irresistible. It considered the experts' plan a French diplomatic success that only the Ruhr occupation could have achieved.[115] That much was true. On 20 April Poincaré instructed Louis Barthou to pronounce France's favorable reaction to the Dawes report. He made no promises about evacuation of the Ruhr. He intended to reserve that card in his hand until the "second peace conference" convened. The grand conference did take place, in London in July and August 1924, but Poincaré was not there.

On 11 May the French electorate repudiated the Bloc National. The parties of the Cartel des Gauches won 328 seats out of 582, and on the eve of the new Chamber's mandate, 31 May 1924, Poincaré resigned. He had consolation in knowing that if the French *position acquise* in Western Germany was to be given up in a questionable compromise, at least it would be his successor who must swallow the defeat. But Poincaré's forced return in 1924 to reconciliation and concession, and the continuity of his reparations goals since January 1922, meant that he could also claim whatever victories his successor might achieve as his own. Finally, by announcing at once his intention to resign instead of fighting the Leftist majority as Millerand would do, Poincaré reasserted his republicanism and avoided too close an association with the Right. The man most responsible for France's financial debacle in

[113] Tel. Poincaré to St. Aulaire, 17 Apr. 1924: MAE Pap. Millerand, vol. 22, no. 162.

[114] Note Seydoux, "Comparaison entre les differents accords de réparations," 19 Apr. 1924: MAE Pap. Millerand, vol. 22, nos. 180-190.

[115] Let. Ministry of Finance (remise par François-Marsal) to PdC, 19 Apr. 1924: MAE Pap. Millerand, Réparations XXII, nos. 191-211.

1924, he would return in 1926 as champion of the franc. The rival of Briand and assassin of his 1921-1922 government, he would return as Briand's great collaborator in the politics of detente after Locarno. But he left office with his mission unfulfilled.

Far from being the ardent defender of the Treaty of Versailles, as historians often portray him, Poincaré was the treaty's bitterest and most incisive political critic. But Poincaré's hope for moderate, internationally sanctioned revisionism was as unrealistic as the treaty itself. He sought a new balance of power, but he was forced to do so at a time when the resources of France, drained by war, were unequal to the task. Instead, Germany herself must be weakened or harnessed if balance was to be maintained. Thus, the system must also be static; the free play of international forces usually providing the dynamic for balance could only work to the detriment of France. The only hope for such a system lay in the full participation of Britain as a European power—and in her acceptance of French leadership on the continent. Tardieu had realized as much in 1919. But France was obliged to court British commitments at a time when imperial and domestic economic pressures pulled Britain away from the continent—and at a time when the balance of power itself was in disrepute.

The task of French postwar diplomacy was to bring Britain to see the short-sightedness of her policy. Poincaré always intended to turn back to London after the Ruhr occupation. But the passive resistance threw off his calculations. It made the Ruhr operation vastly more expensive, thus increasing, not decreasing, France's ultimate dependence on the Anglo-Saxons. Yet at the same time it gave the French reason rightly to expect more from the struggle. So France entered the climactic period of late 1923 all the more out of step with her real international power. Perhaps Millerand was right. Given French dependence, the Anglo-Saxons could always deny France the fruits of victory if given the chance. France might as well scrap her hopes for a "legitimate" settlement and see what she could extort from prostrate Germany. Yet that was a revolutionary foreign policy. It would bespeak the end of hopes for a restoration of something approximating the pre-1914 world and portend instead the authoritarianism and autarky of the 1930s. Poincaré's moderation prohibited such a course. To finance an aggressive foreign policy through domestic inflation and renunciation of the gold standard was unthinkable. But this forces the conclusion that Poincaré's policy was self-defeating. Deeply conservative, he sought peace and stability, but he also sought to restore France to her rightful place among the Great Powers. The goals were incompatible; that does not make them unworthy.

When the Cartel des Gauches took its seats in the Palais Bourbon on 1 June 1924, President Millerand attempted to cling to the presidential authority he had compromised during the electoral campaign. His appointment of François-Marsal as premier moved the Chambers to impeach. On 13 June 1924 they named the president of the Senate, Gaston Doumergue, to be president of the Republic. Seven and a half years before, Doumergue had drafted the treaty with tsarist Russia granting France a free hand on the Left Bank of the Rhine. Now he appointed Edouard Herriot to form a government dedicated to the liquidation of the French Rhineland policy.

·9·

CONCLUSION: THE DEFEAT OF FRENCH REVISIONISM

For France the world war was a struggle for survival. The peacemaking process was her struggle to survive as a Great Power. France was exhausted in 1918, but she refused to play dead. For if the war had drained her strength, victory enhanced her self-image. The greatest battles were fought on French soil and French sacrifices had been the greatest; accordingly, it was the French capital that played host to the world's dignitaries in 1919. No matter that the cost of the ordeal threatened to make of France a second-rate power; to the surviving citizens she was not only the glorious victor, she was again "la grande Nation." Clemenceau proclaimed France the "soldier of Humanity"—Maurice Barrès expected a regenerated France to provide the example of "moral grandeur and disciplined energy" a battered world would need to rebuild. But if publicists, generals, and politicians in that ecstatic spring of 1919 envisioned France as the mistress of Europe, the bureaucrats in the ministries shouldered the responsibility of making that vision real. The confused and desperate policies of treaty execution and revision reflected the enormous goals: not only to make permanent the "victory" of 1918, but to erase the "defeat" of the war itself. Unless France were made a victor, then Germany was not defeated; the alternative to a French peace was a *Paix boche*.

THE FRENCH RHINELAND POLICIES: ALTERNATIVES FOR SECURITY

To Maurice Barrès, Klecker de Balazuc, and Jacques Bainville, to the *Comité de la Rive Gauche du Rhin*, and the expansionist Right, France's mission on the Rhine was an article of faith, a destiny. To Marshal Foch and the thousands for whom his opinion was sacred, the dire military need for the Rhine barrier was also an article of faith. But for the cabinets, France's postwar initiatives in the Rhineland were expressions of policy, and only for special pleaders such as Paul Tirard and Joseph Degoutte was Rhenish policy the unalterable key to postwar strategy. In fact, there was little continuity to the Rhenish policies followed by the Paris governments between 1918 and 1924. Governments changed, so did the hopes and strategies of premiers and permanent advisors in the Quai d'Orsay, so did the policies of the nations with which France was dealing. But all the Rhenish policies followed in those years had some common characteristics. They represented means, not ends in themselves as for the Rhineland myth-makers, and they were all substitute or secondary policies made necessary by the failure of Versailles. Far from being the sole and unswerving goal of French planners, the total control France came to assume over the Left Bank of the Rhine and the Ruhr, and the separatist crisis of 1923-1924, were resorted to out of need and were not entirely deliberate. With the possible exception of Alexandre Millerand, postwar French premiers did not desire to be revisionist, to overthrow the work of the Peace Conference. Rather, all of France desired a treaty that assured security from renewed aggression, reconstruction, and prosperity, commensurate with France's sacrifice—and victory—in the war. The political, financial, and economic clauses of the treaty were designed to satisfy France's postwar needs—as long as the treaty was "integrally implemented," as Tardieu demanded from the Chamber. It was the failure to execute the treaty that rendered his hopes obsolete, and it was the belief that the treaty was impossible of execution, given America's defection and Britain's obstruction, that gave birth to French revisionism.

But was the Treaty of Versailles not the principal barrier to European reconciliation? Were not Germany and the Anglo-Saxon powers justified in jettisoning the treaty and resisting France's futile policy of antagonism? The experiment cannot be re-run, but it is debatable whether French policy was as short-sighted as the British claimed. The Treaty of Versailles cannot be shown to be deleterious, for it was never "tried." It was American, British, and, above all, German revisionism that drove French statesmen beyond the treaty into French revisionism. A true fulfillment policy on the part of Berlin not only would have pacified France by granting the objects of her foreign policy, but the disarmament, economic restructuring, and tax reform required for fulfillment would have gone far to execute the social revolution in Germany that stopped short in 1918.

Which policy best served German democracy: Britain's diplomatic cloak thrown over the Weimar Republic, which only served to defend the power of the great industrialists and parties of reaction, or France's frontal assault on the very elements that worked against treaty fulfillment and domestic social reform? To be sure, French policy was not born of a will for social reform—it aimed at preserving France's own conservative social order as well as her international position. And the triumph of German Social Democracy on the strength of Entente bayonets is equally unthinkable. As Adenauer suggested in 1921, perhaps only a rightist authoritarian regime could marshal the nation's support for fulfillment. But a firmer British stance in the first years of the treaty regime could well have obliged German industrialists to be more accommodating to their French counterparts and to the struggling Berlin regime. They could hardly have been less so as it was. A.J.P. Taylor has argued that it was the Franco-British split, not American defection, that destroyed the postwar dream of lasting peace.[1] The Entente states together did have the power to force German fulfillment, which alone could have stripped Germany of her potential for another bid for hegemony, whatever its influence on German domestic evolution.

Given Allied and German resistance to fulfillment, the French victory of 1918 was inconsummate. Invariably the alternatives sought for the treaty system were found in the only territory where France could exert direct pressure on Germany, and indirect pressure on Britain and the United States—in the occupied Rhineland. The first concern was for military security, without which other accomplishments would be futile. French security thinking was uncoordinated, but essentially all French agencies envisioned a static defense, be it an eternal anti-German coalition of the Western Allies, containment based on the Rhine barrier in the west and the Polish-Czech barrier in the east, or fortifications within France, a Maginot Line. The French did not reject collective security if it could be brought to mean a guarantee of the status quo. But British opposition scotched the plan for an effective security plank in the League of Nations charter and the League Draft Treaty of Mutual Assistance. Briand and Poincaré both considered the virtues of a bilateral alliance or regional pact with Britain, but again found the British unwilling to "put teeth" into a pact. As Curzon explained to St. Aulaire in 1922, it was the French desire for a static Europe that clashed hopelessly with the British concept of normalization. Britain foresaw eventual relaxation of the strictures on Germany until her very integration, economic interdependence, and membership in the League sufficed to ensure her peaceful intent. In practice, this meant compromise on Germany's eastern borders, the effacement of France's eastern barrier. It meant the gradual recovery of German military and economic power within a liberal system committed to loosening, not tightening, the bonds in response to Germany's resurgence. Britain refused to underwrite the Treaty of Versailles, and her revisionism posited a dynamic, fluctuating Europe likely only to change to the detriment of France. French governments had little choice but to pursue a security policy of material guarantees. When the

[1] A.J.P. Taylor, *Origins of the Second World War* (New York, 1961), pp. 34-43.

decisive moment was reached in 1923, however, Poincaré faced the same difficulty as Clemenceau in 1919: he could force a restructuring of Germany, but he could not legitimize such a victory.

The second international dependency of postwar France was financial. Reparations served three purposes for France: they provided the means to rebuild the devastated regions; they provided credits to balance against the huge war debts insisted upon by the United States and Britain; they provided a guarantee against German economic hegemony in postwar Europe. But the manner in which Germany avoided payment, by continuous inflation, defeated these purposes. Paris supported reconstruction herself with huge deficits that weakened the franc and fed domestic inflation. Germany pointed to her bankruptcy as cause for massive reduction of the German debt, imperiling the French war debt position. Yet Germany was recovering economically at an alarming rate. Germany was gaining through the peace, Poincaré feared, all she had aimed for in war. The alternative was sanctions on the Rhine, then seizure of a political guarantee in the Ruhr, to persuade the Anglo-Americans to see the French position, and in any case to harness German economic might.

Finally, a prosperous and independent France required a healthy, expansive heavy industry. The twentieth century, Yves Le Trocquer observed, was the century of steel. The war clearly demonstrated the relation between economic capacity and military potential, and French strategists in the interwar period tended even to overestimate the equation. Again, the Allies granted the legitimacy of French demands for economic handicaps vis-à-vis Germany. Again, the failure of Germany to comply and the unwillingness of Britain to force compliance with the coal deliveries provided French governments with the need and the excuse to pursue an alternate policy based on extension of French control in Western Germany, this time over distribution of Europe's raw materials.

Thus, French Rhenish policies were all in substitution for the decrepit Treaty of Versailles. Like the treaty itself, they represented both French fear and ambition. All were revisionist, and based, to varying degrees, on lucid analysis of the requirements for long-term European stability–all, that is, except the separatist policy. From Clemenceau to Poincaré, French premiers and senior officials of the Quai d'Orsay entertained separatism, even if they despaired of the movement's goals. The policy was not the result of analysis, but of myths and misconceptions. The power of separatism and of Franco-Rhenish affinities was only an element of the propagandists' faith, yet the government adopted the separatist movement, found justifications for it, and allowed it to discredit the entire French effort vis-à-vis Germany. It was not only a political venture, but a cultural venture. It contributed, through the Celtic-Teutonic, Catholic-Protestant, and Latin-Germanic appositions, to the racialism and political Catholicism gaining momentum after the war. It appealed to French cultural chauvinism as well as nationalism, by reawakening old feelings of tutelage over less civilized Germany, feelings that had been purged in 1870-1871. The Rhenish separatist policy also reflected the heightened faith in propaganda that characterized postwar Europe. The war experience trained officials in every belligerent country in the use of propaganda, trained policy makers to think in terms of it; the Russian revolution, perhaps, permitted them to overestimate its effectiveness. The Franco-Rhenish propaganda was self-defeating in the Rhineland, but among Frenchmen it was potent enough for politicians and journalists to proclaim the Franco-Rhenish dream, for officials and intelligence agents to patronize that dream, for ministers and diplomats to permit it to affect their policies.

The French Rhineland policies as a whole exemplified another element of the postwar turmoil that pointed to the triumph of European integration after World War II. The Peace Conference was to be the triumph of liberal internationalism, but it also sought to consecrate national self-determination as the guiding principle of world politics. That very effort sufficed to demonstrate the arbitrariness of national boundaries, the imperfection of the system of the national state sovereignty. Instead of sheltering national rights, the Peace Conference provided for minorities' rights clauses, neutral cities, corridors, and ports, territories under one nation's political control, or under international control, and under the economic control of another. It limited or eliminated sovereign rights of certain nations, and transferred them to other nations, or to international bodies. It engaged not only in the alteration of frontiers and commercial privileges, but in a process of *dévalorisation de frontières*.[2] National sovereignties and economic and political unities overlapped in an attempt to create, self-consciously, a just and functional international system. Foch's "military border on the Rhine," eventually diluted to the Rhenish demilitarization clauses of the treaty, began this process of overlapping sovereignties, which Wilson and Lloyd George came to accept as a practical means of compromise between rival national states. French Rhenish policies in subsequent years fitted this trend. Without purporting to alter Rhenish political ties, French governments assumed

[2] Georges Berlia, *Le problème international de la sécurité de la France*, Cours de grands problèmes politiques contemporains (Paris, 1967), pp. 434-439.

one after another of Germany's sovereign rights until, as Adenauer said in November 1923, Berlin no longer had a single means of making itself felt in the occupied territories. The French were sincere in denying annexationist goals—they sought instead to control German resources, or to deny control to Berlin, to occupy German territory, or to deny occupation to Germany. Together with the efforts at cartelization of heavy industry, the Rhenish policies were integrationist and, in that sense, progressive. But they were based on coercion, not mutual interest, and were backed by insufficient force. As long as the imbalance of economic and demographic strength existed between France and Germany, secure integration required prior political guarantees. Neither Germany nor Britain offered France those guarantees.

The approach of the four principal postwar governments of France between 1918 and 1924 to the Rhenish occupation and the opportunities afforded by it reflected their images of the Treaty of Versailles and its possibility of fulfillment. Clemenceau sacrificed France's Rhenish security demands in favor of the Anglo-American alliances because he accepted Wilson's assurances that the Senate would not repudiate the American president. When the Senate showed signs of doing precisely that, Clemenceau reluctantly approved Tirard's first recommendations for a policy of propaganda and intrigue. The final defeat of the treaty in America early in 1920 destroyed the security settlement in the estimation of all subsequent governments. Millerand and Paléologue also showed little interest in the crippled treaty in other areas. Viewing the sanctions clauses strictly as tools, they pursued a revisionist policy in Germany and in the Danubian basin. A firm hold on the Rhine seemed all the more vital as National Bolshevism and the Soviet advance threatened the existence of Poland.

Aristide Briand continued the emphasis on a continental security system resting on firm alliances in the east, but he and Berthelot otherwise attempted to bring this system into line with the Treaty of Versailles. Briand and Berthelot rejected German and Danubian federalism, and abandoned economic sanctions or favoritism on the Left Bank of the Rhine. Instead, they pursued a policy of fulfillment in cooperation with Germany. It was a novel experiment both for France and Germany, but its fate only confirmed the opinion of revisionists. Fulfillment was a political failure. French and German industrialists, British diplomacy, and the German inflation of 1921 combined to destroy it.

Raymond Poincaré had no faith in the Treaty of Versailles, but he sought also to avoid the coercive revisionist program urged on him by others in the government and by an increasingly restless Chamber. He could not make concessions, he could only threaten an occupation of the Ruhr. From this bargaining position he petitioned Britain for a satisfactory security settlement, the United States for a new reparations plan not threatening Europe with German economic domination on the one hand or American financial domination on the other, and he petitioned Germany to accept defeat and to cooperate in metallurgical reconstruction with France as a co-equal. French pleas were rejected by indignant nations who, beset by their own problems, were unlikely to make national sacrifices on behalf of a French vision of the common good that they did not share in any case. Instead, her own allies accused France of bloody-mindedness and of exploiting the treaty to shape a French hegemony. To break the postwar deadlock, Poincaré occupied the Ruhr. The escalation of the struggle there ended all hope of postwar stabilization on the basis of the treaty. The Rhenish policies of France were forged in 1923 into the cutting edge of French revisionism, the bid for a static European polity based on material guarantees against German military resurgence or economic dominance. In such a polity, the cooperation and goodwill longed for by all nations might proceed free of fear. In such a polity, France might survive as a Great Power.

DAWES, LOCARNO, AND STEEL: PEACEMAKING, 1924-1926

Edouard Herriot undertook at once to liquidate the policy of his predecessor. His starting point was the Rhineland, where he ordered Tirard to restore the whole of the German administration expelled in 1923. The master of bureaucratic survival, Tirard immediately bowed to the new wind from Paris by suggesting a host of "ameliorations" in the conditions of occupation. Having been one of the prime movers of the Rhineland policy, Tirard now advocated a complete return of German sovereignty to the Left Bank and the retreat of the Rhineland Commission from its position of arbiter over Rhenish life. Herriot wired the simple response, "Proceed with your plans," but he refused Tirard's suggested amnesty for separatists.[3] The Rhenish siege was lifted.

French Leftist parties had opposed separatism on principle, but had been unsure whether or not the optimistic ravings of the pro-separatist bloc were justified. Herriot's collaborators now ploughed through the diplomatic files and produced reports on the Rhenish question. With the benefit of hindsight, they diagnosed the myopia characterizing

[3] Tel. Tirard to Herriot, 14 June 1924; Tel. Herriot to Tirard, Degoutte, 17 and 18 June 1924: MAE Rive Gauche, vol. 11, nos. 39-47, 66-69; vol. 45, nos. 268-271.

the Rhenish policies of Millerand, Briand, and Poincaré. Rhenish separatism, said one report, was created out of whole cloth by the Quai d'Orsay and the French occupation authorities. It was doomed to failure, and the resulting alienation of Britain and the United States was especially harmful to French interests. How could this policy have survived for four years? It was possible, the report concluded, because of the systematic misleading of French opinion by propagandists, and because of the government's obligation to take account of that opinion. Especially striking was the "absolute ignorance of realities in the Rhineland found within France's directing circles."[4] The French High Commissariat, another report demonstrated, was bloated and incompetent, with interpreters who hardly knew German, and political agents who encouraged what they thought to be government policy rather than discerning and reporting the truth. The French occupation was rotten, the duty of the Herriot government clear: "Il faut civiliser le Haut-Commissariat Français!"[5] These verdicts passed on French Rhineland policy were never seriously challenged, and its practitioners, Poincaré among them, retreated into silence. The separatist adventure became an episode condemned by mutual agreement to obscurity.

When the grand London Conference on reparations opened on 16 July 1924, Herriot arrived full of doubt, not confidence. His month in office had made him conscious of the weaknesses Poincaré had fought to dissipate through the Ruhr policy. The Dawes Plan would no doubt begin auspiciously, but what if the Germans defaulted again? What freedom of action would France enjoy? Would sanctions again be made possible? Would service of Germany's loan from the United States take precedence over reparations? What would become of the present occupation of the Ruhr—must the Franco-Belgians evacuate at once, before proof of Germany's goodwill? What of the interallied war debts? In sum, would the resumption of reparations by Germany be purchased at the cost of French independence in European politics and world finance?

The only leverage Herriot retained in all these questions was the Ruhr pledge procured by Poincaré in a policy Herriot himself had opposed. Yet he had promised the Chamber that he would not agree to any diminution of French treaty rights. This promise reflected Herriot's buoyant optimism following electoral victory and his faith in

[4] Note Lambert, "Note sur la politique rhénane," June 1924: MAE Rive Gauche, vol. 45, nos. 299-305.

[5] Note, "Notre action en Rhénanie," 1924: Edouard Herriot, unpublished private papers, Ministère des Affaires Étrangères-Paris (hereafter cited as MAE Pap. Herriot), vol. 15, dos. 11.

international liberal cooperation. It could not be fulfilled. On 20 July, he wrote President Doumergue: "What difficulties! The need for German acceptance, the interpretation of the Dawes report, the question of evacuation of the Cologne zone, the evacuation of the Ruhr, the interallied debts—on all these questions we are pressured incessantly. What arms do we have in our hands today? They are few and feeble."[6] Rather than joining hands with the Labourite Ramsay MacDonald in the triumph of internationalist harmony, Herriot found himself isolated, a supplicant. That his bargaining tools were "few and feeble" was due to the weakness of French finances. Poincaré could have done little differently had he been at London instead of Herriot. It was the force of world diplomatic and financial alignment, not Herriot's ideological predilections, that made the Conference of London a French surrender.[7]

The first resolution concerned the problem of future sanctions. American investors refused to lend to Germany under threats of a recurrence of the Ruhr episode. The United States delegation ended by agreeing to participate in the Reparations Commission in case of German default, thus blocking French control of it. Herriot feared the "neutralization" of the Commission, but he could not refuse without losing the loan.[8] Yet the American bankers, seconded by the diplomats who insisted that their hands were tied, still feared further sanctions against Germany and demanded the final emasculation of French treaty enforcement rights. If the Reparations Commission should vote sanctions in the future by a majority decision (i.e., over American and/or British dissent), the question would be appealed to an arbitration commission, thence to the International Court at the Hague.

On the other outstanding issues Herriot was also obliged to surrender. German interest payments on the loan would take precedence over reparations. France would evacuate the Ruhr within twelve months of a reparations agreement, and Allied personnel would relinquish the Rhenish railroads at once. On 16 August 1924, the Allied and German delegates signed the final protocol of the Conference of London. Although the Reichstag quickly ratified, the rancorous protests from every wing of German politics against the "burdens" of the set-

[6] Pers. Let. Herriot to Doumergue, 20 July 1924: MAE Pap. Herriot, vol. 13, dos. Conférence de Londres.

[7] The definitive work on the French currency crisis, the London Conference, and the launching of the Dawes Plan is Stephen A. Schuker, *The End of French Predominance in Europe: The Financial Crisis of 1924 and the Adoption of the Dawes Plan* (Chapel Hill, 1976). See also the works cited in Chapter 7, note 50.

[8] Let. Herriot to President, CdR, 25 Sept. 1924: MAE Pap. Herriot, vol. 5, dos. Réparations.

tlement ought to have left little doubt about the prospects of appeasing even a "democratic" Germany.

Considering the apparent strength of the French position in November 1923, the final reparations agreement can only be judged a crushing defeat for France. American capital would flow to Europe, permitting in time the stabilization of European currencies without a moratorium or debt reduction for Germany. But the war debt question remained untouched, to trouble Allied governments over the next seven years. Germany rebounded handsomely to become the first belligerent to tie its currency to gold, while the franc continued to fluctuate and undergo devaluation over the following years. The sacrifice of French rights to impose sanctions and the planned retreat from the Ruhr and Rhine meant the end of an exclusively French German policy, and reliance upon the increasingly isolationist Anglo-Americans for a balance to Germany. American policy consisted instead of financing Germany's return to industrial dominance, lending her far more than she would pay in reparations, while simultaneously squeezing France to pay her war debts, disarm, and hasten the dismantling of Versailles!

Thus, the occupation of the Ruhr failed in its national object. Perhaps Poincaré was too sanguine in seeking through independent action to educate his allies at a time when both France and Germany, in Seydoux's words, "sat on the same bench" before the creditor nations. He overestimated, certainly, the investment France could afford to make, given the fiscal timidity of the Third Republic, to revise satisfactorily the 1919 settlements. France lacked the means, even if her leaders had had the will to "make Europe." But political security was the *sine qua non* of the kind of economic integration of Germany that Britain and France both desired, each in its own way. Poincaré would have seconded Tardieu's admonition that "there is no longer room for anyone's hegemony." He was engaged in a struggle for long-term parity, then partnership with Germany lest his allies' unwillingness to commit themselves to containment leave France alone against the German Goliath. The Dawes Plan, by reaffirming the Versailles Treaty's ratification of German economic and political unity, and in removing the threat of future French sanctions, only justified French feelings of the insecurity of the continental order.

Herriot's recognition of the immediate security interests of France came as quickly as his understanding of the reparations issues. After all, Peretti, Seydoux, and the military were there to brief him on what was at stake. Herriot took up the cry of previous governments when he announced that France considered no Rhenish evacuations possible until her security claims had been met. Given the failure of the Rhenish policies, this meant a security pact, and Herriot adopted the policy of his predecessors in refusing to permit withdrawal from the Cologne zone until a pact was concluded.

Herriot's pretext for delaying the first evacuation, set for 10 January 1925, was Germany's secret and overt violations of the disarmament obligations. In February 1925 the new government of Stanley Baldwin and Foreign Secretary Austen Chamberlain entertained the notion of a security pact, and Lord D'Abernon dropped the appropriate hint in Berlin. The famous demarche of Gustav Stresemann on 9 February 1925 began the train of events leading to Locarno. Herriot's government fell in April, but Briand returned as foreign minister to carry through the negotiations over the next six months. On 5 October 1925 the Locarno Conference opened.[9] It produced five treaties, of which the most familiar was the Rhineland Pact. Germany, France, Britain, Belgium, and Italy all contracted to maintain the inviolability of Germany's western boundaries and the observance of Articles 42 and 43 of the Treaty of Versailles. Germany, France, and Belgium renounced war among themselves and engaged to submit to arbitration any insoluble differences arising among them. The other four agreements were arbitration conventions between Germany and France, Belgium, Poland, and Czechoslovakia. On the strength of the Locarno accords, Allied troops evacuated the northern Rhenish zone of occupation. Four years later, in connection with negotiations for the Young Plan of reparations, the French agreed to evacuate the remainder of the Rhineland. They did so in 1930, five years before the treaty-stipulated date.

The Locarno treaties and the attending spirit of cooperation between the nations of Western Europe comprised the security solution accepted by a French government after seven years of travail following 11 November 1918. The demographic and economic imbalance between Germany and all her neighbors had not been altered, nor had any material measures been provided by which the Allies could ensure that Germany would not be able to marshal her military resources. Even the Disarmament Control Commission departed from Germany. Collective security was left to depend on German goodwill and con-

[9] The Locarno Conference and the diplomacy of the later 1920s have most recently been treated with insight by Jon Jacobson, *Locarno Diplomacy: Germany and the West, 1925-1929* (Princeton, 1972), and Edward D. Keeton in his excellent, as yet unpublished dissertation, "Briand's Locarno Policy; French Economics, Politics, and Diplomacy, 1925-1929," (Ph.D. dissertation, Yale University, 1975). See also Helmuth Rössler, ed., *Locarno und die Weltpolitik, 1924-1932* (Göttingen, 1969), and transcripts of the symposium "European Security in the Locarno Era," Mars Hill College, North Carolina, 1975.

FIGURE 7. "Vindication: Poincaré to Clemenceau: 'And you there, do you still believe in the Treaty of Versailles?' " H. P. Gassier, 1924. © S.P.A.D.E.M. Paris 1977.

tinued vigilance by the potential enemies of Germany. But as long as that goodwill and vigilance obtained, treaties were unnecessary. Should they lapse, the lack of an intrinsic balance of power meant that collective security lost even its deterrent value.

Observing from his Senate seat in 1925, Poincaré deplored the language of Locarno. "England is no longer the ally of France and Belgium," he wrote, "but the guarantor of Germany as well." If France was "guaranteed" against German aggression, so was Germany guaranteed against French enforcement expeditions. France could still reoccupy the Rhine in case of demilitarization violations, but Poincaré had warned in 1919 that such a reoccupation would probably be a diplomatic impossibility. "England," Poincaré concluded, "becomes the arbiter of Franco-German relations."

A second feature of the Rhineland Pact that Poincaré had fought against during the security negotiations of 1922 was the failure to make German violation of the Rhine *casus foederis*. Locarno recognized Articles 42 and 43 of the treaty, the Rhineland demilitarization, but not Article 44, which declared violation to be "an act of hostility against the signatories." The Locarno treaties were not the "Paix rhénane."[10] Most problematical for European peace was the failure of Locarno to bring Britain to participate in the containment of Germany in central and eastern Europe. The arbitration treaties left open the possibility of revision of Germany's eastern boundaries, while France's retreat from the Rhine left Poland and Czechoslovakia naked before German aggression. The French alliances in the east went hand-in-hand with Foch's offensive military strategy against Germany, which in turn depended on French access to the Rhine. Locarno undermined Foch's position, while it underlined Pétain's defensive strategy. Just two months later the *Conseil Supérieur de la Guerre* entrusted to General Guillaumat the final planning for what became the Maginot Line. In the wake of defeat after defeat at the hands of her own "allies," the *sauve qui peut* psychology, with its destabilizing impact on the rest of Europe, secured its grip on French strategy.

When negotiation for the Dawes Plan reached fruition in 1924, Jacques Seydoux, the Ministry of Commerce, and French businessmen turned their attention to the regulation of Franco-German commercial relations. After 1918, first the French government and then the Ruhr barons refused compromise between the continental metallurgies in the hope of destroying the other's bargaining position. Following the Ruhr struggle, with both industries in turmoil, a will to

[10] Article Poincaré, "Après Locarno," 1925: MAE Grande Bretagne, vol. 72, nos. 7-19.

compromise evidenced itself. A preliminary accord prepared for the end of the treaty commercial regime in January 1925; then by 1926 the negotiations produced the Continental Steel Cartel and the Franco-German commercial treaty. As with the Dawes Plan and Locarno, the cartel seemed a tactical success for France, but a strategic failure.[11]

Robert Pinot of the *Comité des Forges* opened the period of reconciliation in May 1924 by calling for Franco-German industrial cooperation, the "foundation of peace." How much French metallurgy recognized its weakness can be seen in Pinot's reference to a "return to the economic *status quo ante bellum*." His goals were limited, he said, and would pose no threat to Britain. French metallurgy sought no hegemony, only to produce for its own market and to be competitive elsewhere.[12] Although French industry certainly expanded at the expense of Germany as a result of the Treaty of Versailles, it failed to achieve the near parity expected from the recovery of Lorraine. German steel potential dropped by 6.7 million tons after 1918, but by 1925 German metallurgy had recovered from the Ruhr struggle to the point where production levels in the territories in German hands before and after Versailles were 100 percent of the 1913 figures. Owing to the energetic expansion and modernization of the Ruhr plant in the period 1919-1922, however, the total German production in 1925, 12.2 million tons, represented 57 percent capacity. European steel suffered with a shrunken market after the war. If economic recovery should increase demand, Germany was ready to supply it.

French metallurgists were not without some advantages, however. French pig iron production recovered from its low point after the war and by 1925 showed an increase of 39 percent over 1913. But the lack of coke and markets told in the production of steel. French and Saar steel furnaces had a capacity for 12 million tons in 1925. They produced 7.4 million tons, or 61.5 percent capacity. Rolling mills were at 53 percent capacity.[13] Thus, France was unable to exploit the full potential of the liberated territories, but her position was far better than in 1922. The silver lining in the cloud of financial collapse was that the depreciation of the franc improved French competitiveness abroad. For the first time since the war the British had to take measures against French dumping, not German. The tendency continued in 1926 when French

[11] On the Franco-German commercial accord and metallurgical cartel of 1926, see Jacques Bariéty, "Das Zustandekommen der Internationalen Rohstahlgemeinschaft (1926) als Alternative zum misslungenen 'Schwerindustriellen Projekt' des Versailler Vertrages," *Industrielles System*, pp. 552-568; Maier, *Recasting Bourgeois Europe*, pp. 516-545.

[12] Article Robert Pinot, 3 May 1924: MAE Pap. Millerand, vol. 23, nos. 12-13.

[13] Dresdner Bank, *The Economic Forces of the World* (Berlin, 1927), p. 37.

mills worked at about 75 percent capacity, while German mills fell to 50 percent.

Western European syndicates signed a steel accord on 30 September 1926. Germany received a starting quota of 40.46 percent of the market, increasing almost at once to 43.18 percent. France received 31.91 percent and Belgium 12.58 percent. The figures reflected the territorial changes of 1919. In 1913, the ratio of German to French steel production was over 4 to 1 (18.9 million tons to 4.7). In 1926 it was set at 1.3 to 1. The 1926 quotas can only be viewed as an economic recognition of Germany's losses at Versailles, but the political aspects of the cartel and of the commercial treaty were indicative of the defeat of French postwar industrial policy. Instead of the extremely favorable Treaty of Versailles commercial relationship, which French governments hoped to preserve through control of the Rhenish customs regime, the French accepted a freely negotiated regime. France was permitted to export metallurgical goods from Alsace-Lorraine and the Saar totaling 15 percent of the total German production of any item, with no tariff or marketing advantages. In return, the French did confer tariff concessions to German steel products and to the old South German suppliers of industries in Alsace-Lorraine, Luxembourg, and the Saar. The cartel agreement left the Germans room for their own expansion at France's expense. The quotas were reviewed every three months, and if the Germans did not feel the cartel was in their interest, there were no fewer than seven contingencies under which they could break their engagement.

The steel settlement achieved three years after the end of passive resistance ended the deadly competition between the French and German heavy industries. But it offered little security to France, for it demonstrated the same deficiencies as Locarno. France acquired a steady source of coal, but only as long as German goodwill survived. Limits were set on the expansion of German industry, but only for as long as the Germans elected voluntarily to recognize them. Most important, there was no intermixing of ownership between the Ruhr and the industries of Lorraine, Longwy, Luxembourg, and Belgium. The 1926 agreement left the national metallurgies homogeneous and uninterested in each other's fate, free to go their own way should economic emergency or domestic politics make autarky an attractive goal. European economic cooperation did not rest on a perceived community of interest.

The period of European peacemaking from 1924 to 1926 was one of utter defeat for French revisionism, for a stabilization based on material guarantees of a balance of power. Not only was the Versailles status quo not reasserted, the "new era" based on the financial, political, and economic pacts of 1924-1926 was itself meant to be temporary. The Dawes Plan was to regulate German payments for the first few years only, to be replaced by a later plan. War debts were still unsettled. The Locarno treaties failed to stabilize Germany's eastern boundaries, while French financial instability, economic inferiority, and military insecurity undercut France's will or ability to maintain its ambitious Eastern European system against a resurgent Germany. Just two years later Briand privately conceded Eastern Europe as a German economic sphere while hoping to appease Berlin with border rectifications. Revisionism favorable to German expansion was institutionalized; Europe was to be in constant flux.

Germany emerged from the period of peacemaking a political equal and an apparent force for peace and international cooperation. But Germany also emerged free to fall back into nationalism and expansionism should the temptation arise. When the false settlements collapsed in the 1930s, their repudiation could only be countered by full force, by risking the total war, the damnable repetition dreaded above all else by the generation that survived World War I. This fact marked the defeat of French policy, a policy designed to make Europe safe from Germany, whether she came to be governed by republican cabinets, by a restored monarch, or by extremists like the Bavarian Mussolini, Adolf Hitler.

EUROPEAN RECOVERY AND THE NEW DIPLOMACY

Postwar statesmen recognized that the war had changed not only the map of Europe, but the pattern of diplomatic relations. The sophisticated system of communication by written word through permanent representations gave way in part to the practice of personal conference diplomacy. The "democratization of foreign policy" developed concomitantly from the direct participation of prime ministers in the formulation and execution of policy, and from the larger role played by public opinion and interest group lobbying. This "New Diplomacy" certainly received an impetus from the precepts of Woodrow Wilson, but the conference system and "democratization" originated before 1917. The four years' emergency of the war made conference diplomacy carried on by heads of governments in conclave a habit institutionalized in the Supreme Council. Through their efforts to wring further sacrifice from exhausted armies and populations, governments became habituated to propaganda and opinion manipulation. In the war and the complex international economic tangle afterwards, citizens in turn realized how day-to-day foreign policy decisions affected their lives. Foreign policy became everyone's concern, no longer the esoteric pursuit of cosmopolitan cliques within the civil service. Old professionals rued such politicization of diplomacy. Thanks to the war, Camille Barrère noted bitterly, ambassadors had become only agents of transmission. "Politicians have replaced diplomats at these conferences and seem to believe that nations conduct business like deputies in the Palais Bourbon."[14] Historian Ludwig Zimmermann saw in these changes the stumbling blocks to international settlement in the 1920s. "The democratization of foreign policy was pursued without questioning whether this science lent itself to it."[15] Demagogues like Lloyd George and Briand played to home audiences, favored the grand gesture to real progress, and avoided compromise for domestic political considerations.

Certainly the increased imposition of domestic politics limited the flexibility of postwar diplomacy. But diplomatic style is hardly an independent or decisive variable. Poincaré could attempt after 1922 to depersonalize international relations, but he could not erase the politicization of international economics accelerated by wartime passion and postwar scarcity. However one chooses to define the "New Diplomatic" style, it was no more guilty for the spasms of stabilization in the early 1920s than the "Old Diplomacy" was for the greater catastrophe in 1914. The sources of sterility in interwar diplomacy must be sought in the immensity and novelty of postwar problems, in the perceived conflicts of interest between Germany and France, France and Britain, Britain and America, in the corporate and fiscal restraints on government in all the major powers, and, finally, in the very reticence to use state power for the management of the international economic and political system that democratic leaders carried to their tasks.

World War I accelerated the collapse of the European balance of power and the economically "liberal" noninterventionist state. If the strains of rapid industrialization and economic fluctuation with concomitant domestic political tensions, and the full blossoming of German power with concomitant international tensions, increasingly threatened European stability before 1914, how much more unsettling was the world of 1919! Gone was the consciousness of a rough balance of power; gone was the gold standard; in their place was a maze of political upheaval, market disruption, and unprecedented international indebtedness. The recognition by government experts of the magnitude

[14] MS Barrère, "Diplomatie d'hier et d'aujourd'hui," n.d. (1921 or 1922): MAE Pap. Barrère, vol. 2, nos. 184-189.

[15] Zimmermann, *Frankreichs Ruhrpolitik*, pp. 29-30.

of the dislocation, demands by all social groups for state relief and protection, and the experience of war economy all left a sense of state guardianship for national economic power and welfare that calls for business as usual could not wholly erase. But the resurgence of corporate initiative and the abiding repugnance toward state direction in the economy meant that governments were free to pursue international economic solutions only within restrictive limits set by their own distrustful and fragmented economic sectors, and within the bounds of contemporary economic theory. French and German governmental initiatives toward industrial cooperation all broke in part on the opposition of their own elites, while private industrial initiatives were blocked in turn by political considerations: French demands for prior security guarantees, German demands for the dismantling of Versailles. Before 1914 Franco-German economic integration had already raised alarms in France because of the fragility of French security. To rebuild those economic ties so vital to French prosperity and simultaneously to restore a balance of power was the task facing postwar French governments. They were powerless to discharge it.

Thus, the interwar years suffered from the growing pains of the modern directed economy—or from the death rattle of the "liberal state." A few enlightened or ambitious men glimpsed the inadequacy of old political forms and called for continuation of wartime experiments in public management—*dirigisme* at home, transnational state planning abroad. But even if state technocrats had been able to triumph over particularist interests in France and Germany, the shape of the international political and economic settlement depended ultimately on Britain and the United States. Instead of seizing on new forms of international organization, the Anglo-Americans condemned them as unnatural and hearkened back to the models of national self-determination and free international economic competition—models that seemed somehow more "natural" and thus conducive to stability. Wilson, Lloyd George, their successors, and most of the "expert" advisors they deferred to traced the origins of the Great War to the frustration of political forces that needed free expression, and not to the free expression of political and social forces that needed regulation. It was the frustration of nationalism, or the frustration of democracy, or the perverse armaments race, that bred war. To prepare for war seemed to invite it, to repress nationalism seemed to make inevitable its violent release. Economists in turn excoriated Versailles for hindering the natural play of market forces and insisted on the inevitability of Germany's "natural" economic dominance of Europe. These reasonable and humane conclusions, and the further illusion that armaments and warfare would wither away in a world of democratic national states, no doubt stemmed from a deep need to believe that the terrible suffering had had some positive effect. Instead, they only contributed to the syndrome of appeasement, thereby negating the one possible achievement of the war, the elimination of the German threat.

The interwar impotence of the Western democracies is all the more pathetic because their leaders were largely men of goodwill. The image of starving German children was a powerful one, and Allied statesmen cannot be faulted for wanting to believe that the merciful course of action toward Germany was also the realistic one. But the Anglo-American refusal to de-sanctify the national state prohibited the realization that German children could be fed, indeed the German people could again prosper, without a unified or sovereign German Reich. To be sure, Lloyd George argued eloquently that lasting peace was possible only in a political order accepted as legitimate by the German people. But the gradual reconciliation of a defeated power to a new order is unlikely unless its leaders are convinced of the impossibility of overthrowing that order by force. Legitimacy must rest on a balance of power that in turn requires a willingness on the part of the victors to fashion that balance. The year 1919 was the first example of peacemaking on a grand scale by statesmen of democratic societies. Wilson abhorred the thought of violating the "rights" of the defeated power, for it seemingly would make the democracies no more principled than the vanquished autocracies. But refusing to be corrupted by the demands of the international system will not make that system go away.

A fundamental weakness of the "New Diplomacy" derived from the attempt to banish power from the marketplace of international politics while vigorously reaffirming an economy of unrestricted international competition. British and American leaders left it largely to private individuals to manage economic reconstruction,[16] while the British and American people soon lost interest in continental political squabbles. The financiers did their best, according to their own conception of the requirements of stability. But those very requirements precluded a political structure sufficient to channel and control the economic power they endeavored to unleash. To be sure, berating the statesmen of the 1920s for not rebuilding Europe on an integrationist and dirigist model

[16] See Michael J. Hogan, *Informal Entente. The Private Structure of Cooperation in Anglo-American Economic Diplomacy, 1918-1928* (Columbia, Mo. and London, 1977); Charles P. Kindleberger, *The World in Depression, 1929-1939* (Berkeley and Los Angeles, 1973); and Robert Gilpin, *U. S. Power and the Multinational Corporation* (New York, 1975).

such as evolved after 1945 would be to repeat the error of the Whig historians who blamed the Congress of Vienna for not enshrining liberal nationalism. The barriers to such a solution after 1918 were manifold. But the fact remains that the Anglo-Americans spent the interwar years looking for excuses to do nothing. All Bonar Law could respond to Loucheur's sweeping proposals for European stabilization in 1923 was "But will Germany accept it?" Following the failure of the Bankers' Committee in 1922, J. P. Morgan observed: "That there is a great deal to be said for a weak Germany I have always thought, and I should be willing to accept [the French] decision in that direction without any question; only, I fear they will regret it because they will get no more money."[17] Bonar Law refused to see that Germany would accept only what she was obliged to accept. Why should any state act differently? Morgan failed to see that a Germany capable of reparations (and attracting American investment) would also be capable of further mischief unless precautions were taken.

Morgan's incidental remark went far to describe the dilemma faced by postwar France. She could have limited recognition of her financial claims or material guarantees of security, but not both. France's Rhineland diplomacy proved incapable of expanding those narrow options. It meant that the fiscal and economic backwardness at home and the military insecurity and economic dependence abroad, the major social and international problems plaguing France before 1914, persisted—that the sacrifices of the Great War had not availed.

[17] Pers. Let. Morgan (London) to R. W. Boyden, 15 June 1922: HI Logan Papers, Box 2.

BIBLIOGRAPHY

I. UNPUBLISHED DOCUMENTS

A. *France*

The major repository of source material for this study is the archive of the Ministère des Affaires Etrangères, Paris. The records of no single government, particularly the French, can suffice to reveal the narrative of events or policy motivations in diplomatic history. But the mass of new documentation made available by the Quai d'Orsay in 1972 adds significantly to our knowledge of the 1920s and will require fundamental rethinking of some problems. The introductory chapter of this book on French war aims was based largely on the files of the M.A.E. Series Paix, 1914-1920. French documents from World War I suffered egregious damage during the second war—many of the bound documents are photostats of partially burned or water-stained originals. Great gaps in the record do not permit a satisfactory reconstruction of French war aims policy, although the collections Conditions de la Paix A1025, especially volumes 66-67, and La France et la Paix A1155-A1164, especially volumes 162-174, reveal wartime Foreign Ministry thinking on the future of the Rhineland.

Most of the documents cited here for the first time belong to the M.A.E. Series Europe, 1918-1929. This series represents the political correspondence of the "Z" series, and is comprised for the most part of duplicates of telegrams and memoranda produced for the subdivisions and archival service of the ministry. The sheer quantity of newly released material is not, therefore, a measure of its worth. Minutes of French cabinet meetings are, as always, missing. Accounts of other important conferences and memoranda occasionally turn up in private papers but are absent in the ministry files. French politicians have traditionally been less inclined than their German or British counterparts to commit their opinions and acts to paper, but the loss of many of the original documents meant also the loss of whatever minutes or marginal notes they contained. For the period 1920 to 1924, some of the inadequacies of the ministry files are balanced by the extensive Papiers Millerand collection. During his tenure at the Elysée, Millerand insisted on receiving copies of all correspondence and accounts of important meetings. Hence, the papers are largely duplications, but also contain some rare and revealing notes. Unfortunately, no similar collections exist—or are available—for Briand, Poincaré, or key subordinates like Berthelot and Seydoux.

The nearly complete set of telegraphic correspondence in the Series Europe, 1918-1929, nevertheless forms the foundation for reconstruction of the day-to-day conduct of French diplomacy after the Paris Peace Conference. The series is arranged geographically by the name of countries. Rhineland occupation affairs are collected significantly under an autonomous heading *Rive Gauche du Rhin*. The dossiers most significant for this monograph included volumes 1-2, "Dossier général, 1919-1920," Z.29.2; 3-11, "Dossier général, 1921-1924," Z.959.1; 26-47, "Séparatisme Rhénan, 1920-1924," Z.959.2; 63-64, "Rapports mensuels de l'Armée du Rhin, 1921-1922," Z.959.3; 79-82, "Evacuation de la Zone de Cologne, 1924-1925," Z.959.3D; 94-96, "État d'ésprit des populations, 1920-1923," Z.959.5; 110-120, Régime économique et douanière, 1921-1927," Z.959.13; 177-189, "Troupes noires—dossier général, 1920-1924," Z.959.36; 210-217, "Procès-verbaux de la H.C.I.T.R., 1920-1924," Z.959.45.

French relations with other European states are generally centralized under the appropriate heading, *Pologne*, *Italie*, etc. Major international problems, such as security or reparations, are consigned to the rubric of a single key nation, such as *Grande Bretagne* 69-71, "Pacte de Sécurité, 1920-1924," Z. 284.6; *Allemagne* 457-491, "Réparations financières, 1921-1924," Z.39.10; or *Ruhr* 4-37, "Dossier général, Jan. 1923-July 1924," Z.959.44.

The value of the Quai d'Orsay's raw material is greatly enhanced when complemented with the source material of other French and foreign archives. The Service historique de l'Armée de Terre, Château de Vincennes, houses the rich Fonds Clemenceau and Ministère de Guerre archives dating from the war and armistice periods. Especially useful for the reconstruction of French occupation policy in the months after 11 November 1918 were Fonds Clemenceau, 6N53-6N82, and Renseignements Allemagne, 6N114-6N279. The military archives from the 1920s were largely destroyed and the rest are undergoing classification. Of significant value in researching the military's attitudes toward security and the German question were the bound *Procès-Verbaux* of the Conseil Supérieur de Guerre and the Conseil Supérieur de la Défense National for the postwar decade, the Rapports Politiques de l'État-Major, 2eme Bureau, Armée Française du Rhin, 1919-1924, and *L'Occupation de la Ruhr*, personnel et secret, Düsseldorf, Juillet 1924, imprimerie de l'Armée du Rhin. 100 exemplaires. Rapport d'ensemble du Général Degoutte.

A vital source for this project was the archival fund of the Haut

Commissariat Français dans les Territoires Rhénans. These documents from the offices of Tirard's commissariat in Coblenz and Max Hermant's secretariat-general in Paris are in poor condition, jammed in disorderly fashion into loose-leaf binders at the Archives Nationales, and in need of reclassification. Nevertheless, the files under the rubrics "Periode d'Armistice," "Archives du Secrétariat-Général, 1921-1930," "Archives du Cabinet," "Archives des Services des Affaires d'Occupation," and "Archives du Service Économique," contain important information on Tirard's relations with separatists, the Valot mission in Düsseldorf, and particularly the plans and efforts for the creation of a Rhenish bank.

An especially useful source for penetrating the motives and constraints on French policy is the collection of *Procès-Verbaux* of the parliamentary Commissions des Affaires Étrangères to be found in the Archives de la Chambre des Deputés, Palais Bourbon, and the Archives du Sénat, Palais de Luxembourg, Paris. These handwritten minutes of secret sessions of the commissions afford rare opportunities to observe the Président du Conseil-Foreign Minister speak extemporaneously and confidentially on crucial foreign policy issues. Although Poincaré in particular tended to be frank before his Senate colleagues, one must judge to what degree the government representative is speaking his own mind or telling the powerful parliamentary critics what they want to hear.

Whatever the value of these governmental sources, the official documents of the target country must be supplemented with available private papers and key foreign documents. Execution of policy is generally revealed in ministry correspondence; educated hypotheses as to the motivation of policy-makers can often emerge only from the observations and intelligence of allies and adversaries and from the private insights of individual statesmen. The British, Belgian, and German Foreign Ministry documents not only offer insights into the policy differences of French figures and help to place French policy within a European context, but also provide a fascinating opportunity to observe the divergence between French policy and foreign perceptions of it. As always, diplomacy in the 1920s was based as much on misunderstanding as on rational evaluation of accurate intelligence. These sources follow.

B. Great Britain

Public Record Office:
Minutes of the Cabinet (CAB 23)
Cabinet Papers (CAB 24)
Foreign Office—General Correspondence (FO 371)

C. Belgium

Archives du Ministère des Affaires Étrangères et du Commerce Extérieur:

Classement "B" (especially CLB 216-219, "Problèmes d'après-guerre de la Belgique"; CLB 302-316, "Documents diplomatiques sur les Réparations"; CLB 348-349, "Sort de la Rhénanie, 1914-1923"; CLB 351, "Occupation de la Rhénanie, 1922-1924")

Classement numeroté (especially #10, 448, "Allemagne occupée—divergences de vue des autorités militaires et civiles"; #10,469, "Commission des Réparations")

Haut-Commission Interalliée des Territoires Rhènans (especially HCITR 50-53, "Séparatisme rhénan, 1922-1924"; HCITR 100, "Banque rhénane d'émission")

Correspondance Politique, 1919-1923

D. Germany

Records of the German Foreign Office (Microfilm, National Archives). For an inventory of these documents, see George O. Kent, ed., *A Catalog of Files and Microfilm of the German Foreign Ministry Archives, 1920-1945*, 4 vols. (Stanford, 1962).

Büro des Reichsministers

Büro des Staatssekretärs

Abteilung II—Besetzte Gebiete

Geheimakten

Nachlass Stresemann

Referat Deutschland

II. UNPUBLISHED PRIVATE PAPERS

Barrère, Camille. Ministère des Affaires Étrangères. Paris.

Benoist, Charles. Institut de France. Paris.

Cambon, Paul. Ministère des Affaires Étrangères. Paris.

Canet, Louis. Ministère des Affaires Étrangères. Paris.

Curzon, George, Marquess of Kedleston. Public Record Office. London.

Dard, Emile. Ministère des Affaires Étrangères. Paris.

Dawes, Charles G. Deering Library. Evanston, Ill.

Deschanel, Paul. Archives Nationales. Paris.

Dolan, John A. Hoover Institution. Stanford.

Dorten, Hans Adam. Hoover Institution. Stanford.

Doulcet, Jean. Ministère des Affaires Étrangères. Paris.

Dresel, Ellis. Hoover Institution. Stanford.

Hanotaux, Gabriel. Ministère des Affaires Étrangères. Paris.
Harris, David. Hoover Institution. Stanford.
Herriot, Edouard. Ministère des Affaires Étrangères. Paris.
Hymans, Paul. Archives Générales du Royaume. Brussels.
Jaspar, Henri. Archives Générales du Royaume. Brussels.
Jusserand, Jules. Ministère des Affaires Étrangères. Paris.
Logan, James A. Hoover Institution, Stanford.
Loucheur, Louis. Hoover Institution. Stanford.
MacDonald, James Ramsay. Public Record Office. London.
Mangin, Charles. Archives Nationales. Paris.
Mercier, Ernest. Hoover Institution. Stanford.
Millerand, Alexandre. Ministère des Affaires Étrangères. Paris.
Pichon, Stephen. Institut de France. Paris.
———. Ministère des Affaires Étrangères. Paris.
Poincaré, Raymond. Bibliothèque Nationale. Paris.
Requin, Edouard Jean. Hoover Institution. Stanford.
Rolin-Jaequemyns, Edouard. Archives Générales du Royaume. Brussels.
Tardieu, André. Ministère des Affaires Étrangères. Paris.
———. Archives Nationales. Paris.

III. PUBLISHED DOCUMENTS

A. Belgium

Assemblée Nationale. *Annales Parlementaires de Belgique, 1918-1924.* Brussels: Imprimerie du Moniteur belge, 1921-1925.
Ministère des Affaires Étrangères. *Documents diplomatiques relatifs aux réparations (du 26 décembre 1922 au 27 août 1923).* Brussels: Imprimerie Lesigne, 1923.
Ministère des Affaires Étrangères. C. de Visscher and F. Vanlangenhove, eds. *Documents diplomatiques belges, 1920-1940.* Brussels: Palais des academies, 1964-1966.

B. France

Assemblée Nationale. *Journal officiel. Débats parlementaires. Chambre des Députés.*
Assemblée Nationale. *Journal officiel. Débats parlementaires. Sénat.*
Ministère des Affaires Étrangères. *Documents diplomatiques.* Paris: Imprimerie nationale, 1922-1924.
———. *Documents relatifs aux réparations.* Paris: Imprimerie nationale, 1922.

———. *Demande de moratorium du Gouvernement allemande à la Commission des Réparations du 14 novembre 1922.* Paris: Imprimerie nationale, 1923.
———. *Documents relatifs aux notes allemandes du 2 mai et 5 juin 1923 sur les réparations.* Paris: Imprimerie nationale, 1923.
———. *Réponse du gouvernement français à la lettre du gouvernement britannique du 11 août 1923 sur les réparations.* Paris: Imprimerie nationale, 1924.
———. *Documents relatifs aux négociations concernant les garanties de sécurité contre une agression de l'Allemagne (10 janvier 1919–7 décembre 1923).* Paris: Imprimerie nationale, 1924.
Ministère du Commerce. *Rapport general sur l'industrie française.* 2 vols. Paris: Imprimerie nationale, 1919.

C. Germany

Auswärtiges Amt. *Aktenstücke zur Reparationsfrage von 26. Dezember 1922 bis 7. Juni 1923.* Reichstag Wahlperiode no. 1-6226. Berlin: Reichsdruckerei, 1923.
———. *Notenwechsel zwischen der Deutschen und der Französischen Regierung über die separatistischen Umtriebe in den besetzten Gebiete.* Berlin: Reichsdruckerei, 1924.
Reichstag. *Verhandlungen des deutschen Reichstages, Stenographische Berichte.* Berlin: Reichsdruckerei, 1920-1924.
Statistisches Reichsamt. *Statistisches Jahrbuch für das deutsche Reich.* Berlin: Reichsdruckerei, 1925.
Vogels, Werner, ed. *Die Verträge über Besetzung und Räumung des Rheinlandes und die Ordannanzen der Interalliierten Rheinland Oberkommission in Coblenz.* Berlin: C. Heymann, 1925.

D. Great Britain

Foreign Office. E. L. Woodward and Rohan Butler, eds. *Documents on British Foreign Policy, 1919-1939.* London: H.M. Stationery Office, 1946—.
Parliament. *Parliamentary Debates. House of Commons, 1918-1924.* London: H.M. Stationery Office, 1918-1925.

E. Russia

Marchand, René, ed. *Un Livre Noir. Diplomatie d'avant guerre et de guerre d'après les documents des archives russes (1910-1917).* Paris: Librairie du Travail, n.d.
Polansky, J., trans. *Documents diplomatiques secrets russes, 1914-1917.* Paris: Payot, 1928.

Stieve, Friedrich, ed. *Iswolski im Weltkriege. Der diplomatische Schriftwechsel Iswolskis aus den Jahren 1914-1917*, hrsg. im Auftrage des A. A. Berlin: Deutsche Verlagsgesellschaft für Politik und Geschichte, 1925.

F. United States

Department of State. *Foreign Relations of the United States: The Paris Peace Conference, 1919*. 13 vols. Washington, D.C.: Government Printing Office, 1942-1944.

———. *Foreign Relations of the United States*, for 1918-1924. Washington, D.C.: Government Printing Office, 1933-1939.

IV. PERIODICALS

Journée Industrielle
L'Action Française
L'Europe Nouvelle
Le Figaro
Le Journal des Débats
Le Matin
Le Petit Journal
Le Petit Parisien
Le Temps
L'Usine
The Manchester Guardian
The Times (London)

V. MEMOIRS AND BIOGRAPHIES

Allen, Henry T. *My Rhineland Journal*. Boston and New York: Houghton Mifflin, 1923.

———. *The Rhineland Occupation*. Indianapolis: Bobbs-Merrill, 1927.

Bainville, Jacques. *Journal, 1919-1926*. Paris: Plon, 1949.

Baker, Ray Stannard. *Woodrow Wilson, Life and Letters*. 8 vols. Garden City: Doubleday, Page & Co., 1927-1939.

———. *Woodrow Wilson and World Settlement*. 3 vols. Garden City: Doubleday, 1922-1923.

Bardoux, Jacques. *De Paris à Spa, la bataille diplomatique pour la paix française*. Paris: F. Alcan, 1921.

———. *Lloyd George et la France*. Paris: F. Alcan, 1921.

Baruch, Bernard M. *The Making of the Reparation and Economic Sections of the Treaty*. London and New York: Harper & Brothers, 1920.

Baumont, Maurice. *Briand, Diplomat und Idealist*. Göttingen: Musterschmidt, 1966.

Benoist, Charles. *Souvenirs*. 3 vols. Paris: Plon, 1934.

Bonnet, Georges. *Vingt ans de vie politique*. Paris: Fayard, 1969.

Bréal, August. *Philippe Berthelot*. Paris: Plon, 1937.
Bruun, Geoffrey. *Clemenceau*. Cambridge, Mass.: Harvard University Press, 1943.
Caillaux, Joseph. *Mes mémoires*. 3 vols. Paris: Plon, 1947.
Chastenet, Jacques. *Raymond Poincaré*. Paris: Julliard, 1948.
Clemenceau, Georges. *Au soir de la pensée*. 2 vols. Paris: Plon, 1930.
———. *The Grandeur and Misery of Victory*. New York: Harcourt, Brace, 1930.
Clémentel, Étienne. *La France et la politique économique interalliée*. Paris: Carnegie Foundation for International Peace, 1931.
Dawes, Charles G. *A Journal of Reparations*. London: Macmillan, 1939.
Dorten, J. A. *La tragédie rhénane*. Paris: Robt. Laffont, 1945.
Fayolle, Émile. *Cahiers secrets de la grande guerre*. Paris: Plon, 1964.
Foch, Ferdinand. *Mémoires pour servir à l'histoire de la guerre*. Paris: Plon, 1931.
François-Poncet, André. *De Versailles à Potsdam, la France et le problème allemand contemporain*. Paris: Flammarion, 1948.
———. *La vie et l'oeuvre de Robert Pinot*. Paris: Plon, 1927.
———. "Poincaré tel que je l'ai vu." *Figaro littéraire*, 26 June 1948.
Gedye, G.E.R. *The Revolver Republic*. London: J. W. Arrowsmith, 1930.
Hoover, Herbert. *Memoirs of Herbert Hoover: The Cabinet and the Presidency, 1920-1933*. New York: Macmillan, 1952.
House, Edward M., and Charles Seymour, eds. *What Really Happened at Paris: The Story of the Paris Peace Conference, 1918-1919*. New York: Charles Scribner's Sons, 1921.
Huddleston, Sisley. *Poincaré—A Biographical Portrait*. London: T. W. Unwin, 1924.
Joffre, Joseph. *Mémoires du maréchal Joffre*. 2 vols. Paris: Les petits fils de Plon et Nourrit, 1938.
Klotz, Louis. *De la guerre à la paix, souvenirs et documents*. Paris: Payot, 1924.
Lansing, Robert. *The Peace Negotiations: A Personal Narrative*. Boston: Houghton Mifflin, 1921.
Laroche, Jules. *Au Quai d'Orsay avec Briand et Poincaré, 1913-1926*. Paris: Hachette, 1926.
Lloyd George, David. *The Truth about Reparations and War Debts*. London: Heinemann, 1932.
———. *The Truth about the Peace Treaties*. 2 vols. London: V. Gollancz Ltd., 1938.
Loucheur, Louis. *Carnets Secrets, 1908-1932*. Edited by Jacques de Launay. Brussels and Paris: Brepols, 1962.

Mangin, Louis-Étienne. *La France et le Rhin, hier et aujourd'hui.* Geneva: Éditions du milieu du monde, 1945.

Martet, Jean. *Le Tigre.* Paris: A. Michel, 1929.

Middlemas, Keith, and John Barnes. *Baldwin, A Biography.* London: Macmillan, 1969.

Miquel, Pierre. *Poincaré.* Paris: Fayard, 1961.

Mordacq, Jean Jules Henri. *Clemenceau au soir de sa vie, 1920-1929.* Paris: Plon, 1933.

———. *L'armistice du 11 novembre 1918, récit d'un témoin.* Paris: Plon, 1937.

———. *Le mentalité allemande, cinq ans de commandement sur le Rhin.* Paris: Plon, 1926.

———. *Le ministère Clemenceau, journal d'un témoin.* 4 vols. Paris: Plon, 1930-1931.

Nicolson, Harold. *Curzon, the Last Phase, 1919-1925: A Study in Postwar Diplomacy.* Boston and New York: Houghton Mifflin, 1934.

———. *Peacemaking 1919.* New York: Grosset & Dunlap, 1971.

Paléologue, Georges Maurice. *La Russie des tsars pendant la grande guerre.* 3 vols. Paris: Plon-Nourrit, 1921-1922.

Paul-Boncour, Joseph. *Entre deux guerres, souvenirs de la IIIe République.* Paris: Plon, 1945-1946.

Peretti de la Rocca, Emmanuel. "Briand et Poincaré (souvenirs)." *Revue de Paris* 43, no. 4 (1936).

Pershing, John J. *My Experiences in the World War.* 2 vols. New York: F. A. Stokes, 1931.

Persil, Raoul. *Alexandre Millerand, 1859-1943.* Paris: Sociétés d'éditions françaises et internationales, 1949.

Petrie, Charles. *The Life and Letters of the Rt. Hon. Sir Austen Chamberlain.* 2 vols. London: Cassel & Co., 1939-1940.

Pinon, René. *L'avenir de l'entente franco-anglaise.* Paris: Plon, 1924.

Pinot, Robert. *Le Comité des Forges au service de la nation.* Paris: A. Colin, 1919.

Poincaré, Raymond. *Au service de la France: Neuf années de souvenirs.* 10 vols. Paris: Plon-Nourrit, 1926-1933.

Prittie, Terence. *Konrad Adenauer, 1876-1967.* Chicago: Cowles Book Co., 1971.

Pusey, Merlo. *Charles Evans Hughes.* 2 vols. New York: Macmillan, 1951.

Recouly, Raymond. *Le mémorial de Foch, mes entretiens avec le maréchal.* Paris: Les éditions de France, 1929.

Ribot, Alexander. *Journal et Correspondances inédites, 1914-1922.* Paris: Plon, n.d.

Saint-Aulaire, August Felix Charles de Beaupoil, comte de. *Confession d'un vieux diplomate*. Paris: Flammarion, 1953.

Schacht, Hjalmar. *Confessions of the Old Wizard*. Translated by Diana Pyke. Boston: Houghton Mifflin, 1956.

———. *The Stabilization of the Mark*. Translated by Ralph Butler. New York: Adelphi Co., 1927.

Sembat, Marcel. *La Victoire en déroute*. Paris: ed. du Progès civique, 1925.

Seydoux, Jacques. *De Versailles au Plan Young, réparations, dettes interalliées, reconstruction européenne*. Paris: Plon, 1932.

Seymour, Charles, ed. *The Intimate Papers of Colonel House*. 4 vols. New York and Boston: Houghton Mifflin, 1926-1928.

Siebert, Ferdinand. *Aristide Briand, 1867-1932: Ein Staatsmann zwischen Frankreich und Europa*. Zurich: Hentsch, 1973.

Suarez, Georges. *Briand, sa vie, son oeuvre, avec son journal et des nombreux documents inédits*. 6 vols. Paris: Plon, 1938-1952.

———. *Herriot, 1924, revue, corrigée et augmentée, suivie d'un récit historique de R. Poincaré*. Paris: Tallandier, 1932.

Tardieu, André. *The Truth about the Treaty*. Indianapolis: Bobbs-Merrill, 1921.

Tirard, Paul. *La France sur le Rhin, douze années d'occupation rhénane*. Paris: Plon, 1930.

Turner, Henry A. *Stresemann and the Politics of the Weimar Republic*. Princeton: Princeton University Press, 1963.

Watson, David K. *Clemenceau: A Political Biography*. London: Eyre-Methuen, 1974.

Weygand, Maxime. *Mémoires*. 2 vols. Paris: Flammarion, 1957.

VI. CONTEMPORARY POINTS OF VIEW AND UNOFFICIAL DOCUMENTS

Alpha. "Reparation and the Policy of Repudiation." *Foreign Affairs*, September 1923, pp. 58-60.

Bainville, Jacques. *Les consequences politiques de la paix*. Paris: Nouvelle librarie nationale, 1920.

Barker, J. Ellis. *Economic Statesmanship: The Great Industrial and Financial Problems Arising from the War*. New York: E. P. Dutton & Co., 1920.

Barthou, Louis. *Le Traité de Paix*. Paris: E. Fasquelle, 1919.

Baumont, Maurice. *La grosse industrie allemande et le charbon*. Paris: G. Doin et cie., 1928.

Bourgeois, Léon. *Le Traité de Paix de Versailles*. Paris: Alcan, 1919.

Brelet, Marc. *Le crise de la métallurgie; la politique économique et sociale du Comité des Forges.* Paris: Sagot, 1923.

Comité des Forges de France. *La métallurgie et le traité de paix.* Paris, 1920.

Dresdner Bank. *The Economic Forces of the World.* Berlin: Dresdner, 1927.

François-Marsal, Frédéric. *Les dettes interalliées.* Paris: La renaissance du livre, 1927.

Hanotaux, Gabriel. *Le Traité de Versailles du 28 juin 1919: L'Allemagne et l'Europe.* Paris: Alcan, 1919.

Heymann, Carl. *Urkunden zum Separatistenputsch im Rheinlande im Herbst 1923.* Berlin: C. Heymann, 1925.

Keynes, John Maynard. *The Collected Writings of John Maynard Keynes.* 16 vols. New York: St. Martin's Press; London: Macmillan, 1971—.

———. *The Economic Consequences of the Peace.* London: Macmillan, 1920.

Mantoux, Étienne. *The Carthaginian Peace, or The Economic Consequences of Mr. Keynes.* London, New York, Toronto: Oxford University Press, 1946.

Marin, Louis. *Le Traité de Paix.* Paris: Floury, 1920.

Mennevée, Robert. *Documents politiques diplomatiques et financiers, 1921-1923.* Paris: "Les documents politiques," 1923.

———. *Parlementaires et financiers.* Paris: "Les documents politiques," 1923.

Poincaré, Raymond. *Histoire Politique: Chroniques du Quinzaine.* Paris: Plon-Nourrit, 1921.

Rausch, Bernhard. *Geheime Dokumente über die französische Ruhrpolitik.* Berlin: Zentralverlag, 1923.

Stehkämper, Hugo, ed. *Der Nachlass des Reichkanzlers Wilhelm Marx.* 4 vols. Cologne: Neubner, 1968—.

Toynbee, Arnold J. "The So-called Separatist Movement in the Rhineland." *Survey of International Affairs*, 1928.

Wheeler-Bennett, J. W. *Information on the Problem of Security, 1917-1926.* London: G. Allen and Unwin, 1927.

VII. CONTEMPORARY PROPAGANDA ON THE RHENISH QUESTION

A. France

Armée du Rhin. *L'Allemagne en République. Conférences faites aux Officiers de Renseignements à Düsseldorf en 1924.* Düsseldorf: Imprimerie de l'Armée du Rhin, 1924.

Aulard, Alphonse. *La paix future d'après la révolution française et Kant*. Paris: A. Colin, 1915.

Aulneau, Joseph. *Le Rhin et la France; histoire politique et économique*. Paris: Plon-Nourrit, 1921.

Babelon, Ernest. *La grande question d'Occident: Le Rhin dans l'histoire*. 3 vols. Paris: E. Leroux, 1916-1918.

Barrès, Maurice. *L'appel du Rhin, la France dans les pays rhénans*. Paris: Société Litteraire de France, 1919.

———. *La politique rhénane*. Paris: Bloud & Gay, 1922.

———. *Le génie du Rhin*. Paris: Plon-Nourrit, 1921.

———. *Les grands problèmes du Rhin*. Paris: Plon, 1930.

Blondel, Georges. *La Rhénanie, Son Passé, Son Avenir*. Paris: Plon-Nourrit, 1921.

Bourdeaux, Henri. *Sur le Rhin*. Paris: Plon-Nourrit, 1919.

Briey, Renaud de. *Le Rhin et le problème d'occident*. Paris: Plon-Nourrit, 1922.

Chambre de Commerce Française dans les Provinces rhénanes. *Annuaire des Maisons françaises établies en Pays rhénans et des Maisons allemandes recommandées aux Français*. Mainz: Lehrlingshaus, 1923.

Comité de la Rive Gauche du Rhin. *La grande leçon de l'histoire du Rhin*. Paris: Imprimerie Pigalle, 1922.

Coubé, Stephen. *Alsace-Lorraine et France rhénane, exposé des droits de la France sur toute la Rive Gauche du Rhin*. Paris: P. Lethielleux, 1915.

Darsy, Eugène. *Les droits historique de la France sur la rive gauche du Rhin*. Paris: L. Tenin, 1919.

Delaire, Alexis. *Au lendemain de la victoire, le nouvel équilibre européen (avec une preface par M. Barrès)*. Paris: Nouvelle librarie nationale, 1916.

Depuy, Charles. "L'Allemagne à travers les siècles. Ce qu'il faut détruire, ce qu'il faut reprendre." n.d.

Dontenville, J. *Après la guerre—les Allemagnes, la France, la Belgique, et la Hollande*. Paris: H. Floury, 1919.

Dorten, Adam. *Rheinische Politik*. Coblenz: Buchdruckerei "Gutenberg," 1922.

Driault, Édouard. *La France et la guerre, les solutions françaises*. Paris: L. Cerf, 1917.

———. *La République et le Rhin*. Paris: L. Tenin, 1916.

———. *Les traditions politiques de la France et les conditions de la paix*. Paris: F. Alcan, 1916.

Esperandieu, Émile. "Le Rhin français." Paris: Attinger, n.d.

Franck-Chauveau. "La Paix et la frontière du Rhin." n.d.

Funck-Brentano, Franz. *La France sur le Rhin*. Paris: L. Tenin, 1919.

Gaulois, Franc. "La fin de Prusse et le démembrement de l'Allemagne." Geneva: Société Universelle, 1913.

Grailly, F. *La verité territoriale et la rive gauche du Rhin*. Paris: Berger-Levrault, 1916.

Gruben, Hervé de. *La crise allemande et l'occupation rhénane, 1923-1924*. Brussels: J. Lebègne, 1925.

Guyot, Yves. *La province rhénane et la Westphalie*. Paris: Alcan, 1915.

Hayem, Émile. *Au Rhin gaulois*. Paris: Grasset, 1915.

Izoulet, Jean. *. . . et pas de France sans Rhénanie!* Paris: Librarie H. Floury, 1920.

Johannet, René. *. . . Rhin et France*. Paris: Nouvelle Librarie nationale, 1919.

Jullian, Camille. *La Place de la guerre actuelle dans notre histoire nationale*. Paris: Bloud & Gay, 1916.

———. *Le Rhin gaulois*. Paris: Attinger, n.d.

Klecker de Balazuc, Michel. *La république rhénane*. Chroniques parues dans *La Revue d'Alsace et de Lorraine* avec une préface de M. Barrès. Paris: Revue de l'Alsace et Lorraine, 1924.

Laur, Francis. *Une suisse rhénane? La seule garantie contre une guerre future entre la France et l'Allemagne*. Geneva: Rascher, 1918-1919.

Lorin, Henri. *La Paix que nous voudrons*. Paris: Bloud & Gay, 1916.

Marmottan, Paul. *Notre frontière naturelle, le Rhin*. Paris: Berger-Levrault, 1916.

Pange, Jean de. *Les libertés rhénanes: Pays rhénans—Sarre—Alsace*. Paris: Perrin, 1922.

Pinon, René. *La redressement de la politique française, 1922*. Paris: Perrin, 1923.

Privat, Maurice. "Pour en finir avec l'Allemagne: il faut prendre la rive gauche du Rhin." Paris: H. Floury, 1917.

Reclus, Onésime. *Atlas de la plus grande France*. Paris: Attinger, 1915.

———. *L'Allemagne en morceaux*. Paris: Attinger, n.d.

———. *Le Rhin français, annexation de la rive gauche*. Paris: Attinger, n.d.

Recouly, Raymond. *La Barrière du Rhin: Droits et devoirs de la France pour assurer sa sécurité*. Paris: Hachette, 1923.

———. *La Ruhr*. Paris: Flammarion,1923.

Ruelens-Marlier, V. *Le Rhin libre*. Paris: Neuchâtel, 1916.

Sardou, André. *L'indépendance européenne. Étude sur les conditions de paix*. Paris: Plon, 1915.

Savarit, C.-M. *La frontière du Rhin.* Paris: H. Floury, 1915.

Schwob, Maurice. *La question de la Ruhr—une Rhéno-Westphalie indépendante.* Nantes: Édition du Phare de la Loire, 1923.

Stienon, Charles. *La rive gauche du Rhin et l'équilibre européen.* Paris: L. Tenin, 1917.

Tissot, Victor. *L'Allemagne casquée.* Paris, 1876. Reprinted with a preface by Onésime Reclus, 1916.

Vial-Mazel, Georges. *Le Rhin: Victoire allemande.* Paris: E. Chiron, 1921.

B. Germany

Beyer, Franz. *Der Separatistenputsch in Düsseldorf, 30 September 1923.* Berlin: Volk und Reich, 1933.

Boetticher, Freidrich von. *Der Kampf um den Rhein und die Weltherrschaft.* Leipzig: F. Köhler, 1922.

Bruggemann, Fritz. *Die rheinische Republik: Ein Beitrag zur geschichte und Kritik der rheinischen Abfallbewegung während des Waffenstillstandes im Jahre 1918/1919.* Bonn: F. Cohen, 1919.

Coblenz, Hermann. *Frankreichs Ringen um Rhein und Ruhr, eine Schriftenreine zur Abwehr.* Berlin: Trowitsch und Sohn, 1923.

Cuno, Rudolf. *Der Kampf um die Ruhr: Frankreichs Raubzug und Deutschlands Abwehr.* Leipzig: F. Kohler, 1923.

Distler, Heinrich. *Das deutche Leid am Rhein.* Minden: W. Köhler, 1921.

Erdmannsdörfer, H. G. *Der Kampf um Ruhr und Rhein, deutsche Reparation, französischer Rechtsbrüch.* Berlin: Zentralverlag, 1923.

Grimm, Friedrich. *Frankreich am Rhein.* Hamburg: Hanseatische Verlagsanstalt, 1931.

———. *Frankreich an der Saar.* Hamburg: Hanseatische Verlagsanstalt, 1934.

———. *Poincaré am Rhein.* Berlin: Junker & Dünnhaupt, 1940.

———. *Von Ruhrkrieg zur Rheinlandräumung.* Hamburg: Hanseatische Verlagsanstalt, 1930.

Ham, Hermann van. *Rheinland Republik—Rheinlands Untergang.* Trier: Paulinus Druckerei, 1922.

Hartmann, Peter. *Französische Kulturarbeit am Rhein.* Leipzig: K. F. Köhler, 1921.

Hartmann, W. *Frankreichs Militarismus am Rhein im Lichte französischer Kritik.* Berlin: Rheinischer Beobachter, 1925.

Hashagen, Justus. *Das Rheinland und die preussische Herrschaft.* Essen: Baedeker, 1924.

Heyland, Karl. *Die Rechtstellung der besetzten Rheinlands*. Stuttgart: Kohlhammer, 1923.

Jacquot, Paul. *Général Gérard und die Pfalz*. Hrsg. von Dr. Ritter-Mannheim. Berlin: J. Springer, 1920.

Kamper, Walter. *Die Rheinlandkrise des Herbstes 1923, ein politischer Überblick*. Frankfurt/M: Frankfurter Societätsdruckerei, 1925.

Knoch, Sigmund. *Französische Militärjustiz und Militärpolizei im besetzten Gebiete*. Munich: Süddeutsche Monatshefte, 1923.

Köhrer, Erich. *Rheinische Wirtschaftsnot*. Berlin: Deutsche Verlagsgesellschaft für Politik und Geschichte, 1921.

Kraemer, Klaus. *Die rheinische Bewegung*. Wiesbaden: Hermann Rausch, 1919.

Kuske, Bruno. *Rheingrenze und Pufferstaat: Eine volkswirtschaftliche Betrachtung*. Bonn: Marcus & Weber, 1919.

Moldenhauer, Paul. *Die rheinische Republik*. Berlin: Staatspolitischer Verlag, 1920.

Oncken, Hermann. *Die historische Rheinpolitik der Franzosen*. Stuttgart: F. A. Perthes, 1922.

Pyszka, Hannes. *Der Ruhrkrieg*. Munich: Verlag für Kulturpolitik, 1923.

Rheinländer, Anton. *Zentrum und Schulpolitik seit Weimar*. Berlin: Deutsche Zentrumspartei, 1924.

Rheinsche Frauenliga. *Farbige Franzosen am Rhein*. Berlin: Engelmann, 1921.

Schäfer, Oskar. *Die Pirmasenser Separatistenzeit, 1923-1924*. Pirmasens: Schäfer, 1936.

Springer, Max. *Frankreich und seine "Freunde" am Rhein*. Leipzig: R. Hartmann, 1923.

———. *Loslösungsbestrebungen am Rhein, 1918-1924*. Berlin: F. Vahlen, 1924.

Stegemann, Hermann. *Under the Yoke of Foreign Rule: Sufferings of the Rhineland Population*. Leipzig: F. Köhler, 1923.

Stein, Thomas. *Französische Pressestimmen über die Rheinlandpolitik*. Mannheim: Pfalzzentrale, 1921.

Stuplnagel, Otto von. *The French Terror: The Martyrdom of the German People on the Rhine and Ruhr*. Berlin: A. Scherl, 1923.

Süddeutsche Monatshefte. *Terror und Martyrium am Rhein und Ruhr, amtliche Berichte und Dokumente*. Munich, 1923.

Wrochem, Albrecht von. *Die Kolonisation der Rheinlande durch Frankreich*. Berlin: Engelmann, 1922.

VIII. SECONDARY WORKS

Albord, Tony. "L'ère crépusculaire de la stratégie, 1919-1939." *Revue Défense Nationale* 21 (1965).

Albrecht-Carrié, René. *A Diplomatic History of Europe Since the Congress of Vienna.* New York: Harper, 1958.

———. *France, Europe, and Two World Wars.* New York: Harper, 1961.

———. *One Europe: The Historical Background of European Unity.* Garden City: Doubleday, 1965.

Armitage, Susan. *The Politics of Decontrol of Industry: Britain and the United States.* London: Weidenfeld & Nicolson, 1969.

Aron, Raymond. *The Century of Total War.* Garden City: Doubleday, 1954.

Artaud, Denise. "À propos de l'occupation de la Ruhr." *Revue d'histoire moderne et contemporaine* 17 (March 1970): 1-21.

———. *La reconstruction de l'Europe.* Dossiers Clio. Paris: Presses universitaires de France, 1973.

———. "Le gouvernement américain et la question des dettes de guerre, 1919-1920." *Revue d'histoire moderne et contemporaine* 20 (1973).

Baker, Donald. "The Politics of Social Protest in France—the Left Wing of the Socialist Party, 1921-1939." *Journal of Modern History* 43, no. 1 (1971).

Bana, Suda, and Ralph H. Lutz. *The Blockade of Germany after the Armistice, 1918-1919.* Stanford: Stanford University Press, 1942.

Bariéty, Jacques. "Le rôle de la minette dans la sidérurgie allemande et la reconstructuration de la sidérurgie allemande après le Traité de Versailles." *Centre des recherches relations internationales de l'Université de Metz* 3 (1973).

———. "Les réparations allemandes, 1919-1924: objet ou prétexte à une politique rhénane de la France?" *Bulletin de la Société d'Histoire Moderne* 72 (May 1973): 21-33.

Baumont, Maurice. *La faillite de la paix, 1918-1939.* Paris: Presses universitaires de France, 1941.

———. *La grosse industrie allemande et le charbon.* Paris: Gaston Doin, 1928.

———. *Les questions européennes en 1919.* Paris: Centre de documentation universitaire, 1956.

Beau de Lomenie, E. *Le débat de ratification du Traité de Versailles.* Paris: Denoël, 1945.

Bellanger, Claude, et al., directeurs. *Histoire Générale de la Presse Française.* 4 vols. Paris: Presses universitaires de France, 1972.

Bergmann, Karl. *Der Weg der Reparationen.* Frankfurt: Frankfurter Societätsdruckerei, g.m.b.h., 1926.

Berlia, Georges. *Le problème international de la securité de la France.* Cours de grands problèmes politiques contemporains. Paris: Le cours de droit, 1967.

Bischof, Erwin. *Rheinischer Separatismus, 1918-1924.* Bern: H. Lang, 1969.

Böhmer, Leo. *Die rheinische Separatistenbewegung und die französische Presse.* Stuttgart: Deutsche Verlagsanstalt, 1928.

Bois, Jean-Pierre. "L'opinion catholique rhénane devant le séparatisme en 1923." *Revue d'histoire moderne et contemporaine* 21 (1974).

Bonnefous, Édouard. *Histoire Politique de la Troisième Republique.* Vol. 3. *L'après guerre, 1919-1924.* Paris: Presses universitaires de France, 1960.

Brandes, Joseph. *Herbert Hoover and Economic Diplomacy: Department of Commerce Policy, 1921-1926.* Pittsburgh: University of Pittsburgh Press, 1962.

Bühler, Rolf. *Die Roheisenkartelle in Frankreich, Ihre Entstehung, Entwicklung, und Bedeutung von 1876 bis 1934.* Zurich: Girsberger Verlag, 1934.

Bunselmeyer, Robert E. *The Cost of the War, 1914-1919: British Economic War Aims and the Origins of Reparation.* Hamden, Conn.: Archer Books, 1975.

Burnett, Philip M. *Reparation at the Paris Peace Conference from the Standpoint of the American Delegation.* 2 vols. New York: Columbia University Press, 1940.

Campbell, F. Gregory. "The Struggle for Upper Silesia, 1919-1922." *Journal of Modern History* 42 (September 1970): 361-385.

———. *Confrontation in Central Europe. Weimar Germany and Czechoslovakia.* Chicago: University of Chicago, 1975.

Carly, Michael Jobara. "The Origins of the French Intervention in the Russian Civil War, January-May 1918: A Reappraisal." *Journal of Modern History* 48 (September 1976): 413-439.

Carr, E. H. *International Relations Between the Two Wars.* London: Macmillan, 1947.

Carr, J. C., and Walter Taplin. *History of the British Steel Industry.* Cambridge: Harvard University Press, 1962.

Chastenet, Jacques. *L'Histoire de la Troisième Republique.* Vol. 5. *Les années d'illusion, 1918-1931.* Paris: Hachette, 1960.

Craig, Gordon, and Felix Gilbert, eds. *The Diplomats, 1919-1939*. Princeton: Princeton University Press, 1953.

Dahlin, Ebba. *French and German Public Opinion on Declared War Aims*. Stanford: Stanford University Press, 1933.

Dawes, Rufus C. *The Dawes Plan in the Making*. Indianapolis: Bobbs-Merrill, 1925.

Dehio, Ludwig. *Germany and World Politics in the Twentieth Century*. London: Chatto & Windus, 1959.

Dulles, Eleanor Lansing. *The French Franc, 1914-1928*. New York: Macmillan, 1929.

Duroselle, J.-B. *From Wilson to Roosevelt: Foreign Policy of the United States, 1913-1945*. Translated by Nancy Roelker. Cambridge: Harvard University Press, 1963.

———. *Histoire diplomatique de 1919 à nos jours*. Paris: Librairie Alloz, 1957.

———. *La politique extérieur de la France de 1914 à 1945*. Paris: Centre de documentation universitaire, 1965.

———. *Les relations franco-allemandes de 1914 à 1950*. Paris: Centre de documentation universitaire, 1967.

Du Sault, Jean. "Les relations diplomatiques entre la France et le Saint-Siège." *Revue des Deux Mondes* 10 (1971).

Epstein, Klaus. *Matthias Erzberger and the Dilemma of German Democracy*. Princeton: Princeton University Press, 1959.

Erdmann, Karl D. *Adenauer in der Rheinlandpolitik nach dem ersten Weltkrieg*. Stuttgart: Ernst Klett Verlag, 1966.

Eschenburg, Theodor. "Das Problem der deutschen Einheit nach den beiden Weltkriegen." *Vierteljahrshefte für Zeitgeschichte* 5 (1957): 107-134.

Euler, Heinrich. *Die Aussenpolitik der Weimarer Republik, 1918-1923*. Aschaffenburg: Stock und Körber, 1957.

Eyck, Erich. *A History of the Weimar Republic*. 2 vols. Cambridge: Harvard University Press, 1962; Science Edition, New York: John Wiley & Sons, 1963.

Fagerberg, Elliot. *The Anciens Combattants and French Foreign Policy*. n.p.: Presses de Savoie, 1966.

Favez, Jean-Claude. *Le Reich devant l'occupation franco-belge de la Ruhr en 1923*. Geneva: Institut de l'histoire, Université de Genève, 1969.

Feis, Herbert. *The Diplomacy of the Dollar, 1919-1932*. New York: Norton, 1966.

Feldman, Gerald D. *Army, Industry, and Labor in Germany, 1914-1918*. Princeton: Princeton University Press, 1966.

———. "The Economic and Social Problems of the German Demobilization, 1918-1919." *Journal of Modern History* 47, no. 1 (March 1975): 1-47.

———. *Iron and Steel in the German Inflation, 1916-1923*. Princeton: Princeton University Press, 1977.

———. "The Social and Economic Policies of German Big Business, 1918-1929." *American Historical Review* 75, no. 1 (October 1969): 47-55.

Felix, David. *Walther Rathenau and the Weimar Republic: The Politics of Reparation*. Baltimore and London: Johns Hopkins University Press, 1971.

Fischer, Fritz. *Germany's Aims in the First World War*. New York: Norton, 1961.

Fischer, Louis. *The Soviets in World Affairs: A History of the Relations between the Soviet Union and the Rest of the World, 1917-1929*. Princeton: Princeton University Press, 1960.

Fischer, Wolfram. *Die wirtschaftspolitische Situation der Weimarer Republik*. Hannover: Niedersächsische Landeszentrale für politische Bildung, 1960.

Fraenkel, Ernst. *Military Occupation and the Rule of Law: Occupation Government in the Rhineland, 1918-1924*. London and New York: Oxford University Press, 1944.

Frasure, Carl. *British Policy on War Debts and Reparations*. Philadelphia: Dorrance & Co., 1940.

Friedensburg, Ferdinand. *Kohle und Eisen im Weltkriege und in den Friedensschlüssen*. Munich and Berlin: R. Oldenbourg Verlag, 1934.

Gathorne-Hardy, Geoffrey. *A Short History of International Affairs, 1920-1939*. London: Oxford University Press, 1950.

Gatzke, Hans W. *Germany's Drive to the West*. Baltimore: Johns Hopkins University Press, 1950.

Gescher, Dieter. *Die vereinigten Staaten von Nordamerika und die Reparationen, 1920-1924*. Bonn: L. Röhrscheid, 1956.

Gombin, Richard. *Les socialistes et la guerre: La S.F.I.O. et la politique étrangère française entre les deux guerres mondiales*. The Hague: Mouton, 1967.

Greer, Guy. *The Ruhr-Lorraine Industrial Problem. A Study of the Economic Interdependence of the Two Regions and Their Relation to the Reparation Question*. New York: Macmillan, 1925.

Hogan, Michael J. *Informal Entente. The Private Structure of Cooperation in Anglo-American Economic Diplomacy, 1918-1928*. Columbia, Mo. and London: University of Missouri Press, 1977.

Hovi, Kalervo. *Cordon Sanitaire or Barrière de l'Est? The Emergence of the New French Eastern European Alliance Policy, 1917-1919*. Turku, Finland: Turun Yliopisto, 1975.

Howard, John E. *Parliament and Foreign Policy in France, 1919-1939*. London: Cresset Press, 1948.

Hughes, Judith M. *To the Maginot Line: The Politics of French Military Preparedness in the 1920s*. Cambridge: Harvard University Press, 1971.

Hunt, Barry, and Adrian Preston, eds. *War Aims and Strategic Policy in the Great War 1914-1918*. Totowa, N.J.: Rowman and Littlefield, 1977.

Jacobson, Jon. *Locarno Diplomacy, Germany and the West, 1925-1929*. Princeton: Princeton University Press, 1972.

Jones, K. Paul. "Stresemann and the Diplomacy of the Ruhr Crisis, 1923-1924." Ph.D. dissertation, University of Wisconsin, 1970.

Jordan, W. N. *Great Britain, France, and the German Problem, 1919-1939*. London and New York: Oxford University Press, 1943.

Kaplan, Jay L. "France's Road to Genoa: Strategic, Economic, and Ideological Factors in French Foreign Policy, 1921-1922." Ph.D. dissertation, Columbia University, 1974.

Keeton, Edward D. "Briand's Locarno Policy: French Economics, Politics, and Diplomacy, 1925-1929." Ph.D. dissertation, Yale University, 1975.

King, Jere. *Foch versus Clemenceau: France and German Dismemberment, 1918-1919*. Cambridge: Harvard University Press, 1960.

Klein, Peter. *Separatisten am Rhein und Ruhr, die Konterrevolutionäre separatistische Bewegung der deutschen Bourgeoisie in der Rheinprovinz und im Westfalen, November 1918-Juli 1919*. Berlin: Rütten und Loening, 1961.

———. "Zur separatistischen Bewegung der deutschen Bourgeoisie nach dem ersten Weltkrieg." *Deutsche Aussenpolitik* 5 (1961).

Knapton, E. J. *France Since Versailles*. New York: Holt, 1952.

Korbel, Josef. *Poland Between East and West: Soviet and German Policy Toward Poland, 1919-1933*. Princeton: Princeton University Press, 1963.

Krüger, Peter. *Deutschland und die Reparationen 1918-1919*. Stuttgart: Deutschlands Verlagsanstalt, 1973.

Lachapelle, Georges. *Les finances de la III. République*. Paris: Flammarion, 1937.

Laubach, Ernst. *Die Politik der Kabinette Wirth 1921/22*. Lübeck: Matthiesen, 1968.

Lauren, Paul Gordon. *Diplomats and Bureaucrats: The First Institu-*

tional Responses to Twentieth Century Diplomacy in France and Germany. Stanford: Hoover Institution, 1976.

Leffler, Melvyn. "The Origins of Republican War Debt Policy, 1921-1923: A Case Study in the Applicability of the Open Door Interpretation." *Journal of American History* 59, no. 3 (December 1972): 585-601.

———. "Political Isolationism: Economic Expansion or Diplomatic Realism? American Policy Toward Western Europe." *Perspectives in American History* 8 (1974): 413-461.

Lesage, Gerard. "Aspects des rapports entre l'Église et l'État en France, 1921-1932." *Revue du Nord* 53, no. 208 (1971).

Levainville, J. *L'industrie du fer en France.* Paris: A. Colin, 1922.

Levin, N. Gordon, Jr. *Woodrow Wilson and World Politics: America's Response to War and Revolution.* Oxford, London, New York: Oxford University Press, 1968.

Link, Arthur S. *Wilson the Diplomatist.* Baltimore: Johns Hopkins University Press, 1957.

Link, Werner. *Die amerikanische Stabilisierungspolitik in Deutschland, 1921-1932.* Düsseldorf: Droste Verlag, 1970.

———. "Die Ruhrbesetzung und die wirtschafts-politischen Interessen der U.S.A." *Vierteljahrshefte für Zeitgeschichte* 17 (1969): 372-383.

Lowry, Francis B. "Pershing and the Armistice." *Journal of American History* 55 (September 1968): 281-191.

Loyrette, J.E.L. *The Foreign Policy of Poincaré: France and Great Britain in Relation to the German Problem, 1918-1923.* Oxford: Champion Hall, 1956.

Luckau, Alma. *The German Delegation at the Paris Peace Conference.* New York: Columbia University Press, 1941.

Lüthgen, Helmut. *Das Rheinisch-Westfälische Kohlensyndikat in der Vorkriegs-, Kriegs-, und Nachkriegszeit und seine Hauptprobleme.* Würzburg: C. J. Becker, 1926.

Maier, Charles S. *Recasting Bourgeois Europe: Stabilization in France, Germany, and Italy in the Decade After World War I.* Princeton: Princeton University Press, 1975.

Manevy, Raymond. *Histoire de la Presse, 1914-1939.* Paris, 1945.

Mantoux, Paul. *Paris Peace Conference 1919, Proceedings of the Council of Four.* Translated by John B. Whitman. Geneva: Librairie Droz, 1964.

Marks, Sally. "Reparations Reconsidered; A Reminder." *Central European History* 2 (1969).

Marlowe, John. *Perfidious Albion: The Origins of Anglo-French Rivalry in the Levant.* London: Elek, 1971.

Mayer, Arno J. *Political Origins of the New Diplomacy, 1917-1918.* New Haven: Yale University Press, 1959.

———. *The Politics and Diplomacy of Peacemaking: Containment and Counter-revolution at Versailles, 1918-1919.* New York: A. A. Knopf and Random House, 1967.

———. *Dynamics of Counterrevolution in Europe, 1870-1956.* New York: Harper & Row, 1971.

Meinhardt, Günther, *Adenauer und der rheinische Separatismus.* Recklinghausen: Kommunal-Verlag, 1962.

Miller, Jane K. *Belgian Foreign Policy Between Two Wars, 1919-1940.* New York: Bookman, 1951.

Miquel, Pierre. *La Paix de Versailles et l'opinion publique française.* Paris: Flammarion, 1972.

Mommsen, Hans, Dietmar Petzina, and Bernd Weisbrod, eds. *Industrielles System und Politische Entwicklung in der Weimarer Republik.* Düsseldorf: Droste Verlag, 1974.

Morsey, Rudolf. *Die deutsche Zentrumspartei, 1917-1923.* Düsseldorf: Droste Verlag, 1966.

Mowat, R. B. *A History of European Diplomacy, 1914-1925.* London: Edw. Arnold & Co., 1927.

Nelson, Harold I. *Land and Power. British and Allied Policy on the German Frontier, 1916-1919.* London: Routledge & Kegan Paul, 1963.

Nelson, Keith L. "The 'Black Horror on the Rhine': Race as a Factor in Post-World War I Diplomacy." *Journal of Modern History* 42 (December 1970): 606-627.

———. *Victors Divided. America and the Allies in Germany, 1918-1923.* Berkeley, Los Angeles, London: University of California Press, 1975.

Néré, Jacques. *The Foreign Policy of France from 1914 to 1945.* London and Boston: Routledge & Kegan Paul, 1975.

Olivier, M. *La politique du charbon, 1914-1921.* Paris: Felix Alcan, 1922.

Pabst, Klaus. *Eupen-Malmedy in der belgischen Regierungs- und Parteipolitik, 1914-1940.* Aachen, 1964.

Paoli, François-André. *L'Armée Française de 1919 à 1939.* Vol. 2. *La phase de fermeté, 1919-1924.* Ministère des Armées, E.M. de l'Armée de Terre, Service Historique, n.d.

Philippe, Raymond. *Le drame financier de 1924-1928.* Paris, 1931.

Poidevin, Raymond. *Les relations économiques et financières entre la France et l'Allemagne de 1898 à 1914.* Paris: A. Colin, 1969.

Polanyi, Karl. *The Great Transformation: The Political and Economic Origins of Our Time.* Boston: Beacon Press, 1957.

Precheur, Claude. *La Lorraine sidérurgique*. Paris: S.A.B.R.I., 1959.

Renouvin, Pierre. *L'Armistice de Rethondes*. Paris: Gallimard, 1968.

———. "Les buts de guerre du gouvernement français, 1914-1918." *Revue Historique* 235, no. 477 (1966).

———. *Le Traité de Versailles*. Paris: Flammarion, 1969.

———. *War and Aftermath, 1914-1929*. Translated by Remy Hall. New York: Harper & Row, 1968.

Rhodes, Benjamin D. "Reassessing Uncle Shylock: The United States and the French War Debt, 1917-1929." *Journal of American History* 55 (1969).

Rössler, Helmuth, ed. *Die Folgen von Versailles, 1919-1924*. Göttingen: Musterschmidt, 1969.

———. *Ideologie und Machtpolitik, 1919: Plan und Werk der Pariser Friedenskonferenz*. Göttingen, Berlin, Frankfurt, Zurich: Musterschmidt, 1966.

Rupieper, Hermann-Josef. "Politics and Economics: The Cuno Government and Reparations, 1922-1923." Ph.D. dissertation, Stanford University, 1974.

Sauvy, Alfred. *Histoire économique de la France entre les deux guerres*. 4 vols. Paris: Fayard, 1965-1975.

Schmidt, Royal J. *Versailles and the Ruhr, Seedbed of World War II*. The Hague: Martinus Nijhogg, 1968.

Schuker, Stephen A. *The End of French Predominance in Europe. The Financial Crisis of 1924 and the Adoption of the Dawes Plan*. Chapel Hill: University of North Carolina Press, 1976.

Schwabe, Klaus. *Deutsche Revolution und Wilson-Frieden*. Düsseldorf: Droste Verlag, 1971.

Selsam, John P. *The Attempts to Form an Anglo-French Alliance, 1919-1924*. Philadelphia: University of Pennsylvania Press, 1936.

Sontag, Raymond. *A Broken World, 1919-1939*. The Rise of Modern Europe. Edited by William F. Langer. New York: Harper & Row, 1968.

———. *European Diplomatic History, 1871-1932*. New York and London: The Century Company, 1933.

Soutou, Georges. "Die deutschen Reparationen und das Seydoux-Projekt, 1920/21." *Vierteljahrshefte für Zeitgeschichte* 23, no. 3 (July 1975): 237-270.

———. "La politique économique de la France en Pologne, 1920-1924." *Revue historique* 251 (January 1974): 85-116.

———. "Les problèmes du rétablissement des relations économiques entre la France et l'Allemagne, 1918-1929." *Francia* 2 (1973).

Springer, Max. *Der politische Charakter der französischen Kulturpropoganda am Rhein*. Berlin: F. Vahlen, 1923.

Stockder, Archibald H. *Regulating an Industry: The Rhenish-Westphalian Coal Syndicate, 1893-1929*. New York: Columbia University, 1932.

Tawney, R. H. "The Abolition of Economic Controls, 1918-1921." *Economic History Review* 13, no. 1 (1943): 1-30.

Taylor, A.J.P. *The Origins of the Second World War*. New York: Fawcett, 1961.

———. *Struggle for the Mastery of Europe*. London and New York: Oxford University Press, 1971.

———. "The War Aims of the Allies in the First World War." *Politics in Wartime and Other Essays*. London: Hamish Hamilton, 1964.

Tillman, Seth P. *Anglo-American Relations at the Paris Peace Conference of 1919*. Princeton: Princeton University Press, 1961.

Tournoux, P. E. *Défense de frontières: Haut commandement, 1919-1939*. Paris, 1960.

———. "Les origines de la ligne Maginot" *Revue d'histoire de la deuxième guerre mondiale* (1959).

———. "Si l'on a ecouté Foch." *Revue des Deux Mondes* 17 (1959).

Trachtenberg, Marc B. "French Reparation Policy, 1918-1921." Ph.D. dissertation, University of California at Berkeley, 1974.

Ullmann, Richard H. *Anglo-Soviet Relations, 1917-1921: Intervention and the War*. Princeton: Princeton University Press, 1961.

Viallate, Achille. *Le Monde économique, 1918-1927*. Paris: M. Rivière, 1928.

Vietsch, Eberhard von. *Arnold Rechberg und das Problem der politischen West-orientierung Deutschlands nach dem ersten Weltkreig*. Coblenz: Bundesarchiv, 1958.

Wandycz, Piotr. *France and Her Eastern Allies, 1919-1925*. Minneapolis: University of Minnesota Press, 1962.

Weill-Raynal, Étienne. *Les réparations allemandes et la France*. 3 vols. Paris: Nouvelles éditions latines, 1947-1949.

Wentzcke, Paul. *Ruhrkampf, Einbruch und Abwehr im rheinisch-westfälischen Industriegebiet*. 2 vols. Berlin: Reimar Hobbing, 1930-32.

Wolfe, Martin. *The French Franc Between the Wars, 1919-1939*. New York: Oxford University Press, 1951.

Wolfers, Arnold. *Britain and France Between Two Wars: Conflicting Strategies of Peace Since Versailles*. New York: Harcourt, Brace, 1940.

Wright, Gordon. *Raymond Poincaré and the French Presidency*. Stanford: Stanford University Press, 1942.

Yates, Louis. *The U.S.A. and French Security, 1919-1921*. New York: Twayne Publishers, 1957.

Zimmermann, Ludwig. *Deutsche Aussenpolitik in der Ära der Weimarer Republik.* Göttingen, Berlin, Frankfurt: Musterschmidt Verlag, 1958.

———. *Frankreichs Ruhrpolitik von Versailles bis zum Dawesplan.* Hrsg. von Walther Peter Fuchs. Göttingen and Frankfurt: Musterschmidt Verlag, 1971.

Zuylen, Pierre Baron van. *Les mains libres: La politique extérieure de la Belgique, 1914-1940.* Brussels: L'édition universelle, 1950.

INDEX

LIBRARY OF CONGRESS CATALOGING
IN PUBLICATION DATA

McDougall, Walter A. 1946-
France's Rhineland diplomacy, 1914-1924.

Bibliography: p.
Includes index.
1. France—Foreign relations—Germany. 2. Germany—Foreign relations—France. 3. France—Politics and government—1914-1940. I. Title.
DC369.M2 327.44'043 77-85550
ISBN 0-691-05268-9